D1252375

VISUALIZING
GEOLOGY

FOURTH EDITION

DEDICATION

This book is dedicated to Cathy Skinner.

My friend, role model, and inspiration – BWM

My colleague, partner, and soulmate – BJS

REMEMBRANCE

As this book was going to press we learned of the death of Clifford Mills, long-time editor, mentor, and friend.

Thanks and farewell, Cliff. Your skills and judgement live on in this and many other Wiley books.

VISUALIZING
GEOLOGY

FOURTH EDITION

BARBARA MURCK, PhD
University of Toronto

BRIAN SKINNER, PhD
Yale University

WILEY

VICE PRESIDENT AND DIRECTOR	Petra Recter
EXECUTIVE EDITOR	Jessica Fiorillo
MANAGER, PRODUCT DEVELOPMENT	Nancy Perry
EXECUTIVE MARKETING MANAGER	Christine Kushner
PRODUCT MANAGER, MARKET SOLUTIONS	Gladys Soto
SENIOR MARKET SOLUTIONS ASSISTANT	Kathryn Hancox
ASSOCIATE EDITOR	Christina Volpe
SENIOR PRODUCT DESIGNER	Geraldine Osnato
SENIOR CONTENT MANAGER	Elle Wagner
SENIOR PRODUCTION EDITOR	John Curley
SENIOR PHOTO EDITOR	Mary Ann Price
CONTENT TECHNOLOGY SPECIALIST	Jessica Zahorian
MEDIA SPECIALIST	Suzanne Schilit
CREATIVE DIRECTOR	Harry Nolan
SENIOR DESIGNER (INTERIOR DESIGN)	Wendy Lai
SENIOR DESIGNER (COVER DESIGN)	Thomas Nery
COPY EDITOR	Betty Pessagno
PROOFREADER	Christine Cervoni for Camelot Editorial Services, LLC
COMPOSITOR	Sofia Buono for codeMantra

COVER CREDITS
Main Image: Ralph Lee Hopkins/National Geographic Creative
Bottom photos:
Volcano: Greg Vaughn/Alamy
Clouds: Doug Millar/Science Source
Cityscape: Michael S. Yamashita/National Geographic Creative
Moonscape: Jerry Dodrill/Aurora/Getty Images
Algae covered rocks: Raymond Gehman/National Geographic Creative

This book was set in Stix Regular by codeMantra and printed and bound by Quad/Graphics, Versailles. The cover was printed by Quad/Graphics, Versailles.

This book is printed on acid-free paper. ∞

Founded in 1807, John Wiley & Sons, Inc. has been a valued source of knowledge and understanding for more than 200 years, helping people around the world meet their needs and fulfill their aspirations. Our company is built on a foundation of principles that include responsibility to the communities we serve and where we live and work. In 2008, we launched a Corporate Citizenship Initiative, a global eff ort to address the environmental, social, economic, and ethical challenges we face in our business. Among the issues we are addressing are carbon impact, paper specifications and procurement, ethical conduct within our business and among our vendors, and community and charitable support. For more information, please visit our website: www.wiley.com/go/citizenship.

Library of Congress Cataloging-in-Publication Data
Murck, Barbara Winifred, 1954-
 Visualizing geology / Barbara Murck, PhD, University of Toronto, Brian Skinner, PhD Yale University. —Fourth edition.
  pages cm
 ISBN 978-1-118-99651-5 (loose-leaf)
 1. Geology—Study and teaching. I. Skinner, Brian J., 1928- II. Title.
 QE26.3.M87 2015
 550—dc23

                                          2015001930

BRV ISBN: 978-1-118-99651-5
High School Bound Version ISBN: 978-1-119-14751-0

The inside back cover will contain printing identification and country of origin if omitted from this page. In addition, if the ISBN on the back cover differs from the ISBN on this page, the one on the back cover is correct.

Printed in the United States of America

10 9 8 7 6 5 4 3 2 1

HOW IS WILEY VISUALIZING DIFFERENT?

Wiley Visualizing is based on decades of research on the use of visuals in learning (Mayer, 2005).[1] The visuals teach key concepts and are pedagogically designed to **explain, present,** and **organize** new information. The figures are tightly integrated with accompanying text; the visuals are conceived with the text in ways that clarify and reinforce major concepts while allowing students to understand the details. This commitment to distinctive and consistent visual pedagogy sets Wiley Visualizing apart from other textbooks.

The texts offer an array of remarkable photographs, maps, and media from photo collections around the world. Wiley Visualizing's images are not decorative; such images can be distracting to students. Instead, they are purposeful and the primary driver of the content. These authentic materials immerse the student in real-life issues and experiences and support thinking, comprehension, and application.

Together these elements deliver a level of rigor in ways that maximize student learning and involvement. Wiley Visualizing has been proven to increase student learning through its unique combination of text, photographs, and illustrations, with online animations, simulations, and assessments.

1. **Visual Pedagogy.** Using the Cognitive Theory of Multimedia Learning, which is backed up by hundreds of empirical research studies, Wiley's authors create visualizations for their texts that specifically support students' thinking and learning—for example, the selection of relevant materials, the organization of the new information, or the integration of the new knowledge with prior knowledge.

2. **Authentic Situations and Problems.** *Visualizing Geology 4e* benefits from an array of remarkable photographs, maps, and media; these authentic materials immerse the student in real-life issues in geology, thereby enhancing motivation, learning, and retention (Donovan & Bransford, 2005).[2]

3. **Designed with Interactive Multimedia.** *Visualizing Geology 4e* is tightly integrated with *WileyPLUS*, our online learning environment that provides interactive multimedia activities in which learners can actively engage with the materials. The combination of textbook and *WileyPLUS* provides learners with multiple entry points to the content, giving them greater opportunity to explore concepts and assess their understanding as they progress through the course. *WileyPLUS* is a key component of the Wiley Visualizing learning and problem-solving experience, setting it apart from other textbooks whose online component is mere drill-and-practice.

Wiley Visualizing and the *WileyPLUS* Learning Environment a natural extension of how we learn

To understand why the Visualizing approach is effective, it is first helpful to understand how we learn.

1. Our brain processes information using two main channels: visual and verbal. Our *working memory* holds information that our minds process as we learn. This "mental workbench" helps us with decisions, problem-solving, and making sense of words and pictures by building verbal and visual models of the information.

2. When the verbal and visual models of corresponding information are integrated in working memory, we form more comprehensive and lasting mental models.

3. When we link these integrated mental models to our prior knowledge, stored in our *long-term memory,* we build even stronger mental models. When an integrated (visual plus verbal) mental model is formed and stored in long-term memory, real learning begins.

The effort our brains put forth to make sense of instructional information is called *cognitive load*. There are two kinds of cognitive load: productive cognitive load, such as when we're engaged in learning or exert positive effort to create mental models; and unproductive cognitive load, which occurs when the brain is trying to make sense of needlessly complex content or when information is not presented well. The learning process can be impaired when the information to be processed exceeds the capacity of working memory. Well-designed visuals and text with effective pedagogical guidance can reduce the unproductive cognitive load in our working memory.

---

[1] Mayer, R.E. (Ed.) (2005). *The Cambridge Handbook of Multimedia Learning.* Cambridge University Press.
[2] Donovan, M.S., & Bransford, J. (Eds.) (2005). *How Students Learn: Science in the Classroom.* The National Academy Press. Available online at http://www.nap.edu/openbook.php?record_id=11102&page=1.

Wiley Visualizing is designed for engaging and effective learning

The visuals and text in *Visualizing Geology 4e* are specially integrated to present complex processes in clear steps and with clear representations, organize related pieces of information, and integrate related information. This approach, along with the use of interactive multimedia, minimizes unproductive cognitive load and helps students engage with the content. When students are engaged, they're reading and learning, which can lead to greater knowledge and academic success.

Research shows that well-designed visuals, integrated with comprehensive text, can improve the efficiency with which a learner processes information. In this regard, SEG Research, an independent research firm, conducted a national, multisite study evaluating the effectiveness of Wiley Visualizing. Its findings indicate that students using Wiley Visualizing products (both print and multimedia) were more engaged in the course, exhibited greater retention throughout the course, and made significantly greater gains in content area knowledge and skills, as compared to students in similar classes that did not use Wiley Visualizing.[3]

The use of *WileyPLUS* can also increase learning. According to a white paper titled "Leveraging Blended Learning for More Effective Course Management and Enhanced Student Outcomes" by Peggy Wyllie of Evince Market Research & Communications, studies show that effective use of online resources can increase learning outcomes. Pairing supportive online resources with face-to-face instruction can help students to learn and reflect on material, and deploying multimodal learning methods can help students to engage with the material and retain their acquired knowledge.

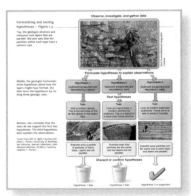

Using the scientific method (Figure 1.3) This matrix visually organizes abstract information to reduce cognitive load.

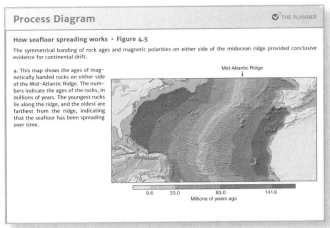

Process Diagram ✓ THE PLANNER

How seafloor spreading works · Figure 4.5

The symmetrical banding of rock ages and magnetic polarities on either side of the midocean ridge provided conclusive evidence for continental drift.

a. This map shows the ages of magnetically banded rocks on either side of the Mid-Atlantic Ridge. The numbers indicate the ages of the rocks, in millions of years. The youngest rocks lie along the ridge, and the oldest are farthest from the ridge, indicating that the seafloor has been spreading over time.

Seafloor spreading (Figure 4.5) Through a logical progression of graphics, this illustration directs learners' attention to the underlying concept. Textual and visual elements are physically integrated. This eliminates split attention—when too many sources of information divide attention.

Earth and lunar "soil"—Not the same! (Figure 7.8) Photos are paired so that students can compare and contrast them, thereby grasping the underlying concept. Adjacent caption eliminates split attention.

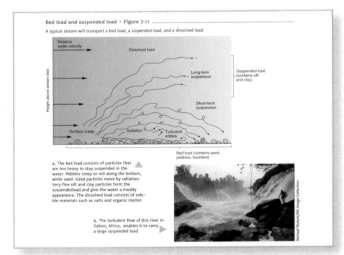

Bed load and suspended load (Figure 7.11) From abstraction to reality: Linking the graph to a photo illustrates how data on the graph relates to an actual river.

---

[3] SEG Research (2009). Improving Student-Learning with Graphically Enhanced Textbooks: A Study of the Effectiveness of the Wiley Visualizing Series.

HOW ARE THE WILEY VISUALIZING CHAPTERS ORGANIZED?

Student engagement is more than just exciting videos or interesting animations—engagement means keeping students motivated to keep going. It is easy to get bored or lose focus when presented with large amounts of information, and it is easy to lose motivation when the relevance of the information is unclear. The design of *WileyPLUS* is based on cognitive science, instructional design, and extensive research into user experience. It transforms learning into an interactive, engaging, and outcomes-oriented experience for students.

Each Wiley Visualizing chapter engages students from the start

Chapter opening text and visuals introduce the subject and connect the student with the material that follows.

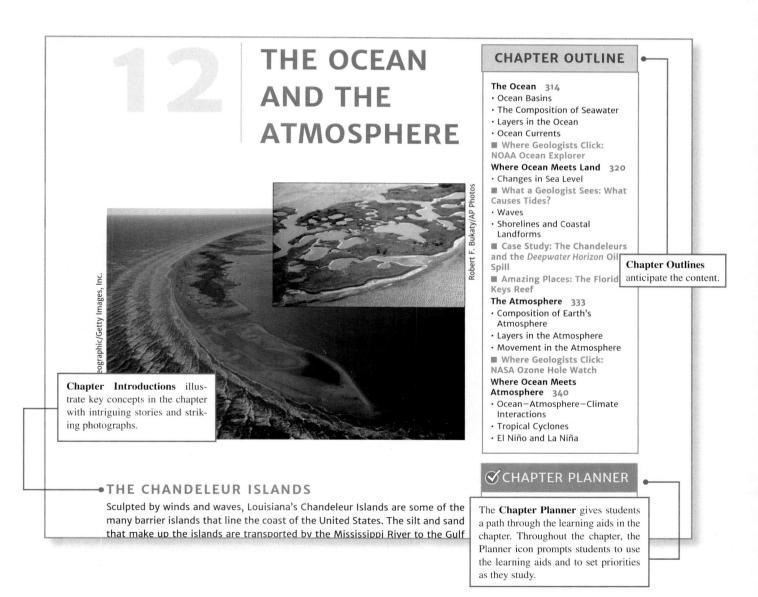

12 | THE OCEAN AND THE ATMOSPHERE

Robert F. Bukaty/AP Photos

...eographic/Getty Images, Inc.

Chapter Introductions illustrate key concepts in the chapter with intriguing stories and striking photographs.

THE CHANDELEUR ISLANDS

Sculpted by winds and waves, Louisiana's Chandeleur Islands are some of the many barrier islands that line the coast of the United States. The silt and sand that make up the islands are transported by the Mississippi River to the Gulf

Chapter Outlines anticipate the content.

✓ CHAPTER PLANNER

The **Chapter Planner** gives students a path through the learning aids in the chapter. Throughout the chapter, the Planner icon prompts students to use the learning aids and to set priorities as they study.

Wiley Visualizing guides students through the chapter

The content of Wiley Visualizing gives students a variety of approaches—visuals, words, interactions, video, and assessments—that work together to provide a guided path through the content.

Learning Objectives at the start of each section indicate in behavioral terms the concepts that students are expected to master while reading the section.

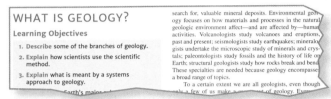

WHAT IS GEOLOGY?

Learning Objectives

1. **Describe** some of the branches of geology.
2. **Explain** how scientists use the scientific method.
3. **Explain** what is meant by a systems approach to geology.

Earth's major

search for, valuable mineral deposits. Environmental geology focuses on how materials and processes in the natural geologic environment affect—and are affected by—human activities. Volcanologists study volcanoes and eruptions, past and present; seismologists study earthquakes; mineralogists undertake the microscopic study of minerals and crystals; paleontologists study fossils and the history of life on Earth; structural geologists study how rocks break and bend. These specialties are needed because geology encompasses a broad range of topics.

To a certain extent we are all geologists, even though only a few of us make a

Geology InSight features are multipart visual sections that focus on a key concept or topic in the chapter, exploring it in detail or in broader context using a combination of photos, diagrams, maps, and data.

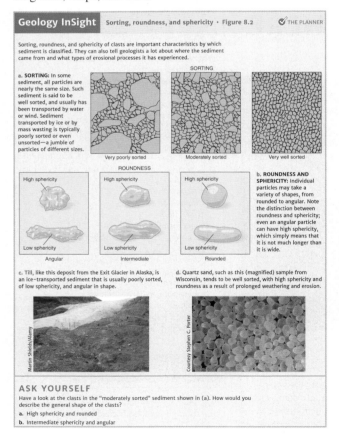

Geology InSight — Sorting, roundness, and sphericity · Figure 8.2 — THE PLANNER

Sorting, roundness, and sphericity of clasts are important characteristics by which sediment is classified. They can also tell geologists a lot about where the sediment came from and what types of erosional processes it has experienced.

a. SORTING: In some sediment, all particles are nearly the same size. Such sediment is said to be well sorted, and usually has been transported by water or wind. Sediment transported by ice or by mass wasting is typically poorly sorted or even unsorted—a jumble of particles of different sizes.

SORTING
Very poorly sorted | Moderately sorted | Very well sorted

ROUNDNESS
High sphericity | High sphericity | High sphericity
Low sphericity | Low sphericity | Low sphericity
Angular | Intermediate | Rounded

b. ROUNDNESS AND SPHERICITY: Individual particles may take a variety of shapes, from rounded to angular. Note the distinction between roundness and sphericity; even an angular particle can have high sphericity, which simply means that it is not much longer than it is wide.

c. Till, like this deposit from the Exit Glacier in Alaska, is an ice-transported sediment that is usually poorly sorted, of low sphericity, and angular in shape.

d. Quartz sand, such as this (magnified) sample from Wisconsin, tends to be well sorted, with high sphericity and roundness as a result of prolonged weathering and erosion.

Martin Shields/Alamy

Courtesy Stephen C. Porter

ASK YOURSELF

Have a look at the clasts in the "moderately sorted" sediment shown in (a). How would you describe the general shape of the clasts?

a. High sphericity and rounded
b. Intermediate sphericity and angular

Process Diagrams provide in-depth coverage of processes correlated with clear, step-by-step narrative, enabling students to grasp important topics with less effort.

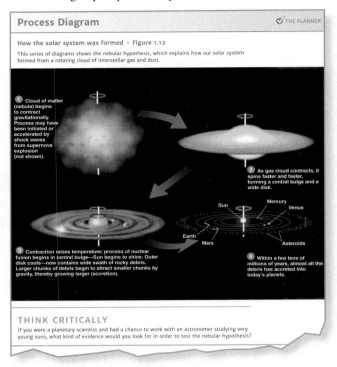

Process Diagram — THE PLANNER

How the solar system was formed · Figure 1.12
This series of diagrams shows the nebular hypothesis, which explains how our solar system formed from a rotating cloud of interstellar gas and dust.

1 Cloud of matter (nebula) begins to contract gravitationally. Process may have been initiated or accelerated by shock waves from supernova explosion (not shown).

2 As gas cloud contracts, it spins faster and faster, forming a central bulge and a wide disk.

Sun | Mercury | Venus
Earth | Mars | Asteroids

3 Contraction raises temperature; process of nuclear fusion begins in central bulge—Sun begins to shine. Outer disk cools—now contains wide swath of rocky debris. Larger chunks of debris begin to attract smaller chunks by gravity, thereby growing larger (accretion).

4 Within a few tens of millions of years, almost all the debris has accreted into today's planets.

THINK CRITICALLY
If you were a planetary scientist and had a chance to work with an astronomer studying very young suns, what kind of evidence would you look for in order to test the nebular hypothesis?

Case Studies are in-depth examinations of fascinating and important issues in geology.

CASE Study — THE PLANNER

The "Little Grand Canyon"

Providence Canyon in Georgia is a gorgeous example of a canyon carved into deeply weathered soil, but it is also a dreadful example of poor soil management. In Figure a, in the canyon wall you can readily spot the dark brown A horizon, the bright red B horizon that is full of clay, and the paler E horizon. This is a good, productive soil, but unfortunately much of it has been washed away.

Some people call Providence Canyon the "Little Grand Canyon" because of its layered appearance, but in reality they are very different. The Grand Canyon was carved into sedimentary rock strata millions of years ago, by natural erosional processes. Providence Canyon is less than 200 years old; it, too, was formed by erosion but greatly accelerated by human activity.

There was no canyon here when settlers from Europe began farming in the early 1800s. The farmers plowed straight up and down the hills, and the furrows rapidly developed into gullies. By 1850, the gullies were 1 to 2 meters deep. The farmers had to abandon their fields, but by then, erosion in the gullies was running amok. The canyon is now more than 50 meters deep. Unfortunately, there are many such locations in North America.

a. Providence Canyon resulted from intense erosion of poorly managed agricultural fields.

In the early 20th century, scientists involved with erosion studies pointed out that water flowing in plowed land needed to be controlled. To fight erosion, farmers now use contour plowing (Figure b). Instead of going in straight lines downhill, the furrows follow the contour of the land. This slows runoff and inhibits the formation of gullies, helping to retain the topsoil on the field.

Kevin Horan/Stone/Getty Images, Inc.

Earthquake Magnitude and Damage

When you hear a radio report about an earthquake, there may seem to be little difference in the seriousness of magnitude 7 or 8 earthquakes. But in fact, the energy released in an earthquake increases exponentially with its magnitude. An earthquake of M7 releases about 32 times as much energy as a quake of M6. An earthquake of M8 releases 32 x 32, or 1000 times as much energy as a quake of M6. And an earthquake of M9, such as the Tōhoku earthquake, releases 32 x 32 x 32, or more than 32,000 times as much energy as a quake of M6. Note that the MMI scale and the moment and Richter magnitude scales are not directly comparable. Modified Mercalli intensity (MMI) differs with distance from the epicenter, whereas the moment and Richter magnitudes do not vary with distance. MMI is also a more subjective measure since it is based on felt and observed damage, whereas the moment and Richter magnitude scales are quantitative and exact.

©AP/Wide World Photos

Parkfield, CA, 2004

Magnitude: 6

Energy released: about the same as 1 atomic bomb

MMI: ≈ VII close to the epicenter

Damage on surface close to the epicenter: In determining the Mercalli Intensity of an M6 earthquake, such as the one that struck Parkfield, California, in 2004, a geologist would notice that some small objects have been broken, sleepers have wakened, and buildings are still standing but bricks have fallen from the walls.

Kobe, Japan, 1995

Magnitude: 7

Energy released: about the same as 32 atomic bombs

MMI: ≈ IX or X near the epicenter

Damage on surface close to the epicenter: The geologist would see that some buildings have shifted, some have collapsed, and damage has been severe. The presence of police suggests panic and the need for control.

©AP/Wide World Photos

San Francisco, CA, 1906

Magnitude: 8

Energy Released: about the same as 1000 atomic bombs

MMI: ≈ XI near the epicenter

Damage on surface close to the epicenter: Widespread destruction is clearly evident. With many buildings collapsed, thousands would be dead or injured in densely populated areas.

Waldemar Lindgren/NG Image Collection

THINK CRITICALLY

Might there be an upper limit to the possible magnitude of an earthquake? If so, what might cause this?

What a Geologist Sees highlights a concept or phenomenon that would stand out to a geologist. Photos and figures are used to improve students' understanding of the usefulness of a geology perspective and to develop their observational skills.

Think Critically questions let students analyze the material and develop insights into essential concepts.

Where Geologists CLICK

Google Earth: Earthquakes and Volcanoes

You can use Google Earth to explore the locations of earthquakes and active volcanoes relative to plate boundaries. First, you will need to download Google Earth to your laptop; it's free. In the menu at left, open "Layers" and then "Gallery." Click "Earthquakes" and "Volcanoes" to show these items on the map.

In the screen capture shown here, we are looking at recent earthquakes and volcanic activity in the Aleutian Islands, between Alaska and Siberia. The Aleutians are volcanic islands that mark a boundary between two plates. As you move through the chapter and learn more about plate boundaries, come back to this figure and see if you can determine what type of boundary it is, and which way the plates are moving. What is the relationship between the volcanic islands and the adjacent deep trench? What is the name of the process that is occurring here? Zoom to some other locations that you think would be tectonically active, and see what you find. Try the Red Sea, the San Andreas Fault, and the Himalaya Mountains to start.

Where Geologists Click showcases a website that professionals use and encourages students to try out its tools.

Monadnock—and Monadnocks

Mount Monadnock (Figure a), a 1156-meter peak in New Hampshire, is one of the world's most frequently climbed mountains—it is easy to climb, yet rewards the climber with a beautiful view of all six New England states. The name **monadnock**, from an Algonquin phrase meaning "mountain standing alone," has become a generic term for a mountain that rises out of a surrounding plain. (A term with similar meaning that is used more often by geologists is **inselberg**.)

© Denis Tangney Jr/iStockphoto

a

Monadnocks are isolated, either because they are unjointed or because they were made of more resistant material than the surrounding landmass. They can be made of any weathering-resistant rock type. Mount Monadnock is made of schist (a metamorphic rock). Another famous example, Uluru (or Ayers Rock), in Australia (Figure b), is made of arkose, a sedimentary rock. Uluru is a remnant of sedimentary strata about 500 million years old. During several periods of tectonic activity, the strata were twisted and uplifted to an almost vertical position. This can be seen in the aerial view of Uluru (Figure c), in which the edges of the vertical strata are visible. After being uplifted, the surrounding rock—less resistant to weathering—was rapidly weathered and eroded away. The part of Uluru that is visible above the surface is just the tip of a much larger rock mass that extends deep underground.

Richard Nowitz/NG Image Collection

b

c

The **Amazing Places** sections take the student to a unique place that provides a vivid illustration of a concept in the chapter. Students could easily visit most of the Amazing Places someday and so continue their geologic education.

GeoDiscoveries Media Library is an interactive media source of animations, simulations, and interactivities allowing instructors to visually demonstrate key concepts in greater depth.

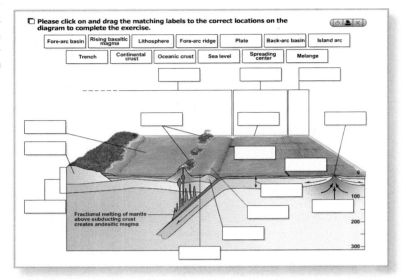

☐ Please click on and drag the matching labels to the correct locations on the diagram to complete the exercise.

| Fore-arc basin | Rising basaltic magma | Lithosphere | Fore-arc ridge | Plate | Back-arc basin | Island arc |

| Trench | Continental crust | Oceanic crust | Sea level | Spreading center | Melange |

Fractional melting of mantle above subducting crust creates andesitic magma

0
100
200
300

CONCEPT CHECK   **STOP**

1. **What** physical and chemical changes happen in rock undergoing metamorphism?

2. **What** distinguishes burial metamorphism from regional metamorphism?

3. **How** does regional metamorphism in a subduction zone differ from regional metamorphism in a collision zone?

4. **What** process changes the chemical composition of a rock, rather than just its texture or mineral assemblage?

Coordinated with the section-opening **Learning Objectives**, at the end of each section **Concept Check** questions allow students to test their comprehension of the learning objectives.

Student understanding is assessed at different levels

Wiley Visualizing with *WileyPLUS* offers students lots of practice material for assessing their understanding of each study objective. Students know exactly what they are getting out of each study session through immediate feedback and coaching.

The **Summary** revisits each major section, with informative images taken from the chapter. These visuals reinforce important concepts.

SUMMARY ✓ THE PLANNER

1 Earthquakes and Earthquake Hazards 107

• **Seismology** relates earthquakes to the processes of plate tectonics. Although the motion of tectonic plates is very gradual, friction causes the rocks in the crust to jam together for long periods and then to break suddenly and lurch forward, causing an earthquake to occur. Earthquakes can cause large vertical or horizontal displacements of the ground, but much of the damage they cause results from the violent shaking that accompanies the displacement.

• The shaking motion experienced during an earthquake can be explained by the **elastic rebound model**, which says that the energy stored in bent and deformed rocks is released as **seismic waves**. After an earthquake, the rocks return to their undeformed state.

• In many cases the destructiveness of earthquakes is magnified by secondary hazards, such as fires, landslides, liquefaction (see the photo), and tsunamis. Proper building design and earthquake preparedness can greatly reduce the loss of life from earthquakes and secondary hazards.

Secondary hazards: Ground liquefaction • Figure 5.4

Courtesy NOAA/NGDC

• Short-term forecasting of earthquakes is still very unreliable. Scientists have concentrated their efforts on finding precursor phenomena, such as foreshocks, but with limited success. However, long-term forecasting can provide a good idea of which regions are at risk. One of the main tools of long-term forecasting is **paleoseismology**, which reveals when past earthquakes occurred in a given region, as well as the periodicity and magnitudes of past earthquakes.

2 The Science of Seismology 115

• **Seismographs** produce recordings of seismic waves that are called **seismograms**. In a basic seismograph (see the diagram), a pen is attached to a heavy suspended mass. Seismic waves cause the paper to shake while the pen stays still and traces a wavy line on the vibrating paper.

Seismograph • Figure 5.7

• Earthquakes produce three main types of seismic waves: **compressional waves**, or P waves (primary waves); **shear waves**, or S waves (secondary waves); and a variety of **surface waves**. Compressional and shear waves are called **body waves** because they travel through Earth's interior.

• Compressional waves travel faster than shear waves and hence arrive at seismographs first. The difference in arrival times between the P and S waves allows seismologists to compute the distance, but not the direction, to the **focus** of an earthquake. To determine the precise location of the **epicenter**, seismologists need measurements from three separate seismic stations. They can then determine the location by triangulation.

• The Richter and moment **magnitude** scales are measures of earthquake intensity that can be determined regardless of the distance to the earthquake or the amount of damage done. Both are logarithmic scales, in which each unit of magnitude corresponds roughly to a 10-fold increase in the amplitudes of seismic waves, but a 32-fold increase in the amount of energy released by the earthquake. The Modified Mercalli Intensity scale is a descriptive scale based on the extent of earthquake damage. On the MMI scale, the intensity is highest near the epicenter.

Critical and Creative Thinking Questions challenge students to think more broadly about chapter concepts. The level of these questions ranges from simple to advanced; they encourage students to think critically and develop an analytical understanding of the ideas discussed in the chapter.

CRITICAL AND CREATIVE THINKING QUESTIONS

1. How did sea-surface temperatures at the peak of the last glaciation differ from those of the present? Why do you think some regions of the ocean have shown more change than others? What influence would these changes have had on atmospheric circulation and weather?

2. How can isotopic analyses of deep-sea sediment reveal changes in global ice volumes?

3. At the height of the most recent ice age, vegetation in North America south of the ice front must have been very different from the vegetation today. Do some research and find out what is known of vegetation changes in your area over the past 20,000 years.

6. Consider the maps in Figure 14.18 a and b. On the left is RCP 2.6, the "peak and decline" scenario for CO_2 emissions; on the right is RCP 8.5, the "continued high emissions" scenario. Locate your home region on the maps. What do the projections hold for RCP 2.6 in this location? Wetter? Warmer? Cooler? Drier? By how much? How different is the RCP 8.5 projection for this location?

Projected effects of increases in atmospheric CO_2 • Figure 14.18

RCP 2.6   RCP 8.5
Change in average surface temperature (1986–2005 to 2081–2100)

What is happening in this picture? presents a photograph that is relevant to a chapter topic and illustrates a situation students are not likely to have encountered previously.

WHAT IS HAPPENING IN THIS PICTURE?

From September 14 to October 4, 2005, a series of earthquakes and eruptions in the Afar Desert in Ethiopia opened up the rift seen in this photograph, which is 60 meters wide at its widest point. The rift is part of a much more extensive depression where two plates, the African and the Somalian plates, are spreading apart. (Older rifts can also be seen in the background.) Compare this photo to the map and satellite image in this chapter's *What a Geologist Sees*.

THINK CRITICALLY
What will happen to Ethiopia if the spreading continues?

Think Critically questions ask students to apply what they have learned in order to interpret and explain what they observe in the image.

SELF-TEST

(Check your answers in Appendix D.)

1. The work of geologists over the years has supported Wegener's contention that the current continental masses were assembled into a single supercontinent, which Wegener called _____.

   a. Pangaea   d. Tethys
   b. Transantarctica   e. Laurasia
   c. Gondwana

2. Which of the following lines of evidence supporting continental drift did Wegener not use when he first proposed his hypothesis?

   a. the apparent fit of the continental margins of Africa and South America
   b. ancient glacial deposits of the southern hemisphere
   c. the apparent polar wandering of the magnetic north pole
   d. the close match of ancient geology between West Africa and Brazil
   e. the close match of ancient fossils on continents separated by ocean basins

3. Analysis of apparent polar wandering paths led geophysicists to conclude _____.

   a. that Earth's magnetic poles have wandered all over the globe in the past several hundred million years
   b. that the continents had moved because it is known that the magnetic poles themselves are essentially fixed

   c. that the apparent wandering path of a continent provides a historical record of the position of that continent over time
   d. Both b and c are correct.

4. _____ is the process through which oceanic crust splits and moves apart along a midocean ridge and new oceanic crust forms.

   a. Continental drift   c. Seafloor spreading
   b. Paleomagnetism   d. Continental rifting

5. This map shows the age of the seafloor, across the northern extent of the Atlantic Ocean. The Mid-Atlantic Ridge can be seen stretching roughly north–south (in the yellow band) down the middle of the map. Yellow through red colors show rocks of similar age. Number them on the map from 1 (oldest) through 5 (youngest).

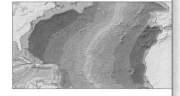

Visual end-of-chapter **Self-Tests** pose review questions that ask students to demonstrate their understanding of key concepts.

WHY *VISUALIZING GEOLOGY 4E?*

The goal of *Visualizing Geology 4e* is to introduce students to geology and Earth system science through the distinctive mode of visual learning that is the hallmark of the Wiley Visualizing series. Students will learn that the geologic features we see and experience result from interactions among three grand cycles, which extend from Earth's core to the fringes of our atmosphere: the tectonic cycle, the rock cycle, and the water cycle. We place special emphasis on plate tectonics because it is an organizing principle and a framework that unifies our understanding of geologic activity on our planet.

Case studies throughout the book bring the science of geology into focus in students' everyday lives. We fit current events into a larger picture that explains how Earth works and why such events happen. Students will also learn about how human actions affect Earth systems and vice versa. The unique format of Wiley Visualizing allows us to reinforce the textual content with arresting images that are, in many cases, the next best thing to being there. Geology invites us to travel outside our familiar environment to distant parts of the world. As in previous editions of *Visualizing Geology*, we have had access to some of the best photos, photographers, and photo researchers in the industry. With such a terrific photography and art program, and with features such as *Amazing Places* and *What A Geologist Sees* in every chapter, we seek to instill what words sometimes cannot: a sense of wonder about the planet we call home.

Organization

Visualizing Geology 4e is organized as follows:

- In Chapters 1 through 4 we outline Earth system science as an approach to the study of our planet and our environment. We describe the various kinds of rocks and minerals, explain the ways in which geologists learn about Earth's changes over time, and present the unifying theory of plate tectonics.

- In Chapters 5 and 6 we discuss the hazards of earthquakes and volcanoes and explain how they relate to the tectonic cycle, and the formation of magma, lava, and igneous rock.

- Chapters 7 through 10 describe the major processes of the rock cycle—weathering, erosion, sedimentation, lithification, and metamorphism. In addition, students will learn about folding, faulting, and structural geology, and the basics of geologic maps and cross-sections.

- In Chapters 11 through 13 we turn our attention to the water cycle and explain the ubiquitous effects of water on Earth's surface, underground, and in the atmosphere. We devote a full chapter to deserts and glaciers, the two

extreme environments that in recent years have become bellwethers of climate change.

- In Chapter 14 we address the record of climate changes, with up-to-date figures, data, and analysis from the IPCC 5th Assessment Report.

- Finally, Chapters 15 and 16 reintegrate the various parts of the Earth system to draw conclusions about two topics of great interest to students and to society as a whole: the history of life on Earth, and the future of the natural resources on which humanity depends.

Changes in the New Edition

The fourth edition has been updated and modified in response to suggestions and reviews by many of our users. We have added many new examples and case studies; refreshed almost all of the *Where A Geologist Clicks* resources; added new material to the Instructor Resources and student Self-Test Questions; and expanded, deepened, and updated the coverage on many topics.

Remember This! is a new feature that appears several times in each chapter, inviting students to think about the connections between the topics in that chapter and previous chapters of the book. It is extremely important for students to think beyond the structure imposed by the book's chapters, to appreciate the fundamental connections between various Earth processes. New *Ask Yourself* and *Think Critically* exercises also will help students develop their critical analytical skills. And of course, as usual, we have added a number of new *Amazing Places*, chapter-opening vignettes, and *Case Studies*.

We have added new vocabulary terms to our basic Glossary, while retaining our goal of avoiding unnecessarily terminology-heavy language. We also have compiled a Glossary of "Level 2" terms—the terms that are italicized (rather than bolded) throughout the book—and these will be available for use by instructors who want to raise the level of scientific terminology in their courses.

This book is intended as a textbook for an introductory college-level course in geology; it is also used in senior high school-level courses. We try to keep the writing accessible and engaging, but rigorous. Because our emphasis is on physical processes, the book could be used as well for an introductory physical geology or physical geography course. We do not expect that most of the students who read this book will go on to become geologists, but we hope that all readers will come to have a better understanding of, and appreciation for, their home planet. For those students do who want to take further courses in geology—and we hope there are many—we aim to provide a solid, sufficient, and challenging background to do so with confidence.

– the Authors

HOW DOES WILEY VISUALIZING SUPPORT INSTRUCTORS?

Wiley Visualizing Site

The Wiley Visualizing site hosts a wealth of information for instructors using Wiley Visualizing, including ways to maximize the visual approach in the classroom and a white paper titled "How Visuals Can Help Students Learn," by Matt Leavitt, instructional design consultant. Visit Wiley Visualizing at www.wiley.com/college/visualizing.

Wiley Custom Select

Wiley Custom Select gives you the freedom to build your course materials exactly the way you want them. Offer your students a cost-efficient alternative to traditional texts. In a simple three-step process create a solution containing the content you want, in the sequence you want, delivered how you want. Visit Wiley Custom Select at http://customselect.wiley.com.

Book Companion Site www.wiley.com/college/murck

All instructor resources (the Test Bank, PowerPoint presentations, and all textbook illustrations and photos available as chapter PowerPoint slides) are housed on the book companion site (www.wiley.com/college/murck). Student resources include self-quizzes and flashcards.

PowerPoint Presentations

(available in *WileyPLUS* and on the book companion site)

A complete set of highly visual PowerPoint presentations—one per chapter—by Karen Savage, California State University, Northridge, and revised for the fourth edition by Amy Mui, University of Toronto, is available online and in *WileyPLUS* to enhance classroom presentations. Tailored to the text's topical coverage and learning objectives, these presentations are designed to convey key text concepts, illustrated by embedded text art. We offer three different types of PowerPoint presentations for each chapter: PowerPoints with just the text art and PowerPoints with text art and presentation notes.

Test Bank (available in *WileyPLUS* and on the book companion site)

The visuals from the textbook are also included in the Test Bank by Richard Josephs, Plymouth State University, who also authored the Pre-Lecture Clicker questions. The Test Bank has a diverse selection of test items, including multiple-choice and essay questions, with at least 20 percent of them incorporating visuals from the book. The test bank is available online in MS Word files, and within *WileyPLUS*.

Art PowerPoints

All photographs, figures, maps, and other visuals from the text are online and in *WileyPLUS* and can be used as you wish in the classroom. These online electronic files allow you to easily incorporate images into your PowerPoint presentations as you choose, or to create your own handouts.

HOW HAS WILEY VISUALIZING BEEN SHAPED BY CONTRIBUTORS?

Wiley Visualizing and the *WileyPLUS* learning environment would not have come about without lots of people, each of whom played a part in sharing their research and contributing to this new approach.

Academic Research Consultants

Richard Mayer, Professor of Psychology, UC Santa Barbara. His *Cognitive Theory of Multimedia Learning* provided the basis on which we designed our program. He continues to provide guidance to our author and editorial teams on how to develop and implement strong, pedagogically effective visuals and use them in the classroom.

Jan L. Plass, Professor of Educational Communication and Technology in the Steinhardt School of Culture, Education, and Human Development at New York University. He co-directs the NYU Games for Learning Institute and is the founding director of the CREATE: Consortium for

Research and Evaluation of Advanced Technology in Education.

Matthew Leavitt, Instructional Design Consultant. He advises the Visualizing team on the effective design and use of visuals in instruction and has made virtual and live presentations to university faculty around the country regarding effective design and use of instructional visuals.

Independent Research Studies

SEG Research, an independent research and assessment firm, conducted a national, multisite effectiveness study of students enrolled in entry-level college Psychology and Geology courses. The study was designed to evaluate the effectiveness of Wiley Visualizing. You can view the full research paper at www.wiley.com/college/visualizing/huffman/efficacy.html.

Instructor and Student Contributions

Throughout the process of developing the concept of guided visual pedagogy for Wiley Visualizing, we benefited from the comments and constructive criticism provided by the instructors and colleagues listed below. We offer our sincere appreciation to these individuals for their helpful reviews and general feedback:

Visualizing Reviewers, Focus Group Participants, and Survey Respondents

James Abbott, Temple University
Melissa Acevedo, Westchester Community College
Shiva Achet, Roosevelt University
Denise Addorisio, Westchester Community College
Dave Alan, University of Phoenix
Sue Allen-Long, Indiana University Purdue
Robert Amey, Bridgewater State College
Nancy Bain, Ohio University
Corinne Balducci, Westchester Community College
Steve Barnhart, Middlesex County Community College
Stefan Becker, University of Washington—Oshkosh
Callan Bentley, NVCC Annandale
Valerie Bergeron, Delaware Technical & Community College
Andrew Berns, Milwaukee Area Technical College
Gregory Bishop, Orange Coast College
Rebecca Boger, Brooklyn College
Scott Brame, Clemson University
Joan Brandt, Central Piedmont Community College
Richard Brinn, Florida International University
Jim Bruno, University of Phoenix
William Chamberlin, Fullerton College
Oiyin Pauline Chow, Harrisburg Area Community College
Laurie Corey, Westchester Community College
Ozeas Costas, Ohio State University at Mansfield
Christopher Di Leonardo, Foothill College
Dani Ducharme, Waubonsee Community College
Mark Eastman, Diablo Valley College

Ben Elman, Baruch College
Staussa Ervin, Tarrant County College
Michael Farabee, Estrella Mountain Community College
Laurie Flaherty, Eastern Washington University
Susan Fuhr, Maryville College
Peter Galvin, Indiana University at Southeast
Andrew Getzfeld, New Jersey City University
Janet Gingold, Prince George's Community College
Donald Glassman, Des Moines Area Community College
Richard Goode, Porterville College
Peggy Green, Broward Community College
Stelian Grigoras, Northwood University
Paul Grogger, University of Colorado
Michael Hackett, Westchester Community College
Duane Hampton, Western Michigan University
Thomas Hancock, Eastern Washington University
Gregory Harris, Polk State College
John Haworth, Chattanooga State Technical Community College
James Hayes-Bohanan, Bridgewater State College
Peter Ingmire, San Francisco State University
Mark Jackson, Central Connecticut State University
Heather Jennings, Mercer County Community College
Eric Jerde, Morehead State University
Jennifer Johnson, Ferris State University
Richard Kandus, Mt. San Jacinto College District
Christopher Kent, Spokane Community College
Gerald Ketterling, North Dakota State University
Lynnel Kiely, Harold Washington College
Eryn Klosko, Westchester Community College
Cary T. Komoto, University of Wisconsin—Barron County
John Kupfer, University of South Carolina
Nicole Lafleur, University of Phoenix
Arthur Lee, Roane State Community College
Mary Lynam, Margrove College
Heidi Marcum, Baylor University
Beth Marshall, Washington State University
Dr. Theresa Martin, Eastern Washington University
Charles Mason, Morehead State University
Susan Massey, Art Institute of Philadelphia
Linda McCollum, Eastern Washington University
Mary L. Meiners, San Diego Miramar College
Shawn Mikulay, Elgin Community College
Cassandra Moe, Century Community College
Lynn Hanson Mooney, Art Institute of Charlotte
Kristy Moreno, University of Phoenix
Jacob Napieralski, University of Michigan—Dearborn
Gisele Nasar, Brevard Community College, Cocoa Campus
Daria Nikitina, West Chester University
Robin O'Quinn, Eastern Washington University
Richard Orndorff, Eastern Washington University
Sharen Orndorff, Eastern Washington University
Clair Ossian, Tarrant County College
Debra Parish, North Harris Montgomery Community
    College District
Linda Peters, Holyoke Community College
Robin Popp, Chattanooga State Technical Community College
Michael Priano, Westchester Community College
Alan "Paul" Price, University of Wisconsin—Washington County
Max Reams, Olivet Nazarene University
Mary Celeste Reese, Mississippi State University
Bruce Rengers, Metropolitan State College of Denver
Guillermo Rocha, Brooklyn College
Penny Sadler, College of William and Mary
Shamili Sandiford, College of DuPage

Thomas Sasek, University of Louisiana at Monroe
Donna Seagle, Chattanooga State Technical Community College
Diane Shakes, College of William and Mary
Jennie Silva, Louisiana State University
Michael Siola, Chicago State University
Morgan Slusher, Community College of Baltimore County
Julia Smith, Eastern Washington University
Darlene Smucny, University of Maryland University College
Jeff Snyder, Bowling Green State University
Alice Stefaniak, St. Xavier University
Alicia Steinhardt, Hartnell Community College
Kurt Stellwagen, Eastern Washington University
Charlotte Stromfors, University of Phoenix
Shane Strup, University of Phoenix
Donald Thieme, Georgia Perimeter College
Pamela Thinesen, Century Community College
Chad Thompson, Westchester Community College
Lensyl Urbano, University of Memphis
Gopal Venugopal, Roosevelt University
Daniel Vogt, University of Washington—College of Forest Resources
Dr. Laura J. Vosejpka, Northwood University
Brenda L. Walker, Kirkwood Community College
Stephen Wareham, Cal State Fullerton
Fred William Whitford, Montana State University

Katie Wiedman, University of St. Francis
Harry Williams, University of North Texas
Emily Williamson, Mississippi State University
Bridget Wyatt, San Francisco State University
Van Youngman, Art Institute of Philadelphia
Alexander Zemcov, Westchester Community College

Student Participants

Karl Beall, Eastern Washington University
Jessica Bryant, Eastern Washington University
Pia Chawla, Westchester Community College
Channel DeWitt, Eastern Washington University
Lucy DiAroscia, Westchester Community College
Heather Gregg, Eastern Washington University
Lindsey Harris, Eastern Washington University
Brenden Hayden, Eastern Washington University
Patty Hosner, Eastern Washington University
Tonya Karunartue, Eastern Washington University
Sydney Lindgren, Eastern Washington University
Michael Maczuga, Westchester Community College
Melissa Michael, Eastern Washington University
Estelle Rizzin, Westchester Community College
Andrew Rowley, Eastern Washington University
Eric Torres, Westchester Community College
Joshua Watson, Eastern Washington University

ACKNOWLEDGMENTS

Our sincere appreciation to the following professionals who provided valuable feedback and suggestions for the first, second, third, and fourth editions of *Visualizing Geology*:

Laura Sue Allen-Long *Indiana University–Purdue University, Indianapolis*
Sylvester Allred *Northern Arizona University*
Laurie Anderson *Louisiana State University*
Jake Armour *University of North Carolina, Charlotte*
Jerry Bartholomew *University of Memphis*
Jay D. Bass *University of Illinois at Urbana-Champaign*
David Basterdo *San Bernardino Valley College*
Barbara Bekken *Virginia Polytechnic and State University*
Gregory Bishop *Orange Coast College*
Ross A. Black *University of Kansas*
Rebecca Boger *Brooklyn College*
Theodore J. Bornhorst *Michigan Technological University*
Michael Bradley *Eastern Michigan University*
Ann Brandt-Williams *Glendale Community College*
Natalie Bursztyn *Bakersfield College*
Michael Canestaro *Sinclair Community College*

Richard L. Carlson *Texas A&M University*
Victor V. Cavatroc *Northern Carolina State University*
Stan Celestian *Glendale Community College*
Chu-Yen Chen *University of Illinois at Urbana-Champaign*
Nehru Cherukupalli *Brooklyn College*
O. Pauline Chow *Harrisburg Area Community College*
Diane Clemens-Knott *California State University, Fullerton*
Mitchell Colgan *College of Charleston*
Constantin Cranganu *Brooklyn CUNY*
Dee Cooper *University of Texas*
Cathy Connor *University of Alaska Southeast*
Peter Copeland *University of Houston*
Linda Crow *Montgomery College*
Michael Dalman *Blinn College*
John Dassinger *Chandler-Gilbert Community College*
Smruti Desai *Cy-Fair College*
Chris DiLeonardo *Foothill College*
Charles Dick *Pasco-Hernando Community College*

W. Crawford Elliott *Georgia State University*
Robert Eves *Southern Utah University*
Mike Farabee *Estrella Mountain Community College*
Mark Feigenson *Rutgers University*
Lynn Fielding *El Camino College*
David Foster *University of Florida*
Carol D. Frost *University of Wyoming*
Tracy Furutani *North Seattle Community College*
Yongli Gao *East Tennessee State University*
William Garcia *University of North Carolina at Charlotte*
Donald Glassman *Des Moines Area Community College*
Richard Goode *Porterville College*
Pamela Gore *Georgia Perimeter College*
Mark Grobner *California State University, Stanislaus*
Paul Grogger *University of Colorado, Colorado Springs*
Erich Guy *Ohio University*
Daniel Habib *Queens College*
Michael Hackett *Westchester Community College*

Duane Hampton *Western Michigan University*
Gale Haigh *McNeese State University*
Duane Hampton *Western Michigan University*
Roger Hangarter *Indiana University–Purdue University, Indianapolis*
Michael Harman *North Harris College*
Frederika Harmsen *California State University, Fresno*
Michael J. Harrison *Tennessee Technological University*
Terry Harrison *Arapahoe Community College*
Javier Hasbun *University of West Georgia*
Michael J. Harrison *Tennessee Tech University*
Stephen Hasiotis *University of Kansas*
Adam Hayashi *Central Florida Community College*
Dan Hembree *Ohio University*
Mary Anne Holmes *University of Nebraska, Lincoln*
William Hoyt *University of Northern Colorado*
Laura Hubbard *University of California, Berkeley*
James Hutcheon *Georgia Southern University*
Scott Jeffrey *Community College of Baltimore County, Catonsville Campus*
Eric Jerde *Morehead State University*
Verner Johnson *Mesa State College*
Marie Johnson *U.S. Military Academy*
Richard Josephs *University of North Dakota*
Amanda Julson *Blinn College*
Matthew Kapell *Wayne State University*
Arnold Karpoff *University of Louisville*

Alan Kehew *Western Michigan University*
Dale Lambert *Tarrant County College, Northeast*
Arthur Lee *Roane State Community College*
Harvey Liftin *Broward Community College*
Walter Little *University at Albany, SUNY*
Steven Lower *Ohio State University*
Ntungwa Maasha *Coastal Georgia Community College*
Ronald Martino *Marshall University*
Anthony Martorana *Chandler-Gilbert Community College*
Charles Mason *Morehead State University*
Ryan Mathur *Juniata College*
Brendan McNulty *California State University, Dominguez Hills*
Joseph Meert *University of Florida*
Mary Anne Meiners *San Diego Miramar College*
Erik Melchiorre *California State University, San Bernardino*
Ken Miller *Rutgers University*
Scott Miller *Penn State University*
Katherine Miller *Florida A&M University*
Keith Montgomery *University of Wisconsin—Marathon*
David Morris *Valdosta State University*
Jane Murphy *Virginia College Online*
Bethany Myers *Wichita State University*
Jacob Napieralski *University of Michigan, Dearborn*
Pamela Nelson *Glendale Community College*
Terri Oltman *Westwood College*
Keith Prufer *Wichita State University*
Steve Ralser *University of Wisconsin—Madison*
Kenneth Rasmussen *Northern Virginia Community College*

Guillermo Rocha *Brooklyn College*
Gary D. Rosenburg *Indiana University–Purdue University*
Ian Saginor *Keystone College*
Karen Savage *California State University, Northridge*
Steve Schimmrich *SUNY Ulster County Community College*
Laura Sherrod *Kutztown University*
Bruce Simonson *Oberlin College*
Jay Simms *University of Arkansas at Little Rock*
Jeff Snyder *Bowling Green State University*
Ann Somers *University of North Carolina, Greensboro*
Debra Stakes *Cuesta College*
Alycia Stigall *Ohio University*
Donald Thieme *Georgia Perimeter College*
Carol Thompson *Tarleton State University*
Kip Thompson *Ozarks Technical Community College*
Heyo Van Iten *Hanover College*
Judy Voelker *Northern Kentucky University*
Arthur Washington *Florida A&M University*
Karen When *Buffalo State University*
Harry Williams *University of North Texas*
Stephen Williams *Glendale Community College*
Feranda Williamson *Capella University*
Thomas C. Wynn *Lock Haven University*
Arif Sikder *Virginia Commonwealth University*
Beth Christensen *Adelphi University*
Stacy Verardo *George Mason University*
Stephen Altaner *University of Illinois Urbana*

ABOUT THE AUTHORS

Barbara Murck is a geologist and associate professor in environmental science at the University of Toronto Mississauga. She completed her undergraduate degree in Geological and Geophysical Sciences at Princeton University and then spent two years in the Peace Corps in West Africa, before returning to Ph.D. studies at the University of Toronto. Her subsequent teaching and research has involved an interesting combination of geology, natural hazards, environmental science, and environmental issues in the developing world, primarily in Africa and Asia. She also carries out practical research on pedagogy. She is an award-winning lecturer who has coauthored a number of books, including several with Brian Skinner.

Brian Skinner was born and raised in Australia, studied at the University of Adelaide in South Australia, worked in the mining industry in Tasmania, and in 1951 entered the Graduate School of Arts and Sciences, Harvard University, from which he obtained his Ph.D. in 1954. Following a period as a research scientist in the United States Geological Survey in Washington D.C., he joined the faculty at Yale in 1966, where he continues his teaching and research as the Eugene Higgins Professor of Geology and Geophysics. Brian Skinner has been president of the Geochemical Society, the Geological Society of America, and the Society of Economic Geologists. He holds an honorary Doctor of Science from the University of Toronto and an honorary Doctor of Engineering from the Colorado School of Mines.

THANKS FOR PARTICIPATING IN A SPECIAL PROJECT

The *Visualizing* series continues to grow, and continues to meet the needs of students and professors in the U.S., Canada, and around the world. The groundbreaking series, demonstrated to improve student learning and engagement, now includes 14 titles, three of them in their fourth edition. With the fourth edition of *Visualizing Geology*, we know that we will find many new ways to engage and inspire our readers.

As usual, many highly professional colleagues at John Wiley & Sons and associated organizations have contributed their efforts and expertise to this book, and we owe them all a huge debt of gratitude. All of these people have been so helpful and so involved, it is difficult to single out any one of them—but we will do it anyway. We just want give a little shout-out to Ryan Flahive as he bids farewell to Geology and Geography to move to his new home as Executive Editor in Biology. We'll miss you, Ryan!

It was great to cross paths with so many great people who have worked on previous projects with the two of us. Some of you we have pestered and irritated more than others (John Curley and Mary Ann Price come to mind). Each person named here has made thoughtful, timely, professional, and often meticulous contributions to making this the best edition yet of *Visualizing Geology*. Thank you so much for your contributions and support:

Petra Recter, Vice President and Director for Market Solutions
Ryan Flahive, Executive Editor
Jessica Fiorillo, Executive Editor
Gladys Soto, Project Manager, Market Solutions
Kathryn Hancox, Market Solutions Assistant
Christina Volpe, Associate Editor
Elle Wagner, Senior Content Manager
John Curley, Senior Production Editor
Mary Ann Price, Senior Photo Editor
Nancy Perry, Product Development Manager
Wendy Lai, Senior Designer
Thomas Nery, Cover Designer
Jessica Zahorian, Content Technology Specialist
Suzanne Schilit, Media Specialist
Christine Kushner, Executive Marketing Manager
Geraldine Osnato, Senior Product Designer
Sofia Buono, Project Manager at codeMantra
Betty Pessagno, Copy Editor
Christine Cervoni, Proofreader at Camelot Editorial Services, LLC
Amy Mui, University of Toronto, Instructional Resources Developer

We also would like to acknowledge the input of our many professional colleagues in geology, who read, thought about, and offered advice on the third edition and our plans for the fourth edition revisions. They are thanked and named elsewhere, but we authors want to thank them for their invaluable contributions. Their input has made the book stronger.

And finally—last, but certainly not least—many thanks to our families for once again putting up with the obsessive focus that is required to bring a project of this complexity to completion. At least it keeps us out of trouble!

– Brian Skinner and Barbara Murck

Contents in Brief

Contents

James P. Blair/ NG Image Collection

Stephen Alvarez/NG Image Collection

Emory Kristof/NG Images Collection

O. Louis Mazzatenta/National Geographic/
NG Image Collection

NASA

©Krafft Explorer/Photo Researchers

Paul C. Dennis/Lost Trio Hiking Association

Robert Sisson/NG Image Collection

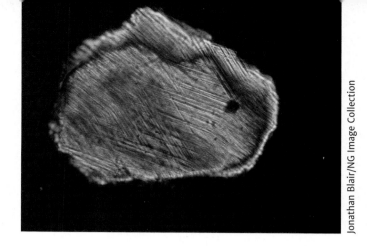

Jonathan Blair/NG Image Collection

Joachim P. Muller

Patrick McFeeley/NG Image Collection

Michael Nichols/NG Image Collection

James L. Stanfield/NG Image Collection

LOOK Die Bildagentur der Fotografen GmbH/Alamy

O. Louis Mazzatenta/NG Image Collection

Marc Moritsch/
NG Image Collection

16 | Understanding Earth's Resources 446

Amazing Places

In every chapter in this book, we take you to an "Amazing Place" that is both beautiful and of geologic interest.

Here is our itinerary:

Chapter 1: Meteorite Impact Craters, to see evidence of the way Earth was assembled

Chapter 2: Naica Mine in Chihuahua, Mexico, for a look at the world's largest crystals

Chapter 3: Famous Unconformities, to see evidence of ancient uplift and erosion

Chapter 4: The Hawaiian Islands, to see plate tectonics and volcanoes in action

Chapter 5: Point Reyes, California, to explore the most famous fault in America, the San Andreas fault

Chapter 6: Sierra Nevada Batholith and Yosemite National Park, for examples of processes that formed the batholith

Chapter 7: Mt. Monadnock—and Monadnocks, for a look at the power of erosion

Chapter 8: The Navajo Sandstone, for its beautiful sedimentary rock formations

Chapter 9: The Canadian Rockies, for spectacular examples of folding and thrusting

Chapter 10: The Source of Olmec jade, for evidence of high-pressure metamorphism

Chapter 11: Lechuguilla Cave, in New Mexico, for incredible shapes made by groundwater

Chapter 12: The Florida Keys Reef, to visit a geologic formation that is also alive

Chapter 13: The Northwest Passage, Alaska, to explore the successful and unsuccessful sailings through the centuries

Chapter 14: Fossil Forests of the High Arctic, to see remarkable preservation of forests that grew in the now-frozen north

Chapter 15: The Burgess Shale, for its fossil record of the first animals on Earth

Chapter 16: Saugus Iron Works, Massachusetts, to see the first iron-smelting operation in North America

The most amazing place of all, however, is Earth itself—the only world in the universe where we know that life exists.

NASA

1 EARTH AS A PLANET

Goddard Institute for SpaceStudies/NASA

☑ CHAPTER PLANNER

- Study the picture and read the opening story.
- Scan the Learning Objectives in each section:
  p. 2   p. 12   p. 20
- Read the text and study all visuals. Answer any questions.

Analyze key features
- Geology Insight, p. 3
- What a Geologist Sees, p. 8
- Case Study, p. 11
- Process Diagram, p. 14
  p. 17   p. 22
- Amazing Places, p. 16
- Stop: Answer the Concept Checks before you go on:
  p. 12   p. 19   p. 24

End of chapter
- Review the Summary and Key Terms.
- Answer the Critical and Creative Thinking Questions.
- Answer What is happening in this picture?
- Complete the Self-Test and check your answers.

THE BLUE MARBLE

Photographs of Earth from space have profoundly influenced our thoughts about Earth. Getting a whole-Earth photograph is difficult—planes don't do the job; you must be out in space, and the Sun has to be directly behind the camera so that Earth is shadow free. A striking whole-Earth photograph was taken by the *Apollo 17* astronauts on their way to the Moon in 1972. When they were 45,000 kilometers out, they looked back, and there was the fully illuminated Earth, like a blue marble suspended in space. The name stuck. NASA now has a stunning group of whole-Earth images called the Blue Marble series.

This particular version of a blue marble image was obtained in 1997. It is one of the most detailed images ever made of Earth. There is a huge storm off the west coast of North America—it is Hurricane Linda—and the Moon is rising over Earth in the upper left. Hurricane Linda reminds us that the different parts of Earth—rocks, water, atmosphere, living things—all interact. The Moon reminds us that Earth is a member of the solar system. To know Earth, we must understand its parts and the system to which it belongs.

WHAT IS GEOLOGY?

Learning Objectives

1. **Describe** some of the branches of geology.

2. **Explain** how scientists use the scientific method.

3. **Explain** what is meant by a systems approach to geology.

4. **Explain** how Earth's major subsystems interact, using the concept of cycles.

The word **geology** comes from two Greek roots: *geo-,* meaning "Earth," and *logis,* meaning "study" or "science." The science called geology encompasses the study of our planet: how it formed; the nature of its interior; the materials of which it is composed; its water, glaciers, mountains, and deserts; its earthquakes and volcanoes; its resources; and its history—physical, chemical, and biological. Scientists who make a career of geology are geologists. Geology, like all other sciences, is based on factual observations, testable hypotheses, reproducible procedures, and open communication of information.

> **geology** The scientific study of Earth.

The Branches of Geology

The study of geology is traditionally divided into two broad subject areas: physical geology and historical geology. **Physical geology** is concerned with understanding the *processes* that operate at or beneath the surface of Earth and the *materials* on which those processes operate. Some examples of geologic processes are mountain building, volcanic eruptions, earthquakes, river flooding, and the formation of ore deposits. Some examples of materials are minerals, soils, rocks, air, and water.

Historical geology, on the other hand, is concerned with the sequence of *events* that have occurred in the past. These events can be inferred from the evidence left in Earth's rocks. Through the findings of historical geology, scientists seek to resolve questions such as the following: When did the oceans form? Why did the dinosaurs die out? When did the Rocky Mountains rise? and When and where did the first trees appear? Historical geology gives us a perspective on the past. It also establishes a context for thinking about present-day changes in our natural environment. This book is concerned mainly with physical geology, but it includes many lessons we can learn from historical geology.

Within the traditional domains of physical and historical geology are many specialized disciplines, some of which are illustrated in **Figure 1.1**. Economic geology, for example, is concerned with the formation and occurrence of, and the search for, valuable mineral deposits. Environmental geology focuses on how materials and processes in the natural geologic environment affect—and are affected by—human activities. Volcanologists study volcanoes and eruptions, past and present; seismologists study earthquakes; mineralogists undertake the microscopic study of minerals and crystals; paleontologists study fossils and the history of life on Earth; structural geologists study how rocks break and bend. These specialties are needed because geology encompasses a broad range of topics.

To a certain extent we are all geologists, even though only a few of us make a career out of geology. Everyone living on this planet relies on geologic resources: water, soil, building stones, metals, fossil fuels, gemstones, plastics (from petroleum), ceramics (from clay minerals), glass (from silica sand), salt (a mineral called halite), and many others. Geologic processes affect us every day. Sometimes we must make decisions based on our understanding of geology, such as how to manage erosion of a coastal property, or whether to buy a home located on a cliff or next to a river. We also influence the geologic environment through our daily activities, whether we are drinking water that came from an aquifer, digging a trench, or planting trees to control soil erosion. This book will help you to become better informed and more mindful of these interactions. As a result, you will be better equipped to make decisions about Earth materials and processes that affect your life.

Science and the Scientific Method

Science is an approach that we use to study, observe, classify, investigate, test, and understand the behavior and characteristics of the world around us. The term *science* also refers to the vast body of knowledge about the natural world that has been built up, little by little, over many centuries of systematic investigation by scientists. **Technology** is the application of scientific knowledge for practical purposes. Civilization and our entire modern way of life are based on this body of knowledge and its applications.

> **science** A systematic approach to studying the natural world.

Scientific knowledge changes constantly; it grows and evolves through testing, interpretation, discussion, and reexamination. When scientists appear to argue or debate their findings, it means that science is working as it should: Scientists tear apart and debate each other's work to test the validity and robustness of the interpretations. It is difficult or even impossible for scientists to be completely detached from the materials and processes they are studying, but they strive to be as objective as they can be. Each new interpretation is grounded in the context of the scientific understanding that preceded it. The entire body of scientific knowledge is open to be studied and tested by anyone who is willing to put in the effort to do so.

Geologists are privileged to work in some of the most exotic places on Earth—and beyond.

NASA

a. Harrison (Jack) Schmitt, a planetary geologist, is the only scientist (so far) to walk on the Moon, for the *Apollo* 17 mission in 1972. Here, he is collecting a lunar sample to take back to Earth.

b. Volcanologists get uncomfortably close to the 2002 eruption of Mount Etna in Sicily, Italy, to record the sounds of the eruption.

Peter Carsten/NG Image Collection

Paleontology Structural Geology
Geophysics Limnology
Hydrology Volcanology Paleobiology
Biogeochemistry
Seismology Geology Economic
Physical Geology
Geochemistry Paleoclimatology
Mining Isotope
Remote Geology
Marine
Environmental Geology
Planetary Sedimentary Gemology
Historical Geology
Geodesy Geochronology Stratigraphy
Sensing Tectonics
Igneous Petrology
Metamorphic Geomorphology
Sedimentology Structural
Oceanography Mineralogy Engineering

Jonathan Blair/NG Image Collection

d. A paleontologist dives into the waters off the Bahama Islands to study stromatolites, a living algal formation reminiscent of Earth's oldest fossils.

Maria Stenzel/NG Image Collection

c. Climatologists collect an ice core from a floe off thecoast of Antarctica. Ice samples can tell us about the changes in Earth's climate over hundreds or thousands of years.

Jim Richardson/NG Image Collection

THINK CRITICALLY

Which of these examples represent physical geology, and which represent historical geology? Do some of them include aspects of both physical and historical geology?

e. A seismologist (expert on earthquakes) inspects one of the fissures that opened up in the Santa Cruz Mountains in California during the Loma Prieta earthquake of 1989.

This is a schematic diagram of the scientific method. The formation of a theory occurs only at the end, after many investigations and confirmation by many different scientists.

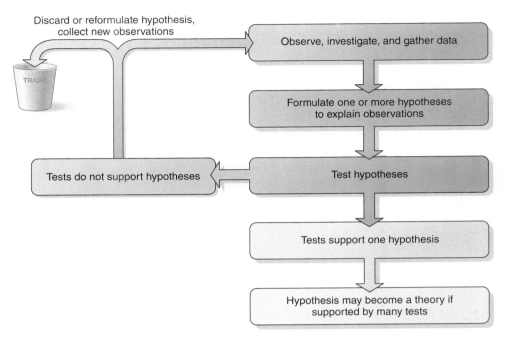

Like all other scientists, geologists use a logical research strategy called the **scientific method**, which has developed through trial and error over many years. The scientific method is based on observations and the collection of evidence that can be seen and tested by anyone who cares to do so. Although it varies in details, it includes the basic steps outlined in **Figure 1.2**.

> **scientific method** The way a scientist approaches a problem; the steps include observing, formulating a hypothesis, testing, and evaluating results.

Let's consider how the scientific method might be applied in a real geologic situation.

Observe and gather data. Scientists start with a question and acquire trustworthy evidence about it, especially measurements. In **Figure 1.3**, a geologist asks the question "How did this group of rocks form?" She observes and measures the sequence of layered rocks in question. She sees that the layers are *horizontal* and *parallel*—important clues. Furthermore, each layer consists of innumerable *small grains*, and the size of the grains varies from layer to layer but is approximately the same within each layer.

Formulate a hypothesis. Scientists explain their observations by developing a **hypothesis**. The geologist in our example develops three hypotheses. She hypothesizes that the rocks were formed from material that was transported and deposited where she has found it; but how was it transported?

> **hypothesis** A plausible but yet-to-be-proved explanation for how something happens.

Hypothesis 1 is that a *glacier* was the transporting agent. Hypothesis 2 is that *wind* did the transporting. Hypothesis 3 is that *water* did the transporting.

A scientist's hypotheses are often influenced by prior experience or knowledge. In Chapters 7 and 8 you will learn why the three hypotheses in our current example are reasonable explanations. Note that the scientist does not have to select one hypothesis at this point. In fact, choosing a "leading candidate" too early may prejudice the scientist and cause her to overlook some relevant clues. T. C. Chamberlin, a 19th-century geologist, argued that scientists should consider *all* reasonable explanations—an approach he called the "method of multiple working hypotheses."

Test the hypotheses. Scientists use a hypothesis—or multiple hypotheses—to make predictions and to develop tests. The tests may involve controlled experiments in a laboratory, further observations and measurements in the field, or possibly the development of a mathematical model. Geologists in particular like to test their hypotheses against real observations. Here's how our geologist tests the hypotheses:

- She travels to a modern glacier and studies the jumble of debris it deposits. She notes that the grains are different sizes, all mixed up, and not in neatly defined layers. So, Hypothesis 1 fails.
- Then the geologist goes to a desert region where she sees wind-transported material deposited in dunes. She observes that particle sizes are approximately the same, but they aren't in parallel layers; the layers are at odd angles. So, Hypothesis 2 fails.

Formulating and testing hypotheses · Figure 1.3

Observe, investigate, and gather data

Raul Touzon/National Geographic Creative

Top, the geologist observes and measures rock layers that are parallel. She also sees that the particles within each layer have a uniform size.

Middle, the geologist formulates three hypotheses about how the layers might have formed. She then tests the hypotheses by visiting three geologic sites.

Bottom, she concludes that the tests do not support the first two hypotheses. The third hypothesis best explains the observations.

(Inset from left to right: Courtesy Stephen C. Porter; University of Washington Libraries, Special Collections, John SheltonCollection, KC9807; Courtesy Stephen C. Porter)

Formulate hypotheses to explain observations

Hypothesis 1	Hypothesis 2	Hypothesis 3
Sediment transported and deposited by a glacier	Sediment transported and deposited by wind	Sediment transported and deposited in water

Test hypotheses

Test:	Test:	Test:
Visit a modern glacier. This is the terminus of Pré de Bar glacier in the Italian Alps.	Look at a sand dune, a modern wind-borne sediment. This is a trench in a dune near Yuma, Arizona.	Look at modern water-laid sediments. These are in a lake in eastern Canada.

Scientist sees a jumble of particles of many sizes. Layers are not parallel.	Scientist sees that particles are the same size but layers are not parallel.	Scientist sees particles are the same size in each layer, and layers are parallel.

Discard or confirm hypotheses

Hypothesis 1 fails Hypothesis 2 fails Hypothesis 3 is supported

---

- Finally, our scientist visits a lake and observes materials transported by a river and deposited in lake water. Now she sees layers that are parallel, and the particles in each layer are approximately the same size. Hypothesis 3 has potential, but more testing is needed.

Retest, test again, and formulate a theory. While visiting the lake, our scientist notes that plants are growing in the lake. To further verify Hypothesis 3, she takes an additional step and hypothesizes that if the material that formed the rocks really was deposited in a lake, the remains of aquatic plants might still be present. If, on further observation, she finds fossilized freshwater plant remains in the layered rocks, she will be even more confident that she is on the right track. Verification of Hypothesis 3 is now stronger.

Once a hypothesis has withstood numerous tests, scientists become more confident in its validity. If it becomes clear that the hypothesis has withstood testing and retesting, and that it has general applicability to more than one specific circumstance, it may be elevated to a **theory**. This is still not

> **theory** A hypothesis that has been tested and is strongly supported by experimentation, observation, and scientific evidence.

Satellite images can reveal interactions among Earth systems. In this photo, dust storms from the Sahara Desert blow far out into the Atlantic. Geologists have found African dust all the way across the Atlantic Ocean, and some think that it might contribute to the death of coral reefs off the coast of Florida and elsewhere.

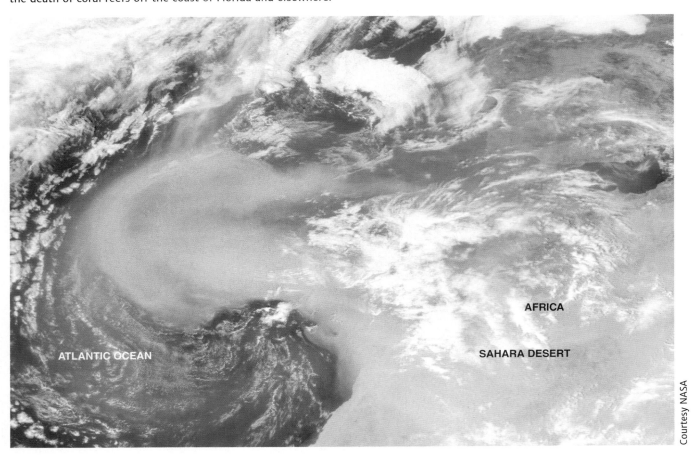

AFRICA

SAHARA DESERT

ATLANTIC OCEAN

Courtesy NASA

the final word, however; a theory is always open to further testing. (*Note*: In everyday speech, people often misuse the term *theory* to mean "hypothesis" by saying dismissively, "That's just a theory." What they really mean is, "That's just a hypothesis." In science, by the time a statement attains the stature of a theory, it is very substantial and must be taken seriously.)

Ultimately, a theory or group of theories that are widely applicable may be formulated into a **law** or **principle**. Laws and principles are statements about some natural phenomenon invariably observed to happen in the same way, and no deviations have ever been observed. For example, in geology the law of original horizontality states that sediment deposited in water is always in horizontal layers (or nearly so, because a lake or seafloor might have slight irregularities) and the layers are parallel to Earth's surface (or nearly so). No exceptions have ever been observed.

Earth System Science

Traditionally, scientists have studied Earth by focusing on separate units—the atmosphere, the oceans, or a single mountain range—in isolation from the other units. However, the first photographs of Earth taken from space (like the chapter-opening photograph) caused a dramatic rethinking of this traditional view. For the first time, it was possible to see the whole planet in one sweeping view. We could see everything at a glance—clouds, oceans, polar ice caps, and continents—all at the same time and in their proper scale. The astronauts, like the rest of us, marveled at Earth's "overwhelming beauty . . . the stark contrast between bright colorful home and stark black infinity" (Rusty Schweikart, *Apollo 9*).

Yet from space it was also clear how small Earth is—just a dust speck compared to the vastness of the solar system and the universe. On such a small planet, it no longer made sense to study all the pieces separately. There was only one geology that mattered, not the geology of America or the Atlantic Ocean but the geology of the whole Earth.

Instruments carried by satellites in space have also given us new ways to study the relationships of the parts on a global scale, as we never could before (**Figure 1.4**). This new, more all-inclusive view of geology is called **Earth system science**.

This figure shows a variety of systems and smaller subsystems. The entire diagram—mountains, river, and lake—illustrates one kind of system: a coastal watershed. The individual pieces enclosed by boxes, such as the river, are also systems. Even small volumes of water or lake sediment (foreground boxes) are systems in their own right.

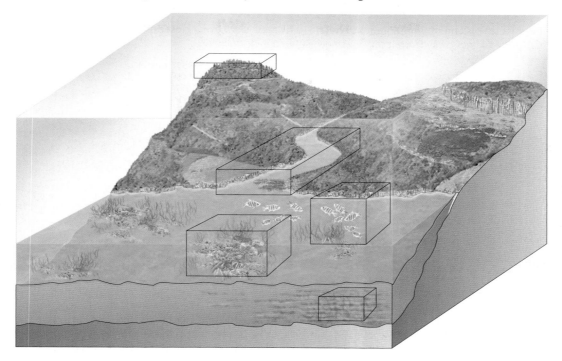

The System Concept A systems approach is a helpful way to break down a large, complex problem into smaller pieces that are easier to study without losing sight of the connections between those pieces. The scientific definition of a system allows the observer to choose the boundaries and limitations of the system. That is why a system is only a concept; you choose its limits for the convenience of your study. A system may be large or small, simple or complex (**Figure 1.5**). It could be the contents of the beaker in a laboratory experiment or the contents of an ocean. A leaf is a system, but it is also part of a larger system (a tree), which is part of a still larger system (a forest).

> **system** A portion of the universe that can be isolated for the purpose of observing and measuring change.

The fact that we distinguish a system from the rest of the universe for specific study does not mean that we ignore its surroundings. In fact, the nature of a system's boundaries is one of its most important defining characteristics, and it helps us understand how a system is influenced by its surroundings. For example, a **closed system** has boundaries that do not allow any matter to enter or escape the system. The boundaries may (and in the real world, always do) allow energy, such as sunlight, to pass through. An example of a closed system would be a perfectly sealed oven, which would allow the material inside to be heated but would not allow any of that material to escape. (Note that in real life, ovens do allow some vapor to escape, so they are not perfect examples of closed systems.)

A second kind of system, an **open system**, can exchange *both* matter and energy across its boundaries. An island offers a simple example (see *What a Geologist Sees* on the next page). The system concept can also be applied to artificial environments. For example, urban geographers and land-use planners sometimes use a systems approach in the study of cities. Enormous flows of energy and materials occur across city borders, both in and out.

The Earth System Earth itself is a very close approximation of a closed system. Energy enters the Earth system as solar radiation. The energy is used in various biologic and geologic processes and then departs in the form of heat. Very little matter crosses the boundaries of the Earth system. We do lose some hydrogen and helium atoms from the outer atmosphere, and we gain some material in the form of meteorites. However, for most purposes, especially over the short term, we can treat Earth as a closed system.

The fact that Earth is a closed system (on the scale of the time that humans have existed) has three important consequences. First, *because the amount of matter in a closed system is fixed and finite,* the mineral and fossil fuel resources on this planet are all we have and all we will ever have until we learn to mine other planets. Second, *all the*

What a Geologist Sees

An Island Is Not a Closed System

To a casual tourist, the island of Bora Bora (shown here, left) may seem like a closed system, isolated from the rest of the world, a great place to "get away from it all." But how isolated is it, really?

Todd Gipstein/NG Image Collection

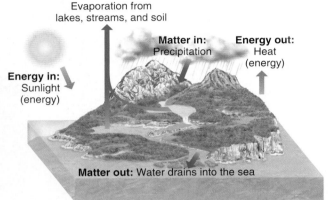

Matter out: Evaporation from lakes, streams, and soil

Matter in: Precipitation

Energy out: Heat (energy)

Energy in: Sunlight (energy)

Matter out: Water drains into the sea

A geologist would look at this volcanic island and see the forested slopes as evidence of abundant precipitation; the flat area between the mountain and the sea as evidence of erosion transferring material from the mountain toward the sea; and, in the foreground, coral reefs growing on the shallow, submerged part of the island as evidence of warm waters and plentiful nutrients. A geologist, like all other scientists, would conclude that the island is an open system.

Recall that an open system allows both matter and energy to cross its boundaries. Energy (in the form of sunlight) and matter (in the form of precipitation) reach the island from outside sources. Energy leaves the island as heat. Matter in the form of water either evaporates or drains into the sea. Birds may fly into and out of the system. In the modern era, humans may also bring materials into and out of the system by importing and exporting resources. In all of these ways, the system exchanges matter and energy with its surroundings.

THINK CRITICALLY

Bora Bora (shown in the photo) is a volcanic island. The volcano is considered to be extinct, but suppose it were just dormant and waiting to erupt again. How would you modify the diagram to describe the inputs and outputs of matter and energy during an eruption?

---

waste materials we develop remain within the confines of the Earth system; or, as environmentalists say, "There is no away to throw things to." Third, *if changes are made in one part of a closed system, the results of those changes eventually will affect other parts of the system.* For instance, when we divert a river to provide drinking water for a city, we may deplete the water resources somewhere else (**Figure 1.6**).

Earth's Interconnected Subsystems

The Earth system can be divided into four very large subsystems: the **geosphere**, **biosphere**, **atmosphere**, and **hydrosphere** (**Figure 1.7**). These can be further subdivided into many

> **geosphere** The solid Earth, as a whole.
>
> **biosphere** The system consisting of all living and recently dead organisms on Earth.
>
> **atmosphere** The envelope of gases that surrounds Earth.
>
> **hydrosphere** The system comprising all of Earth's bodies of water and ice, both on the surface and underground.

subsystems of interest to geologists; for example, the hydrosphere consists of oceans, glacial ice, streams, lakes, groundwater, and so on.

The geosphere may come to mind as being most important for geologists, but in fact all four spheres play important roles in geology. Plants draw nutrients from the lithosphere and incorporate them into the biosphere. When they die and decompose, the material they contain may enter the atmosphere or return to the lithosphere. Rocks erode, and the minerals they contain become salts in the hydrosphere; evaporation returns these salts to the geosphere. The exchanges of materials between spheres never stop.

The four major Earth reservoirs interact most intensively in a narrow **life zone**, a region that extends to about 10 kilometers above and

Upstream changes have downstream impacts • Figure 1.6 _____

The Colorado River and its tributaries provide drinking water to 25 million people and irrigate 1.4 million hectares of agricultural fields. Because of massive upstream diversions, little water makes it all the way to the Gulf of California in Mexico. Consequently, the river has become a broad mudflat where it enters the gulf, as seen in this photo. This demonstrates how changes made in one part of a system eventually affect other parts of the system.

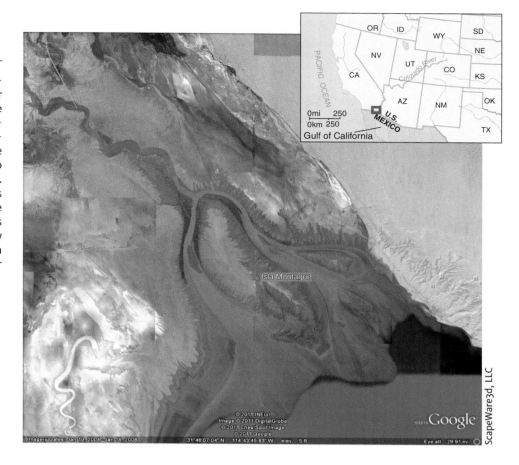

Earth's subsystems: The four "spheres" • Figure 1.7 _____

Earth's four principal subsystems are the geosphere, biosphere, atmosphere, and hydrosphere. Both matter and energy cycle among these subsystems, making them open systems.

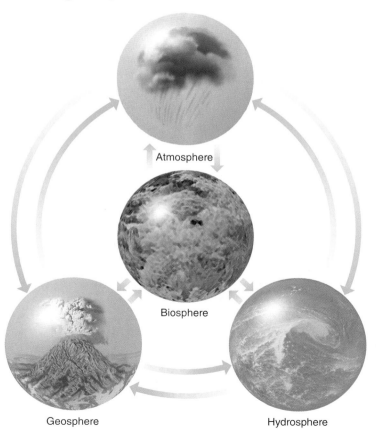

Atmosphere

Biosphere

Geosphere

Hydrosphere

All life on Earth inhabits a zone no wider than 20 kilometers, with the majority in a region no wider than 1 kilometer.

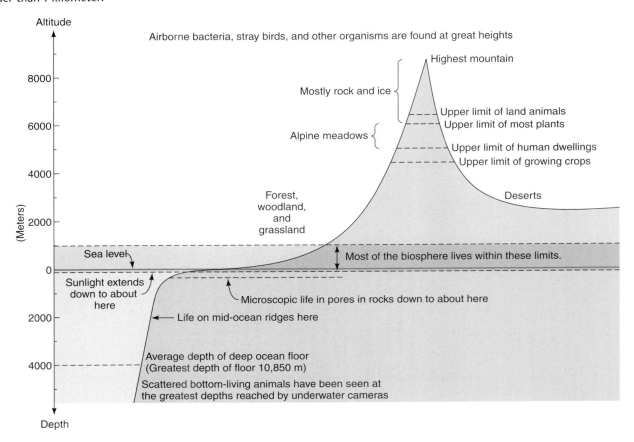

10 kilometers below the Earth's surface (**Figure 1.8**). In this narrow zone, all known forms of life exist. It is only here that conditions favorable for life are created by interactions among the geosphere, hydrosphere, atmosphere, and biosphere. However, recent research is showing that life is highly resilient and can survive in conditions that were thought to be completely inhospitable, as discussed in the *Case Study*.

Figure 1.7 shows the interactions among Earth's reservoirs in a simplistic fashion, but we can be a good deal more precise about the nature of the flows by focusing on the way materials move, or cycle, among the reservoirs. In this book, we will discuss the Earth system as a series of three interrelated cycles that facilitate the movement of materials and energy among the reservoirs. These are the **water cycle**, or **hydrologic cycle**, the **rock cycle**, and the **tectonic cycle**. They are sketched in **Figure 1.9**. It is not necessary for you to understand the details of this diagram yet; we will return to this figure repeatedly in later chapters and label each of the processes that are illustrated with icons

hydrologic cycle A model that describes the movement of water through the reservoirs of the Earth system; the water cycle.

rock cycle The set of crustal processes that form new rock, modify it, transport it, and break it down.

tectonic cycle Movements and interactions in the geosphere and the internal Earth processes that drive them.

lithosphere Earth's rocky outermost layer.

and arrows here. The most important points to understand now are that the interactions form cycles—that is, processes without beginning or end—and that they are closely interconnected.

Because this is a book about physical geology, we will often focus primarily on the **lithosphere**—the outermost part of the geosphere. However, the systems approach tells us that it is unreasonable—even impossible—to consider one part of the Earth system in isolation from the rest. We cannot fully understand where rocks come from without also understanding the hydrologic cycle and the tectonic cycle. Nor can we understand the lithosphere without learning something about the hydrosphere, atmosphere, and biosphere, as well as Earth's deep interior (which is distinct from the lithosphere). Thus, in this course, you will study not only geology but also a little bit of oceanography, hydrology, meteorology, physics, chemistry, biology, and astronomy.

CASE Study

THE PLANNER

Extremophiles: Where Can Life Exist?

Compared to the size of Earth as a whole, the zone that supports life (shown in Figure 1.8) is very limited. But life is resilient, and—as scientists are discovering—more adaptive than we had originally thought. Examples have now been discovered of life existing in physical environments that would previously have been thought far too inhospitable for any living organism.

The life forms that exist in such environments are called **extremophiles** (derived from Latin and Greek words that mean "extreme-loving"). There are many different categories of extremophiles, including *acidophiles* (organisms that can survive in very low-pH, acidic conditions); *alkaliphiles* (very high-pH, alkaline conditions); *thermophiles* and *hyperthermophiles* (extremely high temperatures, such as those found in thermal hot springs); *cryophiles* (extremely cold temperatures, such as in subglacial environments); *halophiles* (extremely salty conditions); *piezophiles* (conditions of extremely high hydrostatic pressure); and *xerophiles* (extremely dry conditions). Some organisms are even called *polyextremophiles*, because they qualify as extremophiles in more than one category!

Many extremophiles—by necessity—acquire their food energy through processes other than photosynthesis, which of course requires access to light energy to convert carbon dioxide into plant tissue. For example, *lithoautotrophs* feed themselves using energy derived from the inorganic oxidation of minerals from rocks. The metabolic processes that utilize energy sources other than the Sun are collectively referred to as *chemosynthesis*. Chemosynthetic organisms are much rarer than photosynthetic organisms, and many of them are extremophiles of one sort or another.

If life can exist on Earth in such extreme environments, there may be implications for the existence of life on other planets, too. On Earth, organisms called *cryptoendoliths* exist in tiny openings in rock, deep underground. They have been studied in gold mines in Canada and South Africa, at depths up to several kilometers below the surface. If such an extreme environment is able to host life on Earth, couldn't a similar environment harbor life on another planet, such as Mars?

Jim Peaco/U.S. National Park Service

Thermophilic organisms (tolerant of very high temperatures) are responsible for the bright colors seen here in Grand Prismatic Hot Spring in Yellowstone National Park.

USGS

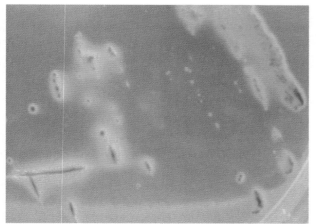

Extremophiles such as those shown here, from a creek that drains mine water from a former uranium mine near Ronneburg, Eastern Germany—are *metallotolerant acidophiles*, adapted to survive conditions of extremely high acidity and toxic metal content.

Richard B. Hoover, Elena Pikuta andAsim Bej, NASA/ NSSTC Universityof Alabama at Huntsville, and the University of Alabama at Birmingham./NASA

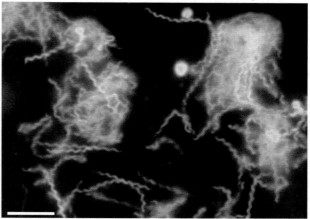

The bacteria shown here are *haloalkaliphilic* (surviving in saline, alkaline conditions), as well as *anaerobic* (surviving in conditions of extremely low oxygen availability). They are found in the highly alkaline, salty, deep water of Mono Lake in California. The red cells are dead; the green cells are living.

THINK CRITICALLY

There is no evidence of life on the surface of Mars, but many scientists still think that life could persist deep in the subsurface rocks. Under what circumstances do you think this might be possible?

In the hydrologic cycle (right), water circulates through various reservoirs, eventually returning to the ocean. The rock cycle (center) describes crustal processes through which rock is uplifted into mountains, then eroded and weathered to form sediment. The tectonic cycle (left) explains where igneous rock comes from, and how new crust is formed and recycled by large-scale motions of Earth's surface and interior. Energy from the Sun powers the hydrologic cycle. Heat from Earth's interior powers the tectonic cycle. Both sources power the rock cycle.

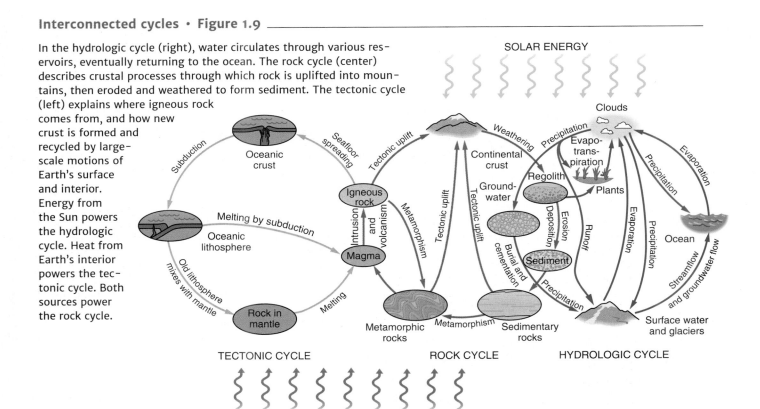

CONCEPT CHECK

1. **What** is the difference between historical and physical geology?

2. **What** distinguishes a theory from a hypothesis?

3. **Why** is the system concept a key part of modern geology?

4. **How** does the geosphere differ from the lithosphere?

EARTH IN SPACE

Learning Objectives

1. **Distinguish** between the rocky planets, the gaseous planets, and the other important nonplanetary objects in our solar system.

2. **Describe** how planetary accretion, meteorite impacts, and chemical differentiation have shaped the solar system.

3. **Identify** several similarities and differences among Earth and the other inner planets.

As geologists, we mainly study the processes that occur on Earth, in isolation from the rest of the solar system. How did Earth become a unique and special place? We must remember that Earth is a planet that is part of a larger system, the solar system. The characteristics of the planet we live on today are linked to the origins of both the planet and the solar system as a whole, as well as to what has happened to the planet over the past 4.56 billion years.

Our Solar System

The **solar system** consists of the Sun and the group of objects in orbit around it. Earth is one of eight large members of our solar system, traditionally called **planets** (from *planetai*, Greek for "wanderers"). In addition to the Sun and the planets, the solar system includes (at this time) 146 known moons and 27 provisional moons, at least eight dwarf planets, a vast number of asteroids and comets, and innumerable fragments of rock and dust. All the objects in our solar system move through space in smooth, regular orbits, held in place by gravitational attraction. The planets, dwarf planets, asteroids, and comets orbit the Sun, and the moons orbit the planets and dwarf planets.

We can separate the planets into two groups on the basis of their physical characteristics and distances from the Sun

Family portrait of the solar system • Figure 1.10

Our solar system's eight recognized planets and other smaller but important objects are shown here to scale against the Sun. (Note, however, that the distances between planets are much greater than shown, and the planets never line up neatly like this.)

(**Figure 1.10**). The innermost planets—Mercury, Venus, Earth, and Mars—are small, rocky, and relatively dense. They are similar in size and chemical composition and are called **terrestrial planets** because they resemble Earth (*Terra* in Latin). Among the terrestrial planets, only Earth is the right size and has the right temperature because of its distance from the Sun to support life. Whether there are other planets in the Milky Way Galaxy or elsewhere that can support life remains an open question. By October 2014, 1832 **exoplanets**—planets in solar systems outside of our own—have been confirmed by NASA, with thousands of additional candidates (**Figure 1.11**). However, only a small handful of these have the physical characteristics that might allow them to support life.

The outer planets of the solar system are much larger and more massive than the terrestrial planets, as shown in Figure 1.10, but they are much less dense. These **jovian planets**—Jupiter, Saturn, Uranus, and Neptune—take their name from *Jove*, the name for Jupiter in Roman mythology. (Jupiter was the king of the gods, and the god of light and weather, among other things. In size, Jupiter is certainly the king of the planets.) The jovian planets probably have small solid centers that resemble terrestrial planets, but much of their planetary mass is contained in thick atmospheres of hydrogen, helium, and other gases. The atmospheres are what we actually see when we observe these planets.

Pluto, considered until recently to be a ninth planet, doesn't fit into either of these planetary groups. It is much smaller and denser than the jovian planets but much less dense than the terrestrial planets. Recent discoveries suggest that Pluto is actually the nearest of a sizeable population of Pluto-like bodies beyond the orbit of Neptune called **Kuiper Belt objects**, some of which are even larger than Pluto. In

Planets in other solar systems • Figure 1.11

This is an artist's rendition of the five exoplanets discovered orbiting around the star 55 Cancri, the brightest dot. The large blue planet is the size of Neptune and is thought to be orbiting within the habitable zone of the star—the right distance to have a temperature that could allow H_2O to be present on the surface in liquid, solid, and vapor forms.

Caltech/Nasa Jet PropulsionLaboratory

How the solar system was formed • Figure 1.12

This series of diagrams shows the nebular hypothesis, which explains how our solar system formed from a rotating cloud of interstellar gas and dust.

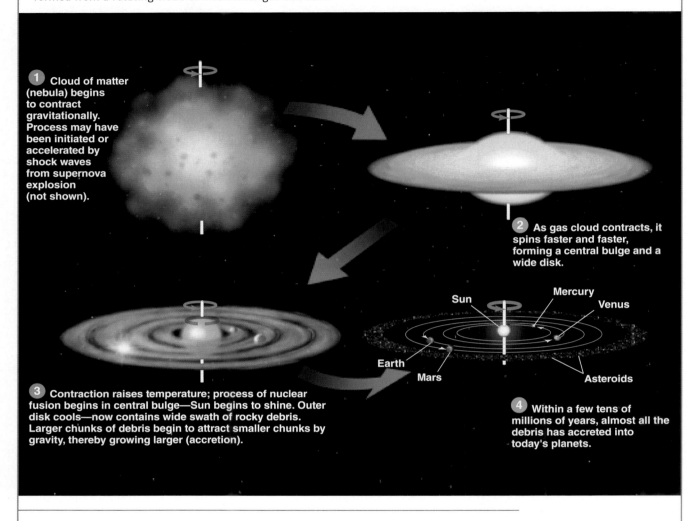

1 Cloud of matter (nebula) begins to contract gravitationally. Process may have been initiated or accelerated by shock waves from supernova explosion (not shown).

2 As gas cloud contracts, it spins faster and faster, forming a central bulge and a wide disk.

3 Contraction raises temperature; process of nuclear fusion begins in central bulge—Sun begins to shine. Outer disk cools—now contains wide swath of rocky debris. Larger chunks of debris begin to attract smaller chunks by gravity, thereby growing larger (accretion).

Sun   Mercury   Venus   Earth   Mars   Asteroids

4 Within a few tens of millions of years, almost all the debris has accreted into today's planets.

THINK CRITICALLY

If you were a planetary scientist and had a chance to work with an astronomer studying very young suns, what kind of evidence would you look for in order to test the nebular hypothesis?

2006, the International Astronomical Union (IAU) adopted a new designation of **dwarf planet** for an object that orbits the Sun, is large enough that its own gravity has pulled it into a spherical shape, but its gravity is too small to have "cleared the neighborhood around its orbit" by gravitational attraction of surrounding debris. Under the new definition, Pluto is a dwarf planet, and so is the large asteroid Ceres. Although the decision aroused controversy (especially among fans of Pluto), it is a normal part of science to adopt new terminology when the old nomenclature has been based on assumptions that later turn out to be flawed.

ASK YOURSELF

Which one of the following pairs does not belong with the others?

a. Jupiter and Saturn

b. gaseous and thick atmosphere

c. Earth and Venus

d. jovian and far from the Sun

e. large and low-density

The Origin of the Solar System

How did the solar system form? The answer to this ancient question is still incomplete, and it is an excellent example of a carefully researched scientific hypothesis. The **nebular hypothesis**, originally formulated by the German philosopher Immanuel Kant in 1755 and now widely accepted as the best description of planetary formation, hypothesizes that the solar system coalesced out of a swirling cloud of interstellar dust and gas called a **nebula** (**Figure 1.12**). This interstellar cloud contained small amounts of all the elements, inherited from earlier generations of stars.

Eventually, the swirling cloud began to collapse in on itself, perhaps because a pressure wave passed through the cloud from a nearby supernova. The collapsing cloud became both hotter and denser at its center. When the gases at the center of the cloud of gas and dust became sufficiently hot and dense, an energy-producing nuclear reaction called **fusion** began, and our Sun was born. The process of fusion, which combines hydrogen atoms to form helium, has powered the Sun for 4.56 billion years and will continue to power it for billions of years into the future.

The nebular hypothesis explains very well why the inner planets are rocky, while the outer planets contain a higher proportion of ice and gas. The temperature was higher in the portion of the nebula that was to become the innermost part of the solar system. Elements with a high melting point (iron, silicon, and so on—the chemicals that make up rock) would have been early to condense from the cloud. Meanwhile, a strong solar wind stripped much of the lighter gases, such as helium and hydrogen, from the inner planets. But the solar wind was not strong enough to do the same to the outer planets, which grew into gas giants. Volatile compounds such as water and methane condense only at lower temperatures. Therefore, water ice, methane ice, and other ices are abundant on the moons and smaller bodies of the outer solar system, where the primordial nebula was cooler.

Planetary accretion, a 20th-century supplement to the nebular hypothesis, accounts for the existence of meteoroids and asteroids. According to the accretion hypothesis, the outer portions of the solar nebula cooled as it flattened out into a disk of rocky, metallic, and icy debris before any of the planets were formed. Through random collisions, the debris began to form clumps. Eventually some clumps grew large enough to pull in the remaining debris by the force of gravity. Thus, the process of accretion accounts for two parts of the IAU's definition of a planet. Planets are round because their gravity overcomes the material strength of the rocks that form the planet. They are isolated because they long ago swept up virtually all the material that was formerly in or near their orbit.

Even so, some stray rocks never managed to be swept up by any planet; these are called **meteoroids**. Sometimes pieces of this debris happen to fall to Earth; they are called **meteors** if they burn up in the atmosphere or **meteorites** if they reach Earth's surface. Meteorites are fascinating relics of the early days of the solar system.

> **meteorite** A fragment of extraterrestrial material that falls to Earth.

A major consequence of the planetary accretion hypothesis is the great importance of violent collisions in the history of the solar system. Every crater on our Moon, as far as we know, was formed by a meteorite impact. (Astronauts and scientists have searched for volcanic craters on the Moon, but none has ever been found.) Scientists recognize impact craters on Earth, too, although they are harder to find because erosion and other geologic processes cover them up or erase them over time (see *Amazing Places*). A meteorite impact in the Yucatán region of Mexico may have been responsible for the catastrophe that killed the dinosaurs more than 65 million years ago.

Even larger impacts than this were commonplace in the early solar system. Most planetary scientists now think it is likely that Earth collided with another planetary body, roughly the size of Mars, around 4.5 billion years ago. The impact tilted Earth's axis of rotation at an angle to the plane of its orbit around the Sun, and that is why we have seasons. The impact must also have melted most of Earth's surface due to the tremendous amount of energy released. The collision completely destroyed the other planet, and it blasted so much debris into orbit that for a little while, Earth had rings much denser than Saturn's. Eventually the rings of debris coalesced into the most familiar of astronomical objects—Earth's Moon (**Figure 1.13**). This hypothesis explains the existence of a magma ocean early in lunar history (shown by rocks retrieved from the Moon). It also explains our Moon's relatively large size in contrast to other moons, which are many times smaller than their parent bodies, and accounts for certain chemical discrepancies and similarities between Earth and its Moon.

Such giant collisions were the inevitable final stage of planetary accretion, when most of the debris has been swept up and only larger objects remain. Signs of giant impacts abound in the solar system. One such impact probably caused Uranus's axis to tip over on its side. Pluto's moon, Charon, was probably created by an impact because it is unusually large compared to Pluto. Perhaps Venus experienced a giant impact, too. Although it lacks a moon, it is the only planet that rotates in the retrograde (east-to-west) direction, an effect that could have been produced by a large glancing blow, essentially tipping the planet upside down.

Why is the accretion history of the planets important to geologists? Because of the heat generated by all of these collisions, every rocky planet probably started out hot enough to melt either partially or completely. During the period of partial melting, terrestrial planets separated into layers of differing chemical composition, a process called **differentiation**. Earth's geosphere differentiated into three layers: a relatively thin, low-density, rocky crust; a rocky, intermediate-density **mantle**; and a metallic, high-density **core**. Similar layers are present in Mercury,

> **crust** The outermost compositional layer of the solid Earth.
>
> **mantle** The middle compositional layer of Earth, between the core and the crust.
>
> **core** Earth's innermost compositional layer.

Gosses Bluff, Australia

Not far from Alice Springs in central Australia, a ring of hills called Gosses Bluff juts up from the endlessly flat landscape. The origin of this curious formation was a puzzle until the 1960s, when it was shown to be the relic of a great meteorite that crashed to Earth 142 million years ago. The impact and explosion blasted out a crater 24 kilometers in diameter, surrounded by a ring of debris (**Figure a**). What we see today is the eroded remnant of the center of the impact site. You can see a ghostly, highly eroded remnant of the outer rim in a photograph from space (**Figure b**).

Evidence for the origin of Gosses Bluff originally came from the study of Meteor Crater, in Arizona (**Figure c**). G.K. Gilbert, a distinguished government geologist, hypothesized in 1891 that Meteor Crater was formed by a great volcanic steam explosion. D.M. Barringer, a mining engineer, disagreed. Barringer thought it was the impact site of

a great iron meteorite, and he was given the right to prospect and mine the iron object. He never found it because, as we now know, the meteorite mostly vaporized as it raced through the atmosphere, and what was left disintegrated into small fragments on impact. Convincing evidence for the impact origin of the crater finally came in 1960, when E.M. Shoemaker, another government geologist, discovered a mineral called *stishovite*, a form of silica that is formed only at super-high pressures, such as those caused by an impacting meteorite.

Our planet formed about 4.56 billion years ago out of innumerable rocks very much like the meteorites that left Gosses Bluff and Meteor Crater. Though impacts of large meteorites are rare in the present era, scars from past impacts remind us that we are not isolated in space but, rather, are still an integral part of an active solar system.

a

Yann Arthus-Bertrand/Science Source

b

Outer rim of crater

Gosses Bluff

Courtesy NASA

c

Stephen Alvarez/NG Image Collection

a. This hilly terrain in Australia, called Gosses Bluff is the remnant of a major meteorite impact that happened 142 million years ago. **b.** The ring-shaped impact crater of Gosses Bluff is more clearly visible when viewed from space. **c.** Meteor Crater, Arizona, shown here, is about 1.2 km in diameter. It was created by a meteorite impact about 50,000 years ago.

THINK CRITICALLY

The presence of stishovite, a high-pressure mineral, confirmed the origin of Barringer Crater as a meteorite impact. What other types of evidence might distinguish this as a crater that formed as a result of a high-speed impact, rather than some other process, such as a volcanic explosion?

Process Diagram

How Earth's moon was formed • Figure 1.13

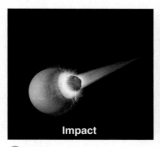

Impact

1 Some 4550 million years ago, the still-forming Earth (unrecognizable because it probably did not yet have oceans) runs into another growing planet, which scientists have named Theia.

Impact + 8 hours

2 Theia is obliterated, and its remnants—along with a good chunk of Earth's mantle—are blasted into orbit around Earth. The off-center impact has knocked Earth's axis of rotation askew.

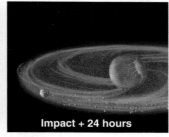

Impact + 24 hours

3 The debris spreads itself into a ring and begins to clump together.

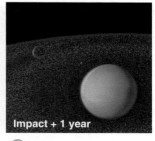

Impact + 1 year

4 The largest clump starts to attract other fragments and is well on its way to becoming the Moon. Its surface is initially molten. Earth has recovered its shape, leaving no trace of the most violent event in its history.

THINK CRITICALLY

What differences would you notice on Earth today if Theia had been a smaller body and, as a result, the Moon were in about the same place as it is today but only one-tenth as large?

Venus, Mars, and the Moon, although they have different proportional sizes and compositions (**Figure 1.14**).

There are other important similarities among the terrestrial planets. All of them have experienced volcanic activity, which means they have or once had internal heat sources. The volcanism is dominated by the eruption of lava that cools to form a volcanic rock called **basalt** (**Figure 1.15**). All of the planets have also been through intense cratering processes, although the signs are well hidden on Venus and Earth. Finally, all have lost their primordial atmospheres. The three that ended up with new atmospheres (Earth, Mars, and Venus) evolved them over time, from material that leaked from their interiors via volcanoes.

Inside the terrestrial planets • Figure 1.14

This figure shows a comparison of the sizes of the terrestrial planets, and the relative amount of total planetary volume represented by the core in each case.

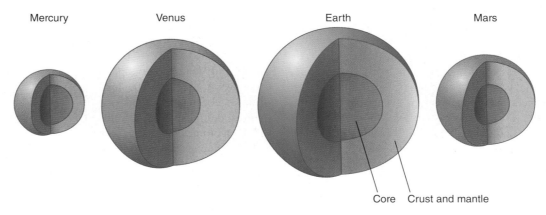

Mercury   Venus   Earth   Mars

Core   Crust and mantle

Basalt: The most common rock in the solar system • Figure 1.15 _____

Lava from Mauna Loa volcano in Hawaii cools to form the volcanic rock basalt, a rock type that also comprises most of the surfaces of Venus and Mars, and the "seas" (dark-colored spots) of Earth's Moon. Though taken only a few years ago, this picture could represent the surface of any of these planets 4.5 billion years ago.

Marc Moritsch/NG Image Collection

What Makes Earth Unique?

Venus and Mars, Earth's nearest neighbors, are in some ways very similar to our planet. In terms of size, Venus is nearly Earth's twin. Yet there is no chance of mistaking either of them for Earth (**Figure 1.16**). Earth's blues, whites, and greens attest that it has three things neither Venus nor Mars, nor any other planet or moon in our solar system, possesses: an oxygen-rich atmosphere; a hydrosphere that contains water in solid, liquid, and vapor forms; and a biosphere full of living organisms.

The nature of Earth's solid surface is another special characteristic. Earth is covered by an irregular blanket of loose debris formed as a result of **weathering**—the chemical alteration and mechanical breakdown of rock caused by exposure to water, air, and living organisms. This layer is called **regolith** (from the Greek words for "blanket" and "stone"). It includes soil, river mud, desert sand, rock fragments, and other unconsolidated debris. Earth's regolith is unique because it teems with life. When material from the biosphere becomes incorporated with rock material, the result is a special type of regolith unique to Earth: **soil**.

Other planets and moons with rocky surfaces have regolith, too (**Figure 1.17**). In the case of the Moon, the regolith has formed from endless pounding by impacting meteorites. Both Venus and Mars have atmospheres that contain water vapor and carbon dioxide, so chemically driven weathering occurs in addition to meteorite pounding, but the key ingredient of Earth-like regolith—life—is not known to be present. In all of these cases, the regoliths are not true soils. (You may read about "lunar soil" and "Martian soil," but such usage of the word "soil" is geologically incorrect. The correct terms are "lunar regolith" and "Martian regolith.")

Another unique property of Earth is the nature and extent of its tectonic activity. **Plate tectonics** has shaped Earth's continents and oceans and governs, to a large extent, the location of Earth's volcanoes and the occurrence of earthquakes. Tectonic activity has given Earth two different kinds of crust—thin, basaltic **oceanic crust** and thick, granitic **continental crust**. Continental crust seems to be unique to Earth—at least Mars and Venus do not appear to have it. Because the location of continents affects oceanic and atmospheric currents, plate tectonics exerts a powerful influence on Earth's climate, which in turn affects the evolution of life. We will have much more to say about plate tectonics in Chapter 4 and later chapters.

> **plate tectonics** The movement and interactions of large fragments of Earth's lithosphere, called plates.
>
> **oceanic crust** The thinner, denser, and younger part of Earth's crust, underlying the ocean basins.
>
> **continental crust** The older, thicker, and less dense part of Earth's crust, the bulk of Earth's landmasses.

Earth and its closest neighbors • Figure 1.16

In spite of their similar origins, Venus, Earth, and Mars have profound geologic differences that have made Earth the only one that is hospitable for life.

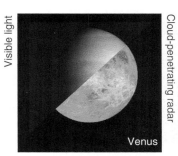

Venus   Earth   Mars

	Venus	Earth	Mars
Atmosphere	97% carbon dioxide; temperature averages a blistering 480°C (hot enough to melt lead)	78% nitrogen, 21% oxygen; average temperature 14.6°C	96% carbon dioxide; thin and insufficient to retain much heat; average temperature −63°C; temperatures usually too low to melt water ice (0°C)
Hydrosphere	Exists only as vapor in the atmosphere due to high temperatures	Contains water as solid, liquid, and vapor	Water cannot exist in liquid form on the surface due to low temperatures and pressure
Biosphere	None	Only known biosphere	None known

(Inset left-top: NASA; left-bottom: Courtesy NASA; middle: Courtesy NASA; right: Courtesy NASA)

Regolith on Mars • Figure 1.17

This photo shows a trench dug on the Martian surface by the Phoenix lander in 2008. The regolith is red, indicating that it has been oxidized—a sign of chemical weathering. The white material is thought to be water ice, and the trench itself is about 20 cm x 30 cm.

STOP CONCEPT CHECK

1. **List** the principal members of our solar system and summarize their basic characteristics.

2. **Summarize** the nebular hypothesis and the planetary accretion model.

3. **How** are Venus, Mars, and Earth similar, and how do they differ from each other and from the jovian planets?

THE EVER-CHANGING EARTH

Learning Objectives

1. **Explain** Hutton's principle of uniformitarianism.

2. **Describe** why the Earth system can be so dynamic and yet appear so stable.

3. **Identify** several key benefits of studying geology.

Geologists study Earth systems, materials, and processes—those of the present day, as well as those of the deep past. One of the most fundamental principles of geology is based on the idea that the processes that we see operating in the Earth system today have operated in a similar manner throughout much of Earth's history. This means, in other words, that there is uniformity in how natural laws operate in space, throughout the Earth system, and in time, over the history of this planet.

Uniformitarianism

This fundamental principle regarding the uniformity of natural laws and processes was most famously articulated by an 18th-century Scottish geologist named James Hutton. Through examinations of layered rock in Scotland, Hutton came to the conclusion that the prevailing biblical view—that all of Earth's rock layers were deposited in one catastrophic flood event—did not fit the evidence in the geologic record. He offered an alternative hypothesis: that each rock layer represented a cycle of erosion and deposition by water, followed by uplift to its present position. He hypothesized that the processes of erosion and deposition that were responsible for the formation of the rock layers must have operated in much the same manner as they do today, and that these processes have been repeated over and over again throughout Earth's history.

The concept was further developed by geologists who followed Hutton, and it came to be referred to as the principle of **uniformitarianism**. One way to express this principle is to state that "the present is the key to the past." We can examine any rock, no matter how old, and compare its characteristics with those of similar rocks forming today. We can then infer that the ancient rock likely formed in a similar environment through similar processes and on a comparable time scale.

uniformitarianism
The concept that the processes governing the Earth system today have operated in a similar manner throughout geologic time.

For example, in many deserts today, we can see gigantic dunes formed from sand grains transported by the wind. Because of the way they form, dunes have a distinctive internal structure (**Figure 1.18**). Using the principle of uniformitarianism, we can infer that a rock composed of cemented grains of sand and having the same distinctive internal structure as modern dunes is the remains of an ancient dune.

Time and Change

The principle of uniformitarianism provides the first step toward understanding Earth's long history. Geologists have used this principle to explain the features preserved in the rock record in a logical manner. In so doing, they have discovered that Earth is incredibly old. An enormously long time is needed to erode a mountain range or for huge quantities of sand and mud to be transported by streams, deposited in the ocean, cemented into rocks, and for the rocks to be uplifted to form a mountain. Yet the rock record tells us that the cycle of erosion, formation of new rock, uplift, and more erosion has been repeated many times during Earth's long history.

Since material is constantly being transferred from one subsystem to another, you may wonder why these systems seem so stable. Why doesn't the sea become saltier or fresher? Why doesn't all the water in the world flow into the sea and stay there? Why should the chemical composition of the atmosphere be mainly nitrogen and oxygen, as it has been for millions of years? How can rock that is 2 billion years old have the same composition as rock that is being formed today? If mountains are constantly being worn down by erosion, why are there still high mountains?

The answers to these questions are all basically the same: Materials cycle from one reservoir to another, but the reservoirs themselves don't change noticeably because the different parts of the cycle balance each other. While a mountain is worn down in one part of the cycle, a new mountain is being built up in another part. This cycling of materials has been going on since Earth was formed, and it continues today. This was one of the most important conclusions about uniformitarianism that grew out of the work of James Hutton.

One important ongoing process that Hutton and those who followed him did not know about is the slow motion of Earth's plates. In a nutshell, plate tectonics involves the motion of about a half dozen large, curved fragments of Earth's lithosphere, plus a large number of smaller ones. Like so much else about Earth, we can now observe the motion of plates from space: **Global Positioning System (GPS)** satellites can measure the shifting of plates in centimeters per year. According to the principle of uniformitarianism, this process should also have operated in the past. When we extrapolate these imperceptibly slow motions over millions of years, we discover a stunning result, which is supported by many decades of scientific observation: Earth's continents were in very different positions in the past (**Figure 1.19**).

The processes that form sand dunes operate in much the same way today as they did millions of years ago.

University of Washington Libraries, Special Collections, John SheltonCollection, KC9807

Melissa Farlow/NG Image Collection

a. A distinctive pattern of wind-deposited sand grains can be seen in a trench dug in this modern sand dune near Yuma, Arizona.

b. A similar pattern can be seen in sandstone rock millions of years old, in the Vermilion Cliffs Wilderness Area in Arizona. We can infer from the similar patterns that these ancient rocks were once sand dunes.

This observation leads us to a more sophisticated understanding of Hutton's principle. The physical processes that occur on Earth and the natural laws that govern them have not changed, but the physical conditions of Earth have changed dramatically over time. Sea levels drop and rise; mountains rise and then are eroded away; the chemical composition of Earth's atmosphere fluctuates, albeit ever so slowly. The cycles maintain a balance, but in doing so the sizes of the reservoirs and the balance among them may change. Modern geologists, while still accepting that the Earth system operates in a context of uniformitarianism, understand that the rates and relative importance of processes can vary over time, and that catastrophic events such as meteorite impacts can have significant consequences, both locally and globally. This is an especially important lesson today, when it appears that our planet has entered a period of human-mediated climatic change that is unprecedented in its rapidity.

Throughout this book we will explore the process of plate tectonics in much greater depth. We will see how virtually every aspect of the Earth system owes its essential character to the existence of plate tectonics. Because plate tectonics has become the overarching theme in geology, it is viewed as a unifying theory. Practically every aspect of geologic science, including the histories of the atmosphere, hydrosphere, and biosphere, is connected to the motion of lithospheric plates.

Process Diagram

How Earth has changed over time • Figure 1.19

These figures show reconstructions of the way Earth's land-masses have changed position over the last 500 million years. Note that Earth had one contiguous super-continent from about 300 million years ago to about 200 million years ago—a point we return to in Chapter 4. The photos on the right show artists' conceptions of some of the major life forms and environments on Earth at each of these times.

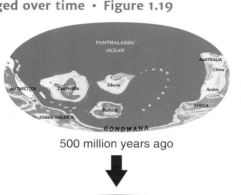

500 million years ago

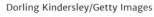 ❶

Marvin Mattelson/NG ImageCollection

300 million years ago

❷

Dorling Kindersley/Getty Images

200 million years ago

❸

Publiphoto/Science Source

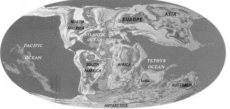

100 million years ago

❹

Publiphoto/Science Source

NG Maps

Present day

❺

THINK CRITICALLY

Based on the movements of plates over the past 300 million years, where do you think the plates will move in the next 100 million years?

Why Study Geology?

With this brief introduction to geology and the Earth system, you have probably deduced some of the reasons why it is important, as well as interesting, to study geology. We need to understand Earth materials because we depend on them for all of our material resources—the minerals, rocks, and metals with which we construct our built environment; the energy with which we run it; the soil that supports agriculture and other plant life; and the air and water that sustain life. Many of Earth's resources are limited and require knowledgeable and thoughtful management. The materials of Earth also have physical and chemical properties that affect us, such as their tendency to flow or fail during a landslide, their capacity to hold or transmit fluids such as water or oil, their ability to absorb waste or prevent it from migrating, or their ability to affect human health if released into the environment in a dangerous manner.

You have learned that Earth is essentially a closed system, which means that all materials remain within the system. It is important to understand how materials move from one reservoir to another. It is also important to understand the time scales that govern these processes in order to gain some perspective on the changes that we see occurring in the natural environment. Some Earth processes are hazardous—that is, damaging to human interests. These geologic hazards include earthquakes, tsunamis, volcanic eruptions, landslides, hurricanes, floods, and meteorite impacts (**Figure 1.20**). Though impacts of large meteorites are rare in the present era, scars from past impacts remind us that we are not isolated in space but, rather, are still an integral part of an active solar system. You can explore some of Earth's most impressive meteorite impact craters using an interactive map online (see *Where Geologists Click* on the next page). The more we know about these hazardous processes, the more successful we will be in protecting ourselves from future natural disasters.

From its beginnings a couple of centuries ago, geology has been an interdisciplinary science because Earth operates through the interactions of biologic, physical, and chemical

Lethal eruption • Figure 1.20

Mount Pinatubo in the Philippines erupted in 1991. Volcanologists predicted the eruption, making it possible to evacuate residents from the area and prevent thousands of deaths. When it erupted, the volcano sent this lethal cloud of searing, dust-laden gases rolling down its flanks, to spread rapidly across the surrounding plains. This particular car and driver escaped, but many houses, trees, and fields were smothered with volcanic ash.

Alberto Garcia/©Corbis

Where Geologists CLICK

Earth Impact Database

The 50 most easily recognizable meteorite impact sites around the world appear on the interactive map at the Earth Impact Database at the Planetary and Space Science Centre of the University of New Brunswick (Canada). These impact sites include Meteor Crater in Arizona, Chicxulub Crater in Mexico, and Manicouagan Crater in Québec. The site provides photos and other information about confirmed impact structures around the world.

processes. Yet we are discovering that the interactions are more complex and dynamic than we would have believed only decades ago. We are still learning about the complexities and interrelationships of subsystems such as climate, ocean currents, and shifting continents. We are now beginning to appreciate our own role in geologic change—for example, rivers, lakes, the atmosphere, soil erosion, and the decline of certain animal species—as well as the need to study the Earth system as a whole rather than in separate fragments.

If you are planning to become a geologist, this book will be an introduction to some of the many fascinating possibilities that await you in your career. If you are taking this course out of personal interest or to fulfill a degree requirement, you will emerge more aware of the geologic nature of our planet and better prepared to make informed decisions about the natural processes that affect your life on a daily basis.

Earth is our home planet. The features that make Earth unique and the powerful geologic processes that characterize the Earth system are a constant source of awe and fascination to those who study them. One of the most important things we can do is to deepen and refine our understanding of our home planet.

 CONCEPT CHECK

1. **Why** do geologists consider the present to be the "key to the past"?

2. **What** are some geologic processes that take place over long periods of time, and some that happen very quickly?

3. **What** are some benefits of understanding geologic processes and principles?

SUMMARY

 THE PLANNER

1 What Is Geology?   2

- **Geology** is the scientific study of Earth, including its formation and internal structure; the materials it is composed of and the properties of those materials; its chemical and physical processes; and its physical, chemical, and biologic history. Physical geology focuses on the materials and processes of the Earth system. Historical geology seeks to establish the chronology of geologic events in Earth's history.

- Geology, like all other **sciences**, employs the **scientific method**, with four major steps: observation and data collection; formulation of a **hypothesis** (or several hypotheses); testing of the hypotheses; and formulation of a **theory** after the hypotheses have been sufficiently tested and revised. A theory is not merely a guess or an opinion but an idea that is well supported by experiment, observation, and logical reasoning.

- Geologists study Earth today using Earth system science. This concept comes from the discovery that Earth is an integrated **system** of interconnected and interdependent parts. Individual systems within the larger Earth system may be classified as open or closed. Earth is, for practical purposes, a closed system, even though some small quantities of matter, such as meteorites, do cross its boundary. The Earth system consists of four principal open subsystems: the **atmosphere**, **hydrosphere**, **biosphere**, and **geosphere**. Materials and energy are stored for varying lengths of time in each of these reservoirs and can move from one to another.

- Three major processes that describe the movement of materials among the subsystems are the **hydrologic cycle**, the **rock cycle**, and the **tectonic cycle**. The term *cycle* indicates that these processes never end as shown in the diagram.

Interconnected cycles · Figure 1.9

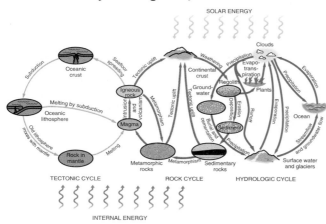

2 Earth in Space 12

- Earth is one of eight bodies in the solar system recognized as planets. The four inner planets, Mercury, Venus, Earth, and Mars, are called the terrestrial planets; they are all small, rocky, and relatively dense, and they have similar sizes and chemical composition. The four outer planets, Jupiter, Saturn, Uranus, and Neptune, are the jovian planets; they consist of huge gaseous atmospheres with small solid cores, giving them very low densities overall. Pluto, until recently considered to be a ninth planet, has been reclassified as a dwarf planet as shown in the diagram.

How the solar system was formed · Figure 1.10

- The nebular hypothesis is the generally accepted hypothesis that the solar system formed from the coalescence and condensation of a nebula, a cloud of interstellar gas and dust. This theory is supplemented by the planetary accretion hypothesis, which states that all of the planets assembled by the accretion of debris within the nebula, and that today's meteoroids and asteroids are fragments that were never swept into the forming planets.

- The processes of planetary accretion, intense early heating, and **meteorite** impacts described by the nebular hypothesis are important to geology because they help explain Earth's beginnings. Early in its history, Earth underwent compositional differentiation into a dense, metallic **core**, a rocky **mantle**, and a brittle, rocky outer **crust**.

- Earth is unique in the solar system in that it possesses an oxygen-rich atmosphere. Earth is also the only planet in the solar system with a hydrosphere in which water exists near the surface in solid, liquid, and gaseous forms, and a biosphere with living organisms. Finally, Earth is the only planet where true soil is formed from regolith by interactions among physical, chemical, and biologic processes, and where life as we know it could exist.

- **Plate tectonics** is a unifying theory in geology. It describes the motion and interaction of large segments of the **lithosphere**. It is because of plate tectonics that Earth has two fundamentally different types of crust: the relatively thin, dense **oceanic crust** of basaltic composition, and the thicker, less dense **continental crust** of granitic composition.

3 The Ever-Changing Earth 20

- The principle of **uniformitarianism** states that the processes we see operating in the Earth system today have operated in a similar manner throughout much of geologic time. In other words, "the present is the key to the past."

- From a human standpoint, most geologic processes are incredibly slow. Earth is roughly 4.56 billion years old, and the rock cycle has been continuous throughout this long history. Though the processes that occur on Earth have not changed, the rates of the different cycles, such as the rock cycle and plate tectonics, have differed over time. The physical conditions on Earth—such as the temperature and composition of the atmosphere, the level of the oceans, and the location of the continents—have also been dramatically different at times in the past as shown in the diagram.

How Earth has changed over time · Figure 1.19

NG Maps

- Earth materials and processes affect our lives through our dependence on Earth resources; through geologic hazards such as volcanic eruptions, floods, and earthquakes; and through the physical properties of the natural environment.

KEY TERMS

atmosphere 8

biosphere 8

continental crust 18

core 15

crust 15

geology 2

geosphere 8

hydrologic cycle 10

hydrosphere 8

hypothesis 4

lithosphere 10

mantle 15

meteorite 15

oceanic crust 18

plate tectonics 18

rock cycle 10

science 2

scientific method 4

system 7

tectonic cycle 10

theory 5

uniformitarianism 20

CRITICAL AND CREATIVE THINKING QUESTIONS

1. Do you think there may be life similar to ours on a planet outside our solar system? What would the atmosphere of that planet be like? Must it have a hydrosphere? Why or why not?

2. Why is the systems approach so useful in studying both natural and artificial processes? Can you think of examples of artificial (i.e., human-built) systems other than those given in the text? Are they open systems or closed systems? (Think about the materials and energy in them.)

3. How do you think the principle of uniformitarianism accounts for occasional catastrophic events such as meteorite impacts, huge volcanic eruptions, or great earthquakes?

4. In this chapter we have suggested that Earth is a close approximation of a natural closed system, and we have hinted at some

of the ways that living in a closed system affects each of us. Can you think of some other ways?

5. In what ways do geologic processes affect your daily life?

6. What are some of the important physical characteristics of environments that lie within the life zone, but outside of the more limited 1-kilometer zone that hosts most of Earth's life? Think about fundamental characteristics, such as temperature, pressure, light availability, and food availability. Why is most of life on Earth restricted to the 1-kilometer zone near the surface? For the more extreme environments, are their constraints similar or do they differ quite a lot?

The life zone • Figure 1.8

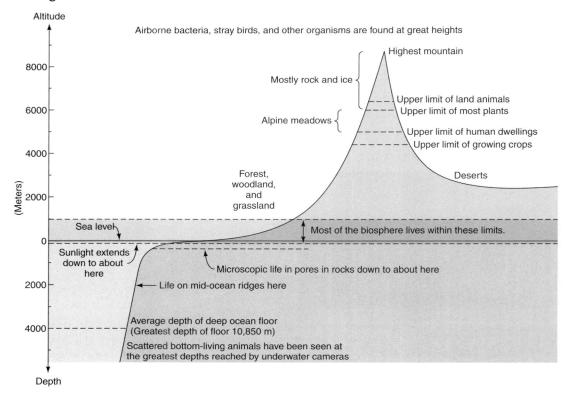

WHAT IS HAPPENING IN THIS PICTURE?

This rock, photographed in Saudi Arabia's Rub' al Khali ("Empty Quarter"), was discovered in 1965. It is believed to be the largest fragment of a meteorite that fell to Earth sometime before 1863 (when the first piece of it was discovered).

Thomas J. Abercrombie/NG ImageCollection

THINK CRITICALLY

1. How do you think these scientists can tell it is a meteorite?

2. Why did it break up into pieces?

3. Why is the desert a good place to look for meteorites? (*Hint*: Think about what would have happened to this rock if it had fallen in a jungle or a mountain range.)

SELF-TEST

(Check your answers in Appendix D.)

1. _____ is fundamentally concerned with understanding the processes that operate at or beneath the surface of Earth and the materials on which those processes operate.

   a. Economic geology

   b. Physical geology

   c. Historical geology

   d. Environmental geology

   e. Planetary science

2. In the scientific method, a theory is _____.

   a. an assumption that cannot be either proven or refuted

   b. a plausible, but yet to be proved, explanation of a phenomenon

   c. a plausible explanation that has been tested and is strongly supported by experimental or observational evidence

   d. the same thing as a hypothesis

   e. a guess that scientists make when they cannot find enough evidence to determine the facts

3. In the scientific method, suppose that an experimental test fails to confirm a certain hypothesis. Which of the following is *never* an appropriate step for a scientist to take?

   a. Discard the hypothesis.

   b. Alter the experimental data to agree with the hypothesis.

   c. Repeat the experiment more carefully.

   d. Formulate and test an alternative hypothesis.

4. The island depicted in the diagram acts as _____.

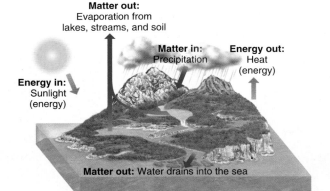

Matter out:
Evaporation from lakes, streams, and soil

Matter in:
Precipitation

Energy out:
Heat (energy)

Energy in:
Sunlight (energy)

Matter out: Water drains into the sea

   a. an intermittent system

   b. a closed system

   c. a solar system

   d. an open system

   e. a isolated system

5. On the time scale of a human lifetime, Earth acts as _____.

   a. an intermittent system

   b. a closed system

   c. a solar system

   d. an open system

   e. an isolated system

6. The _____ is a subset of the Earth system that comprises all of its bodies of water and ice, both on the surface and underground.

   a. atmosphere

   b. hydrosphere

   c. lithosphere

   d. ionosphere

   e. biosphere

7. The _____ explains how new crust is formed and recycled by large-scale motions of Earth's surface and interior.

   a. tectonic cycle

   b. rock cycle

   c. water (hydrologic) cycle

   d. nebular hypothesis

8. According to the planetary accretion model, _____.

   a. planets evolved from molten material condensing from an early solar nebula

   b. planets assembled themselves from meteorite-like debris

   c. most of today's meteorites are the debris that never managed to be swept up by any planet

   d. Both b and c are correct.

   e. Answers a through c are all correct.

9. The inner planets of the solar system are rocky, whereas the outer planets contain a higher proportion of ice and gas. This differentiation occurred in the early solar system because _____.

   a. the rocky and metallic components, which have higher melting points, would have condensed at an early stage and in the innermost region of the solar system

   b. the solar wind was strong enough in the inner solar system to push the lighter gases, such as helium and hydrogen, to the outer solar system

   c. volatile compounds, such as water and methane, condense at lower temperatures common to the outer solar system, where the primordial nebula was cooler

   d. All of the above statements are correct.

10. The photograph is of a basalt flow on the island of Hawaii. Which one of the following statements is correct?

Marc Moritsch/NG Image Collection

   a. Basaltic lava flows have occurred only on Earth.

   b. These types of flows have been common only on Earth and in the early history of the Moon.

   c. Basalt is the most common volcanic rock known in our solar system.

   d. Basaltic lava flows would have been common in the early history of Earth, but in modern times they have largely ceased.

   e. None of the above statements is correct.

11. Earth, Mars, and Venus all have _____.

   a. an oxygen- and nitrogen-rich atmosphere

   b. a core, mantle, and crust

   c. a hydrosphere with liquid water

   d. a biosphere

   e. All of the above answers are correct.

12. These two photographs compare distinctive patterns in windblown sand in a modern dune (a) with similar structures inside an ancient sandstone (b). Our ability to infer that the structures inside the sandstone were formed by the same processes that formed them in a modern sand dune is an application of _____.

a

b

a. the accretionary hypothesis

b. plate tectonic theory

c. Hutton's principle of uniformitarianism

d. the nebular hypothesis

e. planetary differentiation

13. Hutton's principle of uniformitarianism _____.

a. states that the physical processes that act on Earth have not changed over time, even though the physical conditions of Earth have changed dramatically

b. states that the physical processes that act on Earth and the physical conditions of Earth have not changed over time

c. cannot be used to explain rapid fluctuations in the climate system

d. has been rendered obsolete by the modern unifying concept of plate tectonics

14. The rates of some processes involved in the cycles of the Earth system, such as the rock cycle and tectonic cycle, _____.

a. have been constant over time

b. have varied over time

c. have been steadily increasing with time

d. have been steadily decreasing with time

15. The study of geology is important because _____.

a. it helps us understand the processes that govern the Earth system

b. it helps us understand the time scales that govern Earth processes

c. it helps us understand and mitigate the potential threats of geologic hazards, such as earthquakes, volcanic eruptions, landslides, floods, and meteorite impact

d. All of the above answers are correct.

THE PLANNER ✓

Review the Chapter Planner on the chapter opener and check off your completed work.

2 | EARTH MATERIALS

Courtesy Diavik Diamond Mines, Inc.

Jiri Hermann, Courtesy Diavik Diamond Mines, Inc.

Global Locator

Point Lake

NG Maps

DIAMONDS FROM THE DEEP

These diamonds (inset) come from Point Lake, Northwest Territories, Canada, where geologists Charles Fipke and Stewart Blusson discovered diamonds in 1991. They hypothesized that diamonds found in Wisconsin had been pushed from northern Canada by glaciers during the last ice age. They looked for the source and eventually found it. Since 1998, when the mine opened at Point Lake, Canada has become the third largest producer of diamonds in the world.

Apart from its rarity and value, diamond is a remarkable mineral. It is pure elemental carbon, the same chemical composition as graphite and charcoal. Unlike graphite and charcoal, natural diamond forms at extraordinarily high pressures and temperatures, deep under Earth's surface. It is the hardest mineral known and an excellent conductor of heat. Its properties make it valuable for industrial purposes. Artificial diamonds might one day replace silicon in computers; a computer with diamond chips could run at much higher temperatures.

In this chapter you will learn about rocks and minerals. Some are beautiful, some are important economically, and some are vital as nutrients; others are hazardous to human health. By studying rocks and minerals, we can learn to balance their positive and negative effects in our lives.

✓ CHAPTER PLANNER

- Study the picture and read the opening story.
- Scan the Learning Objectives in each section:
  p. 31   p. 35   p. 44   p. 48
- Read the text and study all visuals. Answer any questions.

Analyze key features
- Process Diagram, p. 33
- Geology InSight, p. 34
- What a Geologist Sees, p. 37
- Amazing Places, p. 39
- Case Study, p. 43
- Stop: Answer the Concept Checks before you go on:
  p. 33   p. 44   p. 48   p. 51

End of chapter
- Review the Summary and Key Terms.
- Answer the Critical and Creative Thinking Questions.
- Answer What is happening in this picture?
- Complete the Self-Test and check your answers.

ELEMENTS AND COMPOUNDS

Learning Objectives

1. **Distinguish** between an element and an atom.

2. **Define** atom, isotope, ion, and molecule.

3. **Identify** four kinds of chemical bonding that commonly occur in mineral compounds.

All matter on and in Earth, including the page of text you are reading and the eyes you are reading it with, consists of one or more chemical elements. All of the chemical reactions that control our lives and make life on Earth possible depend on the ways in which these elements interact.

Elements and Atoms

Chemical **elements** are the most fundamental substances

> **element** The most fundamental substance into which matter can be separated using chemical means.

into which matter can be separated and analyzed by ordinary chemical methods (see *Remember This!*). Ninety-two naturally occurring elements are known, and atomic scientists have synthesized a number of other elements. Each element is identified by a symbol, such as H for hydrogen and Si for silicon. Some of the symbols come from the names of the elements in languages other than English, such as Fe for iron, from the Latin *ferrum*, and Na for sodium, from the Latin *natrium*. Others are named in honor of famous scientists, such as element 99, Es, einsteinium. A table of the elements listed in alphabetical order is shown in Appendix B. The table also gives the percentage of each element in the continental crust.

Even the tiniest grain of dust is made of innumerable particles, called **atoms**, which are much too small for the

> **atom** The smallest individual particle that retains the distinctive chemical properties of an element.

eye to see (**Figure 2.1**). In a pure sample of an element, every atom would be the same kind. Atoms are the building blocks of chemistry; they account for all of an element's chemical properties and many of its physical ones, such as density and color. They are so tiny, about one-billionth of a millimeter, that they cannot be seen at all with a conventional optical microscope; only specially designed microscopes have succeeded in imaging atoms.

> **REMEMBER THIS!** The nebular hypothesis tells us that all of the elements in our solar system were inherited from a preexisting interstellar cloud of gas and dust. Can you remember the rest of the nebular hypothesis? Review it by looking back at *The Origin of the Solar System* in Chapter 1.

Chemical reactions produce the rocks, minerals, liquids, and gases of which Earth is made and that geologists study. For this reason, a quick review of chemical elements and atoms is a good place to begin our study of Earth materials. Atoms themselves are composed of even smaller particles, which have no independent chemical properties. The **nucleus** (plural **nuclei**) of an atom contains **protons**, with positive electric charges, and **neutrons**, which are electrically neutral.

The number of protons in an atom—its **atomic number**—determines which element the atom is and gives the atom its chemical characteristics. Atomic numbers range from 1 for the lightest element, hydrogen, to 92 for the heaviest naturally occurring element, uranium. Every element from atomic number 1 to 92 has either been synthesized in the laboratory or found in nature, so there are no new elements to be discovered in that range. However, some laboratories are still working on synthesizing heavier elements, and they have gotten up to element 118 (ununoctium).

Isotopes and Ions

The number of protons plus the number of neutrons in the nucleus of an atom is its **mass number**. Atoms of a given element always have the same atomic number, but they can have variants with different mass numbers. For example, there are three naturally occurring **isotopes** of carbon: carbon-12, carbon-13, and carbon-14. Each of the isotopes of carbon has 6

> **isotopes** Atoms with the same atomic number but different mass numbers.

protons and thus an atomic number of 6. However, the three isotopes contain different numbers of neutrons: 6, 7, and 8 per atom, respectively (thus they have different mass numbers: 12, 13, and 14).

So far we have discussed neutrons and protons, two fundamental components of atoms. The third small, fundamental component of an atom is the **electron**, a negatively charged particle. Electrons orbit the nucleus in complex patterns called **orbitals**, shown schematically in Figure 2.1 as circles of different sizes. An electron has a negative charge

This schematic diagram of carbon-12 shows the main components of a typical atom.

a. A single atom of carbon-12

In a carbon-12 atom, six electrons orbit the nucleus in two complex paths called *orbitals*, rendered here (unrealistically) as circles. The orbitals arrange themselves in energy-level shells, which are more stable when completely filled.

b. Three materials made of carbon

Besides being the sole component of diamond, graphite, and coal, carbon is the most important element in living beings.

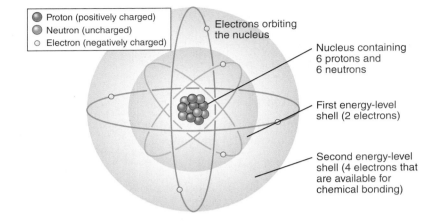

- ● Proton (positively charged)
- ● Neutron (uncharged)
- ○ Electron (negatively charged)

Electrons orbiting the nucleus

Nucleus containing 6 protons and 6 neutrons

First energy-level shell (2 electrons)

Second energy-level shell (4 electrons that are available for chemical bonding)

Diamond

James P. Blair/NG Image Collection

Graphite

John Cancalosi/ NG Image Collection

Coal

James P. Blair/ NG Image Collection

that is equal in magnitude but opposite in sign to the positive charge of a proton.

In its ideal state, an atom has an equal number of protons and electrons and thus is electrically neutral. Under certain circumstances, however, an atom may gain or lose an electron during a chemical reaction. Atoms can exchange electrons; they never exchange protons or neutrons as a result of chemical processes. Thus, electrons play a particularly important role in determining the properties of atoms and in controlling how they may combine with other atoms.

An atom that has lost or gained one or more electrons has a net electric charge and is called an **ion**. If the charge is positive, meaning that the atom has lost one or more electrons, the ion is called a **cation**. If the charge is negative, meaning that the atom has gained one or more electrons, the ion is called an **anion**. A convenient way to indicate ionic charges is to record them as superscripts. For example, Na^+ is the symbol for an atom of sodium that has given up an electron;

> **ion** An atom that has lost or gained electrons.

Cl^- is the symbol for an atom of chlorine that has accepted an electron; and Fe^{2+} is the symbol for an atom of iron that has given up two electrons.

Compounds, Molecules, and Bonding

Chemical **compounds** form when atoms of one or more elements combine with atoms of another element in a specific ratio. For example, sodium and chlorine combine to form sodium chloride (a mineral called halite, also known as table salt), which is written as NaCl. For every Na atom in this compound, there is one Cl atom. The element that tends to form cations is written first; the element that tends to form anions is written second; and the relative numbers of atoms are indicated by subscripts. For example, water forms when hydrogen (a cation, H^+) combines with oxygen

> **compound** A combination of atoms of one or more elements in a specific ratio.

Process Diagram

How ions and compounds form • Figure 2.2

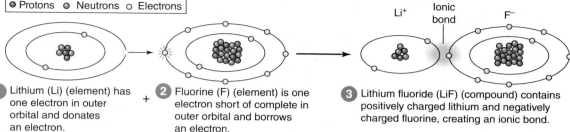

○ Protons ◎ Neutrons ○ Electrons

1 Lithium (Li) (element) has one electron in outer orbital and donates an electron.

\+

2 Fluorine (F) (element) is one electron short of complete in outer orbital and borrows an electron.

3 Lithium fluoride (LiF) (compound) contains positively charged lithium and negatively charged fluorine, creating an ionic bond.

Li⁺ Ionic bond F⁻

THINK CRITICALLY

Suppose the cation in the compound were copper (Cu) and could give up two electrons. Which elements in the Periodic Table (Appendix B) could easily accept the two electrons and complete their outer shell of eight electrons by forming a compound with copper?

(an anion, O^{2-}) in the ratio of two atoms of hydrogen to one atom of oxygen. Thus, for water, we write H_2O. **Figure 2.2** shows how atoms of lithium and fluorine can become ions and then combine to form an ionic compound, lithium fluoride (LiF).

Clearly, the properties of compounds are not the same as the properties of their constituent elements. For example, hydrogen and oxygen are both gases at surface temperature and pressure, whereas water is a liquid. Similarly, elemental sodium and elemental chlorine are both highly toxic, whereas their compound, salt, is essential for life.

The smallest unit that has the properties of a given compound is a **molecule**. Do not confuse a molecule and an atom; the definitions seem similar, but a molecule is a compound that always consists of two or more atoms; the compound H_2O is an example. Molecules are held together by electromagnetic forces known as **bonds**. Bonding involves the transfer of electrons from one atom to another or in some cases the sharing of electrons. There are four principal kinds of bonds, as illustrated in **Figure 2.3**.

> **molecule** The smallest chemical unit that has all the properties of a particular compound.
>
> **bond** The force that holds together the atoms in a chemical compound.

We have spent some time discussing elements, compounds, and bonding because minerals—the main building blocks of the geosphere—occur in the form of chemical compounds (or sometimes as elements). The properties of these minerals depend very much on what chemicals they are made of and how those chemicals are put together. In the next section we will look more closely at the characteristics that define minerals and allow us to identify them.

🛑 **CONCEPT CHECK** STOP

1. **Why** can water be separated into two chemically distinct substances (hydrogen and oxygen), but gold cannot?

2. **How** does a compound differ from an atom, an element, an ion, an isotope, and a molecule?

3. **Which** one of the four main types of bonds is the strongest, and which one is generally the weakest?

Bonding type	Crystal structure	Occurrence	Uses

Ionic bonding: *What happens when one atom transfers an electron to another?* An attractive force is set up between the donor and the receiver that creates an ionic bond. In table salt (NaCl), the positive sodium ions (red) are attracted to all of the negative neighboring chlorine ions (gray), not just to one of them, thus forming a cubic lattice. Compounds with ionic bonds tend to have moderate strength and hardness.

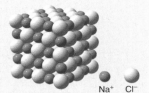

Na$^+$ Cl$^-$

In table salt (sodium chloride, NaCl), each sodium cation is surrounded by chlorine anions.

Crystals of sodium chloride are rectangular, with straight edges.

Salt is a moderately hard solid that dissolves easily in water.

Covalent bonding: *What happens when electrons are shared among different atoms?* The force associated with the sharing is called a covalent bond. Note that electron sharing does not produce ions because electrons have not been lost or gained by the atoms. These are the strongest chemical bonds, and elements and compounds with covalent bonds (e.g., diamond) tend to be strong and hard.

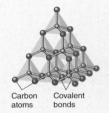

Carbon atoms   Covalent bonds

Diamond consists of carbon atoms connected in a network of covalent bonds. Each atom is connected to four others.

Diamond crystals occur in a rock called kimberlite. Covalent compounds are often strong and hard; diamond is one of the hardest substances known.

Cut and polished diamonds are prized gems. Tiny diamonds are used in industry for cutting and grinding instruments.

Metallic bonding: *Metals bond differently from other materials. Why?* In metals, the atoms are so tightly packed that electrons can be easily shared among several atoms. In fact, the outermost electrons are so loosely held that they can readily drift from one atom to another. This mobility of electrons explains why metals are good at conducting electricity and heat.

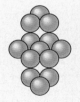

Atoms of gold are packed in the densest possible manner. Each atom is surrounded by, and in contact with, 12 other gold atoms.

This 2.3-kilogram nugget of gold was once embedded in rock, but weathering and erosion have removed most of the rock.

Gold is durable as well as malleable; it has been used as currency since ancient times.

Van der Waals bonding: *Are there any weak kinds of bonds?* Yes, a weak attraction occurs between electrically neutral molecules that have an asymmetrical charge distribution. The positive end of one molecule is weakly attracted to the negative end of the other. For example, carbon atoms in graphite form strong, covalently bonded sheets that are held to one another by weak van der Waals bonds. This is why graphite feels slippery when you rub it between your fingers—you are breaking van der Waals bonds.

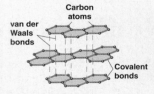

van der Waals bonds   Carbon atoms

Covalent bonds

In graphite, carbon atoms form layers connected by covalent bonds. The layers are weakly held together by van der Waals bonds.

Graphite is not a strong material and can be easily crumbled into small particles.

The "lead" in pencils is not lead, it's really graphite. When you write, the pressure of your hand breaks off a trail of carbon particles.

From left to right and from top to bottom: ©mariusFM77/iStockphoto; Joel Sartore/ NG Image Collection; James P. Blair/ NG Image Collection; Victor R. Boswell, Jr/ NG Image Collection; Nick Norman/NG Image Collection; Bill Curtsinger/ NG Image Collection; John Cancalosi/ NG Image Collection; Richard Nowitz/NG Image Collection.

WHAT IS A MINERAL?

Learning Objectives

1. **Identify** four requirements for a solid material to be classified as a mineral.

2. **Explain** the process of atomic substitution.

3. **Explain** why crystals tend to have flat faces with specific angles between them.

4. **Summarize** the main tests that are used to identify unknown minerals.

To be classified as a **mineral**, a substance must satisfy four criteria; first, it must be a naturally occurring solid; second, it must be formed by inorganic processes; third, it must have a characteristic crystal structure; and fourth, it must have a specific chemical composition. **Figure 2.4** summarizes some of the ways that geologists determine whether or not a material is a mineral.

> **mineral** A naturally formed solid, inorganic substance with a characteristic crystal structure and a specific chemical composition.

Mineral or Not? • Figure 2.4

Can you tell which of the following substances meet all of the requirements to be classified as minerals?

a. Ice is a mineral, though you may not usually think of it this way. It is an inorganic solid material that occurs in nature in the form of hexagonal crystals, and it has a specific chemical formula (H_2O).

b. Water is *not* a mineral because it is not a solid. This criterion also means that naturally occurring substances such as oil and natural gas that are liquids or vapors under "normal" conditions also cannot be considered minerals.

c. Coal fails the second of the four tests for a mineral because it is derived from the remains of plant material and is formed as a result of organic processes. Coal also fails the composition test because it is not a single compound; rather, it is composed of many different compounds.

d. Steel (being produced in the background) fails the first of the four tests for a mineral because it does not occur naturally. It is formed by extensive human processing of naturally occurring ores, which are minerals.

e. Bones contain the same chemical compound found in the common mineral apatite, but bones are *not* minerals because they form by organic processes. Thus the bone in this modern crocodile skull is not a mineral. Solids that are formed by organic processes are often called **biominerals**.

f. This **fossil**, a crocodile skull in the Kenyan National Museum, was once made of bone but is now composed of minerals. During fossilization, the materials of the original bone were replaced in an inorganic process called **mineralization**.

g. Quartz is an easily recognizable mineral, with the simple chemical formula SiO_2. Some minerals have very complex formulas, but the important thing is that the elements combine in specific ratios. In this case, two oxygen atoms bond with one silicon atom to form the mineral quartz.

h. Opal, a gemstone, is typically included in books about minerals, but it is not a true mineral. Opals do not have a specific composition, and they lack a crystalline structure (they are amorphous). Opal is an example of a **mineraloid**.

From left to right and from top to bottom: Robert Sisson/NG Image Collection; Ed George/NG Image Collection; Todd Gipstein/NG Image Collection; BIANCA LAVIES/NG Image Collection; James P. Blair/NG Image Collection; Albert Russ/Shutterstock; James P. Blair/ NG Image Collection; W. Robert Moore/NG Image Collection.

Composition and Structure of Minerals

One of the criteria for a substance to be classified as a mineral is that it must have a specific chemical composition. However, a complication to this rule arises from a phenomenon called **atomic substitution**. In some cases, the ions of two elements can be similar enough in size and in bonding properties that they can substitute for each other in a mineral.

For example, magnesium and iron ions (Mg^{2+} and Fe^{2+}) often can take the place of one another in a mineral lattice because they are similar in size and have identical electrical charge. The mineral olivine (an important component of Earth's mantle) can occur as pure Fe_2SiO_4 or pure Mg_2SiO_4 or an intermediate mixture in which some of the Fe^{2+} cations are replaced by Mg^{2+} cations. The formula for olivine, therefore, becomes $(Mg,Fe)_2SiO_4$, indicating that Mg and Fe can substitute for one another in this mineral. Note that the ratio of cations to anions is not changed by atomic substitution, so the specific composition rule is not violated.

As we have seen, the chemical formula for a mineral must be specific, even if it is not simple. The composition requirements for minerals specifically rule out any material whose composition varies so much that it cannot be expressed by an exact chemical formula. An example of such a material is glass, which is a mixture of many elements and can have a wide range of compositions.

Glass—even naturally formed volcanic glass—also fails the test of having a characteristic **crystal structure**. In a crystal, the atoms are arranged in regular, highly repetitive geometric patterns, as shown in **Figure 2.5a**. By contrast, the atoms in a liquid or in an **amorphous** solid like glass are mixed up or randomly jumbled.

All specimens of a given mineral have an identical crystal structure. Extremely sensitive scanning tunneling microscopes enable scientists to look at the crystal structures of minerals and actually see the orderly arrangement of atoms in the mineral. As you can see in **Figure 2.5b**, the atoms in a crystalline material resemble the regular, orderly rows in an egg carton.

Sometimes two minerals can have the same chemical formula but different crystal structures. A very common example is calcium carbonate ($CaCO_3$), which forms two different minerals called calcite and aragonite. These different forms—with exactly the same chemical composition—are **polymorphs**. Likewise, graphite and diamond are polymorphs of carbon, as explained in Figure 2.3. Remarkably, water ice has 14 different polymorphs that have been discovered so far, all of which have the chemical formula H_2O, but only one of which occurs naturally on Earth. Some of

> **crystal structure** An arrangement of atoms or molecules into a regular geometric lattice. Materials that possess a crystal structure are said to be crystalline.

Atomic structures of crystals · Figure 2.5

The atoms of all crystalline materials are arranged in orderly lattices.

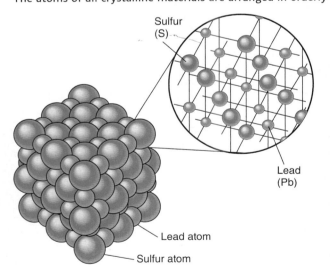

Sulfur (S)

Lead (Pb)

Lead atom

Sulfur atom

b. Atoms are too small to see with an optical microscope, but a scanning tunneling microscope can show the atoms in a crystal. This is an image of a galena crystal; the sulfur atoms look like large bumps and the lead atoms like small ones.

a. Galena (PbS), the main source of lead, has a cubical crystal lattice. The atoms are so small that a 1-centimeter cube of galena would contain 10^{22} atoms. The inset shows an "exploded view" of the arrangement of atoms in a galena crystal. Compare the similar arrangement of atoms in NaCl (Figure 2.3).

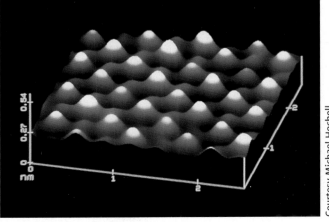

Courtesy Michael Hochell

ASK YOURSELF

Galena (PbS) and halite (NaCl) are

a. atoms.   b. elements.   c. ions.   d. compounds.   e. mineraloids.

the other polymorphs of ice are likely to turn up on the ice-covered moons of other planets, such as Jupiter.

Note that some materials occur in nature as **native elements**; that is, they are not combined in compounds with other elements. Minerals that can occur in this form include some metals, such as gold (chemical formula Au) and silver (Ag), and some nonmetals, such as sulfur (S), graphite (C), and diamond (also C).

Telling Minerals Apart

The compositions and crystal structures of minerals influence their physical properties and characteristics. If we have an unidentified mineral sample, we can apply a few simple tests to determine what mineral it is without taking it to a laboratory or using expensive equipment. The properties most often used to identify minerals are the quality and intensity of light reflected from the mineral, the crystal form and habit of the mineral, its hardness, its tendency to break in preferred directions, its color, and its specific gravity or density. Color, perhaps the most obvious characteristic, is often the least reliable identifier.

Let's look at the properties that are used to identify different minerals and follow the reasoning of a geologist who is attempting to identify the mystery mineral in *What a Geologist Sees*.

What a Geologist Sees

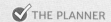 THE PLANNER

A "Mystery Mineral"

Here is a photo of a mineral sample (photo 1). Its identity is—for the moment—unknown to us. What would a geologist see if confronted with a sample of this unknown mineral?

Harry Taylor/Dorling Kindersley/Getty Images, Inc.

The geologist would first note the shiny surface of the specimen, called "metallic luster." The sample is dark gray in color, but the geologist would know that color is generally an unreliable property on which to base a mineral identification.

Next the geologist might make note of the fact that the mineral has grown as a cluster of cubes—it has a "cubic crystal habit." Picking up the specimen, the geologist would discover that it is very heavy; that is, it has a high density.

As we move through this chapter, we will discuss other things that a geologist would see in this mineral sample. You will learn about some of the simple tools (photo) and tests that can help us to figure out the identity of the mystery mineral, which will be revealed at the end of the chapter.

Photo courtesy of Ben Meadows

Geologists use simple tools like these to identify minerals. The bottle contains weak hydrochloric acid (HCl); calcium carbonate ($CaCO_3$) will bubble (or "effervesce") when exposed to a drop of HCl, providing a clue to the mineral's composition. The glass, nail, and penny are used to test hardness. The porcelain block is used to test color. The magnets test for magnetic minerals and the hand lens permits close examination of the mineral's form.

THINK CRITICALLY

Write down the clues as they are revealed to you in this chapter and see if you can use them to figure out the identity of the mystery mineral.

Here are examples that show four common types of luster.

Metallic Pyrite (a form of iron sulfide and a common iron mineral) has a metallic luster.

Vitreous Quartz has a glassy luster.

John Cancalosi/NG Image Collection

Courtesy Brian J. Skinner

Resinous Sphalerite (ZnS, a source of zinc) has a resinous luster, like dried tree resin.

Pearly Talc has a pearly luster.

Courtesy Brian J. Skinner

Courtesy Brian J. Skinner

---

luster The quality and intensity of light that reflect from a mineral.

Luster Minerals reflect light in different ways; we call this property the **luster** of a mineral. The luster of the mystery mineral in *What a Geologist Sees* is **metallic**, meaning that it looks like a polished metal surface. As illustrated in **Figure 2.6**, other kinds of luster you might encounter are **vitreous**, like glass; **resinous**; **pearly**; or **greasy**, as if the surface were covered by a film of oil.

Crystal Form and Habit The ancient Greeks were intrigued by the smooth, planar surfaces of ice needles. The Greeks called ice *krystallos*. Eventually, the word **crystal**

crystal A solid that has grown with crystal faces.

came to be applied to any solid body that has grown with planar faces. The planar surfaces that bound a crystal are called **crystal faces**.

During the 17th century, scientists investigated crystal form as a possible way to identify minerals. But the sizes of crystal faces vary widely from one sample to another. It is apparent in **Figure 2.7** that crystal size and the relative sizes of crystal faces are not the same for these two crystals of quartz. In fact, the relative sizes of crystal faces are not definitive for any mineral.

In 1669 a Danish physician, Nils Stensen (known by his Latin name, Nicolaus Steno) demonstrated that the key property is not the size of faces but rather the angles between them. According to **Steno's law**, the angle between any corresponding pair of crystal faces of a given mineral is constant, no matter what the shape or size of the crystal may be (see Figure 2.7).

Steno suspected that a mineral must have some kind of internal order that predisposes it to form crystals with constant interfacial angles. Proof of a crystal's internal atomic structure finally arrived in 1912, when German scientist Max von Lauë beamed X-rays at crystals and showed that the diffracted rays matched the patterns a geometric array would generate. More recently, scanning tunneling microscopes have given more direct proof of atomic lattice structure, as shown in Figure 2.5b.

Crystals can form either by **crystallization**—essentially, freezing—which occurs when a molten mineral cools to a

Crystal faces and angles • Figure 2.7 _____

Crystals of the same mineral may differ widely in shape, but the angles between faces will remain the same in all specimens. In the two quartz crystals pictured, numbers identify equivalent faces. According to Steno's law, the angle between faces 1 and 3 (for example) is the same in both specimens.

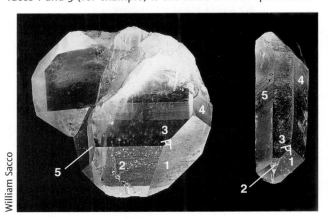

William Sacco

Amazing Places

The Naica Mine, Chihuahua, Mexico

In 2000, two miners in one of Mexico's largest lead and silver mines, the Naica mine near Chihuahua, unexpectedly broke through to a new cave 290 meters below the surface. A similar opening, called the Cave of Swords, had been discovered in 1912, with walls covered by large crystals of gypsum (calcium sulfate). But no one could have expected what they found in the newly discovered cave: crystals, mainly of selenite (a variety of gypsum), that are the largest known crystals of any kind, anywhere in the world.

The giant crystals grew from saline solutions rich in calcium sulfate at a temperature just below 58°C. They grew undisturbed over a period of 600,000 years. When the water was pumped out of the adjacent lead mine, the enormous crystals in this cave were exposed to the air and were seen by people for the first time.

Carsten Petere/ Speleoresearch & Films/ NG Image Collection

Carsten Petere/ Speleoresearch & Films/ NG Image Collection

The Cave of Swords, discovered in 1912, is still in good condition because the mining company has protected it from vandalism.

The largest crystals in the Cave of Crystals can be seen in the foreground. They exceed 11 meters in length and weigh an estimated 55 tons.

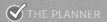

Global Locator

Chihuahua

NG Maps

THINK CRITICALLY

What do you think might happen to these crystals, now that they are no longer surrounded by the fluid in which they grew for so many millennia?

---

temperature where it cannot stay in the liquid state, or by **precipitation**, which occurs when a dissolved mineral becomes sufficiently concentrated that it cannot remain dissolved. Both types of crystals get started by **nucleation**: Molecules of the mineral adhere either to each other, or to any solid object that happens to be present in the liquid, to establish a tiny crystal nucleus. (In this case, a *nucleus* is just a tiny "starter crystal," not a nucleus in the same sense as the nucleus of an atom.) Once the nucleus is established, the crystal grows by attracting more molecules of the same type, as a result of one of the intermolecular forces mentioned earlier (i.e., ionic bonding, covalent bonding, metallic bonding, or van der Waals bonds). As molecules are added, they pack together, following the regular geometric lattice characteristic of the mineral that is forming.

Crystals with planar faces form most easily when mineral grains grow freely in an open space, such as in a cave.

You can see a truly remarkable example of this at the Naica Mine in Chihuahua, Mexico, profiled in *Amazing Places*. Because most mineral grains do not form in open, unobstructed spaces, nicely formed crystals are uncommon in nature. Usually, other mineral grains get in the way. As a result, most mineral grains have an irregular shape. However, in both a crystal and an irregularly shaped grain of the same mineral, all the atoms present are packed in the same strict geometric pattern. This is why we use the term *crystal structure* rather than just *crystal* in defining the characteristics of minerals.

Some minerals grow in such distinctive ways that their shape—called the **habit**—can

habit The distinctive shape of a particular mineral.

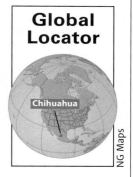

be used as an identification tool. In *What a Geologist Sees* the geologist noted that the mystery sample clearly has a *cubic* habit because it looks like a collection of interlocked cubes. A very different example is the mineral chrysotile, shown in **Figure 2.8**, which takes the form of fine fibers or threads. This **fibrous** habit is characteristic of asbestiform minerals such as chrysotile.

Hardness The **hardness** of a mineral, like habit and crystal form, is governed by crystal structure and by the strength of

> **hardness** A mineral's resistance to scratching.

the bonds between atoms. The stronger the bonds, the harder the mineral. Relative hardness values can be assigned by determining whether one mineral will scratch another, using the **Mohs relative hardness scale**. The scale is divided into 10 steps, each marked by a common mineral listed in **Table 2.1**. Talc, the basic ingredient of "talcum" powders, is the softest

Fibers of asbestos • Figure 2.8

Some minerals have distinctive growth habits without well-formed crystal faces. The mineral chrysotile [$Mg_3Si_2O_5(OH_4)$] grows as fine, cotton-like threads that can be separated and woven into fireproof fabric. This is called an **asbestiform** habit. Several different asbestiform minerals are mined and sold commercially as *asbestos*.

William Sacco

The Mohs scale* of relative hardness of minerals • Table 2.1

Courtesy Brian J. Skinner

These are the 10 reference minerals of the Mohs scale, starting with the softest, talc, in the upper-left corner, and proceeding across two rows to diamond, the hardest mineral in the lower-right corner.

Relative Hardness	Number	Reference Mineral	Hardness of Common Objects
Softest	1	Talc	
	2	Gypsum	
			Fingernail
	3	Calcite	
			Copper penny
	4	Fluorite	
			Carpenter's nail
	5	Apatite	
			Pocketknife; glass
	6	Potassium feldspar	
	7	Quartz	
	8	Topaz	
	9	Corundum	
Hardest	10	Diamond	

*Named for Friedrich Mohs, a German mineralogist, who chose the 10 minerals of the scale.

mineral known and therefore is assigned a value of 1 on the relative hardness scale. Diamond, the hardest mineral, has a value of 10. The 10 steps of the hardness scale do not represent equal intervals of hardness; the important thing is that any mineral on the scale will scratch all minerals below it. For convenience, we often test relative hardness by using a common object such as a penny or a penknife as the scratching instrument, or glass as the object to be scratched. The hardness values of these objects are also shown in Table 2.1.

Our geologist investigating the mystery mineral in *What a Geologist Sees* would find that it is relatively soft and scratches easily with a copper penny, a typical household nail, or a piece of fluorite. It can even be scratched by a fingernail but just barely. This puts its hardness somewhere around 2.5 on the Mohs hardness scale.

Cleavage If you break a mineral with a hammer or drop it on the floor so that it shatters, some of the broken fragments will be bounded by surfaces that are smooth and planar; these are called **cleavage** surfaces. In **Figure 2.9**, the muscovite breaks or

cleavage Breakage of a mineral along preferred planes of weakness.

cleaves easily into thin sheets but does not cleave at all in any other direction. In certain minerals, several cleavage directions are present. The potassium feldspar ($KAlSi_3O_8$) has two cleavages, and the halite (NaCl) has three directions, so that all the fragments of halite shown in Figure 2.9 are bounded by smooth planar surfaces.

Mineral cleavage • Figure 2.9

Geologists use the term *cleavage* to describe how a mineral sample breaks.

©Breck Kent

a. Muscovite (a potassium aluminosilicate mineral), a form of mica, cleaves so easily in one direction that it can be split by hand into flakes that are suggestive of the pages of a book.

John Cancalosi/NG Image Collection

b. Potassium feldspar (another potassium aluminosilicate), one of the most common minerals on Earth, breaks along two directions at right angles.

William Sacco

c. Halite (NaCl, or table salt) has three distinct cleavage directions. No matter how small the bits you break it into, they will always have perpendicular faces.

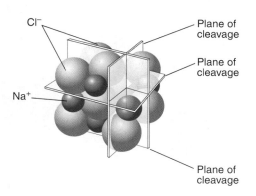

Cl⁻

Plane of cleavage

Plane of cleavage

Na⁺

Plane of cleavage

Don't confuse crystal faces and cleavage surfaces, even though the two often look alike; a cleavage surface is a breakage surface, whereas a crystal face is a growth surface. Also, note the difference between hardness and cleavage: A mineral might be quite hard—that is, resistant to scratching—but it may still cleave easily in one or more directions. Diamond, the hardest mineral, has four directions of cleavage.

The directions in which cleavage occurs are governed by crystal structure. Cleavage takes place along planes where the bonds between atoms are relatively weak, as in the case of muscovite, or where there are fewer bonds per unit area, as in the case of diamond. Because cleavage directions are directly related to crystal structure, the angles between equivalent pairs of cleavage directions are the same for all grains of a given mineral. Thus, the angles between cleavage planes—like the angles between crystal faces—are constant. A small hand lens is usually enough for a geologist to spot these distinctive angles. As we remarked earlier, crystals and crystal faces are somewhat rare; but almost every mineral grain you see in a rock shows one or more breakage surfaces. That is why cleavage is such a useful aid in the identification of minerals.

Our geologist would carefully examine the mystery mineral in *What a Geologist Sees* and discover a place where rough handling has broken off a fragment, revealing three cleavages at right angles.

Color and Streak The color of a mineral, though often striking, is not a reliable means of identification (**Figure 2.10**). A mineral's color is determined by several factors, but the main determinant is chemical composition. Some elements can create strong color effects, even when they are present only as trace impurities. For example, the mineral corundum (Al_2O_3) is commonly white or grayish, but when small amounts of chromium are present as a result of atomic substitution of Cr^{3+} for Al^{3+}, corundum is blood red and is given the gem name *ruby*. Similarly, when small amounts of iron and titanium are present, the corundum is deep blue, producing another gem, sapphire. Many other colors, such as green, gray, white, black, and pink, are not particularly useful in identifying minerals because there are so many minerals that occur in these colors. The *Case Study* discusses the tradition of personal adornment with gemstones of various colors.

Color can be particularly confusing in opaque minerals that have metallic luster. This is because the color is partly a property of the size of the mineral grains. One way to reduce error is to prepare a **streak** by rubbing a specimen of a metallic luster mineral on an unglazed fragment of porcelain called a **streak plate**. The color of a streak is reliable because all the grains in the streak are very small and the effect of grain size is reduced. For example, hematite (Fe_2O_3),

> **streak** A thin layer of powdered mineral made by rubbing a specimen on an unglazed fragment of porcelain.

an important iron-bearing mineral, produces a reddish-brown streak, even though a specimen may look black and metallic (**Figure 2.11**). Our geologist would discover that the streak of the mystery mineral from *What a Geologist Sees* is gray.

Same mineral, different colors • Figure 2.10

Color is not a very reliable property on which to base a mineral identification.

William Sacco

a. These cut gems are all synthetic samples of the mineral corundum (Al_2O_3). They are all the same type of material, but slight differences in chemical composition give them very different colors.

The Natural History Museum

b. Uncut natural specimens of the same mineral, corundum, display a similarly wide range of colors. The red corundum crystals, called rubies, are from Tanzania. The blue crystals, called sapphires, come from New Jersey. The ruby in the upper-right corner is about 2.5 centimeters across.

CASE Study

Minerals for Adornment

The oldest known materials used for personal adornment by our ancestors were shells and fragments of bone, as much as 100,000 years ago. In the Neolithic Period, starting about 10,000 years BCE, people began to rely on hard stones for their utility, and also to value them for their beauty and symbolic meaning.

The wearing of jewelry and gemstones, principally to express status, increased as societies became more complex and as metalworking grew in importance and sophistication. Ancient Egyptians had access to many different gemstones, as well as intricate worked metals in which to set them. They wore gemstones because of their beauty, but also attributed symbolic meaning and power to many of them (**photo 1**).

This gold bracelet from the time of King Tutankhamun is set with turquoise, a symbol of the sky and the goddess Hathor.

DEA/S. Vannini/Getty Images, Inc.

The engagement ring of Kate Middleton, now the Duchess of Cambridge, has a 12-carat sapphire set in white gold and surrounded by diamonds.

WPA Pool/Getty Images, Inc.

Today we still use gemstones for both personal adornment and symbolic meaning (**photo 2**). For many people, it is important to know that the stone they are purchasing is genuine. But all gems can be synthesized; how can you be sure you are buying a natural stone? Trusting reliable jewelers is a good idea, but you can also make your own test. Synthetic stones are usually free of flaws and inclusions, while natural stones—even those of very high quality—almost always have some tiny defects (**photo 3**). Even high-quality diamonds usually contain tiny specks of black graphite. A 10x magnifier is a good way to look for imperfections and make sure your sample is natural.

This 2-carat diamond contains a large inclusion of violet-red garnet.

THINK CRITICALLY

Why do natural minerals tend to have inclusions and impurities, whereas synthetic ones typically do not?

© Mary Evans/Natural HistoryMuseum/Age Fotostock America

Mineral streak · Figure 2.11

Although hematite (Fe_2O_3) is shiny, black or gray, and metallic looking, it makes a distinctive red-brown smear when rubbed on a porcelain streak plate.

William Sacco

Density Another important physical property of a mineral is how light or heavy it feels; this is an indication of its **density**. Two equal-sized baskets have different weights when one is filled with feathers and the other with rocks because the rocks have greater density than the feathers. Minerals that have a high density, such as gold, have closely packed atoms. A sample of gold feels distinctly heavy when you pick it up. Minerals with a low density, such as ice, have less closely packed atoms.

density
Mass per unit of volume.

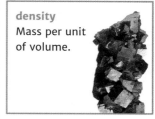

It is not easy to measure the density of a mineral in a laboratory because doing so requires dividing the mass by the volume, and the volume of an irregularly shaped object is difficult to determine. This was the same problem that Archimedes faced more than 2000 years ago, when he was asked to determine whether the gold in a crown was pure or alloyed with a less dense material. Geologists use a modern version of Archimedes' method. First, they measure the weight of the mineral grain in air (W_A). Then they submerge it in water and measure the weight again (W_W). The weight in water is less than that in air, and the difference ($W_A - W_W$) is the weight of water displaced by the mineral grain. The ratio of W_A to ($W_A - W_W$) gives the **specific gravity** of the mineral. Water has a density of 1.0 grams per cubic centimeter (g/cm^3), which means that its specific gravity is numerically equal to its density.

Many common minerals, such as quartz, have specific gravities in the range of 2.5 to 3.0 g/cm^3. Fortunately, fancy equipment is usually not needed to determine the specific gravity of an unknown mineral sample. If a mineral is substantially lighter than 2.5 g/cm^3 or substantially heavier than 3.0 g/cm^3, a geologist can immediately tell this by lifting the sample. Metallic minerals generally feel heavy, whereas minerals with vitreous luster tend to feel light. Our geologist testing the mystery mineral would discover that it feels quite a bit heavier than most other rocks and minerals of the same size; its specific gravity is 7.5 g/cm^3.

Other Mineral Properties We have described the most commonly used properties for identifying a mineral. However, other properties can also be helpful. For example, some minerals are translucent or transparent, while others are opaque. Certain minerals, such as calcite, are **birefringent**; when you look at an object through them, you can see a double image because the mineral's crystal structure splits light beams in two.

If you can afford to destroy some of your sample, dissolving it in acid may provide useful information about its chemical composition. For instance, carbonate minerals such as calcite dissolve readily in dilute hydrochloric acid or even in vinegar; a droplet of the acidic liquid onto the surface of the sample will yield tiny bubbles as the mineral dissolves and releases carbon dioxide gas.

Certain minerals, particularly those that contain iron in their chemical composition, may be **magnetic**; that is, they are attracted by a magnet. Still other minerals, such as scheelite and calcite, have an unusual property—called **luminescence** or **fluorescence**—that causes them to glow when exposed to an ultraviolet light. This property can be easily tested with a handheld "black light" source.

Mystery Mineral Clues What is the identity of the mystery mineral in *What a Geologist Sees?* Our geologist discovered several clues:

1. It has a metallic luster.
2. It has a cubic habit.
3. It is fairly soft, with a hardness of about 2.5 on the Mohs scale.
4. Both the color and the streak are gray.
5. It has three perpendicular cleavage directions.
6. It feels heavy and has an unusually high specific gravity of 7.5 g/cm^3.

Can you figure out the identity of the mineral? In what ways did you apply the scientific method to identify the mineral (see *Remember This!*)? Refer to the table of minerals in Appendix C and see if your identification agrees with that of the geologist. (The answer is given at the end of the chapter.)

> **REMEMBER THIS!** Do you recall the steps of the scientific method? Referring to these steps, explain how you arrived at the identity of our mystery mineral. Go back to *What Is Geology?* in Chapter 1 if you need to review the scientific method.

STOP CONCEPT CHECK

1. **What** requirements must be satisfied if a substance is to be called a mineral?

2. **Why** is it possible for an ion of Fe to substitute for an ion of Mg in minerals such as olivine?

3. **What** is the difference between a cleavage surface and a crystal face, and how are they related?

4. **What** is the difference between luster, color, and streak, and how are they related?

MINERAL FAMILIES

Learning Objectives

1. **Name** the 12 most common chemical elements in Earth's crust.

2. **Identify** the two most common mineral families and four common accessory mineral families.

3. **Describe** the various molecular structures of silicate minerals.

Geologists have identified approximately 4000 mineral species. This number may seem large, but it is tiny compared with the number of synthetic materials, such as ceramics, concrete, drugs like aspirin, and solid chemical reagents. The reason for the disparity between the number of minerals and the millions of solids that have been synthesized in laboratories becomes clear when we consider the relative abundance of the chemical elements in nature (see *Remember This!*).

Out of every kilogram of material in Earth's continental crust, only 12 elements are present in quantities greater than 1 gram, as shown in **Figure 2.12**. The abundant 12 account for 992.3 of the 1000 grams in a kilogram of

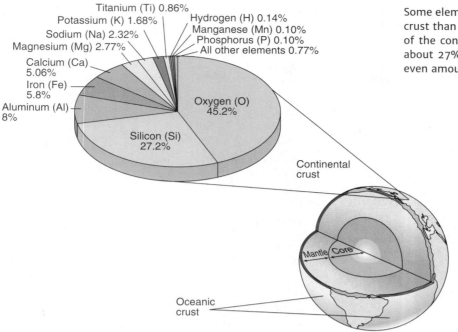

Titanium (Ti) 0.86%
Potassium (K) 1.68%
Sodium (Na) 2.32%
Magnesium (Mg) 2.77%
Calcium (Ca) 5.06%
Iron (Fe) 5.8%
Aluminum (Al) 8%
Hydrogen (H) 0.14%
Manganese (Mn) 0.10%
Phosphorus (P) 0.10%
All other elements 0.77%
Oxygen (O) 45.2%
Silicon (Si) 27.2%
Continental crust
Mantle Core
Oceanic crust

Some elements are vastly more common in Earth's crust than others. Oxygen accounts for about 45% of the continental crust by weight and silicon for about 27%. Carbon, though vital to life, does not even amount to 1 part per 1000.

THINK CRITICALLY

What is the elemental composition of Earth's core? How would the pie chart change if you were to show the elemental composition of the core, or Earth as a whole, instead of just the continental crust?

Earth's continental crust; all common minerals have compositions based on one or more of these abundant elements. The remaining 80 elements, combined, make up less than 1% of the crust by weight and less than 2% by volume. Minerals made of the scarcer elements occur only in small amounts, and valuable, economically exploitable ore deposits of scarce elements such as gold, uranium, and tin are rare and hard to find. However, these scarce elements can be extracted and used to synthesize a wide range of materials in the laboratory and in manufacturing for everyday use.

> **REMEMBER THIS!** Why are Earth's elements so unevenly distributed? Is the same true of the other terrestrial planets? You can remind yourself of the answer to this question by looking back at *The Origin of the Solar System* in Chapter 1.

Minerals of Earth's Crust

Mineral families are groups of minerals that are similar to one another in terms of chemistry, atomic structure, or (more commonly) both. Two elements—oxygen and silicon—make up more than 80% of the atoms in Earth's crust and comprise more than 70% of its mass. Thus it should be no surprise that the great majority of minerals contain one or both of these elements. The most common family of minerals, the silicate minerals, contain a strongly bonded complex anion called the silica anion that contains both silicon and oxygen, $(SiO_4)^{4-}$. The bonding

in most silicate minerals is a mixture of ionic and covalent; as a result, silicates tend to be hard, tough minerals (**Figure 2.13**). The next most abundant family, the **oxide minerals**, contain the simple oxide anion O^{2-}.

> **silicate minerals** The most common mineral family in Earth's crust, based on the silica anion.

A few silicate minerals and a few oxide minerals, together with calcium sulfate and calcium carbonate, comprise the bulk of Earth's crust—an estimated 99.2% by volume. These common minerals, of which there are about 30, are called **rock-forming minerals**. Rock-forming minerals are everywhere—not only in rocks but also in soils and sediments, and even in the dust that we breathe. Rock-forming minerals are common and inexpensive but nevertheless economically vital; you rely on them every day when you drive on a paved road or enter a concrete building.

Less common minerals are called **accessory minerals**. These are widely present in common rocks but usually in such small amounts that they do not determine the properties of the rocks. Though they are less common and typically present in lesser abundance than the principal rock-formers, many are important economically. Some accessory minerals are important **ore minerals**; as mentioned previously, galena (PbS) is the main source of lead, and chalcopyrite ($CuFeS_2$) is the principal source of copper. Others have significant biological functions; the accessory mineral apatite $[Ca_5(PO_4)_3(F,OH)]$ supplies the phosphorus for agricultural fertilizers and is also the fundamental compound in our bones and teeth.

Silicate minerals consist of silicon and oxygen groupings linked together, with other elements in the spaces between them.

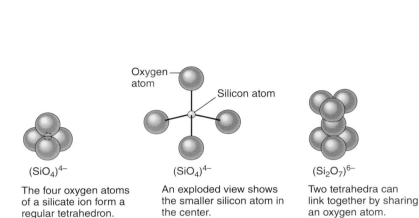

$(SiO_4)^{4-}$	$(SiO_4)^{4-}$	$(Si_2O_7)^{6-}$	$(Si_2O_7)^{6-}$
The four oxygen atoms of a silicate ion form a regular tetrahedron.	An exploded view shows the smaller silicon atom in the center.	Two tetrahedra can link together by sharing an oxygen atom.	Exploded view of the same configuration.

Silicates: The Most Important Rock-Formers

Not only are silicates the most common minerals and the main rock-formers, they also have an unusual diversity of atomic structures. To explain this phenomenon, we begin by looking at the silica anion itself, in which four oxygen atoms are tightly bonded to the single silicon atom. As you saw in Figure 2.13, if we draw a stick figure, joining the centers of the oxygen atoms with lines, we get a regular **tetrahedron** (i.e., a pyramid with a triangular base). The small, ionically bonded silicon atom occupies the space at the center of the tetrahedron, and the oxygen atoms occupy the corners. This is the building block of silicate mineral structures.

Two silica tetrahedra can bond by sharing an oxygen atom. This process can be repeated over and over, with the silica anions assembling themselves into large, complex linked structures called **polymers**. Silica anions only polymerize by joining at corners, never along edges or faces. **Figure 2.14** illustrates the different mineral structures, such as rings, chains, sheets, or three-dimensional frameworks that can be formed out of silica ions through **polymerization**. Different common cations, such as calcium (Ca^{2+}), aluminum (Al^{3+}), magnesium (Mg^{2+}), iron (Fe^{2+}), sodium (Na^+), and others, can fit into the spaces between the polymerized silica tetrahedra.

> **polymerization** The formation of a complex molecule by the joining of repeated simpler units.

The identity of a silicate mineral is determined by three factors: (1) how the silica tetrahedra occur within the mineral (i.e., whether they are single or polymerized); (2) which cations are present; and (3) how the cations are distributed throughout the crystal structure. For example, as shown in Figure 2.14, polymerization in mica produces a sheet, and the pronounced cleavage of mica is parallel to the sheets. In quartz the three-dimensional framework, shown in **Figure 2.15**, is equally strong in all directions, so quartz is a hard, tough mineral that lacks cleavage. The two most common mineral families in the continental crust both have three-dimensional frameworks of polymerized silicate tetrahedra. The two families are the feldspars (most abundant) and quartz.

Other Important Mineral Families

Silicates and oxides are the two main rock-forming mineral families, but other mineral groups are also important as constituents of the crust, as mineral resources, and as life-supporting materials. These groups are based on ions and ionic groupings that are different from those in the silicates and oxides.

For example, **carbonate** family minerals are based on the complex $(CO_3)^{2-}$ anion. The carbonate minerals calcite and dolomite are the main constituents of limestone and marble, as well as the shells of small marine organisms such as mollusks. They are also the principal building blocks of coral reefs. Recall from our discussion of mineral identification that calcite typically dissolves in weak acids; as it turns out, ordinary groundwater is a weakly acidic solution. Thus, most terrains that are underlain by carbonate-bearing rocks have complex systems of underground caves that form in areas where carbonate minerals have been dissolved and carried away by circulating groundwater.

Two other important mineral families are the **sulfates** and **sulfides**, which both contain the element sulfur (or S, which is distinct from Si, silicon). Sulfates are based on the complex $(SO_4)^{2-}$ anion, whereas sulfides are based on the simple S^{2-} anion. One example of an important sulfate mineral is gypsum, used to make plaster, which forms as a salt that precipitates as a result of evaporation of seawater.

Polymerization and the common silicate minerals • Figure 2.14

This chart summarizes the ways in which silica ions can polymerize to form minerals. Typical examples of each type are shown in the photographs. There are many other silicate minerals in each category, but all of the principal categories that occur in nature are illustrated here.

Silicate Structure		Mineral/Formula	Cleavage	Example of a Specimen
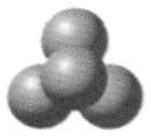	Single tetrahedron	Olivine Mg_2SiO_4	None (breaks with glassy or **conchoidal** fracture)	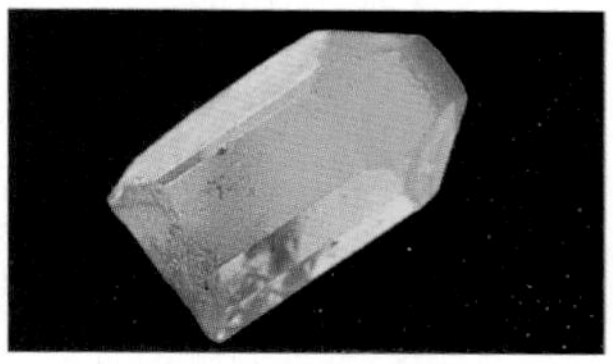 Courtesy Brian J. Skinner
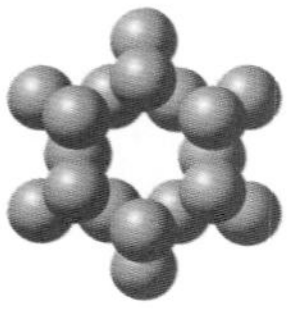	Hexagonal ring	Beryl (gem form is emerald) $Be_3Al_2Si_6O_{18}$	One direction	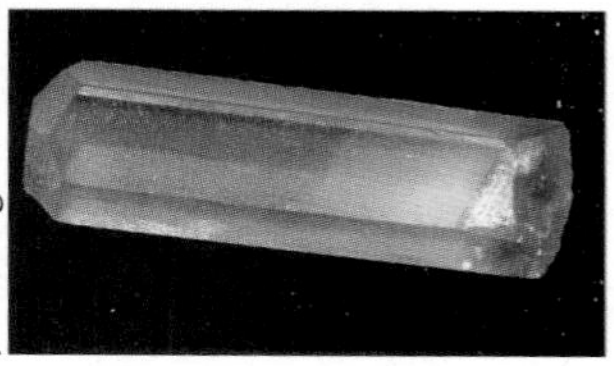 John E. Fletcher & Stewart B. Anthony /NG Image Collection
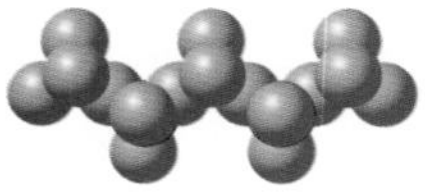	Single chain	Pyroxene group $CaMg(SiO_3)_2$ (variety: diopside)	Two directions at 90°	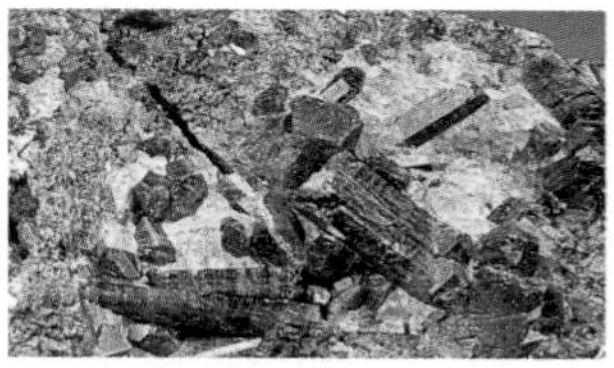 ©Breck Kent
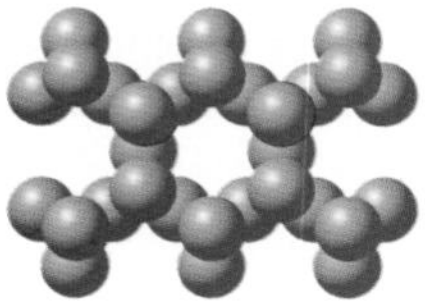	Double chain	Amphibole group $Ca_2Mg_5(Si_4O_{11})_2(OH)_2$ (variety: tremolite)	Two directions at 120°	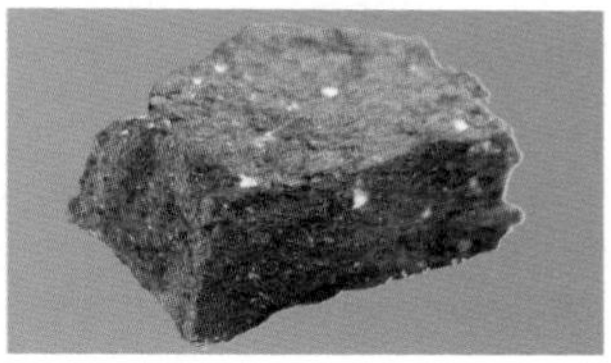 Tyler Boyes/ Shutterstock
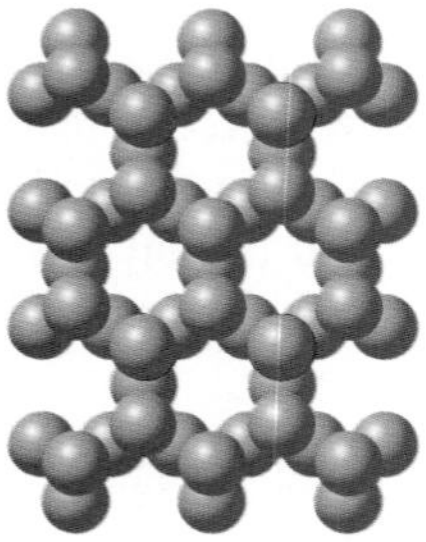	Sheet	Mica $KAl_2(AlSi_3O_{10})(OH)_2$ (variety: muscovite) $K(Mg,Fe)_3(AlSi_3O_{10})(OH)_2$ (variety: biotite)	One direction	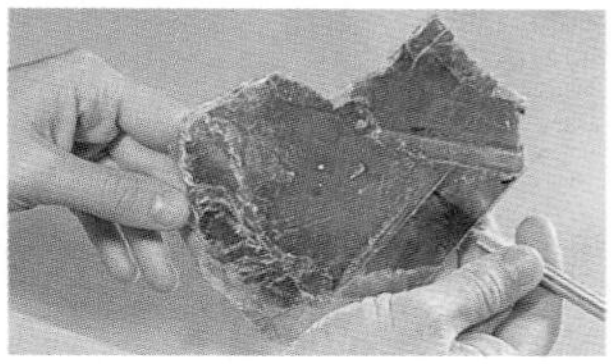 ©Breck Kent
See Figure 2.15 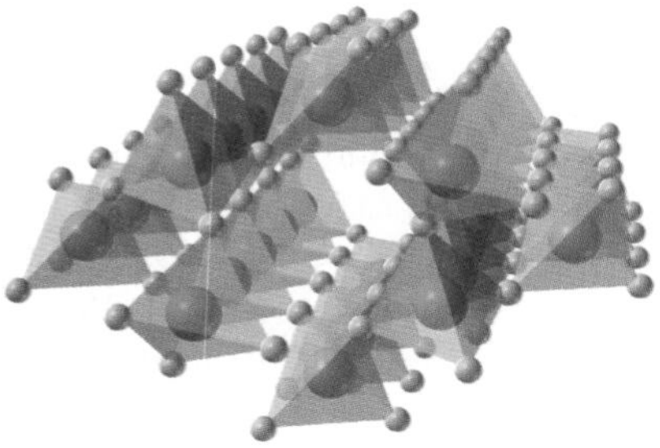	Framework	Feldspar $KAlSi_3O_8$ (variety: orthoclase)	Two directions at 90°	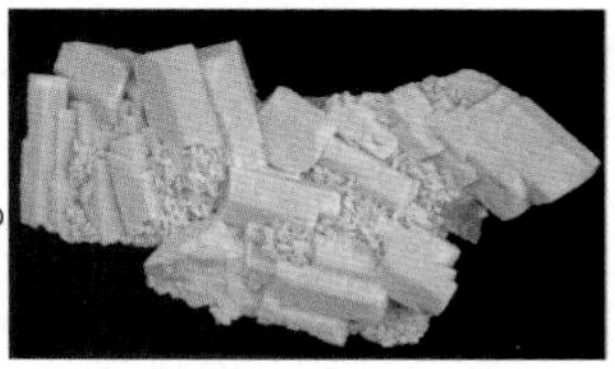 John Cancalosi/ NG Image Collection
		Quartz SiO_2	None (breaks with glassy or conchoidal fracture)	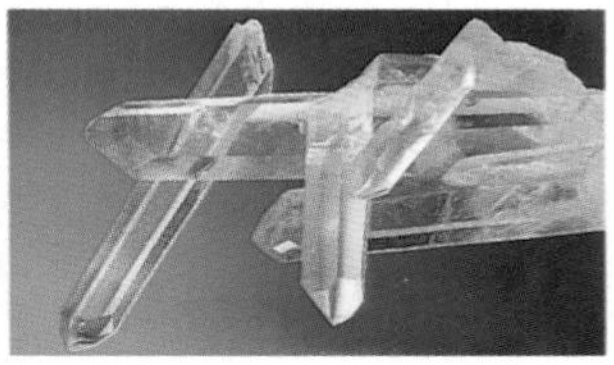 ©Breck Kent

Quartz, one of the most abundant minerals, is composed of silica ions tightly linked in a three-dimensional lattice. It has no cleavage planes and is very resistant to wear. For the purposes of illustration, the oxygen atoms (blue) are shown as being smaller than the silicon atoms (red).

Sulfide minerals typically consist of one or more metal ions (e.g., copper, nickel, or iron) bonded with the S^{2-} anion. Thus, sulfides tend to be important ore minerals from which a wide variety of metals are extracted; galena (PbS) is an example of a sulfide mineral.

Phosphates, another important mineral family, are based on the complex $(PO_4)^{3-}$ anion. Phosphorus is a life-supporting element, and, as mentioned earlier, the phosphate mineral apatite is a central constituent of bones and teeth.

STOP CONCEPT CHECK

1. **Which** two chemical elements make up a little more than 70% of Earth's crust by weight?
2. **Which** two mineral families are the most abundant in Earth's crust?
3. **Describe** how polymerization occurs in silicate minerals and how it can affect the properties of the minerals.

ROCK: A FIRST LOOK

Learning Objectives

1. **Explain** the difference between a rock and a mineral.
2. **Identify** the three major families of rock.
3. **Explain** what holds rock together and why some types of rock are more cohesive than others.

If rocks are the words that tell the story of Earth's long history, minerals are the letters that form the words. An important distinction between a mineral and a rock is that **rocks** are aggregates; this means that rocks are collections of minerals (and sometimes other types

> **rock** A naturally formed, coherent aggregate of minerals and sometimes other nonmineral matter.

of particles) stuck together or intergrown. Rocks usually consist of several different types of minerals, but sometimes they are made of just one type of mineral. In any case, a rock will contain many grains of the constituent mineral or minerals.

Igneous, Sedimentary, and Metamorphic Rock

Rocks are grouped into three large families, according to the processes that form them (**Figure 2.16**). Within each of these major rock families, called *igneous*, *sedimentary*, and *metamorphic*, there is a range of possible mineral assemblages —the types and relative proportions of minerals that constitute the rock. Mineral assemblages help geologists identify and classify rocks, and they reveal much about the geologic environment in which a particular rock formed (see *Remember This!*).

In *Where Geologists Click* you will find a wide range of beautiful photos of rocks, minerals, fossils, and many geologic processes; download them as desktop wallpaper, if you like.

The three rock families are illustrated here.

Courtesy Brian J. Skinner

Raymond Gehman/NG Image Collection

▲ Igneous rock

This granite boulder on Mount Desert Island in Acadia National Park, Maine, was transported to its current location by a glacier. The boulder is sitting on a thick platform of granite that was once part of an enormous magma chamber underlying a volcano. Inset is a close-up photo of granite.

Courtesy Brian J. Skinner

Taylor S. Kennedy/NG Image Collection

▲ Sedimentary rock

This remarkable landscape is in Bryce Canyon National Park in Utah. The horizontal rock layers are mainly sandstone (formed from grains of sand deposited in a beach environment and subsequently cemented together) and limestone (formed when the region was covered by a shallow sea). Sedimentary rock layers like these reveal a great deal about past conditions. The inset photo shows a close-up of sandstone.

Courtesy Brian J. Skinner

James P. Blair/NG Image Collection

◀ Metamorphic rock

The beautiful Lauterbrunnen Valley in Switzerland lies within a great mountain range—the Alps—where the rocks have been uplifted and altered by enormous tectonic forces. In this photo Lauterbrunnen Falls cascades down a steep cliff of metamorphic rock. The inset close-up shows gneiss, a metamorphic rock. This rock may have started as a sedimentary or igneous rock, but it has been altered by heat and pressure, resulting in a new mineral assemblage and distinctive banded appearance.

National Geographic Photo Gallery: Rocks

The National Geographic Society maintains an extensive and beautiful collection of rock and mineral photographs that geologists refer to and enjoy. Elsewhere in National Geographic's Photo Gallery you will find all sorts of information on geologic processes. Try clicking on "Earth" for photos of lava flows, rocks, gems, caves, earthquake damage, and lots more. Under "Prehistoric World" you will find photos of all sorts of fossils.

Igneous Rock Igneous rock (named from the Latin *ignis*, meaning "fire") is formed by the cooling and solidification of **magma**. Magma, or molten rock, often contains mineral grains and dissolved gases. Depending on its environment, magma may cool slowly or very rapidly. When it reaches a temperature that is sufficiently low, mineral grains begin to crystallize from the magma, just as ice crystals form in water as it cools. The physical properties of the rock will differ, depending on whether the cooling process is slow, giving the crystals a lot of time to grow, or fast. We will have much more to say about these differences in Chapter 6.

> **igneous rock** Rock that forms by cooling and solidification of molten rock.
>
> **magma** Molten rock that may include fragments of rock, volcanic glass and ash, or gas.

Sedimentary Rock The next major rock family forms when mineral and rock particles are transported by water, wind, or ice and then deposited. This fragmented, transported, and deposited material is called **sediment**. In certain geologic circumstances, under conditions of low pressure and low temperature near Earth's surface, sediment may be transformed into **sedimentary rock**.

> **sediment** Rock that has been fragmented, transported, and deposited.
>
> **sedimentary rock** Rock that forms from sediment under conditions of low pressure and low temperature near the surface.

"Low temperature" and "low pressure" here are by geologic standards; they may still be higher than the pressure and temperature where we live. Sediment- and soil-forming processes and transportation processes are discussed in detail in Chapter 7, and sedimentary rocks and rock-forming processes are examined in Chapter 8.

Metamorphic Rock The third major rock family is **metamorphic rock**, whose original sedimentary or igneous form and mineral assemblage have been changed as a result of exposure to high temperature, high pressure, or both. The term **metamorphism** comes from the Greek *meta*, meaning "change," and *morphe*, meaning "form"—hence, "change of form." Metamorphism occurs in a variety of tectonic and geologic environments. It can occur as an end result of the processes of burial and compaction through which sediments become transformed into rock. It can also occur when rock is subjected to the extreme pressures and temperatures associated with mountain building along convergent plate boundaries. Temperature-induced metamorphism can occur when rock is heated—essentially baked—by nearby magma. How and why metamorphism occurs, the types of metamorphic rock, and their characteristic mineral assemblages are discussed in detail in Chapter 10.

> **metamorphic rock** Rock that has been altered by exposure to high temperature, high pressure, or both.
>
> **metamorphism** The set of processes by which rock is altered chemically, physically, or both.

REMEMBER THIS! Have a look back at Figure 1.9, which shows the three main interacting Earth cycles. Locate igneous, sedimentary, and metamorphic rock on the diagram; also look for magma and sediment. What processes are shown on the diagram by which one of these materials can be transformed into another?

What Holds Rock Together?

The minerals in some types of rock are held together with great tenacity, whereas in others they are easily broken apart. While the forces that hold minerals together are chemical, the forces that hold rock together are partly mechanical and partly chemical. Igneous and metamorphic rocks are the most cohesive because both types contain intricately interlocked minerals. During the formation of igneous and metamorphic rocks, the growing minerals crowd against each other, filling all spaces and forming an intricate, three-dimensional jigsaw puzzle that will not pull apart very easily. A similar interlocking of grains holds together steel, ceramics, and bricks.

The forces that hold together the grains of sedimentary rock are less obvious. Sediment is a loose aggregate of particles, and it must be transformed into sedimentary rock by one or more rock-forming processes, discussed in detail in Chapter 7. These processes tend to cause the individual grains of the sediment to become interlocking. Sedimentary rock can form by compaction, during which the mineral grains in the sediment are squeezed and compressed by the weight of overlying sediment, becoming compacted into an interlocking network of grains. Second, water may deposit new minerals such as calcite, quartz, or iron oxide into the open spaces that act as a **cement**. A third way that sedimentary rock holds together is by **recrystallization**. As sediment becomes deeply buried and the temperature rises, mineral grains begin to recrystallize. The growing grains interlock and form strong aggregates. The process is the same as that which occurs when ice crystals in a snow pile recrystallize into a compact mass of ice (**Figure 2.17**).

 CONCEPT CHECK

1. **What** is a mineral assemblage?
2. **What** are the principal differences between igneous, sedimentary, and metamorphic rocks?
3. **How** can a loose collection of sediment become a cohesive rock?

Recrystallization · Figure 2.17

When a wolf walked across snow-covered ground in Siberia, its paws caused the ice crystals in the snow to become compacted and to recrystallize. Later, wind eroded away the loosely packed snow. The compacted ice was more resistant to erosion, so the footprints now stand out above the snow surface. A similar process, over a longer period of time and at higher temperatures and pressures, creates sedimentary rock out of loose sediment.

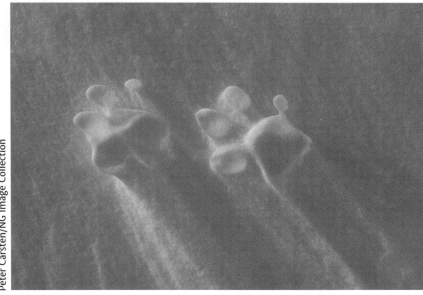

Peter Carsten/NG Image Collection

1 Elements and Compounds 31

- **Elements** are the most fundamental of all naturally occurring substances because they cannot be separated into chemically distinct materials. The minute particles that make up all matter, including elements, are **atoms**. All atoms of a particular element are the same.

- Atoms are made of protons, neutrons, and electrons, which have no independent chemical properties (see diagram). Protons are electrically positive, and electrons are electrically negative. Protons and neutrons reside in the atom's nucleus. The number of protons, the atomic number, identifies the element. The sum of protons and neutrons is the mass number. Most elements have several different **isotopes,** which differ in the number of neutrons. Ordinarily an atom has equal numbers of protons and electrons, but it may gain or lose electrons, in which case it becomes electrically charged and is called an **ion**.

Inside an atom • Figure 2.1

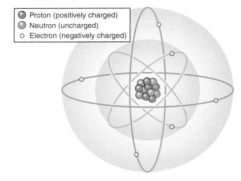

- Proton (positively charged)
- Neutron (uncharged)
- Electron (negatively charged)

- **Compounds** consist of multiple elements and therefore multiple types of atoms. The smallest unit that has the properties of a given compound is a **molecule**. Molecules in a compound are held together by **bonds**. The most common form of bonding is ionic bonding, caused by the electrostatic attraction of two oppositely charged ions. Other forms of bonding are covalent, metallic, and van der Waals bonding.

2 What Is a Mineral? 35

- **Minerals** are naturally occurring solids, each with a unique **crystal structure**. Minerals are formed by inorganic processes and have a fixed chemical composition. One exception to the last-named rule is atomic substitution, in which other atoms of like size and ionic charge may be substituted for specific atoms in a mineral.

- The visible crystal form of a mineral is a direct consequence of its atomic lattice. In some cases, a mineral will not have enough room to grow identifiable crystals, but the underlying geometric lattice remains the same. Crystal faces bound a **crystal**.

- Two minerals can have the same chemical formula but different crystal structures. These different forms are polymorphs. Other minerals occur in nature as *native* elements that are uncombined with other elements.

- Several properties can be used to tell minerals apart, as shown in the photo. Measuring the angles between faces may be useful in identifying a mineral, for although the size and overall shape of crystals may vary, Steno's law states that the angle between corresponding faces remains constant. Other factors that can aid in mineral identification include the mineral's **luster**, **habit**, **hardness**, **cleavage**, and **density**, or specific gravity. Color is often misleading; however, when a mineral is rubbed on a streak plate, it produces a thin layer of powdered mineral, or **streak**, which is more reliable than color for identification.

- Such properties as birefringence, magnetism, and luminescence (or fluorescence) may also be of use in identifying minerals.

Mystery mineral

Harry Taylor/Dorling Kindersley/Getty Images, Inc.

- Identity of the mystery mineral: The mineral is galena (PbS), the main ore mineral of lead.

3 Mineral Families 44

- The distribution of elements in Earth's crust is far from even, as shown in the diagram. Only 12 elements are present at a level of more than 1 part in 1000 by mass, and of these oxygen and silicon dominate. As a result, the number of naturally occurring minerals is relatively small, and the number of important rock-forming minerals is even smaller—only about 30 or so.

Elements of the continental crust • Figure 2.12

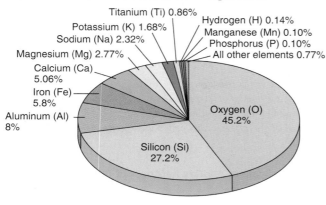

Titanium (Ti) 0.86%
Hydrogen (H) 0.14%
Potassium (K) 1.68%
Manganese (Mn) 0.10%
Sodium (Na) 2.32%
Phosphorus (P) 0.10%
Magnesium (Mg) 2.77%
All other elements 0.77%
Calcium (Ca) 5.06%
Iron (Fe) 5.8%
Aluminum (Al) 8%
Oxygen (O) 45.2%
Silicon (Si) 27.2%

- **Silicate minerals**, based on the $(SiO_4)^{42}$ anion, are the most abundant family of rock-forming minerals. Oxide minerals are the next most abundant family. Other important mineral families include sulfides and sulfates, carbonates, and phosphates. Less abundant accessory minerals usually do not affect the properties of the rock in which they are found, but they may still be of economic importance.

- Silicates can assemble in large, complex structures, such as chains, sheets, and three-dimensional lattices, by **polymerization**, a process in which two silica anions share an oxygen atom. Three factors affect the identity of a silicate mineral: whether the silicate tetrahedra are single or polymerized, which cations are present, and how the cations are distributed.

4 Rock: A First Look   48

- **Rock** is an aggregate of mineral grains, sometimes mixed with other materials such as natural glass or organic matter.

- Rock types are grouped into three major families, shown in the photos. **Igneous rock** is formed by the solidification of **magma,** either slowly beneath Earth's surface or rapidly at the surface. **Sedimentary rock** is formed at or near the surface by the deposition of many layers of **sediment**. **Metamorphic rock** starts as either igneous or sedimentary rocks but changes in form and sometimes in mineral assemblage as a result of the process of **metamorphism** at high temperature, high pressure, or both.

Three kinds of rocks and their natural settings • Figure 2.16

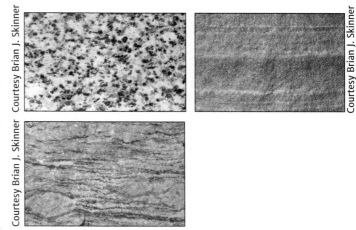

Courtesy Brian J. Skinner

- Igneous and metamorphic rocks are held together by the interlocking of mineral grains. The loose particles of sedimentary rock are held together either by compaction, during which the mineral grains are forced together by the pressure of overlying sediment; cementing of open spaces within a rock; or recrystallization, a process that occurs when growing grains interlock because of increasing pressure and heat.

KEY TERMS

atom   31

bond   33

cleavage   41

compound   32

crystal 38

crystal structure   36

density 43

element   31

habit   39

hardness   40

igneous rock   50

ion   32

isotopes   31

luster   38

magma   50

metamorphic rock   50

metamorphism   50

mineral   35

molecule   33

polymerization   46

rock   48

sediment   50

sedimentary rock   50

silicate minerals   45

streak   42

1. When astronauts brought back rock samples from the Moon, the minerals present were mostly the same as those found on Earth. Can you think of reasons this might be so? Would you expect minerals on Mars or Venus to be the same, or at least very similar, to those on Earth?

2. When a volcano erupts, spewing forth a column of hot volcanic ash, the ash particles are tiny fragments of solidified magma that slowly fall to Earth's surface, forming a layer of sediment. Would a rock formed from cemented particles of volcanic ash be igneous or sedimentary? Can you think of other circumstances that might form rocks that are intermediate between two of the major rock families?

3. Identify which of the following materials are minerals and why: water, beach sand, diamond, wood, vitamin pill, gold nugget, fishbone, and emerald. Should a synthetic diamond be considered a true mineral?

4. The minerals calcite and aragonite have the same chemical formula ($CaCO_3$) but different crystal structures. Are they polymorphs? The materials halite (NaCl) and galena (PbS) have the same geometric patterns in their crystal structures but different compositions. Are they polymorphs?

5. Cubic zirconia is a synthetic substance that is commonly used as a substitute for diamonds in jewelry. Cubic zirconia has a hardness of around 8 on the Mohs scale. Various types of silica glass, such as lead (Pb) glass (or "leaded crystal"), have also been substituted for diamonds; these typically have a hardness of 6 or less on the Mohs scale.

6. If you wanted to test a ring to see if it contained diamond, cubic zirconia, or lead glass, how would you approach the testing? Outline the testing procedure that you propose, making use of the materials in your Mohs hardness scale kit, shown here.

The Mohs scale of relative hardness of minerals • Table 2.1

Courtesy Brian J. Skinner

WHAT IS HAPPENING IN THIS PICTURE?

This geologist is part of a team trying to identify valuable, platinum-bearing minerals near Stillwater, Montana. He is looking at a core sample through a 10× hand lens, one of the simplest and most useful tools in any geologist's backpack.

James L. Amos/NG Image Collection

THINK CRITICALLY

What are some mineral properties that he would be looking for?

SELF-TEST

(Check your answers in Appendix D.)

1. A(n) _____ is an atom that has gained or lost one or more electrons and has a net electric charge.

   a. molecule
   d. ion

   b. isotope
   e. compound

   c. element

2. On this diagram, locate and label the following parts of the atom:

   proton

   nucleus

   electron

   first energy-level electron shell

   neutron

   second energy-level electron shell

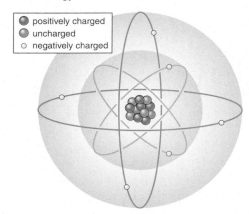

- positively charged
- uncharged
- negatively charged

3. In _____, electrons from different atoms are shared, and the force of this sharing forms the strongest of chemical bonds.

   a. ionic bonding
   c. metallic bonding

   b. covalent bonding
   d. van der Waals bonding

4. In _____, the mobility of electrons in the outermost shell allows materials with these types of bonds to act as good conductors of electricity and heat.

   a. ionic bonding
   c. metallic bonding

   b. covalent bonding
   d. van der Waals bonding

5. To be considered a mineral, a substance must _____.

   a. have a specific chemical composition

   b. be formed by inorganic processes

   c. be a naturally formed solid

   d. have a characteristic crystal structure

   e. have all of the characteristics listed above

6. Volcanic glass is not considered a mineral because it _____.

   a. is amorphous (i.e., it lacks a crystal structure)

   b. is not naturally occurring

   c. does not have enough silicon or oxygen in its chemical composition

   d. All of the above answers are correct.

7. The photograph shows natural samples of the mineral corundum. What best explains the striking difference in color between the red (ruby) and the blue (sapphire) samples?

   a. polymorphism

   b. small variations in composition

   c. differences in crystalline structure

   d. polymerization

The Natural History Museum

8. Which of the following minerals is the hardest?

   a. quartz
   c. muscovite

   b. calcite
   d. feldspar

9. Which of the following physical properties is the least useful in identifying many varieties of common minerals?

   a. cleavage or fracture
   c. color

   b. hardness
   d. density

10. _____ is the most abundant element, by weight, in Earth's continental crust.

    a. Silicon
    d. Aluminum

    b. Iron
    e. Oxygen

    c. Calcium

11. Why is Earth's crust mostly composed of a small number of rock-forming minerals?

   a. Polymorphs are common.

   b. There is an overwhelming abundance of oxygen and silicon.

   c. Igneous rocks lack carbon.

   d. All of the above statements are correct.

12. Gold is an example of a(n) _____, quartz is a _____, and galena is a _____.

   a. native element; silicate mineral; sulfide mineral

   b. oxide mineral; sulfide mineral; phosphate mineral

   c. phosphate mineral; sulfide mineral; carbonate mineral

   d. oxide mineral; silicate mineral; phosphate mineral

13. On the diagram, label each silicate structure with its proper name. For each structure give an example of a mineral (name and chemical formula) and indicate the prominent cleavage.

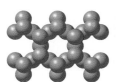

Structure 1

Structure 2

Structure 3

14. The rocks shown in the photographs are examples of _____.

   a. volcanic rock   c. sedimentary rock

   b. plutonic rock   d. metamorphic rock

15. In the rocks depicted in the photographs in question 14, what is most likely holding the mineral grains together?

   a. interlocking crystals formed from cooling magma

   b. compaction and cementation between the mineral grains

   c. interlocking crystals formed from the alteration of preexisting rocks by heat and pressure

   d. van der Waals bonding

THE PLANNER ✓

Review the Chapter Planner on the chapter opener and check off your completed work.

3

HOW OLD IS OLD? THE ROCK RECORD AND GEOLOGIC TIME

Jonathan Blair/NG Image Collection

Global Locator

Jura Mountains

NG Maps

Emmanuel Lattes/Biosphoto

JURA MOUNTAINS

The Jura Mountains separate France from Switzerland. Long inhabited, they derive their name from *juria*, a Latinized form of *iuris*, a word in Gaulish (an extinct language spoken in this region during Roman times) that means "wooded mountain."

The region is famous for fossils of ammonites, nautilus-like sea creatures with coiled and complexly patterned shells (inset photo). Two hundred years ago, as geologists began to study sedimentary rocks, they discovered that certain layers contain characteristic fossils, and those layers were always found in the same position relative to other layers. Fossils in the Jura were distinctive, and the name Jurassic was given to the time when these ammonites lived. Eventually it was discovered that great marine reptiles had swum in the same seas as the ammonites and that dinosaurs had roamed the land during this period as well.

When Michael Crichton published his science fiction novel about the creation of a dinosaur world using genetic residues from fossilized eggs, he called it "Jurassic Park." Steven Spielberg based one of the most successful movies of all time on the book, and the term *Jurassic* became part of everyday vocabulary.

RELATIVE AGE

Learning Objectives

1. **Define** stratigraphy and relative age.

2. **Explain** why gaps are common in the stratigraphic record.

3. **Describe** how fossils make it possible for geologists to correlate strata in different places.

The first scientific attempts to determine the numerical extent of geologic time were made almost three centuries ago. Geologists speculated that they might be able to estimate the time needed to erode away a mountain range by measuring the amount of sediment transported by streams. Their attempts were imprecise, but the inescapable conclusion was that Earth must be millions of years old because of the great thickness of sedimentary rocks. One of the founders of geology, James Hutton, whose work led to the principle of uniformitarianism (Chapter 1), was so impressed by the evidence that in 1788, he wrote that for Earth, there is "no vestige of a beginning, no prospect of an end."

The Stratigraphic Record

Geologists who followed Hutton agreed with his conclusion that Earth must be very ancient, but they lacked a precise way to determine exactly how long ago a particular event occurred. The only thing they could do was figure out the sequence of past events. They could thus establish the **relative ages** of rock formations or other geologic features, which means that they could determine whether a particular formation or feature was older or younger than another formation or feature. By doing so, they took the essential first steps toward unraveling Earth's geologic history. Relative ages are derived from three basic principles of **stratigraphy**, generally attributed to Hutton and Nicolaus Steno (the same scientist we met in Chapter 2 in the context of crystal faces), and the principle of cross-cutting relationships, first stated by Charles Lyell, a Scot like Hutton.

> **relative age** The age of a rock, fossil, or other geologic feature relative to another feature.

> **stratigraphy** The science of rock layers and the process by which strata are formed.

In places where you can find large exposures of sedimentary rock, such as the Badlands of South Dakota and the American Southwest, you will often see that the rocks have a banded appearance (**Figure 3.1**). These bands are called **strata** (an individual band is called a *stratum*), from the Latin word for "layer." The bands are often horizontal, but it is not at all unusual to see that they have been tilted or bent sometime after they were deposited.

All of the rocks in a typical stratified formation are sedimentary, deposited over the ages in water. This observation leads to the first of three key principles of stratigraphy: the **principle of original horizontality**, which states that water-laid sediment is deposited in horizontal strata. You can test this principle yourself: Shake up a bottle of muddy water so that all of the particles are suspended. Let the bottle stand and then examine the result—the mud will be deposited at the bottom of the bottle in a horizontal layer (see Figure 3.1a).

A second key to stratigraphy, which, like the first, is based on common sense, is the **principle of stratigraphic superposition**. This principle states that in any undisturbed sequence of strata, each stratum is younger than the stratum below it and older than the stratum above it (see Figure 3.1b).

The third key to stratigraphy is the **principle of lateral continuity** of sedimentary strata. This principle is based on the observation that sediment is deposited in continuous layers, and a layer of sediment will extend horizontally as far as it was carried by the water that deposited it. Layers of sediment do not terminate abruptly; they get thinner and ultimately pinch out altogether at their farthest edges. The same is true of the sedimentary rock strata that form from sediment layers; they may thin or pinch out laterally, but they usually do not terminate abruptly unless they are cut by a fracture. This important principle allows the geologist to correlate between outcrops of strata when erosion has removed some of the strata (see Figure 3.1c).

It is quite common for once-horizontal strata to be disrupted by later geologic events. This observation led Lyell to formulate a fourth principle that can help geologists determine relative ages: the **principle of cross-cutting relationships**. This principle states that a stratum must always be older than any feature that cuts or disrupts it. Whenever we observe water-laid strata that are bent, twisted, or tilted so that they are no longer horizontal, we can infer that some tectonic force must have disturbed them after they were deposited (see Figure 3.1d). Similarly, if a stratum is cut by a fracture, the stratum must be older than the fracture that cuts across it, as shown in the *What a Geologist Sees* figure on the next spread. When magma fills a fracture, the result is a vein of rock that cuts across the strata. In this case, too, the sedimentary rocks must be older than the cross-cutting vein. Similarly, a "foreign rock" (called a *xenolith* or an *inclusion*) that is encased within another rock unit must predate the rock that surrounds it.

Gaps in the Stratigraphic Record

In the 19th century, geologists tried to estimate the **numerical ages** of rocks—the number of years that have elapsed since a given stratum was deposited. For example, observations

> **numerical age** The age of a rock or geologic feature in years before the present.

might suggest that it would take 1 year for 10 centimeters of sediment to accumulate. If a rock lies 3 meters (300 cm)

The main principles of stratigraphy are illustrated here.

a. The Principle of Original Horizontality
This horizontal layer of sediment was deposited in a lake. The now-dry lakebed is near Death Valley, California. ▼

James Forte/ NG Image Collection

b. The Principle of Stratigraphic Superposition
Horizontal strata like these, in Badlands State Park, South Dakota, can extend for many kilometers laterally, in all directions. The oldest stratum is on the bottom, the youngest on the top. These strata resulted from the deposition of sediment in water. ▼

Annie Griffiths Belt / NG Image Collection

c. The Principle of Lateral Continuity
Even though erosion has removed some of the strata, it is clear that the strata on each side of the valley were originally continuous. ▼

d. The Principle of Cross-Cutting Relationships
These folded strata in the Hamersley Gorge, Western Australia, were originally horizontal; they were crumpled and contorted by plate tectonic movements. The strata themselves are older than the tectonic disruption that caused the folding of the layers. ▼

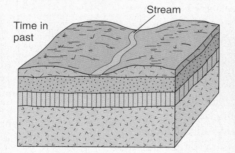

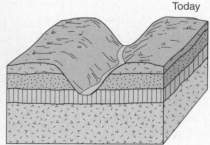

Time in past   Stream   Today

imagebroker.net/SuperStock

THINK CRITICALLY

Sediment poured into a bucket of water settles into a stack of horizontal layers. The oldest layer is on the bottom, the youngest on top. Which two stratigraphic principles are demonstrated by this experiment?

What a Geologist Sees

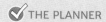

The Principle of Cross-Cutting Relationships

When a geologist visits a rock outcrop for the first time, one of the first tasks is to determine the relative ages of the rock units, using the principles of stratigraphy introduced in this chapter. In these examples, the geologists see clear demonstrations of the principle of cross-cutting relationships.

The horizontal sandstone strata shown here (**photo 1**), in Merseyside, United Kingdom, are cut by large fractures. The fractures have been marked with arrows to show the sense of relative movement of the rock units along the fractures. The geologist examining this roadcut would use the principle of cross-cutting relationships to conclude that the fractures must be younger than the strata.

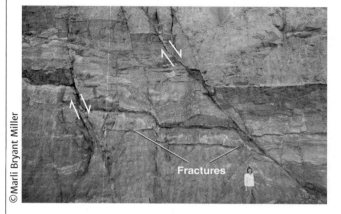

Fractures

©Marli Bryant Miller

Dike

Folded strata of metamorphic rock

Courtesy Lee Gerhard

This geologist (**photo 2**) is looking at a road cut at Three Valley Gap in Alberta, Canada. Here he sees layers of metamorphic rock that are sliced by two darker, cross-cutting igneous rock formations called *dikes*. The geologist can distinguish four stages in the sequence of geological events: (1) deposition of sediment; (2) formation of sedimentary rock from the sediment; (3) metamorphism of the sedimentary rock into a rock called *gneiss*; and (4) intrusion of the dikes. The dikes cut neatly across the folded and contorted layering in the metamorphic rock. By the principle of cross-cutting relationships, the dikes must be the youngest feature.

THINK CRITICALLY

Which other principles of stratigraphy are represented in these photographs, in addition to the principle of cross-cutting relationships? Explain your answer.

below the ground surface under younger sedimentary strata, then its numerical age could be estimated to be about 3000 years (300 cm × 10 cm/year).

Three assumptions must be true for this approach to work. First, the rate of sedimentation must have been constant while the layers were deposited. Second, the thickness of sediment must have been the same as the thickness of the sedimentary rock that eventually formed from it. Finally, all strata must be **conformable**. This means that each layer was deposited on the one below it without any interruptions—in other words, there are no depositional gaps in the stratigraphic record.

There are problems with each of these assumptions, and consequently early estimates of numerical ages using this approach were not very accurate. For example, rates of sedimentation vary greatly from place to place and even from time to time in a given location. Sediment is often compressed while it is turning into rock, resulting in a much thinner stratum than was originally deposited. The conformity assumption also fails: Gaps in the stratigraphic record, called **unconformities**, are common and occur for a variety of reasons (**Figure 3.2**). In *Amazing Places* (see page 63), you can visit some unconformities that played important roles in the development of geology as a science and our understanding of geologic time.

> **unconformity** A substantial gap in a stratigraphic sequence that marks the absence of part of the rock record.

Unconformities: How gaps occur in the stratigraphic record • Figure 3.2

Any boundary that represents a gap in the sedimentary record is called an unconformity. This diagram illustrates the formation of three common types of unconformities: **nonconformity**, **angular unconformity**, and **disconformity**.

Description/Cause	Type of Unconformity
NC Nonconformity	A surface of erosion that separates younger sedimentary strata above from older igneous or metamorphic rocks below.
AU Angular unconformity	A surface of erosion between two groups of sedimentary rocks in which the orientation of older strata, below, is at an angle to younger strata, above.
DC Disconformity	A surface of erosion in which the orientation of older strata, below, are parallel to younger strata, above.

ASK YOURSELF

Let's say that you're looking at a rock outcrop that has flat-lying sedimentary strata overlying twisted and folded sedimentary strata. These, in turn, overlie apparently older metamorphic rock.

What kinds of unconformities are you observing here? It might help if you sketch the outcrop.

a. The lower one is a nonconformity, and the upper one is an angular unconformity.

b. The lower one is a disconformity, and the upper one is a nonconformity.

c. The lower one is an angular unconformity, and the upper one is a disconformity.

d. Both surfaces are disconformities.

e. Neither of these surfaces is an unconformity.

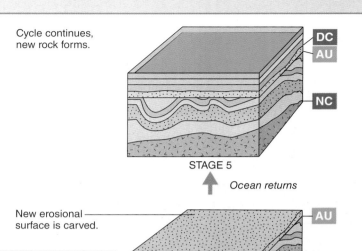
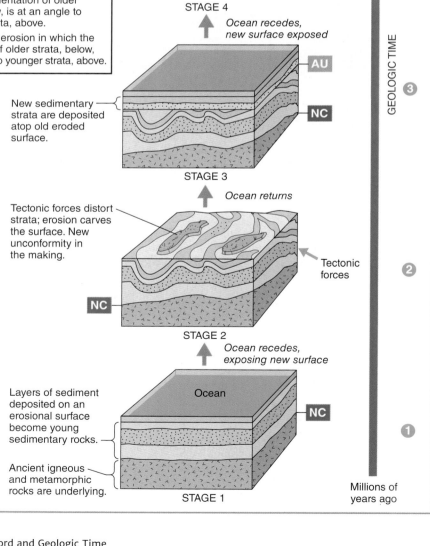

Cycle continues, new rock forms.

STAGE 5

Ocean returns

New erosional surface is carved.

Uplift leads to erosion.

STAGE 4

Ocean recedes, new surface exposed

New sedimentary strata are deposited atop old eroded surface.

STAGE 3

Ocean returns

Tectonic forces distort strata; erosion carves the surface. New unconformity in the making.

Tectonic forces

STAGE 2

Ocean recedes, exposing new surface

Layers of sediment deposited on an erosional surface become young sedimentary rocks.

Ocean

Ancient igneous and metamorphic rocks are underlying.

STAGE 1

Today

GEOLOGIC TIME

Millions of years ago

Famous Unconformities

In 1788, James Hutton sailed along the eastern coast of Scotland, not far from Edinburgh. He was accompanied by John Playfair and James Hall, each of whom would later play important roles in the development of the science of geology. Hutton was struck by what he saw; near-vertical strata had been truncated and overlain by slightly tilted sandy strata—

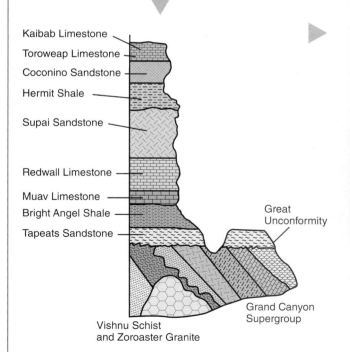

Courtesy Dr. K. Roy Gill

an unconformity. The scientists quickly determined that it would have taken many years to deposit these great thicknesses of sediment— much longer than the accepted age of Earth at that time. In response to this realization, Playfair is famously quoted as having said that "the mind seemed to grow giddy by looking so far into the abyss of time."

Global Locator

Siccar Point

Gran Canyon

NG Maps

a. Hutton's Unconformity

We now know that the vertical strata of Hutton's Unconformity at Siccar Point in Scotland are sandstones of Silurian age, about 425 million years old. The overlying strata are Devonian-aged Old Red Sandstone, about 345 million years old. The surface between the two sets of strata is the unconformity, and it represents an 80-million-year time gap for which there is no rock record.

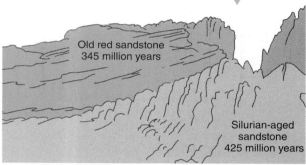

Old red sandstone
345 million years

Silurian-aged sandstone
425 million years

b. The Great Unconformity

In 1869, 81 years after Hutton's voyage along the Scottish coast, John Wesley Powell, an eminent American geologist, led the first recorded boat trip through the Grand Canyon. Powell was so struck by the unconformity below the Tapeats Sandstone that he named it the Great Unconformity. It represents a time gap of several hundred million years. In this panoramic view (right), you can see the Great Unconformity between the horizontally layered sedimentary strata at the top and the older, tilted metamorphic and igneous rock units underneath.

Kaibab Limestone
Toroweap Limestone
Coconino Sandstone
Hermit Shale
Supai Sandstone
Redwall Limestone
Muav Limestone
Bright Angel Shale
Tapeats Sandstone
Great Unconformity
Grand Canyon Supergroup
Vishnu Schist and Zoroaster Granite

Tapeats Sandstone

Great Unconformity

Grand Canyon Supergroup

Ralph Lee Hopkins/ Getty Images

THINK CRITICALLY

What types of unconformities are the ones shown here, in the photos and in the diagram?

Varieties of fossils • Figure 3.3

Some fossils are preserved parts of the organism itself; others are signs or traces of the organism's existence.

James L. Amos/NG Image Collection

▲ **a.** Most fossils begin as hard plant or animal parts, such as the bones of this 23-centimeter-long Pachypleurosaurus, a marine reptile that lived about 200 million years ago and was preserved in rocks of Jurassic age now found in Switzerland.

Courtesy Brian J. Skinner

▲ **b.** These fossil tracks in the Tapeats Sandstone were created when trilobites extended their legs, scooped up some mud, and picked over the mud for food.

Ralph Lee Hopkins/NG ImageCollection

▲ **c.** Other fossils record the imprint of an animal's body on mud that later solidified. This fossil, found on Snow Hill Island in Antarctica, shows the imprint of a snail-like gastropod, made during the Cretaceous Period.

Fossils and Correlation

Many strata contain remains of plants and animals that were incorporated into the sediment as it accumulated. **Fossils** usually consist of "hard parts" such as shells, bones, or wood whose forms have been preserved in sedimentary rock (**Figure 3.3**). In some cases the imprints of soft animal tissues, such as skin or feathers or the leaves and flowers of plants have been preserved. Even the preserved tracks and footprints of animals are considered to be fossils. Many fossils found in geologically young strata look similar to plants and animals living today (**Figure 3.4**).

Ancient and modern • Figure 3.4

A fossilized imprint of a *Lebachia* (**a**), a conifer found in rocks about 250 million years old, strongly resembles a modern Norfolk Island pine (**b**).

a

James L. Amos/NG Image Collection

b

Mark Gibson/Photolibrary/GettyImages, Inc.

Geologists can use fossils to correlate strata at localities (1, 2, and 3) that are many kilometers apart. Strata B, C, D, and E have fossil assemblages that are different from one another but consistent among the three sites.

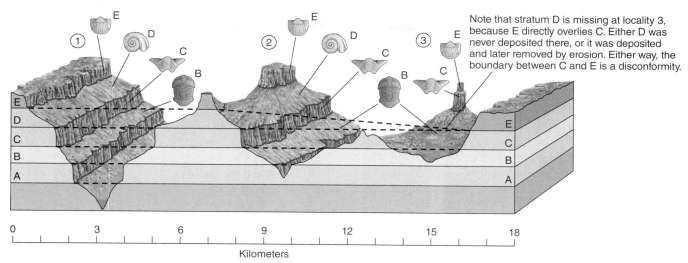

Note that stratum D is missing at locality 3, because E directly overlies C. Either D was never deposited there, or it was deposited and later removed by erosion. Either way, the boundary between C and E is a disconformity.

The farther down in the stratigraphic sequence we go and the older the rock units and life forms are, the more likely we are to find fossils of extinct plants or animals that seem unfamiliar to us. Nicolaus Steno was one of the first scientists to conclude that fossils were the remains of ancient life (see *Remember This!*). He published his ideas in a landmark paper in 1669, in which he also stated the principles of stratigraphic superposition and original horizontality. His conclusions were ridiculed at the time, but by the next century, the idea of the plant and animal origin of fossils was widely accepted.

REMEMBER THIS! Do you remember Steno? In Chapter 2 (*What Is a Mineral?*), you learned about *Steno's law* and the fundamental work of this versatile scientist on the angles between crystal faces. Now you see that he also made central contributions to our understanding of stratigraphy.

The study of fossils, called **paleontology**, is hugely important for understanding the history of life on Earth, and

paleontology The study of fossils and the record of ancient life on Earth; the use of fossils for the determination of relative ages.

we will have much more to say about it in Chapter 15. Aside from their biologic interest, fossils also have great practical value to geologists. About the same time that James Hutton was working in Scotland, a young surveyor named William Smith was laying out canal routes in southern England. As the canals were excavated, Smith noticed that each group of strata contained a specific assemblage of fossils. In time, he

could look at a specimen of rock from any sedimentary layer in southern England and name the stratum and its position in the sequence of strata. This skill enabled him to predict what kind of rock the canal excavators would encounter and how long it would take to dig through it. It also earned him the nickname "Strata."

The stratigraphic ordering of fossil assemblages is known as the **principle of faunal and floral succession**. *Fauna* means "animals," *flora* means "plants;" *succession* means that new species succeed earlier ones as they evolve. William Smith's practical discovery turned out to be of great scientific importance. Floral and faunal successions can be employed in determining the sequence and therefore the relative age of strata. Geologists soon demonstrated that the faunal succession in northern France is the same as that found by Smith in southern England. By the middle of the 19th century, it had become clear that faunal succession is essentially the same everywhere. Thus Smith's practical observations led to a means of worldwide **correlation**, which is the most important way of filling the gaps in the geologic record (**Figure 3.5**).

correlation A method of equating the ages of strata that come from two or more different places.

STOP CONCEPT CHECK

1. **What** are the four basic principles of stratigraphy?
2. **Describe** the three main kinds of unconformities and how they are formed.
3. **How** are fossils used in stratigraphic correlation?

THE GEOLOGIC COLUMN

Learning Objectives

1. **Explain** how worldwide observations of strata and the fossils they contain led to a single sequence of relative ages called the geologic column.

2. **Distinguish** four units of geologic time: eons, eras, periods, and epochs.

Worldwide stratigraphic correlation was one of the greatest successes of 19th-century science. It meant that, by using fossils and stratigraphic correlation, a gap in the stratigraphic record in one place could be filled using evidence from somewhere else. Through worldwide correlation, geologists assembled the **geologic column**, or **stratigraphic time scale**, a composite diagram showing the succession of all known strata, fitted together in chronological order, on the basis of their fossils and other evidence of relative age (**Figure 3.6**).

> **geologic column** The succession of all known strata fitted together in relative chronological order.

Eons and Eras

Even the most cursory inspection of the geologic column reveals how closely our understanding of strata is intertwined with the history of life. The vast majority of Earth's history is divided into three **eons** in which fossils are extremely rare or nonexistent. The earliest eon is the time between Earth's formation and the age of the oldest rocks so far discovered. It

Geology InSight The geologic column • Figure 3.6 ✓ THE PLANNER

The stratigraphic time scale, also called the geologic column, arranges all strata in chronological order and assigns names to the major time units.
My = million years

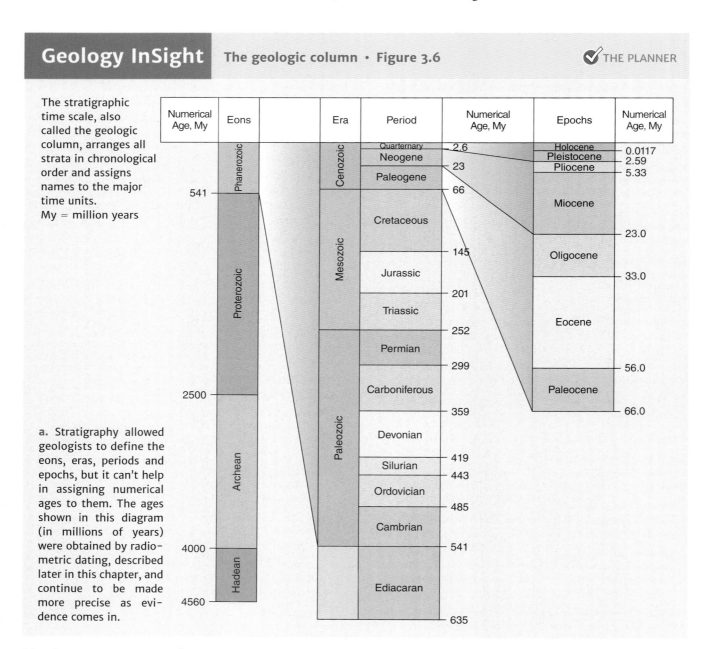

a. Stratigraphy allowed geologists to define the eons, eras, periods and epochs, but it can't help in assigning numerical ages to them. The ages shown in this diagram (in millions of years) were obtained by radiometric dating, described later in this chapter, and continue to be made more precise as evidence comes in.

b. These artist renditions illustrate the changing scenes of plants and animals during the three eras of the Phanerozoic Eon.

Messelobunodon · Bats · Tiny horses · Jewel beetle · Termites and ants · Anteater · Pangolin · Primitive woodpecker

Mark Hallett/NG Image Collection

Cenozoic Era

In the Cenozoic Era, from 66 million years ago until the present day, birds and mammals have flourished. In this scene from 50 million years ago in the Paleogene Period, we can see some ancestors of birds and mammals that are living today.

Mesozoic Era

The Mesozoic Era saw the rise of dinosaurs, the dominant land vertebrates (animals with backbones) for many millions of years. If you look closely in the corners, you can see two harbingers of the future that first appeared in the Mesozoic Era: the first magnolia-like flowering plants (lower left), and the first shrew-like mammals (lower right).

Anchiceratops · *Edmontosaurus* · Bald cypress trees · Ground beetle · Magnolia · Plant beetle · Cockroach · Early mammal

Robert Giusty/NG Image Collection

Paleozoic Era

During the Paleozoic Era, the evolution of life progressed from marine invertebrates (animals without backbones) to fish, amphibians, and reptiles. In this scene from 350 million years ago during the Carboniferous Period, a lobe-finned fish (foreground) swims alongside some early amphibians whose fins have evolved into legs but who still have fishlike tails.

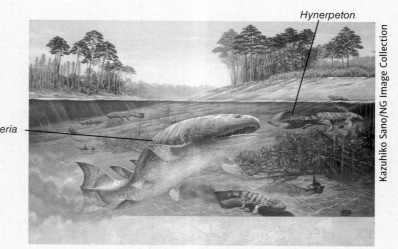

Hynerpeton · *Hyneria*

Kazuhiko Sano/NG Image Collection

THINK CRITICALLY

Many of the names in the geologic column are derived from the "type" localities where strata were first described; examples include Jurassic, Devonian, and Cambrian. Other names are derived from Greek roots, such as Paleogene, from the Greek words *palaios* (long ago) and *genesis* (origin). See how many other word origins you can decipher among the names in the geologic column.

is called the **Hadean** ("deepest") **Eon**. Meteorites and individual ancient mineral grains are the only known physical samples that still survive from this time.

The oldest rocks preserved on Earth mark the base of the **Archean** ("ancient") **Eon**, and the Archean is followed by the **Proterozoic** ("early life") **Eon**. The Archean is roughly the period when single-celled life developed, and the Proterozoic is when multicelled, soft-bodied organisms first emerged. We now know that each eon spanned several hundred million years of time, as shown in Figure 3.6; however, the 19th-century geologists who first worked out the geologic column had no way of determining the length of the eons.

At the beginning of the fourth and current eon, called the **Phanerozoic** ("visible life") **Eon**, the fossil record suddenly becomes much more detailed, thanks to the appearance of the first animals with hard shells and skeletons. Thus, paleontologists of the 19th century divided the Phanerozoic Eon into three shorter units called **eras**: the **Paleozoic** ("ancient life"), **Mesozoic** ("middle life"), and **Cenozoic** ("recent life"). These eras are marked by vastly different faunal and floral assemblages. One reason for the dramatic differences between eras is that they were all separated by major extinction events when more than 70% of the species on Earth perished.

Periods and Epochs

Eras are divided into still shorter units called **periods**. The three eras of the Phanerozoic Eon were the first to be divided into periods, and the divisions were made on the basis of fossils. Geologists named the periods in a somewhat haphazard manner. Some are named for geographic locations (e.g., Jurassic, from the Jura Mountains, as discussed in the chapter-opening essay, and Cambrian, from the Latin word for Wales, where rock of this age was first studied) and others are named for the characteristics of their strata (e.g., Cretaceous, from the Latin word for "chalk").

The earliest period of the Paleozoic Era, the Cambrian Period, is especially noteworthy. This is when animals with hard shells first appeared in the geologic record. It was a time of unprecedented diversification of life, called the **Cambrian explosion** (**Figure 3.7**).

Rocks that formed before the Cambrian Period, in the Proterozoic Eon or earlier, generally cannot be differentiated on the basis of the fossils they contain. With rare exceptions, the fossils are either nonexistent or microscopic. Thus geologists often lump the time that precedes the Cambrian Period, and the rocks formed then, into a single category, called the **Precambrian**.

The one exception to this is the **Ediacaran Period**, which is characterized by remarkable fossils of soft-bodied creatures (**Figure 3.8**). The Ediacaran is the last period of the Proterozoic Eon (and therefore the last of the Precambrian), and it is the only period of the Proterozoic that is defined by macroscopic fossils. All the periods of the Phanerozoic Eon were defined by geologists in the 19th century, but the

The Cambrian explosion • Figure 3.7

Only the sketchiest remains are left of any life forms from Earth's earliest eons. But in the Cambrian Period, life suddenly exploded in a profusion of bizarre and now extinct forms. Trilobites (*below*) ranged from 1 millimeter in size to the largest known specimen, 72 centimeters.

Anomalocaris was the most fearsome predator of the Cambrian seas, a swimming creature up to 1 meter long.

Opabinia, which among other oddities had five eyes, was about 7 centimeters long and would have been a tasty morsel for *Anomalocaris*.

fossils that define the Ediacaran Period were discovered much later. They were first described in Australia in the 1940s, then in Canada, Namibia, and other places around the world. The Ediacaran Period was finally defined in 2004—the first major new addition to the geologic column in 120 years.

Periods, in turn, are split into smaller divisions called **epochs**. The most recent epochs, the Holocene and the Pleistocene, are familiar because humans and their ancestors emerged during these epochs, and their names sometimes

Most ancient macroscopic fossils • Figure 3.8 —

This curious fossil is *Dickinsonia costata*, a soft-bodied creature that lived about 600 million years ago. Lacking hard parts, *Dickinsonia* is only preserved as an imprint in the sediment in which it was buried.

O. Louis Mazzatenta/NationalGeographic/NG Image Collection

appear in the popular press. These recent epochs are not defined by extinction events but by the percentage of their fossils that are still-living species. Many plant and animal fossils found in Pliocene strata, for example, have still-living counterparts, but fossils in Eocene strata have few

Where Geologists CLICK

Lunar and Planetary Institute Timeline

On the website of the Lunar and Planetary Institute, you will find a terrific timeline of life on Planet Earth. A lot of other educational resources are available on the LPI website, too.

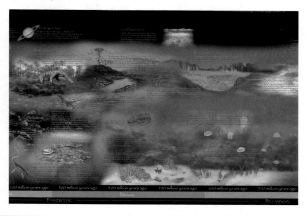

living counterparts. To learn more about the history of life on Earth, see *Where Geologists Click*.

 CONCEPT CHECK

1. **What** is the geologic column, and how were fossils used in its development?

2. **What** major biologic event distinguishes the Phanerozoic Eon from the previous (Precambrian) eons?

NUMERICAL AGE

Learning Objectives

1. **Recount** how scientists attempted to quantify geologic time.

2. **Outline** the process of radioactive decay and its use in determining numerical ages.

3. **Explain** how and why radioactive decay can be used to date igneous rocks.

4. **Describe** how magnetic polarity dating can be used to date both igneous and sedimentary rocks.

The scientists who worked out the geologic column were tantalized by the challenge of numerical time. They wanted to know Earth's age, how fast mountain ranges rise, how long the Paleozoic Era lasted, and, most challenging of all, when life first appeared and how long humans have inhabited Earth.

Early Attempts to Determine Numerical Age

Several methods for solving the problem of numerical time were proposed during the 19th century. All of them were unsuccessful, but the reasons for their failure are nonetheless quite illuminating—and they help explain where our currently accepted estimates came from (**Figure 3.9**). As previously mentioned, early approaches involved estimating rates of sedimentation and multiplying by the thickness of stratigraphic sections. Unfortunately, the resulting estimates for Earth's age varied too widely to be useful, ranging from 3 million to 1.5 billion years.

Early scientists recognized that rivers carry dissolved substances to the sea from the erosion of rocks on land. In

This timeline chronicles some of the major episodes in the long debate over how old Earth is. Even the unsuccessful attempts, such as Kelvin's and Joly's, were useful because they pointed out incorrect assumptions that these scientists and others had made.

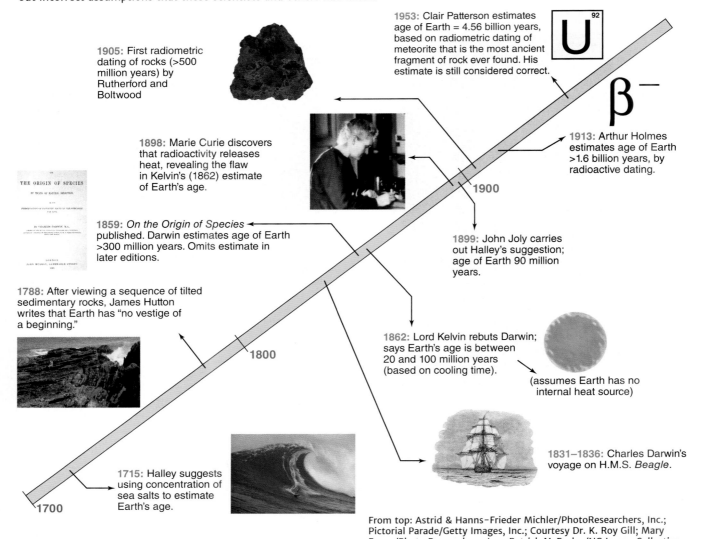

1953: Clair Patterson estimates age of Earth = 4.56 billion years, based on radiometric dating of meteorite that is the most ancient fragment of rock ever found. His estimate is still considered correct.

1905: First radiometric dating of rocks (>500 million years) by Rutherford and Boltwood

1913: Arthur Holmes estimates age of Earth >1.6 billion years, by radioactive dating.

1898: Marie Curie discovers that radioactivity releases heat, revealing the flaw in Kelvin's (1862) estimate of Earth's age.

1900

1859: *On the Origin of Species* published. Darwin estimates age of Earth >300 million years. Omits estimate in later editions.

1899: John Joly carries out Halley's suggestion; age of Earth 90 million years.

1788: After viewing a sequence of tilted sedimentary rocks, James Hutton writes that Earth has "no vestige of a beginning."

1862: Lord Kelvin rebuts Darwin; says Earth's age is between 20 and 100 million years (based on cooling time).

(assumes Earth has no internal heat source)

1800

1831–1836: Charles Darwin's voyage on H.M.S. *Beagle*.

1715: Halley suggests using concentration of sea salts to estimate Earth's age.

1700

From top: Astrid & Hanns-Frieder Michler/PhotoResearchers, Inc.; Pictorial Parade/Getty Images, Inc.; Courtesy Dr. K. Roy Gill; Mary Evans/Photo Researchers, Inc.; Patrick McFeeley/NG Image Collection.

1715, Edmund Halley, for whom Halley's Comet is named, suggested that one could measure the rate at which salts are added to the sea by river input and calculate the time needed to transport all the salts now present in the sea. Halley did not carry out his own suggestion, and it was not until 1899 that John Joly made the necessary measurements and calculations. Using this approach, Joly estimated that the ocean and, therefore, Earth, were 90 million years old. Unfortunately, neither Halley nor Joly realized that the ocean, like other parts of the Earth system, is an open system. Salt is removed by reactions between seawater and volcanic rocks on the seafloor, as well as the evaporation of seawater in isolated basins. The addition and removal of salts have balanced each other for hundreds of millions (even billions) of years.

The 19th century also saw the publication of Charles Darwin's *On the Origin of Species* in 1859. The book intensified the ongoing debate over numerical ages. Darwin understood that the evolution of new species by natural selection must be a very slow process that required vast amounts of time. The first edition of his book contained a rough estimate of Earth's age, based on the erosion rate of a mountain range, of at least 300 million years.

William Thomson (Lord Kelvin), a leading physicist and contemporary of Darwin, emphatically rejected Darwin's estimate. Kelvin used the laws of thermodynamics to calculate how long Earth has been a solid body. Kelvin made two assumptions: (1) Earth was once completely molten, and (2) no heat was added to it after it formed. Once it had cooled enough to form a solid outer layer, Kelvin hypothesized that heat would escape only by conduction (the same way that heat moves through the wall of a coffee cup). He measured the current-day rate of heat loss and extrapolated backward to figure out the age of Earth's solid crust, arriving at a figure of 20 million years. Even Darwin conceded, "Thomson's views on the recent age of the world have been for some time one of my sorest troubles" and removed his age estimate from later editions of *On the Origin of Species*.

Darwin died before geologists vindicated his views on the vast length of geologic time. Kelvin's mistake was his assumption that no heat had been added to Earth's interior since its formation. He did not know about **radioactivity**, a natural physical process that releases heat directly into Earth's interior. Though Earth is a closed system, it does have inputs and outputs of energy, and Kelvin had missed a key input (see *Remember This!*).

> **radioactivity** A process in which an element spontaneously transforms into another isotope of the same element or into a different element.

> **REMEMBER THIS!** Do you remember the definition of a closed system from Chapter 1? A closed system is one in which energy crosses the boundaries, but matter does not. Earth behaves like a closed system, with a few exceptions—small amounts of matter do cross into and out of the Earth system. Can you remember what they are?

What was needed to solve the problem of numerical geologic time was a way to measure events by some process that runs continuously, is not reversible, is not influenced by such factors as chemical reactions and high temperatures, and leaves a continuous record without any gaps. The discovery of radioactivity not only proved that Kelvin's assumptions were wrong but, by fortunate chance, also provided the breakthrough needed to measure absolute time.

Radioactivity and Numerical Ages

To explain how radioactivity allows us to determine the numerical ages of rocks, we need to go back to the fundamentals of chemistry. Recall that most chemical elements have two or more **isotopes** that have the same number of protons per atom but a different number of neutrons per atom (see *Remember This!*). To put it another way, each isotope of an element has the same atomic number but a different mass number.

> **REMEMBER THIS!** Can you remember the difference between an atom and an isotope? How about mass number and atomic number? You can review these by looking back at *Elements and Compounds* in Chapter 2.

Most naturally occurring isotopes have stable nuclei. However, a number of isotopes—such as uranium-238, carbon-14, and potassium-40—are unstable. They spontaneously release particles from their nuclei or absorb particles into their nuclei. In the process, they change their mass number, their atomic number, or both. Any isotope that spontaneously undergoes such a change is said to be **radioactive**, and the process is referred to as **radioactive decay**.

Radioactive decay involves the nucleus of the atom, so it is a nuclear process rather than a chemical process. It releases far more energy than any chemical reaction, which explains why it is still keeping Earth's interior hot after more than 4 billion years. The decay of radioactive isotopes is not influenced by any chemical process, nor by heat or high pressure. Each radioactive isotope has its own rate of decay, so rock that contains several different isotopes has numerous decay timers that can be checked against each other. Thus radioactive decay is a perfect built-in geologic clock.

Radioactive decay can happen in five ways, but two are especially important for determining numerical ages (**Figure 3.10**). One very important decay mechanism is the release from the nucleus of an *alpha* particle, identical to the nucleus of a helium atom, consisting of two protons and two neutrons; this process is called α (alpha) emission. A second important decay mechanism is the release from the nucleus of a *beta minus* particle, the same as an electron but originating from the nucleus, rather than from the electrons that orbit the outer part of the atom; this process is called β⁻ (beta) decay. The isotopes of uranium and thorium, widely used to date geologically ancient rocks, decay to lead isotopes by both alpha and beta decay. The decay of carbon-14 to nitrogen-14, commonly used to date organic remains younger than 70,000 years old, including human fossils, occurs by beta decay.

In any radioactive decay system, the number of original radioactive parent atoms continuously decreases, while the number of nonradioactive daughter atoms produced by the radioactive decay continuously increases. For this reason, many of the radioactive isotopes that were present when Earth was formed have decayed away because they were short-lived. However, radioactive isotopes that decay very slowly are still present.

All decay rates follow the same basic law: The proportion of parent atoms that decay during each unit of time is always the same (**Figure 3.11**). The rate of radioactive decay is determined by the **half-life**.

> **half-life** The time needed for half of the parent atoms of a radioactive substance to decay into daughter atoms.

Here's how it works: Suppose that a given isotope has a half-life of 1 hour. If we start with a sample consisting of 100% radioactive parent atoms, after an hour only 50% of the parent atoms would remain and an equal number of daughter atoms would have formed. At the end of the second hour, another half of the parent atoms would be gone, so there would be 25% parent atoms and 75% daughter atoms. After the third hour, another half of the parent atoms would have decayed, leaving 12.5% parent atoms and 87.5% daughter atoms, and so on. The number of parent atoms decreases as the number of daughter atoms increases, but the total number of atoms—parent plus daughter—remains constant. Determining the proportion of parent atoms that have changed into daughter atoms tells us how long the process has been running, and this is the key to using radioactive decay to determine the age of a rock.

How radioactive decay works · Figure 3.10

In radioactive decay, the nucleus of the radioactive isotope, the **parent**, spontaneously releases or absorbs a particle, changing the parent into a different form, called a **daughter**. Daughter products may be stable, or they may, in turn, be radioactive.

Two important radioactive decay processes are illustrated here: α emission and β⁻ decay.

In α emission, the radioactive parent nucleus releases an alpha particle, which consists of two protons and two neutrons. The atomic number decreases by 2, and the mass number decreases by 4.

In β⁻ decay, the radioactive parent nucleus releases a beta particle, and one of its neutrons turns into a proton. The atomic number decreases by 1, and the mass number is unchanged.

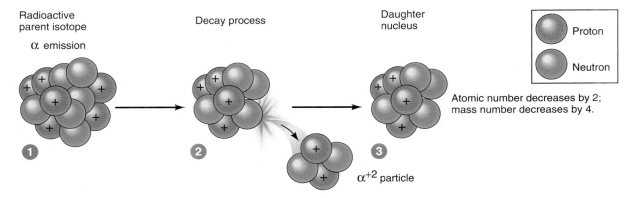

A radioactive nucleus releases an alpha particle, which consists of two protons and two neutrons.

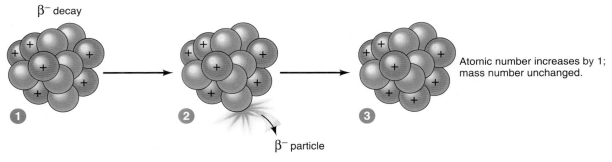

A radioactive nucleus releases a beta particle, and one of its neutrons turns into a proton.

ASK YOURSELF

In what way is a beta particle (β) different from an electron?

a. They are identical.

b. A beta particle is negatively charged, whereas an electron is positively charged.

c. They are the same, but beta particles originate from the nucleus, whereas electrons orbit in the outer part of the atom.

d. Beta particles are significantly larger than electrons.

e. Beta particles are radioactive, whereas electrons are not.

This graph illustrates the basic decay law of radioactivity, for an isotope with a half-life of 1 hour. After an hour, only 50% of the parent atoms remain, and an equal number of daughter atoms have formed. At the end of the second hour, another half of the parent atoms would be gone, and so on. The total number of atoms, parent plus daughter, remains constant.

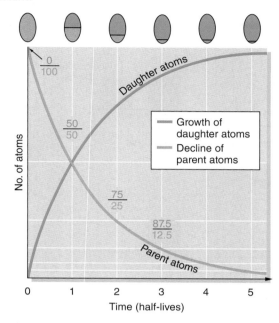

Radiometric Dating

Following the discovery of radioactivity by Henri Becquerel in 1896, and further work by Marie and Pierre Curie, the first estimates of the ages of rocks using radioactive decay were made in 1905. The long-hoped-for "rock clock" was finally available. The results were, and continue to be, remarkable. Radiometric dating has revolutionized the way we think about Earth and its long history.

radiometric dating The use of naturally occurring radioactive isotopes to determine the numerical age of minerals, rocks, or fossils.

A radioactive rock clock measures the amount of time that has elapsed since the minerals in the rock crystallized. When a new mineral grain forms—for example, a grain of feldspar in cooling lava—all the atoms in the grain become locked into the crystal structure and isolated from the environment outside the grain. In a sense, the atoms in the mineral grain, including any radioactive atoms, are sealed in an atomic time capsule. The clock is reset, and the timer starts running. The trapped radioactive parent atoms then begin to decay to daughter atoms at a rate determined by the half-life. By comparing the number of daughter atoms to the number of parent atoms present in the rock today, scientists can determine how much time has passed since the radioactive timer was started, when the mineral grain first formed.

In the simplest case, if no daughter atoms were present in the mineral at the time of formation, we can use Figure 3.11 to work backward and determine how long ago the time capsule was sealed. If the mineral crystal contained some daughter atoms at the time of formation, the process is more difficult. Geologists have developed several ways to estimate the initial content of daughter atoms in a sample. Once that is done, and provided that we know the half-life of the radioactive parent, it is a simple matter to calculate how long ago the mineral crystallized. Geologists use different isotopic systems to study rocks, fossils, and biologic materials of different ages and compositions (**Figure 3.12**).

Radiometric dating has been particularly useful for determining the ages of igneous rocks because the mineral grains in an igneous rock form at the same time as the rock that contains them. On the other hand, most sedimentary rocks consist largely of mineral grains that were formed long before the strata that contain them were deposited. Radiometric dating will tell how old the grains are but not when the strata were deposited. This makes it difficult to directly date most sedimentary rocks and to infer the numerical age of ancient life forms fossilized in the sediments.

As geologists worked out the geologic column, they found many locations where layers of solidified lava and volcanic ash are interspersed with sedimentary strata. Through radiometric dating, they could determine the numerical ages of the lavas and volcanic ash and thereby bracket the ages of the sedimentary strata (**Figure 3.13** see page 75).

Through a combination of geologic relations and radiometric dating, scientists have been able to fill in all the dates in the geologic column, as shown in Figure 3.6. The scale is continually being refined, so the numbers given in the figure are considered the best currently available but are subject to change. Further work will make the numbers more precise. It is a tribute to the work of geologists during the 19th century that the geologic column they established by ordering strata according to their relative ages has been fully confirmed by radiometric dating. At the same time, it is humbling to see how one wrong assumption caused Lord Kelvin to be more than 4 billion years off in his estimate of Earth's age.

Long-lived isotopes such as uranium-238 (right) are especially useful for dating ancient rocks. Short-lived isotopes such as carbon-14 (left) are useless for dating samples that are more than about 70,000 years old. However, carbon-14 is useful for dating geologically recent items of biologic origin, such as human remains and artifacts.

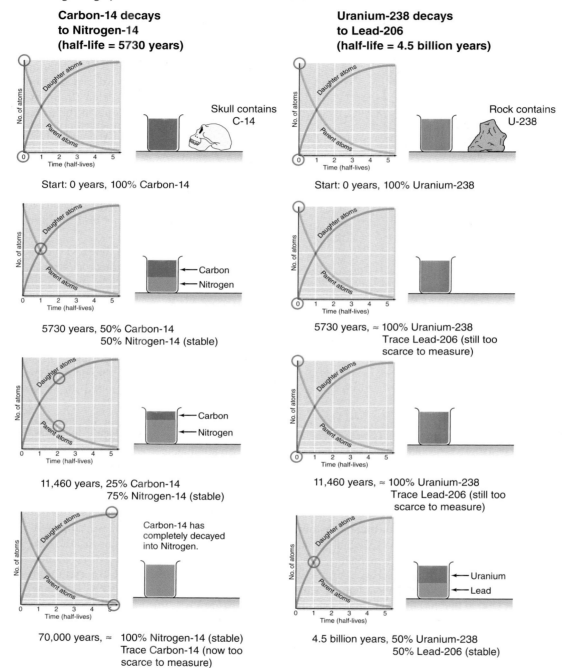

Carbon-14 decays to Nitrogen-14 (half-life = 5730 years)

Skull contains C-14

Start: 0 years, 100% Carbon-14

← Carbon
← Nitrogen

5730 years, 50% Carbon-14
50% Nitrogen-14 (stable)

← Carbon
← Nitrogen

11,460 years, 25% Carbon-14
75% Nitrogen-14 (stable)

Carbon-14 has completely decayed into Nitrogen.

70,000 years, ≈ 100% Nitrogen-14 (stable)
Trace Carbon-14 (now too scarce to measure)

Uranium-238 decays to Lead-206 (half-life = 4.5 billion years)

Rock contains U-238

Start: 0 years, 100% Uranium-238

5730 years, ≈ 100% Uranium-238
Trace Lead-206 (still too scarce to measure)

11,460 years, ≈ 100% Uranium-238
Trace Lead-206 (still too scarce to measure)

← Uranium
← Lead

4.5 billion years, 50% Uranium-238
50% Lead-206 (stable)

Magnetic Polarity Dating

paleomagnetism The study of rock magnetism in order to determine the intensity and direction of Earth's magnetic field in the geologic past.

Time is so central to the study of Earth that geologists are always seeking new ways to determine numerical ages. An exciting newer method of dating, developed in the 1960s, involves **paleomagnetism**, the study of Earth's past magnetic field (**Figure 3.14**). Both igneous and sedimentary rocks "lock in" information about the magnetic field at their time of formation.

Earth's magnetic field reverses its polarity at irregular intervals but, on average, about once every half million years. This means that the magnetic pole that had been in the northern hemisphere moves to a position near Earth's South Pole, and the magnetic pole that had been in the south moves to the north. Note, however, that Earth's geographic

Radiometric dating and the geologic column • Figure 3.13

Radiometric dating can be used to bracket the ages of sedimentary strata. The lava conduit (A) and the igneous intrusion (B) can be dated radiometrically. Conduit A cuts through strata 1, 2, 3, and 4, so it must be younger than all of them. Intrusion B cuts through strata 1, 2, and 3 but not 4, and hence must be older than layer 4. Thus the sedimentary rocks in layer 4 are between 20 million and 34 million years old.

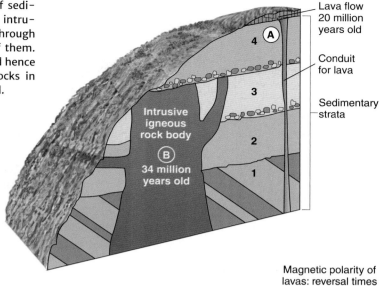

Magnetic reversal time scale • Figure 3.14

Periods of normal polarity, as today, and periods of reversed polarity have been identified and dated, using radiometric dating of lavas, back to the beginning of the Jurassic Period, about 200 million years ago. This figure shows the most recent 7 million years.

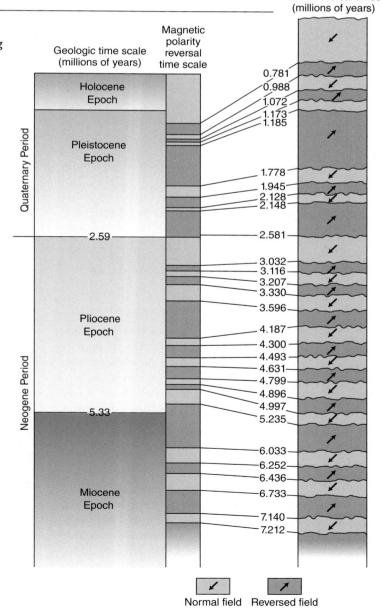

North and South Poles of rotation do not change position. (Earth's magnetic field is explained in additional detail in Chapter 4.)

magnetic reversal A period of time in which Earth's magnetic polarity reverses itself.

Scientists are still working out details of how or why **magnetic reversals** happen. The two important points are that a reversal happens quickly by geologic time standards, and any iron-bearing mineral in an igneous rock retains, or "remembers," the magnetic polarity of Earth at the time that the igneous rock was formed—that is, a change in the magnetic field does not affect already formed minerals. Some sedimentary rocks also retain a record of the magnetic field at the time of formation. As sedimentary particles settle through water, iron-bearing minerals that are already tiny magnets will be oriented by Earth's magnetic field and give the rock in which they lodge a distinct magnetic signal. Through a combination of radiometric dating and magnetic polarity measurements, it has been possible to establish a time scale of magnetic polarity reversals dating back to the Jurassic Period (see Figure 3.14). Still earlier reversals are a subject of ongoing research.

Correlation on the basis of magnetic reversals differs from other geologic correlation methods. One magnetic reversal looks just like any other in the rock record. When evidence of a magnetic reversal is found in a sequence of rocks, the problem lies in knowing which of the many reversals it actually represents. When a continuous record of reversals can be found, starting with the present, it is simply a matter of counting backward. But if there is not a continuous record of reversals, counting backward must be combined with stratigraphic and radioactive dating techniques. Magnetic polarity studies have been used to date strata that contain the fossils of human ancestor species (see *Case Study*). In Chapter 4 you will learn how magnetic polarity studies played a crucial role in the development of plate tectonic theory.

STOP CONCEPT CHECK

1. **What** were some of the early attempts to calculate the age of Earth, and why were they inaccurate?

2. **How** does the process of radioactive decay work?

3. **Why** is radiometric dating more useful for determining the ages of igneous rocks than it is for sedimentary rocks?

4. **How** can magnetic polarity reversals contribute useful information about rock and fossil ages?

THE AGE OF EARTH

Learning Objectives

1. **Explain** why the oldest rocks are not necessarily the same age as the planet.

2. **Summarize** the evidence that has led scientists to conclude that Earth is about 4.56 billion years old.

Throughout this book, we mention examples of actual rates of geologic processes. This would not be possible without the numerical dates obtained through radiometric dating and other numerical age methods. In fact, more than any other contribution by geologists, the ability to determine numerical ages has changed the way humans think about the world and the immensity of geologic time.

Earth's Oldest Rocks

Now that we know how to determine the numerical ages of rocks, can we determine Earth's age? It's not as easy as you might think. The continual recycling of Earth's surface by erosion and plate tectonics means that very few remnants of Earth's original crust, if any, remain. Of the many radiometric dates obtained from Precambrian rocks, the oldest is about 4.0 billion years (**Figure 3.15**). Although no older rocks than this have been found, an individual mineral grain from sedimentary rock in Australia has been dated to 4.4 billion years, so igneous rocks older than 4.0 billion years may someday be located.

Earth as a planet can't be too much older than its oldest mineral grains. However, geologists believe that there is still a gap between the age of the oldest mineral grains, at 4.4 billion years, and the age of Earth. For one thing, shortly after accretion the planet was much hotter than it is today

Earth's oldest rock • Figure 3.15 _____

The Acasta gneiss in northern Canada, shown here, was formed 4 billion years ago. The most ancient rock so far discovered on Earth is located in this rock unit.

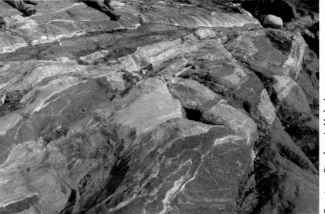

Courtesy Stephen J. Mojzsis

Dating Human Ancestors

The Hadar region of northern Ethiopia (**photo**) has been a fertile site for finding fossils of ancient human ancestors, part of a larger group called *hominids*. Many of the fossils have been found in strata derived from ancient stream gravels, where they were tumbled and battered by long-ago floodwaters. The fossil-bearing gravels are interlayered with sediments that give good magnetic signals.

The problem is to know where in the magnetic polarity time scale the Hadar sediment falls. Geologists answered this question by using the Potassium-Argon (K-Ar) method to establish the ages of a lava flow that lay below

some of the hominid fossils, and a layer of volcanic ash that lay above them. The two radiometric dates determined the magnetic reversal ages unambiguously and indicated that early hominids lived in the region between 3 and 4 million years ago—that is, during the Pliocene Epoch.

Through many studies like this, it is slowly becoming clear that the hominid genus *Homo* (which includes our own species, *Homo sapiens*) evolved a little more than 2 million years ago from an older genus called *Australopithecus*. (Two reconstructed *Australopithecus* skulls from the Hadar are shown here.)

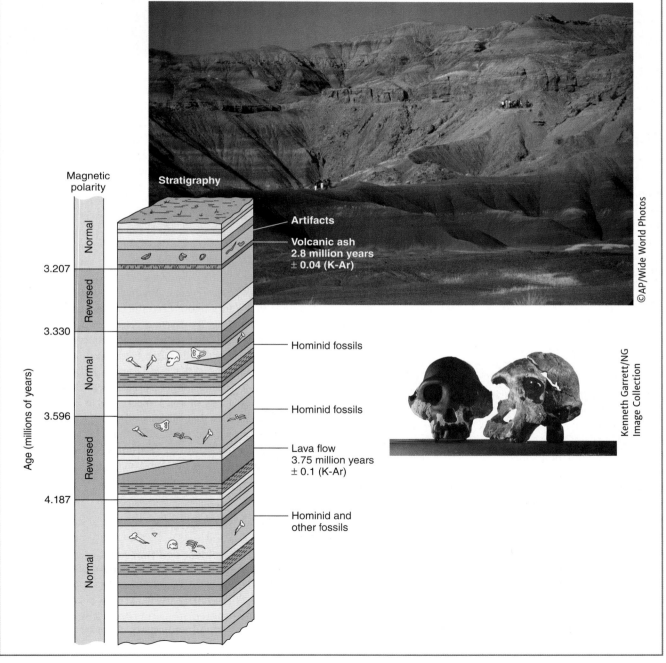

Magnetic polarity

Stratigraphy

Artifacts

**Volcanic ash
2.8 million years
± 0.04 (K-Ar)**

Age (millions of years)

Normal

3.207

Reversed

3.330

Normal

Hominid fossils

3.596

Hominid fossils

Reversed

Lava flow
3.75 million years
± 0.1 (K-Ar)

4.187

Hominid and
other fossils

Normal

©AP/Wide World Photos

Kenneth Garrett/NG
Image Collection

(see *Remember This!*). Where did all of the heat come from? Kinetic energy (that is, energy of motion) associated with accretion and compaction of the materials that comprise our planet, combined with heavy meteorite bombardment, translated into massive amounts of thermal energy—that is, heat. The decay of abundant radioactive material inside the planet contributed further to the internal heating.

> **REMEMBER THIS!** Do you remember the steps outlined in the nebular hypothesis? The nebular hypothesis is the most widely accepted set of ideas concerning the early stages of formation of our solar system, including planet Earth. It is discussed in *Earth as a Planet*, Chapter 1.

As a result of this active heating, Earth was partially or (more likely) completely molten for some time after its materials came together. During that time, the surface was covered by an "ocean" of magma. It took time—millions of years—before the rock that comprises Earth's crust and mantle finally solidified and stabilized. The 4.4-billion-year-old mineral grains from Australia are likely remnants of some of that very early crustal material.

The Extraterrestrial Connection

So far, we have concluded that Earth must be older than its oldest known constituents, dated at 4.4 billion years, but probably not too much older than that. In addition to what the nebular hypothesis tells us about the formation of the terrestrial planets, there is strong geochemical evidence that Earth formed at the same time as the Moon, the other planets, and meteorites. Studies of these materials provide the strongest evidence for the numerical age of our planet.

Through radiometric dating, it has been possible to determine the ages of meteorites and of "Moon dust" brought back by astronauts. The Apollo astronauts found rocks and individual grains of Moon dust that are believed to be pieces of the Moon's original crust. Such rocks are abundant because the Moon has been geologically much less active than Earth.

Meteorite ages are especially valuable because some meteorites have remained virtually unaltered since the formation of the solar system. Melting and other types of geologic alteration reset radiometric clocks. However, some meteorites, such as the Allende meteorite, which fell to Earth in the Mexican state of Chihuahua on February 8, 1969, belong to a rare category called **carbonaceous chondrites**. These very primitive meteorites are believed to contain unaltered material of the kind that accreted to form Earth from the solar nebula. It is "carbonaceous" because it contains tiny amounts of carbon, some of which is in chemical compounds called amino acids—organic components that are essential for life.

A portion of the Allende meteorite is shown in **Figure 3.16**. The dark, fine-grained part of the meteorite is mostly olivine, with a few flecks of metallic iron and some carbon. The clumps of white material are oxides of calcium and aluminum and are thought to be among the first matter to condense from the gas cloud from which the solar system formed. The white clumps are older than Earth itself.

A cosmic interloper • Figure 3.16 _____

The Allende meteorite, which fell to Earth in Mexico, is one of the most famous meteorites in history. Note the white spots on the meteorite. Some of these inclusions, which are slightly older than the black carbonaceous material around them, are more than 4.6 billion years old, making them the oldest objects of any kind ever found on Earth.

James L. Amos/NG Image Collection

A rare class of meteorites, called the SNC meteorites, is of Martian origin. These meteorites originated when large impacts kicked chunks of the crustal rock of Mars into orbit. The oldest one of these ever found on Earth, a meteorite called NWA (North West Africa) 7553 (nicknamed "Black Beauty" because of its glossy black appearance), has yielded radiometric dates of 4.44 billion years from individual mineral grains. This is strong evidence that Mars went through the same solar system-forming processes as Earth and the other terrestrial planets, at about the same time.

What do carbonaceous chondrites, Martian meteorites, and the Moon tell us about the age of the solar system? The ages of carbonaceous chondrites, as a group, cluster closely around 4.56 billion years. Planetary scientists therefore conclude that Earth, and indeed the entire planetary system, formed at that time. Today, more than two centuries after Hutton's Insightful observations at the Siccar Point unconformity that now bears his name (see *Amazing Places*), it is widely agreed that Earth's age is approximately 4.56 billion years. So it is no longer correct to say that Earth has "no vestige of a beginning." When will it cease to exist? Astronomers tell us that billions of years in the future, the Sun will become a red giant, at which point it will expand and engulf Earth. However, Hutton is still correct in one sense: Earth's history is profound, and geologic (as opposed to astronomical) evidence shows no prospect of an end.

STOP CONCEPT CHECK

1. **What** is the oldest age that has been obtained from a material found on Earth? Does this match the presumed age of the planet as a whole? Why or why not?

2. **How** have meteorites and rock samples from the Moon helped geologists determine the age of Earth as 4.56 billion years?

SUMMARY

1 Relative Age 59

- Geologists study the chronologic sequence of geologic events—that is, their **relative age**. Relative age is derived from **stratigraphy**, the study of rock layers and how those layers are formed.

- There are four basic principles of stratigraphy. (1) Strata, or sedimentary rock layers, are horizontal when they are deposited as water-laid sediment (principle of original horizontality). (2) Strata accumulate in sequence, from the oldest on the bottom to the youngest on top (principle of stratigraphic superposition). (3) Strata extend outward horizontally; they may thin or pinch out at their farthest edges, but they generally do not terminate abruptly unless cut by a younger rock unit (principle of lateral continuity). (4) A rock stratum is always older than any geologic feature, such as a fracture, that cuts across it (principle of cross-cutting relationships).

- **Numerical age**, the exact number of years of a geologic feature, is more difficult to determine than relative age. The sequence of strata in any particular location is not necessarily continuous in time. An **unconformity** is a break or gap in the normal stratigraphic sequence. It usually marks a period during which sedimentation ceased and erosion removed some of the previously laid strata. The three common types of unconformities are nonconformities, angular unconformities, and disconformities as shown in the diagram.

Unconformities • Figure 3.2

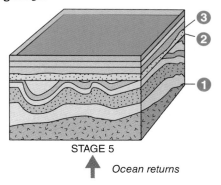

Cycle continues, new rock forms.

STAGE 5

Ocean returns

- **Correlation** of strata is the establishment of the time equivalence of strata in different places. Fossil assemblages, usually consisting of hard shells, bones, and wood, have been the primary key to correlation of strata across long distances. The study of fossils and the record of ancient life on Earth is called **paleontology**. The principle of faunal and floral succession (animals and plants, respectively) says that fossil assemblages will occur in the same sequence, regardless of location.

2 The Geologic Column 66

- The **geologic column**, a stratigraphic time scale, is a composite diagram that shows the succession of all known strata, arranged in chronological order of formation, based on fossils and other age criteria as shown in the diagram.

The Geologic column • Figure 3.6

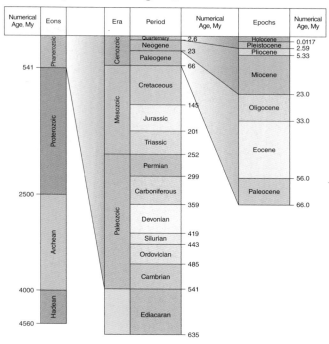

- The geologic column is divided into several different units of time, called eons, eras, periods, and epochs. Earth's history is divided into four eons, each spanning several hundred million years. During the first three, the Hadean, Archean, and Proterozoic eons, fossils are very rare or nonexistent. The exception occurs at the end of the Proterozoic, when soft-bodied fossils allow the Ediacaran Period to be defined. The fourth and most recent eon, the Phanerozoic, is the only eon in which macroscopic fossils are abundant. Very dramatic changes in fossil assemblages occur between the three eras of the Phanerozoic eon—the Paleozoic, Mesozoic, and Cenozoic—which were separated by major extinction events.

3 Numerical Age 69

- Many scientists in the 19th century and earlier proposed different ways to find the age of Earth and came up with widely differing estimates. Though many of those approaches were later shown to be imprecise, each was an important step in finding a method of numerical dating.

- **Radioactivity** is the process in which an element spontaneously transforms itself into another isotope of the same element or into a different element through the release of particles and heat energy. The radioactive decay of isotopes of chemical elements provides a basis for radiometric dating, which gives values for the numerical ages of rock units, and thus values for numerical dates of geologic events. Because radioactive decay is not influenced by chemical processes or by heat and high pressure, it is an extremely accurate gauge of numerical age.

- **Radiometric dating** is based on the principle that in any sample containing a radioactive isotope, half of its atoms of that isotope will change to daughter atoms in a specific length of time, called the **half-life** as shown in the diagram. Radioactive isotopes with long half-lives, such as uranium, are most useful for dating rocks. Carbon-14, which has a much shorter half-life, is most useful for dating organic materials of relatively recent origin (less than 70,000 years).

Radioactivity and time · Figure 3.11

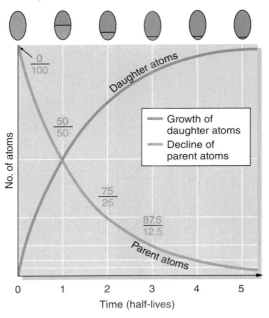

- Though radiometric dating is useful primarily for igneous rocks, a complementary technique called magnetic polarity dating works for sedimentary rocks, too. Magnetic polarity dating involves **paleomagnetism** and the study of reversals in Earth's magnetic field. The cause of these **magnetic reversals** is still not fully understood.

4 The Age of Earth   76

- Through measures of numerical age, it has become clear that most of Earth's history took place in Precambrian time. The oldest Earth rocks discovered are about 4.0 billion years old, as shown in the photo.

Earth's oldest rock · Figure 3.15

Courtesy Stephen J. Mojzsis

- Earth is not a good place to look for the oldest rocks in the solar system because Earth's surface has been subjected to a lot of geologic activity. This has reset some radiometric clocks and destroyed the earliest fragments of the crust. Samples from the Moon and from meteorites indicate that the solar system formed about 4.56 billion years ago, and by inference this is also the age of Earth.

KEY TERMS

CRITICAL AND CREATIVE THINKING QUESTIONS

1. Do the same principles of stratigraphy apply on the Moon as on Earth? Bear in mind that the geologic processes on the Moon have been very different from those on Earth. If you had to determine the relative age of features on the Moon, based entirely on satellite photographs, what would you look for, and how might you proceed?

2. Check the area in which you live to see if there is an excavation—perhaps one associated with a new building or road repair. Visit the excavation and note the various layers, the paving (if the excavation is in a road), and the soil below the surface. Is any bedrock exposed beneath the soil?

3. How old are the rock formations in the area where you live and attend college or university? How can you find out the answer to this question?

4. Choose one of the geologic periods or epochs listed in Figure 3.6 and find out all you can about it. How are rock formations

from that period identified? What are its most characteristic fossils? Where are the best samples of rock from your chosen period found?

5. Even though erosion has cut through the strata shown in this drawing, most of the rock units can still be traced from locality 1 through to localities 2 and 3. Which basic principle of stratigraphy does this illustrate? Which unit can't be traced all the way through? Describe what might have happened to make this so.

Fossils and Correlation • Figure 3.5

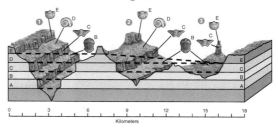

WHAT IS HAPPENING IN THIS PICTURE?

This skier is hauling a sled past a cliff face on Ellesmere Island, Canada.

layersJohn Dunn/Arctic Light/NG Image Collection

THINK CRITICALLY

1. Why do you think the rock strata in the background tilt at such a steep angle?
2. Why are the strata wavy instead of straight?

SELF-TEST

(Check your answers in Appendix D.)

1. A _____ is the age of one rock unit or geologic feature compared to another.

   a. relative age

   b. numerical age

2. The principle of cross-cutting relationships says that _____.

   a. water-borne sediments are deposited in nearly horizontal layers

   b. a sediment or sedimentary rock layer is younger than the layers below it and older than the layers that lie above

   c. a rock unit is older than a feature that disrupts it, such as a fault or igneous intrusion

   d. a sediment or sedimentary rock layer is older than the layers below it and younger than the layers that lie above

3. The _____ states that water-borne sediments are deposited in nearly horizontal layers.

   a. law of superposition

   b. principle of faunal succession

   c. principle of original horizontality

   d. principle of cross-cutting relationships

4. In a conformable sequence, _____.

   a. each layer must have been deposited on the one below it, without any interruptions

   b. there must not be any depositional gaps in the stratigraphic record

   c. Both a and b are correct.

   d. Neither a nor b is correct.

5. An unconformity represents _____.

    a. a gap in the stratigraphic record

    b. a period of erosion or nondeposition

    c. Both a and b are correct.

    d. Neither a nor b is correct.

6. On this diagram, label each unconformity as one of the following:

    nonconformity

    angular unconformity

    disconformity

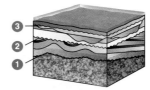

7. Fossils found in strata _____.

    a. are the records of ancient life

    b. allow the correlation of strata separated by many kilometers

    c. have been useful to geologists in creating the geologic column

    d. All of the above answers are correct.

8. The three eras that make up the Phanerozoic Eon are the _____.

    a. Hadean, Archean, and Proterozoic

    b. Paleozoic, Mesozoic, and Cenozoic

    c. Triassic, Jurassic, and Cretaceous

    d. Pliocene, Pleistocene, and Holocene

9. The most distinctive changes in the fossil record occur across the boundaries between _____.

    a. periods   b. eras   c. epochs

10. The dinosaurs were dominant during _____.

    a. the Cenozoic Era   c. the Paleozoic Era

    b. the Mesozoic Era   d. the Precambrian time

11. Label the two decay sequences depicted in this diagram as either alpha emission or beta decay. For each decay sequence, also label the following:

    parent nucleus   daughter nucleus

    alpha particle   (or)   beta particle

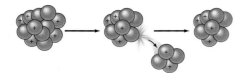

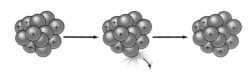

12. Potassium-40 is a naturally occurring radioisotope that decays to Argon-40 and is common in many rocks of the continental crust. The half-life of Potassium-40 is 1.3 billion years. Assuming no contamination, what would be the age of a sample that contains a 1:3 ratio of Potassium-40 to Argon-40?

    a. 1.3 billion years   c. 2.6 billion years

    b. 650 million years   d. 325 million years

13. Why are meteorites—and carbonaceous chondrite meteorites, in particular—useful to scientists in determining the age of Earth?

    a. They date from the origin of the solar system, and there are no rocks left on Earth's surface that are as old as the planet itself.

    b. There are no rocks on Earth's surface that are "datable".

    c. They have been melted and recrystallized many times, so scientists can use them to trace the entire history of the solar system and the planet.

    d. All of the above answers are correct.

    e. None of the above answers is correct.

14. List all of the labeled items (1, 2, 3, 4, A, and B) on the cross section in chronological order from youngest (at the top of your list) to oldest (at the bottom of your list), using the rules of stratigraphy to determine their relative ages.

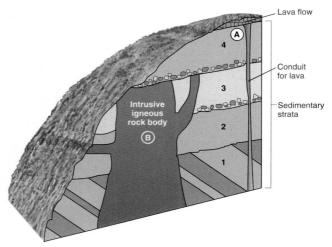

15. Earth is not considered a good place to look for the oldest rocks in the solar system because _____.

    a. contamination from atmospheric tests of nuclear weapons have befouled the crust of Earth

    b. Earth's magnetic field interferes with the radiometric clocks in most igneous rocks

    c. melting has reset radiometric clocks in the rocks of Earth's crust

    d. the earliest crustal rocks have been destroyed by geologic activity

    e. All of the above answers are correct.

    f. Both c and d are correct.

THE PLANNER ✓

Review the Chapter Planner on the chapter opener and check off your completed work.

4 | PLATE TECTONICS

Art Wolfe/Getty Images

Hulton Archive/Getty Images

Global Locator

Mariana Trench

Himalaya

NG Maps

K2 AND THE MARIANA TRENCH

K2, seen here at sunset, is the world's second-tallest peak at 8611 meters. Only Mount Everest (at 8848 meters) is higher. Both mountains are in the Himalaya, a range formed over the past 40 million years by a collision between India and Asia.

More than 300 people have climbed K2, and more than 4000 have climbed Everest (some of them, more than once). But only three—a Swiss oceanographer named Jacques Piccard, a U.S. Navy lieutenant, Donald Walsh, and a Hollywood director, James Cameron—have reached the lowest point on Earth. The Mariana Trench, near Guam, bottoms out at 11,000 meters below sea level. Piccard and Walsh made their historic descent in 1960, in a spherical submersible (inset) capable of withstanding the immense pressures at that depth; Cameron reached bottom on May 25, 2012, in a one-man steel, torpedo-like capsule.

Both Everest and the Mariana Trench are located at the margins of tectonic plates and were created by the same geologic process—the collision of two plates of lithosphere. In the first case, the colliding plates thrust up the world's highest mountain range. In the second, one plate dove beneath the other, dragging the seafloor down with it.

The slow motion of lithospheric plates, known as **plate tectonics**, continually reshapes our world. Over millions of years, it has restructured and relocated continents, built mountain ranges, opened and closed oceans. Without plate tectonics the Himalaya and the Mariana Trench would not exist, and Earth's surface would be an entirely different place.

☑ CHAPTER PLANNER

- Study the picture and read the opening story.
- Scan the Learning Objectives in each section:
  p. 84 p. 92
- Read the text and study all visuals. Answer any questions.

Analyze key features
- Geology InSight, pp. 86−87 pp. 96−97
- Process Diagram, p. 90
- What a Geologist Sees, p. 95
- Amazing Places, pp. 100−101
- Stop: Answer the Concept Checks before you go on: p. 91 p. 104

End of chapter
- Review the Summary and Key Terms.
- Answer the Critical and Creative Thinking Questions.
- Answer What is happening in this picture?
- Complete the Self-Test and check your answers.

A REVOLUTION IN GEOLOGY

Learning Objectives

1. **Describe** Wegener's hypothesis of continental drift.

2. **Identify** the early arguments that supported the hypothesis of continental drift.

3. **Explain** how paleomagnetism provided the definitive evidence for continental drift.

4. **Describe** the process of seafloor spreading.

Scientific revolutions challenge us to look at the world in a new way. They turn accepted ideas upside down. However, they don't take place overnight. For example, for millennia, people thought that Earth was the center of the universe, with the Sun and all the planets revolving around it. In 1543, Nicolaus Copernicus argued that it is the other way around—that the planets revolve around the Sun. It took decades of debate, new inventions such as the telescope, and finally the persuasive writing of such scientists as Galileo and Newton to convince astronomers that Copernicus was right.

Geology, too, underwent a revolution in the 1960s, when geologists discovered new evidence for an old idea called continental drift. Just like Copernicus's theory, the hypothesis that the continents have moved provoked controversy at first. But in recent decades, thanks to supporting evidence from many different sources, including sensitive global positioning systems that measure the actual rates and directions of motion, continental drift has become an integral part of the **theory of plate tectonics**.

> **continental drift** The slow lateral movement of continents across Earth's surface.

Plate tectonics has encouraged us to think of Earth as a system in constant flux, a dynamic world whose appearance and outer surface have changed considerably over the eons. Early geologists gathered information about Earth and its processes painstakingly, one piece at a time; plate tectonics shows us how those pieces fit together.

Continental Drift

In 1912, a German meteorologist named Alfred Wegener began lecturing and writing scientific papers about continental drift. Wegener was not the first to propose that the continents had moved into their present-day positions, but his work in support of the idea was comprehensive and systematic. Wegener hypothesized that the continents had once been joined together in a single "supercontinent," which he called *Pangaea* (pronounced "Pan-JEE-ah"), meaning "all lands" (**Figure 4.1**). He suggested that Pangaea had split into fragments, like pieces of ice floating on a pond, and that the continental fragments had then slowly moved to their present

Pangaea • Figure 4.1 _____

In 1915, Alfred Wegener drew a map much like this one, showing the distribution of the continents about 320 million years ago, in the Carboniferous Period. He proposed that the continents at that time were joined in one supercontinent, which he named Pangaea.

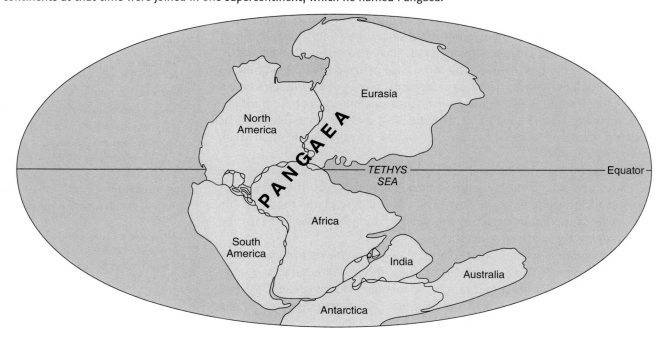

The edge of a continent usually contains several components. The true edge is defined as the point where the continental crust meets the oceanic crust, about halfway down the continental slope.

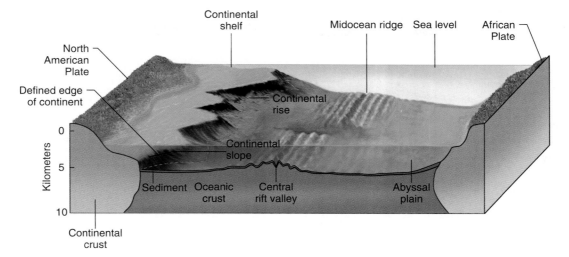

locations. Wegener was the first to refer to this process as "continental drift."

Modern reconstructions of Pangaea differ from Wegener's original 1915 version in some respects, but his basic idea was correct. He went on to marshal a great deal of evidence in favor of the continental drift hypothesis, and he had some powerful supporters in his day. Nevertheless, his work created a storm of protest, hostility, and even ridicule in the international scientific community.

Wegener's Evidence

That debate was to continue for decades among geologists and geophysicists. Some of the criticisms of Wegener's hypothesis were well founded. Contemporary geologists simply could not envision any reasonable mechanism by which continents could be moved. The terminology suggests continents are somehow "adrift" in a sea of water. But the continents are anchored in solid rock, so it seemed that a drifting continent would have to somehow plow through or across a seafloor that was also made of solid rock. Even Wegener could not explain how this could happen.

Let's put aside the problem of *how* plates move for a moment, and look at the evidence for plate motion as the geologists of Wegener's time did. Importantly, no single piece of evidence is conclusive on its own. It took the combined weight of all of these arguments (and more, as you will see later in the chapter) to convince geologists several decades later that Wegener was right.

Matching Coastlines It's easy to see from a map that the Atlantic coastlines of Africa and South America seem to match, almost like puzzle pieces. This apparent close fit of the coastlines of the modern continents had been observed by Leonardo da Vinci, Francis Bacon, and other observers of the natural world as early as the 1500s. Is this an accident, or

does it truly support the hypothesis that the continents were once joined together?

To decide whether the continents really do match, we must first note that there is more to the edge of a continent than meets the eye. The Atlantic coasts of South America and Africa, like those of other continents, do not terminate abruptly at the shoreline but slope gently seaward. This shallow, gently sloping land, partly above sea level and partly below, is called the **continental shelf**. Further offshore, at a water depth of about 100 meters, there is an abrupt change of slope called the *shelf break*, beyond which lies the steeper **continental slope** (**Figure 4.2**). At the base of the continental slope lies the **continental rise**, which is usually covered by a thick layer of sediment. Beyond this, the main part of the ocean floor consists of the flat **abyssal plain**.

The true edge of a continent is defined as the point where the continental crust meets the oceanic crust, which is roughly halfway down the continental slope. In the center of the ocean, between two continents, we often find a submarine mountain range called a *midocean ridge*. (As you will see, this structure turns out to be central to the mystery of what causes continents to move.)

If we fit together South America and Africa along the true edges of the continents (**Figure 4.3a**), we get an even better match than we might expect. In the "best-fit" position, the average gap or overlap between the two continents is only 90 kilometers. In addition, the most significant overlaps consist of wedges of sedimentary or volcanic rock that were added *after* the continents are thought to have split apart.

Matching Geology The close fit between Africa and South America does suggest that they were once joined, like pieces of a jigsaw puzzle. But it is easy to be fooled by jigsaw puzzle pieces that have nearly matching shapes. To be sure that the pieces fit together, you also need to match the designs on the puzzle pieces.

Wegener considered all of the arguments shown here, as he attempted to demonstrate the validity of continental drift. Geologists today continue to refine and build upon these arguments by adding new evidence, new observations, and new analyses.

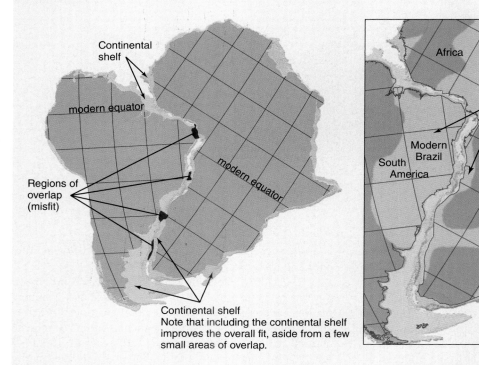

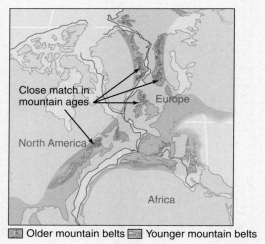

Older than 550 million years
About 550 million years old
Younger than 550 million years

b. Matching geology
When the continents are rotated back together, the ages of similar rock units generally match across the join, particularly in the regions of northeastern Brazil and West Africa.

a. Matching coastlines
This map reconstructs the fit of South America and Africa along the *true* edges of the continents. The darkly shaded areas show overlap. The inclusion of the shallow continental shelf areas improves the fit. Wegener attempted to demonstrate the fit of the coastlines, but he did not have access to detailed information about the continental shelves.

Older mountain belts   Younger mountain belts

c. Matching mountain ranges
In this reconstruction of the northern part of Pangaea, mountain belts of similar ages match up across the join.

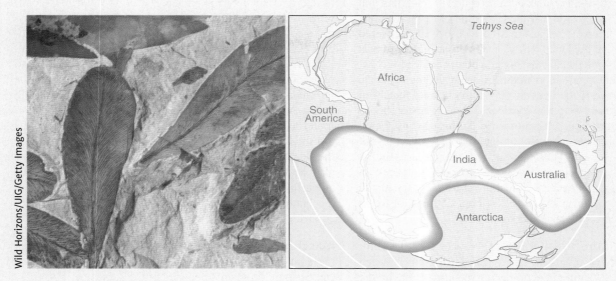

> ◣ **d. Matching fossils**
>
> These tongue-shaped fossil leaves came from a tree of the Permian Period called *Glossopteris*. Similar fossils occur in Africa, India, Australia, and South America, providing strong evidence that these regions were once contiguous. When the continents are moved back to their probable locations in the Permian Period, the *Glossopteris* fossil localities (in green on the map) match nicely.

e. Matching glacial deposits

As glaciers advance, sediment and rock contained within them grind and abrade the bedrock, producing a polished and grooved surface. This surface, at Nooitgedacht, South Africa, was created by the Pangaean ice sheet. The map shows the extent of glacial deposits in the southern continents of Pangaea. Arrows indicate the direction in which the ice was moving, deduced from grooves in the bedrock. ▼

THINK CRITICALLY

In what ways have each of these lines of evidence been improved or expanded upon since Wegener's time?

Similarly, if the continents were once joined together, we should find geologic features that match up from one side of the join to the other. However, matching the geology of rocks on opposite sides of an ocean is more difficult than you might imagine. Erosion and the formation of new rock units since the breakup of Pangaea may have destroyed or covered up some of the evidence, so we will be putting together a puzzle with some pieces missing and others defaced.

A starting point in matching up the geologic puzzle pieces is to see if the ages of similar rock units match up across the ocean. Wegener considered this argument, but in his day the technique of radiometric dating was just being developed, so it was not easy to determine the exact age of a rock. Now we know that there is, indeed, similarity in the ages of rocks and correlation between rock sequences on both sides of the ocean. As shown in **Figure 4.3b**, the match is particularly good between rocks about 550 million years old in northeastern Brazil and West Africa.

Matching Mountain Ranges We can also check for the continuity of mountain chains across the join between the continents. **Figure 4.3c** shows a reconstruction of the northern part of the supercontinent Pangaea. Notice, again, how mountain chains of similar ages seem to line up when the continents are moved back into this position. The oldest portions of the Appalachian Mountains, extending from the northeastern United States through eastern Canada, match up with the Caledonides of Ireland, Britain, Greenland, and Scandinavia. A younger part of the Appalachians lines up with a belt of similar age in Africa and Europe.

Wegener noted the continuity of mountain ranges. He even postulated that the formation of mountain ranges might have something to do with the joining and splitting apart of moving continents, which we now know to be correct. However, it was completely counter to the prevailing ideas about the formation of mountain ranges, which were mostly based on the idea that Earth was contracting and shriveling up, like a drying apple. We now know from the orbital characteristics of the planet that Earth is neither shrinking nor growing in size significantly, so the "contracting Earth" hypothesis does not hold.

Matching Fossils If Africa and South America were really joined together as a supercontinent at one time, then we should expect that they would have similar climates, in addition to similar geologic features. If they had similar climates, then they should have been inhabited by the same types of plants and animals. To check this hypothesis, Wegener looked at fossils. He found that some communities of plants and animals apparently evolved together until the time that Pangaea split apart, and after that time they evolved separately.

For example, Wegener found fossils of an ancient tree, *Glossopteris* (**Figure 4.3d**), in matching areas of southern Africa, South America, Australia, India, and Antarctica. Could the seeds of this plant have been carried by wind or water from one continent to another? Probably not. The seeds of *Glossopteris* were large and heavy, and they would not have traveled far on the wind or water currents. Not only that, *Glossopteris* flourished in a cold climate; it would not have thrived in the warm present-day regions where its fossil remains are found. This, too, is consistent with the idea that these continents were once joined together in a more southerly location.

Certain animal fossils, too, match up well. The fossil remains of *Mesosaurus*, a small, freshwater reptile from the Permian Period, are found both in southern Brazil and in South Africa. The types of rocks in which the fossils are found are very similar. *Mesosaurus* did swim, but it was too small (about 0.5 meters long) to swim all the way across the ocean. Fossil remains of certain types of earthworms also occur in areas that are now widely separated. Since an earthworm could not have hopped across a wide ocean, the landmasses in which they lived must once have been connected.

Matching Glacial Deposits Additional evidence that the southern hemisphere continents were once connected can be found in glacial deposits of the same age (Permian–Carboniferous) in South America, Africa, Australia, and India.

As glacial ice moves, it cuts grooves and scratches in underlying rocks and produces folds and wrinkles in soft sediments (**Figure 4.3e**). These features provide evidence not only of the extent of glaciation, but also of the direction the ice was moving during the glaciation. When today's southern hemisphere continents are moved back together, the direction of ice movement on them is consistent, radiating outward from the center of the former ice sheet. Certain types of glacial deposits around the edges of the former ice sheet also match up across the join.

It's hard to imagine how such similar glacial features could have been created and why they would match up so nicely, if the continents had not been joined together. The glacial deposits also suggest that Africa, South America, Australia, and India were once closer to the South Pole than they are today and that they had cooler climates; this finding is consistent with the fossil assemblages found in these areas.

Paleomagnetism and Apparent Polar Wandering

Wegener had some supporters for his ideas. Two in particular, Arthur Holmes in England and Alexander du Toit in South Africa, were well known and distinguished scientists. Wegener and his supporters gathered more and more evidence in support of continental drift, but most scientists remained unconvinced, mainly because there was no reasonable hypothesis explaining *how* continents could move. Wegener died in 1930 without seeing a resolution to the problem.

Then, in the 1950s, **paleomagnetism** emerged as a new tool for studying Earth's history, and it was destined

Wandering poles • Figure 4.4

This map traces the *apparent* path of the magnetic north pole over the past 600 million years. Rocks in North America point to the magnetic poles on the red curve, and rocks in Europe point to the magnetic poles on the black curve. The *actual* magnetic pole probably never wandered far from the geographic North Pole. The apparent motion is created by the movement of the continents.

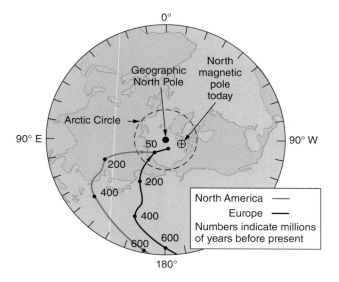

to provide new evidence that would break the intellectual logjam over continental drift (see *Remember This!*). Geophysicists who were studying paleomagnetic pole positions found evidence suggesting that Earth's magnetic poles had wandered all over the globe over the past several hundred million years. They plotted the pathways of the poles on maps like the one shown in **Figure 4.4**, and they called the phenomenon **apparent polar wandering**.

> **REMEMBER THIS!** Do you recall how geologists use paleomagnetism to determine the ages of rocks? In *Magnetic Polarity Dating* in Chapter 3, you learned that reversals in Earth's magnetic field follow a well-established chronology that can be used as a tool for dating.

Geophysicists found the apparent wandering of Earth's magnetic poles puzzling. The origin of Earth's magnetism is related to the planet's rotation about its axis; for this reason, geophysicists knew that it would be impossible for the magnetic poles to wander very far from the axis of rotation. Even more puzzling, they found that the path of apparent polar wandering measured from North American rocks differed from that of European rocks. Earth certainly cannot have two different magnetic north poles at the same time!

The only possible solution to this conundrum is that the magnetic pole is fixed and that the continents themselves had moved, carrying the rocks (and the record of paleomagnetic

poles) along with them. In that case, the apparent motion of the poles would be an illusion, like the apparent motion of trees when you drive by them. In fact, the apparent polar wandering path of a continent, determined from rock units of various ages, provides a historical record of the position of that continent relative to the magnetic poles.

Notice also in Figure 4.4 that the apparent polar wandering paths for Europe and North America actually look quite similar from 600 million years ago to 200 million years ago. In fact, if you rotate Europe and America toward each other so that they are side by side, the two paths overlap exactly. This clearly indicates that Europe and America were moving as a single continent during that time.

The Missing Clue: Seafloor Spreading

By the early 1960s, many clues had been amassed in support of continental drift. The hypothesis made testable predictions, such as matching geology and fossils, and those predictions had been confirmed. The hypothesis was also consistent with evidence that was not known during Wegener's lifetime—the apparent polar wandering paths. But even as the evidence for continental motion continued to build, many scientists remained skeptical. The ripping apart and relocation of an entire continent should have left traces that would still be visible today; where were those traces?

Then, three decades after Wegener's death, geologists found the conclusive evidence they needed—at the bottom of the sea. The missing clue turned up when geophysicists and oceanographers applied the then-new technique of magnetic polarity dating to rocks at the bottom of the Atlantic Ocean.

Magnetic Polarity Banding The scientists were astounded to find that parts of the seafloor consist of magnetized rocks with alternating bands of normal and reversed polarities. The bands are hundreds of kilometers long. More importantly, they are symmetrical on either side of a centerline that coincides with the ridge running down the middle of the Atlantic Ocean (**Figure 4.5**). In other words, if you could fold the seafloor in half along the midocean ridge, the bands on either side would match.

Later evidence would show that not only the paleomagnetic polarities but also the numerical ages of the rocks were symmetrically banded, and they were mirrored on either side of the ridge (as shown in Figure 4.5a). The youngest rocks lie closest to the ridge, and the ages increase in both directions, symmetrically, with distance from the ridge.

The symmetrical pattern of magnetic bands provided powerful support for a hypothesis, first proposed in 1960, called **seafloor spreading**. According

> **seafloor spreading** The process through which the seafloor splits and moves apart along a midocean ridge and new oceanic crust forms along the ridge.

Process Diagram

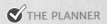

How seafloor spreading works • Figure 4.5

The symmetrical banding of rock ages and magnetic polarities on either side of the midocean ridge provided conclusive evidence for continental drift.

a. This map shows the ages of magnetically banded rocks on either side of the Mid-Atlantic Ridge. The numbers indicate the ages of the rocks, in millions of years. The youngest rocks lie along the ridge, and the oldest are farthest from the ridge, indicating that the seafloor has been spreading over time.

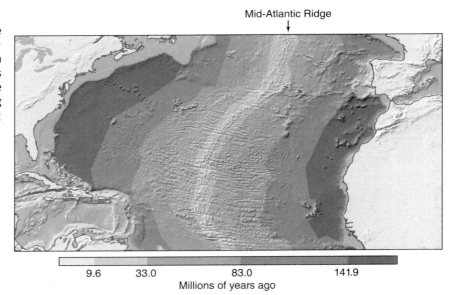

Mid-Atlantic Ridge

9.6   33.0   83.0   141.9

Millions of years ago

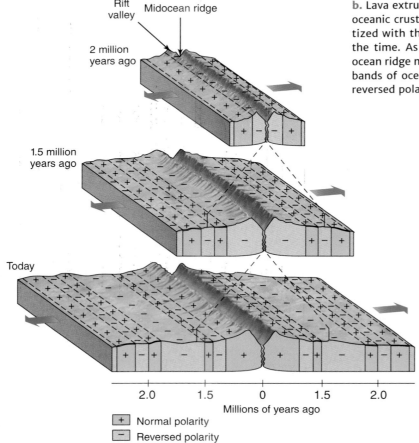

Rift valley   Midocean ridge

2 million years ago

1.5 million years ago

Today

2.0   1.5   0   1.5   2.0

Millions of years ago

+ Normal polarity
− Reversed polarity

b. Lava extruding along a midocean ridge forms new oceanic crust. As the lava cools, it becomes magnetized with the polarity of Earth's magnetic field at the time. As the plates on either side of the midocean ridge move apart from one another, successive bands of oceanic crust have alternating normal and reversed polarities.

THINK CRITICALLY

The paleomagnetic record of the ocean floor shows that the most ancient oceanic crust is only about 200 million years old. Why might this be so?

The arrows show surface motions from continuous GPS measurements on North America. Green lines are plate boundaries. Points on the same plate are generally moving in the same direction, confirming that the plates are rigid. GPS stations on the North American Plate are moving slowly southwest, while those on the Pacific Plate (to the left of the green curve) are moving more rapidly northwest.

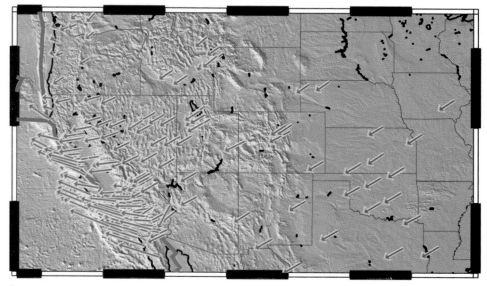

© John Wiley & Sons, Inc.

to this hypothesis, the **midocean ridge** is a place where the seafloor has split apart and the rocks are moving away from one another (as shown in Figure 4.5b). When magma from below wells up into the crack, it solidifies into new volcanic rock on the seafloor. Over time, the expanding seafloor operates as a conveyor belt, carrying the newly magnetized bands of rock away from the ridge in either direction.

The decisive evidence for seafloor spreading is that the ages of seafloor rocks increase with distance from the ridge. The youngest rocks are found along the center of the ridge, where new molten material wells up (as shown in Figure 4.5a). This final piece of evidence convinced the great majority of geologists that seafloor spreading is real. The magnetic evidence of the seafloor also allowed geologists to calculate the spreading rate of the seafloor; it turned out to range between 1 and 10 centimeters a year.

To summarize: Apparent polar wandering paths established that the continents move. Seafloor magnetism showed that the seafloor moves, too, spreading outward from a central rift. Scientists quickly realized that continents are not trundling along on top of a static ocean floor, which would be physically impossible. Instead, they are conveyed in opposite directions by a dynamic ocean floor that is constantly spreading and replenishing itself. Ironically, it was geophysicists—the group that had most vigorously opposed Wegener's ideas—who found the final piece of evidence that proved Wegener correct. The many investigations seeking to test the continental drift hypothesis provide a good example of the scientific method at work.

GPS Measurement of Plate Motion More recently, an even more direct piece of evidence for plate motion became available. In the 1980s, the U.S. Department of Defense declassified the data from a network of satellites that form the Global Positioning System (GPS). GPS receivers help motorists, hikers, boaters, and pilots find their exact location quickly and easily, and they can also be used to track continental drift. Geologists have attached GPS receivers permanently to the ground, so that they do not move unless the ground moves. This allows them to plot maps of Earth's surface velocities (**Figure 4.6**).

The GPS data confirm that the continents are not only moving, but they are moving at the same rates and in the same directions as seafloor spreading. The speeds are too slow for humans to be aware of any movement—they range from 1 to 10 centimeters per year—but they are easily detectable by GPS sensors. They also confirm previous calculations of the rates of plate motion based on magnetic banding.

STOP CONCEPT CHECK

1. **What** does the name *Pangaea* mean?
2. **What** were the main arguments that Wegener gave in support of his hypothesis of continental drift?
3. **How** does apparent polar wandering support the idea of continental drift?
4. **How** does seafloor spreading create paleomagnetic bands on either side of a midocean ridge?

THE PLATE TECTONIC MODEL

Learning Objectives

1. **Outline** the theory of plate tectonics.

2. **Describe** three different types of plate margins.

3. **Explain** the role of mantle convection in plate tectonics.

4. **Summarize** the tectonic cycle: past, present, and future.

Once the evidence for continental drift and seafloor spreading had been established, researchers began seeking a mechanism. A lot of previously puzzling phenomena in geology suddenly began to make sense. For instance, geologists could now explain the location of mountain ranges and deep ocean trenches. They could explain why, in some places (e.g., the Tibetan Plateau), Earth's crust seems to be squeezed together, making high mountains, while in other places (e.g., the East African Rift valleys), it seems to be pulling apart and making deep, steep-sided trenches. Geologists also realized that the distribution of earthquakes and volcanic activity around the planet, which is far from uniform, must somehow be related to the motions (**Figure 4.7**).

Plate Tectonics in a Nutshell

The unifying theory that emerged from all of the research that we have described so far (and much more) is called **plate tectonics**. Note that we call plate tectonics a *theory* rather than a *hypothesis*, because it is so strongly supported by scientific evidence (see *Remember This!*). In later chapters, we will explore in greater detail the many ways that plate tectonics influences the characteristics of this planet; for now, let's take a broad overview of plate tectonics.

> **plate tectonics** The movement and interactions of large fragments of Earth's lithosphere, called plates.

> **REMEMBER THIS!** Can you remember the difference between a *theory* and a *hypothesis*? A hypothesis is a working model based on observations. To become a theory, a hypothesis must be repeatedly tested and supported by many different types of evidence. Revisit *Science and the Scientific Method* in Chapter 1 to review this distinction.

Earth's **lithosphere**, the rocky outer layer that comprises the crust and the outermost part of the mantle, is very thin relative to Earth as a whole, being no more than about 100 kilometers thick. The solid rock that makes up the lithosphere is strong, but it lies on top of a vast mantle of hotter, weaker material that is constantly in motion (albeit very slow motion). The layer of the mantle that lies directly below the lithosphere, called the **asthenosphere**,

Distribution of earthquake epicenters around the world • Figure 4.7

The map shows the locations of earthquakes of magnitude 4.0 and above during 2010, from the U.S. National Earthquake Information Center. The distribution of earthquakes helps geologists locate the edges of tectonic plates. Compare this with Figure 4.8.

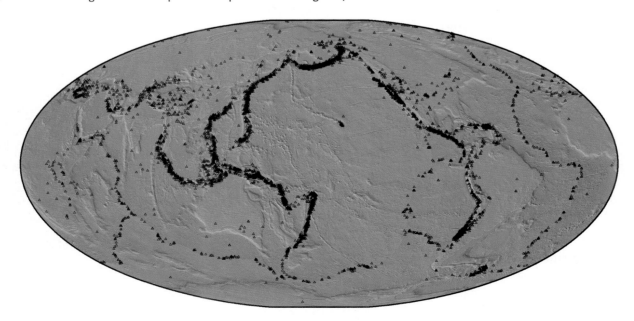

is especially weak because it is close to the temperature at which melting begins. (The lithosphere and asthenosphere will be discussed in greater detail in Chapter 5.) The relationship between these two layers is a condition called **isostasy**, which means that the lithosphere is essentially "floating" on the asthenosphere, like a sheet of ice floating on water.

Why do lithospheric plates exist? A simple thought experiment will help us to clarify the relationship between the brittle lithospheric plates and the underlying mantle.

If you were to place a very thin, cool, brittle shell on top of hot, ductile material that is constantly shifting and moving around, what do you expect would happen? It's almost a certainty that the shell would crack, and that is exactly what has happened to Earth's thin, brittle lithosphere. It has broken into the enormous rocky fragments that we call **plates**. Today there are six large lithospheric plates, extending for thousands of miles, as well as a number of smaller ones (**Figure 4.8**). One important thing to remember is that the plates are fragments of lithosphere, not fragments of crust. However, the characteristics of the plates are controlled, to a great extent, by the type of crust that they are carrying. Thus, plates that carry oceanic crust have different properties and behave differently than plates that carry continental crust.

> **plate** A large fragment of rigid lithosphere bounded on all sides by faults.

It is one thing to realize that the lithosphere has fractured into plates; it is another thing altogether to know where the boundaries of the plates lie. A fracture that separates one piece of moving lithosphere from another is called a **fault**. Geologists have long understood that movement along faults is the main cause of earthquakes. Therefore, to locate the fractures that mark the plate boundaries, geologists turned to evidence from earthquakes. You can investigate the relationship between earthquakes and plate boundaries using Google Earth; see *Where Geologists Click*.

> **fault** A fracture in Earth's crust along which movement has occurred.

Types of Plate Margins

There are three fundamentally different ways in which two adjacent plates can interact. They can move away from each other (or *diverge*), they can move toward each other (or *converge*), or they can slide past each other more or less horizontally, along a long fracture. We will take a look at examples of each of these types of margins and the kinds of earthquakes that happen along them.

Earthquakes occur along faults, where huge blocks of rock are grinding past each other (discussed in greater detail in Chapter 5). Tectonic motions produce directional pressure, which causes rocks on either side of a large fracture to move past each other. The movement is rarely smooth; usually the blocks stick because of friction, which slows their movement. Eventually, the friction is overcome and the blocks slip abruptly, releasing pent-up energy with a huge "snap"—an **earthquake**.

The actual location beneath the surface where an earthquake begins is called the **focus** (plural *foci*). This should not

Tectonic plates · Figure 4.8 _____

These are Earth's major lithospheric plates, as they are currently understood. Compare the plate boundaries to the distribution of earthquake epicenters (Figure 4.7).

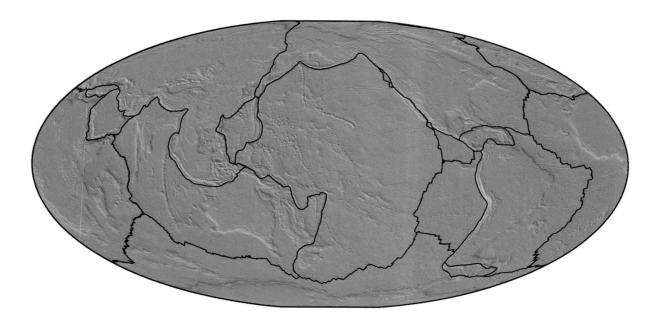

Where Geologists CLICK

Google Earth: Earthquakes and Volcanoes

You can use Google Earth to explore the locations of earthquakes and active volcanoes relative to plate boundaries. First, you will need to download Google Earth to your laptop; it's free. In the menu at left, open "Layers" and then "Gallery." Click "Earthquakes" and "Volcanoes" to show these items on the map.

In the screen capture shown here, we are looking at recent earthquakes and volcanic activity in the Aleutian Islands, between Alaska and Siberia. The Aleutians are volcanic islands that mark a boundary between two plates. As you move through the chapter and learn more about plate boundaries, come back to this figure and see if you can determine what type of boundary it is, and which way the plates are moving. What is the relationship between the volcanic islands and the adjacent deep trench? What is the name of the process that is occurring here? Zoom to some other locations that you think would be tectonically active, and see what you find. Try the Red Sea, the San Andreas Fault, and the Himalaya Mountains to start.

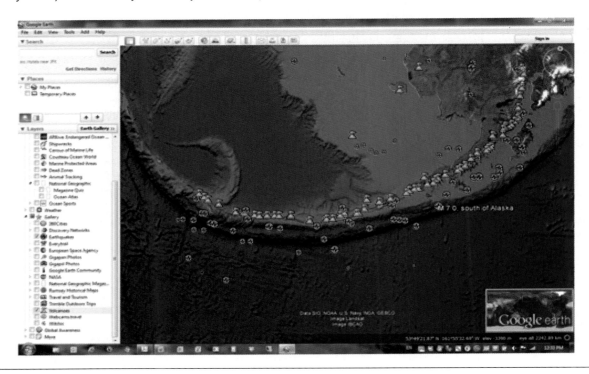

be confused with the better-known **epicenter**, which is the point on Earth's surface that lies directly over the focus. Both the locations of earthquake epicenters and the depths of their foci provide useful information about the characteristics of plate margins (**Figure 4.9**).

Divergent margins, also called **rifting centers** or **spreading centers**, occur where two plates are moving apart (**Figure 4.9a**). They can occur either in continental or oceanic plates. In East Africa, for example, the African Plate is being stretched and torn apart, creating long **rift valleys**. Eventually, a new ocean may form in the widening rift; a modern example of this is the Red Sea (see *What a Geologist Sees*). Where an oceanic plate is splitting apart, the result is a **midocean ridge**, and the one place in the world where a midocean ridge can be seen above the sea is Iceland. Earthquakes are common along divergent margins because the plates are fracturing and splitting apart; however, the earthquakes tend to be weak, with shallow foci.

Along **transform fault margins** plates slide past one

> **divergent margin** A boundary along which two plates move apart from one another.
>
> **rift valley** A linear, fault-bounded valley along a divergent plate boundary or spreading center.

> **midocean ridge** A long submarine ridge in an ocean basin, marking the location of a divergent plate boundary and magma upwelling associated with seafloor spreading.
>
> **transform fault margin** A fracture in the lithosphere where two plates slide past each other horizontally (or laterally).

What a Geologist Sees

The Red Sea and the Gulf of Aden

This spectacular photo, taken by astronauts on the *Gemini 11* mission, shows the southern end of the Red Sea (left) and the Gulf of Aden (right), separating the southern tip of the Arabian Peninsula (right) from the northeastern corner of Africa.

A geologist looking at this scene would realize that two lithospheric plates (the Arabian and African plates; see inset map) are splitting apart. A divergent plate margin runs down the center of the Gulf of Aden and joins another divergent margin that runs down the center of the Red Sea (both underwater). This rift is a continuation of the Great Rift Valley, which marks a continental rift zone in East Africa (see block diagram). The Red Sea is widening at a rate of about 1 centimeter per year.

If the rifting process continues for several million years, the long narrow sea will become a wide gulf; if it continues even longer than that, it may eventually develop into a full ocean with a spreading rift running down the middle. The red dots on the map (inset) show the locations of recent earthquakes and volcanic activity. Compare this photo to the block diagrams in Figure 4.9a that show continental and oceanic rifting.

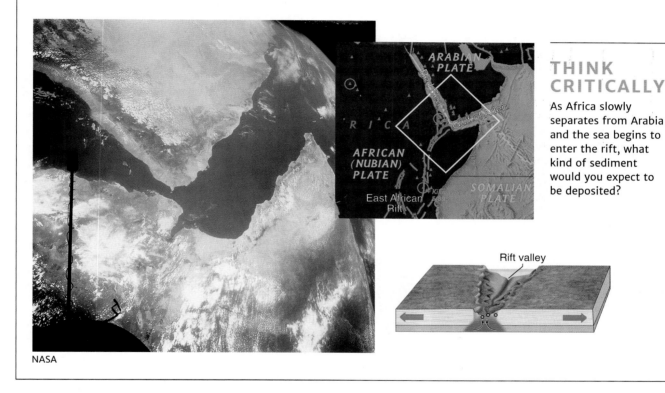

NASA

THINK CRITICALLY

As Africa slowly separates from Arabia and the sea begins to enter the rift, what kind of sediment would you expect to be deposited?

Rift valley

---

another horizontally (**Figure 4.9b**). Transform faults are very common on the ocean floor, and hundreds of them run perpendicular to the midocean ridges. This causes oceanic plates to have very complicated, jagged boundaries, in which spreading centers alternate with transform faults. Transform faults also occur in continental plates; the San Andreas Fault in California is a famous example. Transform-type fault boundaries are also called **strike-slip boundaries**—an alternative term for horizontal or lateral movement of plates.

 Convergent margins occur where two plates move toward each other (**Figure 4.9c**).

> **convergent margin** A boundary along which two plates come together.

Convergence leads to different types of features, depending on whether the boundary is between two oceanic plates, two continental plates, or one of each. When one or both plates of lithosphere are capped by oceanic crust, one plate will typically slide beneath the other plate, plunging into the asthenosphere, in a process called **subduction**. Oceanic plates are the only ones that undergo subduction; plates that are carrying continental crust are too buoyant to be subducted. (Recall that oceanic crust consists mainly of basalt, a denser rock type than the granitic rock that characterizes continental crust.)

Plates interact along their boundaries in three main ways: They spread apart; they move laterally past one another; or they come together. These interactions can occur in both continental and oceanic plates, yielding six major types of plate boundary, illustrated here.

a. DIVERGENT MARGINS Along a divergent margin, the plate splits and the two halves move away from each other in opposite directions. Divergent margins occur in both continental and oceanic crust.

Super Stock/Age Fotostock

Continental: Rift valley When a continent splits, the plates move apart from one another on either side of a main fracture zone, forming a flat-bottomed, steep-sided rift valley. Here in the Great Rift Valley of East Africa, the African Plate is splitting into the Somalian Plate on one side, and the Nubian Plate on the other.

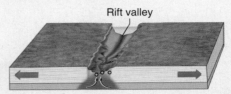

Earthquakes in rift zones: Earthquakes are common in continental and oceanic rift zones, but they tend to be weak and shallow. Strong earthquakes only occur in rock that is cold and brittle. In rift zones the crust is thin and magma rises to the surface, so strong earthquakes are not common.

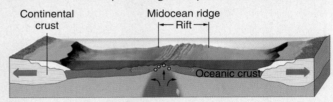

Emory Kristof/NG Image Collection

Oceanic: Midocean rift spreading center If a continental rift widens, it may develop into a linear sea or a full ocean with a spreading rift down the middle. This rift valley in Iceland lies atop the Mid-Atlantic Ridge, a divergent margin where the North American and Eurasian plates are moving apart. It is the only place in the world where a midocean rift rises to the surface. The valley is slowly widening, and part of it has filled with water.

b. TRANSFORM FAULT MARGINS Transform fault margins involve horizontal motion (also called lateral, translational, or strike-slip motion), and they can occur in both oceanic and continental plates.

Along the San Andreas Fault, a transform fault margin in California, the Pacific Plate is slowly grinding past the North American Plate, toward the northwest.

© Craig Aurness/Corbis Images

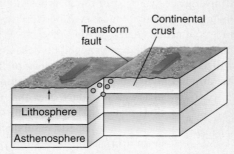

Earthquakes on transform fault margins: Transform fault margins have shallow earthquakes, but they can be very powerful.

c. CONVERGENT MARGINS Plates come together along convergent margins. If oceanic plate is involved, a subduction zone will form. If only continental plates are involved, a collision zone will form.

Ocean–ocean: Subduction zone At an ocean–ocean convergent margin, one oceanic plate sinks downward relative to the other; this is called subduction. The plate melts at depth, and the magma rises to create a chain of volcanic islands. Indonesia is a volcanic island chain, or arc, along an ocean–ocean subduction zone.

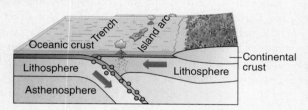

Earthquakes in subduction zones: The deepest and most powerful earthquakes occur in subduction zones. The earthquakes are shallow near the oceanic trench but become deeper along the descending edge of the subducting plate. Zones of shallow- to deep-focus earthquakes, called **Benioff zones**, first alerted scientists to the phenomenon of subduction.

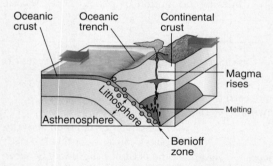

Ocean–continent: Subduction zone When oceanic plate meets continental plate along a convergent margin, the oceanic plate will sink, forming a subduction zone. A chain of volcanoes on the landward side (like the Andes, shown here) marks where the descending plate has melted at depth, and magma has risen to the surface.

Continent–continent: Continental collision zone If both plates at a convergent margin are continental, neither plate will be subducted; instead they will crumple into a great range of mountains. In this photograph, the snow-covered Himalaya Mountains mark the zone where the Australian–Indian Plate (upper left) is colliding with the Eurasian Plate.

Robert Harding/Digital Vision/Alamy

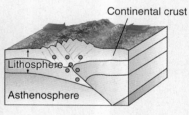

Earthquakes in collision zones: Earthquakes in collision zones can be deep as well as very powerful.

THINK CRITICALLY

Can you explain why earthquakes along divergent and transform plate boundaries are typically shallow, whereas earthquakes along convergent subduction zones and collision zones can be quite deep-seated?

subduction zone A boundary along which one lithospheric plate descends into the mantle beneath another plate.

Subduction zones are marked by very deep **oceanic trenches**—the deepest points in the ocean; the Mariana Trench, mentioned at the beginning of the chapter, is an example. As the plate capped by oceanic lithosphere sinks, it heats up and releases water, causing melting in the overlying mantle. A long line or arc of volcanoes typically forms parallel to the edge of the overriding plate, the result of magma generated by subduction-related melting. Earthquakes along subduction zones are commonly strong—almost all of the "great" earthquakes in history have occurred in subduction zones—and they often have deep foci.

The other type of convergent margin occurs where one continental plate meets another continental plate. In the absence of oceanic plates, no subduction occurs; instead, the plates crumple upward and downward as the lithosphere

continental collision zone A boundary along which two continental plates converge, resulting in the formation of high mountain ranges.

thickens, forming a **continental collision zone**. The Himalaya Mountains, Earth's highest mountain range, were thrust up in just this way by a violent collision between the Australian–Indian Plate and the Eurasian Plate; this collision began over 40 million years ago, and it is

still ongoing. Some continental collision zones were subduction zones in the distant past, but the process of subduction terminated when the overriding plate encountered continental rock that was too buoyant to be subducted.

The types of plate interactions and the plate boundaries that result from them are illustrated schematically in **Figure 4.10**. Note that along some plate boundaries new crust is being created by the emergence of magma at the surface, whereas at others the crust is being consumed—either by compression and crumpling or by subduction into the mantle and subsequent melting. There is no solid evidence to suggest that Earth has either grown or shrunk significantly since its formation; this means that the total area of Earth's crust is constant. Therefore, for every square kilometer of crust that is created at a midocean ridge, somewhere else a square kilometer is consumed by subduction at a convergent margin. Overall, there is a balance between creation and destruction in the tectonic cycle.

A Mechanism for Plate Motion

Although geologists accept the basic theory of plate tectonics, some questions remain. What, exactly, drives plate motion? How does the mantle interact with the crust? What initiates subduction? Scientists have a basic understanding of these processes, but the details have not been completely worked out. Thermal motion in the mantle is at least partially responsible for the motion of plates. This thermal motion

Plate margins: A summary · Figure 4.10

Several different types of plate margins are illustrated schematically in this diagram. (In reality, these different types of margins would not be so close to one another.)

A divergent margin in an oceanic plate is marked by an underwater midocean rift. Offsetting the divergent margin are transform fault margins, along which movement is lateral.

At continental collision zones two plates carrying continental crust collide, the oceanic lithosphere between the continents disappears by subduction; collision thickens the lithosphere and forms a high mountain range.

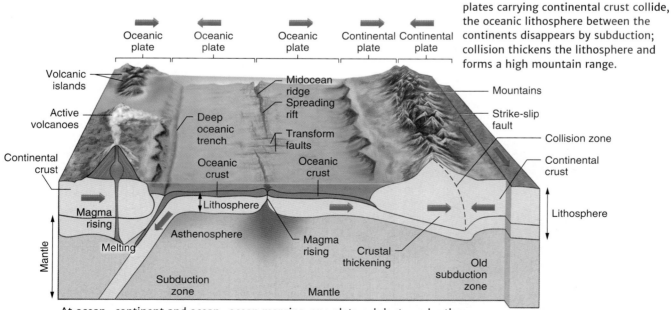

At ocean–continent and ocean–ocean margins, one plate subducts under the other. The subducting oceanic plate begins to melt at a relatively shallow depth. The magma rises to the surface, creating a line of volcanoes along the edge of the overriding plate.

in turn results from the release of heat from Earth's interior. Let's take a closer look at some of the complexities of Earth's heat-releasing processes.

Earth's Internal Heat

Earth gives off heat for two main reasons. First, it is slowly cooling off from its initial formation processes, including accretion and the formation of a molten iron core. Second, heat is constantly being generated by the decay of radioactive elements in the interior, primarily uranium, potassium, and thorium (see *Remember This!*). So much heat comes from this source that if Earth did not release heat into outer space, the entire interior would eventually melt.

> **REMEMBER THIS!** Do you remember how radioactivity works and why it releases so much heat energy? You can review this topic by looking back at the section *Radioactivity and Numerical Ages* in Chapter 3.

Some of Earth's internal heat is released through **conduction**. This is a gentle and slow process of heat transfer; you experience it when you hold a cup of hot coffee in your hands. The heat moves from the coffee through the wall of the cup by conduction, a gradual transfer of energy from atom to atom.

When you boil water in a pot on a stove, you see the water churning up from the bottom of the pot to the top (**Figure 4.11a**). The mass of hot water at the bottom of the pot is slightly less dense than the cooler water at the top, so the hot water rises. When it reaches the surface, it sheds its heat, moves sideways across the surface as it cools, and then sinks back down to the bottom, because cool water is denser than hot water. Back at the bottom of the pot, the water is reheated, and the process repeats in a looping motion called a **convection cell**. This mechanism of heat transfer, called **convection**, is more efficient than conduction. The rising masses of water in the convection cells act like couriers, carrying heat directly from the burner to the top of the pan, instead of laboriously passing heat from atom to atom.

> **convection** A form of heat transfer in a fluid medium by the circulation of currents from one region to another.

Convection as a Driving Force

Even though Earth's mantle is composed mostly of solid rock, it too releases heat through convection. Solid rock, if it is hot enough, can behave as a flowing viscous fluid, just as the solid ice in a glacier flows. Rock deep in the mantle heats up and expands, becoming buoyant. Very, very slowly it moves upward, in huge convection cells (**Figure 4.11b**). Like the water in the boiling pot, the hot rock moves laterally near the surface as it sheds its heat. This lateral movement of rock in the asthenosphere is believed to be one of the causes of the motion of lithospheric plates.

Mantle convection • Figure 4.11

Convection is a very efficient mechanism of heat transfer.

Convection Cell

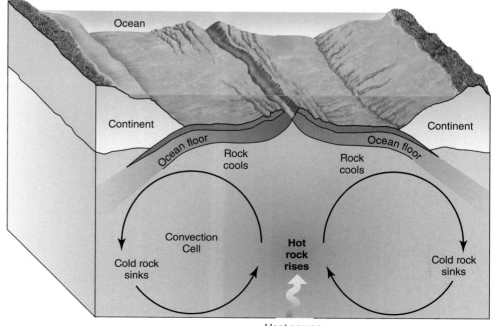

a. An everyday example of convection can be seen when you boil a pot of water. The water closest to the burners heats up, becomes less dense, and rises to the top. At the surface, it cools, moves side-ways, becomes denser, and sinks.

b. Convection also happens in the solid rock of Earth's mantle, on a much grander scale and much more slowly. Hot rock rises slowly from deep in the mantle; then it cools, flows sideways, and sinks. The relationship between convection cells and lithospheric plates is far more complex than what we see in a pot of boiling water.

Convection in the mantle is complex and incompletely understood. Many challenging questions remain unanswered. For example, does the whole mantle convect as a unit, or does the top part convect separately from the bottom, creating rolls upon rolls? In subduction zones, are lithospheric plates pushed down or pulled down, or do they sink into the asthenosphere under their own weight? (Plates with subduction edges move faster than plates without subduction edges, which suggests that the sinking plate edge is pulling the rest of the plate.) How do midocean ridges start, and what role

Amazing Places

The Hawaiian Islands: Hot Spot Volcanoes

The Hawaiian Islands are volcanic islands that lie atop a hot plume of rock and magma rising from deep within the mantle. One of the most striking geologic features of the islands is their increasing ages from southeast to northwest (**Figure a**). The Big Island of Hawaii is currently sitting atop a long, thin plume of hot material, called a **hot spot**, rising from deep within the mantle. The plume itself is stationary, but the lithospheric plate above it (the Pacific Plate) is moving to the northwest (**Figure b**), carrying the older volcanoes along with it. The plume supplies magma to the currently active volcanoes of Mauna Loa and Kilauea. The ongoing eruption of Kilauea (**Figure c**) has added new land to the island almost ceaselessly from 1983 to the present day.

Meanwhile, just 15 kilometers south of Hawaii, the undersea volcano of Loihi appears as a raised topographical feature (**Figure d**). Its peak is just 1 kilometer below the ocean surface, and it is still growing. Loihi erupted as recently as 1996. The older islands, such as Kauai, once lay above the hot spot but were moved off of it as the Pacific Plate moved toward the northwest. Once off the plume, they became inactive. With no new volcanic additions to their landmass, they will eventually erode into the sea. In **Figure e**, the highly eroded cliffs of the Na Pali Coast of Kauai (the northernmost of the major islands), you can see the effects of more than 3 million years of weathering.

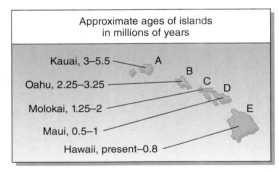

a. **Approximate ages of islands in millions of years:** The oldest islands are in the northwest, and the ages of the islands increase to the youngest in the southeast.

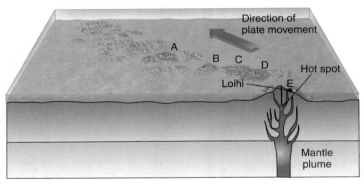

b. **Hot spot:** The plume of hot material rising from the mantle is stationary, but the Pacific Plate is moving over it, toward the northwest.

c. **The youngest Hawaiian island:** Kilauea volcano on the island of Hawaii erupts almost continuously.

Chris Johns/NG Image Collection

do they play in plate motion? What are the shapes and distribution of convection cells?

Scientists also know that hot rock sometimes does not travel in neatly packaged convection cells, but instead may rise in long, thin blobs called **plumes** (see *Amazing Places*).

Do such plumes originate in the middle of the mantle, or even deeper, where the core meets the mantle? How are they related to regular convection cells? Geologists continue to actively research questions such as these, and to refine and expand our understanding of convection in the mantle and plate tectonics.

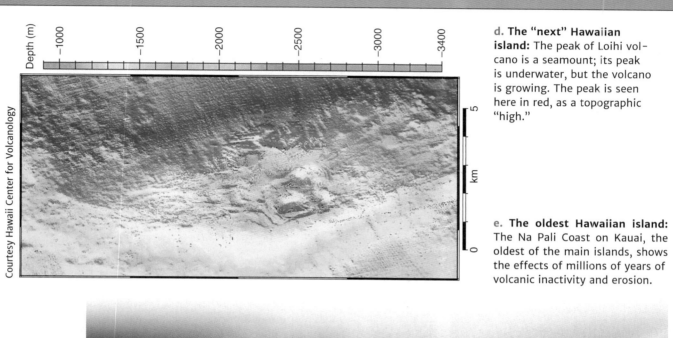

Courtesy Hawaii Center for Volcanology

Depth (m): −1000 −1500 −2000 −2500 −3000 −3400

d. The "next" Hawaiian island: The peak of Loihi volcano is a seamount; its peak is underwater, but the volcano is growing. The peak is seen here in red, as a topographic "high."

e. The oldest Hawaiian island: The Na Pali Coast on Kauai, the oldest of the main islands, shows the effects of millions of years of volcanic inactivity and erosion.

Diane Cook and Len Jenshel/GettyImages, Inc.

THINK CRITICALLY

The block diagram (**Figure b**) shows **seamounts**—topographic highs whose summits are underwater—to the northwest of the oldest island, Kauai (**Figure a**). They are remnants of volcanoes that moved away from the hot spot along with the Pacific Plate. What would you predict to be the ages of these seamounts?

This diagram should look familiar—you saw it in Chapter 1. The first of the three rings is the tectonic cycle, which includes processes that result directly from plate tectonics. It is linked to the rock cycle, primarily through the process of volcanism.

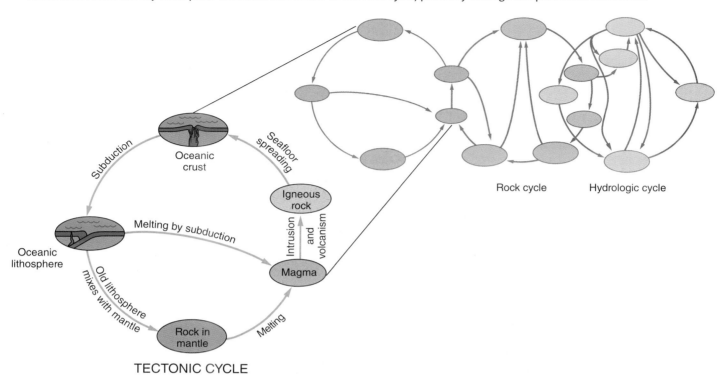

Rock cycle   Hydrologic cycle

TECTONIC CYCLE

The Tectonic Cycle: Past, Present, Future

In Chapter 1 we introduced the concept of interacting cycles in the Earth system (Figure 1.9). In this chapter we focused on the **tectonic cycle**, the left-hand side of the diagram in **Figure 4.12**. New material is constantly added to oceanic crust by volcanism along divergent plate boundaries, while subduction consumes an equal amount of oceanic crustal material at convergent margins. Because of these processes, the seafloor renews itself on the order of every 200 million years. In this chapter, you learned about the processes of seafloor spreading, subduction, and continental collision. In the next two chapters, you will learn more about earthquakes and volcanism, which also play important roles in the tectonic cycle. In subsequent chapters, we will cover the hydrologic cycle and the rock cycle, the two other cycles in this interacting system.

Continental crust lasts much longer than oceanic crust. Because of its lower density (greater buoyancy), it cannot easily be subducted. For that reason, the continental crust preserves a much longer record of the tectonic cycle than does the oceanic crust. While oceanic crust provided the clinching evidence of the breakup and dispersal of the ancient continent Pangaea, the continental crust—interpreted in the light of plate tectonics—shows that Pangaea was not the first supercontinent in Earth's history.

Geologists have discovered that Pangaea itself arose out of a collision between fragments of continental crust between 350 million and 450 million years ago. The collision (or collisions) formed mountain ranges, such as the Appalachians in North America and the Urals in Russia, which are highly eroded now but were once as massive as the present-day Himalayas. These remnants remain as evidence of the assembly of Pangaea.

But even older and more highly eroded remnants of ancient mountain ranges, along with paleomagnetic evidence, reveal an even earlier cycle of supercontinent formation and breakup. Roughly 1100 million years ago, during the Proterozoic Eon, another supercontinent existed, which geologists call Rodinia (**Figure 4.13**). Fragmentary evidence indicates that prior to Rodinia, other ancient supercontinents formed, existed for a few hundred million years, and then broke apart. This repeated process of formation and breakup is called the **supercontinent cycle** or sometimes the **Wilson cycle**, in honor of J. Tuzo Wilson of Canada, one of the major contributors to the plate tectonic revolution.

What will Earth be like in the future? Refer to Figure 1.19 in Chapter 1; the panel showing Earth 500 million years ago shows the scene after Rodinia broke apart, when the pieces were starting to be assembled into Pangaea. Then

tectonic cycle
Movements and interactions in the lithosphere by which rocks are cycled from the mantle to the crust and back; this cycle includes earthquakes, volcanism, and plate motion, driven by convection in the mantle.

Before Pangaea • Figure 4.13

This is a proposed arrangement of continental fragments in the 1100-million-year-old supercontinent Rodinia. The dark red strip marks a mountain chain that formed as a result of collisions as Rodinia was assembled. Pieces of it, now deeply eroded, are dispersed among Earth's present-day continents—scrambled by the breakup of Rodinia and the subsequent assembly and breakup of Pangaea.

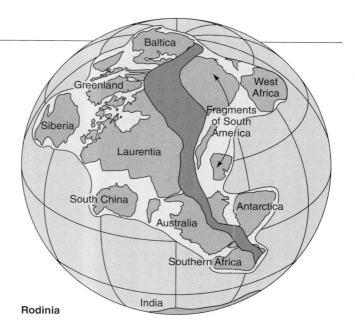

Rodinia

in the panel for 100 million years ago, Pangaea is breaking up, and the fragments are moving toward the world we know today. But the plates are still growing at spreading edges and being consumed at convergent margins. In the future, new spreading edges and convergent margins will form and slowly new supercontinents will arise. Based on much research, **Figure 4.14** illustrates what the world may look like 150 million years in the future.

Plate tectonics affects all life on Earth, sometimes in subtle ways and sometimes in dramatic ways. It influences climate through the distribution of continents and ocean basins, for example. These changes are slow but profound; they can lead to ice ages or periods of unusual warmth, both of which strongly affect the evolution of species. Plate tectonics also controls the distribution of mineral deposits, which we will explore in greater detail in Chapter 16. Other

Earth of the future • Figure 4.14

The world map 150 million years ahead may well look like this. Note the subduction zones on both sides of the Americas, and the welding together of Africa and Eurasia into a giant continent.

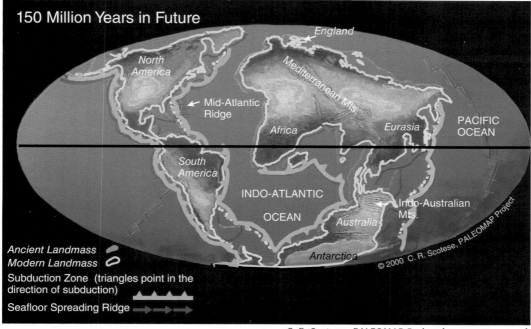

C. R. Scotese, PALEOMAP Project (www.scotese.com)

ASK YOURSELF

If major subduction zones form off the eastern coast of North and South America 150 million years into the future, as suggested on this map, what are the likely consequences?

a. more earthquakes in the coastal areas

b. formation of a deep oceanic trench just off-shore

c. active volcanism along the coast

d. eventual continental collision with Africa (far in the future)

e. All of the above would be likely consequences of a subduction zone off the east coast of the Americas.

effects are more immediately obvious, such as major earthquakes and volcanic eruptions.

At the beginning of this chapter, we described plate tectonics as a "unifying" theory of how the Earth system works. This is because the plate tectonic model brings together many diverse observations of Earth's geologic features and unifies them into a single, reasonably straightforward "story." As a model, plate tectonics is truly representative of the Earth system science approach because it illustrates how internal Earth processes are integrated with all other parts of the Earth system.

CONCEPT CHECK STOP

1. **What** does the theory of plate tectonics tell us about the characteristics of Earth's lithosphere?
2. **How** have geologists determined the shapes of Earth's plates and the locations of the plate margins?
3. **Why** do plates of lithosphere move?
4. **Where** can geologists find evidence of continental assembly and breakup before Pangaea?

SUMMARY

 THE PLANNER

1 A Revolution in Geology 84

- A revolution in geology began almost 100 years ago, with the hypothesis that the continents have not always been in their present positions but moved into their present-day locations after the breakup of a "supercontinent" known as Pangaea, as seen in this reconstruction. This became known as the **continental drift** hypothesis. At first it was quite controversial because scientists could not envision a satisfactory physical mechanism that could move the continents through solid rock.

Pangaea • Figure 4.1

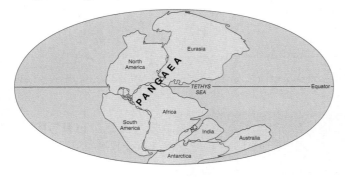

- The evidence for continental drift included the fit between the coastlines of continents. The evidence is stronger when the fit is made along the "true" edge of the continent—where continental crust meets oceanic crust, halfway down the continental slope. Geologic features such as mountain ranges, ancient glacial deposits, and rock types match very closely on both sides of the Atlantic Ocean, which now separates these continents. Matching fossils can be found on both sides of the ocean. Many are from plants and animals that could not have crossed a wide body of water and that would have thrived at different latitudes than the present location of the fossils. In the 1950s, apparent polar wandering was added to the list of evidence in favor of the theory of continental drift.

- The most significant piece of evidence in support of continental drift was the discovery of bands of magnetized rock on the seafloor with alternating normal and reversed polarities, aligned symmetrically on either side of the midocean ridges. The only plausible explanation for this discovery was **seafloor spreading**. Scientists quickly realized that continents and the adjacent seafloor move together. This evidence

was decisive because it finally led to a mechanism that could account for the continents' movement. At midocean ridges, the ocean floor is constantly replenished, pushing older rocks apart. At deep-sea trenches, old ocean floor sinks back into the mantle.

- Global Positioning System (GPS) satellites can now measure the speed and direction of continental drift directly and precisely. They show that the continents are still moving today at the rate of several centimeters per year.

2 The Plate Tectonic Model 92

- According to **plate tectonics** theory, the lithosphere has fragmented into several large **plates**. These plates essentially float on an underlying layer of hot, ductile rock called the asthenosphere. The asthenosphere is in slow but constant motion, and this forces the more rigid lithospheric plates to move around, collide, split apart, or slide past each other. At present there are six major lithospheric plates and many smaller ones.

- Plate tectonics predicts three different kinds of interactions along plate margins, as shown in this diagram. At **divergent margins**, two plates move apart. If the boundary occurs in oceanic crust, a divergent margin coincides with a midocean ridge. When the divergent boundary occurs in continental crust, it produces long and relatively straight rift valleys. Eventually, if the divergence continues for a long enough time, the rift valley will become wide and deep enough to form a sea or an ocean.

- At **convergent margins**, two plates move toward each other. When a plate that is carrying oceanic crust collides with another oceanic plate or with a continental plate, one oceanic plate slides beneath the other plate. This creates a **subduction zone**, which is marked by a deep oceanic trench and a great deal of volcanic activity. A second kind of convergent margin occurs where two continental plates collide over an ancient subduction zone, forming a **continental collision zone**. Plates that carry continental crust are generally too buoyant to subduct, so instead the lithosphere crumples and thickens, building up giant mountain ranges.

- At **transform fault margins**, which are fractures in the lithosphere, two plates slide past each other laterally. Transform faults are common on the ocean floor, where they run perpendicular to midocean ridges.

- Many earthquakes and active volcanoes are located along plate margins. Studies of the locations and depth of earthquakes enable scientists to determine the shapes of lithospheric plates and the type of margin between the plates. Earthquakes occur as a result of motion of rocks along a **fault**. The focus, where the motion starts, is underground; the epicenter is the place on the surface that lies directly above the focus.

- The release of heat from Earth's interior by **convection** is at least partly responsible for driving plate motion. Convection brings hot rock up from deep within the mantle and recycles cold rock back into the mantle. Many unanswered questions remain about convection cells; for example, hot rock also rises in plumes that do not seem to be related to the convection cells.

- Plate tectonics unifies continental drift, seafloor spreading, mountain building, faulting, earthquakes, and volcanism into the **tectonic cycle**. The tectonic cycle creates and recycles

oceanic crust on a time scale of roughly 200 million years. Continental crust lasts much longer, and it preserves earlier cycles of continental assembly and disassembly.

Plate margins: A summary • Figure 4.10

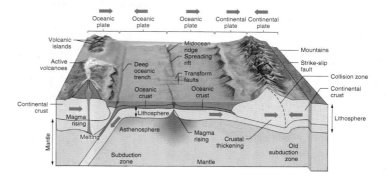

KEY TERMS

continental collision zone 98	fault 93	seafloor spreading 89
continental drift 84	midocean ridge 94	subduction zone 98
convection 99	plate 93	tectonic cycle 102
convergent margin 95	plate tectonics 92	transform fault margin 94
divergent margin 94	rift valley 94	

CRITICAL AND CREATIVE THINKING QUESTIONS

1. Why was the discovery of paleomagnetic bands on the Atlantic Ocean floor such an important turning point in the acceptance of the theory of plate tectonics? Suppose you could rewrite history so that the satellite measurements of continental drift came first. Would the discovery of seafloor spreading still have been important?

2. What are some of the important questions about plate tectonics that remain unanswered today?

3. Why do geologists call plate tectonics a "unifying" theory?

4. We have called plate tectonics a scientific revolution. What other scientific revolutions do you know about? How is the plate tectonics revolution similar to, or different from, other revolutions, such as the Copernican revolution in astronomy?

5. Look at this map of plate boundaries, and see if you can figure out the tectonic environment of the place where you live or attend school. Is it near a plate margin? If so, what type of plate boundary is it? Or do you live in the middle of a plate? If so, which one?

Tectonic plates • Figure 4.8

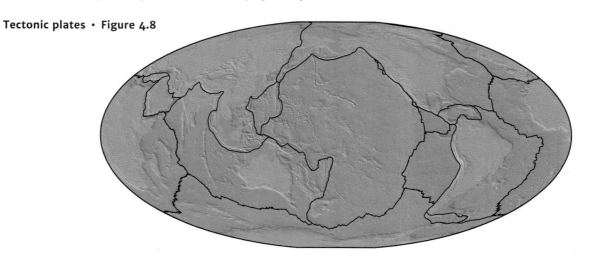

WHAT IS HAPPENING IN THIS PICTURE?

From September 14 to October 4, 2005, a series of earthquakes and eruptions in the Afar Desert in Ethiopia opened up the rift seen in this photograph, which is 60 meters wide at its widest point. The rift is part of a much more extensive depression where two plates, the African and the Somalian plates, are spreading apart. (Older rifts can also be seen in the background.) Compare this photo to the map and satellite image in this chapter's *What a Geologist Sees*.

Courtesy Tony Philpotts

THINK CRITICALLY

What will happen to Ethiopia if the spreading continues?

SELF-TEST

(Check your answers in Appendix D.)

1. The work of geologists over the years has supported Wegener's contention that the current continental masses were assembled into a single supercontinent, which Wegener called _____.

   a. Pangaea
   d. Tethys

   b. Transantarctica
   e. Laurasia

   c. Gondwana

2. Which of the following lines of evidence supporting continental drift did Wegener not use when he first proposed his hypothesis?

   a. the apparent fit of the continental margins of Africa and South America

   b. ancient glacial deposits of the southern hemisphere

   c. the apparent polar wandering of the magnetic north pole

   d. the close match of ancient geology between West Africa and Brazil

   e. the close match of ancient fossils on continents separated by ocean basins

3. Analysis of apparent polar wandering paths led geophysicists to conclude _____.

   a. that Earth's magnetic poles have wandered all over the globe in the past several hundred million years

   b. that the continents had moved because it is known that the magnetic poles themselves are essentially fixed

   c. that the apparent wandering path of a continent provides a historical record of the position of that continent over time

   d. Both b and c are correct.

4. _____ is the process through which oceanic crust splits and moves apart along a midocean ridge and new oceanic crust forms.

   a. Continental drift
   c. Seafloor spreading

   b. Paleomagnetism
   d. Continental rifting

5. This map shows the age of the seafloor, across the northern extent of the Atlantic Ocean. The Mid-Atlantic Ridge can be seen stretching roughly north–south (in the yellow band) down the middle of the map. Yellow through red colors show rocks of similar age. Number them on the map from 1 (oldest) through 5 (youngest).

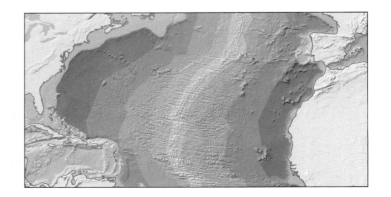

6. _____ technology has allowed scientists to measure the movement of continental crust.

a. Global Positioning System (GPS) c. Magnetometer

b. Seismic recording d. Gravity meter

7. This map shows radiometric ages for the Hawaiian island chain in the middle of the Pacific Plate. These islands formed over a hot spot in Earth's mantle. Draw an arrow on the map to show the direction of movement of the Pacific Plate over this hot spot, as indicated by the ages of the islands in the Hawaiian chain.

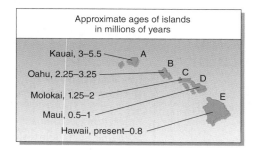

8. At a _____, two lithospheric plates slide past one another horizontally.

a. divergent boundary

b. transform fault boundary

c. subduction zone boundary

d. continental collision boundary

9. At a _____, oceanic crust is consumed back into the asthenosphere.

a. divergent boundary

b. transform fault boundary

c. subduction zone boundary

d. continental collision boundary

10. At a _____, new oceanic crust forms along midocean ridges.

a. divergent boundary

b. transform fault boundary

c. subduction zone boundary

d. continental collision boundary

11. A _____ is a convergent margin along which subduction is no longer active and high mountain ranges are formed.

a. divergent boundary

b. transform fault boundary

c. subduction zone boundary

d. continental collision boundary

12. _____ is the horizontal movement and mutual interaction of large fragments of Earth's lithosphere.

a. Continental drift d. Chemosynthesis

b. Polar wandering e. Plate tectonics

c. Paleomagnetism

13. Heat from the solid mantle is released through a process of _____.

a. polar wandering c. convection

b. paleomagnetism d. magnetic reversal

14. These block diagrams depict different types of plate boundaries. For each block diagram, label the appropriate plate boundary from the following list:

a. Divergent margin c. Transform fault margin

b. Continental collision margin d. Subduction zone margin

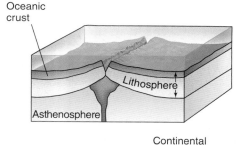

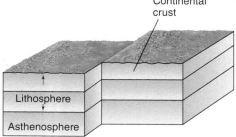

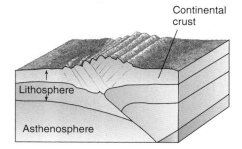

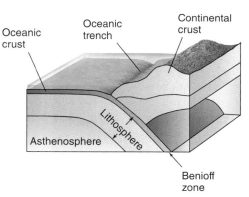

15. On the block diagrams in question 14, indicate the locations of earthquakes for each type of plate boundary. Use a red dot to show the locations of shallow-focus earthquakes and a blue dot to show the locations of deep-focus earthquakes.

THE PLANNER ✓

Review the Chapter Planner on the chapter opener and check off your completed work.

5 EARTHQUAKES AND EARTH'S INTERIOR

By U.S. Navy photo by Mass Communication Specialist 3rd Class Dylan McCord [Public domain]

Global Locator

Japan

NG Maps

THE GREAT TŌHOKU EARTHQUAKE AND TSUNAMI

On March 11, 2011, a massive magnitude 9.0 earthquake shook Japan, the largest Japanese quake ever recorded. The epicenter was offshore of northeastern Honshu Island near the city of Sendai, where the Pacific Plate is being subducted beneath the Eurasian Plate. The overall slippage on the fault between the plates is estimated to have been between 30 and 40 meters over a distance of 300 kilometers.

As the plates moved, the seafloor was suddenly pushed upward, and a great **tsunami**, or seismic sea wave, was generated. On nearby shores water rose in places to heights of almost 40 meters above sea level. Sweeping inland, the wave reduced entire towns to rubble in a matter of minutes.

The earthquake and tsunami killed almost 16,000 people, and more than a million buildings were damaged or destroyed, including the Fukushima Daiichi nuclear power plants. This ultimately led to a Level 7 meltdown of the reactors, the most serious category of nuclear accident. Much of the 5 million tons of ocean-borne debris from the earthquake and tsunami sank, but about 1.5 million tons remained afloat and were carried away by oceanic currents. Some of it has come ashore all the way across the Pacific Ocean in British Columbia, along the northwestern coast of the United States, and as far away as Hawaii.

EARTHQUAKES AND EARTHQUAKE HAZARDS

Learning Objectives

1. **Explain** the connections between earthquakes and plate tectonics.

2. **Describe** several earthquake-related hazards.

3. **Compare** short-term prediction and long-term forecasting of earthquakes.

The Tōhoku tsunami described in the chapter opener occurred as a result of an earthquake in a subduction zone off the eastern coast of Honshu, Japan, where oceanic lithosphere of the Pacific Plate is being subducted beneath continental lithosphere on the leading edge of the Eurasian Plate (see *Remember This!*). It was the seventeenth giant earthquake of magnitude 8.5 or higher that has occurred, worldwide, since 1900 (**Figure 5.1**). Almost all of these giant quakes were in subduction zones and are referred to as **megathrust earthquakes**. The one exception is the Assam, Tibet, quake of 1950, which was located in a continental collision zone.

> **REMEMBER THIS!** Do you remember how the distribution of earthquake locations is related to plate boundaries? You can remind yourself by reviewing Figures 4.7 and 4.8.

The close association between subduction zones and giant earthquakes suggests that the convergent motion of two plates must be responsible for the very largest quakes. But plate motion is very gradual, typically on the order of a few centimeters per year. Why, then, should earthquakes be so sudden and the big ones so catastrophic? And why, after long time intervals, do they recur in the same places? Through the science of **seismology** we seek to answer these and related questions.

seismology The scientific study of earthquakes and seismic waves.

Earthquakes and Plate Motion

Most earthquakes are caused by the sudden movement of stressed blocks of Earth's crust along a fault. If the rocks could slide past one another smoothly, like the parts of a well-oiled engine, big quakes such as the Tōhoku quake would not happen. In the real world, smooth sliding is rare; friction between the huge blocks of rock causes them to seize up, bringing the motion along the locked part of the fault to a temporary stop. While the fault remains locked by friction, energy continues to build up as a result of the plate motion, causing rocks adjacent to the jammed section to bend and

Megathrust earthquakes • Figure 5.1

The largest earthquakes since 1900, including five with magnitudes of at least 9.0, are shown here; almost all were megathrust earthquakes.

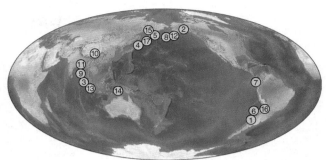

	Location	Date	Magnitude
1.	Chile	1960 05 22	9.5
2.	Prince William Sound, Alaska	1964 03 28	9.2
3.	Off the west coast of Northern Sumatra	2004 12 26	9.1
4.	Near the east coast of Honshu, Japan	2011 03 11	9.0
5.	Kamchatka	1952 11 04	9.0
6.	Offshore Maule, Chile	2010 02 27	8.8
7.	Off the coast of Ecuador	1906 01 31	8.8
8.	Rat Islands, Alaska	1965 02 04	8.7
9.	Northern Sumatra, Indonesia	2005 03 28	8.6
10.	Assam, Tibet	1950 08 15	8.6
11.	Off the west coast of Northern Sumatra, Indonesia	2012 04 11	8.6
12.	Andreanof Islands, Alaska	1957 03 09	8.6
13.	Southern Sumatra, Indonesia	2007 09 12	8.5
14.	Banda Sea, Indonesia	1938 02 01	8.5
15.	Kamchatka	1923 02 03	8.5
16.	Chile-Argentina Border	1922 11 11	8.5
17.	Kuril Islands	1963 10 13	8.5

buckle. Finally, the stress becomes great enough to overcome the friction along the fault. All at once, the blocks slip, and the pent-up energy in the rocks is released as the violent tremors of an earthquake. This cycle of slow buildup of energy followed by abrupt movement along a fault repeats itself many times.

Although movement along a large fault may eventually total many kilometers, this distance is the sum of numerous smaller slips happening over many millennia (**Figure 5.2**). In some places these small slips (collectively called *seismic creep*) are frequent, though they are imperceptible to humans. The largest abrupt vertical displacement on land in recent history occurred in 1899 at Yakutat Bay, Alaska, when a long stretch of the Alaskan shore was suddenly lifted 15 meters above sea level during a major earthquake.

The initial vertical or horizontal motion of plates, dramatic as it may appear, is often not what does the most damage during an earthquake. It is the sustained shaking of the ground that destroys buildings, bridges, and cities, sometimes many kilometers away from the location of the quake. In 1910, Harry Fielding Reid, a member of a commission appointed to investigate the infamous 1906 San Francisco earthquake that destroyed much of the city, proposed the most widely accepted explanation for the shaking.

Over time fault motion can create visible distortion of surface features as well as vertical dislocations of the ground surface.

a. When these orange trees were planted on land that lies over the San Andreas Fault in southern California, the rows were straight. In 1938, earthquake motion along the fault displaced the trees significantly. Arrows show the direction of movement of the plates.

b. The second most powerful earthquake on record, the Alaska "Good Friday" earthquake, struck the Anchorage area on March 27, 1964. Vertical motion along the fault amounted to several meters in some places. Here, the two plates moved apart, and the ground between them subsided by about 2 meters.

©John S. Shelton/University of Washington Libraries, Special Collections

Courtesy USGS

> **elastic rebound model** The proposal that continuing stress along a fault results in a buildup of elastic energy in the rocks, which is abruptly released when an earthquake occurs.

Reid's **elastic rebound model** says that rock, like all other solids, is elastic (within limits). This means that rock stretches or bends when subjected to stress, temporarily changing its shape in a process called **elastic deformation**. The rock snaps back when the stress is removed, which happens when the two blocks on either side of a fault manage to overcome friction and slip past one another. However, like a guitar string after it has been plucked, the rock continues to vibrate even after the process of defor-

> **seismic wave** An elastic shock wave that travels outward in all directions from an earthquake's source.

mation has ceased. These vibrations are called **seismic waves**. Like sound waves from a guitar string, they can travel a long distance from their place of origin. (We will investigate the process of deformation and the related concepts of *stress* and *strain* in greater depth in Chapter 9.)

The first evidence to support Reid's elastic rebound model (**Figure 5.3**) came from studies of the San Andreas Fault, a large, complex fault in California that generated both the 1906 quake and the 1989 "World Series" quake near Oakland. Beginning in 1874, scientists from the U.S. Coast and Geodetic Survey had been measuring the precise positions of many points both adjacent to and distant from the fault. As time passed, movement of the points revealed that at some places, the two sides of the fault were smoothly slipping in opposite directions. Near San Francisco, however, the fault appeared to be locked by friction and did not reveal any slip. Then, on April 18, 1906, the two sides of this

locked section of fault shifted abruptly. The elastically stored energy in the rock was released as the crust snapped to its new position, causing a violent earthquake. Reid's measurements after the quake revealed that the bending, or strain, stored in the crust had disappeared.

Observations show that earthquakes occur in the same places repeatedly. The elastic rebound model tells us that this is just what should be expected. Along a portion of a fault that is locked, stress builds up over time. When the frictional lock is broken, the stress is suddenly and (sometimes) violently relieved, and an earthquake occurs. Tectonic movement of the plates continues, and locked portions of a fault will once again begin accumulating stress over time; a sudden release of energy occurs when the blocks slip past one another. The cycle repeats, and earthquakes happen repeatedly along the same faults.

Earthquake Hazards and Readiness

Each year several million earthquakes occur around the world. Fortunately, only a few are large enough, or close enough to major population centers, to cause much damage or loss of life. A great deal of research focuses on earthquake prediction and hazard assessment. Geologists are working hard to improve their forecasting ability to the point where effective and accurate early warnings can be issued. Let's look briefly at the hazards associated with earthquakes and at efforts to predict them.

Earthquake Hazards Ground motion, with the resulting collapse of buildings, bridges, and other structures, is usually the most significant **primary hazard** to cause damage during an earthquake. In the most intense quakes, the surface of the ground can be observed moving in waves. In

Process Diagram

How the elastic rebound model works • Figure 5.3

The elastic rebound model was developed by Reid after the great 1906 earthquake on the San Andreas Fault. Rock, like any solid, will deform if subjected to stress. If the stress exceeds the material strength of the rock or the strength of the locked segment of a fault, it will break and an earthquake will occur.

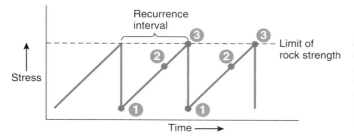

a. Stress builds up until the rock strength at the fault lock is exceeded; then the lock breaks and an earthquake occurs, as shown in this graph. ① corresponds to the unstressed state; ② corresponds to the period during which stress is building up; and ③ is the moment when the frictional lock is broken, the blocks slip past one another, and the fault returns to an unstressed state.

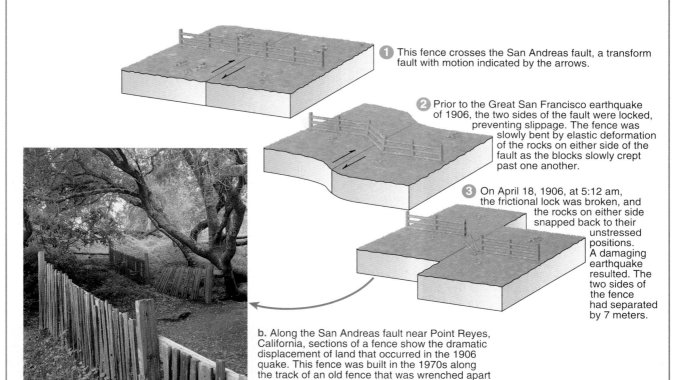

① This fence crosses the San Andreas fault, a transform fault with motion indicated by the arrows.

② Prior to the Great San Francisco earthquake of 1906, the two sides of the fault were locked, preventing slippage. The fence was slowly bent by elastic deformation of the rocks on either side of the fault as the blocks slowly crept past one another.

③ On April 18, 1906, at 5:12 am, the frictional lock was broken, and the rocks on either side snapped back to their unstressed positions. A damaging earthquake resulted. The two sides of the fence had separated by 7 meters.

b. Along the San Andreas fault near Point Reyes, California, sections of a fence show the dramatic displacement of land that occurred in the 1906 quake. This fence was built in the 1970s along the track of an old fence that was wrenched apart by the quake.

Peter Essick/Alamy

THINK CRITICALLY

Scientists have tried to use the elastic rebound theory to predict earthquake (with limited success). With reference to the graph of Stress vs. Time, discuss how you might deploy instrumentation at a potential earthquake site to monitor changes in the rock over time, with the goal of predicting an earthquake. What challenges might you encounter?

cases where the earthquake originates at a shallow depth, shaking can be surprisingly intense. In 2011, nine people were killed in Spain and thousands of buildings were damaged or destroyed by an earthquake of only moderate intensity (magnitude 5.1); ground shaking was intense because the earthquake had originated at only about 1 kilometer depth.

Where a fault breaks the ground surface, buildings can be split, roads disrupted, and anything that lies on or across the fault broken apart. Sometimes large cracks and fissures open in the ground. To make matters worse, movement on one part of a fault can cause stress along another part of the fault, which in turn slips, generating another earthquake, called an **aftershock**. Aftershocks triggered by large earthquakes tend to be on the same fault system as the original quake, though they may be quite far from the original location, causing the damage to be spread more widely as time passes. Some of the hundreds of aftershocks that followed the 2011 Tōhoku earthquake had magnitudes greater than

7; these aftershocks, triggered by the initial great quake, are major earthquakes in their own right.

Ground motion is not the only source of damage in an earthquake. Sometimes the after-effects, or **secondary hazards** related to an earthquake, can cause even more damage than the original quake (**Figure 5.4**). For example, shaking during an earthquake can cause sediment to shift and resettle, which can destabilize roads and buildings. In some cases surface materials may undergo **liquefaction** and flow like a liquid, even if the actual water content of the material has not changed. Other important secondary hazards that can be triggered by earthquakes include landslides, fires, and tsunamis.

Tsunamis are less common than other secondary hazards associated with earthquakes, but they can be even more deadly, as demonstrated by the Tōhoku tsunami of March 2011 (mentioned in the chapter opener) and the great Sumatra–Andaman tsunami in the final week of 2004 (see the *Case Study* on page 114). Tsunamis can also be generated

Earthquake-related hazards • Figure 5.4

Earthquakes can trigger hazards that are sometimes more damaging than the ground motion associated with the earthquake itself.

a. Landslides

Ground motion during an earthquake can shake loose slope materials to cause landslides, such as this one in Huascarán, Peru, in which more than 20,000 people were killed.

b. Cracks and fissures

This deep crack disrupted the road surface after an earthquake in Santa Cruz, California.

c. Fires

Earthquakes can break gas lines and lead to fires such as this one that occurred after the 1989 Loma Prieta earthquake in San Francisco.

d. Ground liquefaction

During an earthquake, some sediments, especially sand or loose fill, can flow like liquid. Ground liquefaction during the 1964 Niigata, Japan, earthquake led to the collapse of buildings.

by submarine landslides and volcanism, but about 85% of all tsunamis are generated by earthquakes in subduction zones.

Earthquake Readiness Earthquakes can cause total devastation in a matter of seconds. The most disastrous quake in history occurred in Shaanxi Province, China, in 1556, killing an estimated 830,000 people. The earthquake caused the caves in which most of the population lived to collapse. In all, 19 earthquakes in history have caused 50,000 or more deaths apiece; those of the past century are shown in **Table 5.1**.

The most powerful quakes are not necessarily the deadliest. The death toll depends to a great extent on the population of the affected region and how well prepared they are for a major quake. The Great Sichuan earthquake of May 12, 2008, in China, and the Haiti earthquake of 2010 were much greater disasters than they need have been because many buildings, including schools, had not been constructed to withstand earthquakes, even though both regions are known to be prone to quakes (**Figure 5.5a**).

Every earthquake hazard, from fires to tsunamis, can be reduced in severity (though not eliminated) with proper design and preparedness. For instance, skyscrapers can be

Earthquakes during the past century that have caused 50,000 or more deaths • Table 5.1		
Place	Year	Estimated number of deaths
Messina, Italy	1908	160,000
Gansu, China	1920	180,000
Tokyo and Yokohama, Japan	1923	143,000
Gansu, China	1932	70,000
Quetta, Pakistan	1935	60,000
T'ang-shan, China	1976	240,000*
Sumatra−Andaman, Indian Ocean	2004	283,000**
Sichuan, China	2008	69,000
Port-au-Prince, Haiti	2010	316,000***

*Unofficial reports list up to 779,000 deaths.
**Most of the deaths due to tsunami.
***This is the official death toll, according to the government of Haiti and the U.S. Geological Survey. The actual casualties could be much lower—some estimates put the death toll under 100,000—but an exact figure will never be known.

Preparing for earthquakes • Figure 5.5

Local circumstances including building codes and education can dramatically affect the casualties resulting from earthquakes.

a. Absent or unenforced building codes can cost lives. Poorly constructed buildings in Port-au-Prince, Haiti, collapsed as a result of the earthquake of January 22, 2010, greatly increasing the death toll there.

© Ron Haviv/VII/Corbis

James A. Sugar/NG Image Collection

© Eriki Sugita/Reuters/Corbis

c. Preparedness can save lives. This 4-year-old boy, wearing a padded protective hood, has taken cover under a table during an earthquake drill in a school in Japan. Drills like these helped save many lives during the Tōhoku earthquake, although the toll of dead and injured was still staggering.

b. A laboratory experiment shows how unreinforced concrete crumbles during earthquake-like conditions.

THINK CRITICALLY

Concrete seems to be a strong material, but in the laboratory experiment (**b**) it crumbles when exposed to earthquake-like conditions. What could be done to make concrete structures like highway support columns, bridges, and buildings stronger or more resilient during an earthquake?

The Great Sumatra–Andaman Earthquake and Tsunami

On December 26, 2004, a 9.1 magnitude earthquake shook the Indian Ocean floor 160 kilometers off the island of Sumatra, Indonesia. The quake caused the most deadly tsunami in history. The quake began when the Indo-Australian Plate, which is being subducted beneath the Burma-Sunda Plate, suddenly moved downward 15 meters (**Figure a**). Along a distance of 1200 kilometers, the rebounding motion pushed the seafloor up by as much as 5 meters. On the surface of the ocean, standing waves generated by the sudden movement of the seafloor swept toward Indonesia, Thailand, Sri Lanka, and India (**Figure b**). When they reached the shore, the waves were amplified to 20 to 30 meters in height, depending on the configuration of each shoreline, and swept far inland, an effect so dramatic that it was visible from space (**Figures c and d**).

Although earthquakes and tsunamis are common in the Indian Ocean, there was no warning system in place when the disaster occurred. The resulting devastation caused hundreds of billions of dollars in damage and at least 283,000 deaths.

a. How the tsunami was unleashed

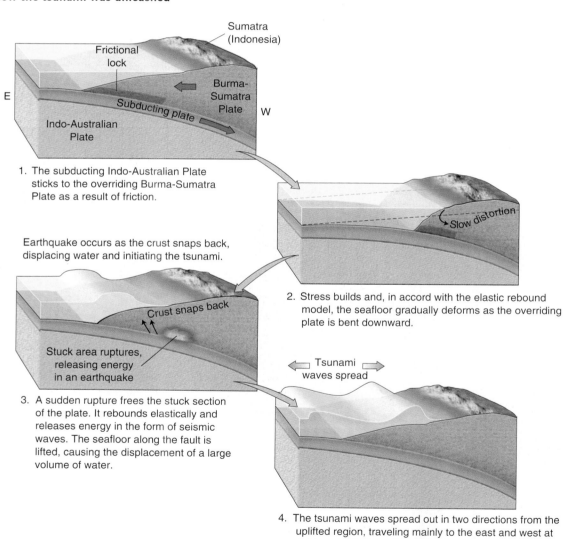

1. The subducting Indo-Australian Plate sticks to the overriding Burma-Sumatra Plate as a result of friction.

Earthquake occurs as the crust snaps back, displacing water and initiating the tsunami.

2. Stress builds and, in accord with the elastic rebound model, the seafloor gradually deforms as the overriding plate is bent downward.

3. A sudden rupture frees the stuck section of the plate. It rebounds elastically and releases energy in the form of seismic waves. The seafloor along the fault is lifted, causing the displacement of a large volume of water.

4. The tsunami waves spread out in two directions from the uplifted region, traveling mainly to the east and west at right angles to the subduction zone.

THINK CRITICALLY

Which kind of wave would you expect to travel faster: a seismic wave or a tsunami wave? Why?

b. Progress of the tsunami

A series of computer-simulated maps shows the progress of the tsunami across the Indian Ocean. The red color indicates wave crests, the blue the wave troughs. ▼

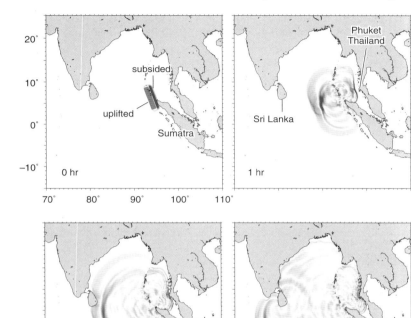

Global Locator

ASIA

Sumatra

NG Maps

c. The tsunami from space

Satellite images show a coast in Sri Lanka ▼ before and during the tsunami.

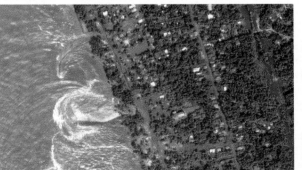

Digital Globe/Zuma Press/NewsCom

HO/AFP/Getty Images/NewsCom

d. The tsunami onshore

In Thailand and other coastal areas around the Indian Ocean, tsunami wave run-up heights of 20-30 meters were observed, and the water came as far as several kilometers inland in some locations. ▼

By David Rydevik, Stockholm, Sweden.

built with reinforced concrete and large counterweights to help them resist shaking. **Figure 5.5b** illustrates the inadequacy of unreinforced concrete during an earthquake. Other aspects of earthquake-resistant design include bolting wood-frame buildings to their foundations; isolating buildings from vibrations by supporting them on steel and rubber pads; enclosing utilities such as water pipes and electric cables in common ducts; and building tunnels with flexible joints. It is also important for people living in earthquake-prone areas to prepare for them—for example, by securing heavy furniture to the walls and by preparing emergency supplies. During an earthquake, your best shelter is underneath a sturdy desk or table (**Figure 5.5c**).

Earthquake Forecasting

Charles Richter, inventor of the Richter scale for quantifying the severity of earthquakes, once said, "Only fools, charlatans, and liars predict earthquakes." Today, unfortunately, this is still more or less correct: No one can predict the exact magnitude and time of occurrence of an earthquake, although many reputable people are trying hard. Scientists' understanding about seismic mechanisms and the tectonic settings in which earthquakes occur has improved greatly since Richter's time, and advances in modern seismology may yet prove him wrong.

There are two aspects to the problem of earthquake prediction. Short-term prediction would identify the precise time, magnitude, and location of an earthquake in advance of the actual event, providing an opportunity for authorities to issue an early warning. Long-term forecasting involves the prediction of a large earthquake years or even decades in advance of its occurrence.

Short-term Prediction and Early Warning

Unfortunately, the short-term prediction of earthquakes has not been very successful to date. Attempts at short-term prediction are based on observations of anomalous precursors—that is, any unusual event or activity preceding and leading up to the occurrence of an earthquake. For example, the magnetic or electrical properties of rock could change, the level of well water could drop, or the amount of radon gas in groundwater could rise in advance of an earthquake; all of these have been observed to precede earthquakes, and any of them could indicate unusual changes and earthquake-related activity in the rock. Strange animal behavior, glowing auras, and unusual radio waves have also been reported as precursors near the sites of large earthquakes; there are plausible scientific explanations for these. Small cracks and fractures can develop in severely strained rock and cause swarms of tiny earthquakes—**foreshocks**—that may presage a big quake. In retrospect, scientists now realize that the Tōhoku earthquake was preceded by several large foreshocks in the days immediately before the event.

The most famous successful short-term earthquake prediction, made by Chinese scientists in 1975, was based on combined observations of slow tilting of the land surface,

changes in groundwater, fluctuations in the magnetic field, and numerous foreshocks that preceded a large quake that struck the town of Haicheng. Half of the city was destroyed, but because authorities had evacuated more than a million people beforehand, only a few hundred were killed. However, less than two years after the successful prediction of the Haicheng earthquake, the devastating 1976 T'angshan earthquake struck, with no apparent precursors. With an official death toll of 240,000 (and unofficial reports suggesting many more), it was the second-most-disastrous earthquake in history. In 1976, and still today, short-term prediction and early warning of earthquakes remain elusive goals for seismologists.

Long-term Forecasting

Long-term earthquake forecasting is based mainly on our understanding of the elastic rebound model, the tectonic cycle, and the geologic settings in which earthquakes occur. In places where earthquakes are known to occur repeatedly, seismologists have detected patterns in the **recurrence intervals** of large quakes—that is, the timing between earthquakes occurring at the same location on a fault. Because historical records seldom go back as far as seismologists would like, scientists also use the information provided by **paleoseismology** to investigate earthquake recurrence intervals.

> **paleoseismology** The study of prehistoric earthquakes.

Prehistoric quakes leave evidence in the stratigraphic record, such as vertical displacement of sedimentary layers, indications of liquefaction, or horizontal offset of geologic features (**Figure 5.6**). If the pattern of recurrence suggests regular intervals of, say, a century between major quakes, it may be possible to predict within a decade or two when a large quake is due to happen next in that location.

By studying ancient earthquakes, scientists have identified a number of **seismic gaps** around the Pacific Rim. A seismic gap is a place along a fault where a large earthquake

Evidence of ancient quakes • Figure 5.6 _____

Offsets in dark, carbon-rich layers of sediment indicate where and how much faults moved during past earthquakes. Using carbon-14 dating, scientists can determine when ancient quakes occurred.

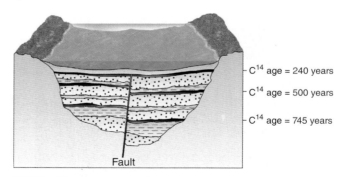

C^{14} age = 240 years

C^{14} age = 500 years

C^{14} age = 745 years

Fault

[:::] Sand layer
[≡] Clay layer
[▬] Carbon-containing layer

has not occurred for a long time, even though tectonic movement is still active and stress is building. Some geophysicists consider seismic gaps to be the places most likely to experience large earthquakes.

Long-term forecasting has met with reasonable success. Seismologists know where most (but not all) of the hazardous areas are located. They can calculate the probability that a large earthquake will occur in a particular area within a given period. They have a model for earthquake generation that successfully unites their predictions and observations in the context of plate tectonic theory. Forecasting helps people who live in seismically active areas to plan and prepare well in advance of a major event. If short-term prediction could advance as much as long-term forecasting has done, many lives could be saved.

STOP CONCEPT CHECK

1. **How** does the elastic rebound model explain the violent tremors that occur very suddenly during earthquakes?

2. **Which** earthquake-related hazards would be of primary concern in the area close to where a quake occurs, and which would have more impacts in locations far away from the quake?

3. **How** do scientists forecast earthquakes?

THE SCIENCE OF SEISMOLOGY

Learning Objectives

1. **Explain** how a seismograph works.

2. **Explain** how surface waves and body waves differ, distinguishing between the two kinds of body waves.

3. **Explain** how seismologists locate the epicenter of an earthquake.

4. **Compare** the different measures of earthquake strength, including the Richter scale, the moment magnitude scale, and the Modified Mercalli Intensity scale.

Seismologists can quickly locate an earthquake anywhere on Earth and tell how strong it is. Even though it is not yet possible to predict an earthquake accurately, scientific understanding of plate tectonics and the response of rock to seismic activity sets the stage for a deeper understanding of Earth's interior.

Seismographs

The earliest known **seismographs** (also called *seismometers*) were invented in China in the 2nd century. The first seismographs in Europe were invented much later, in the 19th century. Modern seismographs are based on the principle of inertia. They provide a printed or digital record of seismic waves, called a **seismogram** (**Figure 5.7**).

seismograph An instrument that detects and measures the vibrations of Earth's surface.

seismogram The record made by a seismograph.

The most advanced seismographs measure the ground's motion optically and amplify the signal electronically. Vibrations as tiny as one-hundred-millionth (10^{-8}) of a centimeter can be detected. Indeed, many instruments are so sensitive that they can sense vibrations caused by a moving automobile many blocks away.

Seismic Waves

The energy released by an earthquake is transmitted to other parts of Earth in the form of seismic waves. The waves elastically deform the rocks they pass through; they leave no record behind them once they have passed, so they must be detected while they pass. The waves, which include **body waves** and **surface waves**, travel outward in all directions from the earthquake's **focus** (**Figure 5.8**).

Body Waves Body waves can be further subdivided into two types. **Compressional waves** can pass through solids, liquids, and gases. They have the highest velocity of all seismic waves—typically 6 kilometers per second in the uppermost portion of the crust—and thus they are the first waves to arrive and be detected by a seismograph after an earthquake. For this reason they are called **P waves** (for **primary waves**).

Shear waves, the other type of body wave, travel through

body wave A seismic wave that travels through Earth's interior.

surface wave A seismic wave that travels along Earth's surface.

focus The location where rupture commences and an earthquake's energy is first released.

compressional wave A seismic body wave consisting of alternating pulses of compression and expansion in the direction of wave travel; also called a P wave, or primary wave.

shear wave A seismic body wave in which rock is subjected to side-to-side or up-and-down forces, perpendicular to the wave's direction of travel; also called an S wave, or secondary wave.

Seismographs have long been used to detect and record earthquake motion.

Jim Mendenhall/NG Image Collection

a. Tremors would cause the central rod in this ancient Chinese seismograph to tilt, releasing a ball from the mouth of the dragon and alerting people to the earthquake danger.

b. In a modern seismograph, seismic waves cause the support post and the roll of paper to vibrate back and forth, while the large mass attached to the pendulum and the pen attached to it barely move because of inertia. The paper moves underneath the pen to create the seismogram.

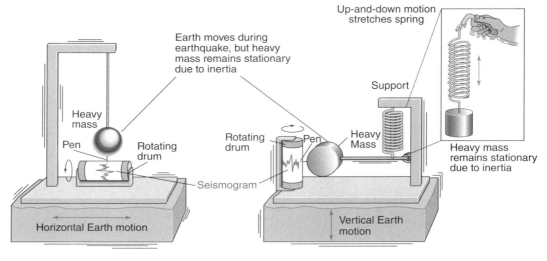

materials by generating an undulating motion in the material. Solids tend to resist a shear force and bounce back to their original shape afterward, whereas liquids and gases do not. Without this elastic rebound, there can be no wave. Therefore, shear waves cannot be transmitted through liquids or gases. This has important consequences for the interpretation of seismic waves, as you will see. Shear waves travel more slowly than compressional waves, at about 3.5 kilometers per second. Because they arrive at a seismograph after the P waves from the same earthquake, they are called **S waves** (for **secondary waves**).

Surface Waves Surface waves travel along or near Earth's surface, like waves along the surface of the ocean. They travel more slowly than P and S waves, and they pass around Earth rather than through it. Thus, surface waves are the last to be detected by a seismograph. Surface waves are responsible for much ground shaking and structural damage during major earthquakes.

Locating Earthquakes

The **epicenter**, or surface location of an earthquake, can be determined through simple calculations, provided that

at least three seismographs have recorded the quake. The first step is to find out how far each seismograph is from the source of the earthquake. S waves travel more slowly, and the greater the distance traveled by the seismic waves, the more the S waves will lag behind the P waves (see Figure 5.8c).

epicenter The point on Earth's surface directly above an earthquake's focus.

After determining the distance from each seismograph to the source of the earthquake, a seismologist draws a circle on a map, with the seismic station at the center of the circle (see Figure 5.8c). The radius of the circle is the distance from the seismograph to the focus. It is a circle because the seismologist knows only the distance traveled by the seismic waves, not the direction from which they came. When this information is calculated and plotted for three or more seismographs, the unique point on the map where the three circles intersect is the location of the epicenter. This process is called **triangulation**. Geologists and others can report information about earthquakes and share information about where and when earthquakes have occurred, through the website maintained by the U.S. Geological Survey (see *Where Geologists Click* on page 120).

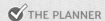

Energy released during an earthquake travels outward in all directions from the focus. Surface waves travel around the outer surface of the planet, and body waves travel through the planet.

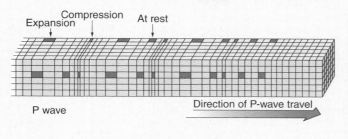

Expansion | Compression | At rest

P wave → Direction of P-wave travel

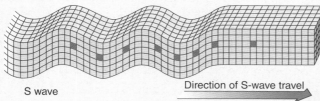

S wave → Direction of S-wave travel

a. Seismic body waves

The grid shows how rock responds to the two types of body waves. The cubes of the grid are modified as the seismic wave passes through them.

Compressional wave A compressional P wave alternately squeezes and stretches the rock as it passes. The cubes of the grid contract and then expand.

Shear wave A shear S wave causes the rock to vibrate up and down, like a rope whose end is being shaken. The cubes do not expand or contract but get distorted, changing shape.

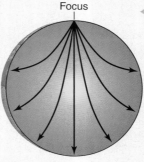

Focus

b. Travel paths of body waves

Seismic waves travel faster through denser rock; hence they travel more quickly at greater depths. This causes their paths to be curved rather than straight. (The increase in rock density and seismic velocity with depth is not smooth; compare these paths to the ones shown in Figure 5.9.)

c. Using seismograms to locate an earthquake

Scientists use seismograms to calculate the distance (in any direction) of a seismograph from an earthquake. By comparing seismograms from three locations, they can determine the location of the epicenter. ▼

① The earthquake happens at time 0. ② The first P waves arrive a little over 2 minutes later. ③ The first S waves arrive 4 minutes later.

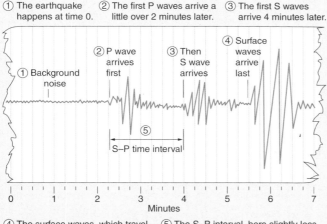

① Background noise
② P wave arrives first
③ Then S wave arrives
④ Surface waves arrive last
⑤ S–P time interval

Minutes

④ The surface waves, which travel the long way around Earth's surface, arrive last. ⑤ The S–P interval, here slightly less than 2 minutes, tells the seismologist how far away the earthquake was.

A typical seismogram Seismograms record both the ground shaking caused by an earthquake and the arrival times of seismic waves at the seismic station.

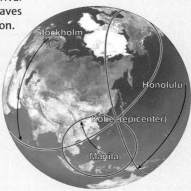

Stockholm
Honolulu
Kobe (epicenter)
Manila

ASK YOURSELF

How does the S–P interval change if the focus of an earthquake is farther from a seismic station?

a. If the focus is farther from a seismic station, the S–P interval is longer.

b. If the focus is farther from a seismic station, the S–P interval is shorter.

c. It doesn't matter how far the focus is; the S–P interval doesn't change.

d. The S–P interval depends on magnitude, not distance of focus from seismic station.

e. The S–P interval varies independently of distance between focus and seismic station.

Triangulation Each of three seismic stations determines its own distance from the earthquake, generating a circle on which the epicenter must lie. The three circles have a unique intersection point, which indicates the location of the epicenter—in this case Kobe, Japan, the site of a major earthquake in 1995.

Measuring Earthquakes

> **magnitude** A measure of the size or intensity of an event.

Geologists use several different scales to quantify the strength, or **magnitude**, of an earthquake, by which we mean the amount of energy released during the quake. The most familiar of these is the **Richter magnitude scale**.

The Richter and Moment Magnitude Scales

Charles Richter developed his famous magnitude scale in 1935. Although it was not the first earthquake intensity scale, it was an important advance because it used data from seismographs rather than subjective estimates of damage. Also, it compensated for the distance between the seismograph and the focus. This means that each seismic station (in principle) calculates the same magnitude for a given earthquake, no matter how far from the epicenter it is located.

Seismologists today determine magnitudes using both the Richter scale and the **moment magnitude scale**, which are similar in many respects but use different starting assumptions. Richter scale calculations are based on the assumption that an earthquake focus is a point. Therefore, the Richter scale is best suited for earthquakes in which energy is released from a relatively small area of a locked fault. In contrast, the calculation of seismic moment takes account of the fact that energy may be released over a large area; this is particularly true of bigger earthquakes. A classic example is the Sumatra–Andaman earthquake of 2004, during which a 1200-kilometer length of fault underwent displacement. Although their methods of calculation differ and the results often differ somewhat, both scales measure the same thing—the amount of energy released, based on the amplitude of seismic waves. In either system, magnitude 9 is catastrophic, and magnitude 2.5 is imperceptible to humans.

The Richter and moment magnitude scales are logarithmic, which means that each unit increase on the scale corresponds to a 10-fold increase in the amplitude of the wave signal. Thus, a magnitude 6 earthquake has a wave amplitude 10 times larger than that of a magnitude 5 quake. A magnitude 7 earthquake has a wave amplitude 100 times larger (10×10) than that of a magnitude 5 quake; and so on.

However, even this comparison understates the difference from one step to the next in the scale, because the amount of damage done by an earthquake is more closely related to the amount of energy released in the quake. Each step in the scale corresponds roughly to a 32-fold increase in energy. The actual amount of damage done by a quake also depends, of course, on local conditions—how densely populated the area is, how the buildings are constructed, how deep the focus is, and how severe the secondary effects are.

Modified Mercalli Intensity Scale Scientists measure the magnitude of an earthquake because they are concerned with the amount of energy released. What is more important for engineers designing buildings and authorities charged with civilian safety is the amount of damage done during an earthquake. Earthquake damage is more effectively measured using the **Modified Mercalli Intensity (MMI) scale**, which was developed by an Italian scientist in 1902 and later modified. The Modified Mercalli scale is based on descriptions of vibrations that people felt, saw, and heard, as well as on the extent of damage to buildings. The scale ranges from I (not felt, except under unusual circumstances) to XII (visible waves on ground, practically all buildings destroyed). The MMI of an earthquake varies with distance from the epicenter; a quake could have an intensity of X near the epicenter, whereas 100 kilometers away the intensity might be only II. The MMI of the Tōhoku earthquake in March 2011 reached IX in some areas, even though the epicenter was located some distance offshore.

The correspondence between MMI and Richter and moment magnitudes is not exact because they are calculated on the basis of very different parameters. In **Table 5.2** and in *What a Geologist Sees* we compare frequency, extent of damage, and MMI for earthquakes of various magnitudes.

STOP CONCEPT CHECK

1. **What** basic physical property does a modern seismograph depend on?

2. **Which** type of seismic wave generally travels the fastest—surface waves, compressional waves, or shear waves?

3. **How** can travel times of body waves be used to reveal the location of an earthquake?

4. **What** is the difference in energy released by a magnitude 6 and a magnitude 7 earthquake?

Earthquake magnitudes, frequencies, and effects · Table 5.2

Richter or moment magnitude*	Number per year	Modified Mercalli Intensity scale*	Characteristic effects in populated areas
<3.4	800,000	I	Recorded only by seismographs
3.5–4.2	30,000	II–III	Felt by some people who are indoors
4.3–4.8	4800	IV	Felt by many people; windows rattle
4.9–5.4	1400	V	Felt by everyone; dishes break, doors swing
5.5–6.1	500	VI–VII	Slight building damage; plaster cracks, bricks fall
6.2–6.9	100	VIII–IX	Much building damage; chimneys fall; houses move on foundations
7.0–7.3	15	X	Serious damage, bridges twisted, walls fractured; many masonry buildings collapse
7.4–7.9	4	XI	Great damage; most buildings collapse
>8.0	<1	XII	Total damage; waves seen on ground surface, objects thrown in the air

*The correspondence between Richter and moment magnitudes and the MMI is not exact because they are calculated on the basis of very different parameters.

STUDYING EARTH'S INTERIOR

Learning Objectives

1. **Explain** how the materials in Earth's interior affect seismic waves.

2. **Explain** what seismic data can reveal about the Earth's interior.

3. **Identify** several ways by which scientists can study Earth's interior indirectly or remotely.

Earthquakes are important because of the damage they can cause, but they also provide us with some of our most detailed information about Earth's interior—including parts that we can never hope to observe directly.

When scientists cannot study something by direct sampling, a second method comes to the forefront: indirect study, or **remote sensing**. Some familiar objects—including the human eye—are actually remote-sensing devices. A camera, for instance, is a remote-sensing instrument that collects information about how an object reflects light. Medical techniques such as X-rays allow doctors to study the inside of the body remotely without opening it up surgically.

The seismic waves from an earthquake are much like X-rays in the sense that they enter Earth near the surface, travel all the way through it, and emerge on the other side. They travel along different paths, depending on the different kinds of materials they encounter. We will first discuss how earthquakes reveal Earth's structure and then describe other sources of information about Earth's interior.

Seismic Methods for Studying Earth's Interior

Before 1906, scientific understanding of seismic waves was limited. But that year, British geologist Richard Dixon Oldham first identified the difference between P waves and S waves and then suggested an explanation for the complicated patterns recorded after an earthquake: Underneath thousands of kilometers of solid rock, he postulated, Earth has a liquid core. Oldham's conclusion is now universally accepted by geologists.

Seismic Discontinuities and the Liquid Core

When a major earthquake strikes, the tremors are measured at seismic stations around the world, and the arrival times of P waves and S waves can be used to determine what kinds of rock the seismic waves passed through. Even a crude diagram of Earth's structure shows that the pattern of arrival times is quite complex. Because Earth's interior is not homogeneous, seismic waves must pass through the boundaries between different materials as they travel through Earth's interior. Seismic waves travel at different velocities and behave differently depending on the properties of the materials they pass through, including the density of the material and whether it is a liquid or a solid.

Three distinct things can happen to seismic waves when they travel through Earth's interior, and especially when they pass through boundaries between different materials:

1. They can be **refracted**, or bent, as they pass from one material into another. This is the same thing that happens to light waves when they pass from air to water.

> **refraction** The bending of a wave as it passes from one material into another material, through which it travels at a different speed.

What a Geologist Sees

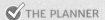

Earthquake Magnitude and Damage

When you hear a radio report about an earthquake, there may seem to be little difference in the seriousness of magnitude 7 or 8 earthquakes. But in fact, the energy released in an earthquake increases exponentially with its magnitude. An earthquake of M7 releases about 32 times as much energy as a quake of M6. An earthquake of M8 releases 32 x 32, or 1000 times as much energy as a quake of M6. And an earthquake of M9, such as the Tōhoku earthquake, releases 32 x 32 x 32, or more than 32,000 times as much energy as a quake of M6. Note that the MMI scale and the moment and Richter magnitude scales are not directly comparable. Modified Mercalli Intensity (MMI) differs with distance from the epicenter, whereas the moment and Richter magnitudes do not vary with distance. MMI is also a more subjective measure since it is based on felt and observed damage, whereas the moment and Richter magnitude scales are quantitative and exact.

Parkfield, CA, 2004

Magnitude: 6

Energy released: about the same as 1 atomic bomb

MMI: ≈ VII close to the epicenter

Damage on surface close to the epicenter: In determining the Mercalli Intensity of an M6 earthquake, such as the one that struck Parkfield, California, in 2004, a geologist would notice that some small objects have been broken, sleepers have wakened, and buildings are still standing but bricks have fallen from the walls.

Kobe, Japan, 1995

Magnitude: 7

Energy released: about the same as 32 atomic bombs

MMI: ≈ IX or X near the epicenter

Damage on surface close to the epicenter: The geologist would see that some buildings have shifted, some have collapsed, and damage has been severe. The presence of police suggests panic and the need for control.

San Francisco, CA, 1906

Magnitude: 8

Energy Released: about the same as 1000 atomic bombs

MMI: ≈ XI near the epicenter

Damage on surface close to the epicenter: Widespread destruction is clearly evident. With many buildings collapsed, thousands would be dead or injured in densely populated areas.

THINK CRITICALLY
Might there be an upper limit to the possible magnitude of an earthquake? If so, what might cause this?

Seismic waves are refracted gradually as they travel into increasingly denser rocks with depth; this results in curved pathways through the interior of Earth. They also can be refracted abruptly as they cross boundaries between materials that have differing seismic characteristics.

reflection The bouncing back of a wave from an interface between two different materials.

2. They can be **reflected**, which means that all or part of the wave energy bounces back, like light from a mirror.
3. They can be **absorbed**, which means that all or part of the wave energy is blocked.

The abrupt changes in velocity that result when seismic waves are refracted or reflected across boundaries or absorbed by materials as they travel through Earth's interior are called **seismic discontinuities**.

seismic discontinuity A boundary inside Earth where the velocities of seismic waves change abruptly.

Refraction, reflection, and absorption all play a role in Oldham's model of Earth's core. P waves are refracted dramatically, and some are reflected when they encounter the boundary between the mantle and the outer core (as shown in **Figure 5.9**). This refraction and reflection creates a ring-shaped **P-wave shadow zone** on the opposite side of Earth from the

Seismic waves in Earth's interior • Figure 5.9

Following an earthquake, the complex pattern of arrival times of seismic waves at distant locations gives scientists a map of Earth's interior.

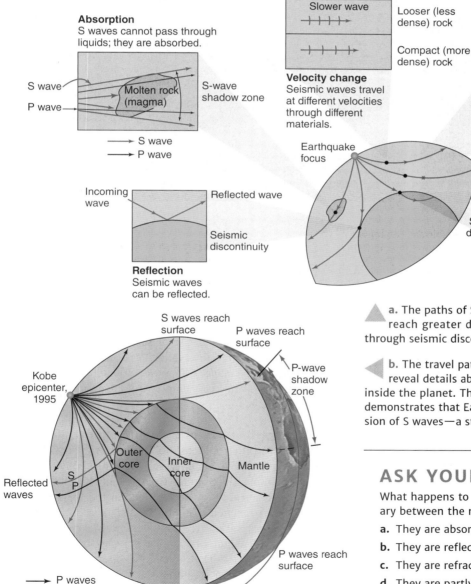

Absorption
S waves cannot pass through liquids; they are absorbed.

S wave
P wave
Molten rock (magma)
S-wave shadow zone

→ S wave
→ P wave

Velocity change
Seismic waves travel at different velocities through different materials.

Slower wave
Looser (less dense) rock
Compact (more dense) rock

Wave bends (refracts in a curve)
Rock is denser at greater depth

Refraction (gradual)
Seismic waves can refract gradually.

Incoming wave
Reflected wave
Seismic discontinuity

Reflection
Seismic waves can be reflected.

Earthquake focus

Seismic discontinuity

Rock 1 (less dense)
Rock 2 (more dense)

Refraction (abrupt)
Seismic waves can refract abruptly.

a. The paths of S and P waves change as they reach greater depths and when they travel through seismic discontinuities.

b. The travel paths and arrival times of S and P waves reveal details about seismic discontinuities and layers inside the planet. The S-wave shadow zone, in particular, demonstrates that Earth's outer core blocks the transmission of S waves—a strong indication that it is liquid.

S waves reach surface
P waves reach surface
P-wave shadow zone
Kobe epicenter, 1995
Outer core
Inner core
Mantle
Reflected waves
S
P
P waves reach surface
→ P waves
→ S waves
S-wave shadow zone

ASK YOURSELF

What happens to P waves when they hit the boundary between the mantle and the outer core?

a. They are absorbed.

b. They are reflected.

c. They are refracted.

d. They are partly refracted and partly reflected.

e. They pass unaltered through the boundary and the outer core.

Two oil-prospecting geologists in Texas are walking through a virtual three-dimensional image of the underground rocks at a potential drilling site in Alaska. The color variations reveal the layers and structures in the rock.

Sarah Leen/NG Image Collection

earthquake. S waves, on the other hand, are blocked completely by the outer core because shear waves cannot pass through liquid. This creates an even larger **S-wave shadow zone** and also provides firm evidence that Earth has a liquid core.

Seismic Tomography The boundary between the liquid outer core and the mantle was the first seismic discontinuity to be identified and explained. Since then, as scientists have developed more sophisticated seismic equipment and more detailed observations, they have discovered many other boundaries and layers within Earth. Today seismologists use seismic waves to probe Earth's interior in much the same way that a doctor uses X-rays and CAT scans to probe the interior of a human body. In CAT (computerized axial tomography) scanning, a series of X-rays along successive planes are used to create a three-dimensional picture of the inside of the body. Similarly, **seismic tomography** allows seismologists to use two-dimensional seismic soundings to build up a three-dimensional picture of Earth's interior (**Figure 5.10**). Geologists don't even have to wait for earthquakes to happen; they can use explosive charges (or large thumper trucks) as a source for seismic waves and then track their passage through the subsurface. These techniques allow scientists to map the locations of seismic discontinuities, the distribution of hot and cold masses, and the distribution of dense and less dense materials inside Earth, and have improved our understanding of plate tectonics.

Other Methods for Studying Earth's Interior

Earthquakes have provided a great deal of information about Earth's interior, but geologists make use of many other tools and techniques to study the deepest parts of our planet. Some of these tools, like the use of seismic information, involve indirect or remote observation of materials and processes deep within the planet. Others are more direct and give geologists access to actual samples from deep in the crust, and even from the mantle.

Direct Observation: Drilling and Xenoliths

Perhaps the most obvious tool for the retrieval and study of samples from Earth's interior is drilling. To date, Earth's deepest mine (in South Africa) is 3.6 kilometers deep, and the deepest hole ever drilled (in the Kola Peninsula of Russia) reached a depth of just over 12 kilometers. Earth's crust varies from an average thickness of 8 kilometers for oceanic crust to an average of 45 kilometers for continental crust. Therefore, a 12-kilometer hole sounds just about right for sampling the top part of the mantle—or does it?

The problem with drilling is that areas where the crust is thin tend to have high heat flow. In other words, if you try to drill a hole through thin oceanic crust all the way to the mantle, you will quickly encounter temperatures that could destroy your drilling equipment. Another problem with oceanic crust is that it is deep underwater, which makes drilling especially difficult. The only place where the rocks are both accessible and cool enough for drilling to great depth is precisely where the crust is very thick—on the continents. The hole in the Kola Peninsula went through more than 12 kilometers of thick continental crust and never even came close to reaching the mantle. Thus, although drilling has yielded much interesting and useful information about the composition and properties of the crust, it hasn't even penetrated to the outermost seismic discontinuity of the mantle (the crust–mantle boundary).

If we can't obtain samples from deep within Earth by reaching in to retrieve them, perhaps we can wait for them to come to us. This does happen—in two different ways. Molten rock, or **magma**, is formed in the upper portions of Earth's mantle, in areas where the temperature is high enough. By studying magma that originates at depth and erupts to the surface, scientists learn about the temperature, pressure, and composition of the mantle in the region where the magma formed. Furthermore, as magma rises toward the surface, it often breaks off and carries with it fragments of the unmelted surrounding rock. We call these fragments **xenoliths**, from the Greek words *xenos* ("foreigner") and *lithos* ("stone"). A xenolith that reaches Earth's surface is a sample of the deep crust or mantle, accessible for direct scientific study (**Figure 5.11**).

Diamonds: Messengers from the deep • Figure 5.11

Diamonds form at extremely high pressures, which only occur naturally at depths of 100 to 300 kilometers below the surface. Although most people treasure diamonds for their beauty and luster, geologists treasure them also as samples from an otherwise inaccessible region of Earth's interior.

Courtesy Dan Schulze

a. The different colors in this diamond—nicknamed the "Picasso" diamond—show zones of differing composition, revealing the complex growth history of this crystal. The variations are captured by a special type of photography that highlights small differences in composition. The diamond is approximately 1 millimeter across.

b. This beautiful large diamond (approximately 2 centimeters across) is the 253.7-carat Oppenheimer Diamond from the Smithsonian Institution's mineral collection. It was discovered in South Africa in 1964. This is a natural diamond that has not been cut, faceted, or polished.

©Smithsonian Institution/Corbis

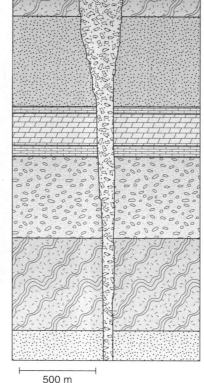

Magma vent is circular when viewed from above.

Xenoliths of mantle rock

Pipe extends 150–200 km down into mantle

c. To reach the surface from great depths, diamonds are carried out by volcanic eruptions of unusual ferocity. These eruptions leave behind long, cone-shaped tubes of solidified magma, called **kimberlite pipes**. Kimberlite eruptions are the only way for diamonds to get from the mantle to the surface.

500 m

THINK CRITICALLY

Would a synthetic diamond grown in a laboratory record a similarly complex growth history to that of the "Picasso" diamond, which grew naturally in the mantle?

Indirect Observation: Magnetism and Planetary Characteristics The characteristics of Earth as a planet, including its orbital characteristics and its magnetic field, provide another powerful indirect source of information to enhance our understanding of Earth's interior. Some of these techniques are also useful in the study of other planets in the solar system.

Earth's magnetic field has provided important tools for dating rocks (Chapter 3) and reconstructing the past motion of lithospheric plates (Chapter 4). It turns out that magnetism also gives us information about Earth's deep interior. **Magnetism** is a force created either by permanent magnets (called *ferromagnets*) or by moving electrical charges. We can try thinking of Earth as having a huge dipole bar magnet with north and south poles at its center, offset slightly from the geographic North and South poles. The problem is that solids, including bar magnets, lose their magnetism at temperatures above a critical transition temperature, called the **Curie point**, which is specific to each material. The Curie point for iron (the material of bar magnets) is about 770°C, but we know that the temperature deep inside Earth is *much* higher than this—at least 5000°C. This means that the bar magnet analogy for Earth's magnetic field must be incorrect, and a different explanation is needed.

Physicists have shown that the movement of an electrically conducting liquid inside a planet could generate a self-sustaining magnetic field, much like a rotating coil of wire in an electric motor (**Figure 5.12**). This is consistent with the observation from seismology that at least the outer part of Earth's core is liquid. However, molten rock is not a good enough electrical conductor to generate a magnetic field in this manner; for this and other reasons, geologists believe that the liquid outer core is made of molten iron and nickel rather than molten rock. This is consistent with evidence from meteorites, as discussed later in this chapter.

We can gain a certain amount of information about any planet's interior—including Earth's—from astronomical observations that reveal the overall characteristics of the planet. The first step is to determine the planet's mass. This can be deduced from the planet's gravitational influence on other planets and satellites. Second, we need to know the diameter of the planet. Once we know the dimensions of the planet and its shape (in the case of Earth, a very slightly flattened sphere), it is a simple matter to figure out its volume and average density (mass divided by volume).

What do these kinds of measurements reveal about Earth's interior? For one thing, we can determine whether material is distributed evenly throughout the planet. The rocks at Earth's surface are very light (low-density) compared to the planet as a whole. Surface rocks have an average density of about 2.8 grams per cubic centimeter (g/cm^3), whereas Earth's overall density is 5.5 g/cm^3. (For comparison, water has a density of 1 g/cm^3 at 4°C.) For the planet as a whole to have such a high density, with such low-density rocks at the surface, there must be a concentration of denser

Earth's magnetic field • Figure 5.12

Earth is surrounded by a magnetic field that provides important clues about the planet's interior.

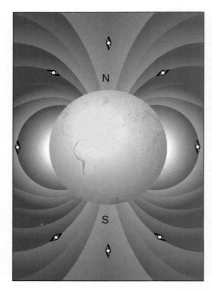

a. Earth's magnetic field causes compass needles to point to the north. More precisely, compass needles align along field lines that lead to the magnetic north and south poles, which are almost—but not exactly—aligned with Earth's geographic North and South poles.

b. Aurora borealis, or the northern lights, seen here from Fairbanks, Alaska, is caused by charged particles from the Sun entering Earth's atmosphere at high latitudes along magnetic field lines.

material somewhere inside the planet. This evidence is consistent with a model where Earth's core is primarily a mixture of two metals, iron and nickel, with a density of about 10 g/cm^3.

A final way to study Earth's interior—last in our summary but definitely not least in importance—is to analyze the building blocks that formed it. Planetary scientists have discovered that many (though not all) meteorites were formed at about the same time and in the same part of the solar system as Earth. Some of these are so-called **primitive meteorites**—that is, they have remained unaffected by melting and other geologic processes since the beginning of the solar system. These meteorites give scientists an idea of the overall composition of the solar system and its constituent bodies (see *Remember This!*). Other meteorite types include the **irons** (primarily composed of iron–nickel metal), **stony-irons** (a mixture of metal and rocky material), and **stony meteorites** (rocky, primarily composed of silicate minerals). All of these show signs of melting and differentiation, and may be more representative of Earth's core and mantle. It is highly significant that a core with the composition of a typical iron meteorite (mostly iron and nickel metal) would bring Earth's overall density up to the observed value of 5.5 g/cm^3.

> **REMEMBER THIS!** Do you recall the nebular hypothesis, which describes how rocky, metallic, gaseous, and icy materials accreted to form the planets and other objects in our solar system? If not, have a look back at the section *Earth in Space* in Chapter 1 to remind yourself.

STOP CONCEPT CHECK

> 1. Why do seismic waves undergo refraction as they pass through Earth?
> 2. What three pieces of evidence indicate that Earth has a molten, iron-rich outer core?
> 3. Why can't geologists drill a hole down to the mantle?

A MULTILAYERED PLANET

Learning Objectives

> 1. **Describe** the formation and composition of Earth's crust.
>
> 2. **Summarize** the composition and layering of Earth's mantle.
>
> 3. **Describe** the composition and types of layering within the core.

By piecing together information from various sources, geologists have arrived at a very detailed understanding of Earth's interior. Let's take a brief tour, starting at the top and working down to the innermost layers. As we proceed, keep in mind that some boundaries inside Earth mark the transition between layers with differing composition, whereas others separate layers with the same composition but different physical properties.

The Crust

Earth's outermost compositional layer is the **crust**. The thickness of the crust varies greatly, from an average of 8

> **crust** The outermost compositional layer of the solid Earth; part of the lithosphere.

kilometers for oceanic crust to an average of 45 kilometers for continental crust (**Figure 5.13**). Even at its thickest spots, the crust is extremely thin compared with Earth as a whole.

It's like a thin, brittle eggshell, or about the same relative thickness as the glass of a light bulb.

Like its thickness, the composition of the crust varies from place to place. About 92% of the crust is igneous rock or metamorphic rock derived from igneous rock (**Figure 5.14**). In general, the rock of the crust is lighter (less dense) than the material in Earth's interior because the crust is composed of material that floated to the top during planetary differentiation. The very outermost surface of the crust, both on land and on the ocean floor, is quite different from the crust as a whole. This surface layer—the ground surface we see around us every day—consists of about 65% sediment and sedimentary rock, formed by the constant action of erosion, weathering, and deposition.

Moving downward through the crust, we encounter the boundary that separates the crust from the mantle. This is a major seismic discontinuity, the next to be discovered after the discovery of the seismic discontinuity that marks the outer liquid core. It was named the **Mohorovičić discontinuity** after the seismologist who discovered it in 1909, but it is usually called the **Moho** for short. Mantle rocks, being denser and compositionally different from crustal rocks, transmit P waves much more quickly. The Moho is thus an example of a boundary between two layers of rock (the crust and the upper mantle) that have different compositions and densities but similar physical characteristics (rigidity).

The Mantle

The **mantle** extends from the Moho to the core (see Figure 5.13). About 80% of Earth's volume is contained in the mantle. Geologists believe, on the strength of evidence from xenoliths, meteorites, and seismic analyses, that the mantle

> **mantle** The middle compositional layer of Earth, between the core and the crust.

Inside view of Earth • Figure 5.13

Seismic studies and other direct and indirect observations have given scientists a good idea of the internal structure of Earth.

a. Earth can be divided into three major compositional layers: the **core**; the **mantle**; and the **crust**. Temperature and pressure increase with depth.

b. The compositional boundaries between layers do not necessarily coincide with the boundaries of zones that differ in strength. For example, the supper mantle includes both a soft, plastic asthenosphere and the rigid lithosphere. The lithosphere includes the rigid portion of the upper mantle as well as the crust above it.

c. The composition and thickness of the crust vary depending on whether the crust is below an ocean or on a continent. Oceanic crust is thinner and denser than continental crust.

Crust
Oceanic crust
Mantle
Asthenosphere
Lithosphere
Crust
Liquid outer core
Mesosphere
Solid inner core
5140 km
2883 km
350 km
100 km
6371 km

Ocean
Oceanic crust
Moho
Continental crust
Kilometers
0
25
50
100
150
200
Vertical scale is 10x the horizontal scale

Continental crust thickness greatly exaggerated

Temperature and pressure increase with depth

350 km
100 km
0

Mesosphere: hot but stronger due to high pressure

Asthenosphere: hot, weak, plastic

Lithosphere: cool, rigid, brittle

---

consists mainly of silicate minerals of iron and magnesium (see *Remember This!*). The upper part of the mantle has a composition similar to that of peridotite, an igneous rock not typically found in the crust, which consists mainly of the iron–magnesium silicate minerals olivine and pyroxene.

> **REMEMBER THIS!** Silicates are by far the most important rock-forming minerals. Do you remember how the crystal structures of silicate minerals are organized and classified? You can remind yourself by revisiting *Mineral Families* in Chapter 2.

Seismic studies have revealed boundaries within the mantle, but not all of them are compositional boundaries. Extending from about 100 to 350 kilometers below the surface is a layer called the **asthenosphere**, from the Greek words meaning "weak sphere." In this zone, some of the rocks are very near the temperatures at which rock melting begins, so they have the consistency of warm tar. The composition of the asthenosphere appears to be the same as that of the mantle just above and below

asthenosphere A layer of weak, ductile rock in the mantle that is close to melting but not actually molten.

lithosphere Earth's rocky, outermost layer, comprising the crust and the uppermost part of the mantle.

it. Thus, the asthenosphere is a layer whose distinctiveness is based on its physical properties—reduced rigidity—rather than its composition.

The outermost 100 km of Earth, which includes the crust and the part of the uppermost mantle just above the asthenosphere, is called the **lithosphere** (see Figure 5.13). The rocks of the lithosphere are cooler, more rigid, and much stronger than the rocks of the asthenosphere. In plate tectonic theory, it is the entire lithosphere—not just the crust—that forms the plates. These plates can move around because they rest on the underlying weaker rocks of the asthenosphere, which slowly deform and flow like an extremely thick, viscous liquid. The asthenosphere deforms by ductile flow, while the lithosphere deforms mainly by fracturing (faulting), as illustrated by the San Andreas Fault at Point Reyes, discussed in *Amazing Places* (see page 130).

The rest of the mantle, from the bottom of the asthenosphere (at about 350 km depth) down to the core–mantle boundary, is the **mesosphere**. Although temperatures in the mesosphere are very high, the rocks are a bit stronger than in the asthenosphere because they are highly compressed. Additional seismic discontinuities exist within the mesosphere, with transitions at about 400 kilometers and at about 670 kilometers below the surface (**Figure 5.15**). These discontinuities are not well understood; they do not seem to be compositional boundaries but rather appear to result from changes in physical properties. For example, when the mineral olivine

Composition of the crust • Figure 5.14

The thin layer of sediment and sedimentary rock at the surface is the interface between the hydrosphere and atmosphere, and the hard rock of the geosphere. The atmosphere and hydrosphere weathers the hard crystalline rock that makes up the crust, causing it to break down.

a. Earth's crust, overall, is composed mainly of crystalline rock—igneous and metamorphic—and less than 8% sedimentary rock.

b. The sedimentary rock forms a thin veneer on top of the igneous and metamorphic rock, so the surface itself is mainly sedimentary.

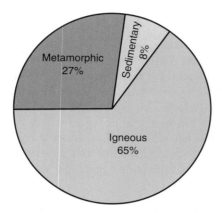

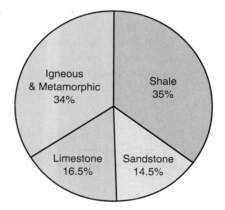

c. Blacktail Canyon in the Grand Canyon shows a sedimentary layer draped over much older granitic rock (darker grey).

National Park Service

Seismic discontinuities in the mantle • Figure 5.15

Earth's mantle is not uniform but has several seismic boundaries within it. Although the exact nature of the boundaries is not completely understood, we know the boundaries exist because P waves and S waves slow down or speed up abruptly and are refracted or reflected at these boundaries.

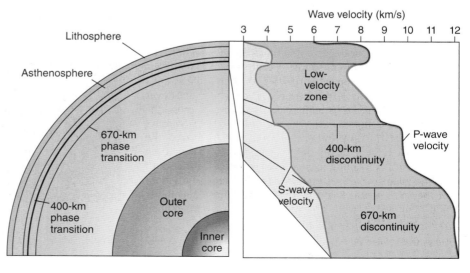

is squeezed at a pressure equal to that found at a depth of 400 kilometers, the atoms rearrange themselves into a more compact structure, or polymorph, of olivine (see Chapter 2). Perhaps this change to a more compact form is responsible for causing the 400-kilometer seismic discontinuity.

It is important to remember that the mantle is mostly solid rock, with the exception of small pockets of melt in the asthenosphere. We know that the mantle must be solid because both P waves and S waves can travel through it. Nevertheless, pressures and temperatures deep within Earth are so high that even solid rock can flow in very, very slow convection currents. Seismologists have recently detected hot regions in the mantle that may coincide with the rising limbs of convection cells that help drive plate motion.

The Core

At a depth of 2883 kilometers, there is a huge decrease in the velocity of P waves, and the velocity of S waves drops to zero. This is the core–mantle boundary (see Figure 5.13),

which represents a change in both the composition and the physical properties of the materials. The core, the innermost of Earth's compositional layers, is the densest part of Earth. It consists of material that "sank" to the center during the process of planetary differentiation. As discussed earlier, geologists believe that Earth's core is composed primarily of iron–nickel metal.

> **core** Earth's innermost compositional layer, where the magnetic field is generated and much geothermal energy resides.

The S-wave shadow zone (and other evidence) tells us that the **outer core**, from 2883-kilometer to 5140-kilometer depth, must be liquid. For three decades geologists thought the core was a homogeneous liquid, but in 1936 the Danish seismologist Inge Lehmann showed that the core, too, has layers. She detected faint seismic waves within the P-wave shadow zone that had reflected off the **inner core**. The pressure in the inner core is so great that iron must be solid there, in spite of the very high temperature. We know this from

Amazing Places

 THE PLANNER

Point Reyes and the San Andreas Fault, California

Point Reyes Peninsula, just north of San Francisco, is a spectacular place to view the history of the San Andreas Fault, one of the world's most famous faults. The fence dislocated by the 1906 earthquake in Figure 5.3 is part of a walking tour at Point Reyes State Park.

Perhaps the most visible evidence of the fault in this location is Tomales Bay, a narrow, straight inlet 20 kilometers long and only 1.4 kilometers wide on the northeast side of the peninsula. The San Andreas Fault runs directly down the center of the bay, which is seen from a satellite in **Figure a**. Over the millennia, earthquakes have ground the rocks on both sides of the fault together and weakened them. Erosion of these weakened rocks formed a linear valley, which has been filled by water from the Pacific Ocean.

The peninsula itself has been on an amazing journey for the past 100 million years, as it has slipped northward along the San Andreas Fault. The ridge on the west side of Tomales Bay contains outcrops of granite and diorite that must have originated in a continental mountain range—possibly the Tehachapi Mountains of southern California 300 kilometers to the south. As it moved northward, the peninsula scraped up souvenirs of the places it passed. The scenic Point Reyes lighthouse (**Figure b**) is built on a rock formation called the Point Reyes Conglomerate. The Point Reyes Fault, another offshoot of the San Andreas system, runs right past the lighthouse (**Figure c**). An identical conglomerate formation is found at Point Lobos, located 180 kilometers to the south on the opposite side of the San Gregorio Fault, an offshoot of the San Andreas Fault. It is very likely that Point Reyes and Point Lobos were adjacent to each other 60 million years ago, when the conglomerate layer formed.

Where will Point Reyes go next?

a. In this satellite view of Tomales Bay and Point Reyes, the trace of the main San Andreas Fault runs diagonally from top left to bottom right. The San Gregorio Fault splits off from the San Andreas Fault farther to the south (off the lower right corner of the photo). ▼

Courtesy Landsat.org

Diane Miller/Photolibrary/Getty Images, Inc.

USGS

b. The Point Reyes Fault runs right past the historic Point Reyes Lighthouse, shown here.

c. This historic photo taken in 1907 shows the surface rupture near Point Reyes that resulted from the 1906 earthquake.

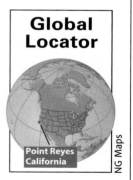

Global Locator

Point Reyes
California

NG Maps

THINK CRITICALLY

As explained above, 60 million years ago Point Reyes was adjacent to Point Lobos, 180 kilometers to the south on the opposite side of the San Gregorio Fault.

1. Given that 180 kilometers of displacement have occurred in 60 million years, calculate the amount of displacement per year along this segment of the fault system.

2. How does the result of your calculation compare with the average rate of displacement along the whole San Andreas Fault system in California—about 33 to 37 millimeters per year? What do you think might account for the difference?

high-pressure experiments on iron. The main difference between the inner core and outer core is thus a difference in the physical state rather than the composition. As heat escapes from the core and works its way to the surface, the core is gradually crystallizing. Thus the solid inner core must be growing larger, though very slowly.

It should be clear by now that what happens deep in the interior of Earth profoundly affects the surface. The release of heat from the interior is an important driving force for plate tectonics, which in turn is the major uplifting force in shaping Earth's varied landscapes and topographies.

SUMMARY

 THE PLANNER

1 Earthquakes and Earthquake Hazards   109

- **Seismology** relates earthquakes to the processes of plate tectonics. Although the motion of tectonic plates is very gradual, friction causes the rocks in the crust to jam together for long periods and then to break suddenly and lurch forward, causing an earthquake to occur. Earthquakes can cause large vertical or horizontal displacements of the ground, but much of the damage they cause results from the violent shaking that accompanies the displacement.

- The shaking motion experienced during an earthquake can be explained by the **elastic rebound model**, which says that the energy stored in bent and deformed rocks is released as **seismic waves**. After an earthquake, the rocks return to their undeformed state.

- In many cases the destructiveness of earthquakes is magnified by secondary hazards, such as fires, landslides, liquefaction (see the photo), and tsunamis. Proper building design and earthquake preparedness can greatly reduce the loss of life from earthquakes and secondary hazards.

Secondary hazards: Ground liquefaction • Figure 5.4

Courtesy NOAA/NGDC

- Short-term forecasting of earthquakes is still very unreliable. Scientists have concentrated their efforts on finding precursor phenomena, such as foreshocks, but with limited success. However, long-term forecasting can provide a good idea of which regions are at risk. One of the main tools of long-term forecasting is **paleoseismology**, which reveals when past earthquakes occurred in a given region, as well as the periodicity and magnitudes of past earthquakes.

2 The Science of Seismology   117

- **Seismographs** produce recordings of seismic waves that are called **seismograms.** In a basic seismograph (see the diagram), a pen is attached to a heavy suspended mass. Seismic waves cause the paper to shake while the pen stays still and traces a wavy line on the vibrating paper.

Seismograph • Figure 5.7

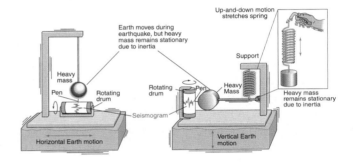

- Earthquakes produce three main types of seismic waves: **compressional waves**, or P waves (primary waves); **shear waves**, or S waves (secondary waves); and a variety of **surface waves**. Compressional and shear waves are called **body waves** because they travel through Earth's interior.

- Compressional waves travel faster than shear waves and hence arrive at seismographs first. The difference in arrival times between the P and S waves allows seismologists to compute the distance, but not the direction, to the **focus** of an earthquake. To determine the precise location of the **epicenter**, seismologists need measurements from three separate seismic stations. They can then determine the location by triangulation.

- The Richter and moment **magnitude** scales are measures of earthquake intensity that can be determined regardless of the distance to the earthquake or the amount of damage done. Both are logarithmic scales, in which each unit of magnitude corresponds roughly to a 10-fold increase in the amplitudes of seismic waves, but a 32-fold increase in the amount of energy released by the earthquake. The Modified Mercalli Intensity scale is a descriptive scale based on the extent of earthquake damage. On the MMI scale, the intensity is highest near the epicenter.

3 Studying Earth's Interior 121

- After an earthquake, seismic waves travel downward into Earth's interior as well as upward and along the surface (see the diagram). Seismic waves travel at different velocities through different materials, and they change velocity and direction when they pass from one material to another material with different physical and/or compositional properties. This understanding of seismic waves has allowed seismologists to identify many **seismic discontinuities** in Earth's interior.

Seismic waves in Earth's interior · Figure 5.9

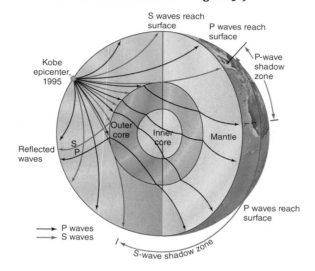

- Seismic discontinuities can result from either a change in composition or a change in physical properties of the material. They may **refract**, **reflect**, or even block seismic waves. P waves are strongly refracted, or bent, when they pass from the mantle to the core. S waves, on the other hand, are completely blocked by the core. This discovery provides evidence that Earth has a liquid outer core.

- Geologists use a variety of remote or indirect techniques to understand Earth's interior, in addition to the study of naturally occurring earthquakes. They can use seismic tomography, analogous to medical tomography, to detect seismic discontinuities underground.

- Other sources of information about Earth's interior include drilling, the magnetic field, the mass and density of Earth, and meteorite studies. Evidence points to the likelihood that Earth has a dense core that consists mainly of iron and nickel.

- So far, geologists have been unable to drill deep enough to sample the mantle directly. However, some mineral samples from the mantle come to the surface as xenoliths, carried along by magma that rises to the surface.

4 A Multilayered Planet 127

- Earth's three main compositional layers are the **crust**, the **mantle**, and the **core**. Each of these layers creates a seismic discontinuity, and this is how geologists can determine their thickness.

- The crust consists of solid rock that is mostly igneous, with a thin veneer of sediment and sedimentary rock at the surface. It varies in average thickness from 8 kilometers (for oceanic crust) to 45 kilometers (for continental crust).

- The mantle contains several physical boundaries (see the diagram). The most important are the boundaries between the **lithosphere**, the **asthenosphere**, and the mesosphere. The lithosphere is about 100 kilometers thick; the asthenosphere begins about 100 kilometers beneath the surface, and ends at a depth of about 350 kilometers; and the mesosphere extends from a depth of 350 to 2883 kilometers.

Seismic discontinuities in the mantle · Figure 5.15

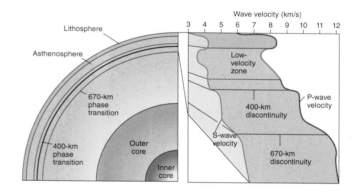

- The core has two layers, a liquid outer core and an inner core that is solid—despite its high temperature—because of the extremely high pressure. The boundary between them is physical, not compositional. The outer core begins at a depth of 2883 kilometers and extends to a depth of 5140 kilometers. The inner core, which was first discovered by its reflection of P waves, is almost certainly growing very gradually as Earth cools down from its formation.

KEY TERMS

CRITICAL AND CREATIVE THINKING QUESTIONS

1. Use the elastic rebound model to describe what happens to rocks at the focus just before, during, and after an earthquake.

2. Why is short-term prediction of earthquakes so much less successful than long-term forecasting? Why do you think seismologists are extremely cautious about making predictions? Do you think it will ever be possible to predict earthquakes accurately and issue effective early warnings? Research your answer.

3. If you were asked to determine the exact shape and size of Earth, how would you go about it? What would you do differently if you were not allowed to use space-age technology such as satellite photographs and orbital data?

4. Some of the boundaries inside Earth represent transitions between layers with differing compositions, whereas others represent transitions between layers with different physical states. Find out more about these different layers and draw a detailed diagram to show the layering.

5. Which of the techniques used to study Earth's interior could also be used to study other planets? Which ones cannot, and why? Scientists know more about the surface of the Sun than about the interior of our own planet; why do you think this is so?

6. Diamond is one of the minerals found in mantle xenoliths in kimberlite pipes. Based on what you know about the composition of the mantle, what other minerals and rock types might you expect to find in xenoliths brought to the surface by kimberlitic volcanism? If you were a prospector trying to find a diamond deposit, what sort of landform would you look for? Can you find some clues from the shape of the kimberlite pipe in the figure?

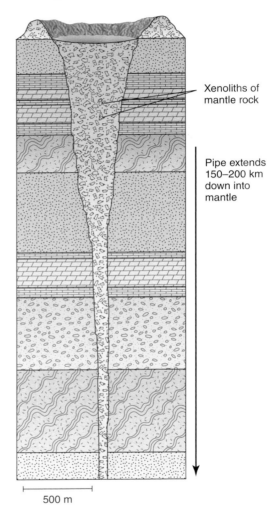

Xenoliths of mantle rock

Pipe extends 150–200 km down into mantle

500 m

WHAT IS HAPPENING IN THIS PICTURE?

This photo shows some of the devastating damage to city infrastructure caused by the Great Hanshin Earthquake of 1995 in Kobe, Japan.

© Reuters/CORBIS

THINK CRITICALLY

1. What happened to the concrete highway supports in the photo? (*Hint:* Have a look at Figure 5.5b.) What could be done to prevent this in the future?

2. Why has the highway toppled over to one side, instead of collapsing straight down? (*Hint:* Consider the picture of the toppled-over buildings shown in Figure 5.4d.)

3. Why do you think the entire stretch of highway collapsed instead of just one or two sections? What implications does this have for engineering approaches to the strengthening of the highway?

SELF-TEST

(Check your answers in Appendix D.)

1. The largest recorded earthquakes have occurred at _____.

   a. divergent boundaries

   b. transform fault boundaries

   c. subduction zone boundaries

   d. continental collision boundaries

2. According to the elastic rebound model, earthquakes are caused by the _____.

   a. slow release of gases from the asthenosphere

   b. sudden release of elastic energy stored in rocks

   c. sudden movement of otherwise stable tectonic plates

   d. rapid release of gases from the asthenosphere

3. _____ and the resulting collapse of buildings, bridges, and other structures are usually the most significant primary hazards that cause damage during an earthquake.

   a. Fire

   b. Tsunami

   c. Ground liquefaction

   d. Ground shaking

4. _____ can provide a good idea of which regions are at risk for severe earthquakes.

   a. Short-term forecasting

   b. Long-term forecasting

   c. Unusual animal behavior studies

   d. Studies of groundwater levels

5. Which of the following are true of body waves?

   a. They move through Earth's interior.

   b. They cannot penetrate Earth's liquid outer core.

   c. They move along Earth's surface, causing great destruction.

   d. Both b and c are correct.

6. Using seismograms from three different seismic recording stations A, B, and C, you determine the epicenter of an earthquake. Stations A and B both had an S–P interval of 3 seconds, and C had an S–P interval of 11 seconds. Which of the following statements most accurately depicts the location of the epicenter?

   a. The epicenter is closest to station A and equally far from B and C.

   b. The epicenter is closest to station B and equally far from A and C.

   c. The epicenter is closest to station C and equally far from A and B.

   d. The epicenter is equally close to A and B and farthest from station C.

7. For the earthquake mentioned in question 6, which seismic station would have recorded the P wave first?

   a. station A

   b. station B

   c. station C

   d. Both stations A and B would have recorded the P wave before station C.

8. This diagram shows a seismogram of a hypothetical earthquake. On the seismogram, label the following:

   S–P interval

   first arrival of P wave

   first arrival of S wave

   background noise

   first arrival of surface waves

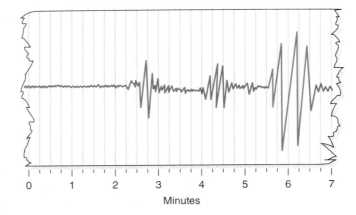

9. Diagrams a and b depict two different types of seismic waves. Which of the following statements can be made about these two seismic waves?

   a. The wave depicted in a is a P wave and has a greater velocity through Earth's crust than other types of seismic waves.

   b. The wave depicted in a is an S wave and has a greater velocity through Earth's crust than other types of seismic waves.

   c. The wave depicted in b is a P wave and has a greater velocity through Earth's crust than other types of seismic waves.

   d. The wave depicted in b is an S wave and has a greater velocity through Earth's crust than other types of seismic waves.

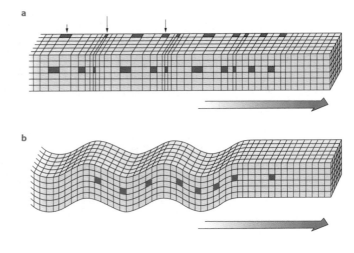

10. A magnitude 8 earthquake releases approximately _____ times more energy than a magnitude 7 event.

a. 2

b. 10

c. 20

d. 21.5

e. 32

11. How does moment magnitude differ from Richter magnitude?

a. Richter magnitude assumes that earthquakes are generated at a point source, whereas moment magnitude takes into account that earthquakes can be generated over a large area of rupture.

b. Moment magnitude assumes that earthquakes are generated at a point source, whereas Richter magnitude takes into account that earthquakes can be generated over a large area of rupture.

c. Moment magnitude uses Roman numerals to designate the strength of an earthquake.

d. Richter magnitude uses Roman numerals to designate the strength of an earthquake.

12. Which of the following is true of seismic waves reaching a discontinuity inside Earth's interior?

a. They can be refracted, or bent, as they pass from the first material into the second.

b. They can be reflected, which means that all or part of the wave energy bounces back.

c. They can be absorbed, which means that all or part of the wave energy is blocked by the second material.

d. All of the above answers are correct.

13. Earth's mantle is composed of _____, which surrounds a(n) _____ core.

a. rock that contains iron- and magnesium–silicate minerals; iron–nickel metallic

b. iron–nickel alloy; rocky iron– and magnesium–silicate

c. rock that contains iron– and magnesium–silicate minerals; molten iron–nickel

d. molten rock; solid iron–nickel metallic

14. On this diagram, label Earth's internal structure using the following terms:

mantle   lithosphere   oceanic crust

asthenosphere   outer core   Moho

inner core   continental crust   mesosphere

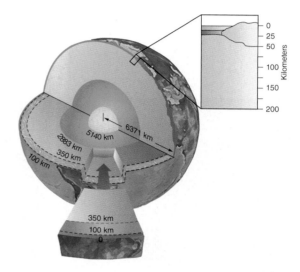

15. The asthenosphere is a layer whose distinctiveness from the rest of the mantle is based on its _____.

a. differences in composition

b. reduced rigidity

c. increased rigidity

d. relatively low temperature

THE PLANNER ✓

Review the Chapter Planner on the chapter opener and check off your completed work.

6 | VOLCANOES AND IGNEOUS ROCKS

Global Locator

Iceland

NG Maps

LUCAS JACKSON/Reuters/©Corbis

EYJAFJALLAJÖKULL ERUPT, EUROPE SHUTS DOWN

Iceland is home to many active volcanoes, and some are covered by ice caps. The consequences of an eruption beneath a glacier can be dangerous. Eyjafjallajökull, a glacier-covered volcano, erupted in 2010 (shown in the photo). The glacier—really an ice cap—covers 100 square kilometers, and the volcano is 1651 meters high.

Eyjafjallajökull began to erupt on April 14, 2010; part of the ice cap melted, causing a *jökulhlaup*—a flood of glacial meltwater. Some of the water flowed into the volcanic vent, causing the eruption to become so explosive that plumes of gas carried volcanic ash high into the atmosphere. Upper atmosphere winds spread the ash cloud across northern Europe and the Atlantic Ocean, shutting down air travel because ash in a jet engine can cause a crash. Hundreds of thousands of passengers were stranded, some for weeks. By May 23 the eruption had settled down, and the worst peacetime travel disruption from natural causes came to an end.

The scenario was repeated in May 2011, with the eruption of Grimsvötn, another subglacial volcano in Iceland. Air travel was not as severely disrupted because lessons from Eyjafjallajökull allowed air traffic controllers to refine their decision-making process about volcanic eruptions and air travel.

VOLCANOES AND VOLCANIC HAZARDS

Learning Objectives

1. **Identify** several different categories of volcanic eruptions and the eruptive styles, landforms, and volcanic materials that are associated with them.

2. **Describe** how volcanic features such as craters, calderas, geysers, and fumaroles arise.

3. **Identify** the hazards associated with volcanoes, as well as the beneficial effects they can have.

4. **Describe** how scientists monitor volcanic activity.

For many people, the thought of a **volcano** conjures up visions of fountains of **lava** spurting up into the air and pouring out over the landscape. Although it's true that most volcanoes produce at least some liquid lava, many other types of materials can emerge from volcanoes as well, such as fragments of rock and glassy volcanic ash. A fragment of rock ejected during a volcanic eruption is called a **pyroclast** (from the Greek words meaning "fire broken"). Collectively, all the **ejecta** (that is, anything that is violently ejected from a volcano) are called **tephra** or pyroclastic material. Pyroclasts can range from car-sized **volcanic bombs** to dime-sized **lapilli** to ultrafine **volcanic ash** whose individual particles can be seen only under a microscope (**Figure 6.1**). To see what's going on right now at an active volcano, see *Where Geologists Click*.

> **volcano** A vent through which lava, solid rock debris, volcanic ash, and gases erupt from Earth's crust to its surface.
>
> **lava** Molten rock that reaches Earth's surface.

The products of volcanic eruptions • Figure 6.1

Volcanic eruptions produce various products, ranging from lava to volcanic ash.

a. Lava
Lava, such as this produced by the eruption of Kilauea that began in 1983, poses minimal danger to humans, although extensive property damage can result if lava flows into populated areas.

Paul Chesley/NG Image Collection

b. Volcanic bombs
The violent release of gas during an eruption ejects volcanic bombs, fist-sized and larger, from Mount Etna in Sicily. ▼

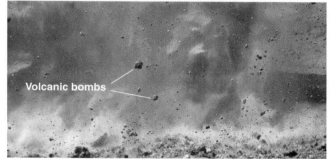

Volcanic bombs

Carsten Peter/NG Image Collection

d. Volcanic ash
Volcanic ash, the smallest tephra, blankets a farm in Oregon after the violent eruption of Mount St. Helens in 1980. Though we call it ash, it is different from what you find in your fireplace because it consists of microscopic pieces of volcanic glass. ▼

Photo Researchers/Getty Images, Inc.

c. Lapilli
These lapilli—pyroclasts that are approximately pea-sized to dime-sized—were erupted from Kilauea volcano and cover the Kau Desert in Hawaii. ▼

J.D. Griggs/USGS

ASK YOURSELF

Aside from molten rock, which one of the following commonly occurs in lava?

a. gas

b. crystals

c. rock fragments

d. All of the above are commonly associated with lava.

e. None of the above answers is correct—lava consists only of molten rock.

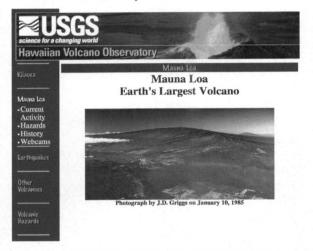
Volcanic gas is another material that is released during eruptions. Stored-up gases can cause a volcano to erupt explosively, covering the surrounding area with a catastrophic shower or flow of tephra. Gases can also seep out silently and poison a whole town overnight, as happened in Cameroon, a country in Central Africa, in 1984. The different kinds of eruptions and the volcanoes they build have much to do with the physical properties of the magma that lies at their source.

> **magma** Molten rock, which may include gas and fragments of rock, volcanic glass, and ash.

We will begin our discussion by taking a look at some of the different kinds of volcanoes.

Eruptions, Landforms, and Materials

All active volcanoes are dangerous on some level, but they have a range of eruption styles. **Figure 6.2** shows several types of volcanoes, arranged in order from most explosive to least explosive. The eruptive style of volcanoes can change from year to year, month to month, or even hour to hour; there is no such thing as an active volcano that is completely safe or completely predictable.

Volcanoes and Eruption Styles The most violent and famous eruptions (**Figure 6.2a**) are **Plinian eruptions**, named after Pliny the Elder, a Roman scholar who died during the eruption of Mount Vesuvius in 79 CE. They produce columns of ash, driven by violent streams of magmatic gas, that reach into the stratosphere 20 kilometers or more and create **pyroclastic flows** of hot cinders and ash that sweep down the mountainside like an avalanche. These flows travel much faster than flowing lava, and they are the most dangerous consequence of a volcanic eruption. **Vulcanian eruptions** are also very explosive. They propel billowing clouds of ash to a height of 10 kilometers or so and produce voluminous pyroclastic material.

> **pyroclastic flow** Hot volcanic fragments (tephra) that flow very rapidly, buoyed by heat and volcanic gases.
>
> **stratovolcano** A volcano composed of solidified lava flows interlayered with pyroclastic material. Such volcanoes usually have steep sides that curve upward.

Both Vulcanian and Plinian eruptions tend to build steep-sided volcanoes, called **stratovolcanoes**. Stratovolcanoes have a somewhat complicated structure, with alternating layers of pyroclastic material and solidified lava flows. Their height and steepness stem from the layers of hardened lava, which act as cement that holds the pyroclasts together.

Strombolian eruptions are mildly explosive, and the magma is typically gas-rich. The volcano may eject showers of pyroclasts hundreds of meters into the air. This type of eruption typically creates cones of loose volcanic rock, generally referred to as **tephra cones**. A **spatter cone** is a tephra cone that is built from irregular gobs of mudlike magma ejected from the volcano, whereas a **cinder cone** (or **scoria cone**) is a loose stack of small, solid pyroclasts, called cinders or (collectively) scoria (**Figure 6.3**). Loose pyroclasts are often welded together during the eruption or cemented together after deposition, forming pyroclastic rock. The rock is called **agglomerate** when the tephra particles are large and **tuff** when the particles are small.

Hawaiian eruptions are the least explosive, as the lava flows quietly over long distances and spreads out in thin, nearly horizontal layers. The flows gradually build up to form broad, flat volcanoes with gently sloping sides, called **shield volcanoes** (**Figure 6.2b**). They resemble a warrior's shield lying flat and may grow

> **shield volcano** A broad, flat volcano with gently sloping sides, built of successive lava flows.

to enormous size. Mauna Kea and Mauna Loa, on the Big Island of Hawaii, rise more than 10 kilometers from their bases (6 km below sea level) to their peaks, 4 kilometers above sea level. That makes them the tallest mountains on Earth, measured from base to peak.

Sometimes lava rises to the surface through long fissures, or linear cracks, rather than venting through a central crater. Some **fissure eruptions** are very voluminous, and produce vast, flat lava plains called **flood basalts** or basalt plateaus. Shield volcanoes, like Mauna Loa, often display some fissure activity as well.

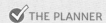
Geologists distinguish several types of eruptions on the basis of their explosiveness and the materials they produce. These differences are also reflected in the kind of landforms they build.

a. Explosive eruptions

Highly viscous magma prevents the release of gas, causing pressure to build. This leads to explosive eruptions with large volumes of pyroclastic ejecta.

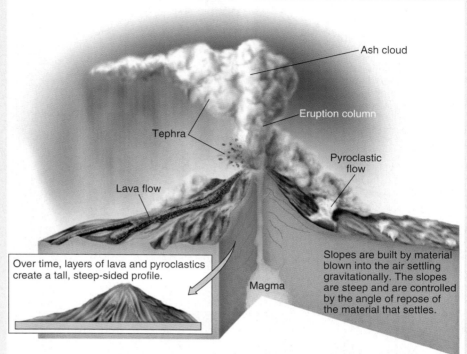

Ash cloud

Eruption column

Tephra

Pyroclastic flow

Lava flow

Magma

Over time, layers of lava and pyroclastics create a tall, steep-sided profile.

Slopes are built by material blown into the air settling gravitationally. The slopes are steep and are controlled by the angle of repose of the material that settles.

The steep-sided stratovolcano is built up over time with layer upon layer of pyroclastic material and less frequent lava flows. Examples of famous stratovolcanoes include Mt. St. Helens, Mt. Pinatubo, Mt. Mayon, and Mt. Fuji.

The 1993 Vulcanian eruption of Mt. Mayon, a stratovolcano in the Philippines, included pyroclastic flows like this one. ▼

©Reuters/Corbis-Bettmann

The Plinian eruption of Mt. St. Helens in May 1980 produced an ash column and released destructive pyroclastic flows and massive landslides and avalanches of rock, trees, and other debris down the steeply sloping sides of the volcano.

InterNetwork Media/Getty Images

Carsten Peter/NG Image Collection

Mt. Etna in Sicily is one of the most active volcanoes in the world. This Strombolian eruption occurred in 2002.

b. Quieter eruptions

No active volcano is completely safe, but some types of eruptions—particularly those associated with very runny lava compositions—are relatively quiet. Such eruptions can still be very large, though, with potentially regional or even global impacts.

Shield volcanoes have shallow, broad slopes, reminiscent of a warrior's shield lying on the ground. The magma is very hot when erupted and has low viscosity, so it flows easily. The slope of the volcano is low. As the magma flows, it cools, becomes more viscous, and flows more slowly. The slope of the volcano may steepen at the edges, creating a gently curved profile. The volcano is built up from successive lava flows, not from solid ejecta.

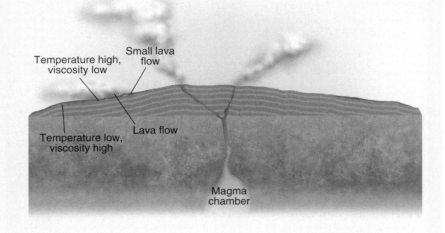

Temperature high, viscosity low

Small lava flow

Temperature low, viscosity high

Lava flow

Magma chamber

Frans Lanting/National Geographic Creative

Mauna Loa

Mauna Kea

Mauna Kea and Mauna Loa are very large shield volcanoes formed by Hawaiian eruptions.

Fissure eruptions, like this one in Hawaii, issue from long cracks in the ground.

Greg Vaughn/Alamy

©John S. Shelton/University of Washington Libraries, SpecialCollections

The Snake River Plains of Idaho are made of flood basalt—a very runny lava that erupts voluminously and flows into broad, flat plains.

THINK CRITICALLY

Why do volcanoes that erupt mostly pyroclastic material typically build steeper-sided landforms than volcanoes that erupt mostly lava?

Cinder cone • Figure 6.3

Cinder cones like this one in Arizona are steep, cone-shaped hills made of accumulated solid pyroclastic material. They are associated with both stratovolcanoes and shield volcanoes and typically result from gas-rich eruptions. Note the lava flow that has emanated from the base of the cone.

USGS

What causes the diversity of eruption types? The answer lies mostly in the kind of magma that provides the source for the volcano. Two factors are important: the viscosity of the magma and the amount of gas dissolved in it. If gas is present in the magma, it must escape somehow. If magma has low viscosity (that is, if it is runny), the dissolved gas can escape relatively easily. The lava may bubble and fountain dramatically, especially at the beginning of an eruption, but the volcano will not explode. However, if the magma is viscous (that is, thick), it is harder for gas bubbles to form and escape. Viscous magmas of the kind that build stratovolcanoes contain 60 to 70% SiO$_2$ by weight. When the gas finally does escape, it usually vents explosively.

> **viscosity** The degree to which a substance resists flow; a less viscous liquid is runny, whereas a more viscous liquid is thick.

Hawaiian eruptions consist of very runny, low-viscosity lava that flows easily from a volcanic vent and contains about 50% silica (SiO$_2$) by weight. The magma is very hot when erupted and has low viscosity, so it flows easily. The slope of the volcano is low. As the magma flows, it cools, becomes more viscous, and flows slowly. The slope of the volcano may steepen at the edges, creating a gently curved profile. The volcano is built up from successive lava slows, not from solid ejecta.

Other Volcanic Features   Near the summit of most volcanoes is a **crater**, a funnel-shaped depression from which gas, tephra, and lava are ejected. Some volcanoes have a much larger depression known as a caldera. Calderas form when the chamber of magma underlying a volcano partially empties due to eruption and the unsupported roof of the chamber collapses under its own weight. Crater Lake in Oregon (**Figure 6.4**) occupies a caldera 8 kilometers in diameter that formed after an immense eruption about 6600 years ago. Tephra deposits from that eruption can still be seen in Crater Lake National Park and over a vast area of the northwestern United States and southwestern Canada.

> **caldera** A roughly circular, steep-walled basin atop a volcano.

Crater Lake • Figure 6.4

Beautiful Crater Lake, Oregon, the deepest lake in the United States, is all that remains of a once-lofty stratovolcano that geologists have named Mount Mazama. Wizard Island, a small tephra cone in the middle of the lake, formed by resurgent activity after the collapse that created the caldera.

DESIGN PICS INC/NG ImageCollection

A resurgent dome of high-viscosity lava forms a small peak in the crater of Mount St. Helens, Washington, in May 1982. The plume rising above the dome is steam.

Volcanoes do not necessarily become inactive after a major eruption. If magma begins to enter the chamber again, it may lift the floor of the caldera or crater and form a **dome** of solidified magma. The caldera of Mount St. Helens contains a dome of magma that has been growing since the eruption of 1980 (**Figure 6.5**); it is referred to as a **resurgent dome** because it results from a resurgence of volcanic activity.

When volcanism finally ceases, the magma chamber still contains hot (though not necessarily molten) rock for hundreds of thousands of years. When groundwater comes into contact with this hot rock, it heats up and may create a **thermal spring**. Many such springs have been turned into famous health spas. Some thermal springs have a natural system of plumbing that allows intermittent eruptions of water and steam. These are called **geysers**, a name that comes from the Icelandic word *geysir*,

The Great Geysir • Figure 6.6 _____

Stokkur geyser, Haukadalur, Iceland, is close to the now dormant Great Geysir from which all geysers take their name. Haukadalur is a literal hotbed of geothermal activity.

meaning "to gush" (**Figure 6.6**). Some volcanic vents emit only gas—usually water vapor that's sometimes mixed with foul-smelling sulfur compounds. These features are known as **fumaroles**.

Volcanic Hazards

Since 1800, there have been 19 volcanic eruptions in which 1000 or more people have died from eruption-related causes (**Figure 6.7**). Note that in many cases, it was not the eruption itself, but rather the secondary and tertiary effects that were responsible for the greatest loss of life. Like other natural hazards, such as earthquakes, a volcanic eruption has **primary effects**, which are directly caused by the eruption itself; **secondary effects**, which are indirectly triggered by the eruption; and **tertiary effects**, which are long-lasting changes brought about by the eruption. Many effects of volcanism are harmful, but some, such as volcanic ash supplying nutrients to the soil, are beneficial.

Primary Effects   Most volcanoes produce at least some lava flows. Because people are usually able to outrun them, lava flows typically cause more property damage than injuries. In Hawaii, where Kilauea has erupted almost continuously for more than three decades, homes, cars, roads, and forests have been buried by lava, but not a single life has been lost (**Figure 6.8**). It is sometimes possible to control a lava flow, at least partially, with retaining walls or a water spray, but otherwise nothing can be done to stop an eruption from occurring.

The greatest threats to human life during volcanic eruptions do not come from lava but from pyroclastic flows and volcanic gases. Unlike slowly moving lava, pyroclastic flows move extremely rapidly and can easily outrace a running (or even a driving) human. The most destructive pyroclastic flow in the 20th century (in terms of lives lost) occurred on the island of Martinique in 1902, when an avalanche of searing ash descended on Mount Pelée at a speed of more than 160 kilometers per hour and killed 29,000 people. (There were two survivors.) In 79 CE, the Italian towns of Pompeii and

Deadly eruptions • Figure 6.7

Since 1800, there have been 19 volcanic eruptions in which 1000 or more people have died from eruption-related causes. These eruptions are marked on the map; they correspond closely to active subduction zones. One major event that doesn't appear on this map is the 1991 eruption of Mount Pinatubo in the Philippines because scientific monitoring and timely evacuations saved thousands of lives.

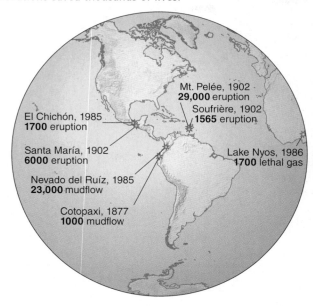

El Chichón, 1985
1700 eruption

Mt. Pelée, 1902
29,000 eruption

Soufrière, 1902
1565 eruption

Santa María, 1902
6000 eruption

Lake Nyos, 1986
1700 lethal gas

Nevado del Ruíz, 1985
23,000 mudflow

Cotopaxi, 1877
1000 mudflow

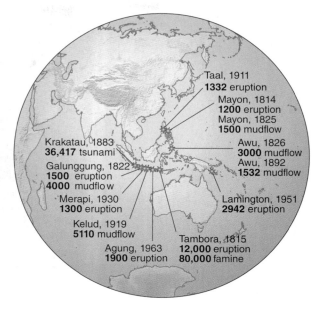

Taal, 1911
1332 eruption

Mayon, 1814
1200 eruption

Mayon, 1825
1500 mudflow

Krakatau, 1883
36,417 tsunami

Awu, 1826
3000 mudflow

Awu, 1892
1532 mudflow

Galunggung, 1822
1500 eruption
4000 mudflow

Merapi, 1930
1300 eruption

Lamington, 1951
2942 eruption

Kelud, 1919
5110 mudflow

Agung, 1963
1900 eruption

Tambora, 1815
12,000 eruption
80,000 famine

Herculaneum were buried under hot pyroclastic material, entombing the bodies and buildings in a natural time capsule (**Figure 6.9**). However, most of these people were dead already, due to another hazard of volcanic eruptions: poisonous gases. More recently, at least 1700 people and 3000 cattle lost their lives when poisonous gas erupted from a volcano at Lake Nyos in Cameroon. In 1783 the Laki eruption in Iceland released so much acidic gas that nearly one-third of the people and half of the domestic animals in the country perished.

Secondary Effects Secondary effects related to volcanic activity but not a direct result of it include fires (which are often caused by lava flows) and flooding (which may happen if a river channel is blocked or a crater lake bursts). The famous

Lava flow • Figure 6.8

This house in Kalapana, Hawaii, is about to succumb to the slow but unstoppable advance of a lava flow (in June 1989). The grass of the lawn burns on contact with the molten rock. As of 2015, lava continued to flow from Kilauea's Pu'u Ōō crater.

Francois Gohier/Photo Researchers,Inc.

Victim of Mount Vesuvius • Figure 6.9

During the eruption of Mount Vesuvius in 79 CE, this resident of Pompeii, Italy, was killed by poisonous gases, and then the body was encased in pyroclastic material. Over the centuries, the body decayed, but a mold of its shape remained in the tephra, later used to create this plaster cast.

Jonathan Blair/NG Image Collection

The basic structure of a volcano and the hazards it creates are illustrated here. These conditions need not all exist at once, but at least some of them occur in any major eruption.

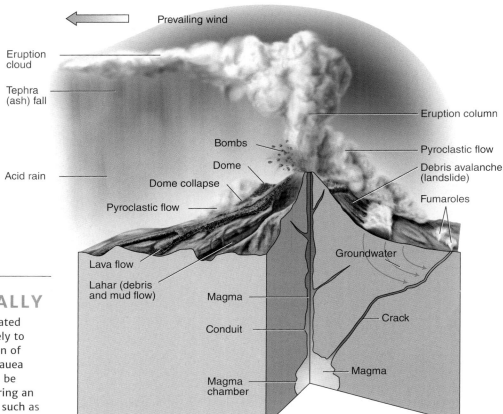

Prevailing wind

Eruption cloud

Tephra (ash) fall

Acid rain

Eruption column

Bombs

Dome

Dome collapse

Pyroclastic flow

Pyroclastic flow

Debris avalanche (landslide)

Fumaroles

Lava flow

Lahar (debris and mud flow)

Groundwater

Magma

Conduit

Crack

Magma

Magma chamber

THINK CRITICALLY

Which of the hazards illustrated here would you be most likely to encounter during an eruption of a shield volcano, such as Kilauea in Hawaii? Which would you be most likely to encounter during an eruption of a stratovolcano, such as Mount Pinatubo or Mount St. Helens?

eruption at Krakatau, Indonesia, in 1883 claimed most of its victims due to a tsunami, the same kind of ocean wave that can also be caused by earthquakes. Volcanoes can also produce **volcanic tremors**, a type of seismic activity that helps scientists predict eruptions but rarely poses a threat itself.

Mudslides have often been a major cause of volcano-related deaths. A deadly mudflow called a **lahar** can result from volcanic ash mixing with snow at the volcano's summit or rain falling on recently deposited volcanic ash. **Figure a** in the *Case Study* shows a lahar from the eruption of Mount Pinatubo. Lahars can occur months after the eruption. A related phenomenon is a volcanic **debris avalanche**, in which many different types of materials, such as mud, pyroclastic material, and downed trees, are mixed together. A devastating debris avalanche caused much of the damage from the 1980 eruption of Mount St. Helens. **Figure 6.10** summarizes the various primary and secondary hazards from an eruption.

Tertiary Effects   Volcanic activity can change a landscape. Eruptions can block river channels and divert the flow of water. They can dramatically alter a mountain's appearance, as in the 1980 eruption of Mount St. Helens. They can form new land, such as the black sand beaches of Hawaii, which are made of dark pyroclastic fragments, or the volcanic island of Surtsey, which emerged from the ocean near Iceland in 1963 and is composed of both lava flows and pyroclastic cones.

Volcanoes can also affect the climate on regional and global scales (**Figure 6.11**). Major eruptions can cause toxic rain and acid rain, spectacular sunsets, or extended periods

of darkness. Sulfur dioxide (SO_2), a common gaseous emission of volcanoes, forms small droplets, or **aerosols**. If they get into the stratosphere, these aerosols spread around the world, absorb sunlight, and cool Earth's surface. An example from recent times is the 1815 eruption of Mount Tambora in Indonesia, which caused three days of near darkness as far away as Australia. The following year was so cool in Europe and North America that it was called "the year without a summer." Farther back in time, the eruption of flood basalts, such as the Deccan Traps in India and the Siberian Traps in Russia, may have caused or contributed to several of the mass extinctions that divide geologic periods.

Beneficial Effects   Not all the effects of volcanic eruptions are negative, and it is no accident that many people choose to live near active volcanoes. Volcanic eruptions renew the mineral content of soils and replenish their fertility; some of the most fertile soils of the world are adjacent to active volcanoes (**Figure 6.12**). Volcanism also provides geothermal energy and some types of mineral deposits. One rare kind of volcanism brings up diamond-bearing magma from deep in the mantle. All natural gem-quality diamonds on Earth reach the surface through volcanism.

Predicting Eruptions

It isn't possible to stop volcanic eruptions, but it is sometimes possible to predict them. Prediction is based on a combination of understanding the geologic history of a volcano and monitoring present activity for any changes or anomalies.

Plinian Eruption in the Philippines

Mount Pinatubo is 90 kilometers northwest of Manila, in the Philippines. In 1990 Pinatubo was a vegetation-covered mountain that had not erupted for 500 years. Then, in July 1990, the region was rocked by a 7.8 magnitude earthquake, suggesting that Pinatubo might be waking up. By March 1991 villages around the volcano were feeling quakes, and on April 2 a small eruption of volcanic ash occurred.

Geologists knew that the plains around the volcano were underlain by thick layers of fertile volcanic ash, thousands of years old. Pinatubo had once been a dangerous volcano; could a cataclysmic eruption be on the way? On June 7 a dome-shaped mass of lava began to form. On June 9 geologists made a gutsy call: they recommended evacuation for everyone in a 20-kilometer radius; 25,000 people departed. The following day, 18,000 people were evacuated from Clark Airfield, the main U.S. Air Base in the Philippines. Concerns rose, and on June 13, the danger radius was extended to 30 kilometers; the number of evacuees from nearby towns rose to 58,000.

The main eruption commenced on June 15, 1991. It was the second-largest volcanic eruption of the 20th century. (The largest was Novarupta, Alaska, in 1912.) The top of the mountain exploded (**Figure a**), blasting a hole 2.5 kilome-ters in diameter and propelling volcanic ash and sulfurous gases more than 30 kilometers into the atmosphere. The cloud lingered in the stratosphere and lowered worldwide temperatures for the next year by half a degree.

By unfortunate coincidence, Tropical Storm Yunya was bearing down on the island at the time of the eruption. The rain-soaked ash caused roofs to collapse, and the unstable mud continued to flow downhill for months, burying towns, wiping out bridges, and causing more damage than the eruption itself. **Figure b** shows the town of Bamban, 30 kilometers away from Mount Pinatubo, being inundated with a hot volcanic mudflow one month after the eruption, and **Figure c** is a scene of the same area 3 months later.

Thanks to early warnings from geologists, most of the area around the volcano had been evacuated, so the eruption killed relatively few people. Although 847 people died (mainly due to mudflows), scientists estimate that up to 20,000 lives were saved by the timely evacuation.

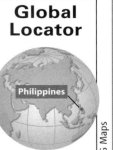

Global Locator

Philippines

NG Maps

a

Photri/The Image Works

b

Chris Newhall/USGS

c

Chris Newhall/USGS

THINK CRITICALLY

1. What do you think might have happened to local residents if the geologists had issued their warning too late?

2. What if they had issued the warning too early and the eruption had not occurred as predicted?

The eruption of Laki, a volcano in Iceland, from 1783 to 1784 had dramatic effects on global climate.

a. The fissure eruption of Laki produced the largest flow of lava in recorded history.

b. In the winter after Laki's eruption, the average temperature in the northern hemisphere was about 1°C below normal. In the eastern United States, the decrease was closer to 2.5°C. At the same time, ice cores from Greenland recorded a dramatic spike in acidity due to acid precipitation.

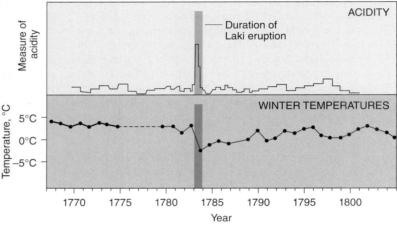

Establishing a Volcano's History

The first step in prediction is to identify a volcano as active, dormant, or extinct. An **active volcano** has erupted within recorded history, whereas a **dormant volcano** has not erupted in recent history. For example, Mount Pinatubo in the Philippines had been dormant for about 500 years prior to its awakening in 1991. An **extinct volcano** shows no signs of activity and is deeply eroded.

Another important step in prediction is identifying the volcano's past eruptive style. For example, Mount Pinatubo is surrounded by thick deposits of pyroclastic material, a sign that the volcano has erupted violently in the past. Subduction zone stratovolcanoes such as Mount Pinatubo and Mount St. Helens are more likely to erupt explosively than are shield volcanoes, so understanding the tectonic setting of the volcano is also important. The type of rock that has solidified from past eruptions, either silica rich or silica poor, also indicates the volcano's style of eruption.

Monitoring Changes and Anomalies

When a volcano starts to show signs of increasing activity, scientists begin to monitor it more closely (**Figure 6.13**). They watch for changes—sudden as well as gradual, cumulative ones—and anomalies—things that don't fit the pattern of activity that the volcano had previously established.

Many of these changes can be detected and monitored from space through remote sensing. Ground temperature

Fertile but dangerous • Figure 6.12

Farming villages speckle the slopes of Mount Merapi, an active volcano on the island of Java, Indonesia. Merapi has a long history of dangerous, often fatal, eruptions, but the fertility of its soils lures farmers to its hazardous slopes. Although volcanic soils cover just 1% of Earth's land surface, they support 10% of the world's population.

Process Diagram

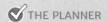

How scientists monitor volcanic activity • Figure 6.13

a. Volcano monitoring from the ground

Volcanic eruptions are almost always preceded by a host of physical changes that geologists can monitor, such as tremors, releases of gas, and changes in the slopes of the volcano.

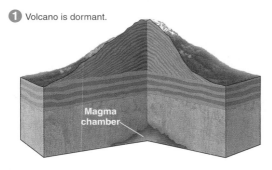

1 Volcano is dormant.

Magma chamber

2 Chamber receives an influx of magma, which begins to move upward into the volcano's feeder channel.

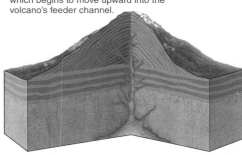

3 Many physical changes occur as magma moves up into the volcano. Monitoring allows geologists to track the movement of magma and note any sudden or significant changes that may signal an iminent eruption.

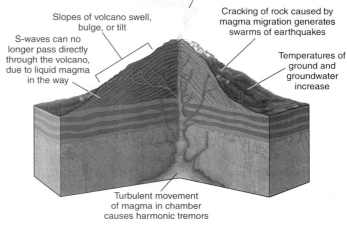

Volume and composition of gases emitted from volcano change

Slopes of volcano swell, bulge, or tilt

Cracking of rock caused by magma migration generates swarms of earthquakes

S-waves can no longer pass directly through the volcano, due to liquid magma in the way

Temperatures of ground and groundwater increase

Turbulent movement of magma in chamber causes harmonic tremors

b. Volcano monitoring from orbit

Recent lava flows around Mount Vesuvius show up bright red in this false-color satellite image, which records infrared radiation (indicating heat). Older lavas and volcanic ash show up in shades of yellow and orange. West of Naples lies a cluster of smaller volcanoes called the Flegreian Fields. By comparing successive satellite images, geologists can detect changes in ground temperature.

THINK CRITICALLY

How much time do you think would typically elapse between Step 1 and Step 3 in this series?

Naples

Mount Vesuvius

Flegreian Fields

National Remote Sensing Centre Ltd/ Photo Researchers, Inc.

changes can be detected using infrared imaging, for example (**Figure 6.13b**). Even changes in the shape of the land can be detected remotely: Scientists obtain two images of the area taken days or weeks apart and compare them digitally, highlighting even tiny changes in slope or orientation of the ground surface.

The first indications of forthcoming volcanic activity do not indicate the likely time of eruption—it might be weeks or months ahead. However, as more and more information is obtained, the predicted timing often can be refined. Eventually, geologists monitoring a volcano may reach a point where they can recommend that civil authorities evacuate nearby settlements until after the eruption. As a consequence, volcanic eruptions—even very large ones—tend to cause fewer fatalities than earthquakes because earthquakes are much more difficult to predict.

Volcanoes and Volcanic Hazards **149**

As magma intrudes upward from an underlying magma chamber, the crust is stressed and cracked by the intrusion, causing small earthquakes. Therefore, the first indication of a forthcoming eruption is usually the onset of swarms of small earthquakes. As an eruption approaches, the volcanic edifice swells in response to the intrusion of magma. Warning signs include changes in shape or elevation, such as bulging or tilting, or the formation of a dome. Swelling can be detected using tiltmeters, lasers, and other instruments that measure the shape and orientation of the ground surface. The presence of these features indicates that the underground reservoir of magma is growing.

Rising magma releases volcanic gases, and careful monitoring of changes in the rate of emission (volume per unit of time) and composition of gases is often helpful in predicting how soon an eruption will occur. In particular, an increase in the ratio of sulfur to chlorine in volcanic gas emissions is often an indication of an imminent eruption. Changes in ground temperature and changes in the temperature or composition of water in crater lakes, wells, or hot springs can also be warning signs.

STOP CONCEPT CHECK

1. **Why** do stratovolcanoes tend to erupt more explosively than shield volcanoes?
2. **What** is the difference between a crater and a caldera?
3. **Which** volcanic hazards pose the greatest risk to humans?
4. **What** physical changes are precursors to a volcanic eruption?

HOW, WHY, AND WHERE ROCK MELTS

Learning Objectives

1. **Describe** how temperature, pressure, and water content affect a rock's melting point.
2. **Explain** the processes of fractional melting.
3. **Identify** three properties that distinguish one lava or magma from another.
4. **Describe** the tectonic settings in which major magma types occur.

Underneath every active volcano lies a reservoir of magma, called a **magma chamber**. Understanding volcanism involves understanding how rock melts to become magma. Fortunately, rock can be melted artificially as well as naturally (**Figure 6.14**). Scientists have learned a lot about the behavior of molten rock from laboratory experiments and from practical work in metal foundries.

At Earth's surface, rock begins to liquefy when it is heated to a temperature between about 800°C and 1000°C. However, rock (unlike ice, for example) typically consists of many different minerals, each with its own characteristic melting temperature. Thus we cannot talk about a single melting point for a rock. Complete melting is commonly attained by about 1200°C, although some rock compositions have melting temperatures as high as 1500°C. Two other factors also strongly affect the melting temperature: pressure and the presence of water in the rock.

Heat and Pressure

If you descend into a mine, it becomes apparent that the farther down you go, the hotter it gets. The rate at which temperature increases with depth, called the **geothermal gradient**, is quite different underneath continental surfaces than it is under the seafloor. In the continental crust, temperature rises initially at about 30°C per kilometer; at depth, temperature rises increasingly slowly, for an average of about 6.7°C per kilometer, reaching 1000°C at a depth of more than 100 kilometers. Underneath the ocean floor, the rate of increase is about twice as rapid. The temperature increases by 13°C per kilometer, reaching 1000°C at a comparatively shallow depth. This is shown by the dashed lines in **Figure 6.15a**, which are lines of equal temperature, called **isotherms**. Below the asthenosphere–lithosphere boundary, the geothermal gradient becomes more gradual (0.5°C/km) and the temperature difference between suboceanic and subcontinental rock disappears (**Figure 6.15b**).

As you can see in Figure 6.15, the temperature in the upper mantle is higher than the temperature at which most rock types melt at Earth's surface. Yet the upper mantle is mostly solid. How is this possible? The answer is that the pressure also rises very dramatically with increasing depth, and increasing pressure causes rock to resist melting (**Figure 6.16a**). For example, albite, a common rock-forming mineral (a feldspar), melts at 1104°C at the surface. At a depth of 100 kilometers, the pressure is 35,000 times greater than it is at sea level. At that pressure, the melting temperature of albite rises to 1440°C, which still slightly exceeds the normal temperature at that depth. Thus albite remains solid when it is beneath the surface. In contrast, a decrease in pressure (for example as magma rises to the surface) lowers the dry melting temperature and can lead to an effect called **decompression melting**. This is why solid rock sometimes melts as it rises from depth in Earth's interior, and why some magmas stay molten all the way to the surface.

The presence of water (or water vapor) in rock can dramatically reduce the melting temperature (**Figure 6.16b**). By analogy, as anyone who lives in a cold climate knows, salt can melt the ice on an icy road because a mixture of salt and ice has a lower melting temperature than pure ice. Similarly, a mineral-and-water mixture typically has a lower melting

Molten rock: Artificial versus natural • Figure 6.14

Melting rock in foundries and laboratories has helped scientists to understand the natural behavior of molten rock.

a. In a foundry, steelworkers heat metal ores to the melting point in order to separate the metal from the surrounding rock. People first figured out how to melt rock to extract useful metals more than 8000 years ago.

b. A geologist in a protective suit measures the temperature of lava erupting from Mauna Loa, Hawaii. Bright orange, yellow, and white lava is hotter, whereas dull red, brown, and black colors indicate cooler lava.

temperature than the dry mineral alone. The effect of water on the melting of rock becomes particularly important in subduction zones, where water is carried down into the mantle by oceanic crust.

Fractional Melting Most rock is composed of many different minerals, and each mineral melts at a different temperature, so rock typically melts over a temperature range of 200 degrees or more. This means that the boundary between solid rock and melt (molten rock) is not well defined, as in

Geothermal gradient • Figure 6.15

Both graphs indicate how temperature increases with depth below the surface.

a. The lines of equal temperature, or *isotherms,* seem to sag underneath the continental crust because the rate of increase of temperature is slower there, compared to the increase in temperature under oceanic crust. The isotherms level off deeper under the surface.

b. Earth's surface is at the top of this graph, so depth (and pressure) increase as you move down. The dashed curve shows the geothermal gradient under oceans, and the solid curve shows the gradient under the continental crust. Note that the two curves merge below 200 kilometers.

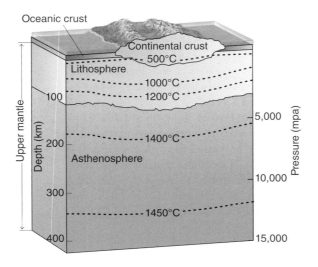

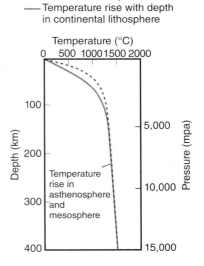

Increasing pressure with depth below the surface raises the melting temperature of rock. The presence of water can counteract this effect.

a. The melting temperature of a dry mineral (albite, in this case) increases at high pressures. A mineral at depth (shown by the small square) can melt in two different ways: either by an increase in temperature (red arrows) or by a decrease in pressure (blue arrows).

b. The melting temperature of a mineral in the presence of water typically decreases as pressure increases. This is exactly the opposite of what happens to dry minerals.

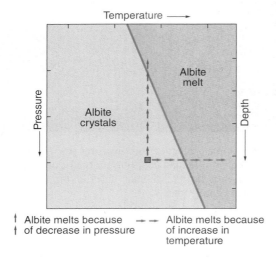

Albite melts because of decrease in pressure
Albite melts because of increase in temperature

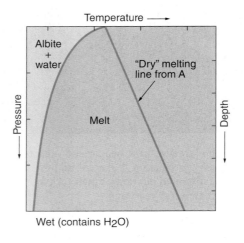

the melting of an ice cube, but blurry, as in **Figure 6.17**. When the temperature rises enough for part of the material in the rock to melt and part to remain solid, it becomes a **fractional melt**. Only if the temperature continues to increase or the pressure decreases will the rock melt completely. **Fractionation**, an important process that can lead to the development of a diversity of rock types, is caused by fractional melting. This kind of mechanical separation of melt from solid residue can occur in the lithosphere as a result of tectonic forces.

> **fractional melt** A mixture of molten and solid rock.
>
> **fractionation** The separation of melted materials from the remaining solid material in the course of melting.

hydrogen, and oxygen—Earth's most abundant elements. Oxygen combines with the other elements to form oxides, such as silica (SiO_2), Al_2O_3, CaO, and water vapor (H_2O). Silica usually accounts for 45 to 75% of the magma, by weight. In addition, a small amount of dissolved gas (between 0.2 and 3% of the magma, by weight) is usually present, primarily water vapor and carbon dioxide (CO_2). Despite their low abundance, these gases strongly influence the properties of magma. The proportion of silica also has a strong effect on magma's appearance and properties.

Temperature We know from direct measurements at erupting volcanoes that lavas vary in temperature from about 750°C to 1200°C. From laboratory experiments with synthetic magma, geologists know that magma temperatures in the mantle must rise as high as 1400°C. They also know that magmas with high H_2O contents tend to melt at lower temperatures.

Magma and Lava

As mentioned earlier, molten rock below the surface is called *magma*. When magma reaches the surface, it is called *lava*. A lot of magma never reaches the surface but instead remains underground, trapped in a magma chamber, until it crystallizes and hardens to igneous rock. We cannot study magma underground in its natural setting, but we can study lava, and we can experiment with synthetic magma. From our direct observations of lava, we know that magmas differ in composition, temperature, and viscosity.

Composition Most magma is dominated by silicon, aluminum, iron, calcium, magnesium, sodium, potassium,

Viscosity All magma is liquid and has the ability to flow, but magmas differ to a marked extent in how readily they flow. This is certainly true for lavas. As shown in **Figure 6.18**, some lava is very fluid, almost like a stream of water, but other lava creeps along slowly and steadily, like molasses.

Two properties in particular control viscosity: temperature and silica content. The higher the temperature, the lower the viscosity of lava. In **Figure 6.18b** the two lavas have the same composition, but the runny pahoehoe flow was erupted at higher temperature than the sticky aa flow. Lavas with high silica contents tend to flow slowly because of the tendency of silica molecules to polymerize, or form long chains

Process Diagram

How fractional melting and fractionation occur • Figure 6.17

Because most rock types contain a mixture of materials, they do not melt all at once, at a single temperature.

a. There is a range of temperatures and pressures in which the rock consists of a mixture of melted and unmelted crystals, called *fractional melting*. The numbered circles on this diagram correspond to the stages in the melting process, which are illustrated in part **b.**

b. Two minerals in a mixture melt at different rates. This can lead to fractionation (Step 4), the separation of melt from solid material of a different composition.

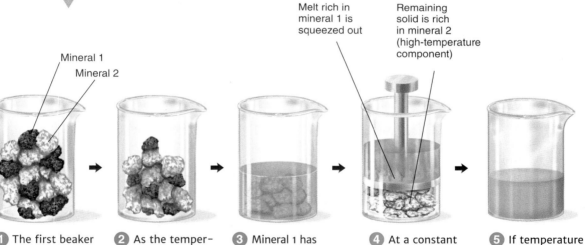

1. The first beaker shows a mixture of two minerals. At a low temperature, both are solid.

2. As the temperature increases, mineral 1 (the dark mineral) begins to melt.

3. Mineral 1 has totally melted and has dissolved some of mineral 2 in the process; the remainder of mineral 2 remains solid.

4. At a constant temperature, we have mechanically compressed the sample, separating the solid from the melt.*

5. If temperature were to continue to increase, the material in the beaker would eventually become completely melted.

*This kind of mechanical separation of melt from solid residue can occur as a result of tectonic forces.

THINK CRITICALLY

If you were to heat up a glass beaker full of crushed rock, the beaker would melt before you could finish studying the rock-melting process. How do you think geologists study rock melting in a laboratory?

Shield volcanoes commonly produce two kinds of basaltic lava: Low-viscosity **pahoe-hoe** lava (pronounced "pah-hoy-hoy") flows freely, whereas high-viscosity **aa** lava (pronounced "ah-ah") flows more slowly.

a. High-temperature, low-silica lavas tend to flow freely. This stream of low-viscosity (runny) pahoehoe lava was erupted in Hawaii in 1983, at a temperature of about 1100°C. ▼

J.D. Griggs/USGS

J.D. Griggs/USGS

▲ **b.** Two strikingly different lava flows are visible here at Kilauea, Hawaii. The smooth, ropy rock on which the geologist is standing formed from low-viscosity pahoehoe lava. The rough, chunky rock that the geologist is sampling is aa; it came from a more viscous, slow-moving flow that erupted years later.

(see **Remember This!**). Thick, slow-moving lavas have high viscosity, and these lavas have the greatest tendency to erupt explosively.

> **REMEMBER THIS!** Can you recall how and why polymer chains form in silicate materials? Review the section on *Mineral Families* in Chapter 2 to remind yourself.

The Three Main Kinds of Magma Fractionation leads to a wide diversity in magma compositions, but observations indicate that three compositions are predominant. **Basaltic magma** contains between 45 and 50% SiO_2 by weight, with a little dissolved gas. Formed in the mantle by decompression melting, basaltic magma has low viscosity, flows readily, and forms shield volcanoes.

In a subduction zone, oceanic crust on top of sinking lithosphere contains water and hydrous minerals; at a depth of about 100 kilometers, water is released, and wet fractional melting in the mantle produces magma that is of intermediate composition. **Andesitic magma** contains about 60% SiO_2 by weight and 2 to 4% by weight of dissolved gases—mainly H_2O. Such magmas are viscous and tend to be

erupted explosively with a lot of pyroclasts, forming tephra cones and stratovolcanoes.

When wet fractional melting occurs within the continental crust, the **rhyolitic magma** so formed contains between 70 and 75% SiO_2 by weight plus 3 to 8% by weight of dissolved H_2O. Rhyolitic magma is extremely viscous; it erupts violently and forms masses of volcanic ash. When most of the gas has escaped from a rhyolitic magma chamber, the remaining magma may be extruded as a sticky, slow-moving lava.

Tectonic Setting and Volcanism The location of a volcano has a great deal to do with the type of lava or magma that is found there and, hence, with the type of volcanic rock that is formed. Volcanoes are mostly found in two tectonic settings: near plate margins and above so-called hot spots in the mantle (see *Remember This!*). **Figure 6.19** illustrates the types of lava associated with these different locations.

> **REMEMBER THIS!** Can you describe the characteristics of the tectonic settings that are important locations for volcanic activity? Review the section on *The Plate Tectonic Model* in Chapter 4 to remind yourself.

At oceanic divergent margins, such as along midocean ridges (**Figure 6.19a**), the oceanic crust is quite thin, and the geothermal gradient is steep. This setting favors the eruption of hot, low-viscosity basaltic lavas. Basalt is generated by fractional melting of the underlying mantle. The magma rises through crustal fissures along the midocean range, creating new oceanic crust.

At ocean–ocean or ocean–continent subduction zones (**Figures 6.19b and c**), the subducting rock has a high water content and therefore melts at a lower temperature, as shown in Figure 6.16. Such magma will often solidify before reaching the surface, but it may stay molten for a variety of reasons. For example, fractional melting may separate the minerals with a higher melting point from those with a lower melting point and allow the latter to erupt to the surface. The resulting andesitic lava is cooler and more viscous than basaltic lava. Andesitic lava is more likely to erupt explosively, producing pyroclastic deposits and building stratovolcanoes.

The lava generated at mantle hot spots (**Figure 6.19d**) tends to be hot and basaltic, and it builds giant shield volcanoes by layering one fluid lava flow on top of another.

Finally, the lava formed in continental crust as a result of heat supplied from below by a hot spot (**Figure 6.19e**) tends to be rhyolitic and especially high in silica. Eruption of such material produces abundant pyroclasts, particularly in the form of volcanic ash.

STOP **CONCEPT CHECK**

1. **What** effect does H_2O have on the melting properties of rocks?

2. **How** does fractional melting contribute to the formation of a wide range of magma and lava compositions?

3. **Summarize** the properties that distinguish basaltic magma from andesitic and rhyolitic magma.

4. **How** do different tectonic settings lead to the formation of different kinds of magma?

COOLING AND CRYSTALLIZATION

Learning Objectives

1. **Explain** how different rock textures are produced in volcanic and plutonic rock.

2. **Identify** the three main compositional categories of igneous rock, based on their silica content.

3. **Explain** how different types of igneous rock can form from the same magma, through fractional crystallization.

Whereas melting influences the properties of magma, cooling and **crystallization** influence the properties of igneous rock. For example, the rate of cooling determines how large the individual mineral grains in the rock will grow. Grain size affects the appearance or

> **crystallization** The process whereby mineral grains form and grow in a cooling magma (or lava).

texture of the rock. The composition of the magma determines the final mineral assemblage in the solidified rock. Let's examine each of these factors more closely.

Cooling Rates and Rock Textures

Even a quick study of igneous rock types reveals that there are two large families. **Volcanic rock** forms from magma extruded at Earth's surface and is therefore also referred to as **extrusive rock**. **Plutonic rock** forms when magma crystallizes deep underground. This process is much slower and therefore gives the mineral grains time to grow larger, giving the rock an easily distinguishable texture. Because the rate at which magma cools influences the sizes of mineral grains that form, volcanic rock tends to have smaller mineral grains than more slowly cooled plutonic rock.

> **volcanic rock** Igneous rock that solidifies on or near the surface, from lava.
>
> **plutonic rock** Igneous rock that solidifies underground, from magma.

Rapid Cooling: Aphanitic Igneous Rock Sometimes magma cools so rapidly that mineral grains do not have a chance to form at all. The result is a naturally occurring, noncrystalline rock called **volcanic glass** (known as *obsidian* if it is rhyolitic in composition) (**Figure 6.20a**). Volcanic glass, like other types of glass, breaks along curved or wavy surfaces because it lacks a crystal structure to provide preferred planes of weakness; this wavy fracture pattern is called **conchoidal fracture**.

Often, mineral grains do form in rapidly solidifying magma, but they are extremely small and can be seen only with magnification (see *What a Geologist Sees*). Rock with this very fine-grained crystalline texture is said to be **aphanitic** (**Figure 6.20b**). Volcanic rock usually cools rapidly, so the texture is commonly aphanitic.

> **aphanitic** An igneous rock texture with mineral grains so small they can be observed only under a magnifying lens.

Dissolved gases, too, can affect the texture of volcanic rock. An erupting lava may froth and bubble; if the froth is blasted into the air and cools quickly, it forms **pumice**, a glassy rock that is full of bubbles.

Different lava types are generated in different tectonic settings.

a. Midocean ridge
Submarine pillow lavas such as these on the East Pacific Rise are typical of low-viscosity basaltic volcanism along divergent midocean ridges. The basaltic magma is generated by partial melting of the mantle. ▶

OAR/National Undersea Research/ Photo Researchers, Inc.

b. Ocean–ocean subduction zone
Ocean-ocean subduction zones are characterized by stratovolcanism, with andesitic lava flows and abundant pyroclastic material, as shown here in Gunung Semeru, Indonesia. ▼

Stocktrek Images/Getty Images, Inc.

c. Ocean–continent subduction zone
Andesitic lava flows and explosive pyroclastic eruptions are typical of volcanoes that form in subduction zones along ocean–continent convergent margins, as shown here in Vulcan Osorno, Chile. ▼

Pablo Corral Vega/NG Image Collection

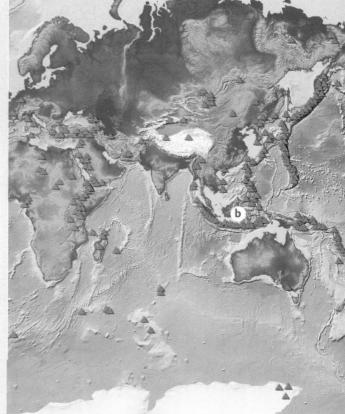

d. **Hot spot under a shield volcano**
Mantle hot spots typically erupt with low-viscosity basaltic lava flows, as shownhere at Kilauea Volcano, Hawaii. ▶

Philippe Bourseiller/The Image Bank/Getty Images

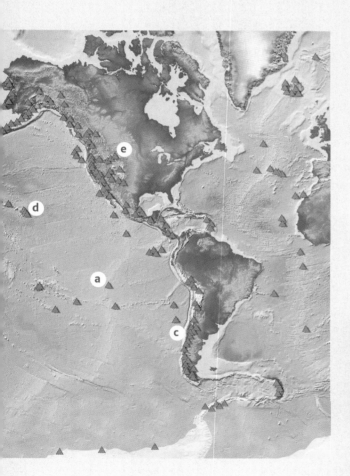

e. **Hot spot causing continental melting**
When mantle hot spots underlie continents, the magma must pass through thick continental rock of approximately granitic composition to reach the surface. The result is high-viscosity rhyolitic magma and explosive eruptions, as shown here in Yellowstone National Park. ▼

Raymond Gehman/NG Imag eCollection

The rate at which lava cools determines the size of grains in the resulting volcanic rock, with slower cooling producing larger grains.

a. Glassy texture Volcanic glass is a naturally occurring, noncrystalline material that forms when magma cools extremely quickly, preventing the formation and growth of crystals. It is often called *obsidian*, but that term technically refers to volcanic glass that is specifically rhyolitic in composition. Volcanic glass breaks with conchoidal fracture, as shown in this photo.

b. Aphanitic texture In this fine-grained rock, individual mineral grains cannot be discerned with the naked eye. The holes, or vesicles, are caused by trapped volcanic gas. In this sample from Hawaii, each of the largest vesicles is about the size of a small pea.

c. Porphyritic texture This volcanic rock sample from Nevada contains large mineral grains, or phenocrysts, suspended in an aphanitic groundmass. The largest grains visible in the photo are approximately 6 millimeters in length.

Siim Sepp/Shutterstock.com

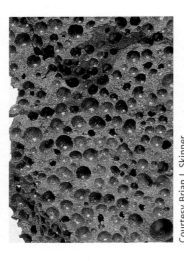

Courtesy Brian J. Skinner

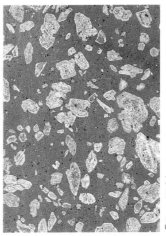

©Tony Waltham

As a gas-rich lava cools, the viscosity increases and it becomes increasingly difficult for gas bubbles to escape. When the lava finally solidifies into rock, the last bubbles may become trapped, leaving holes called **vesicles**. In basaltic lava, this process can create a vesicular rock that resembles Swiss cheese, as shown in Figure 6.20b.

In some cases, large grains begin to form while magma is still underground. Then, when it is erupted, the remaining magma solidifies quickly to form a fine-grained, aphanitic texture. The result is called **porphyritic** texture, and it is illustrated in **Figure 6.20c**. The large mineral grains are called **phenocrysts**, and the surrounding fine-grained material is the **groundmass** (see *Remember This!*).

> **REMEMBER THIS!** Sedimentary rock also can have large mineral grains encased in finer-grained material. What would such a rock be called, and how could you distinguish it from an igneous rock? Turn back to *Rock: A First Look* in Chapter 2, and then check out the section on *Sedimentary Rock* in Chapter 8.

Slow Cooling: Phaneritic Igneous Rock

> **phaneritic** An igneous rock texture with mineral grains large enough to be seen by the unaided eye.

Unlike aphanitic rock with its tiny mineral grains, **phaneritic** rock usually has time to form mineral grains that can be readily seen by the unaided eye (**Figure 6.21**). Plutonic rock is commonly phaneritic in

Plutonic rock textures • Figure 6.21

Two distinct phaneritic textures can be seen in this granite specimen from California's Sierra Nevada. The two outside layers have small but visible grains of quartz (clear), feldspar (white), and biotite (black). Sandwiched between them is a vein of pegmatite, which contains the same minerals in much larger grains.

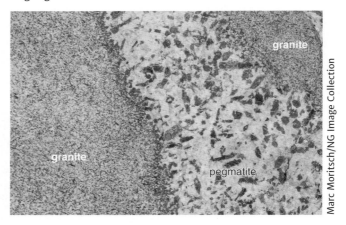

granite

granite

pegmatite

Marc Moritsch/NG Image Collection

THINK CRITICALLY

You know that volcanic rock can have porphyritic texture (as seen in Figure 6.20c), but what about plutonic rock? Can porphyritic texture occur in plutonic rock, and what would this indicate?

What a Geologist Sees

Putting Rocks under a Microscope

Faced with identifying the minerals present in an aphanitic igneous rock, a geologist turns to a microscope for help. The geologist first polishes a flat surface on a small fragment of the rock sample and then glues the polished surface to a glass plate. Careful grinding of the free surface of the sample to a thickness of just 0.03 millimeter makes the fragment thin enough for light to pass through

(**Figure a**). Geologists call these mounted rock slices *thin sections*.

Next, our geologist puts the thin section on the stage of a microscope and examines it under polarized light (**Figure b**). Different minerals appear differently in polarized light. The geologist identifies this sample as aphanitic vesicular basalt.

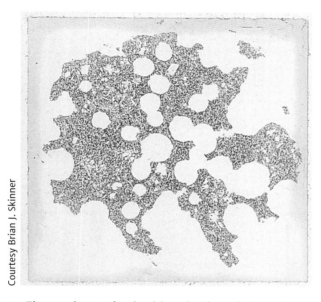

Courtesy Brian J. Skinner

a. The specimen of aphanitic volcanic rock from Figure 6.20b has been cut and polished to a thin section about 3.5 millimeters across.

William Sacco

b. In this specimen, the geologist has focused on an area about 0.05 millimeter across and can see white, needle-shaped plagioclase feldspar grains and smaller, brightly colored pyroxene gains. The dark background is volcanic glass.

THINK CRITICALLY

Notice that the individual mineral grains in the igneous rocks shown in the photographs in this chapter have irregular, interlocking boundaries.

1. Why would this be so?
2. Would a metamorphic or sedimentary rock look different? In what ways?

---

texture, because the magma cools and solidifies slowly; in contrast, rapidly cooled volcanic rock is more commonly glassy, aphanitic, or porphyritic. **Pegmatite** is a phaneritic igneous rock with mineral grains larger than 2 centimeters. Pegmatite with exceptionally large mineral grains (sometimes up to several meters!) may form in the last stage of crystallization of a plutonic rock body, when gases build up in the remaining magma. The vapor facilitates the growth of large crystals because chemicals can migrate quickly to the growing crystal faces.

Chemical Composition

Geologists subdivide the most common igneous rock types into three broad compositional categories, based on their silica contents. Rock that contains a large amount of silica (about 70% SiO_2 by weight) is usually light colored. Geologists call such rock **felsic** (a word formed from "feldspar" and "silica") because feldspar is typically the most abundant mineral. At the other end of the scale is **mafic** rock (a word formed from "magnesium" and "ferric," or iron rich), with a large amount of dark-colored minerals rich in magnesium and iron. Mafic rock is usually lower in silica content (about 50% SiO_2 by weight). Finally, igneous rock with about 60% SiO_2 by weight is said to be **intermediate**, in both composition and color.

Geologists thus organize igneous rock types in two ways: by grain size and by composition, especially silica content. The results are shown in **Table 6.1**. The rock samples on the left are volcanic (generally aphanitic), and the ones on the right are plutonic (almost always phaneritic). The ones on the top contain the most silica and are lightest in color, and the ones on the bottom contain the least silica and are darkest in color.

The composition of any igneous rock is closely related to the composition of its parent magma. Basaltic magma flows freely, tends to contain less trapped gas, and erupts less explosively. Rhyolitic magma, because of its high silica content, flows less freely, traps more gas, and thus tends to erupt

explosively. Therefore, the rock composition associated with a volcano gives an important clue to its history, showing how it has erupted in the past and how it is likely to erupt in the future.

Fractional Crystallization

Although the six igneous rock types summarized in Table 6.1 are the most common, there are literally hundreds of other kinds of igneous rock on Earth. The reason for this diversity is that a single magma source can differentiate into several kinds of igneous rock through **fractional crystallization**, a sort of reversal of fractional melting (**Figure 6.22**). Crystallization occurs over the same range of

> **fractional crystallization** The separation of crystals from liquids during crystallization.

Volcanic and plutonic equivalents · Table 6.1

Grain Size →

Silica Content of Magma	Resulting Volcanic Rocks		Resulting Plutonic Rocks	
High (= 70%–75%)	**Rhyolite** lies at the felsic, high-silica end of the scale, and consists largely of quartz and feldspars. It is usually pale, ranging from nearly white to shades of gray, yellow, red, or lavender.	 *Courtesy Brian J. Skinner*	**Granite** Granite, the plutonic equivalent of rhyolite, is common because felsic magmas usually crystallize before they reach the surface. It is found most often in continental crust, especially in the cores of mountain ranges.	 *Courtesy Brian J. Skinner*
Intermediate (= 60%)	**Andesite** is an intermediate silica rock, with lots of feldspar mixed with darker mafic minerals such as amphibole or pyroxene. It is usually light to dark gray, purple, or green.	 *Courtesy Brian J. Skinner*	**Diorite** is the plutonic equivalent of andesite, an intermediate silicarock.	 *Courtesy Brian J. Skinner*
Low (= 45%–50%)	**Basalt**, a mafic rock, is dominant in oceanic crust, and the most common igneous rock on Earth. Large-volume, low-viscosity lava flows from shield volcanoes and fissures are usually basaltic. Dark-colored pyroxene and olivine give it a dark gray, dark green, or black color.	 *Courtesy Brian J. Skinner*	**Gabbro** is the plutonic equivalent of basalt, a low-silica rock.	 *Courtesy Brian J. Skinner*

Silica Content ↑

During fractional crystallization, early-formed crystals can become separated from the remaining magma in several different ways, resulting in different rock compositions.

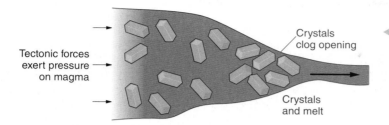

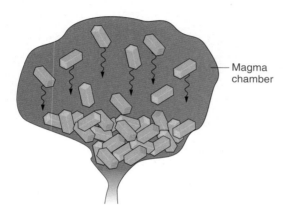

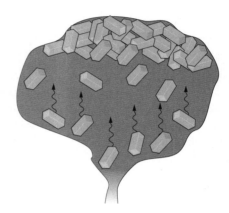

▷ **a. Filter pressing** Magma is squeezed through a small opening by tectonic forces. Only the liquid gets through, and the newly formed crystals are left behind.

▲ **b. Crystal settling** The first minerals to crystallize are denser than the melt and may sink to the bottom.

▲ **c. Crystal flotation** The first crystals are lighter than the liquid and may rise to the top.

THINK CRITICALLY

Can you think of some tectonic circumstances in which these crystal separation processes might happen?

temperatures as melting, and the last minerals to melt are the first to crystallize. If the early-formed crystals become separated from the remaining melt, the result is a rock and magma with different compositions, both of them different from the original magma.

Fractional crystalization was first investigated experimentally by Norman Bowen in the early 1900s. Bowen melted powdered rock samples and observed the sequence of minerals that crystallized from the melts. He hypothesized that rock types with widely varying compositions could form by differentiation from a single, homogeneous starting melt of basaltic composition. The sequence of mineral assemblages and resulting rock compositions, from early-crystallizing mafic to late-crystallizing felsic assemblages, is called **Bowen's reaction series**. Although real

crystallization is more complex than this, Bowen's model helps to explain the wide range of igneous rock types on Earth.

STOP CONCEPT CHECK

1. **How** does a rock form a porphyritic texture?
2. **What** are the plutonic equivalents of basalt, andesite, and rhyolite?
3. **How** does filter pressing lead to a separation of crystals from melt?

PLUTONS AND PLUTONISM

Learning Objectives

1. **Describe** the most common plutonic formations.

2. **Explain** why volcanoes create plutonic rock and plutons, in addition to volcanic rock.

Although perhaps less familiar than volcanic rock, plutonic rock gives rise to some dramatic geologic formations, known as **plutons** (**Figure 6.23**). Plutons are **intrusive** bodies, different from the rock that surrounds them (and different from volcanic rock, which is extrusive). They originate as magma, solidify while still underground, and are eventually exposed as plutons at the surface by erosion.

> **pluton** Any body of intrusive igneous rock, regardless of size or shape.

Many large plutonic bodies are granitic, or between granite and diorite in composition. The magma that forms the largest plutons probably results from extensive fractional melting of the lower continental crust. The magma migrates upward, squeezing into preexisting fractures and pushing overlying rock out of the way (**Figure 6.24**).

Batholiths and Stocks

> **batholith** A large, irregularly shaped pluton that cuts across the layering of the rock into which it intrudes.

Plutons are named according to their shapes and sizes. The largest type of pluton is a **batholith** (from the Greek words meaning "deep rock"). Some batholiths exceed 1000 kilometers in length and 250 kilometers in width. The Sierra Nevada, a very large batholith that forms the core of the Sierra Nevada Mountains and Yosemite National Park in California, is described in *Amazing Places*.

How magma rises • Figure 6.24

Magma forces its way upward by three main mechanisms: by wedging open preexisting cracks, by wedging off fragments of rock, called **xenoliths**, and by melting and assimilating some of the invaded rock.

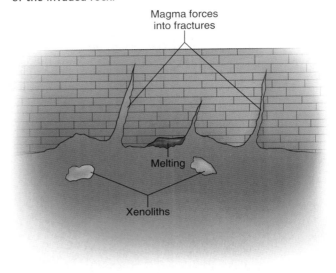

Magma forces into fractures

Melting

Xenoliths

THINK CRITICALLY

You encountered xenoliths in Chapter 5, as part of our discussion about how geologists use xenoliths to learn more about the mantle. Could the same approach be applied to xenoliths like the ones shown here, even though they didn't come all the way from the mantle?

Where they are visible at the surface as a result of erosion, the walls of batholiths tend to be nearly vertical. This early observation led geologists to believe that batholiths extend downward to the base of Earth's crust. However, geophysical measurements suggest that this perception is incorrect. Most batholiths seem to be only 20 to 30 kilometers thick. A smaller version of a batholith, only 10 kilometers or so in its maximum dimension, is called a **stock**. In some cases, as shown in Figure 6.23, a stock may be just a small part of a much larger batholith that lies underneath it.

Plutons • Figure 6.23

Volcanic necks are vertical plutons, whereas sills run parallel to the layering in the surrounding rocks, and dikes cut across the surrounding rock layers. Batholiths, the largest of all plutonic rock bodies, are deeply rooted.

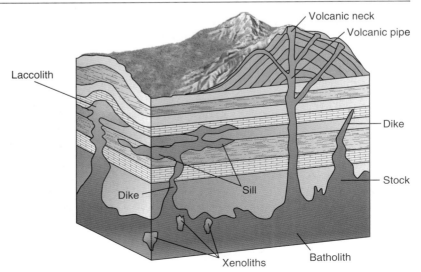

Laccolith

Volcanic neck

Volcanic pipe

Dike

Stock

Dike

Sill

Xenoliths

Batholith

Amazing Places

Sierra Nevada Batholith and Yosemite National Park

The Sierra Nevada Range, one of Earth's most striking mountain ranges, separates California from Nevada. At the core of the mountain range, approximately 650 kilometers in length overall, is the giant Sierra Nevada Batholith (see **Figure a**). Rather than one enormous pluton, the batholith is actually a composite body that consists of many smaller plutons, each one intruding previously emplaced plutonic bodies.

The melting and intrusion processes that produced the batholith commenced about 200 million years ago, at the end of the Triassic Period. At that time, the North American Plate began to override the Farallon Plate, an ancient oceanic plate that lay to the west of the continent. As the Farallon Plate was subducted under the continent, melting began to occur. Magma rose through the overlying continent, some of it reaching the surface through volcanism, and some of it cooling and solidifying underground as plutons. The formation of the intrusive bodies that comprise the batholith took about 100 million years overall. Subsequently, uplift and erosion exposed the parts of the batholith that are now revealed at the surface (see **Figure b**). Today, only fragments of the Farallon Plate remain, each with its own name—Juan de Fuca, Rivera, and Cocos. The Juan de Fuca

Plate, for example, is a small fragment of oceanic plate that is currently being subducted under the west coast of North America in British Columbia and Washington.

Granitic rocks of the batholith can be seen throughout the Sierra Nevada Range, but they are most strikingly displayed in Yosemite National Park, where soaring walls of granite confine the Merced River within Yosemite Valley (see **Figure c**). The valley has a long history of erosion dating back to the Cretaceous. Capped by glacial scouring during the most recent ice age. Yosemite—a National Park since 1864 and a UNESCO World Heritage Site since 1984—is a truly amazing place for its history and scenery, as well as for its geology.

Global Locator

Sierra Nevada

NG Maps

NASA

a. The Sierra Nevada Batholith is an enormous complex of plutons underlying the Sierra Nevada Mountain Range in the eastern part of California.

By Jon Sullivan [Public domain], viaWikimedia Commons

b. Half Dome, seen here from Glacier Point, is the exposed top of an enormous mass of granite that is just one small part of the Sierra Nevada Batholith.

c. Yosemite Falls, located just west of Half Dome, barrels more than 700 meters through massive granite to the Yosemite Valley below.

© Matej Hudovernik/ Shutterstock

THINK CRITICALLY

How deep are the roots of a batholith like the Sierra Nevada? (*Note:* This is not as simple a question as you might think! Scientists are still trying to figure out the exact answer, which requires grappling with a lot of questions about the processes of subduction and subcrustal melting, and how they work.)

Intrusion of magma into fractures forms smaller plutons such as dikes, sills, and volcanic necks, which are later exposed by erosion.

a. Dike
A dike of gabbro cuts across horizontal sedimentary rock strata in Grand Canyon National Park, Arizona.

b. Sill
The Palisades Sill, shown here, is a 100-meter-thick intrusive body of gabbroic composition. It was intruded along the contact between sedimentary rock strata of Triassic age, and it forms steep, high cliffs along the Hudson River.

c. Volcanic neck
This volcanic neck called Devil's Tower, in Wyoming, is all that remains of an ancient eroded volcano. You might remember this location for the role it played in the movie *Close Encounters of the Third Kind*.

Dikes and Sills

Smaller plutons tend to take advantage of fractures in the surrounding rock. Two of the most obvious indicators of past igneous activity are dikes and sills (**Figure 6.25**). A **dike** forms when magma squeezes into a cross-cutting fracture and then solidifies. If the magma intrudes between two layers and is parallel to them, it forms a **sill**. Sometimes this intrusion causes the overlying rock to bulge upward, forming a mushroom-shaped pluton called a **laccolith**. As shown in Figure 6.23, all of these intrusive forms may occur as part of a network of plutonic bodies.

Dikes and sills can be very large. For instance, there is a large and well-known sill-like mass made of gabbro that is visible in the Palisades, the cliffs that line the Hudson River opposite New York City. The Palisades Intrusive Sheet is about 300 meters thick. It formed from multiple charges of magma intruded between layers of sedimentary rock about 200 million years ago. The sheet is visible today because tectonic forces raised that portion of the crust upward, and then the covering sedimentary rock strata were largely removed by erosion.

As Figure 6.23 shows, plutons can also be connected to volcanoes. Beneath every volcano lies a complex network of channels and chambers through which magma reaches the surface. When a volcano becomes extinct, the magma in the channels solidifies into various kinds of plutons. A **volcanic pipe** is the remnant of a channel that originally fed magma to the volcanic vent; when exposed by erosion, it is called a **volcanic neck** (**Figure 6.25c**).

STOP CONCEPT CHECK

1. **What** are the names and characteristics of two commonly observed smaller tabular plutons?

2. **How** do plutons become exposed at Earth's surface, if they are formed underground?

 THE PLANNER

1 Volcanoes and Volcanic Hazards 139

- **Volcanoes** eject a wide variety of materials, including **lava** (molten rock, or **magma**, that has reached Earth's surface), gases, volcanic ash, larger pebbles, and rocks. The solid fragmental ejecta are collectively called tephra. Large tephra particles are called volcanic bombs, intermediate-sized particles are called lapilli, and the smallest particles are called volcanic ash. When tephra is consolidated into a rock, it is called agglomerate if the particles are large and tuff if they are small.

- The diversity of volcanic eruption types is mostly due to two factors: the **viscosity** of the magma and the amount of gas present in it. The viscosity of the magma in turn depends on its chemical composition, temperature, and gas content.

- **Shield volcanoes** and fissure eruptions tend to be quiet and nonexplosive. They gradually build up the volcano through a series of lava flows. **Stratovolcanoes** tend to erupt explosively. They are built up from a series of layers of lava and pyroclastic material.

- Funnel-shaped craters and much larger depressions known as **calderas** are common features at the summits of volcanoes. New magma may push up the floor of a crater or caldera and form a resurgent dome. If groundwater in the vicinity of an active magma chamber becomes heated, it may form thermal springs or geysers.

- Direct, or primary, volcanic hazards of volcanoes are hazards directly caused by the volcanic eruption. They include **pyroclastic flows**, lava flows, and poisonous gases (see the diagram). Secondary hazards are those triggered by the eruption, such as volcanic tremors or lahars. Some extremely large eruptions produce tertiary effects, long-lasting and even permanent changes brought about by the eruption. One example is a worldwide drop in temperature because of aerosols in the upper atmosphere. Tertiary effects can also be beneficial—for example, the creation of new land or rich volcanic soil.

Volcanic hazards · Figure 6.10

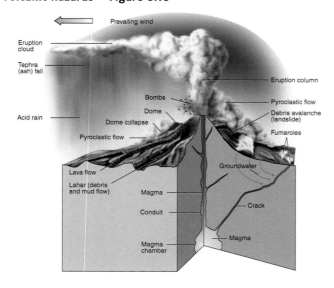

- For purposes of prediction, volcanoes are categorized as active, dormant, or extinct. The past eruption style of a volcano is a guide to its future behavior. Scientists can often tell an eruption is coming because of changes in seismic activity, gas emissions, ground and water temperatures, and the slope of a volcano's sides. They cannot yet predict exact eruption times, but by monitoring a volcano and watching for signs of anomalies, they can often recommend evacuation of the area days or weeks before an eruption.

2 How, Why, and Where Rock Melts 150

- Both temperature and pressure increase with depth. The geothermal gradient is the increase of temperature with depth. The rate of increase with depth is less through and under the continental crust than it is through and under the oceanic crust, as shown on the graph.

Geothermal gradient · Figure 6.15

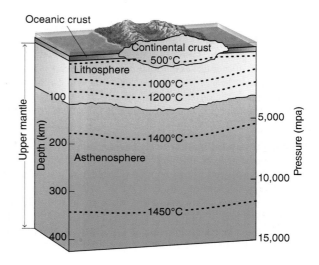

- Minerals can melt in two ways: through an increase in temperature or through a decrease in pressure (known as decompression melting). The presence of water in a rock typically lowers its melting point.

- Rock-forming minerals melt at different temperatures, so rocks do not have a single melting point; rather, they melt over a range of temperatures. A **fractional melt** is a body of rock in which some materials have melted and others have not. Fractional melting often separates minerals through a process called **fractionation.** When rock begins to melt, only a small volume of melt—a partial melt—forms at first. In some circumstances, the melt may become segregated from the remaining solid rock (e.g., by filter pressing), which may then continue to melt on its own. The separated material will have a different mineral composition from the original rock.

- Magmas can be distinguished from one another by composition, temperature, and viscosity. Magma that has a high silica content usually has a low melting temperature and high viscosity. Medium- to high-silica magma typically forms at convergent margins, where one plate subducts under another and where water is involved in the melting process. Very high-silica magma may have passed through continental crust on its way to the surface. Low-silica basaltic magma commonly forms at divergent margins, such as midocean ridges, and at hot spots.

3 Cooling and Crystallization   155

- **Crystallization**, the process whereby mineral grains form and grow in cooling magma or lava, influences some properties of igneous rock, such as texture and grain size. The crystallization process and the final mineral assemblage in turn depend on factors such as the magma composition and rate of cooling. Magma that cools from the molten state more rapidly will have smaller grains because the grains do not have as much time to crystallize.

- Igneous rock can be classified as **volcanic** or **plutonic**. Volcanic rock crystallizes from lava; plutonic rock crystallizes underground, from magma. Because volcanic rock cools rapidly, the crystals are usually small, microscopic, or even absent, with a texture known as **aphanitic**. Plutonic rock is typically **phaneritic**, with easily visible crystal grains.

- Felsic rock is typically light in color, with high silica content; mafic rock is typically darker, with lower silica and higher iron contents. The most common volcanic rock is basalt, a dark, low-silica (mafic) rock that is the main constituent of oceanic crust. Granite, a light-colored, high-silica (felsic) plutonic rock, is a dominant constituent of continental crust.

- **Fractional crystallization** occurs when mineral grains become separated from the melt from which they are crystallizing. This separation can happen if the crystals sink to the bottom (crystal settling) or float to the top of the magma (crystal flotation). If magma flows through an opening that is too constricted to allow the crystals to pass through, separation by filter pressing may occur. The combination of different magma compositions, rates of cooling (see the photo), and fractional crystallization leads to the great diversity of igneous rock types on Earth.

Plutonic rock textures · Figure 6.21

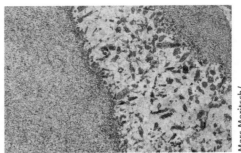

Marc Moritsch/
NG Image Collection

4 Plutons and Plutonism   162

- Plutonic rock bodies, or **plutons**, form underground when magma intrudes into preexisting rock strata, either cutting through them or flowing between them, as shown in the diagram.

Plutons · Figure 6.23

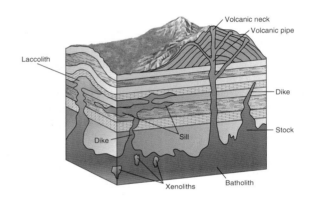

- Plutons, which occur in a variety of sizes and shapes, can be exposed at the surface when surrounding rock is stripped away by weathering and erosion. The largest type of pluton is a **batholith**, an irregularly shaped igneous body more than 50 kilometers in diameter, which cuts across the rock it intrudes on. A stock is a smaller version of batholith. Two smaller types of plutons, dikes and sills, are indicators of past magmatic activity.

KEY TERMS

CRITICAL AND CREATIVE THINKING QUESTIONS

1. For many years, scientists debated the reasons for the existence of Earth's geothermal gradient. What explanations can you think of for the hotter temperatures toward the center of Earth? Why is the geothermal gradient steeper under the oceans than elsewhere?

2. Volcanic rock is sometimes called *extrusive*, and plutonic rock is sometimes called *intrusive*. Why do you think geologists describe them this way? (You might want to look up these words in a dictionary.)

3. What factors might prevent magma from reaching Earth's surface?

4. The slopes of active volcanoes tend to be populated. What reasons can you think of for living near a volcano? Do you think the advantages outweigh the disadvantages? Why or why not?

5. Several flood basalt eruptions apparently occurred at roughly the same time as mass extinctions that divide geologic eras or periods. But geologists are not sure yet whether volcanic activity actually causes mass extinctions. What are some arguments for and against this theory?

6. Which line in Figure 6.16a illustrates decompression melting? Sketch this line onto the graph in Figure 6.16b (assuming that the two axes are the same). Note that the line no longer illustrates decompression melting when it is transposed to Figure 6.16b; why is this? Is it possible to show decompression melting using Figure 6.16b?

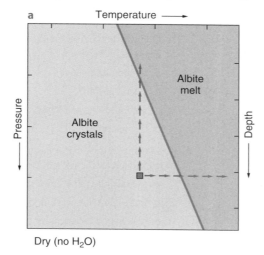

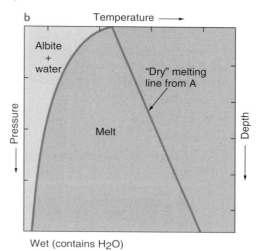

WHAT IS HAPPENING IN THIS PICTURE?

Pumice, a volcanic rock, is so light that this person has no trouble lifting a large mass over their head.

THINK CRITICALLY

1. How can rock be this light?

2. What does this rock sample tell us about the magma from which it came?

SELF-TEST

1. _____ are explosive eruptions characterized by pyroclastic flows and ash plumes that extend into the stratosphere.

   a. Vulcanian eruptions

   b. Hawaiian eruptions

   c. Plinian eruptions

   d. Strombolian eruptions

2. _____ consist of low-viscosity lava that flows easily from a volcanic vent.

   a. Vulcanian eruptions

   b. Hawaiian eruptions

   c. Plinian eruptions

   d. Strombolian eruptions

3. These two photographs show the Mauna Loa, Mauna Kea, and Mount St. Helens volcanoes. Of these volcanoes, which has the greatest potential for an explosive eruption?

   a. Mauna Loa

   b. Mount St. Helens

   c. Mauna Kea

   d. They all have equal potential for an explosive volcanic eruption.

4. Which of the volcanoes shown in the photos in question 3 is being fed by magma with the highest viscosity?

   a. Mauna Loa

   b. Mount St. Helens

   c. Mauna Kea

   d. The magma composition is probably identical for all of these volcanoes.

5. _____ form when the chamber of magma underlying a volcano empties due to eruption and the unsupported roof of the chamber collapses under its own weight.

   a. Fumaroles

   b. Geysers

   c. Calderas

   d. Craters

6. The greatest threats to human life during volcanic eruptions do not come from lava but from _____ and _____.

   a. pyroclastic flows; mudflows

   b. pyroclastic flows; ash fall

   c. ash fall; mudflows

   d. ash fall; volcanic gases

7. One way geologists monitor volcanic activity is by studying changes in the shape of volcanic features by using _____.

   a. temperature gauges

   b. seismographs

   c. geologic studies of past eruptions

   d. tiltmeters

8. Melting of rock can occur because of _____ and can be facilitated by the presence of water.

   a. increasing temperature or increasing pressure

   b. increasing temperature or decreasing pressure

   c. decreasing temperature or decreasing pressure

   d. decreasing temperature or increasing pressure

9. These two photographs are close-up views of two igneous rock samples. Label each appropriately with the following terms:

   porphyritic texture   volcanic rock

   phaneritic texture   plutonic rock

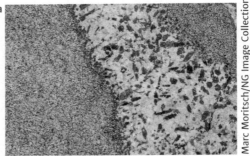

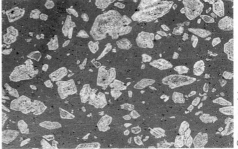

10. Which of the samples depicted in the photographs in question 9 cooled more slowly?

    a. The sample labeled **a**.

    b. The sample labeled **b**.

    c. Both rocks cooled quickly.

    d. Both rocks cooled slowly.

11. Which of the samples depicted in the photographs from question 9 records two distinct phases of cooling—slow followed by rapid?

    a. The sample labeled **a**.

    b. The sample labeled **b**.

    c. Neither. Both rocks cooled at the same rate.

12. These six photographs show volcanic rock samples paired with their plutonic equivalents. Identify each and label the photograph with the proper rock name from the following list:

    basalt   andesite

    granite   gabbro

    rhyolite   diorite

Courtesy Brian J. Skinner

1. _____   2. _____

Courtesy Brian J. Skinner

3. _____   4. _____

5. _____   6. _____

13. In the process of _____, crystals that have already formed in magma become separated from the remaining melt.

    a. magmatic redistribution

    b. distributed crystallization

    c. fractional crystallization

    d. fractional melting

14. Label this block diagram, depicting various plutonic bodies, using the following terms:

    dike   volcanic neck

    sill   stock

    batholith   xenoliths

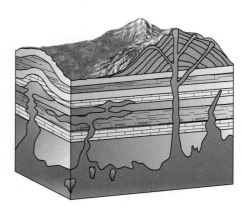

15. The plutonic features depicted in the block diagram in question 14 will become exposed at Earth's surface _____.

    a. through continued volcanic eruptions

    b. through uplift and erosion

    c. through melting of the overlying rock

    d. only after an explosive volcanic eruption

THE PLANNER ✓

Review the Chapter Planner on the chapter opener and check off your completed work.

7 WEATHERING AND EROSION

Global Locator

Bryce Canyon National Park

NG Maps

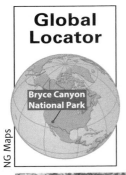

Taylor S. Kennedy/NG ImageCollection

Frank Krahmer/Masterfile

☑ CHAPTER PLANNER

- Study the picture and read the opening story.
- Scan the Learning Objectives in each section:
  p. 171   p. 181   p. 186
- Read the text and study all visuals. Answer any questions.

Analyze key features
- Process Diagram, p. 172
- What a Geologist Sees, p. 173
- Amazing Places, p. 174
- Geology InSight, p. 178–179
- Case Study, p. 185
- Stop: Answer the Concept Checks before you go on:
  p. 180   p. 184   p. 191

End of chapter
- Review the Summary and Key Terms.
- Answer the Critical and Creative Thinking Questions.
- Answer What is happening in this picture?
- Complete the Self-Test and check your answers.

HOODOOS OF BRYCE CANYON

Utah's Bryce Canyon National Park is a fantastic landscape of multicolored spires called *hoodoos*. The Paiute believed the shapes were people who had been turned to stone as punishment for evil deeds.

Hoodoos are a testament to the relentless geological processes of weathering and erosion. They form from the narrow rock walls, or fins, seen in the photograph. Water seeps into fractures and by repeatedly freezing and thawing pries the cracks open. Boulders come loose and break away from the fin, creating a window or an arch. Eventually the roof of the arch collapses, leaving a spire on either side.

Many of the hoodoos at Bryce Canyon have names such as "The Rabbit" or "Three Wise Men." But they are among the most short-lived of geological features—each hoodoo loses about 1 meter of height per century. In a few centuries, the hoodoos of today will be completely weathered away.

WEATHERING—THE FIRST STEP IN THE ROCK CYCLE

Learning Objectives

1. **Describe** how and where the breakdown of rock occurs.

2. **Describe** the main processes that contribute to mechanical weathering.

3. **Explain** the three main types of chemical reactions involved in chemical weathering.

4. **Summarize** the conditions of climate, topography, and rock composition that are conducive to different types of rock weathering.

Earth's surface is a meeting place. It is where the activities of Earth's internally driven processes—plate motion, seismicity, rock deformation, and volcanism—confront the quicker-paced activity of Earth's surface layers: the atmosphere, hydrosphere, and biosphere. The external forces of wind, water, and ice constantly modify the surface, cutting away material here, depositing material there, and sculpting the landscapes that surround us.

All of this activity is part of the **rock cycle**, one of the three great cycles that drive the Earth system, as shown in **Figure 7.1**. (This figure also appears in Chapters 1, 4, and 11; compare the four versions of the diagram.) The Earth system has three interconnected parts: the hydrologic cycle, the rock cycle, and the tectonic cycle. The rock cycle is in the middle because it is directly affected by the other two. The tectonic cycle is the subject of Chapters 4 through 6, and the rock cycle is the subject of this chapter and Chapters 8 through 10. Then in Chapters 11 through 14 we will turn our attention to the hydrologic cycle.

The rock cycle has no beginning or end; it is an endless set of processes, powered by Earth's internal heat energy and by incoming energy from the Sun. Nevertheless, we have to jump in somewhere, so we will begin our discussion with **weathering**, the set of processes that break bedrock into smaller rock and mineral fragments. Later in the chapter we will look more closely at **erosion**, the set of processes that pick up and transport weathered rock fragments.

> **rock cycle** The set of crustal processes that form new rock, modify it, break it down, transport it, and deposit it anew.

> **weathering** The chemical and physical breakdown of rock exposed to air, moisture, and living organisms.

> **erosion** The transport of loosened particles of rock, either downslope by the pull of gravity, or by a fluid, such as water, air, or moving ice.

The rock cycle • Figure 7.1

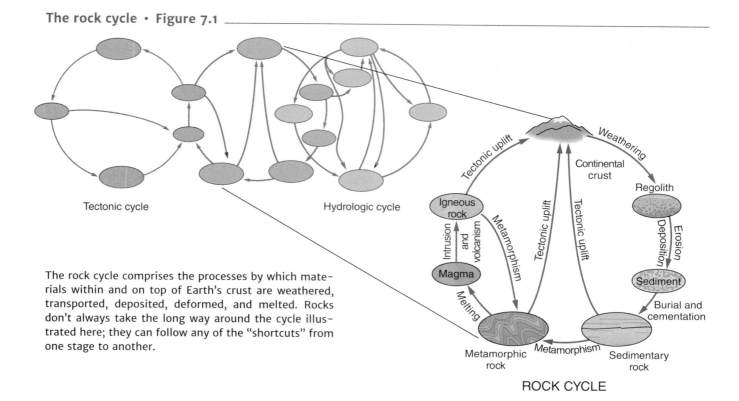

The rock cycle comprises the processes by which materials within and on top of Earth's crust are weathered, transported, deposited, deformed, and melted. Rocks don't always take the long way around the cycle illustrated here; they can follow any of the "shortcuts" from one stage to another.

Tectonic cycle

Hydrologic cycle

ROCK CYCLE

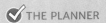

How rock disintegrates • Figure 7.2

Weathering causes the progressive breakdown of rock into smaller units. Each time a cube (**a**) is subdivided, the available surface area doubles (**b**) This renders the rock more susceptible to attack by agents of weathering. Little by little, the corners and edges become rounded, and the particles become smaller as the rock disintegrates.

a

1

1 unit

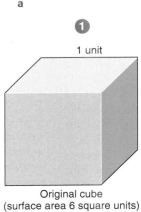

Original cube
(surface area 6 square units)

2

¹/₂ unit

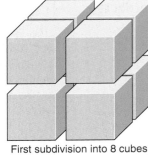

First subdivision into 8 cubes
(surface area 12 square units)

3

¹/₄ unit

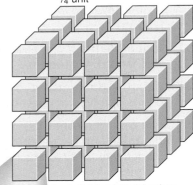

Second subdivision into 64 cubes
(surface area 24 square units)

b

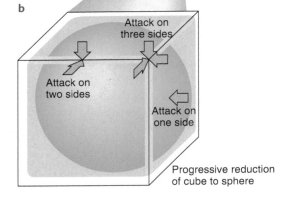

Attack on three sides

Attack on two sides

Attack on one side

Progressive reduction of cube to sphere

THINK CRITICALLY

What additional steps have to happen in order to complete the transformation of this disintegrated rock into soil?

Animals Animals/National Geographic Creative

Rock in this outcrop in Kansas has become fragmented, forming regolith. Water and air have penetrated the fractures and reacted with the minerals; rock near the surface is heavily weathered because it is more exposed to water and air. At the surface, the regolith has completely turned to soil.

Weathering: How Rock Disintegrates

Weathering takes place throughout the zone in which materials of the geosphere, hydrosphere, atmosphere, and biosphere can mix. This zone extends downward, below Earth's surface as far as air, water, and microscopic organisms can readily penetrate, and it ranges from 1 meter to hundreds of meters in depth. Rock in the weathering zone usually contains numerous **fractures** (cracks) and **pores** (small spaces between mineral grains) through which water, air, and organisms can enter. Given enough time, they produce major changes in the rock (**Figure 7.2**).

The product of weathering is fragmented rock. This material forms a loose layer that unevenly covers Earth's surface; it is called **regolith**, from the Greek words meaning "blanket" and "stone." Fragments in the regolith range in size from microscopic to many meters across, but all of them have formed by chemical and physical breakdown of bedrock. As the particles of rock get smaller and smaller, plants become capable of growing roots into the regolith and extracting mineral nutrients from it. Organisms—both microscopic and macroscopic—begin to carry out biological activity in the fragmented rock, and contribute organic matter to it. At this point, the regolith becomes **soil**.

> **regolith** A loose layer of broken rock and mineral fragments that covers most of Earth's surface.
>
> **soil** The uppermost layer of regolith, which can support rooted plants.

Joint Formation

a. Looking at this rock outcrop in Joshua Tree National Monument in California, a geologist would notice the uniform texture, lack of layering, and abundant fractures. The geologist would see that some of the fractures, called *joints*, have been widened by weathering, to the point of detaching some stones from the main rock body. ▼

Jeff Foott /Getty Images, Inc.

b. The geologist would understand that the joints originally formed underground, where the rock mass was subjected to great pressure from the overlying and surrounding rock. Squeezing and twisting by tectonic forces caused the rock to fracture and form joints.

c. Now that the rock is at the surface, the geologist would wonder about the sequence of events after the fracturing happened. The rock mass slowly rose to the surface as the overlying rock eroded away. This caused pressure on the rock mass to be decreased, allowing the rock to expand and crack. Later, weathering rounded off and widened the joints even further. ▼

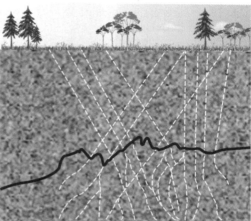

Ancient surface

Removed by erosion

Modern surface

THINK CRITICALLY

How would the presence or absence of joints affect the rate of weathering of a rock mass?

---

mechanical weathering The breakdown of rock into solid fragments by physical processes that do not change the rock's chemical composition.

chemical weathering The decomposition of rock and minerals by chemical and biochemical reactions.

The breakdown processes involved in weathering fall into two general categories. In **mechanical weathering**, the rock physically breaks down into pieces, but there is no change in its mineral content. **Chemical weathering** involves the dissolving of minerals or chemical reactions that replace the original minerals with new minerals that are stable at Earth's surface. Although mechanical weathering is distinct from chemical weathering, the two processes almost always occur together, and their effects are sometimes difficult to separate.

Mechanical Weathering

Rock in the upper half of the crust is brittle, and like any other brittle material, rock breaks when twisted, squeezed, or stretched, as it commonly is by tectonic forces. Although we cannot always determine the timing and origin of tectonic forces, we can see the results in the form of **joints**. *What a Geologist Sees* examines how joints commonly form.

joint A fracture in rock, along which no appreciable movement has occurred.

Joints are the main passageways through which rainwater, air, and small organisms enter the rock and lead to mechanical and chemical weathering, as you see in **Figure 7.3**. Joints differ from faults (Chapter 5) in that there has not been any noticeable slippage along the fracture; a fault, by definition, is a fracture along which movement has occurred in the masses of rock on either side.

Some of the world's most scenic and best-loved peaks are joint-free rock masses that resist mechanical weathering because water cannot find an entry. A **monadnock** (or **inselberg**) is a mountain that stands above the surrounding low-lying plain, as a result of its resistance to weathering and erosion. The formation of monadnocks is described in *Amazing Places*.

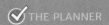
Monadnock—and Monadnocks

Mount Monadnock (**Figure a**), a 1156-meter peak in New Hampshire, is one of the world's most frequently climbed mountains—it is easy to climb, yet rewards the climber with a beautiful view of all six New England states. The name **monadnock**, from an Algonquin phrase meaning "mountain standing alone," has become a generic term for a mountain that rises out of a surrounding plain. (A term with similar meaning that is used more often by geologists is **inselberg**.)

a

© DenisTangneyJr/iStockphoto

Monadnocks are isolated, either because they are un-jointed or because they were made of more resistant material than the surrounding landmass. They can be made of any weathering-resistant rock type. Mount Monadnock is made of schist (a metamorphic rock). Another famous example, Uluru (or Ayers Rock), in Australia (**Figure b**), is made of arkose, a sedimentary rock. Uluru is a remnant of sedimentary strata about 500 million years old. During several periods of

tectonic activity, the strata were twisted and uplifted to an almost vertical position. This can be seen in the aerial view of Uluru (**Figure c**), in which the edges of the vertical strata are visible. After being uplifted, the surrounding rock—less resistant to weathering—was rapidly weathered and eroded away. The part of Uluru that is visible above the surface is just the tip of a much larger rock mass that extends deep underground.

Richard Nowitz/NG Image Collection

b

NASA

c

THINK CRITICALLY

Monadnocks are formed when the rock around them is eroded. If the resistant rock mass was in the form of a long, horizontally continuous stratum, what would the resulting feature look like after the surrounding material eroded away?

Joints are not always straight. In a process called **sheet jointing** or **exfoliation** (**Figure 7.3a**), large, curved slabs of rock peel off from the surface of a uniformly textured igneous rock. As with other types of joints, sheet jointing may be due to pressure release or a combination of forces that contribute to mechanical weathering.

Mechanical weathering takes place in four main ways—through freezing of water, formation of salt crystals,

Mechanical weathering occurs when rock disintegrates into smaller fragments by physical means, rather than as a result of chemical reactions.

a. Sheet jointing

Sheet jointing, or exfoliation, results in curved domes, like the famous Half Dome in Yosemite National Park, California.

b. Frost wedging

This granite boulder in the San Andres Mountains of New Mexico has been split apart by repeated freezing and thawing of water that penetrated along the joints.

George F. Mobley/NG Image Collection

Tim Laman/NG Image Collection

Maria Stenzel/NG Image Collection

Paul C. Dennis/Lost Trio Hiking Association

c. A geology student takes notes on a steep scree slope in Victoria Land, Antarctica. All of the loose rubble in this photograph was separated from the bedrock by frost wedging.

d. Root wedging

This tree began growing in a crack in the hard limestone of the Niagara Escarpment in southern Ontario. The tree's roots have widened the crack over time.

penetration by plant roots, and abrasion. By far the most widespread type of mechanical weathering involves the freezing of water.

Water is an unusual substance. Most liquids contract when they freeze, and the volume of the resulting solid is smaller than the volume of the liquid. However, when water freezes, it expands, increasing in volume by about 9%. If you put a full, capped bottle of water in the freezer, the bottle will burst when the water freezes because it cannot contain the larger volume of ice. Wherever temperatures fluctuate around the freezing point for part of the year, water in the ground will alternately freeze and thaw. If the water gets inside a joint in the rock, the freeze–thaw cycles act like a lever, prying the rock apart, and eventually the rock shatters. This process is known as **frost wedging** (see **Figure 7.3b and c**).

The formation of salt crystals can also cause mechanical weathering. Water moving slowly through rock fractures will dissolve soluble (that is, easily dissolved) material, which may later precipitate to form salt crystals. The force exerted by growing crystals within rock cavities or along grain boundaries can cause rock to fall apart. This process occurs mostly in desert regions, where calcium carbonate and calcium sulfate salts are precipitated from groundwater as a result of evaporation. Another type of mechanical weathering is caused by penetration by plant roots. Trees are very resourceful and can grow where there seems to be hardly any soil. A tree may become rooted in a crack in the bedrock, eventually widening the crack and wedging apart the bedrock, as shown in **Figure 7.3d**. Large trees swaying in the wind can also cause fractures to widen. When trees are blown over, they can cause additional fracturing. Although it is difficult to measure, the total amount of rock breakage caused by plants must be very large.

The final method of mechanical weathering is **abrasion.** This is the gradual wearing-away of bedrock by the constant battering of loose particles transported by water, wind, or ice.

Chemical Weathering

Chemical weathering is primarily caused by slightly acidic water. As raindrops fall through the air, they dissolve atmospheric carbon dioxide:

$$H_2O + CO_2 \rightarrow H_2CO_3$$

Rainwater thus is a weak solution of carbonic acid (H_2CO_3)—like Perrier water! When weakly acidified rainwater becomes soil water or groundwater, it may dissolve additional carbon dioxide from decaying organic matter, becoming more strongly acidified. Another way that rainwater can become acidified is by interacting with **anthropogenic** (human-generated) sulfur and nitrogen compounds released into the atmosphere, which produces **acid rain.** Human-caused acid rain is stronger than natural acid rain and causes accelerated weathering.

Through **dissolution**, minerals can be completely removed without leaving a residue. Some common rock-forming minerals, such as calcite (calcium carbonate) and dolomite (calcium magnesium carbonate), dissolve readily in slightly acidified water (**Figure 7.4a, b**).

> **dissolution** The separation of a material into ions in solution by a solvent, such as water or acid.

Water can also alter the mineral content of rock without dissolving all of it. One reaction of special importance in chemical weathering is **ion exchange**. Ions, which have a positive or negative electric charge, exist both in solution and in minerals (see *Remember This!*). Ions in minerals are tightly bonded and fixed in a crystal lattice, but ions in solutions can move about randomly and cause chemical reactions. Ion exchange is important in a common chemical weathering process known as **hydrolysis**, in which hydrogen ions (H^+) released from acidic water enter and alter a mineral by displacing larger positively charged ions such as potassium (K^+), sodium (Na^+), and magnesium (Mg^{2+}) (**Figure 7.4c**). This type of weathering alters the composition of both the minerals and the water solutions that fill the pore spaces and fractures in the rock.

> **REMEMBER THIS!** Do you remember what ions are? They are formed when an atom either gives up or accepts an electron. You can review this by looking back at *Isotopes and Ions* in Chapter 2.

Where do the potassium and other ions go after they are replaced by hydrogen ions? Some remain in the groundwater, accounting for the taste of "mineral water" that some people find pleasant and others do not, and some flow out to sea and form part of the ocean's reserve of dissolved salts. On the other hand, if the water evaporates, the dissolved materials can precipitate out again as solid evaporites, such as halite and gypsum.

Another very important process of chemical weathering is **oxidation**, a reaction between minerals and oxygen dissolved in water. Oxidation and hydrolysis often operate together (**Figure 7.4d**). Iron and manganese, in particular, are present in many rock-forming minerals; when such minerals undergo chemical weathering, the iron and manganese are released into the solution and are immediately combined with oxygen. Oxidized iron commonly forms an insoluble yellowish hydrous material called limonite, and manganese forms an insoluble black mineral called pyrolusite.

Factors Affecting Weathering

Many factors influence the susceptibility of rock to chemical and mechanical weathering, as shown in **Figure 7.5**. The most important factors are tectonic setting, composition of the rock, rock structure (especially the abundance of openings such as joints), topography, amount of vegetation and biological activity, and climate (especially temperature and rainfall).

In chemical weathering, minerals dissolve or change their composition as a result of reactions with rainwater or groundwater.

a. Dissolution

This 19th-century marble tombstone in a New England cemetery has gradually been dissolved by rainwater. The once sharply chiseled inscriptions are barely legible. Marble, which contains the soluble mineral calcite, is vulnerable to dissolution.

© David Wells/The Image Works

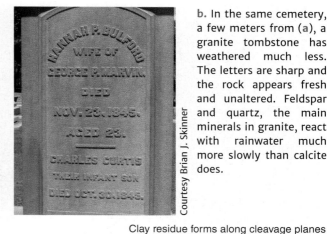

Courtesy Brian J. Skinner

b. In the same cemetery,
a few meters from (a), a granite tombstone has weathered much less. The letters are sharp and the rock appears fresh and unaltered. Feldspar and quartz, the main minerals in granite, react with rainwater much more slowly than calcite does.

c. Ion exchange

The diagrams below show how acidified water enters a mineral along fractures and cleavage planes, allowing alteration by ion exchange to occur. The photo (right), looking down a microscope, shows where a feldspar grain has been altered by ion exchange. The clay residue has been removed to make the pattern of alteration more visible.

Clay residue forms along cleavage planes

Unaltered feldspar

Courtesy Brian J. Skinner

Acidified water containing hydrogen ions (H^+) enters feldspar crystal along existing fractures.

Potassium ion (K^+) leaves in solution.

Unaltered feldspar

Alteration products (clay)

Where potassium has washed away, an insoluble residue of clay remains.

d. Hydrolysis and oxidation

This photo shows two types of igneous rock: pale granite and darker gabbro. The granite is resistant to chemical weathering, but groundwater seeped into joints and chemically attacked the gabbro. Chemical alteration of the gabbro happened first by hydrolysis, in which the original minerals are gradually altered to produce clay and soluble salts; and then by oxidation of iron in the minerals.

David Leveson

THINK CRITICALLY

On Earth, clay minerals are the most common products of weathering. Samples from the surface of the Moon brought back by astronauts do not contain any clay minerals. Why?

Pablo Galán Cela/Age Fotostock America, Inc.

a. Tectonic setting

Young, rising mountain ranges, such as those of the Himalaya, weather very rapidly. This view of the Indus River in Pakistan shows many boulders that have separated from the bedrock because of mechanical weathering.

Unjointed rock weathers slowly.

Stephanie Maze/NG Image Collection

b. Rock structure

The pace of weathering is also strongly affected by the closeness of joints. Sugarloaf Mountain in Rio de Janeiro, Brazil, is a large, unjointed mass of granite, and it stands out against an otherwise deeply eroded landscape.

Steep slope weathers quickly.

Medford Taylor/NG Image Collection

c. Topography

Weathering proceeds more quickly on a steep slope than on a gentle one. This rockslide on the island of Madeira in the Atlantic Ocean will expose new bedrock to weathering.

Courtesy Amy L. Rhodes, Smith College

Bacterial activity can promote chemical weathering.

d. Biological activity

Animals—even microorganisms—contribute significantly to the breakdown of rock. Here, a student lifts a mat of algae. The algae feed on a bacterium, *Thiobacillus ferrooxidans*, that thrives in acidic runoff from abandoned sulfur- and iron-bearing mines.

Raymond Gehman/NG Image Collection

Resistant quartzite knob weathers slowly.

e. Composition

Different minerals weather at different rates. Calcite weathers quickly by dissolution, and feldspar weathers at an intermediate rate by ion exchange. Quartz is very resistant to weathering because it dissolves slowly and is not affected by ion exchange. The knob atop Pilot Mountain, in North Carolina, is made of quartzite that has weathered much more slowly than the surrounding sedimentary rock.

© Frans Lanting/Corbis

Deforestation accelerates weathering and erosion.

f. Vegetation

Plants contribute to both mechanical and chemical weathering. They tend to hold a deeper regolith in place, which promotes weathering because it retains water. However, the removal of plants through slash-and-burn agriculture, clear-cut logging, or natural landslides can also accelerate weathering, as seen here in a photo of Madagascar.

THINK CRITICALLY

Chemical and mechanical weathering commonly occur together, although one or the other is normally dominant. Can you think of an environment where purely mechanical or purely chemical weathering could occur?

Different climates cause rock to weather at different rates and by different types of weathering.

a. Different types of weathering are shown on this graph of Temperature versus Rainfall. Warm, wet conditions (lower left corner) favor chemical weathering, whereas cold, dry conditions (upper right corner) favor mechanical weathering.

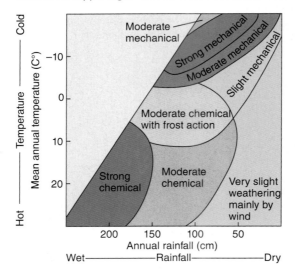

b. This map of North and South America illustrates some locations where the climate corresponds to the different zones of weathering shown in (**a**)

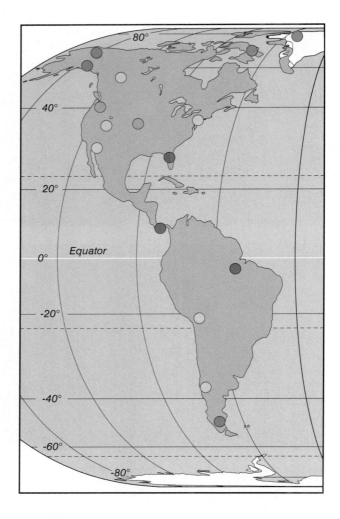

ASK YOURSELF

In (**a**), what type of environment is represented by the bottom righthand corner of the graph?

a. polar ice cap

b. tropical rain forest

c. mountainous alpine

d. hot desert

e. tundra

From the perspective of a human lifespan, weathering generally happens very slowly. For example, granite and other hard bedrock surfaces in New England, Canada, and Scandinavia still display polish and fine grooves made by the scraping of glaciers of the last ice age, which ended more than 10,000 years ago. In such regions, which have plentiful rainfall but cool climates, it takes hundreds of thousands of years for regolith to develop.

Climate affects the rate of weathering in two main ways. Chemical weathering is more intense in warm, wet, tropical climates than in cold, dry, arctic climates. In warmer, wetter regions, chemical weathering occurs quickly and extends to depths of many tens of meters. Even so, it has been estimated that deep tropical weathering of 500 meters or more requires many millions and possibly tens of millions of years. In cold, dry climates, such as in Greenland or Antarctica, chemical weathering proceeds very slowly. On the other hand, mechanical weathering can be fairly rapid in these harsh environments, especially in the presence of steep slopes and intense seasonal freeze–thaw cycles. The main type of environment where both kinds of weathering proceed very slowly is in hot, dry climates (**Figure 7.6**).

STOP CONCEPT CHECK

1. **Why** does weathering mainly occur near Earth's surface?

2. **How** do joints contribute to mechanical weathering?

3. **What** are three processes that contribute to chemical weathering?

4. **Why** is mechanical weathering prevalent in arctic regions?

PRODUCTS OF WEATHERING

Learning Objectives

1. **Identify** the end products of weathering.

2. **Describe** the process of soil formation.

3. **Explain** why soils that form in different climates have different characteristics and profiles.

4. **Discuss** the links between human activity and soil loss.

Have you ever wondered where a boulder in a mountain stream or the sand on a beach or the mud in a swamp actually comes from? The answer is the same in each case: from the mechanical and chemical weathering of rock exposed at Earth's surface.

Sediment

When rock is fragmented by weathering, the resulting material is regolith. If regolith is significantly altered by organic activity, it may become soil. These two processes happen primarily in place, or what geologists call *in situ*. But very often the fragments of rock undergo a process of erosion, in which they are picked up, transported, and deposited somewhere far from the location of the parent bedrock. When that happens, we refer to the resulting material as **sediment**. In Chapter 8 we will investigate the characteristics of sediment, and the processes whereby sediment becomes sedimentary rock, in much greater detail.

> **sediment** Rock that has been fragmented, transported, and deposited.

> **clay** A family of hydrous alumino-silicate minerals; also, tiny mineral particles of any kind that have physical properties like those of clay minerals.

Chunks of rock freshly broken loose from bedrock are usually similar to the original parent bedrock from which they were derived. However, with prolonged exposure to chemical weathering, minerals that are stable at higher temperatures and pressures begin to decompose, while new minerals, stable at the conditions of Earth's surface, are formed. For example, the feldspar crystals in granite break down to form **clay** minerals (**Figure 7.7**). Although tiny (the grains are typically less than 0.004 mm in diameter), clay minerals are some of the most stable minerals on Earth's surface. For this reason, they are a major component of soil and sediment, both on land and in the sea.

On the other hand, some minerals, such as quartz, are more resistant to weathering and hence do not break down into grains as small as those found in clay. Instead, quartz usually ends up as **sand**, which has grain sizes as coarse as 1–2 millimeters—roughly 100 to 1000 times larger than the grains in clay. Sediment with grain sizes between those of sand and clay is called **silt**. The grain sizes of particles weathered from bedrock decrease with the distance traveled by the sediment from its source. Some of the finest sand is found at coastal beaches because it has had an especially long journey from the mountains.

Soil

Perhaps the most complex product of weathering is also the most familiar: soil. As you know, soil forms when regolith is extensively altered by both chemical and biological activities. It usually contains a mixture of minerals with different grain sizes, all the way from fine clay to coarse sand, along with some material of biologic origin. If you look at soil under a magnifying glass, you will find fragments of **humus**, and possibly some tiny insects and worms. With a very strong microscope, you might even observe bacteria living on the humus.

> **humus** Partially decayed organic matter in soil.

Soil is a complex medium in which all parts interact and play important roles. Humus retains some of the chemical nutrients released by decaying organisms and by the chemical weathering of minerals. Humus is critical to soil fertility, which is the ability of a soil to provide nutrients such as phosphorus, nitrogen, and potassium needed by growing plants. All of the processes that involve living organisms and other soil constituents produce a continuous cycling of plant nutrients between the regolith and the biosphere.

Kaolin—From rock to fine china • Figure 7.7

White clay from Kao Ling, China, has for centuries been used to produce some of the finest porcelain in the world. The same kind of clay is now found in many other places, but it is still called *kaolin* in honor of the place that made it famous. Here, a worker fashions cups from kaolin clay.

Hiroji Kubota/Magnum Photos, Inc.

These microscopic views of Earth soil (a) and lunar regolith (b) show some significant differences. Earth soil contains organic material and hydrous minerals such as clay, while lunar regolith contains none of either.

a

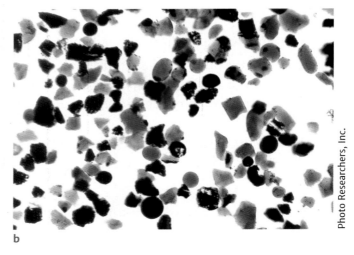

b

THINK CRITICALLY

Can you think of two reasons why Earth is the only planet (that we know of) where true soils occur?

Soil formation and the properties of the resulting soil are influenced by five main factors, which of course are very similar to the factors that influence weathering. These are (1) the characteristics of the parent material (that is, the bedrock from which the soil is formed); (2) climate; (3) topography; (4) the activity of living organisms (both microscopic and macroscopic); and (5) time. The combined influence of these soil-forming factors determines the main properties of any soil. To learn more about soil formation, see *Where Geologists Click*.

Of these factors, the composition of the parent material exerts the most fundamental influence on the chemical composition of the soil. Climate and topography greatly influence the rate and type of weathering that occurs. Climatic factors such as the amount of precipitation and humidity also control soil chemistry, color, and other properties to a great extent. Living organisms and the organic matter that they contribute form the crucial link between regolith or sediment and true soil. And finally, the length of time that soil formation has been operating controls the degree to which all of these processes contribute to the development of a deep soil layer (see *Remember This!*).

REMEMBER THIS! How long has there been soil on planet Earth? To answer this question, think about what is required for soil formation (weathering, water, biological activity); then think about Earth's history. Revisit *The Geological Column* (Chapter 3) and *The Origin of the Solar System* (Chapter 1) to see if you can determine when soil-forming processes might have begun.

Because of the central role of biological activity in soil formation, Earth is the only planet in the solar system that has true soil. Other rocky bodies in the solar system have blankets of loose rocky material (regolith) that have been pulverized to a very fine texture, but their regoliths lack humus (**Figure 7.8**).

Where Geologists CLICK

Virtual Soil Science Learning Resources

The *Virtual Soil Science Learning Resources* website, coordinated through the University of British Columbia Faculty of Land and Food Systems, provides access to a broad network of online soil-related resources. These include virtual laboratory exercises, soil maps, land impact assessment tools, and educational activities that focus on basic soil principles.

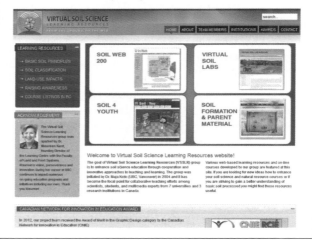

Soil Profiles and Horizons

Soil evolves gradually, from the top down. As erosion removes the top layer, weathering of the underlying material continually creates new soil. When fully developed, soil consists of a series of **soil horizons**, each of which has distinct physical,

> **soil horizon** One of a succession of zones or layers within a soil profile, each with distinct physical, chemical, and biologic characteristics.
>
> **soil profile** The sequence of soil horizons from the surface down to the underlying bedrock.

chemical, and biologic characteristics. All of the soil horizons in a particular location, from the surface down to the bedrock, together comprise the **soil profile**. Soil profiles (**Figure 7.9**) vary considerably from one location to another. However, certain kinds of horizons are common to many soil profiles.

The uppermost horizon in many soil profiles, the **O horizon**, is an accumulation of organic matter. Below it lies the **A horizon**, which is typically dark in color because of the humus present. An **E horizon**, which is sometimes present below A, is typically grayish in color because it contains little humus, and the mineral grains do not have dark coatings of iron and manganese hydroxides. Both the A and E horizons have had the soluble minerals leached out of them. E horizons are most common in the acidic soils of evergreen forests.

The **B horizon** underlies the A horizon (or E, if one is present). B horizons are brownish or reddish in color because of the presence of iron hydroxides that have been transported downward from the horizons above. The B horizon is a zone of accumulation, where materials that were leached from the A horizon are redeposited. Clays

are usually abundant in the B horizon. The **C horizon** (commonly known as the **subsoil**) is deepest, consisting of parent rock material in various stages of weathering. Oxidation of iron in the parent rock gives the C horizon a yellowish or rusty color.

Beneath the C horizon is unweathered bedrock. Geologists studying the rock of a region search for samples of "fresh," unweathered bedrock in order to form a true picture of the rock's original properties. Such samples can be found in natural outcrops along stream banks, in steep sides of mountains, in cliff faces where the soils are thin, and at artificial exposures such as highway road cuts, quarries, or mines.

As we have emphasized repeatedly in this chapter, all of Earth's systems interact at the surface. You might not think that the climate above the ground would have anything to do with a soil profile that develops underground, but in fact they are closely related. As **Figure 7.10** shows, soil horizons and profiles are strongly influenced by the climatic zone in which they form. The soil profile in an arid region will be quite different from the soil profile in a region that gets plenty of rainfall.

For example, a hard layer of carbonate minerals is a common horizon in desert soils. The hot, dry conditions cause groundwater to evaporate. The resulting precipitation of dissolved minerals forms a crusty layer in the soil, called **hardpan** or **caliche**. If the hardpan layer is near the surface, plant roots may not be able to grow to their normal depth. In forested areas in cold, dry climates, like the great boreal forests of the northern hemisphere, a thick layer of organic matter will often accumulate at the surface. This spongy O horizon, consisting of needles and cones dropped from coniferous trees, accumulates because organic decomposition is very slow in cold, dry conditions. In contrast, organic matter that falls to the floor of a hot, humid rainforest will degrade very rapidly. As a result, soils in tropical rainforests are typically poor in organic matter and lack an O horizon.

Soil profile • Figure 7.9 _____

This is a typical sequence of soil horizons that would commonly develop in moist, temperate climates. The A horizon, which lies within reach of plant roots, is commonly called the **topsoil**.

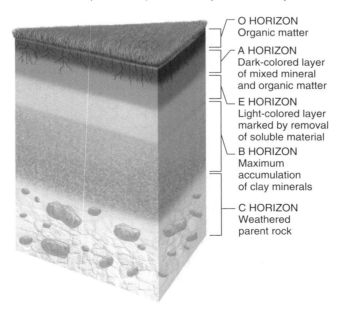

O HORIZON
Organic matter

A HORIZON
Dark-colored layer of mixed mineral and organic matter

E HORIZON
Light-colored layer marked by removal of soluble material

B HORIZON
Maximum accumulation of clay minerals

C HORIZON
Weathered parent rock

Soil Management

Because it is part of the never-ending rock cycle, soil is not static. Soil is constantly being formed, and it ceaselessly moves from place to place by natural processes. Unlike some other parts of the rock cycle, which are beyond our control, soil is very strongly affected by human activities. Natural erosional processes can be greatly accelerated by human activities that clear land and expose the soil to wind or water. Soil is the foundation of our entire agricultural system, and its health is crucial for global food security. This makes proper soil management a vital concern (see *Case Study* on page 185).

To protect agricultural fields from topsoil loss, farmers can utilize techniques such as contour plowing, to prevent the downslope flow of water; shallow tillage, to prevent exposure of the subsoil to wind and water; mulching, to introduce organic content and preserve moisture in the soil; crop rotation, to preserve the nutrient content and health of the soil; and the construction of wind breaks.

Soil horizons are strongly influenced by the climatic zone in which they form. Here are some of the variations in soil profiles that you might see in a forest, a grassland, and a desert. In the dry desert climate, for example, a carbonate-rich hardpan layer may form.

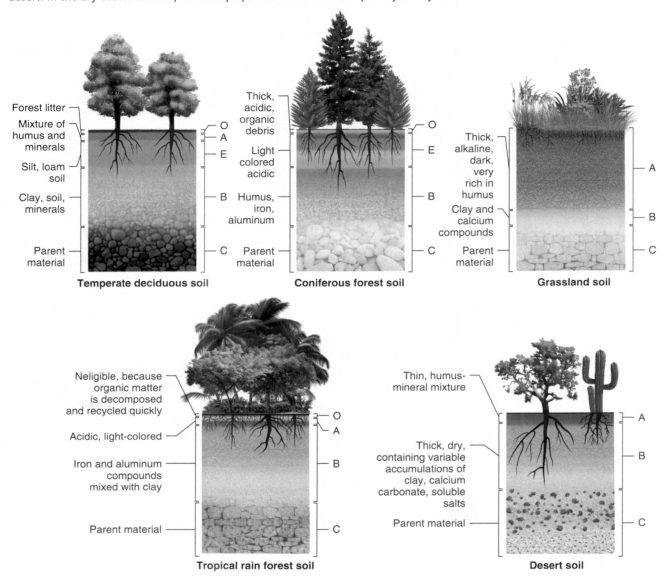

Temperate deciduous soil

Forest litter — O
Mixture of humus and minerals — A
— E
Silt, loam soil
Clay, soil, minerals — B
Parent material — C

Coniferous forest soil

Thick, acidic, organic debris — O
Light colored acidic — E
Humus, iron, aluminum — B
Parent material — C

Grassland soil

Thick, alkaline, dark, very rich in humus — A
Clay and calcium compounds — B
Parent material — C

Tropical rain forest soil

Neligible, because organic matter is decomposed and recycled quickly — O
— A
Acidic, light-colored
Iron and aluminum compounds mixed with clay — B
Parent material — C

Desert soil

Thin, humus-mineral mixture — A
Thick, dry, containing variable accumulations of clay, calcium carbonate, soluble salts — B
Parent material — C

Despite such measures, the erosion of farmland topsoil is a massive worldwide problem. In the United States, the amount of agricultural soil eroded each year exceeds the amount of replenished soil by about 1 billion tons. For every kilogram of food we eat, the land loses 6 kilograms of soil. This is clearly unsustainable. The rapid loss of soil as a result of overly intensive land use or other human activities is a costly form of land degradation. In Chapter 13 we will look more closely at land degradation and related problems, especially in drylands.

Although there is a small but growing "sustainable farming" movement, on a global scale we are very far from consuming only as much soil as can be regenerated in a reasonable amount of time by natural soilforming processes. A lot more critical thinking and action are needed in order to control soil erosion. Luckily, many of the techniques that can protect topsoil are relatively inexpensive and require few technological inputs; political will is the main necessity.

STOP CONCEPT CHECK

1. **What** are the primary differences between sediment, regolith, and soil?

2. **What** are the main factors that influence soil formation?

3. **What** is the difference between a soil profile and a soil horizon?

4. **How** do good soil management practices slow the loss of topsoil from farmlands?

The "Little Grand Canyon"

Providence Canyon in Georgia is a gorgeous example of a canyon carved into deeply weathered soil, but it is also a dreadful example of poor soil management. In **Figure a**, in the canyon wall you can readily spot the dark brown A horizon, the bright red B horizon that is full of clay, and the paler E horizon. This is a good, productive soil, but unfortunately much of it has been washed away.

Some people call Providence Canyon the "Little Grand Canyon" because of its layered appearance, but in reality they are very different. The Grand Canyon was carved into sedimentary rock strata millions of years ago, by natural erosional processes. Providence Canyon is less than 200 years old; it, too, was formed by erosion but greatly accelerated by human activity.

There was no canyon here when settlers from Europe began farming in the early 1800s. The farmers plowed straight up and down the hills, and the furrows rapidly developed into gullies. By 1850, the gullies were 1 to 2 meters deep. The farmers had to abandon their fields, but by then, erosion in the gullies was running amok. The canyon is now more than 50 meters deep. Unfortunately, there are many such locations in North America.

a. Providence Canyon resulted from intense erosion of poorly managed agricultural fields.

USDA/Soil Conservation Service

In the early 20th century, scientists involved with erosion studies pointed out that water flowing in plowed land needed to be controlled. To fight erosion, farmers now use contour plowing (**Figure b**). Instead of going in straight lines downhill, the furrows follow the contour of the land. This slows runoff and inhibits the formation of gullies, helping to retain the topsoil on the field.

Kevin Horan/Stone/Getty Images, Inc.

b. Farmers today use contour plowing to prevent soil from washing away.

EROSION AND MASS WASTING

Learning Objectives

1. **Distinguish** between weathering, erosion, and mass wasting.

2. **Define** turbulent and laminar flow.

3. **Describe** how water, wind, and ice transport regolith across Earth's surface.

4. **Define** and give examples of mass wasting by slope failures and by flows.

The term *erosion* encompasses the set of processes whereby regolith is picked up and transported from one place to another. Weathering, in contrast, happens in place and mainly concerns the processes involved in the breakdown of rock. The two sets of processes can, of course, happen together, and they often do; for instance, rock can be abraded (a weathering process), and the particles that break off the bedrock will be transported elsewhere by the wind (an erosional process).

The fluids that are mainly responsible for causing erosion on Earth are water, wind, and ice. (Even though we usually think of ice as a solid, it does flow when it forms a glacier or an ice sheet.) Different fluids have different resistance viscosities. Ice, which flows so slowly that its motion cannot be seen by the human eye, behaves as an extremely viscous fluid (see *Remember This!*). Water, which flows freely, is much less viscous, and air is the least viscous of the three.

> **REMEMBER THIS!** Do you recall what *viscosity* is? It is a measure of the extent to which a fluid is resistant to flow. You can review our discussion of viscosity by turning back to *Eruptions, Landforms, and Materials* in Chapter 6.

A fluid's viscosity partly determines whether its flow is **laminar** or **turbulent**. In laminar flow, all fluid particles travel in parallel layers. Turbulent flow is erratic and complex, full of swirls and eddies. Turbulent flow is more effective at picking up particles off the ground. Air flow is almost always turbulent; water flow is usually turbulent, except when the velocity of flow is very low.

Erosion by Water

Erosion by water begins even before a distinct stream channel has formed on a slope. This happens in two ways: by impact, which occurs when raindrops hit the ground and dislodge small particles of soil; and by overland flow, which occurs during heavy rains. Overland flow involves water moving as sheets over the ground, not in channels.

When the water starts flowing in a channel, particles are moved in several ways: The largest particles, which form the **bed load** (boulders, cobbles, and pebbles), roll or slide along the stream bed due to the force of the flowing water. Smaller (sand-sized) particles move along the stream bed by **saltation** (**Figure 7.11**).

The particles in the **suspended load**—silt and clay—are small. Although they do not actually float, they do not sink to the bottom as long as the water is flowing. If you took a sample of water from a muddy stream and let it stand, the silt and clay would settle to the bottom as mud. But in the turbulent environment of a stream, the upward-moving currents keep them from sinking. Thus mud deposits form only where velocity decreases and turbulence ceases, as in a lake, the sea, or a reservoir.

Streams also carry a **dissolved load** of soluble materials released by chemical weathering. The dissolved load may also contain organic matter, which accounts for the infamous "black water" found in rivers that drain swamps.

> **bed load** Sediment that is moved along the bottom of a stream.
>
> **saltation** A mechanism of sediment transport in which particles move forward in a series of short jumps along arc–shaped paths.
>
> **suspended load** Sediment that is carried in suspension by a flowing stream of water or wind.
>
> **dissolved load** Soluble material that is carried in solution by water.

Erosion by Wind

Saltation and suspension are the main processes by which flowing water is able to pick up and transport particles; the same processes also occur in flowing air. Because the density of air is about 800 times less than that of water, however, air cannot move the large particles that water flowing at the same velocity can move. In exceptional cases, such as hurricanes and tornadoes, winds can reach speeds of 300 kilometers per hour and sweep up coarse rock particles and other debris several centimeters in diameter, and even larger.

In most regions, however, wind speeds rarely exceed 50 kilometers per hour, a velocity that is described as a "strong" wind. As a result, most (at least 75%) of the sediment transported by wind occurs through saltation of sand grains. Only the finest particles, the grains of dust, remain aloft long enough to be moved by suspension. Even so, enough suspended particles are moved during a dust storm that visibility can be greatly reduced (**Figure 7.12**). We will revisit wind erosion in Chapter 13, when we consider processes that are particularly important in drylands.

Erosion by Ice

Ice is a solid. However, it flows downslope under the influence of gravity, albeit very slowly, in parts of the world where there is enough year-round ice to form a **glacier** (discussed further in Chapter 13). Compared with water and

Bed load and suspended load • Figure 7.11

A typical stream will transport a bed load, a suspended load, and a dissolved load.

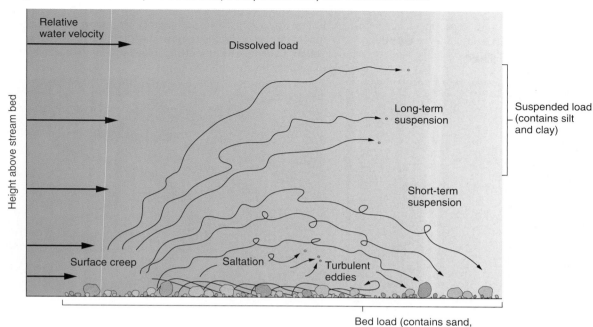

a. The bed load consists of particles that are too heavy to stay suspended in the water. Pebbles creep or roll along the bottom, while sand-sized particles move by saltation. Very fine silt and clay particles form the suspendedload and give the water a muddy appearance. The dissolved load consists of soluble materials such as salts and organic matter.

b. The turbulent flow of this river in Gabon, Africa, enables it to carry a large suspended load.

Michael Nichols/NG Image Collection

Massive dust storm • Figure 7.12

In this photo a wall of dust approaches Lubbock, Texas, the result of a massive dust storm on the afternoon of October 17, 2011.

Courtesy NOAA

air, ice is extremely viscous. Glacial ice therefore moves only by laminar flow, but its high viscosity also means that it is capable of carrying a wide range of sediment sizes—even very large boulders (**Figure 7.13**).

Glaciers contribute both to mechanical weathering and to the erosion of weathered material. Flowing ice scrapes up weathered rock and soil, and plucks out large blocks of bedrock. The glacier transports the load of sediment that it scrapes up, along with any additional material that falls onto its surface from adjacent slopes. The load of rock fragments carried at the bottom of the glacier—essentially the glacier's bed load—rasps and polishes the bedrock, carving long grooves that are indicative of the direction of ice flow. You saw an example of glacial grooves in Chapter 4, when we discussed the evidence Alfred Wegener used to determine the extent of glaciation on the supercontinent Pangaea (see Figure 4.3e).

Flowing glacial ice transports rocky fragments in a wide range of sizes.

a. This rocky debris, ranging from large boulders to tiny pebbles, was deposited by the Ngozumpa Glacier in the Himalaya Mountains. The very blue color of the lake comes from suspended rock flour.

b. Two ice streams, transporting rock fragments from adjacent mountain slopes, merge to form the Kaskawulsh Glacier in the Yukon, Canada. The smooth, parallel streams are a hallmark of laminar flow.

The constant grinding of glacial ice and rock fragments against the bedrock surface also creates finely pulverized sediment called **rock flour**. Transported away from the glacier by wind or by streams of meltwater, suspended rock flour is responsible for the bright blue color typically associated with glacial lakes.

Gravity and Mass Wasting

Landscapes may seem fixed and unchanging, but if you made a time-lapse movie of almost any hillside for a few years, you would see that the slope changes constantly as a result of **mass wasting**. There is no such thing as a static hillside—a lesson learned all too often by people who live at the top, the bottom, or on the side of a steep slope.

> **mass wasting** The downslope movement of regolith and/or bedrock masses due to the pull of gravity.

> **slope failure** The falling, slumping, or sliding of relatively coherent masses of rock.

> **flow** Any mass-wasting process that involves a flowing motion of regolith containing water and/or air within its pores.

Most erosional processes require a fluid to pick up and transport the weathered material. In mass wasting, regolith moves downslope under the pull of gravity, with no transporting fluid required (although fluids are sometimes present). Exactly how the downslope movement happens, and how fast it happens, are controlled by the composition and texture of the regolith and bedrock, the amount of air and water in the regolith, and the steepness of the slope. For convenience, we divide mass wasting into two categories: **slope failures** and **flows**.

Slope Failures The important aspects and terminology associated with slope failures are summarized in **Figure 7.14**. Slope failures occur as one of three basic types. A **slump** involves rotational movement of rock and regolith—that is, downward and outward movement along a curved surface. Slumps often result from poor engineering practices, such as after slopes have been oversteepened for construction of buildings or roads. **Slides** involve rapid displacement of a mass of rock or sediment in a straight line down a steep or slippery slope. A **fall** is a sudden vertical, or nearly vertical, drop of rock fragments or debris. Rockfalls and debris falls are sudden and usually very dangerous.

Flows Flowing regolith can be either wet or dry (**Figure 7.15**). **Slurry flows** occur when the regolith is saturated with water; they can occur either rapidly or slowly. Rapid slurry flows can move at speeds up to 160 kilometers per hour and are very dangerous. Slow slurry flow, a process known as **solifluction**, is common in areas with high rainfall, where soil is thin over bedrock, and in areas where the ground is frozen at depth. Mudflows are another type of water-saturated flow, usually faster-flowing than solifluction.

Flowing regolith that is not water saturated is called a **granular flow**. Like slurry flows, granular flows can be either slow or fast. The most common kind of granular flow (and the most common kind of mass wasting) is called **creep**. One type of rapid granular flow is **debris avalanches**, which are rare, spectacular, and extremely dangerous. A debris

> **creep** The imperceptibly slow downslope granular flow of regolith.

avalanche is likely to start as a rockfall or slide but gains speed when the material pulverizes and begins to flow

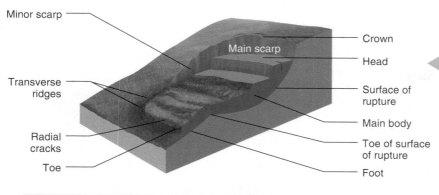

Minor scarp

Transverse ridges

Radial cracks

Toe

Crown

Main scarp

Head

Surface of rupture

Main body

Toe of surface of rupture

Foot

a. Slope failures can be slow or fast. The head refers to the top of the failure, and the toe is at the farthest end of the failed mass. The three main types of slope failure, shown below, are slumps, slides, and falls.

© Marli Bryant Miller

Direction of motion

b. A slump is a slower kind of failure in which the debris moves rotationally (as shown by the curved arrow). This slumping failure occurred in central California.

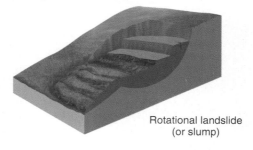

Rotational landslide (or slump)

Courtesy Stephen C. Porter

Site of detachment

Rockslide deposit

c. In this rockslide in the Andes Mountains in Argentina, the rocks moved in a roughly straight line from the point of detachment to the valley floor.

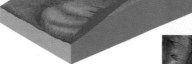

Translational landslide

d. Kaibito Canyon in Arizona has been the site of repeated rockfalls, as you can see both from the debris at the base of the cliff and from the scars on the cliff face where rocks have detached themselves in the past.

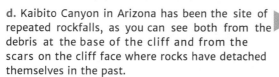

Rockfall

Bill Hatcher/NG Image Collection

How regolith flows • Figure 7.15

Downslope movement of regolith in flows is controlled by the amount of water present, the steepness of the slope, and the particle size.

Slurry (wet) flows

a. These solifluction lobes are in the Tien Shan Mountains of Kyrgyzstan.

Marli Bryant Miller

b. A mudflow poured from unstable cliffs around the Dorset/ Devon border, UK.

© Ian White/ Alamy

Solifluction sheets

Solifluction

Solifluction lobes

Wet, slow

Mudflow

Wet, fast

Granular (dry) flows

Marli Bryant Miller

c. Tree trunks on this hillslope in Nevada are curved as a result of creep.

d. This massive debris avalanche in Caraballeda, Venezuela, killed many thousands of people and left deposits up to 6 m in thickness.

Lawson Smith/U.S. Army Corps of Engineers

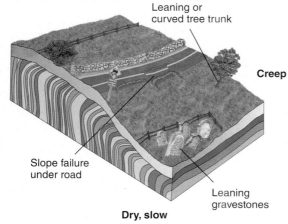

Leaning or curved tree trunk

Creep

Slope failure under road

Leaning gravestones

Dry, slow

← 1–10 km →
Larger than slide

Debris avalanche

Material becomes airborne, flows downslope like a fluid

Dry, fast

downslope like a fluid. Debris avalanches can be triggered by earthquakes or volcanic eruptions.

Factor of Safety   It is usually not possible to stop a large landslide, but with sufficient warning it may be possible to move people and sometimes property out of harm's way. As with other natural hazards, landslide prediction relies on close monitoring of potentially unstable slopes, in an effort to identify any sudden changes or anomalies that could indicate an upcoming failure.

For landslides, the central concern is the balance between destabilizing forces (pushing the material downhill) and stabilizing, or resisting, forces (holding the material in place). The downslope forces cause **shear stress** on the slope materials. The resisting forces result from the **shear strength** of the slope materials. The ratio of shear strength to shear stress for a given slope is the **factor of safety (FS)**. If FS > 1, shear strength is greater than shear stress, and the slope is stable. If FS < 1, the slope is unstable because shear stress is greater than shear strength.

The factors that contribute to shear stress and shear strength are numerous and complex. The cohesive strength of the soil or regolith—that is, the force that binds together the particles—is the main resisting factor; this, in turn, depends on rock or soil properties such as the mineral composition, water content, pore spaces, type of cement, and presence or absence of fractures. Downslope drivers include the weight of the soil or regolith itself, the steepness of the slope, the load on top of the slope (e.g., a building), water saturation, and many other factors. The role of a factor can sometimes vary. For example, plant roots typically bind soils and contribute to slope stability. However, vegetation can become a destabilizing influence, as when a large tree at the top of a slope is caught and pulled by the wind.

The possibility of a triggering event, such as an earthquake, also contributes to the potential for slope instability. The world's major historic and prehistoric landslides tend to cluster along belts that lie close to the boundaries between converging lithospheric plates. One reason is that most large earthquakes occur along plate boundaries. Earthquakes often trigger landslides in areas where the regolith is unstable (**Figure 7.16**). Also, the world's highest mountain chains lie at or near plate boundaries. These mountains typically consist of jointed rock strata that were strongly fractured and deformed as they were uplifted. Both the joint planes and the bedding surfaces are potential zones of failure. Finally, stratovolcanoes, also common along plate boundaries, have steep slopes that are conducive to landslides.

It may seem as if landslides and mass wasting should ultimately level all of the world's mountains and leave the continents as flat, featureless plains. That will never happen

Why landslides occur near plate boundaries
• **Figure 7.16** _____

Earthquakes, particularly those close to plate edges, often trigger landslides. The subduction-related quake of March 27, 1964, the Great Alaska Earthquake, caused many slides. One of them, shown here, covered part of the Sherman Glacier.

W.E. Garrett R./NG Image Collection

because uplift is always taking place at the same time. For example, at Nanga Parbat, a Himalayan mountain that lies at the boundary between the Indian and Eurasian plates, uplift rates are as high as 5 millimeters a year. At such rates, the mountain should increase in altitude by 5000 meters every million years. However, high mountains also mean high erosion rates, and weathering and erosion tear down the mountain almost as rapidly as it rises. Much of this destruction is a result of mass wasting.

STOP CONCEPT CHECK

1. **How** are weathering, erosion, and mass wasting related, and in what ways are they distinct?

2. **What** are the differences between a stream's bed load, suspended load, and dissolved load?

3. **What** are the main differences and similarities in how sediment is transported by water, by wind, and by glacial ice?

4. **Which** kind of mass wasting is the most common, and which kinds are the most dangerous?

1 Weathering—The First Step in the Rock Cycle 171

- The **rock cycle** is the continuous cycle of processes by which rock is formed, modified, transported, decomposed, and re-formed. Most of Earth's surface is covered by a blanket of weathered rock, which we call **regolith**. Regolith fragments can range in size from many meters to microscopic (see figure). When small regolith particles are altered by biological processes, the result is **soil**, a material from which rooted plants can extract nutrients.

How rock disintegrates • Figure 7.2

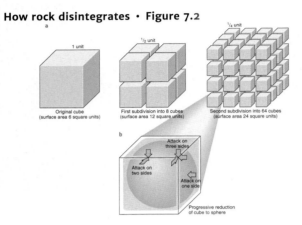

- When rock is exposed at Earth's surface, it is constantly subjected to **weathering**, the process by which air, water, and microbes break down bedrock into smaller rock and mineral fragments. Weathering extends as far down as air, water, and living organisms can readily penetrate Earth's crust. Weathering may be **mechanical**, or **chemical**. The agents of weathering enter bedrock along **joints** and via pores.

- Joints are fractures along which no appreciable movement has occurred. Mechanical weathering takes place in four main ways: by frost wedging, or the freezing of water; by the growth of salt crystals in confined spaces; by the prying action of roots; and by abrasion.

- Chemical weathering involves the removal of some minerals in solution and the transformation of others into new minerals that are stable at Earth's surface. This type of weathering is caused primarily by water that is slightly acidic. Acid rain can be naturally occurring or human generated. Human-generated acid rain, which is created when rainwater interacts with anthropogenic sulfur and nitrogen compounds, is stronger than natural acid rain and causes accelerated weathering.

- There are several important processes by which chemical weathering occurs, including **dissolution**, in which minerals are completely dissolved and carried away in solution; ion exchange and hydrolysis, in which hydrogen ions from acidic water enter and alter a mineral by displacing larger, positively charged ions; and oxidation, a reaction between minerals and oxygen dissolved in water.

- From a human perspective, chemical and mechanical weathering occur very slowly, over many thousands of years. The effectiveness of weathering depends on the type and structure of rock, the tectonic setting, the steepness of the slope, the local climate, and the amount of biological activity. Chemical weathering is most active in moist, warm climates, whereas mechanical weathering is most active in cold, dry climates.

2 Products of Weathering   181

- Regolith is the first product of weathering. If regolith is picked up and transported, it becomes **sediment**. With time, weathering eventually breaks down rock into very fine particles known as **clay**, silt, or sand. Clay refers to a family of hydrous aluminosilicate minerals, but it is more commonly used to describe any tiny mineral particles that have physical properties similar to those of clay minerals. Silt particles are larger than clay, and sand is larger than silt.

- Soil is regolith that can support rooted plants. Earth's soil is different from the "soil" of other planets because it contains **humus**, or partially decayed organic matter, as well as many small living organisms. Humus retains some chemical nutrients released by decaying organisms and the chemical weathering of minerals. These nutrients, such as phosphorus, nitrogen, and potassium, are critical for soil fertility.

- Soils weather from top to bottom and develop distinctive **soil horizons**, whose properties are a function of the duration, intensity, and nature of the weathering process. In a typical **soil profile** (see figure), the O horizon is the topmost layer of accumulated organic matter. The A horizon is rich in humus; the A and E horizons are layers from which soluble material, especially iron and aluminum, has been lost through leaching. Farther down, clay minerals accumulate in the B horizon. Deeper still, the C horizon consists of slightly weathered parent rock. Soil profiles can vary greatly from location to location, as they are strongly affected by climate.

Soil profile • Figure 7.9

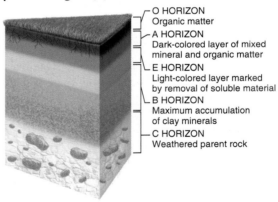

O HORIZON
Organic matter

A HORIZON
Dark-colored layer of mixed mineral and organic matter

E HORIZON
Light-colored layer marked by removal of soluble material

B HORIZON
Maximum accumulation of clay minerals

C HORIZON
Weathered parent rock

- Soil is critical for food security, but it is easily influenced by human actions. To prevent the loss of topsoil from agricultural fields, farmers use a variety of methods, including contour plowing and crop rotation, to preserve soil health and protect it from the erosive action of wind and water.

3 Erosion and Mass Wasting   186

- **Erosion** involves the removal and transport of regolith through the combined actions of ice, water, wind, and gravity. This is different from weathering, which happens in place, though both processes can occur at the same time. Most processes of erosion involve a fluid picking up and transporting material.

- Both air and water move particles by the process of **saltation**, a mechanism of sediment transport in which particles move forward in a series of short hops along arc-shaped paths. Only the smaller sand-sized particles move along the bottom of a stream by saltation, whereas the larger particles move by rolling or sliding. These larger particles are known as the **bed load**; lighter particles carried in suspension form the **suspended load** and organic matter and dissolved ions released by chemical weathering typically form the **dissolved load**.

How slopes fail · Figure 7.14

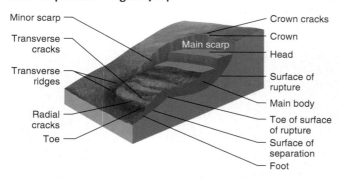

Minor scarp
Transverse cracks
Main scarp
Transverse ridges
Radial cracks
Toe
Crown cracks
Crown
Head
Surface of rupture
Main body
Toe of surface of rupture
Surface of separation
Foot

- Air and water carry suspended particles most effectively through turbulent flow. Turbulent flow is dynamic, nonlinear, and generally more effective at picking up particles off the ground. Glaciers, however, transport particles by laminar flow, in which the particles move in parallel layers. A glacier is a permanent body of ice consisting largely of recrystallized snow. A glacier plays a significant role in erosion and transport by acting in three ways: as a plow, as a file, and as a sled.

- **Mass wasting** is the en masse downslope movement of rock or regolith under the pull of gravity. In contrast to other types of erosion, in mass wasting the materials moved do not need to be transported by a fluid. **Slope failures** (see figure) involve downslope movement of relatively coherent masses of rock or regolith. Slope failures can be one of three types: a fall, or a sudden vertical drop of rock fragment or debris; a slide, which involves rapid displacement of a mass of rock or sediment in a straight line down a steep slope; or a slump, a slower type of slope failure that involves rotational movement of rock.

- **Flows** are mixtures of regolith and water or air. Flowing regolith can be wet or dry. Wet flows include slurry flows that can occur rapidly or slowly; a slow slurry flow is also known as solifluction. Granular flows can be rapid, as in debris avalanches, or slow. The most common type of granular flow, which is also the least noticeable because of its slow motion, is called **creep**.

- Both weathering and erosion are controlled by climate and topography. Mass-wasting processes—especially landslides—tend to be particularly frequent along plate boundaries, where earthquakes commonly act as triggering mechanisms.

KEY TERMS

bed load 186

chemical weathering 173

clay 181

creep 188

dissolution 176

dissolved load 186

erosion 171

flow 188

humus 181

joint 173

mass wasting 188

mechanical weathering 173

regolith 172

rock cycle 171

saltation 186

sediment 181

slope failure 188

soil 172

soil horizon 183

soil profile 183

suspended load 186

weathering 171

CRITICAL AND CREATIVE THINKING QUESTIONS

1. Look around for evidence of mechanical and chemical weathering. How might you determine their relative importance in the area where you live?

2. Many features have recently been discovered on Mars that are suggestive of erosion by water. What is the evidence that Mars once had a hydrosphere? How long ago did it have a hydrosphere? Where did the water go?

3. The Moon lacks an atmosphere, a hydrosphere, and a biosphere, but when the first astronauts landed, they discovered that the Moon has a deep regolith. How might the regolith have been formed, and how does it differ from Earth's regolith?

4. What kinds of mass-wasting processes occur where you live? Can you identify any evidence that suggests how rapidly or how slowly mass wasting is moving regolith downslope? Look especially for signs of creep, which occurs almost everywhere. Some clues are bent tree trunks, curved fences, lobes of soil on grassy slopes, and tilted gravestones.

5. Keep an eye out for the structures in your town used to stabilize slopes or protect property from mass wasting. Are the slopes in your area engineered, or have they been left more or less in their natural state? Where you find retaining walls, do they appear to have stabilized the slope as intended?

6. Figure 7.11 shows surface creep, saltation, and suspension of particles in a flowing stream of water. All of these processes also work if the transporting medium is air or ice. In what ways would the diagram be different if it showed air as the transporting medium? What if the diagram showed ice as the transporting medium—in what ways would it be the same, or different?

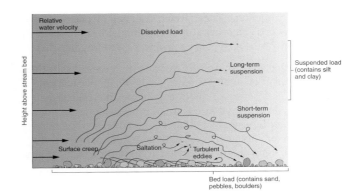

WHAT IS HAPPENING IN THIS PICTURE?

Mudflows are a particularly rapid and dangerous form of mass wasting. In January 2005, 400,000 tons of mud cascaded down on the California town of La Conchita, killing 10 people.

THINK CRITICALLY

From a geological point of view, a town should never have been built in this location. Why? What do you think might have caused the mudslide? How might this hazard have been foreseen?

SELF-TEST

(Check your answers in Appendix D.)

1. On this diagram locate and label the following processes in the rock cycle:

   weathering   burial and cementation

   melting   erosion and deposition

   tectonic uplift   intrusion and volcanism

   metamorphism

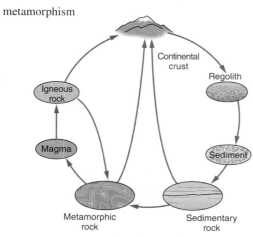

ROCK CYCLE

2. In _____, rock breaks down into solid fragments by physical processes that do not change the rock's chemical composition.

   a. chemical weathering   c. mass wasting

   b. mechanical weathering   d. erosion

3. This diagram shows the chemical weathering of a common feldspar mineral. The process shown depicts _____.

   a. a strong chemical reaction

   b. a moderate chemical reaction

   c. dissolution

   d. ion exchange

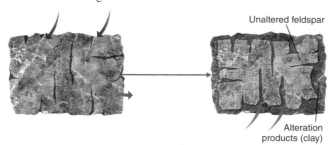

Unaltered feldspar

Alteration products (clay)

4. Death Valley in California is one of the hottest and driest spots in North America. Summer air temperatures commonly reach 50°C, and rainfall averages less than 5 centimeters per year. In this desert environment, what type of weathering would you expect to find?

   a. strong chemical weathering

   b. strong mechanical weathering

   c. moderate chemical weathering

   d. moderate mechanical weathering

   e. very slight weathering, mostly by wind

5. Which of the following is true of sediments found on Earth's surface?

   a. They are one product of the mechanical weathering process.

   b. They are one product of the chemical weathering process.

   c. They are the result of a combination of mechanical and chemical weathering processes.

   d. None of the above statements is correct.

6. A dark-colored layer of mixed mineral and organic matter defines the _____ soil horizon.

   a. O   c. E   e. C

   b. A   d. B

7. This diagram shows five soil profiles. On the basis of the vegetation and soil characteristics shown, match the correct environment to each soil profile:

   Coniferous forest   Grassland   Desert

   Tropical rainforest   Temperate deciduous forest

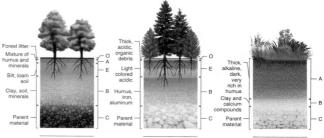

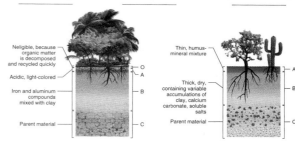

8. _____ is one method modern farmers can use to fight soil erosion.

   a. Uphill plowing   c. Contour plowing

   b. Plowing along natural drainage systems   d. Downhill plowing

9. _____ involves the removal and transport of regolith through the combined actions of ice, water, wind, and gravity. This is different from _____, which happens only in place, though both processes can occur at the same time. The process of _____ further alters Earth's surface by the downslope displacement of regolith due to the pull of gravity.

   a. Erosion; mass wasting; weathering

   b. Weathering; erosion; mass wasting

   c. Mass wasting; weathering; erosion

   d. Erosion; weathering; mass wasting

   e. Mass wasting; erosion; weathering

10. _____ is dynamic, nonlinear, and generally more effective at picking up particles off the ground than is _____, in which particles travel in parallel layers.

   a. Viscous flow; laminar flow

   b. Viscous flow; turbulent flow

   c. Laminar flow; turbulent flow

   d. Turbulent flow; laminar flow

11. Air and water tend to carry suspended particles most effectively through _____.

   a. a combination of viscous and laminar flow

   b. turbulent flow

   c. laminar flow

   d. a combination of turbulent and laminar flow

12. _____ transport regolith through laminar flow.

   a. Streams

   b. Winds

   c. Debris flows

   d. Glaciers

13. _____ are a form of slope failure involving rapid displacement of a mass of rock or sediment in a straight path down a steep or slippery slope.

   a. Rockfalls

   b. Slumps

   c. Slides

   d. Slurries

14. _____ involve rotational movement of rock or regolith.

   a. Rockfalls

   b. Slumps

   c. Slides

   d. Slurries

15. This illustration shows block diagrams of mass wasting of hill slopes through sediment flow. Identify each block diagram based on processes related to rate and degree of wetness from the following list:

   wet, slow   dry, slow

   wet, fast   dry, fast

THE PLANNER ✓

Review the Chapter Planner on the chapter opener and check off your completed work.

8 | FROM SEDIMENT TO SEDIMENTARY ROCK

Global
Locator

The Bahamas

NG Maps

WES C. SKILES/National Geographic Creative

Courtesy NASA

DIVING THE BLUE HOLE

The Bahamas offers spectacular diving, and particularly legendary is Dean's Blue Hole (photo). A blue hole is an underwater sinkhole, like a vertical cave. The rock formation that hosts this blue hole is the Great Bahama Bank, a giant pillar of limestone that rises 8 kilometers from the bottom of the ocean. Geologists call the top of the pillar, which we see at the surface as the Bahama Islands, a **carbonate platform**. A photo from space (inset) shows several platforms in light blue, comparable in area to the peninsula of Florida (left); the largest is the Great Bahama Bank.

The pillars grew slowly from the accumulation of coral and other marine debris. About 200 million years ago, when the Atlantic Ocean began to form, this region was a shallow sea, perfect habitat for corals. As the ocean deepened, the coral kept growing, with the top remaining below the sea surface. Eventually, the accumulated coral debris became cemented into limestone.

During the last ice age, sea level dropped and the platform was exposed. The limestone was chemically weathered by rainwater, and deep cave systems formed. When the ice age ended and the glaciers melted, sea level rose and the platform was inundated.

Dean's Blue Hole is now a favorite place for those who like to dive without any artificial breathing apparatus; three world records for free-diving were established here.

SEDIMENT

Learning Objectives

1. **Describe** clastic sediment in terms of size, sorting, and roundness.

2. **Explain** where and how chemical sediment is formed.

3. **Explain** where and how biogenic sediment is formed.

Nearly every geological process leaves its mark in the sedimentary record. Tectonic forces raise mountain ranges, which contribute source materials for sediment. Climatic processes control the way rock weathers and how the resulting sediment is transported. Both sets of processes influence the characteristics of the sites where sediment is precipitated or deposited; we will consider these processes and sites later in the chapter. To understand the complicated record these events leave, we first have to know more about the different kinds of sediment. Geologists separate sediment into three broad categories: clastic, chemical, and biogenic.

Clastic Sediment

Clastic sediment derives its name from **clasts**, individual grains of mineral or fragments of rock. Clasts range in size from large boulders down to clay particles finer than flour. In fact, the size of the clasts is the primary basis for classifying clastic sediment (**Figure 8.1**).

> **clastic sediment**
> Sediment formed from fragmented rock and mineral debris produced by weathering and erosion.

Two other important characteristics used to describe clastic sediment are the shape and size distribution of the grains (**Figure 8.2**). The main components of shape are **roundess** (contrasted with angularity); and **sphericity** (contrasted with elongation). Other terms, such as "platy," are sometimes used to describe certain types of mineral grains in the sediment, such as micas. With regard to size distribution, the most important characteristic is **sorting**, which is a measure of the uniformity of grain sizes in the sediment.

Volcaniclastic sediment is a type of clastic sediment in which all of the clasts are volcanic in origin (see *Remember This!* on page 200). Explosive volcanic eruptions blast out large quantities of fragments during an eruption. An old saying describes the unique nature of volcaniclastic sediment: "Igneous on the way up but sedimentary on the way down."

From clasts to rock • Figure 8.1

Sediment with different-sized clasts produces sedimentary rock with different characteristics and names.

SEDIMENT

...WITH COMPRESSION AND TIME, CAN BECOME...

ROCK

Gravel	Sand	Silty mud	Clayey mud
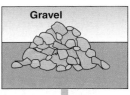	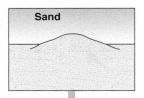	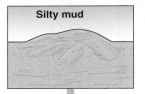	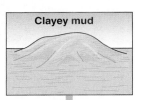

A sediment with pea-sized or larger particles is called *gravel*. When gravel is cemented, the rock so formed is a **conglomerate**.

Sand consists of somewhat smaller particles, each about the size of a pinhead. When compacted and cemented, sand becomes **sandstone**.

Sediment with even finer particles, the size of grains of table salt, is called *silt*. The corresponding rock type is **siltstone**.

The finest sedimentary particles, the size of flour or smaller, are called *clay*.* The corresponding rock type is **shale** or **mudstone**.

Fletcher & Baylis/Photo Researchers, Inc.

©Marli Bryant Miller

G. R. Roberts/Photo Researchers, Inc.

Courtesy Brian J. Skinner

This shows a pebble-rich strata of conglomerates interbedded with sandstone; the area photographed, which is about 1 m wide, is exposed in the walls of a canyon eroded by the Tsauchab River in Namibia.

This sandstone from Montana was deposited atop a stratum of pebble-rich conglomerate of Cretaceous age. This sandstone is about 7.5 cm across. The colors of depositional layers vary because of different iron contents.

Siltstone is interlayered with sandstone here, near Adelaide, Australia; the field of view is about 20 cm across.

This shale sample is about 10 cm across. The colors are caused by different contents of organic matter.

*Note that *clay* in this context refers only to particle size, not composition.

Sorting, roundness, and sphericity of clasts are important characteristics by which sediment is classified. They can also tell geologists a lot about where the sediment came from and what types of erosional processes it has experienced.

SORTING

a. SORTING: In some sediment, all particles are nearly the same size. Such sediment is said to be well sorted, and usually has been transported by water or wind. Sediment transported by ice or by mass wasting is typically poorly sorted or even unsorted—a jumble of particles of different sizes.

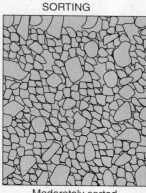

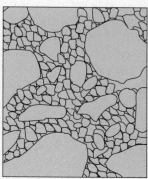

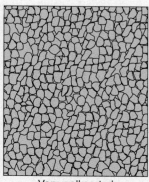

| Very poorly sorted | Moderately sorted | Very well sorted |

ROUNDNESS

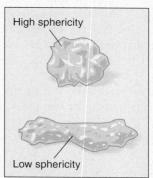

High sphericity

Low sphericity

Angular

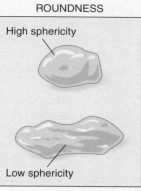

High sphericity

Low sphericity

Intermediate

High sphericity

Low sphericity

Rounded

b. ROUNDNESS AND SPHERICITY: Individual particles may take a variety of shapes, from rounded to angular. Note the distinction between roundness and sphericity; even an angular particle can have high sphericity, which simply means that it is not much longer than it is wide.

c. Till, like this deposit from the Exit Glacier in Alaska, is an ice-transported sediment that is usually poorly sorted, of low sphericity, and angular in shape.

d. Quartz sand, such as this (magnified) sample from Wisconsin, tends to be well sorted, with high sphericity and roundness as a result of prolonged weathering and erosion.

Martin Shields/Alamy

Courtesy Stephen C. Porter

ASK YOURSELF

Have a look at the clasts in the "Moderately sorted" sediment shown in (a). How would you describe the general shape of the clasts?

a. High sphericity and rounded

b. Intermediate sphericity and angular

c. Low sphericity and rounded

d. High sphericity and angular

Because the fragments are hot when formed, they are also called **pyroclasts** (from the Greek *pyro*, meaning "fire"). Pyroclasts are also classified by size as **bombs, lapilli,** and **ash**, from largest to smallest.

> **REMEMBER THIS!** Do you remember the definitions and characteristics of the various types of pyroclasts? You can review this by returning to *Volcanoes and Volcanic Hazards* in Chapter 6.

Chemical Sediment

All surface water and groundwater contains dissolved chemicals; there is no natural water on or in Earth that is completely free from dissolved matter. When dissolved matter separates from water by **precipitation**, the result is a **chemical sediment**. In a strict sense, chemical sediment refers to material that separates from water as a result of inorganic (that is, nonbiological) processes. As you will see, however, some chemical and biological processes in water are closely intertwined, and it can be difficult to differentiate them.

> **precipitation** The separation of a solid from a solution.
>
> **chemical sediment** Sediment formed by inorganic precipitation of minerals dissolved in lakewater, riverwater, or oceanwater.

Inorganic precipitation happens, among other ways, as a result of the evaporation of water. For example, if an inland sea is subjected to an increasingly warm and dry climate, or if the inflow of fresh water is restricted for some reason, the rate of evaporation may exceed the rate of input of fresh water into the water body. As the water evaporates, the sea may become so shallow and saline that salts that were dissolved in the water will begin to precipitate as solids. Modern examples of this process are found in the Aral Sea (Uzbekistan); California's Mono Lake; and Utah's Great Salt Lake (**Figure 8.3**).

Precipitation of solids also can occur if the chemical conditions in the water change. Changes in water chemistry can affect the solubility of a substance, causing it to either precipitate (if the solubility goes down) or dissolve (if the solubility goes up). Temperature, pressure, and the presence of other chemical substances dissolved in the water all can have an impact. For example, calcium carbonate ($CaCO_3$) is more soluble—that is, more easily dissolved—in ocean water at low temperatures and high pressures. The solubility of $CaCO_3$ also increases if the amount of dissolved carbon dioxide (CO_2) in the water increases (because—for the chemists—CO_2 and $CaCO_3$ are both reactants in the equation that causes dissolution). The interplay of these three factors has the result that calcium carbonate can be precipitated in shallow ocean water but dissolves in deeper ocean water.

Both carbon dioxide and calcium carbonate are generated in ocean water by biological processes, but the actual

Chemical sediment • Figure 8.3 _____

Utah's Bonneville Salt Flats is a desolate landscape. Chemical sediment containing magnesium and potassium chloride, in addition to ordinary salt, sodium chloride, has been deposited over the past 14,000 years by the evaporation of prehistoric Lake Bonneville. Great Salt Lake is a small remnant of Lake Bonneville.

John Burcham/NG Image Collection

Biogenic sediments are composed of the remains of organisms.

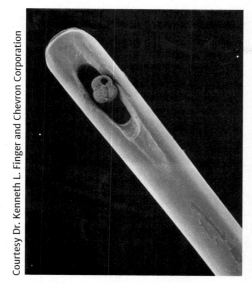

Courtesy Dr. Kenneth L. Finger and Chevron Corporation

a. In the eye of this needle is the shell of a **foraminifer** (or *foram*), a one-celled plankton that is abundant in the ocean. The shells of forams cover one-third to one-half of the ocean floor, accumulating to form biogenic deposits of calcareous ooze, which are especially abundant in warmer ocean water.

Jan Hinsch/Getty Images

b. Diatoms are a group of algae with outer casings made of amorphous silica. After accumulating on the ocean floor, they become an important constituent of siliceous ooze. Most diatoms are microscopic, including the wide variety of species shown here, but they range up to 2 millimeters in size.

precipitation or dissolution of calcium carbonate occurs inorganically, as a result of changes in the chemical or physical conditions in the water. Thus this is a good example of the overlap between chemical sediment and a third important category, *biogenic sediment.*

Biogenic Sediment

Biogenic sediment is composed of the accumulated remains of plants and animals, or of material that precipitates as a result of biological activity. The accumulated organic matter typically includes the hard parts of animals, such as shells, bones, and teeth, as well as fragments of plant matter, such as wood, roots, and leaves. These can be large fragments, or they can be microscopically small. In terrestrial environments, an important class of biogenic sediment begins with the accumulated remains of plants in swampy environments. Over time and with pressure, this accumulated plant matter gradually becomes **peat**, the precursor material to coal.

> **biogenic sediment**
> Sediment that is composed primarily of plant and animal remains or that precipitates as a result of biological processes.

In the ocean, biogenic sediment comes in two principal varieties. **Calcareous ooze**, made of calcium carbonate ($CaCO_3$), comes from the remains of tiny sea creatures (**Figure 8.4a**). While they are alive, these creatures float, but after they die, their calcareous shells drop to the bottom of

the ocean, where they accumulate. Calcareous ooze forms only in areas where the water is relatively warm. Calcium carbonate is extracted from seawater by organisms, but it can be precipitated (or dissolved) inorganically as a result of changing chemical or physical conditions in the water; thus, it can be considered both biogenic and chemical.

In colder, deeper waters, calcareous sediment dissolves and the biogenic sediment that accumulates is often siliceous in composition. Much of the deep ocean floor is mantled with **siliceous ooze**, which comes from silica-secreting organisms such as **diatoms** and **radiolarians** (**Figure 8.4b**) Siliceous ooze is chemically similar to quartz but differs in mineral structure. The silica casings of diatoms are actually composed of amorphous silica, like the mineraloid opal; they are made of the same material as the mineral quartz, but they lack its orderly crystal structure.

STOP CONCEPT CHECK

1. **What** terms are used to describe the individual particles that compose clastic sediment?
2. **How** do chemical and biogenic sediments differ from clastic sediment?
3. **What** are the main differences and similarities in the way chemical sediment and biogenic sediment are formed?

DEPOSITIONAL ENVIRONMENTS

Learning Objectives

1. **Define** deposition and describe the conditions that commonly lead to the deposition of sediment.

2. **Describe** the principal environments where deposition takes place on land.

3. **Describe** the principal environments where deposition takes place in and near the ocean.

Think back to the rock cycle (Figure 7.1), and what you have learned about the processes by which rock disintegrates. Weathering by mechanical, chemical, and biological mechanisms transforms rock into regolith. To become sediment—the next step in the rock cycle—the broken-up rock must be picked up, transported by any of several possible erosional mechanisms, and eventually deposited. In this section we review the mechanisms by which sediment can be transported, and then we consider the main environments where it is commonly laid down, or deposited.

Transport and Deposition of Sediment

As you learned in Chapter 7, particles of regolith generated by the weathering of rock can be transported erosionally by water, ice, and wind, or they can move downslope under the influence of gravity, with or without the involvement of a fluid medium, by mass wasting. Many of the important mechanisms of sediment transport are summarized in **Figure 8.5**.

Wherever the carrying capacity of the transporting agent decreases sufficiently for sediment to settle out, **deposition** occurs. This typically happens where the energy of the flowing medium suddenly declines. Thus, common environments for the deposition of sediment include stream

| deposition The laying down of sediment. |

channels and floodplains, where flowing water comes to an abrupt stop; lakeshores and lake bottoms, where currents are slow; the margins of glaciers, where ice flow ceases; and areas where the wind is intermittently strong, such as beaches and deserts. Offshore, sediment is deposited where rivers enter the ocean and where oceanic currents move seafloor sediment.

Since the term *deposition* refers generally to the laying down of sediment, it can be applied to chemical and biogenic sediment, as well as to clastic sediment. The gravitational settling of clasts carried by flowing water, air, or ice is deposition. The precipitation of dissolved matter from water in a lake or ocean also is a type of deposition.

Let's look more closely at the principal environments where the deposition of sediment occurs on land, in the ocean, and in coastal zones. Many of the important depositional environments are summarized in **Figure 8.6**.

Depositional Environments on Land

There are four principal sites of deposition on land (**Figure 8.7**): along the margins of glaciers; in streams; in lakes; and wherever winds blow strongly and intermittently.

Glacier Margins Sediment transported by a glacier is either deposited along the glacier's base or released along its margins as melting and retreat of the glacier occur. The sediment may then be subjected to further reworking by running water. Debris that has been deposited directly from ice commonly forms a random mixture of particles that range in size from clay to boulders and consist of all the types of rock over which the ice has passed. This type of sediment is called **till** (**Figure 8.7a**). Glaciers and glacial deposits are discussed in greater detail in Chapter 13.

Streams and Floodplains Streams are the main transporters of sediment on land. Streams tend to deposit their load of sediment wherever the flow velocity decreases rapidly, such as along the margins of the channel, upon entering a large standing body of water, or upon emerging from a steep mountain slope onto a flat plain. Sediment deposited by streams also varies in its characteristics from place to place, depending on the type of stream, the strength of flow, and the sediment load.

Generally speaking, stream-carried sediment becomes better sorted and more rounded with distance from the source. Thus, a typical large, smoothly flowing stream may deposit well-sorted coarse and fine particles as it slowly migrates back and forth across its valley. During spring floods, fine silt and clay are deposited on the floodplain. In contrast, an energetic mountain stream flowing down a steep valley transports a wide range of particles, including boulders, and a high proportion of angular rock fragments. Such "immature" sediment may contain chemically less-stable minerals, such as amphiboles and feldspars that have not yet had enough time to undergo chemical weathering.

When a stream flowing in a steep channel reaches the front of the mountain and is no longer constrained by valley walls, it may spread out into an **alluvial fan**, in which the sediment ranges from coarse, poorly sorted gravel upstream to well-sorted sand downstream.

Lakes and Swamps Sediment that is deposited in a lake typically accumulates on the lakeshore and in quiet waters on the lake floor. The sediment load of a stream entering

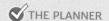
Sediment can be transported by flowing wind, water, and ice. It also can move downslope under the influence of gravity, without the requirement of a transporting medium. The major modes of sediment transport are illustrated here.

a. Wind: A dust storm strikes the Darfur region of Sudan, 2007.

STEPHEN MORRISON/EPA/NewsCom

b. Water: Sediment is carried alongshore by waves and currents in Irian Jaya, Indonesia.

Wayne G. Lawler/Photo Researchers, Inc.

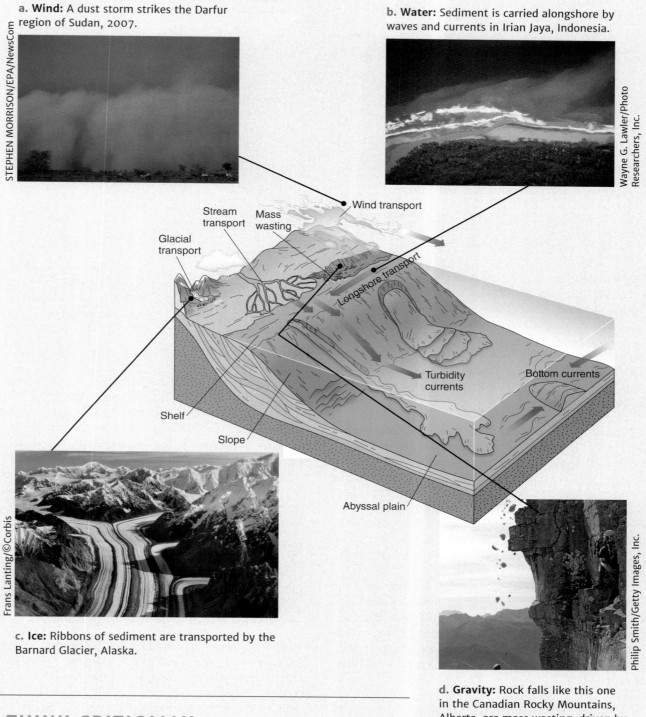

Wind transport

Stream transport

Mass wasting

Glacial transport

Longshore transport

Turbidity currents

Bottom currents

Shelf

Slope

Abyssal plain

Frans Lanting/©Corbis

Philip Smith/Getty Images, Inc.

c. Ice: Ribbons of sediment are transported by the Barnard Glacier, Alaska.

d. Gravity: Rock falls like this one in the Canadian Rocky Mountains, Alberta, are mass wasting, driven by gravity.

THINK CRITICALLY

How would you distinguish between gravity-driven mass wasting in which the moving material is water-saturated (such as a mudflow), and sediment (mud) that is transported by a flowing stream of water?

Many of the important depositional environments for sediment, both on land and in the ocean, are shown here. Each environment has its own unique collection of sediment.

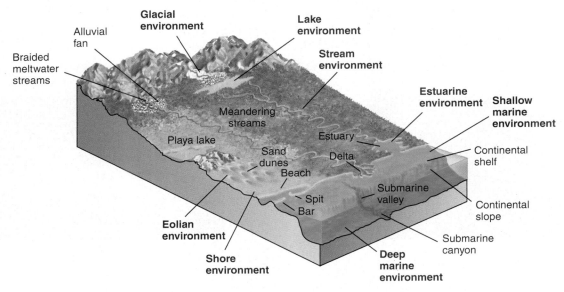

a lake will be dropped just after it enters the lake, because this is where the stream's velocity and transporting ability suddenly decrease. This typically leads to the formation of a **delta** (**Figure 8.7b**). Inclined, generally well-sorted layers on the front of the delta pass downward and fan outward into thinner, finer-grained, evenly laminated layers on the lake floor.

> **delta** A sedimentary deposit, commonly fan-shaped, that forms where a stream enters a standing body of water.

In arid regions, seasonal lakes called **playas** are common (**Figure 8.7c**). These ephemeral lakes fill up with water for part of the year and then leave deposits of evaporated salts when they dry out. As discussed above, evaporation is an important inorganic process that leads to the deposition of chemical sediments. Ponds, swamps, and wetlands are also sites of sediment deposition on land. Swamps and wetlands can actually be considered as stages in the life cycle of a mature lake, characterized by infilling of the water body with accumulated mineral and plant matter.

Lake deposits may appear similar in many ways to marine deposits. Among the distinguishing characteristics are the generally smaller extent of lake deposits (lakes are typically smaller than seas), and the presence of freshwater fossils instead of marine fossils. As you might expect, lake deposits are much less common in the geological record than marine sediment.

Dry, Windy Environments
Sediment transport and deposition in dry environments tends to be dominated by wind, or **eolian** processes, named after Aeolus, the Greek god of wind. **Eolian sediment** tends to be finer than that moved by other erosional agents (see *Remember This!*). Grains of sand are easily transported in places where strong winds are blowing and vegetation is too sparse to stabilize the land surface, such as seacoasts and deserts.

> **eolian sediment** Sediment that is carried and deposited by wind.

Sand carried in suspension by the air is deposited whenever the wind velocity decreases, so areas where wind is intermittent are likely sites for deposition. In such places, windblown sand may pile up to form dunes composed of well-sorted grains (**Figure 8.7d**), with bedding inclined in the downwind direction (i.e., the direction toward which the air is flowing). Using these characteristics, geologists can easily identify ancient dune sand in the rock record.

> **REMEMBER THIS!** Why is windblown sediment typically finer-grained than sediment transported by swiftly-flowing water or by ice? What characteristic of air is responsible for this? If you can't remember, try looking back at *Erosion and Mass Wasting*, Chapter 7.

Powdery dust that has been picked up and moved by the wind may travel great distances and be deposited thousands of kilometers away. For example, oceanographers have discovered windblown sediment from the Sahara Desert of North Africa on the other side of the Atlantic Ocean. One important type of windblown sediment is **loess** (a German word meaning "loose" and pronounced "luhss"). Consisting predominantly of yellow-brown silt, loess is windblown

Wind, water, and ice typically deposit their sediment load in locations where the energy or velocity of their flow decreases suddenly.

a. Glacier margins: Sediment of all sizes has been deposited in this moraine at the end of the Ghiacciaio Dei Forni glacier in the Italian Alps. Unsorted glacial sediment like this is called *till*.

b. Delta: A river on Russia's Kamchatka Peninsula contributes sediment that forms a classic fan-shaped delta where the river enters the ocean.

Alamy

Peter Carsten/NG Image Collection

c. Playa: Playas, or dry lakebeds, like this one in Nevada, may intermittently be covered with water, but normally they have the salt-encrusted appearance seen here.

d. Dunes: Sand dunes, like these in the Namib Desert, tend to form in dry environments dominated by aeolian (wind) transport of sediment.

James P. Blair/NG Image Collection

Werner Hilpert/Getty Images, Inc.

The Loess Plateau of northern China, here in Shaanxi Province, is a thick sequence of fine, buff-colored, wind-blown sediment that accumulated in periglacial areas during the last ice age. Loess is very soft; the arch-shaped openings visible in the photo are dwellings carved into the hillside. It is also easily eroded; the farmers have terraced the slopes to prevent the soil from washing away.

Jim Richardson/NG Image Collection

dust transported from deserts, the surfaces and edges of glaciers, and glacial streams during times of ice-sheet retreat (**Figure 8.8**).

Depositional Environments in and near the Ocean

Sediment can be deposited anywhere in and around the edges of the ocean (see Figure 8.6). As on land, deposition in the ocean commonly occurs wherever the velocity of the current decreases suddenly (**Figure 8.9**). Chemical and biogenic sediment deposition is also very important in the oceanic environment, blanketing much of the ocean floor.

Deltas and Estuaries As on land, delta deposits form where streams flow into the ocean and lose energy, dropping their suspended load of sediment. Large marine deltas are complex deposits that consist of coarse stream-channel sediment, fine sediment deposited between channels, and still finer sediment deposited farther out on the seafloor.

Where the load of sediment carried by a stream to the sea is smaller, much of it may be trapped in an **estuary** (**Figure 8.9a**). In estuaries, coarse sediment tends to settle close to land, whereas fine sediment is carried farther seaward. Tiny individual particles of clay carried in suspension settle very slowly to the seafloor. As a transitional environment between land and sea, estuarine sediment often contains a large amount of organic matter, including fossils of organisms from both land and sea.

> **estuary** A semi-enclosed body of coastal water, in which fresh water mixes with seawater.

Beaches Quartz, the most durable of the common minerals in continental rock, is the most common component of beach sand. However, not all ocean beaches are sandy. Any beach consists of the coarsest rock particles contributed by the erosion of adjacent sea cliffs, together with materials carried to it by rivers or by currents moving along the shore. Beach sediment tends to be better sorted than stream sediment of comparable coarseness. Particles of beach sediment, dragged back and forth by the surf and turned over and over, become rounded by abrasion. Though beach sands are often buff colored, they don't have to be; they may also be white, black, or even green, reflecting the presence of different minerals (**Figure 8.9b**).

Continental Shelves Most of the world's sedimentary rocks originate as sediment deposited on continental shelves. As fresh water flows out to sea through an estuary or a river mouth, it continues seaward across the continental shelf. It will deposit most of its sand-sized sediment, whether river derived or formed by erosion of the shore, within about 5 kilometers of the land. However, some sand can be found 100 kilometers or more offshore. Otherwise, continental shelf sediment tends to consist of silty or sandy mud that contains marine fossils.

On the continental shelf of eastern North America, up to a 14-kilometer thickness of fine sediment has accumulated over the past 150 million years. Shelves, in effect, catch weathered continental crust in such a way that it is continually recycled by the processes of plate tectonics and the rock cycle. Because of the abundance of marine life in shallow shelf waters, continental shelf sediment generally contains a high percentage of organic matter.

Depositional environments in and near the ocean • Figure 8.9

Clastic, chemical, and biogenic sediments are all important in different oceanic and near-ocean depositional environments.

Brackish water from mixing of ocean and river water

Sandbar

Seagulls

Raymond Gehman/NG Image Collection

Pavel Tvrdy/Shutterstock

Courtesy NASA

a. Estuary

Where the Tijuana River (between the United States and Mexico) flows into the Pacific Ocean, it deposits sediment—as well as sewage and trash from both sides of the border—into an estuary. Here, seagulls congregate on sandbars formed by sediment.

b. Beach

The unusual color of Hawaii's Green Sand Beach comes from a high concentration of the mineral olivine in its sand (inset). The beach is surrounded by the eroded walls of a volcano. The volcanic basalt contains olivine, which washes down onto the beach. Olivine is not very resistant to weathering, so we would only expect to find a green sand beach very close to its volcanic source.

c. Carbonate shelf

Carbonate sediment accumulates in the warm, shallow offshore waters of these islands in the Bahamas. The fine sediment appears white and consists of fine skeletal debris from tiny sea creatures.

d. Deep-sea turbidites

Turbidites are deposited by swiftly flowing currents, in the deep ocean where the continental slope transitions to the flat abyssal plain. These turbidite beds from the ocean floor have been tilted, uplifted, and exposed in a wave-eroded bench along the coast of the Olympic Peninsula in Washington.

Bruce Dale/NG Image Collection

Courtesy Stephen C. Porter

Carbonate Platforms and Reefs Where the climate and surface temperature are warm enough to nurture abundant carbonate-secreting organisms, biogenic sediment composed of calcium carbonate may accumulate on continental shelves or broad, flat carbonate platforms that rise from the seafloor (**Figure 8.9c**). The carbonate platforms and submarine cave systems of the Great Bahama Bank are profiled in the chapter-opener. A **reef** is a wave-resistant structure built from the skeletons of marine invertebrates. Reefs are generally restricted to warm, sunlit waters of normal marine salinity; they are discussed in greater detail in Chapter 12.

Marine Evaporite Basins In coastal areas with a sufficiently warm and dry climate, ocean water may evaporate fast enough to leave behind the salts that were dissolved in it, as a marine **evaporite** deposit. These deposits can be distinguished from lake-derived evaporite deposits because they have a different mineral composition. Marine evaporite deposits are very common, reflecting the many times that shallow seas have flooded large areas of continents in the past. They underlie as much as 30% of the land area of North America. The Great Salt Lake and its salt flats, such as Bonneville Salt Flats shown in Figure 8.3, is one example of this.

> **evaporite** A rock formed by the evaporation of lakewater or seawater, followed by lithification of the resulting salt deposit.

If you visit the website highlighted in *Where Geologists Click*, you will find a video that describes how marine evaporite deposits eventually resulted in the formation of the distinctive geological features of Arches National Park, Utah.

Continental Slope and Abyssal Plain Thick sediment deposits are found at the foot of the continental slope, at depths as great as 5 kilometers beneath the surface of the ocean. The origin of these deposits was difficult to explain until marine geologists discovered that **turbidity currents**—essentially, underwater landslides that originate on the continental shelf—deposit them. These currents of sediment, sometimes started by the shaking from an earthquake, rush swiftly down the continental slope at velocities of up to 90 kilometers per hour. When a turbidity current reaches the flat abyssal plain of the ocean floor, it slows down and deposits a graded layer of sediment called a **turbidite**. At any site on the continental slope and rise, a major turbidity current is a rare event that happens perhaps once every few thousand years. Nevertheless, over millions of years, turbidites can slowly accumulate and form thick deposits consisting of many layers (**Figure 8.9d**).

> **turbidity current** A turbulent, gravity-driven flow consisting of a mixture of sediment and water, which conveys sediment from the continental shelf to the deep sea.

As mentioned earlier, a large part of the flat abyssal plain of the deep ocean floor is covered with biogenic sediment. Calcareous ooze forms mainly at low to middle latitudes, where the water is relatively warm; in colder water,

Where Geologists CLICK

The National Park Service: Arches National Park

The U.S. National Park Service provides much useful information about science and nature in all of the national parks. Here, at the Arches National Park website, you can watch an interesting video that describes the formation of the distinctive geological features of the park, highlighting the connections between sedimentation, rock formation, and tectonic activity.

Geology of Arches

as you recall, $CaCO_3$ dissolves before reaching the bottom. Siliceous ooze is more common in the deeper, colder waters of the Pacific and Indian oceans, and in the Southern Ocean encircling Antarctica. In these areas the biological productivity of surface waters is high, due to the upwelling of deep ocean water rich in nutrients. A large volume of organic matter is generated at shallow depths, which then rains down and accumulates in a blanketing layer on the ocean floor.

🛑 **CONCEPT CHECK**

1. **What** are the main mechanisms of sediment transport and the main environments in which they deposit sediment?

2. **What** are some of the differences and similarities in the main depositional environments on land?

3. **What** are some of the differences and similarities between the main depositional environments near and in the ocean, and those on land?

SEDIMENTARY ROCK

Learning Objectives

1. **Relate** the appearance of sedimentary rock to its mode of formation.

2. **Summarize** three processes that lead to the lithification of sediment.

3. **Identify** the most common clastic, chemical, and biogenic sedimentary rock types.

4. **Explain** how features such as ripple marks, cracks, and fossils can tell geologists about the environment in which a rock originated.

5. **Describe** the concept of sedimentary facies.

Lithification, the group of processes by which sediment is transformed into rock, is an important step in the rock cycle (see Figure 7.1). After sediment has been picked up, transported, and deposited, it may be buried by more overlying sediment. Then—depending on conditions at the site of deposition and burial—it may undergo lithification to become sedimentary rock. In this section, we discuss how lithification occurs and how the appearance of the new rock depends on both the materials and the processes by which it is created.

> **lithification** The group of processes by which loose sediment is transformed into sedimentary rock.

Rock Beds

When you look at an outcrop of sedimentary rock, such as the one shown in **Figure 8.10**, one of the first things you notice is the **bedding**. As discussed in Chapter 3, the banded appearance comes from the fact that sedimentary particles are deposited in distinct strata. Over time, the mineral composition of the sediment being transported to a particular location may change, or the sediment may be deposited in different ways. This causes the individual beds to look different. The boundary between adjacent strata is called a **bedding surface**. The presence of bedding and bedding surfaces tells geologists that the rock was once sediment.

> **bedding** The layered arrangement of strata in a body of sediment or sedimentary rock.

The appearance of a bed can tell a geologist a great deal about how the sediment was deposited. For example, in a **graded bed**, the coarse clasts are concentrated at the bottom, grading up to the finest clasts at the top (**Figure 8.11**). Graded beds often form where a stream or river enters a lake or an ocean.

Turbulent flow in streams, wind, or ocean waves produces a type of bedding called **cross bedding**. The thick strata of sandstone contain many thin beds that are inclined with respect to the stratum in which they occur, as shown in *Amazing Places*. The direction in which the cross bedding is inclined can tell geologists the direction in which the water or air currents were moving when they deposited the sediment.

Lithification

In order for newly deposited, loose sediment to be lithified and turned into rock, the individual particles must somehow be bound together into a cohesive unit. When a layer of sediment is buried, either by the accumulation of more sediment or by tectonic processes, it is placed under higher pressure, leading to **compaction**.

> **compaction** Reduction of pore space in a sediment as a result of the weight of overlying sediment.

Bedding • Figure 8.10

Nicole Duplaix/NG Image Collection

The alternating red and black beds of the Bungle Bungle Range in north-western Australia derive their unique coloration from layers of sandstone with different permeabilities. Algae grow in the more permeable strata, tinting the rock black.

The appearance of a bed can say a lot about its origin.

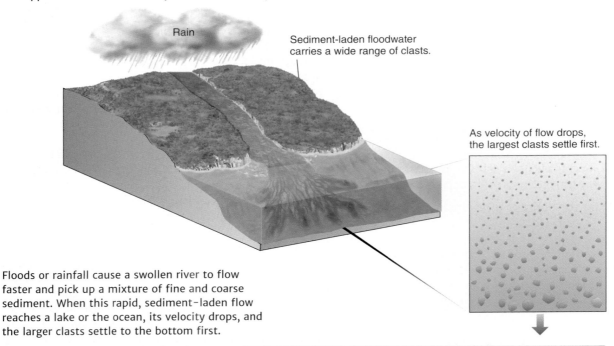

Rain

Sediment-laden floodwater carries a wide range of clasts.

As velocity of flow drops, the largest clasts settle first.

Floods or rainfall cause a swollen river to flow faster and pick up a mixture of fine and coarse sediment. When this rapid, sediment-laden flow reaches a lake or the ocean, its velocity drops, and the larger clasts settle to the bottom first.

The center stratum in this rock from California is a graded bed, which was produced very quickly, by a single flood. After the sediment was deposited, it lithified into rock with a graded bed, like the one shown here. The largest clasts, which settled first, are on the bottom.

Fine grains

Coarse grains

©Marli Bryant Miller

---

cementation The process in which substances dissolved in pore water precipitate out and form a matrix in which grains of sediment are joined together.

Compaction is generally the first step in lithification, which can proceed in several ways. One common process that often happens during lithification is **cementation**, in which the grains of sediment are joined together. Cementation can happen in various ways, such as the evaporation of groundwater under desert conditions. As the water evaporates, chemicals such as silica, calcium carbonate, and iron hydroxide precipitate and cement the grains of sediment together.

Another important lithification process is **recrystallization**, which is especially common in limestone formed by coral reefs. Calcium carbonate crystals in the fossilized reef change from their original form (aragonite) to the more stable mineral, calcite. In the process of recrystallizing, crystals that were separate can grow together.

Pressure caused by sediment accumulation or tectonic forces initiates the lithification process, as you can

recrystallization The formation of new crystalline mineral grains from old ones.

The Navajo Sandstone

George F. Mobley/NG Image Collection

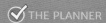

Global Locator

Zion National Park

Eolian transport

Sand sea

Stream

Transport

〰 Appalachians   ▨ Grenville Mountains

Many rock formations in Utah's Zion National Park resemble sand dunes—because they originally were dunes. The imposing cliffs and hills (see photos, top and right) were once part of a vast sea of sand, larger than the Sahara Desert is today. The dunes lithified into sandstone and subsequently eroded into the formations you see today. The sedimentary formation they belong to, the Navajo Sandstone, extends over several states in the American Southwest and attains a thickness of 700 meters in Zion National Park.

If all of this rock was once sand, where did the sand come from? Dune patterns indicate that the prevailing winds came from the north, but no mountain ranges of suitable size or age can be found there. The mountain range we call the Rockies did not yet exist in the Lower Jurassic Period, 190 million years ago, when the Navajo sand was deposited.

However, the Appalachian Mountains and remnants of the more ancient Grenville Mountains did exist then. Uplifted by a tectonic collision that began 500 million years ago, they were once as tall as the Himalaya and extended all the way into what is now Texas. By the Lower Jurassic, the Appalachians had eroded considerably; it was likely their sediment that formed the Navajo Sandstone. Rivers flowing westward carried the sediment westward (inset map). As the climate became arid, winds transported the now-dried river sands southward, where they became one of the largest sand seas that ever existed on Earth.

THINK CRITICALLY

What was the tectonic environment in which the Appalachian Mountains were uplifted?

Robert Sisson/NG Image Collection

Process Diagram

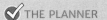 THE PLANNER

How lithification occurs • Figure 8.12

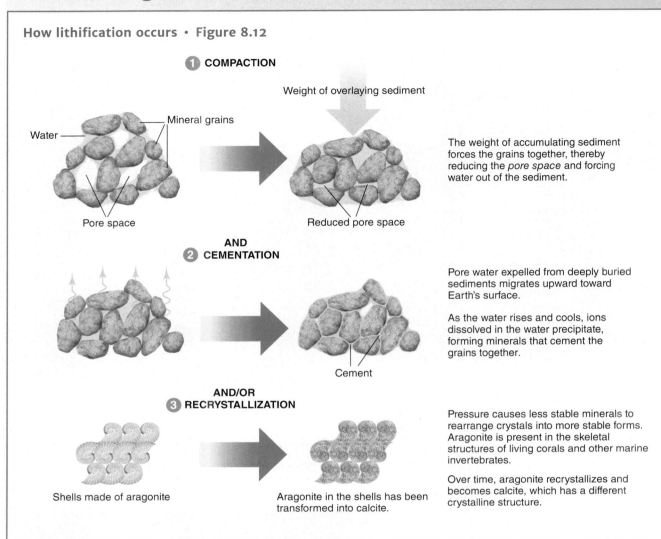

① COMPACTION

Weight of overlaying sediment

Mineral grains

Water

Pore space

Reduced pore space

The weight of accumulating sediment forces the grains together, thereby reducing the *pore space* and forcing water out of the sediment.

AND
② CEMENTATION

Cement

Pore water expelled from deeply buried sediments migrates upward toward Earth's surface.

As the water rises and cools, ions dissolved in the water precipitate, forming minerals that cement the grains together.

AND/OR
③ RECRYSTALLIZATION

Shells made of aragonite

Aragonite in the shells has been transformed into calcite.

Pressure causes less stable minerals to rearrange crystals into more stable forms. Aragonite is present in the skeletal structures of living corals and other marine invertebrates.

Over time, aragonite recrystallizes and becomes calcite, which has a different crystalline structure.

THINK CRITICALLY

Consider the chemical composition of Earth's crust (Chapter 2). What would you predict is the most common mineral cement in clastic sedimentary rock?

---

see in **Figure 8.12**. The pressures involved in lithification are high by everyday human standards, but they are low pressures by geological standards, and they are very low in comparison with the pressures that induce metamorphism (Chapter 10). All of the relatively low-temperature, low-pressure changes that happen to sediment after deposition are collectively called **diagenesis**. They include lithification as well as processes involving chemical reactions or microbial activity that are not part of lithification.

Types of Sedimentary Rock

Our first task as geologists is to determine whether a rock is, in fact, sedimentary. This can be more challenging than

it might seem. For example, if a sedimentary rock is made up of particles derived from the weathering and erosion of igneous rock, it may contain many of the same minerals as the source rock. How, then, can we tell for sure that it is sedimentary rather than igneous? In addition to such clues as bedding, the texture of the rock provides evidence (**Figure 8.13**).

Clastic Sedimentary Rock When clastic sediment lithifies, it produces a rock with properties that reflect the type of sediment it came from. The four basic classes are conglomerate, sandstone, mudstone, and shale. These are the rock equivalents of gravel, sand, silt, and clay-rich sediment (see Figure 8.1).

Two of these rocks are sedimentary, and one is igneous. How can you tell which is which?

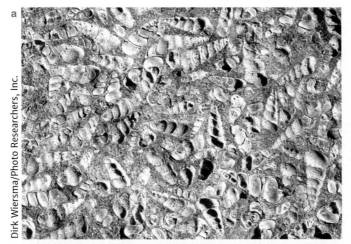

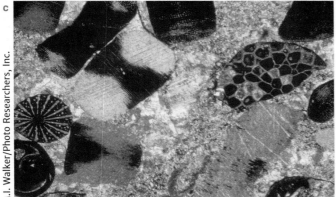

Dirk Wiersma/Photo Researchers, Inc.

M.I. Walker/Photo Researchers, Inc.

Grey Wall Studio/ Shutterstock

Answers

a. The fossils in this specimen are a give-away. No organism can survive the high temperatures at which igneous rock are formed, so the presence of ancient shells means the rock (limestone) is sedimentary.

b. Looking at this sample, we see interlocking, irregularly shaped crystals without any cement. This rock is granite, an igneous rock.

c. In the magnified view of this sample, we see mineral grains rounded by abrasion. The grains do not abut one another; they have gaps between them that are filled by cement. This rock is sedimentary. (It is sandstone, held together by calcite cement.)

To be classified as **conglomerate**, a sedimentary rock must have clasts larger than 2 millimeters. In a typical conglomerate, the large clasts are surrounded by much finer-grained material, called the **matrix**. If the clasts are angular, rather than rounded, the rock is called **breccia**. The presence of angular clasts means that the sediment has been transported only a short distance and was not subjected to a long abrasion process.

The medium-sized grains in **sandstone** range from 0.05 to 2 millimeters in size. They are usually dominated by quartz because quartz is a tough mineral that resists weathering. If the sediment has not been transported very far from its source, it may still contain a lot of feldspar or rock fragments. Geologists would call such a sandstone "immature."

> **conglomerate** Clastic sedimentary rock with large fragments in a finer-grained matrix.
>
> **sandstone** Medium-grained clastic sedimentary rock in which the clasts are typically, but not necessarily, dominated by quartz grains.

Mudstone, often called **mudrock**, consists primarily of silt- and clay-sized particles; these include tiny pieces of rock and mineral grains, as well as clay minerals. Mudrock, as a group, includes the rock types **siltstone, mudstone**, and **claystone**—all very fine-grained sedimentary rock types that are distinguished from one another on the basis of their relative proportions of silt-sized to clay-sized particles. Rock that is classified as mudrock breaks into blocky fragments. In contrast, **shale**, a subvariety of mudrock, is **fissile**, which means that it splits into sheet-like fragments.

> **mudstone** A group of very fine-grained, nonfissile sedimentary rock types with differing proportions of silt- and clay-sized particles.
>
> **shale** Very fine-grained fissile or laminated sedimentary rock, consisting primarily of silt- or clay-sized particles; a fissile mudstone.

Chemical Sedimentary Rock

Chemical sedimentary rock results from the lithification of chemical sediment.

As we have seen, such sediment is formed by the chemical precipitation of minerals from water. Most chemical sedimentary rock types contain only one important mineral, such as calcite, dolomite, gypsum, or halite. These **monomineralic** compositions, together with their modes of precipitation, provide the basis for classification of these rock types.

Chemical sedimentary rock often forms from evaporite deposits. Calcite, gypsum, and halite typically form from the evaporation of seawater, while the evaporation of lakewater may yield more exotic minerals (e.g., sodium carbonate, borax). Many evaporite minerals are mined because they have industrial uses; for example, gypsum is used to make plasterboard. In addition, most of the salt we eat comes from evaporite deposits.

An unusual but economically important kind of chemical sedimentary rock is a **banded iron formation**. Such rock

> **banded iron formation** A type of chemical sedimentary rock rich in iron minerals and silica.

is the source of most of the iron mined today. Not only are banded iron formations valuable for their ore, they also tell the story of a critical period in Earth's history. Almost all banded iron formations are about the same age—1.8 to 2.5 billion years old. This strongly suggests that unique conditions existed on Earth during that period (see *What a Geologist Sees*).

Biogenic Sedimentary Rock The most abundant biogenic sedimentary rock is **limestone**. It is formed from lith-

> **limestone** A sedimentary rock that consists primarily of the mineral calcite.

ified shells and skeletal material from marine organisms, and from the lithification of calcareous ooze. Limestone is a very common rock type, which tells us something about the massive abundance of tiny marine organisms. It is also an extremely important rock type in the history of our planet because it provides a long-term storage reservoir for carbon that would otherwise reside in the atmosphere in the form of carbon dioxide. We will look at atmospheric carbon dioxide in greater detail in Chapter 14.

Some marine organisms build their shells or skeletons from calcite, but most construct them from the mineral aragonite, which, like calcite, is composed of calcium carbonate ($CaCO_3$). During diagenesis, the aragonite is transformed into the more stable mineral calcite, the main ingredient of limestone. Calcite is sometimes replaced by the mineral dolomite (a carbonate mineral that contains both magnesium and calcium); the resulting rock is called **dolostone**.

Another marine biogenic rock, **diatomite**, consists of the lithified remains of diatoms. (Recall that microscopic diatoms, which have casings made of amorphous silica, are a common constituent of siliceous ooze on the ocean floor; see Figure 8.4b.) **Chert**, another silica-rich marine rock, originates from a combination of chemical and biogenic processes. The silica in some chert is derived from silica-rich shells and casings from microscopic sea animals, like

radiolarians (see Figure 8.4b). In other kinds of chert, such as the chert layers that commonly occur in banded iron formation, remnants of radiolarians and diatoms may be sparse or even absent. In those cases, it can be speculated that the silica may have precipitated directly from seawater, forming chemical rather than biogenic sediments.

Our last important biogenic sediment, peat, forms in terrestrial swampy environments. Eventually, given enough time and pressure, peat may lithify to become **coal**. The process of lithification (in this case, called **coalification**) involves further compaction, release of water, and slow chemical changes that

> **coal** A combustible rock formed from the lithification of plant-rich sediment.

weld the plant fragments together, thereby making the coal relatively lower in water and richer in carbon than the original peat.

Interpreting Environmental Clues

Just as history books record the changing patterns of civilization, layers of sediment, like pages in a book, record how environmental conditions have changed throughout Earth's history. Geologists are able to "read" this story by interpreting the evidence in the sedimentary rock that forms from the sediment.

We have already seen that the size, shape, and arrangement of particles in sediment (the **texture** of the sediment), preserved in rock, provide evidence about the transport of the sediment and the geological environment in which sediment was deposited and accumulated. These and other clues enable us to demonstrate the existence of past oceans, coasts, lakes, streams, deserts, glaciers, and wetlands.

Ancient sedimentary deposits bear a striking resemblance to sedimentary environments on Earth today (**Figure 8.14**). Note that this is an excellent example of the principle of uniformitarianism (see *Remember This!*). Patterns formed by currents of water or air moving across sediment can be preserved and later exposed on bedding surfaces. For example, bodies of sand that are moved by wind, streams, or coastal waves are often rippled; these wavy structures may be preserved in sandstone as **ripple marks** (**Figure 8.14a and b**). Similarly, mud cracks (**Figure 8.14c and d**), fossil tracks (**Figure 8.14d and e**), and even raindrop impacts can be recorded on bedding surfaces, attesting to moist surface conditions at the time they were formed.

> **REMEMBER THIS!** Can you state the principle of uniformitarianism and discuss its importance for the science of geology? Review this by looking back at *The Ever-Changing Earth*, Chapter 1.

Fossils also provide significant clues about former environments. Some animals and plants inhabit warm, moist climates, whereas others can live only in cold, dry climates. Using the climatic ranges of modern plants and animals as guides, we can infer the general character of the climate

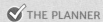
Atmospheric Change, Recorded in Rock

The geologist studying this rock outcrop notices the reddish color, typical of iron-rich rock. Closer examination (inset) shows that it is composed of thin red and black iron-rich layers alternating with white silica-rich layers made of the rock type **chert**. The rock type is **banded iron formation**. There are no obvious clastic grains, suggesting that the rock formed from a chemical precipitate. Our geologist hypothesizes that this 2.5-billion-year-old stratum in the Hamersley Range in Australia was formed when iron that was dissolved in seawater precipitated as chemical sediment.

Today, seawater contains only slight traces of iron because oxygen in the atmosphere reacts with it to form insoluble iron compounds. If the ocean was once rich in dissolved iron, there must have been very little oxygen in the atmosphere at that time.

The geologist would then ask the obvious question: How did Earth make the transformation from an oxygen-poor atmosphere 2.5 billion years ago to the oxygen-rich atmosphere of today?

In some 2.5-billion-year-old rocks, there are microscopic fossils of cyanobacteria. These bacteria are thought to be the first organisms on Earth to extract energy from sunlight by photosynthesis, a chemical process that releases oxygen. Scientists hypothesize that algae might have oxygenated Earth's atmosphere very rapidly—and possibly more than once, as they proliferated and then poisoned themselves by producing too much oxygen. Each time the oxygen concentration changed, an iron mineral would precipitate out of the seawater, creating a new band of iron-rich sediment. Eventually, about 2.0 to 1.8 billion years ago, the oxygen level of the atmosphere reached a point where the ocean could no longer retain much iron, and banded iron formations could no longer form.

Courtesy Brian J. Skinner

Black layers are rich in reduced iron (Fe^{2+}).

Red layers are rich in oxidized iron (Fe^{3+}).

White layers are rich in silica.

Close-up of layers in a banded iron formation

THINK CRITICALLY

The photo of the banded iron formation reveals both iron-rich and silica-rich layers. If oxygen from cyanobacteria caused iron to precipitate, what is your hypothesis as to why silica precipitated?

Ancient features preserved in rock often look very similar to their modern equivalents, giving scientists important clues about ancient environments. Note that the modern environment may be nothing like the ancient environment in which the sediment first accumulated.

a. Ripples are forming in a shallow-water environment near the shore of Ocracoke Island, North Carolina.

Courtesy Stephen C. Porter

b. Almost identical ripple marks are exposed on a bedding surface of sandstone at Artist's Point, Colorado National Park, Colorado.

© Marli Bryant Miller

c. Mud cracks are forming on this modern river bed as the river dries up.

Medford Taylor/NG Image Collection

d. Similarly shaped mud cracks are preserved on the surface of shale exposed at Ausable Chasm, New York. We can infer that this rock formation was deposited in an intermittently wet environment, such as a seasonal lakebed or a tidal flat.

Courtesy Stephen C. Porter

e. A yellow-eyed penguin made these footprints in soft sand on the beach at Otago Peninsula, South Island, New Zealand.

Bill Hatcher/National Geographic Creative

f. Fossilized footprints are preserved in sandstone. The animals that left these prints may have been hunting for prey stranded by the falling tide, just like the present-day seagulls in Alaska.

© age fotostock/Alamy

This now-extinct fossilized seed fern, from the genus Pecopteris, dates from the Carboniferous Period. Fossils of tropical, moisture-loving plants, such as horsetails, seed ferns, and tree ferns, can be found in Carboniferous-aged sedimentary rock from all over the world, even in areas that now have cooler or drier climates.

Kevin Schafer/Corbis Images

in which similar ancestral forms lived (**Figure 8.15**). Even microscopic fossils are important; for example, the shells of foraminifera can tell us about former temperatures and salinity conditions in the oceans. Fossils are also the basis for determining the relative ages of strata. As you learned in Chapter 3, fossils have played an essential role in efforts to reconstruct the past 635 million years of Earth's history.

Even the color of fresh, unweathered sedimentary rock can provide clues to the environmental conditions in

which the rock originated. The color of a particular rock is determined by the colors of the minerals, rock fragments, and organic matter of which it is composed. For example, iron sulfides and organic detritus buried with sediment are responsible for most of the dark colors in sedimentary rock. The presence of these materials implies that the sediment was deposited in an oxygen-poor (reducing) environment. Reddish and brownish colors result mainly from the presence of iron oxides, occurring either as coatings on mineral grains or as very fine particles. These minerals point to oxygen-rich (oxidizing) conditions in the environment.

Sedimentary Facies

If you examine a vertical sequence of exposed sedimentary rock, you may notice differences as you move upward from one bed to the next. You may note changes in sedimentary rock type, color, fossil content, and thickness. The differences indicate that the environmental conditions in that location changed over time. If you trace a single bed laterally for a few kilometers, you may also notice changes indicating that conditions differed from one place to another at any given time during deposition of the sediment.

Changes in the character of sediment from one environment to another are referred to as changes of **sedimentary facies**. One facies may be distinguished from another by differences in grain size, grain shape, stratification, color, chemical composition, depositional structure, or fossils. Adjacent facies can merge into each other either gradually or abruptly (**Figure 8.16**). For example, coarse gravel and sand

Sedimentary facies • Figure 8.16 _____

Each depositional environment leaves its own kind of sedimentary record, which may change over time. This section shows a variety of depositional environments in which distinctive facies are deposited.

On the land surface, the facies lie side by side, but in a vertical section they lie one above another. The seaward dip of the boundaries between facies indicates that, over time, the boundaries have migrated in the landward direction, due to a rise in sea level.

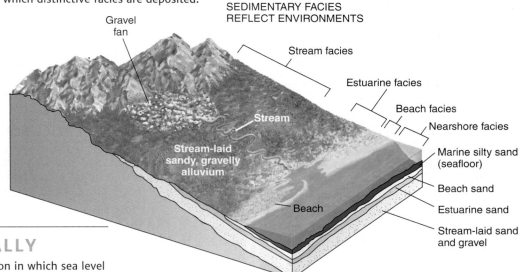

THINK CRITICALLY

This diagram shows a situation in which sea level steadily increased, causing the facies boundaries to migrate in a landward direction. What would happen if sea level rose, then fell, then rose again? What would the resulting deposits look like in a vertical section, like the front face of the block diagram?

Sediment Deposition and Human History

About 30 years ago, in Ethiopia, geologists were looking for fossils in the rocky hills south of the Awash River, near a place called Dikika. Today the region is dry, hot, and barren (**Figure a**). But the tiny set of bones that emerged from these rocks is the oldest and most complete fossil of a human-like (**hominid**) child ever found (**Figure b**).

The paleontologists who found the girl's remains named her Selam—"peace," in Amharic. The strata of the Hadar Formation that held her bones reveal much about how Selam lived—and died. The sedimentary facies revealed that Selam and others of her species, *Australopithecus afarensis* (including the famous fossil "Lucy," found not far away in 1974), lived in an environment of rapidly fluctuating, ephemeral lakes and fast-moving streams, in a deltaic depositional system.

The paleontologists hypothesize that about 3.3 million years ago, a little girl wandered near a stream. Around her were open grasslands and shaded woodlands, home to elephants, hippos, rhinoceroses, and antelopes; this is known from fossils in the area. Study of the girl's skeleton indicate that the tiny 3-year-old walked upright on two feet, but had strong muscles and gorilla-like shoulders so that she could climb trees to escape predators, take shelter, and forage for fruit.

Flooding must have been common in this constantly shifting terrain. Perhaps the little girl died by falling into a swiftly flowing stream—her bones were found encased in river channel deposits of gravel and sand, with clear evidence of rapid sedimentation. Her small body would have been buried quickly by sediment-laden water, protected from predators and the elements for millennia.

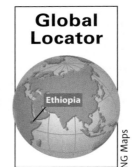

Global Locator

Ethiopia

NG Maps

NewsCom

a. Members of the scientific team sift loose sediment, looking for small fossils. Sedimentary strata of the Ethiopian badlands are in the background.

Lealisa Westerhoff/Getty Images

b. The paleontologist who headed the Dikika research team holds the baby Selam's fossilized skull, which fits easily into the palm of his hand.

THINK CRITICALLY

The Dikika girl's remains were fossilized because she was quickly covered by sediment, which then became sedimentary rock. What geological processes had to take place after that, in order for her remains to eventually be exposed at the surface?

on a beach may gradually pass into finer sand, silt, and clay on the floor of the sea or a lake. Coarse, boulder-like glacial sediment, on the other hand, may end abruptly at the margin of a glacier.

By studying the relationships among different sedimentary facies and using these characteristics to identify original depositional settings, we can reconstruct a picture of the environmental conditions that prevailed in a region during past geological times (see *Case Study*).

🛑 **CONCEPT CHECK** STOP

1. **What** can cross bedding and graded bedding tell us about the conditions under which a particular sedimentary rock was formed?

2. **How** does sediment become sedimentary rock?

3. **Which** kind of sediment becomes shale when it lithifies?

4. **What** are some clues about past environments that can be preserved in sedimentary rock?

5. **How** do geologists use the concept of sedimentary facies to learn about past environments?

HOW PLATE TECTONICS AFFECTS SEDIMENTATION

Learning Objectives

1. **Explain** how divergent plate margins influence sedimentation.

2. **Describe** what happens to sediment during continental collisions.

3. **Describe** how and why sediment accumulates in subduction zones at convergent plate margins.

Overall, clastic sediment is far more abundant than chemical sediment or biogenic sediment. The locations where clastic sediment is commonly formed and deposited are largely controlled by plate tectonics. Clastic sediment originates from the rock and mineral debris produced by weathering and erosion of continental masses. The eroded sediment accumulates in low-lying areas—troughs, trenches, and basins of various types. **Figure 8.17** summarizes the plate tectonic settings where clastic sediment is most likely to accumulate. Chemical and biogenic sediment are not as strongly influenced by plate tectonics, although the locations of the ocean basins where many of these deposits occur, as well as the size and depth of the basins, are controlled by plate tectonics.

Divergent Plate Boundaries—Rift Valleys

Low-lying rift valleys are formed when a continent splits apart as a result of tensional forces (see *Remember This!*). The East African Rift is an example of a rift that is still active in a continent that is spreading apart; the Red Sea is a young rift where a new ocean is already forming; and the Atlantic Ocean is a mature (i.e., well-developed) rift. A rift valley may eventually become a continental margin bordering an ocean, or the tensional forces may stop at some point, and the valley would then become a failed rift, such as the Newark Basin of New Jersey, or the similarly aged Hartford Basin of Connecticut, down which the Connecticut River flows for much of its way to the sea.

> **REMEMBER THIS!** Do you recall how a continent splits apart along a divergent plate margin, eventually widening into a linear sea and then an ocean? How about processes at subduction zone and continental collision zone margins? You can review by looking back at *The Plate Tectonic Model*, Chapter 4.

Both the East African Rift and the ancient Newark Basin hold deep wedges of immature clastic sediment deposited by streams. In the Red Sea, marine sediment now covers the clastic sediment that was deposited before the Red Sea was wide enough for the sea to enter and before the evaporite deposits that formed while the seawater was still shallow. On the Atlantic Ocean Margin of North America, sediment that has eroded from the adjacent continent has accumulated over many millions of years to a thickness of over 14 kilometers (see **Figure 8.17a**).

The trailing edge of a continent that is moving away from a rift is called a **passive continental margin**. Most of the strata deposited on the continental shelf of a passive margin are composed of mature, shallow-water marine sediment. The continental shelf slowly subsides as accumulation takes place, and the pile of sediment grows thicker and thicker. Lithification occurs as sediment is buried progressively deeper in the pile.

Convergent Plate Boundaries— Continental Collisions

A variety of low-lying areas are found within and along the edges of high mountain ranges. Many of these are structural basins or troughs caused by faulting and folding of rock associated with the process of mountain building. Coarse, immature (and thus angular and poorly sorted) stream sediment erodes from a rising mountain range and is transported quickly down the steep slopes. The sediment accumulates in low-lying areas as vast thicknesses of conglomerate, gravel, and sand (see **Figure 8.17b**). In the Himalaya, for example, thick sequences of conglomerate and coarse sandstone flank the southern edge of the range, while the finest-grained sediment has been transported all the way to the sea by the many streams that flow to the Indian Ocean.

Convergent Plate Boundaries— Subduction Zones

The lowest-lying points on Earth's surface are the long, deep oceanic trenches that form on the seafloor in subduction zones (see **Figure 8.17c**). The subduction of oceanic lithosphere results in melting and the subsequent creation of a line (or arc) of volcanoes on the overriding plate. The elevation plunges dramatically from the top of the volcanic arc to the bottom of the trench, within a lateral distance of a few hundred kilometers. Because erosion proceeds most rapidly where the slopes are steep, we would expect to find rapid erosion and deposition of sediment here—and we do. Sediment is transported to the trench by streams and turbidity currents, accumulating as turbidite deposits. Sediment also accumulates in low-lying areas on either

Clastic sediment accumulates in low-lying areas, which occur in specific locations that are strongly controlled by plate tectonics.

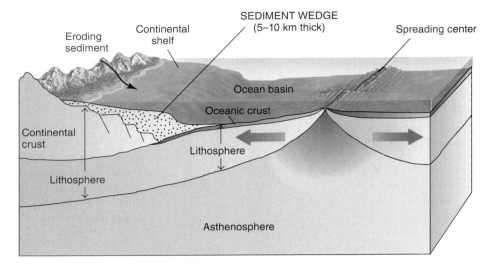

a. Rift valleys: Thick sedimentary wedges accumulate in rift valleys and along passive continental margins that are formed when continental crust rifts and a new ocean basin opens.

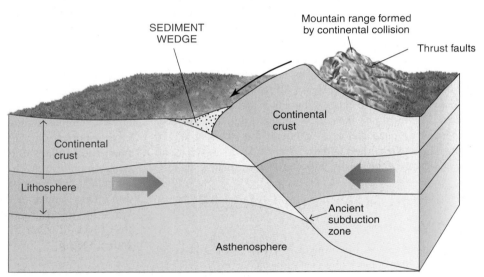

b. Structural basins: Sediment accumulates in structural basins along the edges of mountain ranges thrust up by continental collisions.

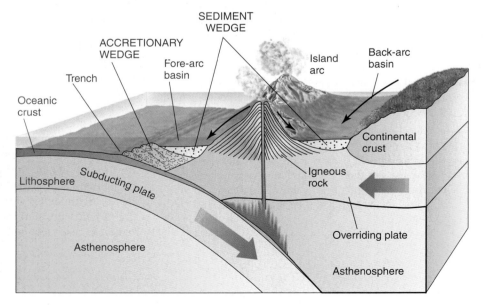

c. Accretionary wedges: Sediment is shed from continents into deep-sea trenches at subduction zones, forming an accretionary wedge in the **fore-arc basin** that is compressed as the oceanic plate subducts. Sediment also accumulates in the **back-arc basin** that forms behind the subduction zone.

Accretionary wedge • Figure 8.18

In oceanic subduction zones, the volcanic arc forms a back-arc basin between the volcanic island arc and the mainland. Though not as dramatic topographically as deep ocean trenches, these basins are places where ocean-floor sediment accumulates.

AgeFotostock/SuperStock

a. The eastern edge of Taiwan is an active accretionary wedge in a back-arc basin. This chaotic terrain of rock broken during accretion is near Taitung, at the southern end of the wedge.

Creatas/SuperStock

b. Steep gorges can result from rapid uplift during accretion. This is Taroko Gorge, Hualien, at the northern end of the Taiwan accretionary wedge.

side of the volcanic arc, called the **fore-arc** and **back-arc basins**.

At some convergent margins, sediment is scraped off the subducting plate in thick slabs, separated by faults, which pile up like a stack of playing cards on the overriding plate. Adjacent volcanic arcs ensure that a lot of volcanic debris is present in the sediment. These wedge-shaped accumulations of volcaniclastic sediment are called **accretionary wedges** (**Figure 8.18**). For example, the islands of Taiwan and Barbados largely consist of accretionary wedge sediment thrust up above sea level. At other subducting margins, the sediment travels down into the mantle, along with the subducting plate. The water contained in the sediment is released there, and it facilitates wet partial melting at depths of 100 kilometers and greater. These partial melts fuel the

explosive volcanic eruptions that are characteristic of subduction zones.

The chaotic mix of volcaniclastic sediment, fragments of oceanic lithosphere, and rock metamorphosed under the low-temperature, high-pressure conditions of the accretionary wedge in a subduction zone is called a **mélange**, from the French word for "mixture." Mélanges give geologists a close look at processes that occur along subducting margins—geological environments that are otherwise impossible to access.

The fragments of oceanic lithosphere that are sometimes incorporated into a mélange are particularly significant. These fragments, called **ophiolites**, are of immense geological interest because they expose oceanic crust and underlying mantle at the surface. A complete ophiolite suite typically consists of mantle rock at the base, overlain by complexes of gabbro dikes (remnants of the feeder system for the basaltic magma that formed the oceanic crust), with pillowed oceanic basalt and seafloor sediment at the top. Pillows are balloon-like volcanic structures that form when lavas are extruded underwater. These unusual rock suites provide a rare opportunity for geologists to see oceanic crust from top to bottom, to sample the mantle, and—perhaps most importantly—to study the Moho (crust–mantle boundary) itself.

STOP CONCEPT CHECK

1. **Why** is clastic sediment deposition more strongly influenced by plate tectonics than chemical and biogenic sediment deposition?

2. **What** kind of depositional environments are found in continental collision zones?

3. **What** happens to sediment that is scraped off of a subducting plate?

SUMMARY

 THE PLANNER

1 Sediment 198

- Sediment and sedimentary rock provide a record of how climates and environments have changed throughout geological history. Geologists use three broad categories to distinguish sediment types: clastic, chemical, and biogenic.

- **Clastic sediment** consists of fragmented rock and mineral debris produced by weathering, together with broken remains of organisms. The fragments, called clasts, are classified on the basis of size (see figure). Clasts may become rounded and sorted during transport by water and wind, but they typically remain unsorted during transport by glaciers or as a result of mass wasting. Volcaniclastic sediment is a type of clastic sediment in which the fragments, also called pyroclasts, are volcanic in origin.

From clasts to rock · Figure 8.1

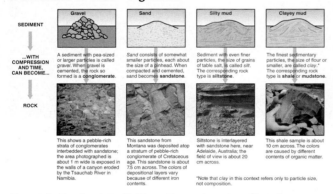

From left: Fletcher & Baylis/Photo Researchers, Inc.; ©Marli Bryant Miller; G. R. Roberts/Photo Researchers, Inc.; Courtesy Brian J. Skinner

- **Chemical sediment** is formed when substances carried in solution in lakewater or seawater are **precipitated**, generally as a result of evaporation or other processes that concentrate the dissolved substances.

- **Biogenic sediment** is composed of the accumulated remains of organisms. Plants, animals, and microscopic life-forms may all contribute skeletal and/or organic material to biogenic sediments such as calcareous ooze, siliceous ooze, and peat.

2 Depositional Environments 202

- Sediment can be transported by flowing wind, water, or ice, and it can move downslope under the influence of gravity.

- Stream, lake, glacial, and eolian sediments are common on land. **Eolian sediment**, which is transported by wind, tends to be finer than sediment moved by other erosional agents. We can interpret environmental clues, such as ripple marks, mud cracks, and fossil tracks, to deduce past surface conditions.

- Streams and lakes are common transporters of sediment on land and can form several types of depositional environments, including alluvial fans and **deltas**, triangle-shaped deposits that form where streams enter a standing body of water.

- Other depositional environments are near the ocean (see figure). Some sediment may be trapped in **estuaries**, semi-enclosed bodies of water along the coast, where fresh water and ocean water mix. Beaches tend to comprise finer sediment, as the particles have been repeatedly abraded by surf.

Deposition of sediment · Figure 8.6

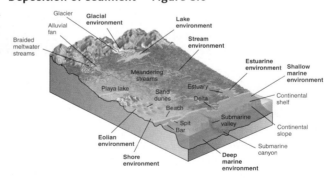

- Sediment is also deposited in the ocean. Reefs are deposits made of the skeletons of marine invertebrates. **Turbidity** currents are underwater landslides that transport sediment from the edge of the continental shelf to the deeper water at the foot of the continental slope. Another type of depositional environment in the ocean is the seafloor, which commonly hosts two types of deposits: calcareous ooze and siliceous ooze.

3 Sedimentary Rock 209

- When sediment is turned into sedimentary rock, the **bedding**, or layered arrangement of the strata, is generally preserved. The presence of bedding and bedding surfaces, the boundaries between adjacent strata, indicates that the rock was once sediment. In a graded bed, the coarsest clasts are at the bottom, and the finest are at the top. Cross bedding is produced by turbulent stream or wind flow or by ocean waves.

- **Lithification** (see figure) is the group of processes that transforms loose sediment into sedimentary rock (see figure). Lithification takes place through a variety of changes, including **compaction**, the reduction of pore space as a result of increased pressure; **recrystallization**, the formation of new minerals from old ones; and **cementation**, the process by which substances dissolved in pore water precipitate out and cement grains of sediment together. The low-temperature, low-pressure changes that happen to sediment after **deposition** are called diagenesis.

How lithification occurs• Figure 8.12

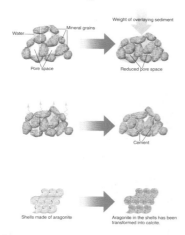

- Clastic sedimentary rock, like sediment, is classified mainly on the basis of clast size. **Conglomerate**, **sandstone**, and **mudstone** are the common rock equivalents of gravel, sand, and mud (silt- and clay-rich sediment), respectively. Conglomerate has large clasts in a fine-grained matrix, sandstone contains medium-sized grains, and mudstone consists of very small particles. **Shale** is mudstone that readily splits into thin layers.

- **Evaporite** is a chemical sedimentary rock formed by evaporation of lake or ocean water. **Banded iron formations**, though uncommon, are significant both economically and for understanding the history of our planet. **Limestone** is the most common biogenic sedimentary rock.

- Sedimentary rocks contain clues that help geologists understand the environments in which they formed. We can interpret clues such as ripple marks, mud cracks, and fossil tracks to deduce past environmental conditions.

- A sedimentary facies is a single geological unit consisting of sedimentary rock strata deposited at more or less the same time. Geologists learn about the history of a region by studying the way that different sedimentary facies adjoin and grade into each other in space and in time.

4 How Plate Tectonics Affects Sedimentation 219

- Clastic sediment, which originates from the rock and mineral debris produced by weathering and erosion, is the most abundant type of sediment. Clastic sediment tends to collect in low-lying areas whose location is strongly affected by plate tectonics (see figure). Chemical and biogenic sediment deposition is less strongly influenced by plate tectonics.

Tectonic environments for sediment deposition • Figure 8.17b

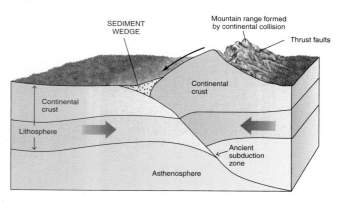

- Divergent margins create rift valleys and passive continental margins, both of which are common environments in which sediment accumulates.

- Colliding tectonic plates create structural basins and valleys associated with mountain ranges, as a result of the folding and faulting of rock. Low-lying basin topography combined with high mountains that provide a source of sediment typically leads to active sedimentation.

- Subducting plates form deep oceanic trenches along with volcanic arcs that may have back-arc basins. Sediment can be quickly buried in this environment, allowing it to be recycled into the mantle.

KEY TERMS

CRITICAL AND CREATIVE THINKING QUESTIONS

1. Estuaries are generally shallow, yet there are thick accumulations of estuarine sediment in the geological record. What hypothesis can you suggest to explain this?

2. Do any sedimentary rocks outcrop in the area where you live? If so, see if you can recognize the kinds of rock present and identify the environment in which the sediment was deposited.

3. Exploration for oil has led to the discovery of up to 14 kilometers of sedimentary rock on the continental shelf of North America. If the oldest of the strata were deposited 150 million years ago, during the Jurassic Period, and the youngest are still being deposited today, what is the average rate of deposition?

4. Investigate the formation of graded bedding by filling a large beaker with a half-and-half mixture of water and sediment. The sediment should have a variety of grain sizes, including fine clays, sand, and gravel. Shake up the mixture and let it settle quietly until the water is completely clear. Which grains settle first, and which settle last? What does the final sediment deposit look like?

5. Examine all photos in this chapter that show sediment or sedimentary rock. In each case, see if you can figure out which transport mechanism was responsible for moving the sediment (from Figure 8.5), and the type of environment where the sediment was deposited (from Figure 8.6).

Transport of sediment • Figure 8.5

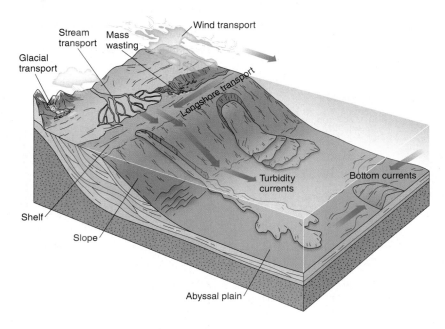

Deposition of sediment • Figure 8.6

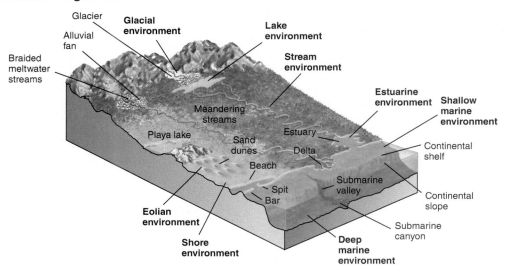

WHAT IS HAPPENING IN THIS PICTURE?

This slab of rock from the Cambrian Period was collected in Quebec, Canada. It contains fossilized tracks of an animal called *Climactichnites*.

O. Louis Mazzatenta/NG Image Collection

THINK CRITICALLY

1. The rock displays ripple marks, in addition to the animal tracks; can you distinguish them from each other?

2. What kind of animal could have made tracks like these, and what kind of environment did it live in? (By the way, no one knows exactly what *Climactichnites* looked like.)

SELF-TEST

(Check your Answers in Appendix D.)

1. _____ sediment forms from loose rock and mineral debris produced by weathering and erosion.

   a. Clastic

   b. Biogenic

   c. Chemical

2. These photographs are close-up views of two sediment samples labeled **a** and **b**. Which sediment shows a greater degree of rounding?

   a. Sample A

   b. Sample B

   c. Neither sample is well rounded.

   d. Both samples are well rounded.

3. Which of the two sediments in the photographs shows a greater degree of sorting?

   a. Sample A

   b. Sample B

   c. Neither sample is well sorted.

   d. Both samples are well sorted.

4. Examine the middle sedimentary bed depicted in the photograph. This bed is a best described as _____.

   a. cross bedded

   b. glacial

   c. graded

   d. eolian

a

b

Alamy

Courtesy Stephen C. Porter

Fine grains

Coarse grains

©Marli Bryant Miller

5. Three separate processes can lead to the lithification of sediment. During _____, the weight of accumulating sediment reduces pores space and forces out water from sediment. _____ occurs when ions dissolved in solution precipitate out, forming minerals that hold the grains together. Pressure can lead to _____, which causes less-stable minerals to rearrange crystals into more-stable forms.

a. compaction, Cementation, recrystallization

b. compaction, Recrystallization, cementation

c. dehydration, Recrystallization, cementation

d. dehydration, Cementation, recrystallization

6. Which of the three rock samples in these photographs is *not* a sedimentary rock?

a. Sample A

b. Sample B

c. Sample C

d. All of the rock samples displayed are sedimentary rock.

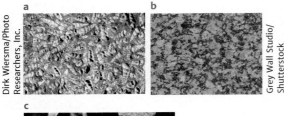

a

b

c

7. _____ is a sedimentary rock that is typically composed entirely of calcite.

a. Sandstone

b. Limestone

c. Shale

d. Conglomerate

e. Evaporite

8. _____ is a medium-grained sedimentary rock of clastic origin.

a. Sandstone

b. Limestone

c. Shale

d. Conglomerate

e. Evaporite

9. Which one of the following rocks is most likely to have formed in a desert playa?

a. sandstone

b. limestone

c. shale

d. conglomerate

e. evaporite

10. If mud cracks are found on a bedding surface of sedimentary rock, what can we deduce about the environmental conditions during deposition of the original sediment?

a. Deposition occurred during a strong windstorm.

b. The environment was subject to strong currents.

c. The environment was moist and then dried out.

d. Deposition occurred as a result of glaciation.

11. In which of the following sedimentary environments would you expect to find siliceous and calcareous oozes?

a. shallow marine environment

b. stream environment

c. deep marine environment

d. estuarine environment

12. Given the vertical association of depositional facies presented in this block diagram, what can we deduce about sea level over time?

a. Sea level was rising during deposition.

b. Sea level was falling during deposition.

c. Sea level was stable during deposition.

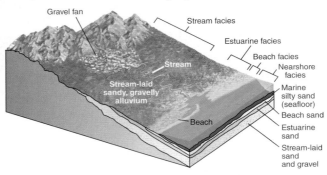

13. In what type of tectonic setting would you expect to find voluminous amounts of arc-derived volcaniclastic sediment?

a. divergent margin–rift valley

b. convergent margin–subduction zone

c. convergent margin–continental collision

d. passive continental margin

14. Accretionary wedges composed of sediment scraped off the oceanic crust are typical of what type of tectonic setting?

a. divergent margin–rift valley

b. convergent margin–subduction zone

c. convergent margin–continental collision

d. passive continental margin

15. In what type of tectonic setting would you expect to find sediment in structural basins adjacent to mountain ranges?

a. divergent margin–rift valley

b. convergent margin–subduction zone

c. convergent margin–continental collision

d. passive continental margin

THE PLANNER ✓

Review the Chapter Planner on the chapter opener and check off your completed work.

FOLDS, FAULTS, AND GEOLOGIC MAPS

ANCIENT MOUNTAINS IN EAST GREENLAND

This dramatic photo shows an island in King Oscar Fjord, one of many oceanic inlets along the coast of East Greenland (map); the boat to the left of the island provides scale. **Fjords** are formed when glacially-carved valleys become flooded.

The rock of East Greenland was deformed during the Caledonian **Orogeny**, an extensive period of tectonic activity and mountain-building that lasted from about 490 to 390 million years ago. The major continental landmasses that collided have been named Laurentia, Baltica, and Avalonia. The collision of these continents (inset) formed Laurussia, which included much of the land that now makes up Europe and North America.

During the Caledonian Orogeny, the lithospheric plates that carried Laurentia, Baltica, and Avalonia came together, slowly squeezing the Iapetus Ocean which separated them. The collision uplifted high mountain ranges, much like the Himalayas of today. The eroded remnants of these mountains are visible today in Greenland, Scandinavia, Scotland, Ireland, eastern Canada, and New England ("Acadian Orogen," inset map). Laurussia eventually combined with other continents to form the northern continent Laurasia. About 300 million years ago Laurasia collided with the southern continent Gondwana, resulting in the formation of Pangaea (Chapter 4). Pangaea combined virtually all continental landmasses of Earth at that time into one great supercontinent.

This intense folding shows how the tectonic forces of mountain-building are preserved in the rock record.

Ralph Lee Hopkins/NG Image Collection

ROCK DEFORMATION

Learning Objectives

1. **Differentiate** between uniform, tensional, compressional, and shear stress.

2. **Describe** the differences between elastic, brittle, and ductile deformation.

3. **Discuss** the importance of cratons and orogens.

As you learned in Chapters 4 and 5, lithospheric plates are constantly moving around, colliding with one another, and interacting along their margins. Crustal rock is recycled into the mantle at subduction zones, and new crust is created at divergent margins. At convergent margins in collision zones, enormous forces deform huge masses of continental crust and uplift them into great mountain ranges. We can't actually see the rock being twisted and bent by tectonic forces because it happens very slowly and deep underground. However, the aftermath is easily visible in locations where the deformed rock has been uplifted by tectonic forces and exposed by erosion, such as in our chapter-opening photo of East Greenland.

In **Figure 9.1**, originally flat and horizontal beds of sedimentary rock in the Himalaya Mountains have been folded, faulted, and tilted into a spectacular zigzag. To understand how this occurs, we rely on both laboratory measurements and field studies of deformed rock. The processes involved in rock deformation are the subject of this chapter.

Stress and Strain

In discussing rock deformation, we use the word **stress** rather than **pressure**. These two words are related in meaning but different in connotation. Both are defined as the force acting on a surface per unit area. The term *pressure*, as used in geology, implies that the forces on a body of rock are essentially uniform in all directions. Sometimes this is

also called **uniform stress** or **confining stress**. These are appropriate terms to describe, for instance, the stress on a small body immersed in a liquid such as water or magma.

Rock, however, is solid; unlike liquid or gas, solids can resist different pressures in different directions at the same time. For this reason, *stress* is a more versatile term for discussing rock deformation because it does not imply that the forces are necessarily the same in all directions. To be even more precise, we sometimes use the term **differential stress** when the force is greater from one direction than from another. The stresses that cause rock to change shape are differential. They can be classified into three different kinds, as illustrated in **Figure 9.2**: **tension**, **compression**, and **shear**.

In response to stress, rock will experience **deformation**, or **strain**. Strain can involve a change in the volume of the

> **stress** The force acting on a surface, per unit area, which may be greater in certain directions than in others.
>
> **pressure** A particular kind of stress in which the forces acting on a body are the same in all directions.
>
> **tension** A stress that acts in a direction perpendicular to and away from a surface.
>
> **compression** A stress that acts in a direction perpendicular to and toward a surface.
>
> **shear** A stress that acts in a direction parallel to a surface.
>
> **strain** Deformation; that is, a change in the shape or volume of rock in response to stress.

The core of a great mountain range • Figure 9.1 _____

These tightly folded rock strata in the Himalaya Mountains of southwestern Tibet bear witness to the intense geologic stresses that bent them into a zigzag shape.

SuperStock

The shape of a cube of rock changes, depending on the type of stress applied to it. The arrows indicate tensional, compressional, and shear stress. Rock subjected to differential stress—stress that is stronger in one direction than another—typically responds by changing shape, as shown by these blocks.

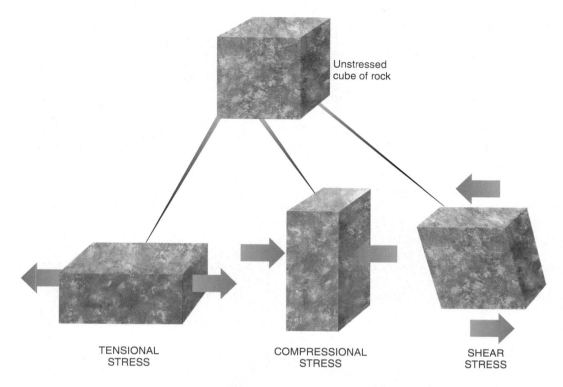

Unstressed cube of rock

TENSIONAL STRESS

COMPRESSIONAL STRESS

SHEAR STRESS

rock, or a change in the shape of the rock, or both. Uniform stress causes a change in volume only. For example, if a body of rock is subjected to uniform stress by being buried deep in Earth, its volume will decrease; that is, the rock will be compressed. If the spaces (or **pores**) between the grains become smaller as water is expelled from them, or if the minerals in the rock are transformed into more compact structures, the volume change may be quite large. As you saw in Figure 9.2, however, strain caused by differential stress is more likely to involve a change in the shape of the rock.

Brittle and Ductile Deformation

The way rock responds to differential stress depends not only on the amount and kind of stress but also on the nature of the rock itself. For example, rock may stretch like a metal spring and then return to its original shape when the stress is removed. Such a nonpermanent change is called **elastic deformation**. For most solids, including rock, there is a degree of stress—called the **elastic limit**—beyond which the material is permanently deformed. If the rock is subjected to more stress than this, it will

> **elastic deformation** A temporary change in shape or volume from which a material rebounds after the deforming stress is removed.

not return to its original size and shape when the stress is removed (see **Figure 9.3**).

When rock is stressed past its elastic limit, it can deform in two different ways. **Ductile deformation**, also called **plastic deformation**, is one type of permanent deformation in rock (or other solid) that has been stressed beyond its elastic limit (beyond point Y in **Figure 9.3a**). Alternatively, the rock may undergo **brittle deformation**.

> **ductile deformation** A permanent but gradual change in shape or volume of a material, caused by flowing or bending.
>
> **brittle deformation** A permanent change in shape or volume, in which a material breaks or cracks.

A brittle material deforms by fracturing, whereas a ductile material deforms by changing its shape. Drop a piece of chalk on the floor, and it will break; drop a piece of modeling clay and it will bend or flatten instead of break. Under the conditions of room temperature and atmospheric pressure, chalk is brittle, and modeling clay is ductile. Similarly, some rock behaves in a brittle manner and some in a ductile manner (see **Figure 9.3g**). However, rock that is brittle in one set of conditions may be ductile in different conditions.

The main factors that affect how rock deforms are temperature, confining pressure, rate of deformation, and composition of the rock. Let's look briefly at each of these.

Laboratory studies, practical work with substances like glass, and field observations all have helped geologists understand how solids are deformed.

a. A sample of rock tested in a laboratory will exhibit a straight-line relationship between stress and strain (change of shape or volume) when being deformed elastically.

This straight-line relationship (*X* to *Y*) is known as Hooke's law. If the stress is removed at any point between *X* and *Y*, the rock will return to its original size and shape.

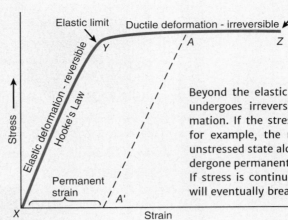

Beyond the elastic limit (*Y*), the rock undergoes irreversible ductile deformation. If the stress is removed at *A*, for example, the rock returns to an unstressed state along *AA'* and has undergone permanent strain equal to *XA'*. If stress is continued past *A*, the rock will eventually break, at *Z*.

b. A paper clip that is holding only three sheets of paper is deformed elastically and returns to its original shape after the papers are removed. This corresponds to a position anywhere along the line *XY* in (**a**).

c. The same paper clip becomes permanently bent when used to hold together a 50-page document. Its elastic limit is somewhere between 3 and 50 pages. Beyond the elastic limit, the clip has suffered permanent strain. This corresponds to point *A'* in (**a**).

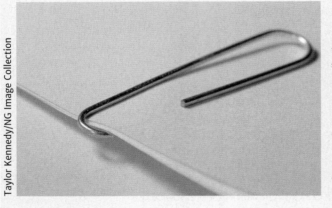

Taylor Kennedy/NG Image Collection

Taylor Kennedy/NG Image Collection

Temperature As shown in Figures 9.3d and 9.3e, glass is brittle at room temperature but becomes ductile at a higher temperature. Rock behaves like glass in this respect; it is brittle at the surface but becomes ductile deep inside the planet, where temperatures are higher.

Confining Pressure The effect of (uniform) confining pressure on deformation is not familiar from our everyday experience. High confining pressure reduces the brittleness of rock because it hinders the formation of fractures. **Figure 9.4** shows the results of a series of experiments that demonstrate

d. At room temperature, glass deforms in a brittle manner, as shown by this light bulb shattering when it hits the floor. Very little ductile deformation occurred, which means the elastic limit and the point of fracture are very close together. This corresponds to point *Z* in (**a**). ▼

e. If glass is heated slowly over a flame, it can bend and flow in a ductile manner, as in this glassmaker's studio. This means that at high temperature, glass has an extensive range of ductile deformation. This corresponds to any point along the line *YZ* in (**a**). ▼

Ted Kinsman/Photo Researchers/Getty Images, Inc.

Sam Abell/NG Image Collection

f. This rock responded to stress by folding and flowing, a ductile deformation, so the deformation occurred between points *Y* and *Z*. At room temperature, the deformation is permanent, and this corresponds to point *A′* in (**a**). ▼

g. This rock exhibits both brittle fracture and ductile deformation. The yellow rock has been deformed by brittle fracture, corresponding to point *Z* in (**a**). The white and blue-gray rock units have been deformed by ductile deformation, corresponding to a point on line *YZ*. Each of the three rock types was subjected to the same stress regime, so composition plays a role in how rock deforms. ▼

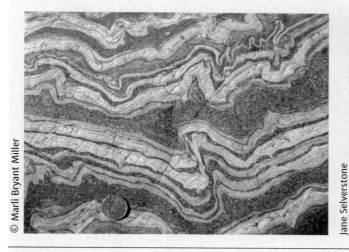

© Marli Bryant Miller

Jane Selverstone

THINK CRITICALLY

Can you think of another material used in daily life that could become deformed as a result of exposure to stress? What kind of deformation does it undergo? Is it elastic (i.e., reversible)? Ductile or brittle?

this effect. Near Earth's surface, where confining pressure is low, rock exhibits brittle behavior and develops many fractures. At great depth, however, where confining pressure is high, rock tends to be ductile and deforms by flowing or bending.

Rate of Deformation The rate at which stress is applied to a solid is another important factor in determining how a material will deform. If you take a hammer and suddenly whack a piece of ice, it will fracture. But if you apply stress to the ice little by little over a long period, it will sag,

These cylinders show the results of a series of experiments on the effects of confining pressure on rock.

a. This is an undeformed cylinder of rock.

b. This cylinder was subjected to high confining pressure and, at the same time, compression from above. It deformed in a ductile manner, becoming shorter and fatter.

c. An identical cylinder was subjected to the same amount of compression from above but lower confining pressure. It deformed in a brittle manner, with many fractures.

Courtesy Mervyn Paterson

bend, and behave in a ductile manner. The same is true of rock. If stress is applied quickly, the rock may behave in a brittle manner, but if small stresses are applied over a very long period, the same rock may behave in a ductile manner. The term **strain rate** refers to the rate at which rock is forced to change its shape or volume. The lower the strain rate, the greater the tendency for ductile deformation to occur (**Figure 9.5**).

To summarize, low temperature, low confining pressure, and high strain rates tend to enhance the brittle behavior of rock. Low-temperature and low-pressure conditions are characteristic of Earth's crust, especially the upper crust. As a result, fracturing is common in upper-crustal rock. High temperature, high confining pressure, and low strain rates, which are characteristic of the deeper crust and the mantle, reduce the brittle properties of rock and enhance the ductile properties. The depth below which ductile properties predominate is referred to as the **brittle–ductile transition**. Fractures are uncommon deep in the crust and in the mantle because rock at great depths (below about 10–15 km) tends to behave in a ductile manner.

Composition The composition of a material determines the exact point at which its brittle–ductile transition will occur. For example, both chalk and modeling clay are brittle at −50°Celsius. When warmed to room temperature, the modeling clay behaves in a ductile manner, but the chalk is still brittle. This is because they have different chemical compositions and, therefore, different properties. The same is true of different rocks and their mineral constituents. Some minerals—notably quartz, garnet, and olivine—are strong and brittle, as are the rocks that contain these minerals (e.g., sandstone and granite). For the most part, quartz-bearing rocks control the depth of the brittle–ductile transition. Other minerals—notably mica, calcite, and gypsum—are more often ductile under natural conditions. Thus, the rocks that contain them (e.g., limestone, marble, shale, slate) also tend to deform in a ductile manner.

Water is another component that enhances the ductile properties of rock. It reduces the friction between mineral grains and dissolves material at points of high stress, which permits the material to move to places where the stress is lower. Trace amounts of water can also enter strong minerals such as quartz and olivine and significantly weaken them, through a process called **hydrolytic weakening**.

The effects of different strain rates can be demonstrated with Silly Putty.

© Cambridge Polymer Group, Boston, MA (2001). Photograph by Gavin Braithwaite

a. At very slow strain rates, Silly Putty flows like a liquid. Starting from an apparently solid ball shape, it changes to the shape of a liquid drop over a few hours.

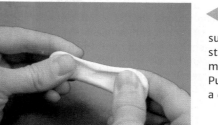

© Cambridge Polymer Group, Boston, MA (2001). Photograph by Gavin Braithwaite

b. At medium strain rates, such as when stretched by human hands, Silly Putty deforms in a ductile manner.

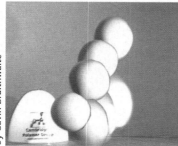

©Cambridge Polymer Group, Boston, MA (2001). Photograph by Gavin Braithwaite

c. At high strain rates, Silly Putty deforms elastically. (Bouncing is an elastic effect, caused by the material's tendency to return to its original shape.)

Courtesy Dr. James Bales, Assistant Director of the MIT Edgerton Center, and Dr. Stephen Spiegelberg, Cambridge Polymer Group, Inc.

d. At extremely high strain rates, such as when shot by a bullet, Silly Putty shatters like glass.

Where Rock Deformation Occurs

In which tectonic environments can the different types of stress—tension, compression, and shear stress—be expected to occur? Tensional stress involves a pulling-apart motion; it is characteristic of environments in which divergent motion is occurring, such as a continental rift or midocean ridge. Shear stress occurs where lithospheric plates are sliding past one another, such as along the boundary between the Pacific Ocean Plate and the North American Plate. Compression is characteristic of environments in which convergent motion is occurring, such as subduction zones and continent–continent collisions.

The deformation of rock in continent–continent collisions provides some of the best evidence that Earth has been tectonically active for billions of years. Seafloor spreading—the conclusive evidence for plate tectonics—occurs in oceanic crust (see *Remember This!*). However, all of today's oceanic crust is relatively young—less than 200 million years old. Therefore, evidence for earlier plate tectonics comes from continents and how they are put together (**Figure 9.6**), including the placement of **cratons** and **orogens**. A period of mountain-building during which an orogen forms is called an **orogeny**. For example, the collision of Avalonia and Laurentia described in our chapter opener resulted in the Acadian

craton A region of continental crust that has remained tectonically stable for a very long time.

orogen An elongate region of crust that has been deformed and metamorphosed through a continental collision.

Orogeny, one of four major orogenies that contributed to the uplifting of the great mountain belt known as the Appalachians. Some orogens, including the Alps and the Himalayas, are still active today; others, including the Appalachians, are inactive and now highly eroded. Through radiometric dating, some orogens have been found to be as old as 4 billion years.

> **REMEMBER THIS!** Can you describe how seafloor spreading works and why it was the conclusive piece of evidence that convinced geologists about continental drift and plate tectonics? If not, you can return to *The Missing Clue: Seafloor Spreading* in Chapter 4 to review.

Orogens such as the Appalachians still display some topographic relief even after hundreds of millions of years of erosion, because of a phenomenon called **isostasy** (**Figure 9.7**). Isostasy is the process in which a floating object automatically adjusts to a position of equilibrium with the medium in which it is floating. From everyday experience, you know that a block of wood floating in water will sink if a weight is put on top of it, and it will bob up if the weight is removed. The same thing happens with icebergs floating in the ocean. Icebergs are partially visible above the ocean surface, but every iceberg has a deep root that keeps it floating in balance. As the exposed top of an iceberg melts, the entire block of ice will bob upward to maintain this flotational balance.

isostasy The flotational balance of the lithosphere on the asthenosphere.

Cratons and orogens • Figure 9.6

Today all of North America lies on one plate, but a closer look shows that the North American continent has been assembled like a jigsaw puzzle from older parts. The cratons are the oldest tectonic units in the core of the continent. Between the cratons lie elongate orogens, with highly deformed and metamorphosed rock (Chapter 10)—signs that these were once sites of intense mountain-building activity.

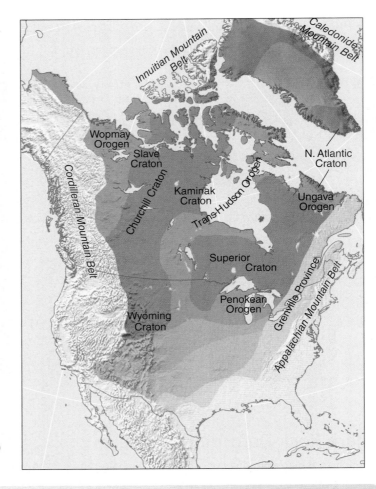

Billions of years old

> 2.5	1.8–1.7	1.2–1.0
1.9–1.8	1.7–1.6	< 1.0

Process Diagram

✓ THE PLANNER

How continents adjust to loads • Figure 9.7

The rigid lithosphere "floats" on the ductile asthenosphere.

1 In a collision of two cratons, the lithosphere thickens—both upward and downward—and the lithosphere–asthenosphere boundary is pushed down, creating a mountain belt (an orogen) with a deep root.

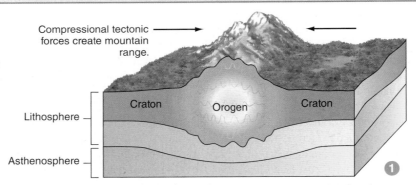

2 As erosion slowly reduces the height of the mountains in the orogen, the root slowly rises to compensate for the removal of mass. This continuing adjustment to maintain buoyancy, like a cork finding its level in water, is called isostasy.

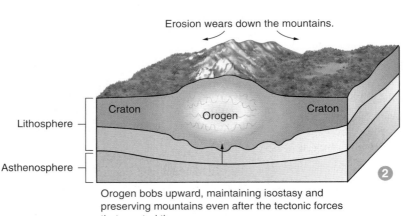

Orogen bobs upward, maintaining isostasy and preserving mountains even after the tectonic forces that created them are gone.

THINK CRITICALLY

Which orogens in North America would you expect to have the deepest roots, and how could you test your hypothesis?

Isostasy plays an important role in shaping Earth's topography, particularly in orogens. Continental collisions cause the entire continental crust to thicken; as a result, beneath every great mountain range is a root of thickened continental crust that dips down into the asthenosphere, similar to the root of an iceberg. This root keeps the entire orogen in flotational balance with respect to the underlying hot, weak asthenosphere. As erosion weathers away the top of the mountain range, the root pushes upward, like the root of a melting iceberg (as shown in Figure 9.7). But unlike an iceberg, which floats in seawater, an orogen is solid rock that floats in the hot, ductile asthenosphere, which makes the process extremely slow. The Appalachian Mountains are still adjusting isostatically after more than 300 million years of weathering.

STRUCTURAL GEOLOGY

Learning Objectives

1. **Define** strike and dip.

2. **Identify** which kinds of stress are associated with various types of faults.

3. **Define** and describe synclines, anticlines, and other types of folds.

The concepts of stress and strain play a central role in **structural geology**. Structural geologists attempt to decipher the geologic history of a region by identifying and mapping deformational features in rock. These features are also important from a practical perspective. For example, faults control the locations of certain types of ore deposits. Other rock structures can affect slope stability, influence the flow of groundwater, or trap oil and natural gas deep underground (**Figure 9.8**).

Many practical applications, such as oil prospecting and groundwater flow mapping, require geologists to make inferences about rock units and structures that lie underground, hidden from view. Most of their information comes from observations made at the surface, with additional information from drilling and other methods of subsurface study. A systematic program of measurements and mapping can give structural geologists a very good idea of what might lie beneath the surface.

structural geology The study of stress and strain, the processes that cause them, and the deformation and rock structures that result from them.

Strike and Dip

The **principle of original horizontality** tells us that sedimentary strata are horizontal when they are first deposited (see *Remember This!*). Where such rocks are tilted, we can

Structural geology and oil • Figure 9.8

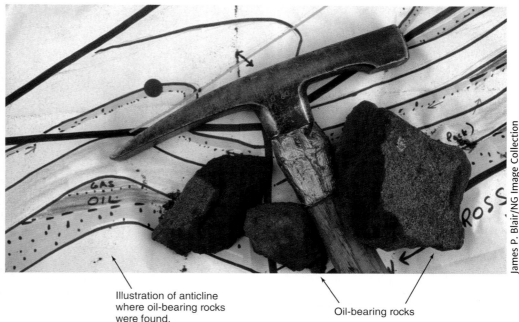

These rocks, which contain oil, are from an exploratory oil well on the North Slope of Alaska. The diagram underneath the rock hammer shows a typical rock formation that harbors oil. A layer of porous rock (in yellow) forms an arch-shaped fold with impervious rock overlying it. Oil and natural gas rise through the porous rock, becoming trapped at the top of the arch.

Illustration of anticline where oil-bearing rocks were found.

Oil-bearing rocks

James P. Blair/NG Image Collection

infer that deformation has occurred. To describe this deformation, a geologist starts by measuring the orientation of the tilted rock layer. This information is given by the **strike**. It is a basic fact of geometry that a sloping plane—in this case, the tilted rock layer—intersects a horizontal plane along a line (**Figure 9.9a**). The strike of the rock layer is the compass direction of that line (measured in degrees north, south, east, or west).

strike The compass orientation of the line of intersection between a horizontal plane and a planar feature, such as a rock layer or fault.

dip The angle between a tilted surface and a horizontal plane.

is 90°, which represents a layer that has been tipped so that it is completely vertical. When rock layers are tilted even further than the vertical orientation, we say they are **overturned**.

It is important to remember that strike and dip describe the orientation and slope of the rock layer, specifically its **bedding surface**, not the ground surface itself. Strike and dip are also used to describe the orientation of other types of planar structural features, including faults.

> REMEMBER THIS! Do you remember the principle of original horizontality, and the other important basic principles of stratigraphy? You can review them by looking back at *Relative Age* in Chapter 3.

We need an additional measurement to fully describe the orientation of a tilted rock layer. **Dip** is measured as an angle downward from the horizontal plane in degrees, using an instrument similar to a protractor. Dip is always measured in a direction perpendicular to strike. In **Figure 9.9b**, the rock strata are tilted at 30°. If they were dipping more shallowly, the angle would be smaller; if they were dipping more steeply, the angle would be greater. The maximum possible dip

Faults and Fractures

Fractures, or cracks, are characteristic of brittle rock deformation. Fractures occur in all sizes. Some are so tiny that you would need a microscope to see where an individual mineral grain has cracked. Cracks this small are sometimes called **microfractures**. Recall that a **fault** is a fracture in rock along which differential movement has occurred in the blocks of rock on either side of the fracture surface. Some faults are small, only meters long, but other faults and fault systems are hundreds or even thousands of kilometers long.

There are many types of faults, caused by different kinds of stress. The major types are summarized in **Figure 9.10**.

Strike and dip · Figure 9.9 _____

Geologists use the terms *strike* and *dip* to describe the orientation of a tilted layer of rock.

a. The strike is formed by the intersection of a rock layer and a (sometimes imaginary) level plane. The dip is the angle of tilt of the rock stratum, measured from the horizontal plane.

b. In this drawing, the top of the water provides a suitable horizontal plane. The shoreline indicates the strike. The dip is the angle at which the rock layers are tilted. In this drawing, they are tilted 30° from horizontal. The patterns in the diagram are commonly used to distinguish different rock types.

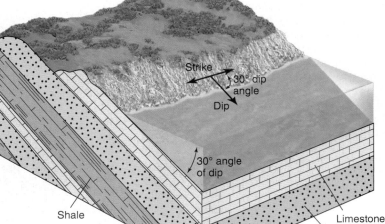

ASK YOURSELF

The rock strata shown in this figure have a dip of 30°. What would be the orientation of a stratum with a dip of 90°?

a. vertical

b. horizontal

c. It would be impossible to determine this without additional information.

Tensional stress—Normal fault

a. When the crust is stretched by tension, normal faults occur. The **hanging-wall block** overhangs the fault and moves down relative to the **footwall block**, underneath the fault. This may expose a cliff-like landform at the surface called a **scarp**. The photo shows a normal fault in sedimentary rock layers exposed in a roadcut in Guatemala.

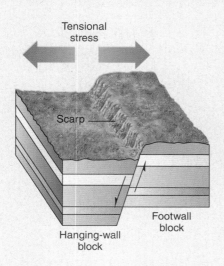

J.K. Nakata/USGS

Tensional stress—Horst and graben

b. Normal faults often occur in pairs. In a **graben**, two faults dip toward each other, and the block between them drops down. In a **horst**, the faults dip away from each other, and the block between them rises. The photo shows the Great Rift Valley of Kenya, under tensional stress because it is on a divergent plate margin. The stretching has created a series of paired horsts and grabens.

Emory Kristof/NG Image Collection

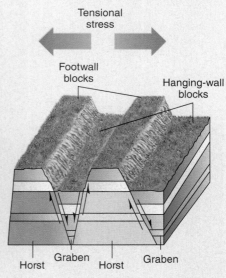

Compressional stress—Reverse fault

c. In a reverse fault, compressional stress pushes the hanging-wall block up and over the footwall block. The direction of movement along the fault is opposite that on a normal fault. The rock hammer shows the scale of the small reverse fault in the strata in the photo.

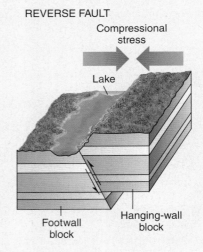

REVERSE FAULT

Compressional stress

Lake

Footwall block

Hanging-wall block

Compressional stress—Thrust fault

d. A thrust fault is a reverse fault with a very shallow dip. Geologists indicate this with a row of triangles pointing toward the hanging-wall block. The photo shows the Lewis Overthrust at the eastern edge of the Rocky Mountains.

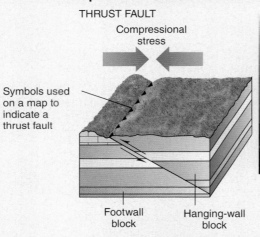

THRUST FAULT

Compressional stress

Symbols used on a map to indicate a thrust fault

Footwall block

Hanging-wall block

Bobak Ha'Eri (Own work) [CC BY 3.0 (http://creativecommons.org/licenses/by/3.0)], via Wikimedia Commons

Shear stress—Strike-slip fault

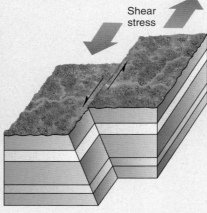

Shear stress

e. In a strike-slip fault, the movement is mostly horizontal and prallel to the strike of the fault. Such faults are created by shearstresses. The photo shows the Denali Fault in Alaska, where recent movement has offset a road by several meters. The TransAlaska Pipeline is in the background.

THINK CRITICALLY

For the photos in which strata are discernible, can you see which units are offset by the fault and in which direction?

Normal Faults Tensional (or extensional) stress, stress that stretches or pulls apart the crust, causes normal faults (**Figure 9.10a**). Normal faults sometimes occur in pairs, as shown in **Figure 9.10b**, creating a distinctive pairing of uplifted and downdropped blocks called horsts and grabens. For example, the East African Rift Valley is a huge system of roughly parallel faults that extends for more than 6000 kilometers through the countries of East Africa. In North America, the region lying between the Sierra Nevada and the Rocky Mountains, known as the Basin and Range Province, is also made up of alternating horsts and grabens.

Reverse Faults Compressional stress is responsible for **reverse faults** and **thrust faults** (**Figure 9.10c, d**). In reverse faults, the hanging-wall block is pushed over the footwall block, shortening and thickening the crust. The reverse fault in Figure 9.10c dips steeply. When a reverse fault dips more shallowly, less than 45°, it is called a thrust fault (see Figure 9.10d). Thrust faults are common in mountain chains along convergent plate boundaries. The ranges

normal fault A fault in which the block of rock above the fault surface moves downward relative to the block below.

reverse fault A fault in which the block on top of the fault surface moves up and over the block on the bottom.

thrust fault A reverse fault with a shallow angle of dip.

strike-slip fault A fault in which the direction of the movement is mostly horizontal and parallel to the strike of the fault.

in the Canadian Rockies, described in *Amazing Places*, were formed by thrust faults.

In large thrust faults, the hanging-wall block may move thousands of meters, coming to rest on top of much younger rock in the foot-wall block. The principle of superposition says that in any undisturbed sequence of strata, the younger strata are deposited on top; a thrust fault represents a disturbance of the original stratigraphic sequence.

Strike-Slip Faults Shear stress typically creates **strike-slip faults**, along which two adjacent blocks are displaced translationally (that is, horizontally) relative to one another. The name comes from the fact that the blocks slip in a direction parallel to the strike of the fault (not the strike of the rock layers), as shown in Figure 9.10e. Transform faults, discussed in Chapter 4, are strike-slip faults.

One strike-slip fault is so famous that almost everyone has heard of it: the San Andreas Fault in California. Along this fault, the Pacific Plate is moving toward the northwest relative to the North American Plate (**Figure 9.11**). The word *relative* is very important here. In fact,

The San Andreas Fault system · Figure 9.11

The San Andreas Fault is part of a complicated system of faults 1300 kilometers in length, along which the Pacific Plate is moving in a north-westerly direction relative to the North American Plate. This map shows major faults in the vicinity of San Francisco along which motion has occurred in the past 10,000 years.

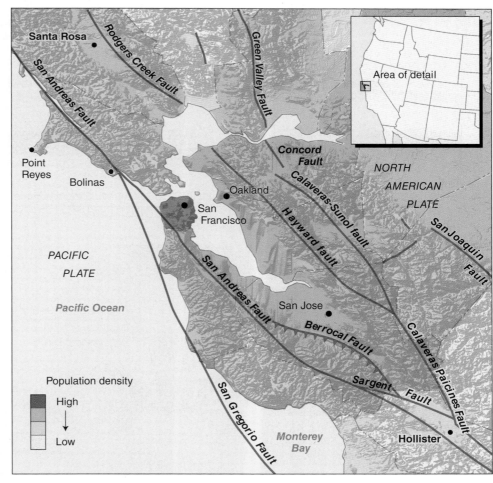

Global Locator

NG Maps

Canadian Rockies

The Canadian Rockies

The Canadian Rockies in western Alberta and eastern British Columbia offer many beautiful views of folding and faulting.

a. This dramatic fold at Mount Kidd marks the end of the Lewis Thrust Fault into folded rock.

Design Pics/ NG Image Collection

Joachim Mueller

b. Visible from the Kananaskis Highway west of Calgary Opal Mountain is a combination of folded and faulted strata.

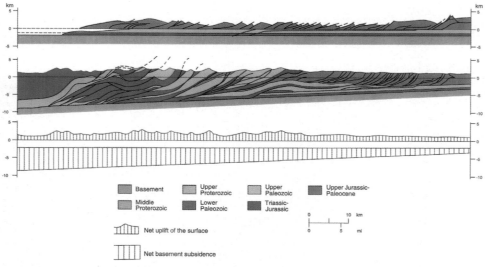

▓ Basement	▓ Upper Proterozoic	▓ Upper Paleozoic	▓ Upper Jurassic-Paleocene
▓ Middle Proterozoic	▓ Lower Paleozoic	▓ Triassic-Jurassic	

⊓⊓⊓ Net uplift of the surface

⊓⊓⊓ Net basement subsidence

0   10 km
0   5   mi

c. The Canadian Rockies are part of a great **fold-thrust belt** that resulted from **thin-skinned tectonics**, in which compressional forces moved great slabs of the uppermost crust along thrust faults from west to east. The vertical lines show uplift, and the horizontal lines show how the root of the mountain range was depressed isostatically to compensate for the uplift (compare to Figure 9.7).

d. Imagine a snowplow pushing a layer of snow, which compresses horizontally and thickens vertically. A series of thrust faults form in front of the plow, and the snow is highly folded between the faults. The geologic cross section of the Rockies (**Figure c**) ear Opal Mountain and Mount Kidd shows the folds and thrusts very clearly.

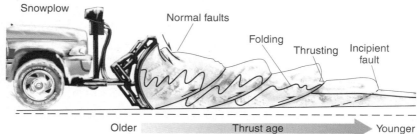

Snowplow   Normal faults   Folding   Thrusting   Incipient fault

Older   Thrust age   Younger

both the Pacific Plate and the North American Plate are moving in a roughly northwesterly direction, but the Pacific Plate is moving more quickly, about 10 centimeters/year, like a fast runner overtaking a slower one. Over the past 15 million years, the Pacific Plate may have moved more than 600 kilometers northwest relative to the North American Plate, which is moving at about 5 centimeters annually.

Strike-slip faults can be described according to the direction of relative horizontal motion of the fault blocks, as follows: To an observer standing on either block, the movement of the other block is **left lateral** if it has moved to the left, and **right lateral** if it has moved to the right. The San Andreas Fault is right lateral because to an observer standing on the Pacific Plate, the North American Plate appears to be moving to the right (i.e., toward the southeast). Note that it does not matter which plate you stand on; if you stand on the North American Plate, the Pacific Plate will still appear to be moving toward your right (i.e., toward the northwest), so the San Andreas is still a right-lateral fault.

Folds

When rock deforms in a ductile manner, it bends and flows, creating folds. A fold may be a broad, gentle warping over

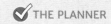

fold A bend or warp in layered rock.

many hundreds of kilometers, a tight flexing of microscopic size, or anything in between.

What a Geologist Sees

☑ THE PLANNER

Monocline

The geologist viewing this scene in southern Utah would take measurements of the strike and dip of the strata, and would be able to conclude that this structure is a **monocline**.

© Corbin17/Alamy

Approximate area of photo

Alamy

a. The reddish-colored strata are deformed. The flat-lying strata at the top of the photo dip downward at an increasingly steep angle, toward the right-hand side of the photo. This is a fold, but only one limb is evident, so it is a monocline.

b. The geologist prepares a schematic drawing of the area in the photo. You can see that the strata become nearly vertical on the right side of the monocline. The land surface cuts across the rock strata on the right, but it lies almost parallel to the rock strata on the left.

In a monocline like this one, the strata might be draped over an underlying feature, such as a fault; alternatively, the geologist might actually be looking at one limb of an anticline. In that case, she would expect the strata to dip downward again in the area to the left of the photo and the block diagram. What could the geologist do to figure out which one of these is the correct interpretation?

THINK CRITICALLY

Which strata in the photograph are the oldest, and how can you tell?

The simplest type of fold is a **monocline**, a local steepening in otherwise uniformly dipping strata (see *What a Geologist Sees*). An easy way to visualize a monocline is to lay a book on a table and drape a handkerchief over one side of the book. So draped, the handkerchief forms a monocline. However, most folds are more complex than monoclines, and, a monocline that is visible at the surface may be just one part of a larger and more complicated fold that is partially hidden underground. Folds are often combinations or variations of two basic types: **anticlines** and **synclines**. If you push the edge

> **anticline** A fold in the form of an arch, with the rock strata convex upward and the older rock in the core.
>
> **syncline** A fold in the form of a trough, with the rock strata concave upward and the younger rock in the core.

of a rug with your foot, it will form a series of anticlinal and synclinal folds.

Several measurements are needed to describe the geometry and orientation of a fold. Imagine a plane dividing the fold in half, as symmetrically as possible (**Figure 9.12**). This is the **axial plane** of the fold. The two halves of the fold, on either side of the axial plane, are the **flanks**, or **limbs**. Axial planes can be vertical, as in Figure 9.12b, or tilted if the two limbs dip at different angles. The axial planes of simple folds are planar, but in a complicated fold, the axial plane itself can be a curved surface.

Notice that the axial planes in Figure 9.12b connect the most strongly curved parts of each rock layer—in other words, the axial plane passes through the crests of the rock layers in the anticline and the troughs of the rock layers in the syncline. The line where the axial plane intersects the

Simple folds • Figure 9.12

Most folds—even very complicated ones—can be described as some combination of the two simple fold types, anticline and syncline.

Youngest rocks

Syncline

Anticline

Oldest rocks

© Marli Bryant Miller

a. On the left in this photo of the Old Red Sandstone in Wales is an anticline, an arch-shaped fold in which the layers of rock are convex upward, with the oldest rock underneath. On the right is a syncline, a trough-like fold with the youngest rock on top.

b. The axial plane separates the two limbs of a fold. The fold axis corresponds to the line of maximum curvature in the folded rock layers—usually along the crest of the arch in an anticline or the deepest part of the trough in a syncline. The axial trace is the horizontal projection of the axis.

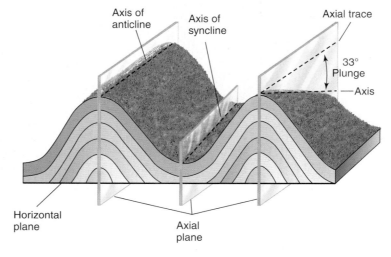

Axis of anticline

Axis of syncline

Axial trace

33° Plunge

Axis

Horizontal plane

Axial plane

Upwarping and downwarping of the crust can cause domes and basins to form.

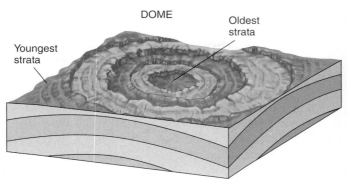

DOME

Oldest
strata

Youngest
strata

a. This is a dome in northern Flinders Range, South Australia. The strata are late Proterozoic in age. Note from the block diagram that when domes erode, they expose older rock at their centers.

Bernhard Edmaier/Photo Researchers, Inc.

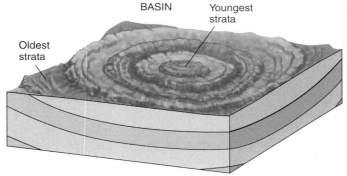

BASIN

Youngest
strata

Oldest
strata

b. Downwarping of the crust causes basins to form. In a basin, the youngest rock is at the center, and the oldest rock is around the outer edge.

fold is called the **axis**, or **hinge**. The axis of a simple fold may be horizontal (as in the anticline on the left in Figure 9.12b), but some fold axes are tilted. A fold in which the axis is not horizontal is said to be **plunging** (like the anticline on the right in Figure 9.12b).

Note that synclines do not always form valleys, even though their strata are concave-upward, and anticlines do not always form ridges, even though their strata are convex-upward. Sometimes an anticline may expose a rock stratum that is more susceptible to erosion than the surrounding layers; in that case, the anticline will erode away quickly and form a valley. In general, the contours of the land do not always follow the bedding surfaces and, in fact, can be misleading. The shapes and orientations of the bedding surfaces matter much more for geologists because they record the long-term deformational history of the rock.

Sometimes a large area of crust undergoes upwarping or downwarping, which forms broad, gentle folds. Upwarping of strata forms **domes**, while downwarping forms large, bowl-like **basins** (**Figure 9.13**). Folds can also be **asymmetrical**, with one limb dipping more steeply than the other, or even **overturned**, with one limb tilted so far over that it is upside down. Folds that are so strongly overturned that they are almost lying flat are called **recumbent**. This is another way in which rock deformation can change the normal sequence of strata.

STOP CONCEPT CHECK

1. **What** information do the strike and dip of a rock layer provide?

2. **What** is the difference between a normal fault and a reverse, or thrust, fault?

3. **What** are the main parts of a fold?

GEOLOGIC MAPS

Learning Objectives

1. **Distinguish** between a topographic map and a geologic map.

2. **Describe** how a geologist makes a geologic map.

3. **Explain** what kind of information can be shown on a geologic cross section.

Geologists cannot see all the structural details of deformed rock strata in a given area; soil, water, vegetation, and buildings cover much of the evidence. Through field observations and measurements, sometimes combined with drilling or laboratory analysis, geologists gather information and portray in two-dimensional format as much of the geology as they can see or extrapolate. The result is a **geologic map**.

You can learn more about geologic maps and about the mapping work of the U.S.

> **geologic map** A map that shows the locations, kinds, and orientations of rock units, as well as structural features such as faults and folds.

Where Geologists CLICK

National Geologic Maps Database

For a more extensive discussion of geologic maps, go to the National Geologic Maps database, maintained by the USGS, where you can view geologic maps in progress and see areas where geologic mapping is still being done.

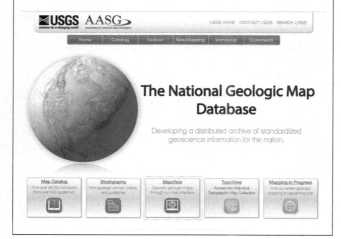

Geological Survey by visiting the National Geologic Maps Database (*Where Geologists Click*).

Topographic Maps

Commonly, a **topographic map** is used as the base for a geologic map (**Figure 9.14**). You may have used a topographic map if you have ever gone backpacking or hiking. An important aspect of topography is **relief**, the difference between the lowest and highest elevations in the area. A mountainous region has high relief, whereas a flat plain has low relief. Topographic maps use **contour lines**, lines of equal elevation, to portray topography.

> **topographic map** A map that shows the shape of the ground surface, and the location and elevation of surface features, usually by means of contour lines.

The height information from a topographic map can be used to plot a **topographic profile** of the landscape, as shown in Figure 9.14. First, pick a line along which you would like to construct the topographic profile (e.g., the line labeled $A–A'$ on the map). Next, set up your topographic profile: Use the line $A–A'$ as the horizontal axis, and draw and label a vertical axis to represent height or elevation. Directly below each point where $A–A'$ crosses a contour line on the map, place a dot at the appropriate height on the profile. Finally, connect the dots with a smooth curve. This curve represents the topography of the mountain. (In Figure 9.14 we exaggerated the height in order to make the differences in elevation stand out.)

Making and Interpreting Geologic Maps

Topography is the starting place, but geologists also need to know about the rock that makes up the topography. To do this, they must construct a geologic map (**Figure 9.15**). In general, the first step is to carry out field work to gather geologic information from **outcrops**. They note the exact location of the outcrop, the type of rock that is present, the orientation of the layers, and the presence of structural features such as faults or folds. They may need to employ additional sources of information, such as satellite imagery, drilling, seismic studies, or microscopic or chemical analysis of rock samples. The goal is to determine, as much as possible, what lies hidden beneath soil, vegetation, water, and buildings in the areas between the outcrops.

> **outcrop** A place where bedrock is exposed at the surface.

The various types of rock that are identified by the geologist are portrayed on the map as geologic **formations**. A formation is a unit of rock that can be distinguished from units above and below it, on the basis of differences in rock

Topographic maps contain information about the ups and downs of the land. Contour lines indicate points of equal height; for example, every point on the line labeled "1100" is 1100 feet (335 m) above sea level. The topographic profile at the bottom shows the topography along line A–A'.

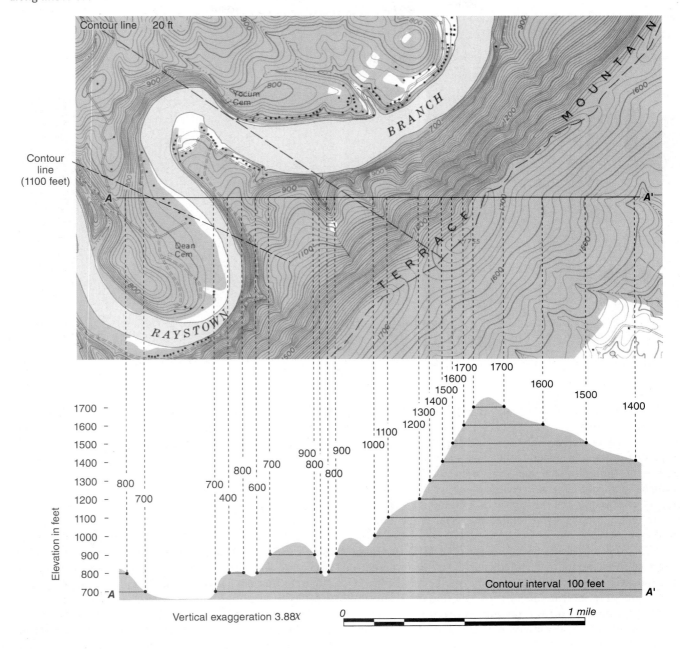

type or characteristics, and recognizable boundaries with other rock units.

The different rock formations are portrayed on the geologic map with different colors, and often with standard symbols. However, the colors and symbols do not reveal whether the underlying strata are vertical or horizontal, or folded or tilted in one direction or another. This information is indicated using symbols that show the locations and strike-dip orientations of folds, faults, and other geologic features. The colors and symbols most commonly used to

To make a geologic map, the geologist begins by taking mea-surements such as strike and dip at rock outcrops.

a. This block diagram shows a landscape with tilted rock stra-ta. Much of the rock is covered at the surface by grass and soil, but there are some outcrops where bedrock is exposed and where the geologist can take the necessary measurements.

b. The geologist transfers the information about rock types and boundaries (called **geologic contacts**) onto a map of the area. Where the bedrock is covered, the geologist makes an educated guess about the types of rock and locations of boundaries. This can be used to construct a geologic cross sec-tion—a vertical profile of the strata, shown here as the front panel in the block diagram.

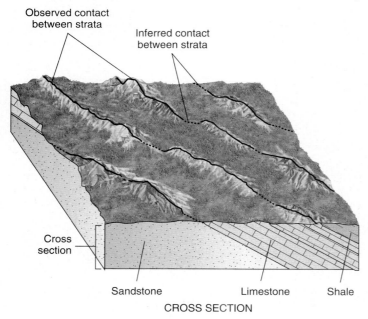

Observed contact between strata

Inferred contact between strata

Cross section

Sandstone   Limestone   Shale

CROSS SECTION

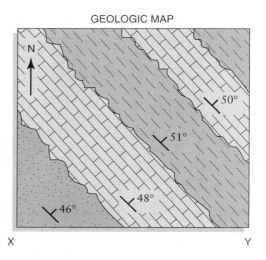

GEOLOGIC MAP

N

50°

51°

48°

46°

X   Y

portray rock formations on maps are shown in **Figure 9.16**. The finished product will look something like the map shown in **Figure 9.17**.

It is particularly challenging to represent folds on a geologic map. In general, the most convenient way to represent three-dimensional structures like folds is to project them onto the horizontal plane of the map sur-face. For example, the projection of a fold axis or an axial plane onto a map is a line, called the **axial trace** (shown on Figure 9.12).

To fully represent the geometry of a fold, the map needs to show the following elements: (1) a line represent-ing the axis and the axial plane (that is, the axial trace); (2) a symbol to indicate the type of fold (anticlines are il-lustrated using two arrows pointing away from the axial trace; synclines are illustrated using two arrows pointing toward the axial trace); (3) an arrow to show the direction in which the axis is plunging; and (4) a number (measured in degrees from horizontal) to show the plunge angle. **Figure 9.18** gives an example of how these symbols are used on a map.

The oldest-known geologic map—possibly the first one ever made—was drawn on a papyrus scroll in ancient Egypt. Evidently, it was used to show the locations of cer-tain rock types for quarrying purposes. Probably the most important geologic map ever produced was made by an English surveyor, William Smith (see *Case Study*). Today,

geologic maps still help geologists interpret the geologic history of an area. Geologists from mining companies, oil companies, engineering firms, environmental agencies, consulting firms, and government agencies refer to such maps regularly.

Geologic Cross Sections

A geologic map shows the locations of all rock outcrops on the ground surface, as well as the orientations of layering, structures, and other geologic features. It also shows the ge-ologist's educated guess (combined with any other available data) as to what lies under the soil, vegetation, and build-ings between the outcrops. A geologic map also can be used to make inferences about what happens to the rock layers just under the ground. Do they bend completely around and come back to the surface? Do they level out and become flat? Do they grade into a different type of rock?

To answer these questions, geologists must try to visu-alize the area in three dimen-sions, even if they only have information concerning the rocks at the surface. Geologists do this three-dimensional vi-sualization by constructing a **geologic cross section** like

> **geologic cross section** A diagram that shows geologic features that occur underground.

Symbols commonly used on geologic maps • Figure 9.16

Representative patterns and symbols are commonly, but not universally, used to show various kinds of rock in geologic maps and cross sections.

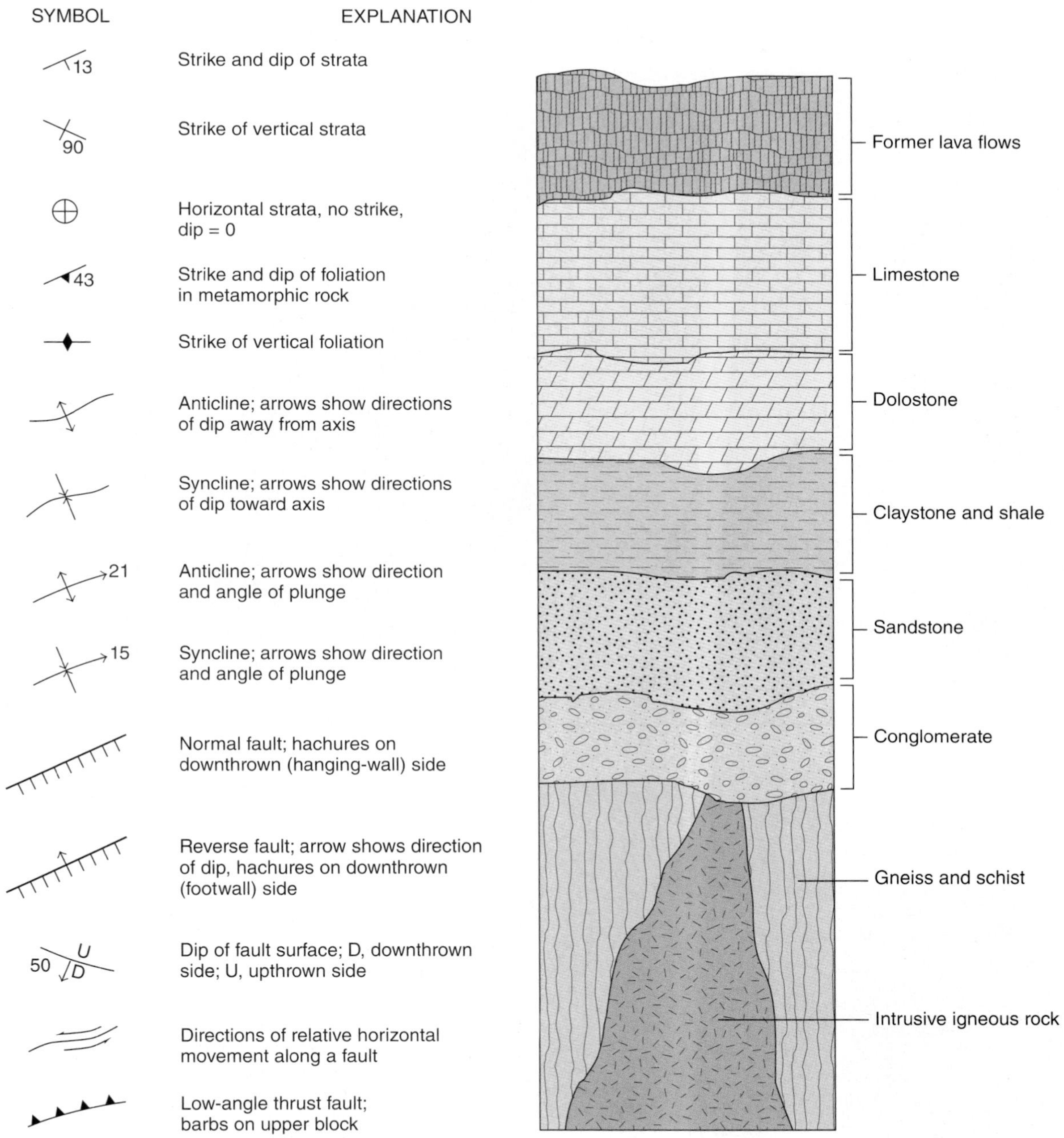

SYMBOL
EXPLANATION
13
Strike and dip of strata
90
Strike of vertical strata
Horizontal strata, no strike, dip = 0
43
Strike and dip of foliation in metamorphic rock
Strike of vertical foliation
Anticline; arrows show directions of dip away from axis
Syncline; arrows show directions of dip toward axis
21
Anticline; arrows show direction and angle of plunge
15
Syncline; arrows show direction and angle of plunge
Normal fault; hachures on downthrown (hanging-wall) side
Reverse fault; arrow shows direction of dip, hachures on downthrown (footwall) side
50 U D
Dip of fault surface; D, downthrown side; U, upthrown side
Directions of relative horizontal movement along a fault
Low-angle thrust fault; barbs on upper block
Former lava flows
Limestone
Dolostone
Claystone and shale
Sandstone
Conglomerate
Gneiss and schist
Intrusive igneous rock

the one shown in **Figure 9.19** and in *Amazing Places*. Constructing a geologic cross section is challenging; it requires not only knowledge of the surface geology, but a good deal of basic expertise about stratigraphy and structural geology. The geologist starts with a detailed geologic map and then adds his or her best guess as to how the strata fold and fault underneath the ground. As you can see from Figure 9.19, the layering in a major fold-and-thrust belt like the Alps or the Rockies can be very complicated.

A typical geologic map • Figure 9.17

This is part of a geologic map that shows the Canmore Quadrangle in Alberta, Canada. Mount Rundle and Mount Kidd, described in *Amazing Places: The Canadian Rockies*, are located nearby, just to the north and south, respectively. The colors indicate the age and type of rock, and the contour lines show the topography. In the magnified inset you can see the symbols for thrust fault, strike and dip, syncline, and anticline.

Showing folds on maps • Figure 9.18

It is challenging to portray three-dimensional subsurface structures like folds on the two-dimensional surface of a map.

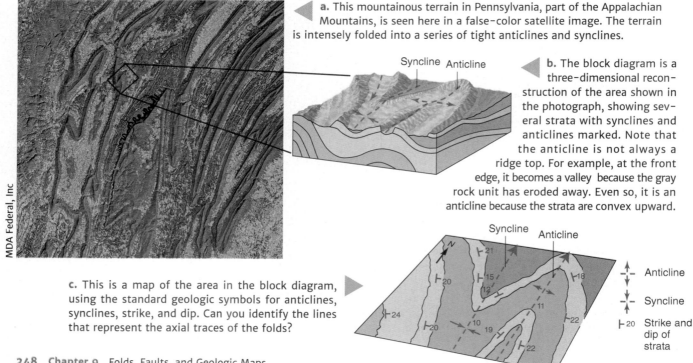

a. This mountainous terrain in Pennsylvania, part of the Appalachian Mountains, is seen here in a false-color satellite image. The terrain is intensely folded into a series of tight anticlines and synclines.

b. The block diagram is a three-dimensional recon-struction of the area shown in the photograph, showing several strata with synclines and anticlines marked. Note that the anticline is not always a ridge top. For example, at the front edge, it becomes a valley because the gray rock unit has eroded away. Even so, it is an anticline because the strata are convex upward.

c. This is a map of the area in the block diagram, using the standard geologic symbols for anticlines, synclines, strike, and dip. Can you identify the lines that represent the axial traces of the folds?

Geologists use cross sections to illustrate what happens to rock formations under the ground surface.

a. The map shows part of the Alps, a great mountain chain that borders Italy, France, and Switzerland, which was formed by crustal deformation and compressive forces. The points labeled A and A′ are the beginning and end of the cross section shown here.

b. The cross section A–A′ reveals the intense folding and faulting that have resulted in the mountainous landscape of the Alps. Features you should be able to spot in the cross section include several faults, an enormous anticlin like structure (called a **nappe**), and the remnants of a subduction zone.

Helvetic Alps Pennine Alps Southern Alps

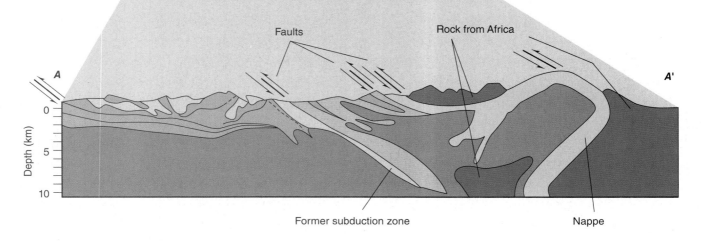

Faults

Rock from Africa

A A'

Depth (km)

0

5

10

Former subduction zone

Nappe

🛑 STOP CONCEPT CHECK

1. **What** types of information are included on geologic maps that are not included on topographic maps?

2. **How** can a geologist illustrate the characteristics of rock strata that extend under the surface?

3. **How** does a geologist differentiate a reverse fault from a normal fault on a map?

The Map That Changed the World

In 1815, the English geologist and surveyor William "Strata" Smith (**Figure a**) published this immense geologic map of England (**Figure b**), described in a recent history as "the map that changed the world." The map was a major step in the emergence of the modern science of geology.

The map is literally a work of art. It was printed in 15 sections, measures 2 meters by 3 meters, and includes more than 1000 place names. Smith used 23 different colors to depict where each stratum was exposed at the surface. Every copy of the map was hand-painted with watercolors, and only 400 copies were printed. (Only 43 are known to still exist.)

Even more important than the map's size and detail was its organization. From his studies of fossils (**Figure c**), Smith understood that all 23 strata lie in a definite vertical sequence, and the sequence is the same anywhere in England. In other words, he had discovered the key to understanding all geologic processes: the geologic column.

a

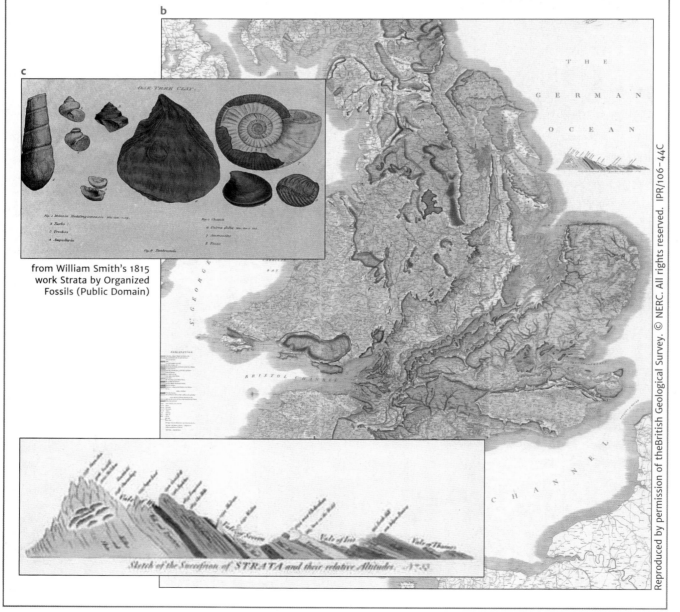

b

c

from William Smith's 1815 work Strata by Organized Fossils (Public Domain)

Sketch of the Succession of STRATA and their relative Altitudes.

SUMMARY

1 Rock Deformation 228

- In response to **stress**, a rock may undergo **strain**; that is, it may change its shape, volume, or both. A nonpermanent change is **elastic deformation**. A permanent change that involves folding or flowing is **ductile** (or plastic) **deformation**. A permanent change that involves fracturing is **brittle deformation**.

- Rock deformation results from **pressure** or stress placed on rock by the movements and interactions of lithospheric plates.

- Stress can be uniform (the same in all directions) or differential (stronger in one direction than in another). As shown in the figure, **compression** results from forces that squeeze a body of rock; **tension** results from forces that stretch the rock, or pull it apart; and **shear** stress causes rock to be twisted and to change shape.

Three types of stress • Figure 9.2

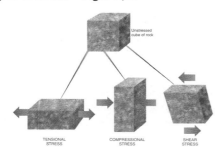

- Low temperature, low confining pressure, and high rate of strain enhance the brittle properties of rock. Failure by fracture is common in upper-crustal rock, where temperature and pressure are low. High temperature, high confining pressure, and low rate of strain, which are characteristic of the deeper crust and the mantle, enhance the ductile behavior of rock. The composition of rock also influences its deformational properties.

- Deformed rock is commonly found in **orogens**, where former tectonic plates collided. Today's continents are complicated assemblages of orogens and **cratons**—regions of ancient crust eroded to near sea level. Orogens are collision zones between cratons, and, because of **isostasy**, they remain subject to vertical movement long after the collisions that produced them have ended.

2 Structural Geology 235

- **Structural geology** deals with the processes and structures associated with stress and strain, such as faults, fractures, and **folds**.

- The **strike** of a stratum, a fault, or another geologic surface is the orientation of the line marking the intersection of the surface with a horizontal plane. The **dip** is the angle between the tilted surface and a horizontal plane, measured down from the horizontal in degrees. Any planar features in rock can be described using these two measurements.

- **Normal faults**, in which the hanging-wall block moves down relative to the footwall block, are caused by tensional (pull-apart) stress. In **reverse faults**, caused by compressional (squeezing) stress, the hanging-wall block moves up and over the footwall block. Shallowly dipping reverse faults are called **thrust faults**. In **strike-slip faults**, caused by shear stress, the movement is mainly horizontal and parallel to the strike of the fault (as shown in the figure).

Stresses and the faults they cause • Figure 9.10

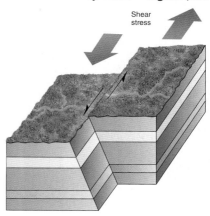

- An **anticline** is an upward fold in the form of an arch, with the oldest rock in the core of the arch. A **syncline** is a downward fold in the form of a trough, with the youngest rock in the concave "valley" of the trough. Many folds are combinations or variations of these two basic types. To fully portray the geometry of a fold, we must describe the fold axis and (if necessary) the direction in which the axis is plunging, as well as the dip of the plunging axis.

3 Geologic Maps 244

- Geologists use **geologic maps** to portray rock units and structures found at Earth's surface. It is common to use a **topographic map** (see figure) as the base for a geologic map. Topographic maps give information about the relief, or "ups and downs," of the land surface, using contour lines to connect points of equal elevation.

Creating a topographic profile • Figure 9.14

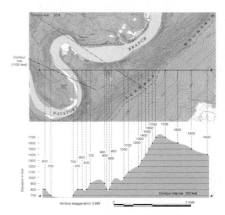

- Geologic maps provide information about the distribution, locations, and orientations of rock formations and structures that occur as **outcrops** at the surface, using standardized symbols, colors, and fill textures to portray various geologic features.

- Sometimes it is important to be able to visualize an area in three dimensions in order to understand what happens to the geologic structures in the subsurface and to interpret the geologic history of the area. This is done by constructing a **geologic cross section**. Geologic cross sections are based partly on the surface geology, as revealed by geologic mapping, and partly on other sources of information about underground geology, such as drilling or seismic studies.

KEY TERMS

anticline 242

brittle deformation 229

compression 228

craton 233

dip 236

ductile deformation 229

elastic deformation 229

fold 241

geologic cross section 246

geologic map 244

isostasy 233

normal fault 239

orogen 233

outcrop 244

pressure 228

reverse fault 239

shear 228

strain 228

stress 228

strike 236

strike-slip fault 239

structural geology 235

syncline 242

tension 228

thrust fault 239

topographic map 244

CRITICAL AND CREATIVE THINKING QUESTIONS

1. Find real examples of plate boundaries along which each of the following types of stress predominates: (a) compression, (b) tension, and (c) shearing. Try to find examples different from those used in the text.

2. To construct geologic cross sections, geologists use the information on topographic maps, often supplemented with information about the subsurface provided by remote study techniques. What are some of the techniques geologists use to study rock structures hidden beneath Earth's surface? (*Hint*: Look back at Chapter 5.)

3. In this chapter we mentioned the role of structural geology in determining the locations of mineral ores, oil, and natural gas. Try to find out about some other practical uses and applications of structural geology, geologic maps, and cross sections.

4. Imagine that you are taking a field course in the Alps. From geologic cross sections, you expect to find some very large folds (see Figure 9.19) where the rock layers have been bent over backward. What kinds of evidence could you look for that would help you determine whether a particular sequence of rock is right-side up or upside down? In other words, how would you determine whether a trough-shaped fold was a right-side up syncline or an upside down (i.e., overturned) anticline?

5. Examine the magnified portion of the geologic map from Figure 9.17. Can you see the symbols that refer to thrust faulting? In each case, identify which unit has been thrust over the top of the other; you may need to refer back to Figure 9.18 to review the meanings of the various map symbols. Also look at the strike-and-dip symbols on the map; in which direction are most of the strata dipping, and at what angle?

A typical geologic map • Figure 9.17

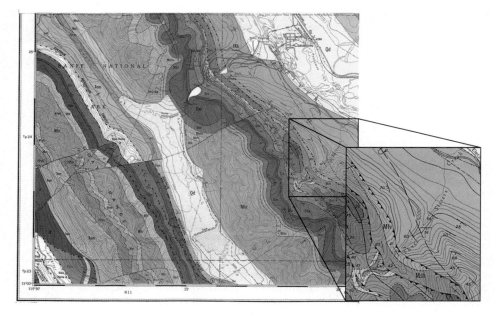

WHAT IS HAPPENING IN THIS PICTURE?

Chief Mountain, in Glacier National Park in Montana, is a huge chunk of Precambrian rock that lies on top of a layer of much younger Cretaceous shale and sandstone (underneath the arrow).

National Park Service

THINK CRITICALLY

The arrow points to a fault. Can you determine what kind of fault it is? *Hint*: Chief Mountain is part of the same fault system as Mount Kidd, described in *Amazing Places*.

SELF-TEST

(Check your answers in Appendix D.)

1. _____ is a type of stress that acts in a direction perpendicular to and away from a fault surface.

    a. Shear stress

    b. Compression

    c. Tension

2. _____ is a type of stress that acts in a direction parallel to and along a fault surface.

    a. Shear stress

    b. Compression

    c. Tension

3. In _____ deformation, rock will bend as long as stress is applied to the crust but will resume its original shape if the stress is released.

    a. elastic

    b. brittle

    c. ductile

4. What type of crustal deformation is depicted in this photograph?

    a. elastic

    b. brittle

    c. ductile

SuperStock

5. The structure depicted in the photograph in question 4 could have formed as a result of stress, under conditions that have any combination of _____.

   a. high confining pressure, low temperature, and high strain rate

   b. low confining pressure, low temperature, and high strain rate

   c. high confining pressure, low temperature, and high strain rate

   d. high confining pressure, high temperature, and low strain rate

6. A(n) _____ is an elongate region of crust that has been deformed and metamorphosed by a continental collision. By contrast, a(n) _____ is a region of continental crust that has remained undeformed for a very long time.

   a. syncline; anticline

   b. anticline; syncline

   c. orogen; craton

   d. craton; orogen

7. On this block diagram of tilted strata, draw symbols to show the direction of strike and dip and indicate the 30° angle of dip.

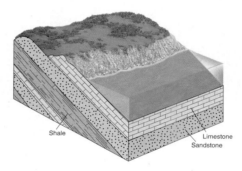

Shale
Limestone
Sandstone

8. This diagram shows a faulted block of Earth's crust. What type of fault is depicted in the diagram?

   a. normal fault

   b. thrust, or reverse, fault

   c. strike-slip fault

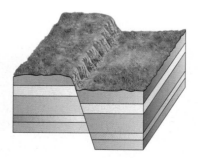

9. The fault depicted in the diagram in question 8 must have formed in response to what kind of stress?

   a. tension

   b. compression

   c. shear

10. A _____ fault is a product of compression of Earth's crust, whereas a _____ fault is a product of tension. _____ faults result from shear stress.

   a. strike-slip; normal; Thrust (reverse)

   b. normal; thrust (reverse); Strike-slip

   c. thrust (reverse); strike-slip; Normal

   d. thrust (reverse); normal; Strike-slip

   e. strike-slip; thrust (reverse); Normal

11. Label this diagram with the following terms:

   anticline   axial plane

   syncline   plunge

   axial trace

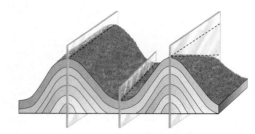

12. A(n) _____ is a local steepening in otherwise uniformly dipping strata.

   a. anticline

   b. syncline

   c. monocline

   d. dome

   e. basin

13. A _____ would allow a geologist to locate the steepest cliff face in a region.

   a. geologic map

   b. topographic map

   c. geologic cross section

14. A _____ can be used to show the subsurface structure of an orogen.

   a. geologic map

   b. topographic map

   c. geologic cross section

15. The areal distribution of rocks and structures in an area is best depicted on a _____.

   a. geologic map

   b. topographic map

   c. geologic cross section

THE PLANNER ✓

Review the Chapter Planner on the chapter opener and check off your completed work.

10 METAMORPHISM: NEW ROCK FROM OLD

James L. Stanfield/NG Image Collection

Federico Rostagno/Shutterstock

Global Locator

Carrara

NG Maps

✓ CHAPTER PLANNER

- Study the picture and read the opening story.
- Scan the Learning Objectives in each section: p. 256   p. 264   p. 268   p. 272
- Read the text and study all visuals. Answer any questions.

Analyze key features
- Geology InSight, p. 258–259
- What a Geologist Sees, p. 260
- Process Diagram, p. 262
- Case Study, p. 263
- Amazing Places, p. 266
- Stop: Answer the Concept Checks before you go on: p. 264   p. 267   p. 272   p. 273

End of chapter
- Review the Summary and Key Terms.
- Answer the Critical and Creative Thinking Questions.
- Answer What is happening in this picture?
- Complete the Self-Test and check your answers.

PIETÀ

To carve the *Pietà*, Michelangelo Buonarroti needed a block of perfect marble 2 meters wide. The year was 1498, in Rome. Michelangelo had resigned himself to a visit to the quarries in distant Carrara (inset photo), when word reached him that a block had arrived in Rome but had not been paid for. Irving Stone writes in *The Agony and the Ecstasy*:

> *He watched the rays of the rising sun strike the block and make it transparent as pink alabaster, with not a hole or hollow or crack or knot in all its massive white weight. It tested out perfect against the hammer, against water, its crystals soft and compacted with fine graining. His* Pietà *had come home.*

White marble starts as marine sediment, composed of the accumulated fragments of shells made of calcite. The sedimentary rock that forms from this sediment is limestone. When subjected to heat and pressure, the calcite recrystallizes, all traces of the shells disappear, and the limestone becomes a crystalline white marble. This transformation is called metamorphism.

Which is more remarkable: the metamorphism from calcareous sediment to pristine marble, or the transformation from raw quarried marble block to finished sculpture? We are amazed by them both.

WHAT IS METAMORPHISM?

Learning Objectives

1. **Describe** the conditions required for metamorphism.

2. **Discuss** how temperature, pressure, pore fluid, stress, and rate of deformation affect the results of metamorphism.

Metamorphism is the set of processes by which rock is altered chemically, physically, or both. One of the most important characteristics of metamorphism is that it happens in solid rock, and solids—unlike liquids and gases—preserve clues about the events that changed them. For example, if you throw a stone into a pond, the splash and resulting ripple soon disappear. Throw a stone at a window, however, and the result is permanently cracked glass.

> **metamorphism** The mineralogical, textural, chemical, and structural changes that occur in rock as a result of exposure to elevated temperatures and/or pressures.

Metamorphic rock, too, preserves a record of all the heating, stretching, fracturing, and grinding that has happened to it throughout its geologic history. When we encounter an area with a lot of metamorphic rock, we can be certain that it has been geologically busy. Decoding the record of that activity is challenging, but the rewards are great because the decoding can tell us about long-ago collisions of continents, the breakup of ancient supercontinents, and whether rich mineral deposits might be present as a result of such activity.

The Physical Limits of Metamorphism

Perhaps the best analogy for metamorphism is simple, everyday cooking—a process that takes, for instance, flour, salt, sugar, yeast, and water and transforms them into a completely new substance called bread, or turns raw meat into a medium-rare steak (**Figure 10.1a**). Like cooking, and like **diagenesis**, metamorphism involves heat and pressure, but the temperatures and pressures involved are considerably higher (see *Remember This!*).

> **diagenesis** Chemical and physical changes that happen to sediment before, during, and after lithification to sedimentary rock.

Metamorphism and cooking • Figure 10.1

Metamorphism and cooking are similar in some respects; they both involve physical and chemical changes that happen to solid materials.

©Marli Bryant Miller

a. In the thermal metamorphism of beef, the outer layers have been subjected to higher temperatures, and therefore a higher degree of metamorphism, than the inner portion, causing changes in texture and color. ▶

Alex Vasilescu/Getty Images, Inc.

b. Here at the Purcell Sill in Montana, an intrusion of hot magma (solidified now as basalt, the darkest material along the center of the photo) exposed the surrounding lighter-colored limestone to high temperatures, "cooking" the limestone and causing changes in its mineralogy and texture.

c. This rock has been metamorphosed by exposure to high pressure and high temperature deep in the crust. The original mineral suite has been converted into a new metamorphic rock: gneiss. The extreme folding indicates that the rock, from Sand River, South Africa, underwent ductile deformation during metamorphism.

Courtesy Brian J. Skinner

Some of the same physical processes that occur in diagenesis, such as compaction and recrystallization, continue during metamorphism—but in a more intense way. In metamorphism, these processes are accompanied by chemical reactions that change the rock's mineral assemblage and texture and sometimes its chemical composition as well. Metamorphism also takes place at greater depths than diagenesis—typically between about 5 and 40 kilometers, which is most of the extent of the thickness of the crust. However, there is one important kind of change that does not take place during metamorphism: The rock does not melt, and that is what makes metamorphic rock so interesting. The rock may have been squeezed, stretched, heated, and altered in complex ways (**Figure 10.1b, c**), but it has remained solid.

The heat that causes metamorphic reactions is Earth's internal heat. We know from drilling deep gas and oil wells, and from deep gold mines, that temperature in the continental crust increases with depth at a rate of about 30°C per kilometer. At a depth of about 5 kilometers, the temperature is about 150°C. This temperature represents the dividing line between the processes of diagenesis, which change sediment into sedimentary rock (below 150°C), and the processes of metamorphism (above 150°C). Geologists have settled on 150°C as the "official" boundary between diagenesis and metamorphism, but the actual transition from diagenesis into metamorphism is more gradational; some rocks begin to show distinct signs of metamorphic changes at 150°C, but others do not.

The upper temperature limit of metamorphism is about 800°C. The onset of melting above this temperature marks the transition from metamorphic processes to magmatic processes. As discussed in Chapter 6, the beginning of melting can occur at a variety of temperatures, depending on the pressure, the composition of the rock, and the amount of fluid present, particularly water and carbon dioxide. Thus, 800°C is only a generalization of the temperature at which fractional melting typically begins in the crust.

Just as pressure influences the temperature at which melting begins, it also influences the kind of metamorphic changes that occur at temperatures below the onset of melting. The air pressure at sea level on Earth's surface is defined to be 1 atmosphere (atm)—about half the pressure of the air inside an automobile tire. However, rock is heavier than air. In the crust, pressure increases with depth at a rate of about 300 atm per kilometer, or about 30 megapascals per kilometer. Therefore, the pressure 5 kilometers below the surface is 1500 times greater than the surface atmospheric pressure—that is, 1500 atm, or 150 MPa. This is the depth at which both temperature and pressure are high enough for recrystallization and growth of new minerals to start.

Figure 10.2 shows the range of temperatures and pressures over which metamorphism occurs. The pressure and temperature conditions under which sediment is changed into sedimentary rock during diagenesis occupy the upper-left corner of the graph (Figure 10.2b). Below this, and down to a depth of about 15 kilometers, where the pressure reaches 400 MPa (4000 atm) and the temperature is about 400°C, metamorphism occurs but is not very intense. In this region **low-grade** metamorphic rock is formed; the minerals change, but the appearance is still similar to that of sedimentary rock. At higher temperatures and pressures, extending to the onset of melting,

low-grade Rock metamorphosed in temperature and pressure conditions up to 400°C and 400 MPa.

Temperature and pressure conditions for metamorphism • Figure 10.2

Throughout much of the crust, elevated temperatures and pressures lead to metamorphism. The vertical scale is given in units of both pressure and depth beneath the surface; temperature increases with increasing depth in the crust and is shown to be increasing from left to right on the graph.

b. Colored bands illustrate the temperature and pressure conditions for diagenesis, low-grade and high-grade metamorphism, and melting. The cross-hatched diagonal band indicates the conditions most commonly found in continental crust.

a. This diagram shows schematically where in the crust metamorphism and melting occur.

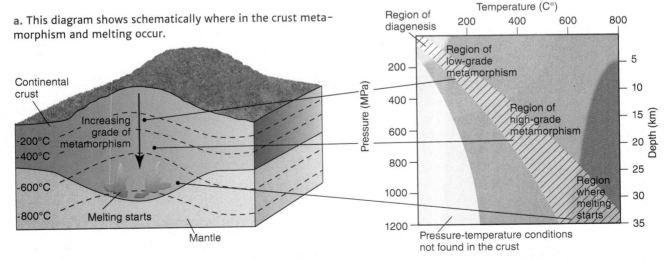

high-grade Rock
metamorphosed in
temperature and
pressure conditions
higher than about
400°C and 400 MPa.

high-grade metamorphic rock is formed. In the lower-right corner of the diagram, representing the hottest temperatures and highest pressures, rock may begin to melt and would no longer be considered metamorphic.

rate at which high pressures and temperatures are applied, and the presence or absence of fluid. The directionality of pressure also plays an important role in metamorphism. As explained in Chapter 9, geologists use the term **stress** to refer to pressures that are greater in one direction than in others. Many metamorphic rocks clearly show the effects of directional stress. Let's look at all these factors.

Factors Influencing Metamorphism

As in cooking, the end product of metamorphism is controlled by the ingredients (the composition of the rock) and the surrounding temperature. However, metamorphism is also influenced by pressure, the duration and

Temperature and Pressure When rock is heated, some of the original minerals recrystallize but don't change composition; others are involved in chemical reactions that form new minerals. **Figure 10.3** shows the effect of increasing temperature and pressure on shale, the most common variety of sedimentary rock. Notice that as the

Geology InSight   From Sedimentary Rock to Metamorphic Rock • Figure 10.3   ✓ THE PLANNER

Increasing temperature and pressure

As shale is subjected to higher and higher temperatures and pressures, it develops into a sequence of metamorphic rocks that have different mineral assemblages. The figure shows rock samples as they appear to the unaided eye. All of the specimens are about 8 centimeters across.

Courtesy Brian J. Skinner

Courtesy Brian J. Skinner

▲ **a. Shale** from Linden, New York. The shale breaks readily along bedding surfaces but irregularly between the surfaces. Individual mineral grains are too small to be resolved.

▲ **b. Slate** from Pawlett, New York. Slaty cleavage has developed as a result of low-grade metamorphism, but minerals are still too small to be resolved by the unaided eye.

Minerals present

Clay

Chlorite

Muscovite (white mica)

Feldspar

Quartz

grade of metamorphism increases, completely new minerals appear—and, in some cases, disappear again at higher grades. Thus, identifying the component minerals is a good way to tell these metamorphic rocks apart. Notice also that as the temperature and pressure of metamorphism increase, the mineral grains become progressively larger. Rock subjected to low-grade metamorphism tends to be fine-grained, while high-grade metamorphism produces coarse-grained rock.

Pore Fluid An important factor that affects metamorphism is the presence of open spaces, called **pores**. The same term is used for any small, intergranular spaces in rock or sediment, such as those between the grains in a sedimentary rock, as well as small fractures in igneous and metamorphic rock.

Most pores are filled with either a watery fluid or a gaseous fluid, such as carbon dioxide. The watery, or aqueous, fluid is never just pure water; it has small amounts of gases and salts dissolved in it, along with traces of all the mineral constituents present in the enclosing rock. At high temperatures, the pore fluid is likely to be entirely gaseous. Regardless of its specific characteristics, pore fluid plays a vital role in metamorphism.

Pore fluid enhances metamorphism in two ways. First, the presence of pore fluid permits material to dissolve from one place, move quickly via the fluid, and be precipitated in another place. In this way, pore fluid speeds up recrystallization and generally leads to the formation of rock with relatively large mineral grains.

c. Phyllite from Orange County, New York. The grade of metamorphism is higher than that of a slate, and the mica grains that have grown can just be seen by the unaided eye. ▼

d. Garnet-mica schist, from Gassetts, Vermont. This mica-rich rock has been subjected to high-grade metamorphic conditions. Individual mineral grains are readily visible. ▼

Courtesy Brian J. Skinner

Courtesy Brian J. Skinner

e. Biotite gneiss from Uxbridge, Massachusetts. This rock was formed under the same metamorphic conditions as schist, but it differs in composition, containing less mica and more quartz and feldspar. All mineral grains are large enough to be readily visible. ▶

Courtesy Brian J. Skinner

THINK CRITICALLY

Make a list of the key minerals shown at the bottom of the page, listing them in the order in which they first appear in the rocks. Later, you will use this to answer question 5 in Critical and Creative Thinking Questions at the end of the chapter.

Muscovite (white mica)

Biotite (dark mica)

Garnet

Kyanite

Sillimanite

Feldspar

Quartz

Second, pore fluid enhances metamorphism by acting as a reservoir during the growth of new minerals. When the temperature and pressure of a rock undergoing metamorphism change, so does the composition of the pore fluid. Some of the dissolved constituents move from the fluid to the new minerals growing in the metamorphic rock. Other constituents move in the other direction, from the minerals to the fluid. Pore fluid speeds up chemical reactions in the same way that water in a stew pot speeds up the cooking of a tough piece of meat. Because of this, metamorphism proceeds rapidly when pore fluid is present, but when pore fluid is absent or present in tiny amounts, metamorphic reactions occur very slowly.

As pressure increases and metamorphism proceeds, the amount of pore space decreases, and the pore fluid is slowly driven out of the rock. The escaping pore fluid carries with it small amounts of dissolved minerals. As the fluid flows through fractures in the rock, some of the dissolved minerals may precipitate, creating veins (**Figure 10.4**). Veins are quite common in metamorphic rock.

Quartz vein • Figure 10.4 _____

This sample of gneiss contains many quartz veins (white) that crisscross the rock. The quartz precipitated out of pore fluid that was expelled from the rock during metamorphism.

Courtesy Jay Ague, Dept. of Geology and Geophysics at Yale University

What a Geologist Sees

THE PLANNER

Metamorphic Geology at the Roadside

A geologist who looks at this road cut, (**Figure a**), in central Connecticut would see dark-colored rock with a nearly vertical direction of breakage. The geologist suspects metamorphic rock that has suffered ductile deformation, with the principal direction of compressive stress perpendicular to the plane of breakage.

Looking more closely the geologist sees rock in which all the mineral grains are large enough to be readily visible, so he concludes that he is looking at high-grade metamorphic rock. Examination of the outcrop reveals the presence of quartz, feldspar, amphibole, and biotite, so he concludes further that the rock is a gneiss.

Cutting through the gneiss is a white dike. On close examination (**Figure b**), it is apparent that the dike consists mainly of quartz and feldspar (the pink colored mineral in (**Figure c**) is a potassium feldspar 15 centimenters across), and that the texture is that of an igneous rock—there is no platy fabric or plane of breakage as there is in the gneiss. The geologist concludes that the dike is granite was intruded into a fracture in the metamorphic rock after the main phase of metamorphic deformation.

b

Courtesy Brian J. Skinner

c

Courtesy Brian J. Skinner

a

Courtesy Brian J. Skinner

THINK CRITICALLY

What characteristics would the geologist use to distinguish the granite dike (igneous rock) from the gneiss (metamorphic rock)?

The two rock samples in these photos have similar mineral assemblages but look very different because of their different stress histories.

a. This granite consists of quartz (glassy), feldspar (white), and biotite (dark), which crystallized from magma (a liquid) under conditions of uniform stress. Note that the biotite grains are randomly oriented.

b. This gneiss, a high-grade metamorphic rock, contains the same minerals as the granite, but they developed entirely in the solid state and under differential stress. The biotite grains are aligned, giving the rock a pronounced layered texture.

The presence of pore fluid also greatly influences the onset of rock melting. The effect of fluid on rock is to lower the melting temperature of the rock. The upper temperature limit of metamorphism therefore depends in part on the amount of pore fluid present. When a tiny amount of fluid is present, only a small amount of melting occurs, and the magma remains trapped in small pockets in the metamorphic rock. When the rock cools, so do the pockets of magma. The result is a composite rock, part igneous and part metamorphic, called **migmatite**.

When abundant pore fluid is present and large volumes of magma develop, the magma rises and intrudes into overlying metamorphic rock. In such cases, we observe batholiths of granitic rock closely associated with large volumes of metamorphic rock. This igneous–metamorphic rock association occurs along subduction and collision margins of tectonic plates (see *What a Geologist Sees*).

Stress   As you learned in Chapter 9, rock that is buried deep underground typically experiences differential stresses that have a strong effect on its appearance (**Figure 10.5**). Differential stress causes rock undergoing metamorphism to develop a distinctive layered or planar texture called **foliation**.

> **foliation**   A planar arrangement of textural features in metamorphic rock that give the rock a layered or finely banded appearance.

Figure 10.5a shows a nonfoliated rock, and Figure 10.5b shows a foliated rock. Foliation is particularly evident when minerals belonging to the mica family are present. This is because micas are platelike minerals in which the silicate anions link together to form flat sheets. Under differential stress, micas grow so that the sheets of the crystal structure are perpendicular to the direction of maximum stress (**Figure 10.6**).

Low-grade metamorphic rock tends to be so fine grained that the new mineral grains can be seen only under a microscope (see the slate specimen in Figure 10.3). Foliation in these rocks produces a distinctive style of fracture, called **slaty cleavage**. The orientation of the cleavage planes says a great deal about the conditions under which metamorphism occurred, as explained in **Figure 10.7**.

> **slaty cleavage**   Foliation in low-grade metamorphic rock, which causes the rock to break into flat, plate-like fragments.

Slaty cleavage is similar to cleavage in a mineral (Chapter 2) but with a very important difference. A mineral grain is a single crystal, and cleavage occurs because the

Foliation under the microscope • Figure 10.6

This image was created by making a thin section of rock, then viewing it in polarized light under a microscope. This sample of foliated metamorphic rock (schist) consists mostly of muscovite (a mica, the colored grains) and quartz (the black grains). The direction of maximum stress is indicated by the arrows.

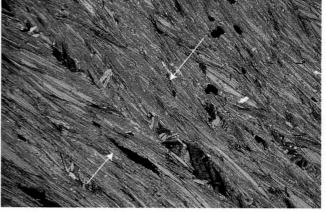

How slaty cleavage and schistosity develop • Figure 10.7

Slaty cleavage is a foliation that develops in low-grade metamorphic rock, as a result of differential stress. At higher grades of metamorphism, slaty cleavage is replaced by schistosity.

▼ **a.** In low-grade metamorphism, the maximum stress comes from the weight of overlying rock and, therefore, is perpendicular to the bedding. This creates foliated rock with cleavage planes parallel to the bedding.

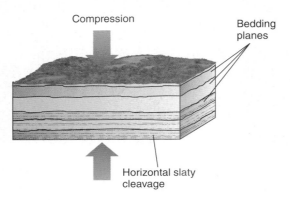

▼ **b.** The slaty cleavage in this red slate from Granville, New York, is parallel to the bedding, indicating that the maximum stress was perpendicular to the bedding. The sample shows a cleaved surface.

a. Slaty cleavage: This view shows a cleaved surface.

▼ **c.** During a collision of tectonic plates, strata are squeezed and folded, causing a ripple-like appearance. The maximum stress is from the compression of the colliding plates; it is horizontal, as shown by the arrows. This causes the rock to develop cleavage in the vertical direction, at an angle to the bedding.

Specimen a viewed perpendicular to the cleavage direction. Note the numerous small parallel steps and ridges; they are parallel to the direction of slaty cleavage.

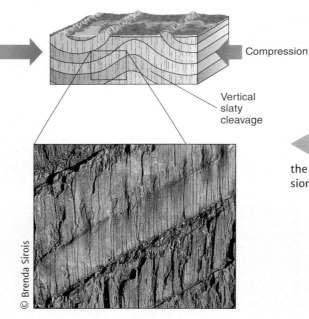

◀ **d.** In this sample from the Martinsburg Formation in Pennsylvania, slaty cleavage has developed at an angle to the bedding, indicating that this region was under compression when the rock was metamorphosed.

▲ **e.** As metamorphism continues to a higher grade, schistosity replaces slaty cleavage. This specimen of mica schist is from Manhattan in New York City. The photo shows the sample viewed perpendicular to the plane of schistosity.

THINK CRITICALLY

What are the main differences between slaty cleavage and schistosity?

bonds between atoms in the crystal are weaker in some directions than in others. In contrast, cleavage in a rock involves a great many crystal lattices, and it happens because the crystals themselves are roughly parallel. The flat cleavage planes that result make slate an excellent material for roofing and paving tiles, blackboards, billiard tables, and other uses that require a durable natural material with a flat surface (see the *Case Study*).

Another kind of foliation, **schistosity**, forms under conditions of high-grade metamorphism, which causes mineral grains to grow large enough to be seen with the naked eye (see Figure 10.7e). This kind of foliation differs from slaty cleavage primarily in the size of the mineral grains. Another difference is that schistose rock generally breaks along wavy or distorted surfaces, while slaty cleavage is strictly planar.

> **schistosity** Foliation in coarse-grained metamorphic rock.

Duration and Rate of Metamorphism Chemical reactions can occur rapidly or slowly. Some reactions, such as the burning of natural gas to produce carbon dioxide and water, happen so fast that they can cause an explosion if not handled carefully. At the other end of the scale are reactions that take thousands or even millions of years to complete. Most of the reactions that happen during metamorphism are the latter kind.

CASE Study

✓ THE PLANNER

Metamorphism and Billiards

Billiards is played on tables made from slate, a metamorphic rock. Early billiard tables, like modern ones, were rectangular, surrounded by cushions, and fitted with six pockets. However, they were made of wood, which tended to vibrate and warp, and thus interfered with the accuracy of players.

Around 1825, during the Industrial Revolution, an Englishman named John Thurston invented the slate bed. Manufacturers of billiard tables discovered that using the slaty cleavage surface for the table top ensured a surface that was smooth and free of vibrations. Slate tables were also sturdier and less prone to wear than wooden tables. Slate comes from the low-grade metamorphism and compression of shale (**Figure a**). In North America, a belt of slate (**Figure b**) runs along the eastern seaboard from Georgia to Maine formed by the same continental collision that created the supercontinent of Pangaea 400 million years ago. Here, shepherds in western China (**Figure c**) work on their skills at billiards while their flocks graze in the background.

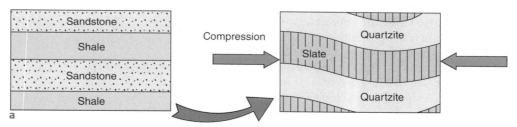

Metamorphism converts shale to slate.

Brian Skinner

b

Natalie Behring/News Com

c

THINK CRITICALLY

Billiard table surfaces need to be very flat and smooth. What conditions—both in the deformational process, and in the rock itself—would lead to the development of such a smooth, flat surface?

Despite the slowness of most metamorphic reactions, scientists have been able to use laboratory experimentation to demonstrate that high temperatures, high pressures or stresses, abundant pore fluid, and long reaction times produce large mineral grains. Coarse-grained rock—with mineral grains the size of a thumbnail or larger—is formed under long-sustained metamorphic conditions (possibly over millions of years) with high temperature, high stress, and abundant pore fluid. On the other hand, fine-grained rock—with mineral grains the size of a pinhead or smaller—is either produced under conditions involving lower temperature and lower stress or under conditions where pore fluid was scarce or reaction times were short.

STOP CONCEPT CHECK

1. **What** is the approximate depth where diagenesis ceases and metamorphism starts?
2. **What** three variables, besides rock composition, are most important in causing metamorphism?

METAMORPHIC ROCK

Learning Objectives

1. **Identify** the common foliated metamorphic rocks.

2. **Identify** the common nonfoliated metamorphic rocks.

The names of metamorphic rocks are based mostly on their textures and mineral assemblages (see *Where Geologists Click*). The most widely used names apply to metamorphic rock derived from the sedimentary rock shale, sandstone, and limestone, and from the igneous rock type basalt. This is because shale, sandstone, and limestone are the most abundant sedimentary rocks, and basalt is the most abundant igneous rock. We will first describe the metamorphic rock types that have some degree of foliation; then we will move on to describe metamorphic rocks that tend to occur without foliation.

Metamorphic Rocks with Foliation

As mentioned earlier in this chapter (see Figure 10.3), the metamorphic products of shale form a sequence of rock types, beginning with slate, a low-grade product. As the metamorphism proceeds to higher grades, the rock looks less and less like its parent rock, shale, and develops larger and larger mineral grains. Foliation is often apparent in the metamorphic products of shale, because platy mica minerals are commonly present (see *Remember This!*).

REMEMBER THIS! Micas are minerals in which the silicate anions link together in flat sheets. Can you remember what it's called when silicate anions link together in chains or sheets? You can remind yourself by looking back at *Mineral Families* in Chapter 2.

There are some subtleties of terminology in the sequence of rock derived from shale. The names **slate** and **phyllite** describe textures. They are usually used without adding mineral names as adjectives because their mineral assemblages are not easy to see. On the other hand, the mineral grains in

slate A very fine-grained, low-grade metamorphic rock with slaty cleavage; the metamorphic product of shale.

phyllite A fine-grained metamorphic rock with pronounced foliation, produced by further metamorphism of slate.

Where Geologists CLICK

Imperial College Rock Library: Metamorphic Rocks

The Imperial College of London maintains a large collection of photographs of minerals and rocks from the collections of the Imperial College Department of Earth Science and Engineering and the Royal School of Mines. The photographs are paired with in-depth descriptions, glossaries, and learning tools and activities that can help you to improve your skills in sample identification and interpretation.

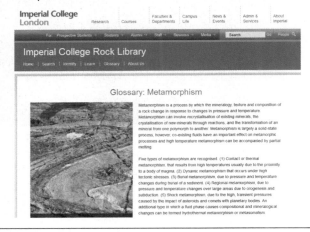

schist and **gneiss** (pronounced "nice") are large enough to be identified, so geologists usually add the mineral assemblage to the name, as in "garnet-mica schist."

Metamorphic rock doesn't always develop from sedimentary rock; igneous rock also can undergo metamorphism. The names given to metamorphosed igneous rocks differ from those used for the metamorphic rocks that develop from shale and other sedimentary rocks.

Basalt—the most abundant igneous rock—is a very common parent rock. Note that the metamorphism of basalt generally requires the presence of a hydrous pore fluid, to allow for the formation of hydrous minerals such as micas and amphiboles. The metamorphism of basalt produces several distinct mineral assemblages, depending on the metamorphic conditions to which it is subjected (**Figure 10.8**).

Under the conditions of high stress and low to moderate temperature that occur in subduction zones, the metamorphic rocks blueschist and eclogite are produced. Eclogite is an important source for such semiprecious gemstones as garnet and jadeite (see *Amazing Places*). Under moderate to intermediate metamorphic grades in continental collision zones, particularly where pore fluid is available, the metamorphic rocks greenschist and

Metamorphism of basalt • Figure 10.8

When basalt is metamorphosed under conditions in which pore water can enter the rock, distinctive textures and mineral assemblages develop.

a. Low-grade metamorphism produces greenschist, so named because of the presence of a green, mica-like mineral called chlorite. Greenschist is fine-grained, with pronounced foliation. This specimen is from Minnesota.

b. Under high-grade metamorphism, chlorite is replaced by amphibole, and the resulting rock is amphibolite. Foliation is present but not pronounced, because mica is usually absent. The elongate crystals of hornblende (an amphibole group mineral) in this specimen from North Carolina are all parallel.

c. Under conditions of very high stress, as in subduction zones, the low-grade metamorphic product of basalt is blueschist, which owes its color to the mineral glaucophane. This strongly foliated specimen is from Greece.

d. At even higher pressures and moderate temperatures, blueschist is replaced by the high-grade metamorphic rock eclogite, which contains such minerals as jadeite and garnet. In this specimen from Greece, the red garnets are obvious; the dark green mineral surrounding the garnets is a pyroxene. Eclogite may have weak foliation, or may lack foliation.

The Source of Olmec Jade

Jade, in both of its common mineral forms, jadeite and nephrite, is beautiful but exceedingly tough, which makes it suitable for cutting with tools and ideal for intricate carving. Jade-bearing rocks are developed by metamorphism under high pressure and moderate temperature conditions in subduction zones.

The largest jadeite deposits are in Myanmar and Central America. Until recently, the Central American deposits posed a mystery. From roughly 1200 to 400 BCE, the Olmec people lived in the region that today is eastern Mexico and Guatemala. They are known, among other things, for beautiful jade carvings such as the axe shown here (**Figure a**).

However, geologists and archaeologists did not know where the Olmec jade had come from. They did know about a band of jadeite deposits along the northern bank of the Motagua River in Guatemala, where local miners called *jaderos* made a good living extracting jadeite. However, this jadeite is inferior to the Olmec jade, which has a distinctive blue-green color; this could not have been the source for the real Olmec jade.

Global Locator

Guatemala

All this changed in 1998 when Hurricane Mitch eroded the slopes on the other side of the Motagua River and exposed more extensive jadeite deposits. In (**Figure b**), a geologist stands on a newly exposed outcrop of the jadeite-bearing rock. Subsequent explorations have revealed that the jade-bearing area is six times larger than geologists previously knew. The newly discovered jadeite is a very close match to the Olmec jade, with the same translucent blue-green color and white inclusions (**Figure c**).

Mystery solved!

a

Universal History Archive/Getty Images, Inc.

b

Courtesy George E. Harlow

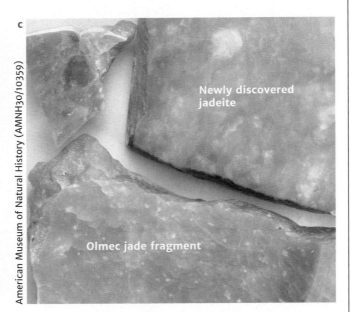

c

American Museum of Natural History (AMNH30/10359)

Newly discovered jadeite

Olmec jade fragment

THINK CRITICALLY

What kinds of analysis might scientists undertake to determine whether the Olmec jade came from the same source as the newly exposed jadeite deposits?

Marble, from metamorphosed limestone, and quartzite, from metamorphosed sandstone, are the two most common nonfoliated metamorphic rock types. The smaller photos show the samples in polarized light under a microscope.

a. Quartz-rich sandstone becomes quartzite when its pore spaces are filled with silica and the entire mass recrystallizes as a result of metamorphism. The specimen shown here is from Minnesota.

b. Marble is a metamorphic rock composed mainly of calcite. Pure marble is snow white. The pink color of this sample (from Tate, Georgia) and the common "marbled" pattern come from mineral impurities other than calcite in the marble.

amphibolite develop from igneous rocks of the same basaltic composition.

Metamorphic rocks made from basalt are less foliated than the series of rocks formed by the metamorphism of shale, because they do not contain as much mica. Amphibole—the mineral that typically defines the foliation in amphibolites—is not as sheet-like as the mica minerals and so forms a weaker foliation.

Metamorphic Rocks Without Foliation

Two kinds of sedimentary rock consist almost entirely of a single mineral species and therefore are said to be **monomineralic**. The first is sandstone, a clastic sedimentary rock that is usually dominated by quartz grains. The second is limestone, a chemical sedimentary rock whose only essential constituent is calcite. Neither of these rocks contains the ingredients (mainly aluminum, potassium, and iron) necessary to form micas and other minerals that might impart foliation to a metamorphic rock.

quartzite The product of metamorphism formed by recrystallization of sandstone.

marble The product of metamorphism formed by recrystallization of limestone.

As a result, **quartzite** and **marble**—the metamorphic rocks derived from quartz-rich sandstone and limestone, respectively—usually lack foliation (**Figure 10.9**). (In contrast, those ingredients are present in sedimentary rock such as shale, where they occur in clay minerals; therefore, the metamorphism of shale does lead to the formation of micas, resulting in a foliated texture.) Under a microscope, the individual mineral grains in quartzite and marble tend to be uniform in size and closely packed together, showing few or no signs of their sedimentary origin, such as bedding planes or fossils.

STOP CONCEPT CHECK

1. **How** do the metamorphic conditions of temperature and pressure differ between greenschist and blueschist?

2. **What** are the two common nonfoliated metamorphic rocks and their parent rocks?

TYPES OF METAMORPHISM

Learning Objectives

1. **Describe** the processes and circumstances involved in contact metamorphism.

2. **Distinguish** burial metamorphism from diagenesis.

3. **Identify** the tectonic settings where regional metamorphism occurs.

4. **Describe** the unusual circumstances in which cataclastic and shock metamorphism occur.

5. **Define** metasomatism and explain how it differs from metamorphism.

The processes that cause changes in texture and mineral assemblages in metamorphic rock are **mechanical deformation** and **chemical recrystallization**. Mechanical deformation includes grinding, crushing, bending, and fracturing. **Figure 10.10a** shows a conglomerate in which the pebbles have not been mechanically deformed. By contrast, **Figure 10.10b**, which shows flattened pebbles in a conglomerate, is an example of mechanical deformation.

Chemical recrystallization includes changes in mineral composition, growth of new minerals, recrystallization of old minerals, and changes in the amount of pore fluid due to chemical reactions that occur when rock is heated or squeezed. Metamorphism typically involves both mechanical deforma-

tion and chemical recrystallization processes, but their relative importance varies greatly. We can distinguish several kinds of metamorphism on the basis of the importance of mechanical deformation and chemical recrystallization, and the tectonic environments in which they occur.

Contact Metamorphism

Where hot magma intrudes into cooler rock, high temperatures cause chemical recrystallization in surrounding rock. The magma itself may also release pore fluid—chiefly heated water—as it cools. The fluid, in turn, transports materials and accelerates the growth of new minerals. **Contact metamorphism** is primarily temperature driven; mechanical deformation—and therefore foliation—are minor.

An igneous intrusion is commonly surrounded by a zone or **aureole** of contact metamorphism (**Figure 10.11**). If the rock is relatively impervious, such as shale, or if the magma contains little water, then the aureole may extend only a few centimeters. However, a large intrusion contains more heat energy than a small one and may also release a large volume of pore fluid as it cools.

> **contact metamorphism** Metamorphism that occurs when rock is heated and chemically changed adjacent to an intruded body of hot magma.

When intrusions are very large (the size of stocks and batholiths), and when they intrude into highly reactive and relatively pervious rock, such as limestone, the effects of contact metamorphism may extend for hundreds of meters. Unlike other kinds of metamorphism, contact metamorphism is not associated with any particular tectonic setting; it may occur wherever magma intrusions occur.

Mechanical deformation • Figure 10.10

Mechanical deformation involves processes such as grinding, crushing, bending, and fracturing.

a. This undeformed conglomerate contains pebbles rounded from stream transport.

Michael P. Gadomski/Photo Researchers, Inc.

b. In the deformed conglomerate, differential pressure has squeezed the once-rounded pebbles to such an extent that they are now flat.

Courtesy Brian J. Skinner

A layer of limestone undergoes contact metamorphism when granite magma intrudes into it. The intrusion is surrounded by an aureole of altered rock, with several distinct zones.

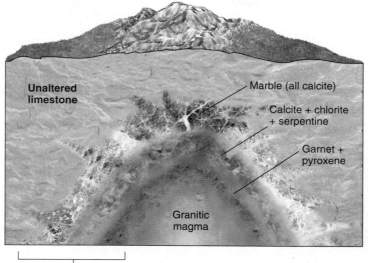

In the outermost zone, farthest from the heat of the granite intrusion, the limestone has been metamorphosed to marble.

Unaltered limestone

Marble (all calcite)

Calcite + chlorite + serpentine

Garnet + pyroxene

Granitic magma

Inside the marble is a zone where chemicals dissolved in the pore fluid have reacted with the limestone to form chlorite and serpentine.

Aureole of metamorphic rock

Closest to the magma is a zone of high-grade metamorphism containing garnet and pyroxene.

Burial Metamorphism

The first stage of metamorphism to occur in sedimentary rock after diagenesis is **burial metamorphism**. The metamorphic processes caused by burial begin at about 150°C, when a sedimentary rock has been buried at a depth of about 5 kilometers. The maximum stress exerted during burial metamorphism tends to be vertical; foliation, if present, is thus parallel to bedding.

> **burial metamorphism** Metamorphism that occurs after diagenesis, as a result of the burial of sediment in deep sedimentary basins.

Burial metamorphism requires a relatively thick layer of overlying rock or sediment, so it is usually observed in deep sedimentary basins such as those found along passive margins or fore-arc basins (see *Remember This!*). Burial metamorphism is primarily a matter of chemical recrystallization—mechanical deformation occurs but is minor. Because the temperature of the rock in these basins seldom exceeds 300°C, burial metamorphism tends to be low grade. As temperature and pressure increase beyond this point, or as sediment on a continental margin is deformed during a tectonic collision, burial metamorphism grades into regional metamorphism.

> **REMEMBER THIS!** Do you recall what a passive margin is and where fore-arc basins are located? You can remind yourself by reviewing *How Plate Tectonics Affects Sedimentation* in Chapter 8.

Regional Metamorphism

The most common kinds of metamorphic rock in the continental crust—slate, phyllite, schist, and gneiss—are found in areas extending over tens of thousands of square kilometers. They are formed by a process called **regional metamorphism**, which involves both intense mechanical deformation and extensive chemical recrystallization.

> **regional metamorphism** Metamorphism of an extensive area of the crust, associated with plate convergence, collision, and subduction.

Regional metamorphism occurs only at convergent plate margins. Regionally metamorphosed rock is found in mountain ranges and in the eroded remnants of former mountain ranges (**Figure 10.12**). It is formed as a result of subduction, or through collisions between masses of continental crust. Rock at convergent margins is subjected to

The theory of plate tectonics provides a unified view of burial metamorphism (1), regional metamorphism in a subduction zone (2), and regional metamorphism in a collision zone (3). Contact metamorphism (4) can occur adjacent to an igneous intrusion in any tectonic setting. The dashed lines are **isotherms** (lines of equal temperature).

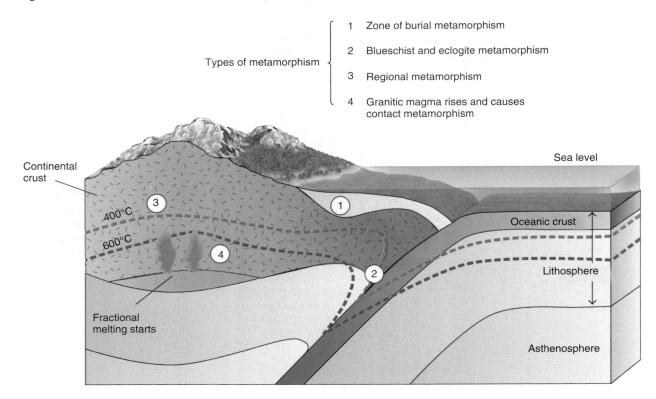

Types of metamorphism
1   Zone of burial metamorphism
2   Blueschist and eclogite metamorphism
3   Regional metamorphism
4   Granitic magma rises and causes contact metamorphism

ASK YOURSELF

Examine the points labelled "2" and "3" on this diagram. Note that "2" is at much greater depth than "3". What are the relative temperatures of these two locations?

a. The point labelled "2" would be at a higher temperature, since it is at a much greater depth in the crust.

b. The two points are at roughly the same temperature (about 400°). This can be determined by looking at the isotherm, or line of equal temperature. Both points fall close to the 400-degree isotherm.

c. It would be impossible to determine this from the diagram, without additional information.

intense differential stresses; the foliation that is characteristic of regionally metamorphosed rock is a consequence of such stresses, although, as discussed above, the full development of foliation depends on the composition of the rock.

Regionally metamorphosed rock can also be found in places where no plate collisions are occurring today, but where plate tectonic activity was intense at some time in geologic history—that is, in orogens. These are regions where plates have collided in the past, and their fragments have been assembled into the lithospheric plates we see today. Orogens provide some of our best evidence that plate tectonics and regional metamorphism have been active on Earth for billions of years (see *Remember This!*).

> **REMEMBER THIS!** How do orogens form, and what do they tell us about the geologic history of an area? What is the relationship between deformation and metamorphism in these regions? Remind yourself about orogens by looking back at *Rock Deformation* in Chapter 9.

A special kind of regional metamorphism occurs at subduction margins. In region 2 of Figure 10.12, you can see the isotherms bend down steeply, indicating that these rocks are much cooler than the surrounding crust. This phenomenon occurs because the solid, cold oceanic crust dives rapidly (by geologic standards) into the hot, weak asthenosphere. The

Quick pressure, slow heat • Figure 10.13 ─────

When a block of rock is squeezed, the entire block "feels" the stress immediately. When the rock is heated on one side, however, it takes a long time for the other side to get hot. A thermometer on the side away from the heat source will still register a low temperature after a fairly extended period of heating.

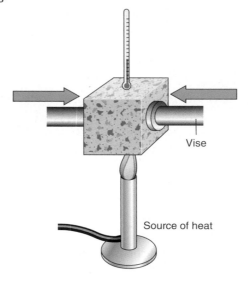

Vise

Source of heat

pressure on the subducting rock rises quickly, but the temperature of the rock cannot rise at the same rate. This conclusion follows from a basic property that can be observed in a laboratory: Rock transmits pressure immediately but conducts heat slowly (**Figure 10.13**). Therefore, in a subduction zone, metamorphism occurs at very high pressures but low to moderate temperatures. This produces a distinctive series of rocks, including blueschist and (at higher grades) eclogite.

Shock and Cataclastic Metamorphism

Occasionally metamorphism occurs in other geologic settings where very special conditions occur, even if only briefly or sporadically. These include fault zones, meteorite impact craters, and even the sites of large fires.

One such process is called **cataclastic metamorphism**, which is almost completely dominated by mechanical deformation. It occurs when bodies of rock grind past one another in a fault zone, pulverizing the rock in a narrow zone along the fault plane, and generating some heat as a result of friction. Cataclastic metamorphism is rare and generally localized in extent.

Geologists use the term **shock metamorphism** to refer to circumstances in which the pressure that causes metamorphism is extremely high for a short period of time; it is mainly identified at the sites of meteorite impacts, although there may be some other extremely rare and limited occurrences. As geologists have become more aware of the role of meteorite impacts in our planet's geologic history, the unique kinds of metamorphism produced by these rare events have become important diagnostic tools for detecting highly eroded ancient impact sites (**Figure 10.14**).

Metasomatism

Metamorphic processes may dramatically change the appearance of a rock and may cause its chemical constituents to move and crystallize into new mineral assemblages. However, they have little effect on the overall

Shock metamorphism • Figure 10.14 ─────────────────────

Shock metamorphism has been found to occur almost exclusively at the sites of meteorite impacts.

a. Nördlingen Cathedral in Germany sits in the center of an ancient impact crater. The cathedral was constructed of local rock that was metamorphosed by the heat and high pressure associated with a meteorite impact.

b. This microscopic view of shock-metamorphosed quartz of the type found in the Nördlingen building stone has lines that record very high-pressure deformation. The stones also contain tiny diamonds, which were formed here instantaneously by the extreme pressure in the blast wave from the exploding meteorite.

Alamy

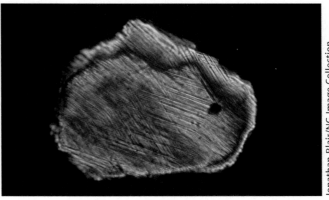

Jonathan Blair/NG Image Collection

chemical composition of the rock. This is one reason geologists can tell the identity and composition of metamorphic parent rock.

There is an important exception to this general rule. Pore fluids, chiefly water and carbon dioxide, can be squeezed into or out of a body of rock during metamorphism. Most metamorphic environments have a small fluid-to-rock ratio, which means the amount of fluid present compared to the amount of rock is less than about 1:10. That is enough fluid to facilitate metamorphism but not enough to dissolve much of the rock and thus change its composition noticeably.

In a few circumstances, though, large fluid-to-rock ratios of 10:1 or even 100:1 can occur. One example of such a circumstance is a large, open rock fracture through which a lot of fluid flows. The rock adjoining the fracture can be drastically altered by the addition of new material, the removal of material into the fluid solution, or both. The term **metasomatism**, which comes from the Greek words for "change" and "body," is applied in such cases. Note that *metamorphism* refers to a change of form (*morph* is the Greek word for "shape," or "form"), often accompanied by a redistribution of chemical constituents. *Metasomatism*, on the other hand, refers to a change in the chemical composition of the rock as a whole.

> **metasomatism** The process whereby the chemical composition of a rock is altered by the addition or removal of material by solution in fluids.

Figure 10.15 is a photograph of a contact metamorphic rock that was originally a limestone. Without the addition of new material, the limestone would have become a marble, dominated by calcite. Through metasomatism, however, it gained the constituents needed to crystallize garnet and a pyroxene called diopside, in addition to calcite. Metasomatic fluids may also carry valuable minerals in solution, which can lead to the formation of ore deposits, discussed in Chapter 16.

Metasomatism • Figure 10.15

Metasomatism of limestone produced this colorful rock from the Gaspé Peninsula in Quebec. The white is calcite, the red is garnet, and the dark brown is pyroxene. The sample is 2.5 by 1.5 centimeters.

William Sacco

🛑 CONCEPT CHECK

1. **What** physical and chemical changes take place in rock undergoing contact metamorphism?

2. **What** distinguishes burial metamorphism from regional metamorphism?

3. **How** does regional metamorphism in a subduction zone differ from regional metamorphism in a collision zone?

4. **Why** are cataclastic and shock metamorphism rare and limited in extent?

5. **What** process changes the chemical composition of a rock, rather than just its texture or mineral assemblage?

METAMORPHIC ZONES AND FACIES

Learning Objectives

1. **Define** metamorphic zones, index minerals, and isograds.

2. **Explain** the concept of metamorphic facies and show how facies correlate with the temperature and pressure the rock is exposed to.

Much of the early research on regional metamorphism and metamorphic rock assemblages was done in the Scottish Highlands in the late 1800s (see *Remember This!*). Geologists discovered that mineral assemblages varied a great deal from place to place but that the overall chemical composition of the rocks was essentially the same as that of shale. Their research on the progressive metamorphism of shale provided the basis for future studies of metamorphism and metamorphic rocks.

> **REMEMBER THIS!** Much of the pioneering work of establishing the science of geology in the 18th and 19th centuries was done in Scotland. For example, do you remember James Hutton, considered to be the "father of geology"? What were some of his important contributions? You can review by looking back at *Relative Age* in Chapter 3.

Metamorphic Zones and Index Minerals

Geologists realized that even though the bulk chemical composition of the Scottish Highland rocks did not vary from place to place, the mineral assemblages differed

**Regional metamorphic zones and isograds •
Figure 10.16** _____

This map shows an area of regionally metamorphosed rock (shale) in Scotland, where the concept of metamorphic zones was first described. Isograds mark the first appearances of index minerals. Rock lying between two isograds is said to be in a particular metamorphic zone. For example, rock between the biotite and garnet isograds would contain the index mineral biotite but would not yet have reached the metamorphic conditions in which garnet would appear; it is in the "biotite zone."

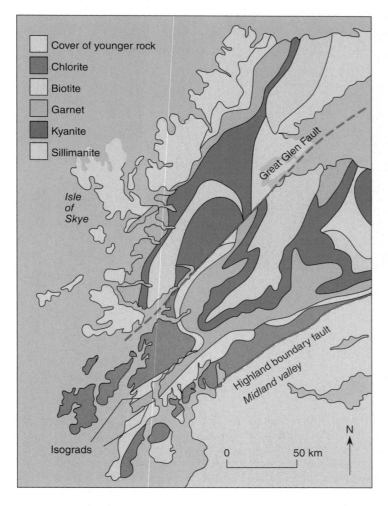

because the grade of metamorphism differed from place to place. The geologists identified characteristic **index minerals** that marked the appearance of each new mineral assemblage in a progression from low-grade to higher-grade metamorphic rock. They drew lines, called **isograds** (lines of equal grade), connecting the map locations where a given index mineral first appeared (**Figure 10.16**). Rock lying between one isograd and the next would thus have similar mineral assemblages, indicating that they formed under similar metamorphic conditions; they were defined as belonging to the same **metamorphic zone**. This method of mapping, first used in Scotland over

a century ago, has been successfully tested on different types of rock around the world.

Metamorphic Facies

The metamorphic rocks in Scotland came from source rock of similar composition (shale) that was exposed to a range of metamorphic conditions—same composition, differing conditions. It is also possible to group together metamorphic rock of differing compositions that have all been exposed to the same temperature and pressure conditions of metamorphism; such a grouping is called a **metamorphic facies**.

> **metamorphic facies** The set of metamorphic mineral assemblages that form in rock of different compositions under similar temperature and stress conditions.

Each of the metamorphic facies has been named, as you can see in **Figure 10.17**. Each facies is representative of a specific set of metamorphic conditions. For example, the blueschist facies represents relatively high-pressure, low-temperature metamorphism, while the hornfels facies represents relatively high-temperature, low-pressure metamorphism. The names of the facies typically reflect some obvious feature that is common to that particular facies, such as the color of a common rock (e.g., blueschist, greenschist); the presence of a distinctive mineral (e.g., zeolite, amphibole); an unusual type of rock (e.g., eclogite); or a distinctive texture (e.g., granulite).

The pressure–temperature diagram in Figure 10.17 shows the characteristic pressure and temperature ranges for each metamorphic facies and how they relate to specific tectonic settings. The zeolite facies is characteristic of burial metamorphism, and the hornfels facies is characteristic of contact metamorphism. Blueschist and eclogite facies are typical for subduction zones. Greenschist, amphibolite, and granulite facies occur in the regional metamorphism of continental crust thickened by plate collisions. For any given composition of source rock, it is possible to prepare a pressure–temperature grid like the one in Figure 10.17 that shows the specific mineral assemblages characteristic of each metamorphic facies. This allows geologists to compare the influence of particular tectonic environments and pressure–temperature conditions across a variety of rock types.

STOP **CONCEPT CHECK**

1. **What** is an index mineral, and how are index minerals used in mapping metamorphic zones?

2. **Outline** the metamorphic facies concept and the conditions that characterize the major facies.

This graph shows the regions of pressure and temperature that characterize the different metamorphic facies. The lines indicate how pressure and temperature change under conditions of (A) contact metamorphism, (B) regional metamorphism in continental plate collisions, and (C) regional metamorphism in subduction zones.

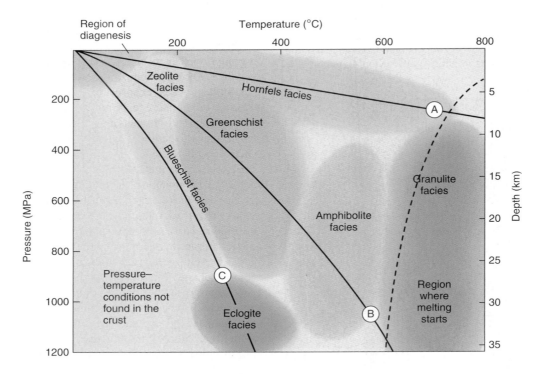

SUMMARY

1 What Is Metamorphism?   256

- New rock textures and new mineral assemblages develop when rock is subjected to elevated temperatures and stresses. **Metamorphism** is a term that describes all such processes that occur at higher temperatures and pressures than diagenesis, but without melting the rock.

- The transition from diagenesis to metamorphism is gradual, but the dividing line between the two is customarily taken to be a temperature of around 150°C, which typically occurs at a depth of about 5 kilometers. The temperature and pressure are both high enough at that depth to initiate the formation of new minerals. Between 5 and 15 kilometers beneath the surface, rock is subjected to **low-grade metamorphism**. The region of **high-grade metamorphism** lies from 15 kilometers to the depth at which melting occurs, often between 30 and 40 kilometers. The kind of metamorphism that occurs depends on temperature and pressure as well as composition.

- Pore fluid enhances metamorphism by permitting material to dissolve, move around, and be precipitated somewhere else

in the rock, as well as speeding up some chemical reactions. Pore fluid is driven out of rock as metamorphism progresses. Veins in metamorphic rock mark the passageways through which pore fluid once flowed. At the high-temperature limit of metamorphism, pore fluid can reduce the melting point of rock to the point where small pockets of magma form. The resulting rock, with small pockets of igneous rock surrounded by metamorphic rock, is called migmatite.

- Differential stress during metamorphism produces a distinctive texture known as **foliation**, marked by parallel cleavage planes and plates formed by crystals that are all aligned in the same direction. It is particularly noticeable in rock containing minerals of the mica family. Foliation developed in low-grade metamorphic rock is termed **slaty cleavage**; in coarser-grained, higher-grade metamorphic rock, it is called **schistosity** as seen in the photo. The orientation of the foliation is perpendicular to the direction of maximum stress. Under conditions of low-grade metamorphism, the maximum stress is usually downward, and the slaty cleavage is horizontal and parallel to bedding. Under conditions of compression, produced by plate tectonics, the maximum stress is horizontal, and the slaty cleavage is vertical.

Foliation under the microscope • Figure 10.6

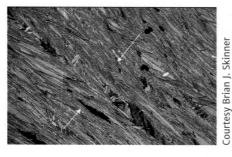

Courtesy Brian J. Skinner

- High temperature, high pressure, abundant pore fluid, and long reaction times tend to produce metamorphic rock with large mineral grains. Metamorphic rock containing small mineral grains usually forms at lower temperatures and pressures but can also form if pore fluid is scarce or reaction time is short.

2 Metamorphic Rock   264

- The names of metamorphic rocks are based partly on texture and partly on composition. Foliated metamorphic rocks derived from shales are **slate**, **phyllite**, **schist**, and **gneiss**, in order of increasing metamorphic grade. The first two terms refer to textures of fine-grained rock. In schist and gneiss, where the mineral grains are large enough to see, it is customary to identify rock further by its mineral composition, as in "biotite schist" or "quartz-biotite-amphibole gneiss." Gneiss is characterized by a coarsely foliated texture, with alternating bands of mica-rich and mica-poor material, giving the rock a banded appearance.

- Foliated rock can derive from igneous rock, the most common of which is basalt. Rock derived from basalts include greenschists (low-grade metamorphic rock) and amphibolites (high-grade metamorphic rock). Under conditions of high pressure and moderate temperature, which occur in subduction zones, a different series of metamorphic rock forms from basalts. These are blueschists (low grade) and eclogites (high grade).

- Two common kinds of metamorphic rock have no foliation. These are **marble** (see photo), a metamorphic product of limestone, and **quartzite**, a metamorphic product of sandstone. These tend to be monomineralic, or nearly so; the main mineral present in marble is calcite, and the main mineral present in quartzite is quartz.

Nonfoliated metamorphic rock • Figure 10.9

Siim Sepp / Shutterstock

Dirk Wiersma/Photo Researchers, Inc.

Pasieka/ Photo Researchers, Inc.

3 Types of Metamorphism   268

- The processes that are primarily responsible for changes in texture and mineral assemblages in metamorphic rock are mechanical deformation and chemical recrystallization. Typically, both sets of processes are involved in metamorphism, but their relative importance depends on the specific pressure and temperature conditions of metamorphism.

- **Contact metamorphism**, shown in the diagram, is caused by the intrusion of hot magma or fluid (primarily water) into cooler rock. Because contact metamorphism is caused by high temperatures, the main process involved is chemical recrystallization, and there is little mechanical deformation of the rock.

Contact metamorphism • Figure 10.11

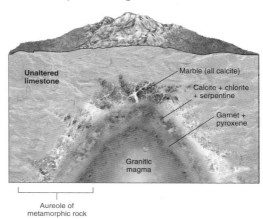

Unaltered limestone

Marble (all calcite)

Calcite + chlorite + serpentine

Garnet + pyroxene

Granitic magma

Aureole of metamorphic rock

- Sedimentary rock that is subjected to sufficiently high temperatures and pressures due solely to the weight of overlying strata undergoes **burial metamorphism**. Burial metamorphism is a low-grade metamorphic process. If the resulting rock is foliated, the foliation is usually parallel to the bedding planes.

- **Regional metamorphism** occurs under the conditions of differential stress and elevated temperature that result from collisions between tectonic plates. A special kind of regional metamorphism occurs at subduction zones, where pressures are high but temperatures are moderate, due to the very rapid burial of the rock.

- Very high pressures and temperatures caused by meteorite impacts produce a unique kind of high-pressure metamorphism, called shock metamorphism. The intense grinding of rock along a fault zone combined with frictional heating can produce cataclastic metamorphism.

- **Metasomatism** occurs when a large volume of fluid flows into or out of a rock. It is a process that changes the overall chemical composition of the rock by moving chemical components into or out of the rock rather than just altering the texture or mineral assemblage.

4 Metamorphic Zones and Facies   272

- For a given rock composition, the assemblages of minerals that are formed under a given set of temperature and stress conditions, as shown in the diagram, are the same, regardless of where in the world the metamorphism happens.

Metamorphic facies • Figure 10.17

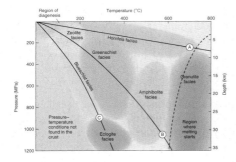

- Rock of different chemical compositions that are metamorphosed under the same temperature and stress conditions are said to belong to the same **metamorphic facies**, even though they will develop different mineral assemblages.

- Each metamorphic facies is associated with a particular tectonic setting. Blueschist facies and eclogite facies conditions occur in the high-pressure environment characteristic of subduction zones. Greenschist, amphibolite, and granulite facies conditions occur along convergent margins where continental masses collide. The zeolite facies is characteristic of burial metamorphism, and the hornfels facies is characteristic of contact metamorphism.

KEY TERMS

burial metamorphism   269

contact metamorphism   268

diagenesis   256

foliation   261

gneiss   265

high-grade   258

low-grade   257

marble   267

metamorphic facies   273

metamorphism   256

metasomatism   272

phyllite   264

quartzite   267

regional metamorphism   269

schist   265

schistosity   263

slate   264

slaty cleavage   261

CRITICAL AND CREATIVE THINKING QUESTIONS

1. Briefly describe how pressure and temperature might change over time in rock being subjected to contact metamorphism, burial metamorphism, and subduction-related regional metamorphism.

2. Examining the texture of a rock is an important process for geologists because the texture can reveal whether the rock has been metamorphosed and under what conditions. Explain why. Would this process work for both foliated and nonfoliated rock? Why (or why not)?

3. Compare the concept of metamorphic facies to that of sedimentary facies (see Chapter 8). In what ways are they similar? In what ways are they different?

4. Let's say that you have bought a property in a hilly area, and you are going to build a new house on the property. You like the idea of building on a hill slope with a view, but you are concerned about safety issues. One of the hills on the property is composed of gneiss, another is slate, and a third is a marble in which there are caves. Which one of these hill slopes do you think would provide the most stable location for your home, and why? Try sketching the hill slope keeping in mind the different rock types and how they might be distributed.

5. Compare the metamorphic zones shown on the map of Scotland to the sequence of metamorphic rock that forms as a result of the progressively higher grade metamorphism of shale, shown in Figure 10.3. Describe the correspondence

between the metamorphic zones and index minerals (Figure 10.16) and the mineral ranges shown at the bottom of Figure 10.3.

Regional metamorphic zones and isograds • Figure 10.16

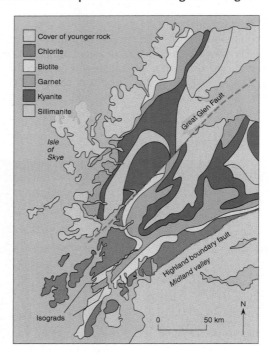

WHAT IS HAPPENING IN THIS PICTURE?

This roof in France was made from a commonly occurring planar metamorphic rock.

Photononstop/SuperStock

THINK CRITICALLY

1. What kind of rock do you think it is?
2. What properties of this rock would make it very suitable for use as a roof tiling material?
3. Do you think this rock is used in modern roofing? Why or why not?

SELF-TEST

(Check your answers in Appendix D.)

1. How does metamorphism differ from diagenesis and lithification?

    a. Diagenesis and lithification occur at higher temperatures and pressures.

    b. Diagenesis and lithification occur at lower temperatures and pressures.

    c. Metamorphism requires melting of preexisting rock.

    d. Diagenesis and lithification do not cause any significant changes in the rock or sediment.

2. Under which of the following conditions does contact metamorphism occur?

    a. high temperature and high pressure

    b. high temperature and low pressure

    c. low temperature and low pressure

    d. All of the above answers are correct.

3. For this diagram locate and label the areas on the temperature–pressure diagram that correspond to regions of Earth's crust listed below.

    region of diagenesis   region of high-grade metamorphism

    region where melting   region of low-grade metamorphism
    starts

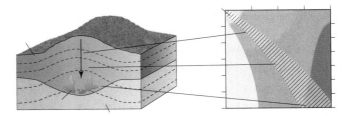

4. Pore fluids enhance metamorphism by _____.

    a. permitting material to dissolve

    b. permitting chemical components to move around and be precipitated somewhere else

c. speeding up some chemical reactions

d. All of the above answers are correct.

5. _____ is the planar alignment of minerals due to differential stress during metamorphism.

a. Ionization

c. Foliation

b. Metasomatism

d. Diagenesis

6. Foliated metamorphic rock derived from shales, in order of increasing metamorphic grade, are _____.

a. phyllite, slate, and schist or gneiss

b. phyllite, gneiss, and schist or slate

c. slate, phyllite, and schist or gneiss

d. slate, gneiss, and phyllite or schist

7. Basalt can be metamorphosed to form a series of foliated rocks ranging from greenschists (low grade) to amphibolites (high grade). It is also possible for a different series of metamorphic rocks to form, ranging from blueschists (low grade) to eclogites (high grade). Under what conditions does this latter series form?

a. low pressure and moderate temperature

b. low pressure but high temperature

c. high pressure but moderate temperature

d. high pressure and high temperature

8. The two rock samples shown in these photographs are nonfoliated metamorphic rock. Sample A was formed through the metamorphism of sandstone, and Sample B is composed of calcite. Which of the following correctly identifies the two samples?

a. Sample (a) is quartzite, and Sample (b) is schist.

b. Sample (a) is quartzite, and Sample (b) is marble.

c. Sample (a) is marble, and Sample (b) is quartzite.

d. Sample (a) is marble, and Sample (b) is schist.

9. Metamorphism involves two main groups of processes: _____.

a. fractional melting and chemical recrystallization

b. fractional melting and fractional crystallization

c. fractional melting and mechanical deformation

d. mechanical deformation and chemical recrystallization

10. _____ occurs over an extensive area of the crust and is associated with plate convergence, collision, and subduction.

a. Regional metamorphism

c. Contact metamorphism

b. Burial metamorphism

d. Diagenesis

11. _____ occurs when rocks are heated and chemically changed adjacent to an intruded body of hot magma.

a. Regional metamorphism

c. Contact metamorphism

b. Burial metamorphism

d. Diagenesis

12. On this diagram, label the areas designated 1 through 4 from the following choices:

regional metamorphism

blueschist- and eclogite-facies metamorphism

burial metamorphism

zone where fractional melting starts, granite magma rises, and contact metamorphism occurs

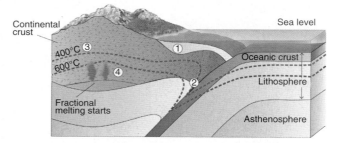

13. Metasomatism is a process by which the chemical composition of rock is altered. What is the mechanism of this chemical alteration?

a. addition or removal of material by solution in fluids

b. loss of chemical material during fractional melting

c. loss of chemical material during fractional crystallization

d. None of the above answers are correct.

14. Label this diagram with the proper metamorphic facies.

zeolite facies   granulite facies

blueschist facies   greenschist facies

amphibolite facies   hornfels facies

eclogite facies

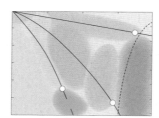

15. In the diagram in question 14, the three lines labeled A, B, and C represent temperature and pressure pathways for different types of metamorphism. Which of these three pathways describes the suite of metamorphic facies that you would expect to see in an area of regional metamorphism due to continental collision?

a. A   b. B   c. C

THE PLANNER

Review the Chapter Planner on the chapter opener and check off your completed work.

11

WATER ON AND UNDER THE GROUND

Author Skinner (dark helmet) views the Falls from above.

Courtesy Brian Skinner

Vadim Petrakov / Shutterstoc

THE SMOKE THAT THUNDERS

Mosi-oa-Tunya, or "the smoke that thunders," as it is called by the local Makololo people, is the largest single sheet of falling water in the world—over 100 meters tall and 1.5 kilometers wide. Today, we know it as Victoria Falls.

The falls are formed as the Zambezi River, in southern Africa, flows across basaltic lava plains and then plummets into a chasm about 120 meters wide, carved by its waters along a fracture in the basalt. The river forms the border between Zambia on the north (to the right in the photograph) and Zimbabwe to the south. The waterfall converts the calm river into a ferocious torrent; the roar can be heard from 40 kilometers away. Enough water passes over these falls every hour to supply a city of 2 million people for a year.

Humans harness the power of water for electricity, as well as for drinking and other uses. The first power station was set up at Victoria Falls in 1938. In North America, the Niagara Power Project exploits the 52-meter drop over Niagara Falls, plus a further 55-meter drop down the Niagara Gorge, by withdrawing water upstream of the waterfalls and carrying it through tunnels to generating plants located downstream. It's easy to imagine how the immense force of these waterfalls can mold and shape the land below.

THE HYDROLOGIC CYCLE

Learning Objectives

1. **Define** and describe the hydrologic cycle.

2. **Identify** the main pathways and reservoirs in the hydrologic cycle.

Four great reservoirs make up the Earth system: the geosphere, hydrosphere, atmosphere, and biosphere. Water moves—and helps move materials—among all four spheres. Water vapor is an important part of the atmosphere. Water is a constituent of many common minerals (e.g., micas, clays) in the geosphere, where it is tightly bonded in their crystal structures. And, of course, water is a fundamental component of living things in the biosphere (see *Remember This!*).

> **REMEMBER THIS!** How are the four major spheres of the Earth system related to the life zone? You can remind yourself about this by reviewing *Earth's Interconnected Subsystems* in Chapter 1 and looking back at Figure 1.8.

Water in the Earth System

hydrologic cycle A model that describes the movement of water through the reservoirs of the Earth system; the water cycle.

evaporation The process by which water changes from a liquid into a vapor.

transpiration The process by which water taken up by plants passes directly into the atmosphere.

condensation The process by which water changes from a vapor into a liquid or a solid.

precipitation The process by which water that has condensed in the atmosphere falls back to the surface as rain, snow, or hail.

The **hydrologic cycle**, also called the **water cycle**, describes how water moves among these four reservoirs (**Figure 11.1**), and the scientific study of water is called **hydrology**.

Water moves through the hydrologic cycle along numerous pathways from one part of the Earth system to another (**Figure 11.1a**). The processes by which it moves include **evaporation** and **transpiration**, both of which are powered by energy from the Sun. Depending on local conditions of temperature, pressure, and humidity, some of the water vapor in the atmosphere will undergo **condensation**, changing to a liquid or a solid. It will then fall back to the land or ocean as rain, snow, or hail via the process of **precipitation**. Some precipitation becomes **surface runoff**, and some trickles directly into the ground via **infiltration**.

The schematic representation of the hydrologic cycle (**Figure 11.1b**) will look familiar to you if you have read Chapters 1, 4, and 7, which introduced the tectonic cycle and the rock cycle. The water cycle is linked to both of these other cycles. Like them, it is a closed cycle that consists of interconnected open systems. Because

surface runoff Precipitation that drains over the land or in stream channels.

infiltration The process by which water works its way into the ground through small openings in the soil.

it is a closed cycle, the total amount of water in the system is fixed. However, all the local reservoirs within the cycle, such as rivers, lakes, and trees, are free to gain or lose water. They sometimes do so quite dramatically, as during a flood or drought.

Pathways and Reservoirs

Unlike many aspects of the tectonic cycle and the rock cycle, most of the water cycle is easily observable to us. We can measure the amount of global precipitation; using satellite monitoring, we can even measure the amount of evaporation. With these measurements, along with the overall mass balance of the water cycle, geologists can roughly deduce how much water is exchanged along each of the pathways shown in Figure 11.1b.

It is also instructive to compare the sizes of each of the reservoirs in the water cycle (**Figure 11.2**). The largest reservoir in the hydrosphere—by far—is the world ocean, which holds 97.5% of Earth's water. Thus, the vast majority of Earth's water is saline (salty), not fresh. This has important consequences for humans because we depend on fresh water as a resource for drinking, agriculture, and industrial use.

The other numbers in Figure 11.2 may surprise you. Most of Earth's fresh water (almost 74%) is locked up in polar ice sheets, where it is almost inaccessible to humans. The vast majority of unfrozen fresh water (98.5%) lies underground. Historically, human settlement has concentrated along lakes or rivers, where the other 1.5% of the world's fresh water—namely, surface water—is readily available (**Figure 11.3**). But in most rural areas and quite a few urban areas as well, underground water sources are much more plentiful.

There is a correlation between the size of a reservoir and the **residence time**, the average length of time that a water molecule spends in that reservoir. Residence times in the large-volume reservoirs, such as the ocean and ice sheets, are several thousands of years. The time spent by water in the groundwater system may amount to hundreds of years or more. In small-volume reservoirs, the residence time of water is much shorter—weeks in streams and rivers, days in the atmosphere, and hours in some living organisms.

Process Diagram

How water moves around the Earth system • Figure 11.1

The hydrologic cycle is one of the three interconnected cycles that make up the Earth system. Compare to Figures 1.9, 4.12, and 7.1.

a. The hydrologic cycle describes the movement of water through the Earth system.

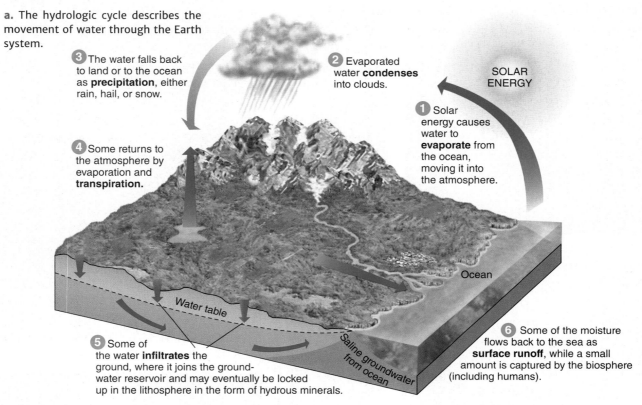

3 The water falls back to land or to the ocean as **precipitation**, either rain, hail, or snow.

2 Evaporated water **condenses** into clouds.

SOLAR ENERGY

1 Solar energy causes water to **evaporate** from the ocean, moving it into the atmosphere.

4 Some returns to the atmosphere by evaporation and **transpiration.**

Water table

Ocean

5 Some of the water **infiltrates** the ground, where it joins the ground-water reservoir and may eventually be locked up in the lithosphere in the form of hydrous minerals.

Saline groundwater from ocean

6 Some of the moisture flows back to the sea as **surface runoff**, while a small amount is captured by the biosphere (including humans).

b. The hydrologic cycle links the rock cycle and the tectonic cycle to the surficial processes of the hydrosphere and atmosphere. This diagram depicts the same information as shown in **a.**

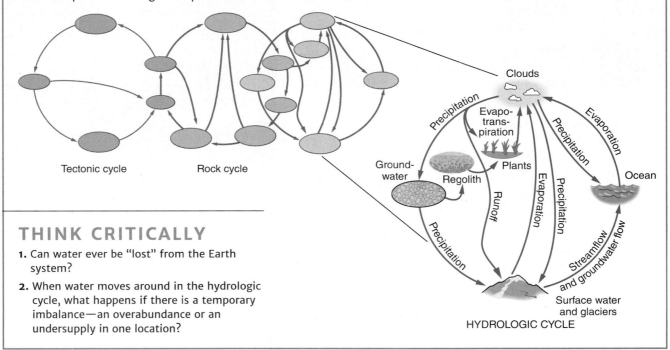

Tectonic cycle

Rock cycle

Clouds

Precipitation

Evapo-trans-piration

Evaporation

Precipitation

Precipitation

Evaporation

Ground-water

Regolith

Plants

Runoff

Precipitation

Ocean

Streamflow and groundwater flow

Surface water and glaciers

HYDROLOGIC CYCLE

THINK CRITICALLY

1. Can water ever be "lost" from the Earth system?

2. When water moves around in the hydrologic cycle, what happens if there is a temporary imbalance—an overabundance or an undersupply in one location?

Reservoirs in the hydrologic cycle • Figure 11.2

The vast majority of Earth's water is salty (**a**), frozen (**b**), or underground (**c**). The most visible everyday sources of fresh water, such as rivers (**d**), lakes, and the atmosphere, together comprise less than one-hundredth of a percent of Earth's water budget.

a

Bill Curtsinger/NG Image Collection

b

Emory Kristof/NG Image Collection

c

Alex Saber/ NG Image Collection

d

Bates Littlehales/NG Image Collection

The world's water resources (in proportion):
97.5 liters salt water (A)

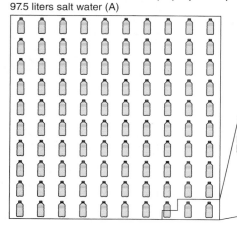

1.85 liters frozen water (B)

0.64 liters groundwater (C)

10 milliliters surface water (D)*
(= 2 teaspoons)

*includes water in biosphere and atmosphere

Living on the water's edge • Figure 11.3

Many of the world's great cities are built on riverbanks or coastlines. St. Louis has long benefited from its proximity to the Mississippi River. In the foreground, a towboat pushes barges upstream; in the background, the *Mississippi Queen* riverboat brings tourists to the Gateway Arch.

Annie Griffiths Belt/NG Image Collection

Although water is continuously cycling from one reservoir to another, the total volume of water in each reservoir is approximately constant over short time intervals. However, the volume of water in each reservoir can change dramatically over longer intervals. During glacial ages, for example, vast quantities of water evaporate from the ocean and are precipitated on land as snow. The snow slowly accumulates to build ice sheets that are thousands of meters thick and cover vast areas. At such times, the amount of water removed from the ocean is so large that the global sea level can fall by many meters, and the expanded glaciers increase the ice-covered area of Earth.

STOP **CONCEPT CHECK**

1. **What** are the major reservoirs in the hydrologic cycle?
2. **How** does the residence time of water correlate to the size of a reservoir in the hydrologic cycle?

HOW WATER AFFECTS THE LAND

Learning Objectives

1. **Identify** the basic characteristics of streams and straight, braided, and meandering channels.
2. **Identify** three common land formations made by stream deposits.
3. **Define** drainage basin.
4. **Describe** how lakes form and disappear.

If you stand outside during a heavy rain, you can see that, initially, water tends to move downhill in a process called **overland flow** (or **sheet flow** because the flowing water often takes the form of a thin, broad sheet). After traveling a short distance, overland flow begins to be concentrated into well-defined passageways, thereby becoming **streamflow**. Overland flow and streamflow together constitute surface runoff, one of the main pathways in the water cycle. Let's look more closely at streams and streamflow, the passageways of streams, and the interactions of streams with the land.

Streams and Channels

Every **stream** or river has a **channel**, and several factors affect the shape of the channel and the landforms it creates. Streams create landforms through two main processes: erosion (see Chapter 7) and deposition (see Chapter 8). Both processes go on throughout a stream's existence and along its entire length, but one or the other may predominate at a particular location or during a particular time, depending on a variety of factors.

The three most important factors controlling the development of a stream channel are the **gradient**, **discharge**, and **load**. The three factors are interrelated. For example, if the gradient of a stream becomes steeper along a particular stretch of channel, the velocity of flow is likely to increase as well. If the velocity is high, a greater load can be carried (see *Remember This!*). If the discharge increases, the channel

stream A body of water that flows downslope along a clearly defined natural passageway.

channel The clearly defined natural passageway through which a stream flows.

gradient The steepness of a stream channel.

discharge The amount of water passing by a point on a channel's bank during a unit of time.

load The suspended and dissolved sediment carried by a stream.

Different channel types occur in different locations, depending on the physical characteristics of the flow, topography, and underlying rock. Pools are places along a channel where the water is deepest. Arrows indicate the direction of streamflow and trace the path of the deepest water.

The three main types of stream channels are straight, meandering, and braided streams.

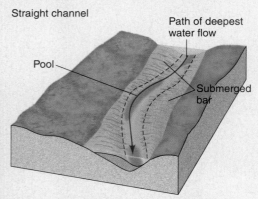

a. Straight channels, such as this stream that drains a glacier in Alaska, occur only in relatively short stretches. They are often found where streams have a high gradient (near the stream's headwaters), and they generally have a classic V-shaped valley.

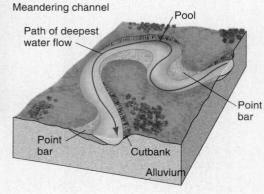

b. A meandering stream near Phnom Penh, Cambodia, shows several typical features: a low gradient, light-colored sandy bars on the inside edge of the bends, and oxbow lakes marking previous watercourses that have been cut off.

---

must handle more water in a given period; as a result, both the velocity of flow and the depth of the water in the stream will increase. (Note that this is the first of two different meanings of *discharge* used in this chapter.) In some cases, the channel itself will increase in width and depth as the water scours the banks and the bottom. This scouring, in turn, adds new sediment to the load. When the velocity of the water eventually decreases, the sediment settles out and allows the channel to return to its original size.

> **REMEMBER THIS!**   Do you remember all of the various components of a stream's load? You can remind yourself by revisiting *Erosion by Water* in Chapter 7.

While gradient, discharge, and load are the most important determinants of a channel's size and shape, other factors are also important. Topography, for example, determines the gradient, and climate determines the amount of precipitation, and hence the discharge. The geologic characteristics of the underlying rock are also important. For example, a stream may suddenly bend, or its gradient may increase when it passes from erosion-resistant rock into rock that is easily eroded. Because these factors interact in different ways, no two stream channels are exactly alike. Nevertheless, we can classify them into three broad categories, as shown in **Figure 11.4**.

Unlike engineered aqueducts and canals, natural streams are never really straight from start to finish. **Straight channels**

c. The Tasman River in New Zealand's Southern Alps has the classic profile of a braided stream, with a low gradient and a large and variable load of sediment—produced in this case by the influence of the Tasman Glacier just upstream. ▶

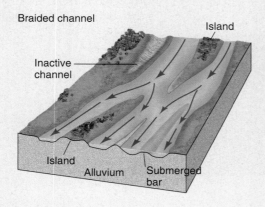

Braided channel

Island

Inactive channel

Island

Alluvium

Submerged bar

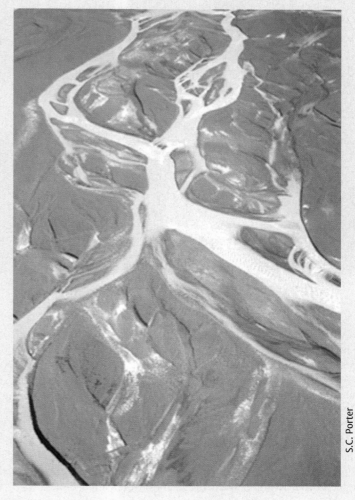

S.C. Porter

THINK CRITICALLY
Why are straight channels rare in nature?

(**Figure 11.4a**) may occur over short distances, particularly in **upstream** areas (that is, near the **headwaters**, or **source**, of the stream), where the gradient is high and the channel deeply incised. Even in a "straight" channel, close examination will show that the deepest part of the channel oscillates from side to side.

Meandering channels tend to develop where the stream gradient is low, typically in the lower, or **downstream**, parts of a stream system (close to the **mouth**, where the stream empties into another surface water body). The erosion in a meandering stream concentrates along the sides of the channel rather than the bottom. As water sweeps around a bend, it flows more rapidly along the outer bank, undercutting and steepening it to form a **cut bank**. Meanwhile, along the inner

side of each meander, where the water is shallow and velocity is low, sediment accumulates to form a **point bar**, as shown in **Figure 11.4b**. Thus, meanders slowly change shape and shift their position along a valley as the stream erodes material from one bank and deposits sediment on the other. Sometimes the water finds a shorter route downstream, bypassing a meander by cutting across the narrow part of the loop. As sediment is deposited along the banks of the new channel route, the former meander is cut off and converted into a curved **oxbow lake**.

Braided channels arise when a stream's ability to move its sediment load varies over time. At times of high flow, a stream can carry more sediment. If the discharge decreases but the load does not, the stream deposits the excess sediment in its own channel as bars or islands. These variations in flow

In this photograph, taken several months after the Mount St. Helens eruption in 1980, you can see the braided form of the Toutle River. In the foreground, engineers have built an artificial levee to straighten the river's course and control erosion.

Braided flow created by high bed load upstream

Muddy water due to high rate of erosion upstream

Straight channel flow created by artificial levees

Steve Raymer/NG Image Collection

over time cause the channel to repeatedly divide and reunite, as shown in **Figure 11.4c**. Braided patterns tend to form in streams with highly variable discharge and large loads of coarse sediment. Braided patterns can form in streams with discharge that varies seasonally (e.g., following rapid snowmelt) and in streams with easily eroded banks.

As an extreme example of dramatic changes in a river channel, Washington's Toutle River changed almost overnight from a meandering stream to a braided stream in 1980, when Mount St. Helens erupted (**Figure 11.5**). The debris avalanche that resulted from the eruption deposited huge amounts of loose and easily eroded pyroclasts and volcanic ash into Toutle Valley, dramatically increasing the river's load. In addition, there were no longer any living trees to hold the old riverbanks in place. Changes in an ancient river's flow patterns (as revealed in sedimentary strata) can tell geologists about the geologic history of a region.

Stream Deposits

Stream deposits form along channel margins, valley floors, mountain fronts, and at the stream's mouth, where it opens into the ocean or a lake. These are all places where a stream typically loses energy and, therefore, its ability to carry a load. A point bar, described previously, is one example of a stream deposit.

floodplain The relatively flat valley floor adjacent to a stream channel, which is inundated when the stream overflows its banks.

When a stream rises during a flood, water overflows the banks of the stream's channel and inundates the **floodplain** (**Figure 11.6a**). As sediment-laden water flows out of the channel, its depth, velocity, and turbulence decrease abruptly at the margins

of the channel. This results in sudden, rapid deposition of the coarser part of the load along the margins, which builds up a broad, low ridge of **alluvium** atop each bank, called a **natural levee**. Farther away, the finer particles settle out in the quiet water covering the valley. This creates the broad, flat, fertile land that is typical of floodplains.

alluvium Unconsolidated sediment deposited in a recent geologic time by a stream.

Another kind of alluvial structure develops where a stream draining a steep upland region suddenly emerges onto the floor of a much broader lowland valley. The stream will slow down and lose some of its ability to carry sediment. It will deposit the coarser part of its load (the part that can no longer be transported) in an **alluvial fan** (**Figure 11.6b**). Such fans are typical of semiarid conditions where vegetation is sparse and infrequent rainfall creates streams that are heavily laden with sediment.

A similar situation occurs when a stream flows into a standing body of water, such as the ocean or a lake. It quickly loses velocity and fans out, dropping its sediment load (the heaviest particles first and the finer particles farther seaward). Over time, the sediment builds up a deposit called a **delta** (so named because of its triangular shape, which resembles the Greek letter delta, Δ). Most of the world's great rivers, including the Nile, Ganges-Brahmaputra, Huang He, Amazon, and Mississippi, have built massive deltas (**Figure 11.6c**).

Prominent deltas do not form in places where strong wave, current, or tidal action redistributes sediment as quickly as it reaches the coast. If the rate of sediment supply exceeds the rate of coastal erosion, a delta will form. However, the converse holds, too: If the rate of deposition slows down, the delta will disappear. This has been observed

a. Some of the main types of landforms created by sediment deposition in streams are shown here.

Oxbow lakes are abandoned channel segments – former meanders, cut off from the main channel when the stream found a shorter, more direct path of flow.

Floodplains are formed when the stream overflows its banks. The finest particles in the suspended load settle out on the valley floor, creating the broad, flat, fertile floodplain.

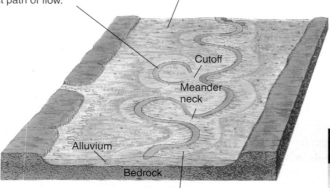

Cutoff

Meander neck

Alluvium

Bedrock

Natural levees are created when water flows over the banks during a flood. The water immediately loses energy, depositing the coarsest particles from its load along the stream banks.

b. Where this stream emerges from the mountains into Death Valley, California, it abruptly slows and deposits its sediment load. This has created a symmetrical alluvial fan, covered by a braided system of channels. The stream was dry at the time the photograph was taken.

© Marli Bryant Miller

Courtesy Visible Earth/NASA

c. Where the Nile River empties into the Mediterranean Sea, the sediment it deposits has formed a fan-shaped delta that supports the green vegetation seen in this satellite.

in the Mississippi River Delta over time (**Figure 11.7**). Modifications of the river channel have caused a decline in sediment load and delivery of sediment to the delta, where the river emerges into the Gulf of Mexico. This, in turn has caused the delta to shrink. Marshes have given way to open water, ponds have turned into lakes, and barrier islands have shrunk. The degradation of the delta is at least partly responsible for the increased vulnerability of New Orleans and other coastal areas of Louisiana to the impacts of hurricanes.

Large-Scale Topography of Stream Systems

Streams are governed by a simple principle: Water flows downhill. Rainwater that falls on the land surface will move from higher to lower elevations under the influence of gravity. A stream's headwater region is an area of relatively higher elevation. Small, high-gradient **tributary** streams carry water downslope from the headwater region, combining their flow to form a larger stream. The gradient gradually decreases toward the low-lying region of the stream's mouth.

> **drainage basin** The total area from which water flows into a stream.

Every stream is surrounded by a **drainage basin** (sometimes called a **catchment** or **watershed**). Drainage basins range in size from less than a square kilometer to areas the size of subcontinents. In general, the greater a stream's annual discharge, the larger its drainage basin. The vast drainage basin of the Mississippi River encompasses more than 40% of the total area of the contiguous United States (**Figure 11.8**). From an environmental perspective, a drainage basin is a more natural geographic entity than a country or a state because issues of water supply, pollution, and wildlife management that affect one part of a watershed are likely to affect it all. (See *What a Geologist Sees*.)

If you have driven across North America, you may have seen highway signs marking the **continental divide**. This

> **divide** A topographic high that separates adjacent drainage basins.

major **divide** separates streams that drain toward one side of the continent from streams that drain toward the other side. The continental divide of western North America lies along the length of the Rocky Mountains (**Figure 11.9**). Any two adjacent drainage basins are separated by a divide that directs runoff in one direction or another, even if streams flowing from the basins ultimately flow into the same ocean.

Lakes

A **lake** is a standing body of water that has an open surface, in direct contact with the atmosphere. Water enters lakes from

> **lake** A standing body of water with an open surface.

streams, overland flow, and groundwater, and it exits either by evaporation or by flowing through an outlet. All freshwater

Disappearing coastline • Figure 11.7

The taming of the Mississippi River with levees and artificially modified channels has slowed the deposition of new sediment in its delta downstream. As a result, the entire Mississippi Delta has been shrinking. In this time series of maps, land areas are in brown and yellow, marshes and wetlands are in green, and open water is in blue tones.

1839

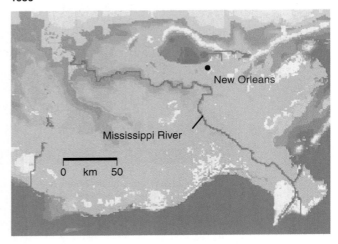

1993

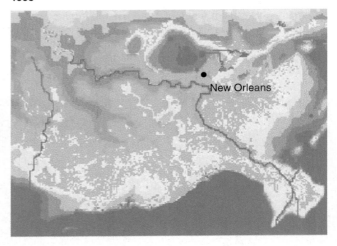

2090 *projection*

The Mississippi River drainage basin • Figure 11.8

The drainage basin of the Mississippi River encompasses most of the midwestern United States and extends into southern Canada. In this diagram, the widths of the rivers are exaggerated to represent the discharge in cubic meters per second.

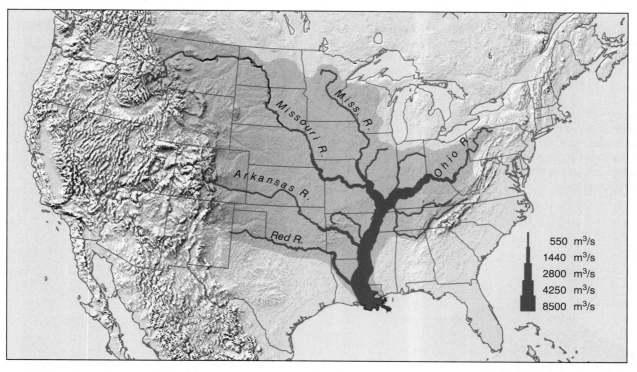

550 m³/s
1440 m³/s
2800 m³/s
4250 m³/s
8500 m³/s

Continental drainage in the Americas • Figure 11.9

This map of North and South America shows the location of continental drainage basins and divides.

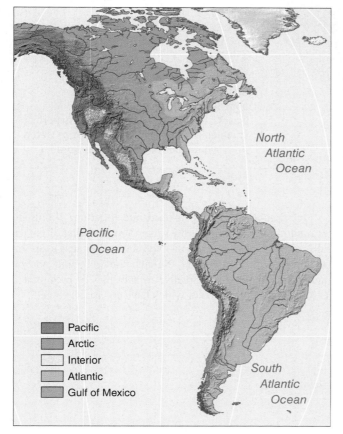

North Atlantic Ocean

Pacific Ocean

Pacific
Arctic
Interior
Atlantic
Gulf of Mexico

South Atlantic Ocean

lakes have outlets; however, some saline lakes lack outlets and therefore lose water only through evaporation, which inevitably leads to a buildup of salt. The Great Salt Lake in Utah and the Aral Sea on the border between Kazakhstan and Uzbekistan are important examples of inland saline lakes.

Lakes are important to us as sources of fresh water and food, as well as for transportation and recreation. The majority of lakes in the United States have been altered by, and in some cases even created by humans. Sometimes the changes are deliberate, as when a **reservoir** lake is created by the construction of a dam, or a wetland is drained to make it accessible for human development. In other cases, the human effects are unintentional. For example, runoff of sewage or fertilizer into a lake can cause **eutrophication**, which can kill most of the life in the lake (**Figure 11.10**). Eutrophication also occurs as a natural part of the process of swamp formation.

Lakes can form as a result of several different geologic processes. Crustal faulting creates many large, deep lakes. A lava flow may form a dam in a river valley, causing water to back up as a lake. Landslides suddenly create lakes by blocking valleys. Throughout formerly glaciated regions of North America and Europe, plains of glacial sand and gravel contain natural pits and hollows left by the melting of stagnant ice masses that were buried in the sand and gravel deposits. Kettle lakes, a common landform in New England, form when such pits fill with water.

An important characteristic of lakes is that they are short-lived features on the geologic time scale. They disappear through one of two processes or a combination of both.

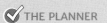
Drainage Basins

The drainage basins of many rivers are hard to see from a satellite because they are covered by vegetation. However, a geologist looking at this satellite image (**Figure a**) of Wadi Al Masilah in South Yemen, adjacent to the desert of Rub' al Khali, would not have any trouble drawing in the drainage basin of one tributary of the river. The geologist has used a dashed line to outline the boundary—that is, the divide—that surrounds and defines the drainage basin of the tributary. It is fairly simple to identify the divide because streams on either side of it flow in opposite directions, as shown in (**Figure b**). Note that the outlined basin would itself be a part of the drainage basin of the larger river at the top of the photograph.

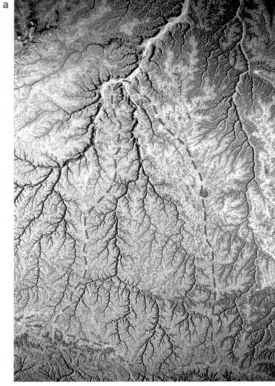

a

b

Rill

Gully

Sheetflow

Interfluves

Drainage divide

Valley

Drainage basin

THINK CRITICALLY

The stream channels in the outlined drainage basin in the satellite image appear to be completely dry. But look closely, and you can see that the main river channel, at the top of the photo, has water in it. Where did the water come from?

First, lakes that have stream outlets will be gradually drained as the outlets are eroded to lower levels. Second, lakes accumulate inorganic sediment carried by streams entering the lake and organic matter produced by plants within the lake. Eventually, they fill up, forming boggy **wetlands** with little or no free water surface.

In arid climates, many lakebeds are either dry or intermittently filled with shallow water. Streams bring dissolved salts to these ephemeral (short-lived) lakes. Because evaporation removes only pure water, the salts remain behind, and salinity levels increase. Eventually, the salts may be precipitated as solid evaporites, some of which have economic value.

A dying river • Figure 11.10

This river in Florida has turned green and mucky because of eutrophication. The growth of algae has been stimulated by excessive nutrients, possibly from sewage or fertilizer. Eventually, the algae will use up all the oxygen in the water, making it impossible for other life to survive in the river.

Environmental Images/Age Fotostock America, Inc.

STOP **CONCEPT CHECK**

1. **How** do the three main types of stream channels develop?

2. **What** are the major types of stream deposits, and in what environments do they typically occur?

3. **What** separates a drainage basin from adjacent drainage basins?

4. **Why** are lakes geologically short-lived?

WATER AS A HAZARD AND A RESOURCE

Learning Objectives

1. **Describe** how floods occur and what factors may help to control them, or make them worse.

2. **Summarize** the global importance of fresh water as a resource.

Although water is a vital resource, it can also be a dangerous force. Uneven distribution of rainfall through the year causes some water bodies to dry up, but others rise and overflow their banks, creating hazardous circumstances for people who live in the area.

Floods

Under natural circumstances, all water bodies undergo changes in the volume of water they hold or transport. From time to time, when the discharge or water level becomes too much to handle, the water body will **flood** (**Figure 11.11**).

> **flood** An event in which a water body overflows its banks.

During a stream flood, the "extra" water flowing in the channel, contributed by excess precipitation, is called **storm runoff**. The greatest discharge of a flood usually comes well after the rains that produced it. Geologists record the development of a flood with a **hydrograph**, a graph that shows the stream's discharge as a function of time. **Figure 11.12** shows an example of a hydrograph in which a passing storm generated a brief interval of intense rainfall. As the runoff moved into the stream channel, the discharge quickly rose. The **crest** or **peak** of the resulting flood—when the highest flow passed by the hydrologic station where the measurements were made—occurred about two hours after the storm. You can see from the graph that it took another eight hours for the flood runoff to pass through the channel and for the discharge to return to its normal level.

Lakes also flood, as do oceanic coastal zones. In the case of coastal flooding, it may be the inflow of water from the ocean, rather than the runoff of water from the land, that does most of the damage. The **storm surge** associated with Hurricane Katrina in 2005, in which water from the Gulf of Mexico was blown onshore by high winds of the hurricane, temporarily raised the water level near New Orleans by 6 meters or more. The storm surge breached the levees even before the main force of the storm winds and rain hit the city (**Figure 11.13**).

Coastal flooding and stream flooding often take people by surprise, but geologists view them as normal and inevitable. The geologic record shows that floods have been occurring throughout Earth's history, for as long as there has been a hydrosphere. Even though flooding is a natural geologic process, it can quickly become a human catastrophe when it affects population centers. The Huang He in China, called the Yellow River because of its heavy load of yellowish-brown silt, has a long history of catastrophic floods (see *Remember This!*). In 1887, the river

Great Mississippi River floods • Figure 11.11

Satellite images and aerial photography show the region where the Missouri River joins the Mississippi River at St. Louis, Missouri.

a. The satellite image on the left shows a dry summer with low flows (July 1988). On the right is the same region in July 1993. Weeks of rain hundreds of kilometers away caused the rivers to overflow their levees. Numerous towns, along with 44,000 square kilometers of farmland in nine states, were flooded by 3 cubic kilometers of floodwater.

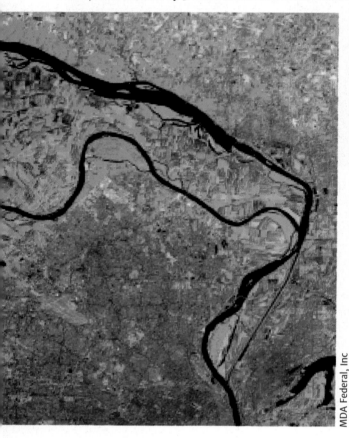

MDA Federal, Inc

MDA Federal, Inc

b. Flooding of the Mississippi River occurred again in 2011, rivaling the great historical floods of 1993 and 1927. Here, on May 3, 2011, flood-waters have swamped the region just north of New Madrid, Missouri.

ASSOCIATED PRESS

This diagram illustrates the hydrograph of a stream after a brief, intense storm.

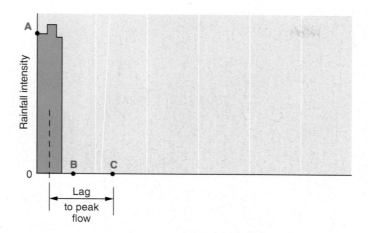

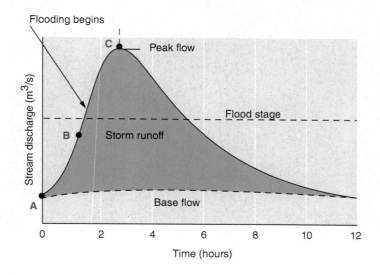

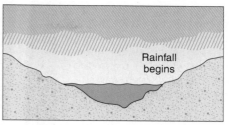

A. Onset of storm (0 hours):
The peak discharge is delayed as the runoff collects and runs down the stream channel.

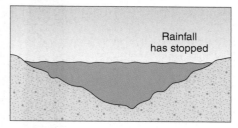

B. 1 hour:
One hour after the cloudburst, the stream can still contain the increased volume.

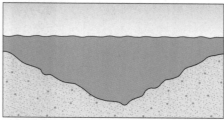

C. 2 hours:
After two hours, the stream reaches its peak flow and cannot be contained by its banks any more.

Base flow is the "normal" flow of water in a stream, contributed by groundwater.

inundated 130,000 square kilometers and swept away many villages in the heavily populated floodplain. In 1931, another Huang He flood killed a staggering 3.7 million people. Yet these same floods help replenish the soil in the floodplain, which explains why people keep moving back to the area.

REMEMBER THIS! What is *silt*? If you can't remember, review *Products of Weathering* in Chapter 7. The yellowish-brown silt carried by the Huang He is very fine-grained and wind-deposited, derived from the surfaces of glaciers in northern China. Do you remember what this type of sediment is called? Remind yourself by looking back at *Depositional Environments on Land*, Chapter 8.

Human interventions sometimes increase the chance that flooding will occur (instead of decreasing it). Urban development can exacerbate flooding in a variety of ways. Urban construction on compressible sediment, often accompanied by withdrawal of groundwater, can lead to **subsidence**, which increases the danger of flooding (as it

subsidence A drop in the surface of the land.

did in New Orleans during Hurricane Katrina). The impermeable ground cover associated with urbanization can add substantially to surface runoff in urban areas. Storm sewers also contribute to flooding because they allow runoff from paved areas to reach the river channel more quickly. As a result, floods in urbanized basins often have higher

High water breached the protective levees of New Orleans when Hurricane Katrina struck in August 2005. St. Bernard Parish was protected by a levee, but it was not sufficient to withstand the storm surge. Ten days after the storm, when this photo was taken, the subdivision was still under almost 2 meters of water.

Tyrone Turner/NG Image Collection

peak discharges and reach their peaks more quickly than do floods in undeveloped basins.

Because floods can be so damaging, predicting and preparing for them is essential (**Figure 11.14**). To do this, scientists plot the frequency of past floods of different sizes on a graph to produce a **flood-frequency curve**. The average time interval between two floods of the same magnitude is called the **recurrence interval**. For example, a "10-year flood" has a recurrence interval of 10 years, which means that there is a 1-in-10 (or 10%) chance that such a flood will occur in any given year. A flood with an even greater discharge having a recurrence interval of 50 years would be termed a "50-year flood" for this particular stream, and there would be a 1-in-50 (2%) chance of such a flood occurring in any given year. Regional planners should (and do) keep these intervals in mind when planning development on or near a floodplain.

Another aspect of flood prediction is real-time monitoring of storms and water levels. Hydrologists can combine information about the weather with their knowledge of a river basin's geology and topography to forecast the peak height of a flood and the time when the crest will pass a particular location. Such forecasts, which are often made with the aid of computer models and **geographic information systems (GIS)**, can be very useful for planning evacuation or defensive measures.

Understandably, many people throughout history have been unsatisfied with simply predicting floods and have attempted to prevent them. River channels are often modified, or "engineered," for the purposes of flood control and protection as well as to increase access to floodplain lands, facilitate transport, enhance drainage, and control erosion. The modifications usually consist of some combination of widening, deepening, straightening, clearing, or lining of the natural channel. All of these approaches are collectively called **channelization**.

Like dams, channelization projects can contribute to the economic well-being of a community—but often at a price. Channel modifications interfere with natural habitats and ecosystems. Such modifications can degrade the aesthetic

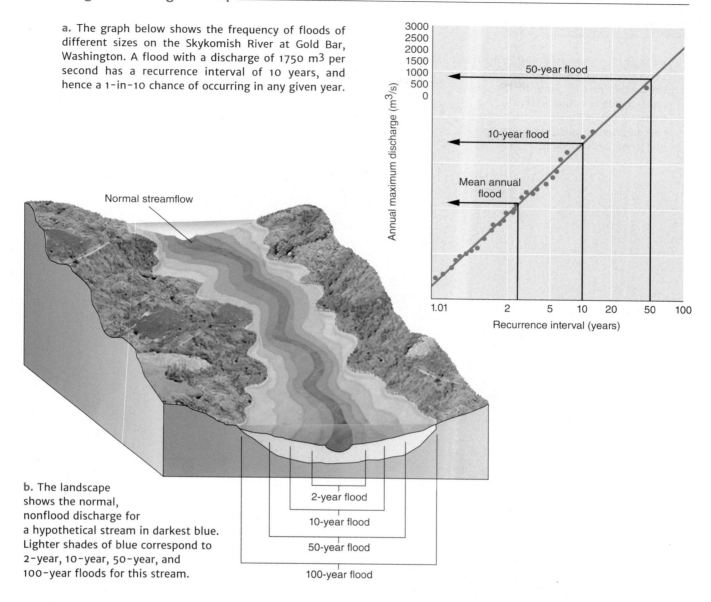

a. The graph below shows the frequency of floods of different sizes on the Skykomish River at Gold Bar, Washington. A flood with a discharge of 1750 m3 per second has a recurrence interval of 10 years, and hence a 1-in-10 chance of occurring in any given year.

b. The landscape shows the normal, nonflood discharge for a hypothetical stream in darkest blue. Lighter shades of blue correspond to 2-year, 10-year, 50-year, and 100-year floods for this stream.

value of a river and aggravate water pollution. Projects sometimes control flooding in the immediate area but contribute to more intense flooding downstream. Perhaps most importantly, any modification of a channel's course or cross section renders invalid the hydrologic data collected there in the past. During the Mississippi River floods of 1973 and 1993, experts could not account for water levels that were higher than predicted by the historical data; the likely cause was extensive upstream modifications of the river channel by humans.

Surface Water Resources

A reliable water supply is critical—not only for human survival and health but also for the role it plays in industry, agriculture, and other economic activities (**Figure 11.15**). According to the United Nations, 43 countries worldwide,

with a total population of almost 700 million people, are today designated as **water-scarce**; by 2025, this could increase to 1.8 billion people. The lack of water in these countries places serious constraints on agricultural production, economic development, health, and environmental protection.

Globally, crop irrigation accounts for about 73% of the demand for water, industry for about 21%, and domestic use for the remaining 6%, though the proportions vary from one region to another. Demand in each of these sectors has more than quadrupled since 1950. Population growth is partly responsible for the increasing demand, but improvements in standards of living around the world have also contributed to the large increase in water use per capita over the past few decades. The total amount of water being withdrawn (i.e., diverted from rivers, lakes, and groundwater) for worldwide human use is about eight times the annual streamflow of the Mississippi River.

The large map shows the world's main watersheds in terms of the amount of renewable water available per person, per year. The smaller map and graphics show access to improved drinking water, as well as the main purposes of water withdrawals in different world regions.

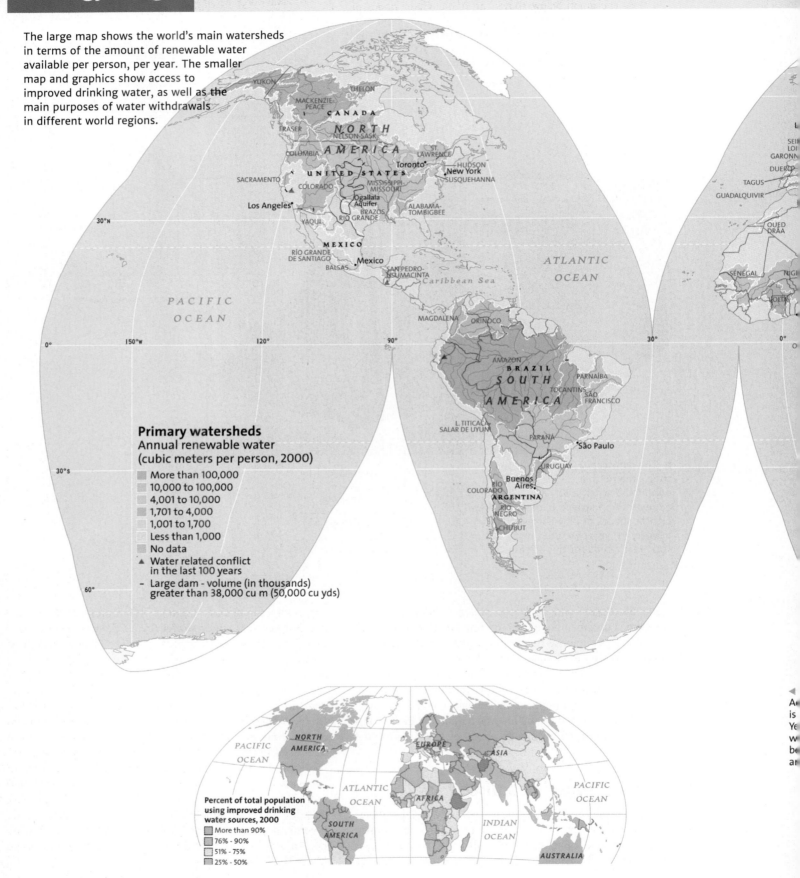

Primary watersheds
Annual renewable water
(cubic meters per person, 2000)

- More than 100,000
- 10,000 to 100,000
- 4,001 to 10,000
- 1,701 to 4,000
- 1,001 to 1,700
- Less than 1,000
- No data
- ▲ Water related conflict in the last 100 years
- – Large dam - volume (in thousands) greater than 38,000 cu m (50,000 cu yds)

Percent of total population using improved drinking water sources, 2000

- More than 90%
- 76% - 90%
- 51% - 75%
- 25% - 50%

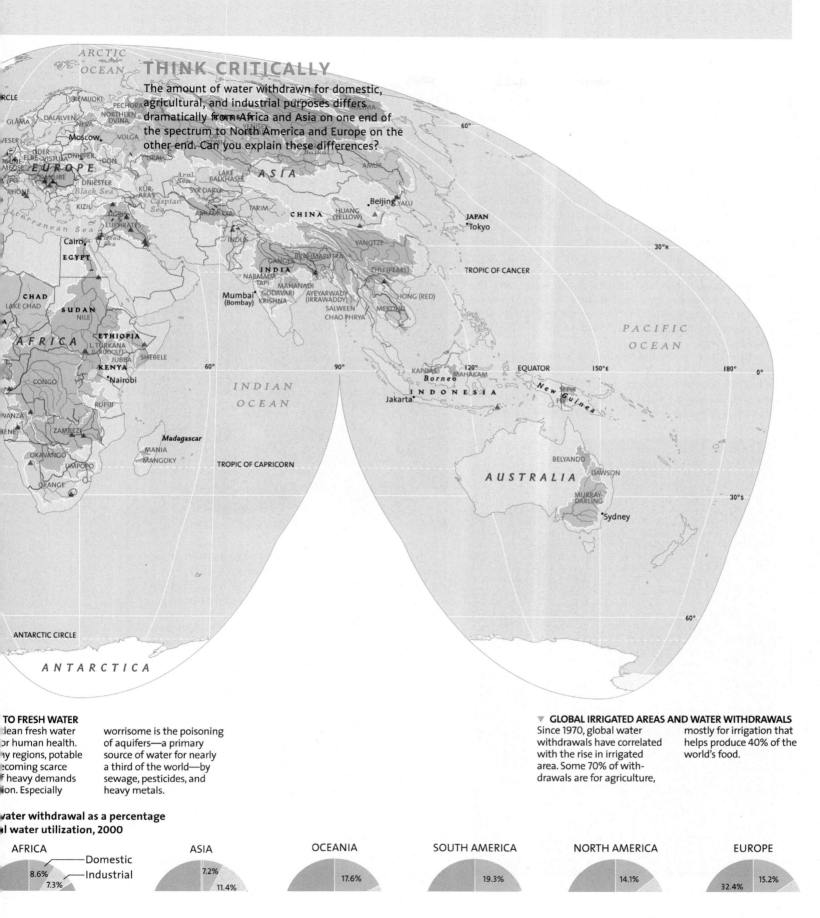

THINK CRITICALLY

The amount of water withdrawn for domestic, agricultural, and industrial purposes differs dramatically from Africa and Asia on one end of the spectrum to North America and Europe on the other end. Can you explain these differences?

TO FRESH WATER

lean fresh water
or human health.
y regions, potable
coming scarce
f heavy demands
ion. Especially

worrisome is the poisoning
of aquifers—a primary
source of water for nearly
a third of the world—by
sewage, pesticides, and
heavy metals.

▼ **GLOBAL IRRIGATED AREAS AND WATER WITHDRAWALS**

Since 1970, global water
withdrawals have correlated
with the rise in irrigated
area. Some 70% of with-
drawals are for agriculture,

mostly for irrigation that
helps produce 40% of the
world's food.

ater withdrawal as a percentage
l water utilization, 2000

AFRICA	ASIA	OCEANIA	SOUTH AMERICA	NORTH AMERICA	EUROPE
8.6% Domestic 7.3% Industrial	7.2% 11.4%	17.6%	19.3%	14.1%	32.4% 15.2%

Mono Lake and the Los Angeles Water Supply

California's Mono Lake, in the Sierra Nevada Mountains, has been the site of a collision between human needs for reliable supplies of fresh water and the needs of a unique habitat and its wildlife.

Seventy years ago, the water level of the lake was 1956 meters above sea level, and these calcium carbonate spires (called *tufa*, **Figure a**) were underwater. But in 1941, the Los Angeles Aqueduct began diverting water from four of the six streams that empty into Mono Lake. With insufficient input to make up for its evaporation losses, the water level dropped, the lake shrank to half its original volume, and the salinity doubled. Migratory birds, such as the nation's second-largest colony of California gulls (**Figure b**), were placed in jeopardy. Their food supply (brine shrimp) was dying because of the high salinity of the water, and the islands on which the birds nested were in danger of being connected to the mainland because of the retreating water. This made the birds increasingly vulnerable to predators, mainly coyotes.

By the late 1980s, the lake and its ecosystem were nearing collapse. In 1994, after a court battle between the city of Los Angeles and environmental groups, both sides agreed to a plan to raise the water level by 5 meters and compensate Los Angeles for the loss of part of its water supply.

b

NG Maps

Craig Aurness/© Corbis

a

Gordon Wiltsie / NG Image Collection

By May 2011, water levels in the lake had risen to 1945 meters, about halfway to the target of 1948 meters set by the agreement. The lake is expected to reach its target level in 15 to 20 years. Dams that once diverted streams into the aqueduct have been reengineered to do the opposite: They maintain a steady flow into Mono Lake and divert water into the aqueduct only if there is an overflow. For the California gulls, the change may have come just in time.

ASK YOURSELF

The tufa towers seen in (Figure a) are formed by the precipitation of calcium carbonate, when calcium-rich fresh water bubbles up from underground sources into the carbonate-saturated water of Mono Lake. Based on what you know about sediment deposition from Chapter 7, how would you classify the material of which the towers are constructed?

a. clastic sediment

b. chemical sediment

c. evaporite

d. soil

e. All of the above answers are correct.

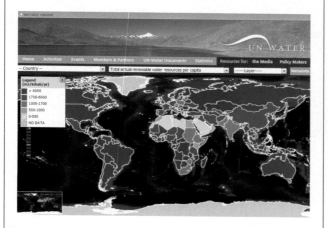
Sometimes, because of population growth and development, regions with the greatest demand for water do not have abundant and readily available supplies of surface water. For this reason, surface water is often transferred from one drainage basin to another, sometimes over long distances. Besides raising political issues related to water rights, such **interbasin transfer** can have negative environmental impacts (see *Case Study*).

You can learn more about the global importance and status of freshwater resources, and about the United Nations' efforts to ensure safe and abundant water resources, by visiting *Where Geologists Click.*

STOP **CONCEPT CHECK**

1. **What** is channelization, and how does it influence flooding?
2. **What** are some consequences of transferring water from one drainage basin to another?

FRESH WATER UNDERGROUND

Learning Objectives

1. **Explain** how the porosity and permeability of rock affect the motion of groundwater.

2. **Identify** two major types of aquifers.

3. **Discuss** some of the causes and challenges of groundwater contamination and depletion.

4. **Describe** how subsidence and cave formation are related to groundwater.

Less than 1% of all water in the hydrosphere cycle is **groundwater**. Although this sounds small, the volume of groundwater is 40 times greater than that of all the water in freshwater lakes and streams.

> **groundwater**
> Subsurface water contained in pore spaces in regolith and bedrock.

Water is everywhere beneath the land surface, even beneath parched deserts. About half of it is near the surface, no more than 750 meters below ground. At greater depths, the pressure exerted by overlying rock reduces the pore space, making it difficult for water to flow freely. Water that occurs at great depths tends to be briny, that is, rich in dissolved mineral salts and not well suited for human use. Therefore, from a practical perspective, we can think of groundwater as the water found between the land surface and a depth of about 750 meters, even though an equally large amount of water is present at greater depths.

How Groundwater Moves

Most groundwater is in motion. Unlike the swift flow of rivers, however, which is measured in kilometers per hour, the movement of groundwater is so slow that it is measured in centimeters per day or meters per year. The reason is simple: Whereas the water of a stream flows through an open channel, groundwater must move through small, constricted passages. Therefore, the rate of groundwater flow depends on the nature of the rock or sediment through which the water moves.

The Water Table Much of what we know about groundwater has been learned from the accumulated experience of generations of people who have dug or drilled millions of wells. This experience tells us that a hole penetrating the ground ordinarily first encounters a zone in which the spaces between the grains in regolith or bedrock are filled mainly with air, although the material may be moist to the touch. This is the **zone of aeration**, also known as the **vadose zone (Figure 11.16)**.

> **zone of aeration** Soil and sediment above the water table, which holds both air and moisture.

Underground water exists everywhere, and water flows out wherever the ground surface intersects the water table. A drilled well passes first through the zone of aeration, where pore spaces are filled with both air and water. Eventually it reaches the water table, where the pore spaces are completely filled with water.

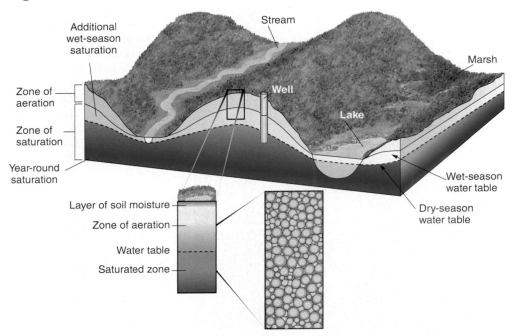

Additional wet-season saturation

Stream

Marsh

Zone of aeration

Zone of saturation

Well

Lake

Year-round saturation

Wet-season water table

Dry-season water table

Layer of soil moisture

Zone of aeration

Water table

Saturated zone

---

water table The top surface of the saturated zone.

saturated zone Water-saturated rock and sediment that underlies the water table.

After passing through the zone of aeration, the well (if it's deep enough) reaches the **water table** and then enters the **saturated zone**, also known as the **phreatic zone**, in which all openings are filled with water. This means that, technically, the water table is a two-dimensional surface—it is the top surface of the saturated zone.

The water table is high beneath hills and low beneath valleys. This may seem surprising, because the surface of a glass of water or a lake is always level. But water underground flows very slowly and is strongly influenced by surface topography. If all rainfall were to cease, the water table would slowly flatten. Seepage of water into the ground would diminish and then stop entirely, and streams would dry up as the water table fell. During droughts, the depression of the water table is evident from the drying up of springs, stream beds, and wells. Repeated rainfall, which soaks the ground with fresh supplies of water, maintains the water table at a normal level and keeps surface water bodies replenished.

Whether it is deep or shallow, the water table marks the upper limit of readily usable groundwater. For this reason, a major aim of groundwater specialists and well drillers is to determine the depth and shape of the water table. To do this, they must first understand how groundwater moves and what factors and forces control its distribution underground.

porosity The percentage of the total volume of a body of rock or regolith that consists of spaces (pores).

Porosity and Permeability Porosity determines the amount of fluid a sediment or rock can contain. The porosity of sediment is affected by the size and shape of the particles and the compactness of their arrangement (**Figure 11.17a, b**). The porosity of a sedimentary rock is also affected by the extent to which the pores have been filled with cement (**Figure 11.17c**). Plutonic igneous rock and metamorphic rock, which consist of many closely interlocked crystals, generally have lower porosities than do sediment and sedimentary rock (see *Remember This!*). However, joints and fractures may increase their porosity.

REMEMBER THIS! Can you summarize the characteristics of igneous, metamorphic, and sedimentary rock that could affect their porosity and permeability? Review *Rock: A First Look* in Chapter 2 for a discussion about what holds grains together in different types of rock. Chapters 6, 8, and 10 have additional specific details about the characteristics of the various rock types.

A rock with low porosity is likely also to have low **permeability**. However, high porosity does not necessarily mean high permeability because both the sizes and continuity of the pores (i.e., the extent to which the pores are interconnected) influence the ability of fluids to flow through the material.

permeability A measure of how easily a solid allows fluids to pass through it.

Percolation After water from a rain shower soaks into the ground, or infiltrates, some of it evaporates, while some is taken up by plants. The remaining water continues to **percolate** under the influence of gravity until it reaches the water table. The "perc test" that must be carried out

Porosity in sediment and rock • Figure 11.17 _____

In these examples of porosity, all of the pore spaces are filled with water, as they would be in the saturated zone.

a. The porosity is about 30% in this sediment with particles of uniform size.

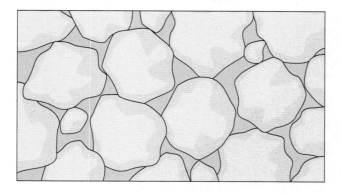

b. This sediment, in which fine grains fill the space between larger grains, has a lower porosity, around 15%.

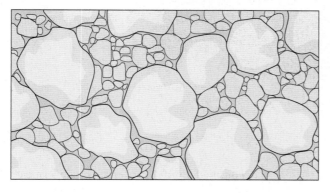

c. In sedimentary rock, the porosity may be reduced by cement that binds the grains together and fills the pores.

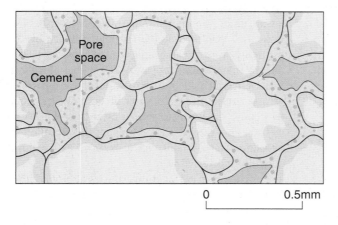

Pore space

Cement

0   0.5mm

when a new septic system is being installed is a measure of **percolation**.

The movement of groundwater in the saturated zone is similar to the flow of water that occurs when you gently squeeze a water-soaked sponge. Water moves slowly through very small pores along thread-like paths. The water flows from areas where the water table is high toward areas where it is lower. In other words, it generally flows toward surface streams or lakes (**Figure 11.18**). Some of the flow paths turn upward and enter the stream or lake from beneath, seemingly defying gravity. This upward flow occurs because groundwater is under greater pressure beneath a hill than beneath a stream or lake. Because water tends to flow toward points where pressure is low, it flows toward bodies of water at the surface.

Recharge and Discharge Recharge of groundwater occurs when rainfall and snowmelt infiltrate the surface and percolate downward to the saturated zone (see Figure 11.18). The water then moves slowly along its flowpath toward zones where **discharge** occurs. (Note that earlier in the chapter, we used the term *discharge* for a somewhat different concept—the flow of water along a stream channel.) In discharge zones, subsurface water either flows out onto the ground surface as a **spring** or joins bodies of water such as streams, lakes, ponds, swamps, or the ocean. Groundwater discharge into streams maintains the base flow of the stream. Pumping groundwater from a well with a mechanical pump also creates a point of discharge, where water moves from the subsurface to the surface. The amount of time water takes to move through the ground to any discharge area depends on distance and rate of flow; it may take as little as a few days or as long as thousands of years.

Where Groundwater Is Stored

When we wish to find a reliable supply of groundwater, we search for an **aquifer** (Latin for "water carrier"). An aquifer is not a body of water—it is a body of rock or regolith that is water saturated, which means that it must be porous. Gravel and sand units generally make good aquifers; many sandstones are also good aquifers, as are fractured or cavernous limestone and granite. An aquifer in which the water is free to rise to its natural level is called an **unconfined aquifer** (**Figure 11.19**). In a well drilled into an unconfined aquifer, the water will rise to the level of the surrounding water table. Bringing it to the surface requires a pump or a bucket.

This diagram illustrates the flow paths of water as it seeps in through the ground surface, flows downward to the zone of saturation, and then percolates along curved pathways under the influence of gravity, eventually emerging at the surface once again.

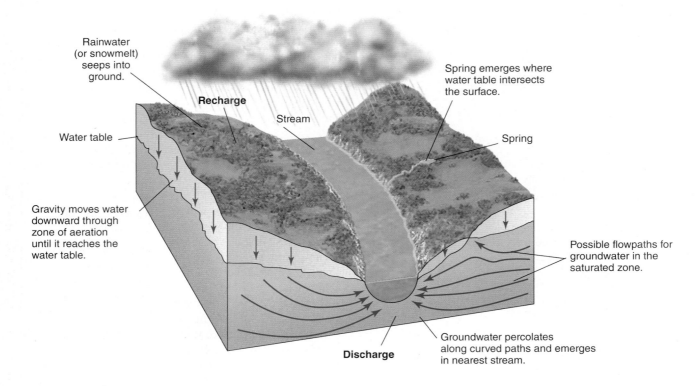

Rainwater (or snowmelt) seeps into ground.

Spring emerges where water table intersects the surface.

Recharge

Stream

Water table

Spring

Gravity moves water downward through zone of aeration until it reaches the water table.

Possible flowpaths for groundwater in the saturated zone.

Discharge

Groundwater percolates along curved paths and emerges in nearest stream.

Aquifers, confined and unconfined • Figure 11.19

An unconfined aquifer is open to the atmosphere through pores in the rock and soil above the aquifer. In contrast, the water in a confined aquifer is trapped between impermeable rock layers.

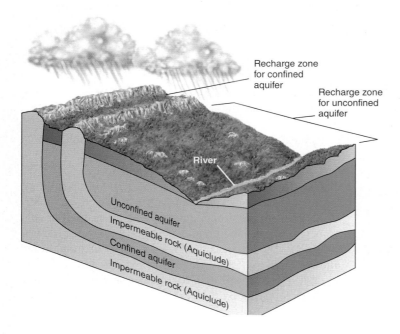

Recharge zone for confined aquifer

Recharge zone for unconfined aquifer

River

Unconfined aquifer

Impermeable rock (Aquiclude)

Confined aquifer

Impermeable rock (Aquiclude)

A **confined aquifer** is overlain by impermeable rock units, called confining layers or **aquicludes** (see Figure 11.19 and **Figure 11.20**). Common aquicludes are shale and clay layers, as well as

> **aquiclude** A layer of impermeable rock.

unfractured, nonporous, impermeable bedrock. The water in a confined aquifer is held in place by the overlying impermeable unit, and its recharge zone may be many kilometers away at a higher elevation. If a well is drilled into the aquifer, the high water pressure due to the elevation of the recharge zone will cause the water to rise or even flow out of the well without having to be pumped; this is called an **artesian well**. A fault can also serve as a natural conduit for artesian water.

A change in permeability of rock at ground level may give rise to a spring, which is a natural analogue of an artesian well. Such a change may be due to the presence of an aquiclude (**Figure 11.21**), or it may happen along the trace of a fault (Figure 11.20a).

Artesian water • Figure 11.20

An artesian well or spring flows out (or sometimes gushes) from under the ground on its own, without the need for pumping.

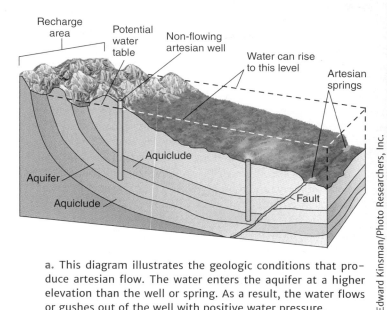

a. This diagram illustrates the geologic conditions that produce artesian flow. The water enters the aquifer at a higher elevation than the well or spring. As a result, the water flows or gushes out of the well with positive water pressure.

Edward Kinsman/Photo Researchers, Inc.

b. This flowing artesian well in Letchworth State Park, New York, freezes during the winter to form a core of ice that sometimes grows as high as 20 meters.

What causes springs? • Figure 11.21

Springs flow wherever the water table is intersected by the ground surface.

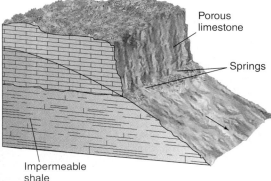

a. Water flows from a spring in a limestone, along its contact with an underlying impermeable shale unit that functions as an aquiclude.

Courtesy Brian J. Skinner

b. This spring in the Grand Canyon is fed by water from the porous Redwall and Muav Limestones, cavernous limestone units that are the water source for many springs. The underlying aquiclude is the impermeable Bright Angel Shale.

Groundwater Depletion and Contamination

A well will supply water if it is deep enough to intersect the water table. As shown in **Figure 11.22**, a shallow well may become dry during periods when the water table is low, whereas a deeper well may yield water throughout the year. When water is pumped from a well, a **cone of depression** (a cone-shaped dip in the water table) will form around the well. In most small domestic wells, the cone of depression is hardly discernible. Wells pumped for irrigation and industrial uses, however, sometimes withdraw so much water that the cone may become very wide and steep and can lower the water levels in surrounding wells. When large cones of depression from pumped wells overlap, the result is regional depression of the water table.

If the rate of withdrawal of groundwater regularly exceeds the rate of natural recharge, the volume of stored water steadily decreases; this is called **groundwater mining**. It may take hundreds or even thousands of years for a depleted aquifer to be replenished. The results of excessive withdrawal include lowering of the water table, drying up of springs and streams, compaction of the aquifer, and subsidence, a decline in land surface elevation.

Sometimes it is possible to recharge a depleted aquifer by pumping water into it. In other cases, the effects of depletion may be permanent. For example, when an aquifer suffers **compaction**—that is, when its mineral grains collapse on one another because the pore water that held them apart has been removed—it is permanently damaged and may never be able to hold as much water as it originally held.

Urban development can increase the rate of depletion of groundwater, not only by increasing the demand for water but also by increasing the amount of impermeable ground cover in the area. When roads, parking lots, buildings, and sidewalks cover a recharge area, the rate of infiltration and groundwater recharge can be substantially reduced. Subsidence caused by withdrawal of groundwater (**Figure 11.23**) is a problem in many urban areas, such as Mexico City, Bangkok, and Venice. The weight of buildings also contributes to the compaction of compressible sediment.

Laws and policies relating to water rights are very complicated, and the application to groundwater is even more complicated than it is for surface water. Because groundwater is hidden from view, it is difficult to monitor its flow and regulate its use. If you drill a well into an aquifer underlying your property, are you entitled to withdraw as much water as you need from that well? Should you withdraw water only for your own purposes, or should you be permitted to withdraw the water and sell it elsewhere? What happens if withdrawing the groundwater depletes the aquifer and your neighbor's well runs dry?

Similar problems arise when a landowner's actions cause an aquifer to become contaminated. In some jurisdictions, it is technically legal to contaminate groundwater; it becomes illegal only when the contaminated groundwater flows into a neighboring property. To make matters worse, because of the slow movement of groundwater, those responsible for the problem may be long gone before their actions begin to affect their neighbors.

Many of the types and sources of contaminants that affect surface water also cause groundwater contamination.

Year-round and seasonal wells • Figure 11.22

Seasonal changes affect the height of the water table. A well will produce year-round only if it extends into the year-round zone of saturation.

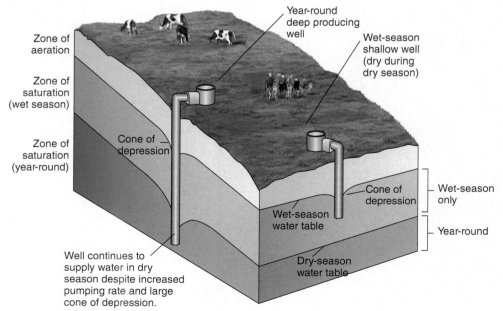

Subsidence and flooding • Figure 11.23

In Galveston, Texas, these homes had to be abandoned because pumping of groundwater lowered the level of the land, allowing seawater to flow in from the Gulf of Mexico. The snapshot in the foreground shows the same neighborhood, high and dry, years earlier.

Ted Spiegel/NG Image Collection

Because of its hidden nature, however, groundwater contamination can be much more difficult to detect, control, and clean up than surface water contamination. The most common source of water pollution in wells and springs is untreated sewage. Agricultural pesticides and fertilizers, significant sources of surface water pollution, are also common contaminants of groundwater. Harmful chemicals leaking from waste disposal facilities can also infiltrate groundwater reservoirs and contaminate them.

Probably the most serious groundwater contamination problem in North America is caused by leaking underground storage tanks at gas stations, refineries, and other industrial settings (**Figure 11.24**). Such sources can continue to cause groundwater contamination for decades and can be exceedingly difficult to detect and remediate.

When Groundwater Dissolves Rock

In regions underlain by rock types that are highly susceptible to chemical weathering, especially limestone and dolostone (Chapter 7), groundwater typically creates extensive systems of underground caverns. These, in turn, have noticeable impacts on surface topography.

Caves and Sinkholes
Caves are formed when circulating groundwater at or below the water table dissolves carbonate rock. The process begins with dissolution along interconnected fractures and bedding planes. A cave passage then develops along the most favorable flow route.

> **cave** An underground open space; a cavern is a system of connected caves.

The development of a continuous passage by slowly moving groundwater may take up to 10,000 years, and the further enlargement of the passage by more rapidly flowing groundwater needed to create a fully developed cave system may take an additional 10,000 to 1 million years. Finally, the cave may become accessible to humans after the water table drops below the floor of at least some of the chambers. The deepest cave yet discovered in the United States is Lechuguilla Cave, in Carlsbad Caverns National Park in New Mexico, where there are more than 100 known caves (see *Amazing Places*).

In the parts of the cave that lie above the water table (in the vadose zone), groundwater continues to percolate downward, dripping from the ceiling to the floor. Calcium carbonate dissolved in the water precipitates out of solution and builds up beautiful icicle-like decorations on the cave walls, ceilings, and floor. These include **stalactites** (hanging from the ceiling) and **stalagmites** (projecting upward from the floor), as well as columns, draperies, and flowstones. In the saturated zone, below the water table, water movement is largely horizontal, creating tubular passages.

Caves are dissolution cavities that are closed to the surface or have only a small opening. In contrast, a **sinkhole**

> **sinkhole** A dissolution cavity that is open to the sky.

is a dissolution cavity that is open to the sky. Some sinkholes are formed very abruptly, when the roofs of caves collapse.

A forgotten oil spill • Figure 11.24

The surface of Newtown Creek in New York is fouled with oil from an underground spill that happened in 1948, when approximately 65 million liters of oil leaked from a refinery owned by the Standard Oil Company of New York. This is more than the amount of oil spilled in the infamous *Exxon Valdez* accident in 1989. The successor company, ExxonMobil, was sued for $25 million by the state and has now cleaned up part of the mess, but oil continues to contaminate the groundwater and ooze to the surface.

Lechuguilla Cave

In 1986, cavers (also known as spelunkers) discovered the deepest-known cave in the United States, called Lechuguilla Cave, in Carlsbad Caverns National Park. Its entrance had been known for decades, but it had been considered a dead end until cavers dug through the floor to a huge network of passages on the other side.

Lechuguilla Cave has now been explored to a depth of 475 meters, and it has almost 160 kilometers of mapped passages. It is as spectacular as it is deep, but it is closed to the public to preserve its unusual formations.

a. A "bush" made of fragile aragonite pokes out of a stalagmite made of calcite. Aragonite and calcite are polymorphs of calcium carbonate (see Chapter 2).

b. "Soda straws" reach down from the ceiling in this small chamber. Water flows down through the center of each straw. If water starts flowing down the outside, it will build a stalactite.

c. Gypsum crystals provide a clue to this cave's unusual history. Unlike most limestone caves, which are formed by carbonic acid carried by rainwater, Lechuguilla formed from the bottom up. Hydrogen sulfide from underlying oil deposits percolated up into the groundwater and formed sulfuric acid, which dissolved the rock. As the water table dropped, gypsum (calcium sulfate) deposits precipitated from the acidic water.

Most sinkholes, though, develop much more slowly and less catastrophically, simply growing wider over time as the carbonate bedrock slowly dissolves. Dean's Blue Hole, profiled in the opener for Chapter 8, is an undersea sinkhole that formed by dissolution of rock in the carbonate platform of the Great Bahama Bank. Sinkholes also can form as a result of human activity, most commonly from collapse of the surface into an underground cavity left by the mining of coal or salt, or, less commonly, as a result of oil extraction.

Sinkholes were in the news a lot in 2013. One man was killed in Florida when part of his house suddenly collapsed into a sinkhole; later in the year, part of a Florida resort was swallowed up by a sinkhole. Another sinkhole in the middle of an intersection left about 50 homes and businesses in Santa Fe, New Mexico, without power or water. Flooding caused sinkholes to open up in Colorado and Alberta that year as well. Sinkhole activity and associated damages are common in the southern states and other areas around the world that are underlain by carbonate rock, but deaths are a relatively rare occurrence.

Karst Topography In regions where underground dissolution and cavern formation are extensive, a distinctive landscape typically forms on the surface. **Karst** topography is a complex landscape that is characterized by many small, closed basins, sinkholes, cave openings, and disrupted drainage patterns (**Figure 11.25**).

> **karst** Topography characterized by sinkholes and disrupted drainage patterns, typical in carbonate regions.

Karst • Figure 11.25

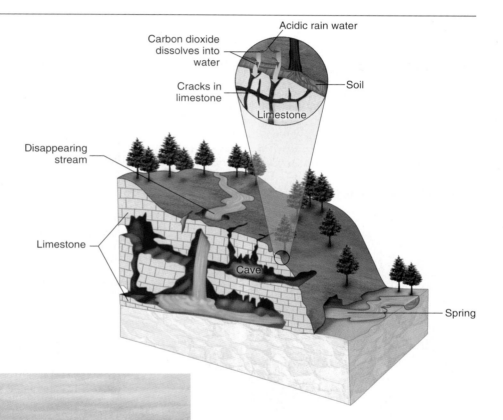

a. Karst topography is characterized by disappearing streams, sinkholes, and underground dissolution caves and caverns.

b. This is karst terrain near Guilin, China. The limestone pillars remained after a major cavern collapse created the valley in which the village is located. The pillars themselves are riddled with caves and passageways.

Pyty/Shutterstock

Streams disappear into the ground and join the groundwater. Large springs form downstream, where the water table intersects the land surface, or along favorable routes of escape, such as faults.

Karst is most typical of regions underlain by soluble carbonate rock (limestone or dolostone), although it can also occur in regions with extensive evaporite (salt) deposits. In carbonate terrains with karst topography, the rate of dissolution is faster than the average rate of erosion of surface materials by streams and mass wasting.

STOP CONCEPT CHECK

1. **How** does permeability differ from porosity?
2. **What** is the geologic difference between an unconfined and a confined aquifer?
3. **Why** is ground subsidence sometimes related to groundwater withdrawal?
4. **How** and why do caves and sinkholes develop in certain regions?

SUMMARY

 THE PLANNER

1 The Hydrologic Cycle 280

- The water cycle, or **hydrologic cycle**, describes the movement of water from one reservoir to another in the hydrosphere as shown in the figure. The ocean is the largest reservoir, followed by the polar ice sheets. The largest reservoir of unfrozen fresh water is groundwater. Surface water bodies, the atmosphere, and the biosphere are much smaller water reservoirs.

How water moves around the Earth system • Figure 11.1

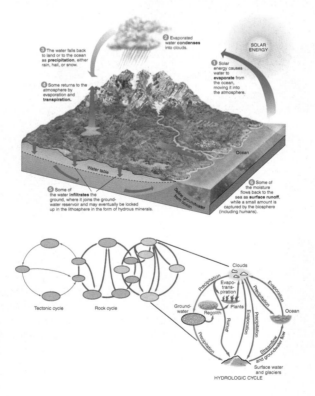

- The pathways or processes by which water moves from one reservoir to another include **evaporation**, **condensation**, **precipitation**, **transpiration**, **infiltration**, and **surface runoff**.

- Like the tectonic and rock cycles, the hydrologic cycle is a closed cycle of open systems. Because it is closed, the global hydrologic cycle maintains a mass balance.

2 How Water Affects the Land 283

- **Streams** and rivers flow downslope along a clearly defined natural passageway, the **channel**. Interrelated factors that influence the behavior of a stream include the **gradient**, **discharge**, **load**, and velocity of the water.

- Streams create landforms through erosion and deposition. Straight, braided, and meandering channels, as shown in the diagram, and oxbow lakes are erosional landforms. Point bars, alluvial fans, deltas, and **floodplains** are depositional landforms made of recently deposited sediment, or **alluvium**.

- Every stream is surrounded by its **drainage basin**, the total area from which water flows into the stream. The topographic "high" that separates adjacent drainage basins is a **divide**. Streams originate in a headwater region, where they collect water from a large number of smaller tributary streams. Water exits a stream system from the stream's mouth, which may empty either into a larger river, a lake, or the ocean.

- **Lakes** form in topographic basins created by faults, glacial debris, landslides, and lava flows, as well as in areas of poor drainage. Lakes are usually short-lived geologic features because they tend to disappear by erosion of the outlet or by silt deposition.

Three kinds of streams • Figure 11.4

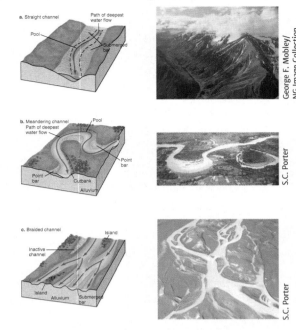

George F. Mobley/
NG Image Collection

S.C. Porter

S.C. Porter

3 Water as a Hazard and a Resource 291

- A **flood** occurs when a stream's discharge becomes so great that it exceeds the capacity of the channel, causing the stream to overflow its banks. The risk of floods is increased by subsidence, and flooding can be exacerbated by human activity.

- Prediction of flooding is based on analysis of the frequency of occurrence of past events, as shown in the diagram, and on real-time monitoring of storms using a hydrograph. River channel modifications made for purposes of flood control and protection, as well as for navigation and other purposes, are collectively known as channelization.

Predicting floods • Figure 11.14

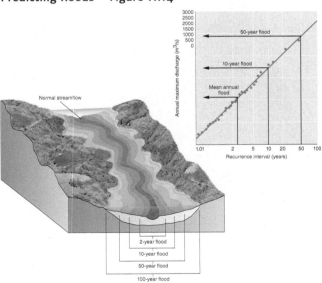

- Agriculture is by far the largest consumer of fresh water. Surface water can be transported from one drainage basin to another, but only at the risk of long-term environmental changes in the affected basins.

4 Fresh Water Underground 299

- **Groundwater** is subsurface water contained in spaces within bedrock and regolith. In the **zone of aeration**, water is present but does not completely saturate the ground. In the phreatic or saturated zone, all openings are filled with water. The top of the **saturated zone** is the **water table**.

- The rate of groundwater flow is dependent on the characteristics of the rock or sediment through which the water must move. **Porosity** is the percentage of the total volume of a body of rock or regolith that consists of open spaces. **Permeability** is a measure of how easily a solid allows fluids to pass through it. Groundwater in the saturated zone moves slowly by **percolation** through very small pores from areas where the water table is high to where it is lower.

- Groundwater **recharge** occurs when rainfall and snowmelt infiltrate and percolate downward to the saturated zone. **Discharge** occurs where subsurface water leaves the saturated zone and becomes surface water in a stream, lake, or **spring**.

- An **aquifer** is a body of permeable rock or regolith in the zone of saturation. An unconfined aquifer is in contact with the atmosphere through the pore spaces of overlying rock or regolith, while a confined aquifer lies between layers of impermeable rock, called **aquicludes,** as shown in the diagram. The water pressure in a confined aquifer may be high enough to force the water partway or all the way to the surface when a well is drilled into it. Such a well is called artesian. Excessive withdrawal from an aquifer can cause the water table to drop, springs and streams to dry up, and regolith to compact and subside.

Aquifers, confined and unconfined • Figure 11.19

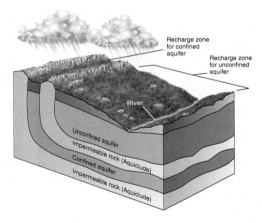

- Many of the types and sources of contaminants that affect surface water also cause groundwater contamination. These include untreated sewage, agricultural pesticides and fertilizers, and leaks or spills of chemicals from commercial and industrial sites.

- **Caves**, caverns, **sinkholes**, and **karst** topography are formed when rock—most commonly carbonate rock—is dissolved by circulating groundwater, creating underground cavities. Stalactites and stalagmites are built up from calcium carbonate precipitated from percolating groundwater.

KEY TERMS

alluvium 286	floodplain 286	recharge 301
aquiclude 302	gradient 283	saturated zone 300
aquifer 301	groundwater 299	sinkhole 305
cave 305	hydrologic cycle 280	spring 301
channel 283	infiltration 280	stream 283
condensation 280	karst 307	subsidence 293
discharge (1) 283	lake 288	surface runoff 280
discharge (2) 301	load 283	transpiration 280
divide 288	percolation 301	water table 300
drainage basin 288	permeability 300	zone of aeration 299
evaporation 280	porosity 300	
flood 291	precipitation 280	

CRITICAL AND CREATIVE THINKING QUESTIONS

1. Investigate the ways in which water shortages, floods, or other processes associated with water (e.g., erosion and deposition of sediment) have affected human history. How did societies respond, and what effects did those responses have?

2. The concept of residence time is very important in geology. It applies not only to water but also to any substance that moves from one reservoir to another in the Earth system. What other substances, besides water, move around in the Earth system? Are those substances typically transported by water? Why would we want to monitor these substances and keep track of their residence times?

3. Where does your community obtain its water supply? Is it a groundwater or a surface freshwater source? Is either the quantity or the quality of the water threatened?

4. Visit a stream before and after an intense rainfall. Observe the gradient, discharge, load, and velocity of the streamflow. What changes do you notice?

5. Consider the flood hydrograph shown here. How much time elapsed between the start of rainfall and flood stage at this particular location? How much time did authorities have in which to issue an early warning to residents of the area, before flooding began? If you were in a position of authority, how would you have handled this situation?

Hydrograph of stream discharge • Figure 11.12

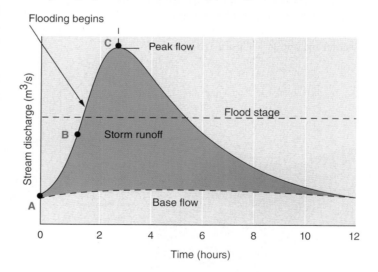

WHAT IS HAPPENING IN THIS PICTURE?

This 100-meter-wide sinkhole opened up one day in Winter Park, Florida, and grew to the point where it eventually swallowed up part of a house, six commercial buildings, and the municipal swimming pool.

THINK CRITICALLY

1. What could have caused this to happen?

2. What kind of rock do you think might underlie a location that is prone to this sort of collapse?

SELF-TEST

(Check your answers in Appendix D.)

1. On this diagram, label each stage of the hydrologic cycle (1 through 6) using the following terms:

precipitation	cloud formation through condensation
surface runoff	surface evaporation and transpiration
infiltration and groundwater flow	evaporation from the ocean

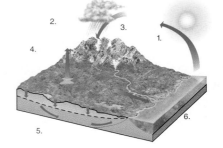

2. The diagram with question 1 depicts Earth's hydrologic cycle. Which reservoir in the hydrologic cycle holds *most* of the freshwater resources of the planet?

a. the ocean

b. ice sheets

c. lakes

d. groundwater

3. The _____ of a stream will have a large influence over channel development and the evolution of associated landforms.

a. discharge

b. gradient

c. sediment load

d. All of the above answers are correct.

4. _____ channels will form in streams when there is a low slope gradient and large and variable sediment load.

a. Straight

b. Meandering

c. Braided

5. Lakes are ephemeral features that disappear by _____.

a. the accumulation of inorganic sediment carried in by streams

b. the accumulation of organic matter produced by plants within the lake

c. gradually being drained by stream outlets eroding to lower levels

d. All of the above answers are correct.

6. On this diagram, label each of the landforms associated with a meandering stream system:

alluvium   cutoff

oxbow lake   meander

floodplain   natural levees

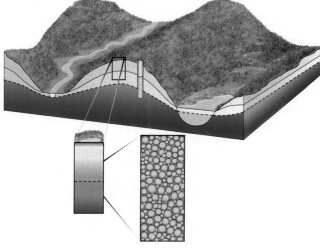

7. A(n) _____ is the total area from which water flows into a stream.

a. alluvial fan

b. braided channel

c. water cycle

d. drainage basin

8. Urban development can lead to increased risk of flooding by _____.

a. compressing underlying sediment, causing subsidence

b. increasing surface runoff

c. channeling runoff more quickly to rivers through storm drains

d. All of the above answers are correct.

9. There is a _____ chance of a "50-year flood" occurring in any given year.

a. 1%

b. 2%

c. 5%

d. 10%

e. 50%

10. Although the proportions vary from one region to another, what accounts for the greatest demand for water globally?

a. industry

b. domestic use

c. crop irrigation

11. The _____ controls the porosity of an aquifer.

a. size of the particles in the material

b. shapes and uniformity of the material

c. amount of cementing agent in the pore space of the material

d. All of the above factors control the porosity of an aquifer.

12. A(n) _____ is an underground reservoir of water that is overlain by impermeable rock units.

a. aquiclude

b. aquifer

c. confined aquifer

d. unconfined aquifer

13. In a well drilled into a(n) _____, the water will rise to the level of the surrounding water table.

a. aquiclude

b. aquifer

c. confined aquifer

d. unconfined aquifer

14. Placing a well in a position where Earth's surface intersects the water table will result in a well that does not require pumping to produce water.

a. True

b. False

15. On this diagram, label each groundwater feature using the following terms:

dry-season water table   wetland (marsh)

wet-season water table   zone of aeration

zone of saturation

THE PLANNER ✓

Review the Chapter Planner on the chapter opener and check off your completed work.

12 | THE OCEAN AND THE ATMOSPHERE

Annie Griffiths/National Geographic/Getty Images, Inc.

Robert F. Bukaty/AP Photos

THE CHANDELEUR ISLANDS

Sculpted by winds and waves, Louisiana's Chandeleur Islands are some of the many barrier islands that line the coast of the United States. The silt and sand that make up the islands are transported by the Mississippi River to the Gulf of Mexico. Hurricanes occasionally carve channels through the islands or wash sand over the top, creating dunes on the seaward side (left in this photo) and flat, marshy ground on the landward side. The Chandeleurs and their wetlands protect the shore against the battering of storm waves, filter and store groundwater, and provide habitat for countless species.

Barrier islands are constantly reshaped. The erosive effects of weather and waves are balanced by deposition of new sediment. Human intervention can alter this balance. The Chandeleurs have been eroding for half a century, as levees altered the flow of the Mississippi River and deprived the islands of sediment.

In 2005, Hurricane Katrina struck a devastating blow, submerging the entire north end of the island in the foreground of this pre-2004 photo. The islands lost 50% of their overall area (inset). In 2010, the islands were struck again when the BP *Deepwater Horizon* exploded, spilling 4.9 million barrels of oil. Some of this oil washed up onto the Chandeleurs. We will explore the fate of that oil, and its impacts on the Gulf and the Chandeleur Islands, later in this chapter.

THE OCEAN

Learning Objectives

1. **Explain** where Earth's ocean water came from and what controls the shape and distribution of ocean basins.

2. **Summarize** the processes that add and remove salts from seawater.

3. **Identify** the ocean's three main layers and describe the differences between them.

4. **Describe** the overall pattern of surface and deep ocean currents.

> **REMEMBER THIS!** Can you recall why there are no rocks on Earth that are older than about 4 billion years, and what methods scientists have used to determine the actual age of Earth? You can review these by returning to *The Age of Earth* in Chapter 3.

In Chapter 11 we introduced the hydrologic cycle and described the events in this cycle that take place on land. If we stopped there, we would be left with a rather distorted view of the hydrologic cycle as a whole. The **world ocean** is by far Earth's largest reservoir of water. The atmosphere, a much smaller reservoir than either the ocean or fresh water on land,

> **world ocean** The interconnected body of salt water that covers 71% of Earth's surface.

also plays a critical role in redistributing Earth's water. In fact, it is best to think of the ocean and the atmosphere as a linked system. Atmospheric circulation drives ocean waves and currents; in turn, the ocean regulates the temperature and humidity of the lower atmosphere. The atmosphere is also the conveyor that transfers water vapor from the ocean to the land.

In this chapter we will discuss the atmosphere and ocean individually, and then we will consider how they are linked to each other and to the land as parts of one great system.

Ocean Basins

Water has been present on Earth's surface since its earliest days. In fact, we do not have any geological record of a time before water. The oldest rock so far discovered on Earth (about 4.0 billion years old) is gneiss that was once a sedimentary rock. These sedimentary strata were deposited in water and are similar to strata being deposited today. We can be reasonably certain, then, that the ocean formed sometime between 4.56 billion years ago (when Earth was formed) and 4.0 billion years ago (see *Remember This!*). We also know that early in Earth's history the surface was much too hot for liquid water to persist, with active volcanism and even a magma ocean. It took hundreds of millions of years—from 4.56 billion years ago to perhaps 4.0 billion years ago—for the planet to cool sufficiently for liquid water to pool in depressions on the surface, and for the ocean to begin to form.

A bigger uncertainty is exactly where all the water in the ocean came from (**Figure 12.1**). Some water was present from the beginning, trapped inside the planet along with other volatile elements among the materials from which Earth was formed. During the first few hundred million years after the planet was formed, water was actively released to the atmosphere in the form of steam from volcanoes (it still is today, but volcanism is not as active now as it was in Earth's early history). Consequently, one hypothesis is that the water in the hydrosphere came primarily from Earth's interior. A more recent hypothesis (based on studies of comets and meteorites) suggests that at least some of the water in our hydrosphere arrived from outer space via cometary impacts. Possibly both processes contributed water to our planet.

Before we consider the characteristics of the water in the ocean, let's have a look at the "containers" that hold this water. Most of the water on the surface of our planet is contained in four huge interconnected ocean basins (shown in **Figure 12.1b**). The Pacific, Atlantic, and Indian oceans are connected with the Southern Ocean, the body of water that encircles Antarctica. (The Arctic Ocean is considered a northern extension of the Atlantic Ocean.) Collectively, these four bodies of water, together with a number of smaller ones, such as the Mediterranean Sea, Hudson Bay, and the Persian Gulf, cover 71% of Earth's surface.

The ocean basins are topographically low, separated by the continents, which are topographically high. Recall from Chapter 4 that the ocean basins are underlain by relatively dense rock of basaltic composition, whereas the continents consist of relatively less-dense rock that is approximately granitic in composition. The shape of the ocean basins is controlled by plate tectonics. An ocean begins as a rift, widening into a linear sea and then a full ocean basin as plates diverge along midocean ridges. On the other hand, ocean basins can close and disappear altogether when two continents converge and collide.

From subduction zone trenches—the deepest locations on our planet's surface—to the chains of volcanic mountains that snake the lengths of entire ocean basins, to the flat expanses of the abyssal plains, the ocean floor is characterized by a wide variety of dramatic topographic features, as shown in Figure 12.1b. The volcanic island of Mauna Kea extends 10,203 meters from its base on the ocean floor to its summit, making it the tallest mountain on Earth (considerably taller than Mount Everest, whose summit, at 8840 meters above sea level, is the highest location on Earth).

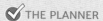

The world ocean is by far the largest reservoir in the hydrosphere. Scientists do not fully agree on where Earth got all of its water.

Where did the water come from?

Some water was trapped inside the planet along with other volatile elements. In the first few hundred million years after the planet formed, some of this water was released by volcanoes. ▼

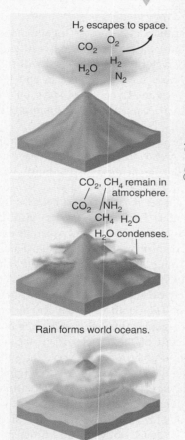

H_2 escapes to space.

CO_2 O_2
H_2O H_2
  N_2

CO_2, CH_4 remain in atmosphere.

CO_2 NH_2
CH_4 H_2O

H_2O condenses.

Rain forms world oceans.

Possible external sources for Earth's water

Additional water may have been brought in by comets from the outer regions of the solar system. As the surface slowly cooled, liquid water began to be retained in lowlying basins. ▼

©Don Dixon

NG Maps/Marie Tharp

▲ **Where is Earth's water today?**

Most of Earth's water today is in the ocean basins, which are topographically low compared to the continents. The distribution of continents and oceans has changed dramatically over the course of Earth's history as a result of plate tectonics. The four great water bodies that comprise the world ocean today are the Pacific, Atlantic, Indian, and Southern oceans.

THINK CRITICALLY

Early in Earth's history, when the surface was still very hot, what would have happened to water released from Earth's interior by volcanic eruptions?

The Composition of Seawater

If you have ever swum in the ocean, you know that seawater contains a lot of salt, which makes it not only unpalatable but also dangerous for human consumption. (If you tried living on salt water, you would become dehydrated, as your body would try to rid itself of the excess sodium and potassium ions.)

The **salinity** of seawater ranges between 3.3 and 3.7%.

> **salinity** A measure of the salt content of a solution.

This may seem quite small, but it is about 70 times the salinity of tap water. Not surprisingly, when seawater is evaporated, more than three-quarters of the dissolved matter that remains behind is sodium chloride—that is, table salt. Seawater contains most of the other natural elements as well, but it contains many of them in such low concentrations that only extremely sensitive analytical instruments can detect them.

The elements dissolved in seawater come from several sources, and the salinity of seawater varies from place to place. Chemical weathering of rock releases soluble materials such as salts of sodium, potassium, and sulfur. The soluble compounds are leached out of the weathered rock and become part of the dissolved load in river water flowing to the sea. Volcanic eruptions, both on land and beneath the sea, also contribute soluble compounds via volcanic gases and hot springs. The "so called 'black smoker' vents" found at spreading centers (see Chapter 6) also add dissolved minerals to the water. Two other processes, evaporation of surface water and freezing of seawater, tend to make seawater saltier because they remove fresh water while leaving the salts behind.

A river in the ocean · Figure 12.2 _____

This satellite photo uses false colors to represent the amount of living plant material (chlorophyll) at the sea surface, where fresh water flows from the Amazon River into the Atlantic Ocean. The freshwater "plume" (shown here in blue-green) extends hundreds of kilometers off the coast of Brazil.

Fresh water plume

Mouth of the Amazon

NASA

Why, then, doesn't the sea continue to become saltier and saltier? The answer is that it is an open system and constantly receives fresh water from precipitation and river flow (**Figure 12.2**). Also, aquatic plants and animals withdraw some elements, such as silicon, calcium, and phosphorus, to build their shells or skeletons. Other elements precipitate out in mineral form and settle to the sea bottom. All of these processes balance each other, keeping the composition of seawater essentially unchanged. This is the problem that John Joly ran into when he tried to use the salinity of seawater to estimate the age of Earth (Chapter 3); he assumed, incorrectly, that the salinity of seawater had been changing more or less continuously since the planet was formed.

Layers in the Ocean

The salinity and temperature of seawater together control its density: Cold, salty water is dense and will sink, whereas warm, less salty water is less dense and will rise. Figure 12.2 shows this very clearly; the warm and less salty water from the Amazon River water stays on top of the cold, salty Atlantic Ocean water for hundreds of kilometers.

There are three major layers, or zones, in the ocean, in which the density of the water differs. The differences are caused by changes in both temperature and salinity, with temperature being the major factor (**Figure 12.3**).

Water in the **surface layer** is the warmest because it is directly exposed to sunlight. The surface layer is also the **photic zone**, where most wavelengths of light penetrate easily, and photosynthetic organisms can be supported. This is a well-mixed layer; the water is churned by constant wind, wave, and current activity. It is also in constant contact with the atmosphere, and freely exchanges gases with the atmosphere across its surface. The depth to which the surface layer extends varies geographically; in tropical regions, where the sun shines directly on the ocean surface, the surface layer is thicker than in polar regions, where the sun's energy is less intense, and the air temperature is very cold.

Below the surface layer is a transition called the **thermocline**, in which the temperature drops rapidly to just above the freezing point of water. Because of the steep decline in temperature, the density of water also drops precipitously. The steep decline in density has its own name; it is called the **pycnocline**. This transitional layer is also a **dysphotic zone**, where there is enough light for organisms to exist but generally not enough for photosynthesis to occur. The term *dysphotic* comes from the Greek root words *phot* for "light" and *dys*, meaning "to alter." This is particularly apt because light does penetrate to this depth in the ocean, but not unaltered—only the blue and green wavelengths make it this far; yellows, reds, and violets are blocked. Organisms here live in a constant state of twilight.

In the **deep zone**, extending to the ocean floor, the water temperature is cold and nearly constant. Water density is high and so is pressure, which increases at a rate of about 1 bar (100 kPa, or about 1 atm) for every meter of

Variations in water temperature and salinity with depth define the three major zones in the ocean. The penetration of light also controls the zones where life is able to survive.

a. The three major zones, shown here, are the **surface layer**, well-mixed and of relatively low density; **thermocline**, where both temperature and density change quickly with depth; and **deep zone**, cold, and of relatively high density.

b. Light penetration is crucial for the survival of most oceanic life. The surface layer is the **photic zone**, where light penetrates fully and photosynthesis can occur. The deep **aphotic zone** is dark most of the time; life there requires special adaptations. In the transitional **dysphotic zone**, twilight is the normal condition.

c. The life-supporting zones of the ocean are shown here. The characteristics of life forms in each zone are a function of light, temperature, and pressure, and the composition and density of the water. Note that the term **benthic** refers to the bottom—at depths ranging all the way from very shallow to very deep.

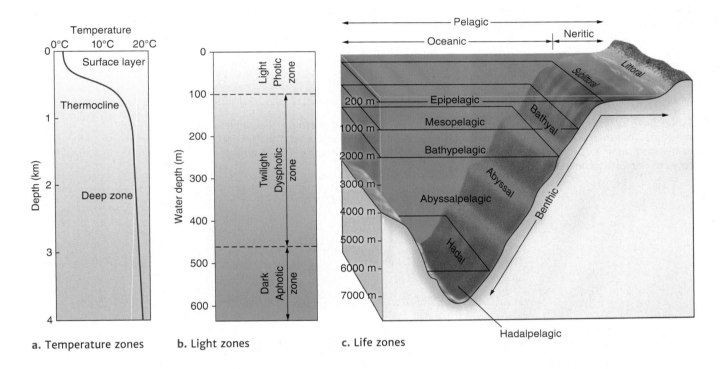

a. Temperature zones   **b.** Light zones   **c.** Life zones

depth. If you bring to the surface an organism that lives in one of the deep zones of the ocean, it is likely to explode! This is because these organisms are specifically adapted to manage the extreme pressure of the deep ocean. This is also the **aphotic zone**, where little or no light penetrates. The deepest zone of the ocean may seem wholly inhospitable, but it is also a region with abundant nutrients. Organisms that are unable to carry out photosynthesis can derive food energy from dissolved organic matter or from dissolved minerals near seafloor hydrothermal vents.

The life-supporting zones of the ocean are shown in **Figure 12.3c**. The characteristics of ocean-dwelling organisms are finely adjusted to the physical properties of the zone in which they live, including temperature; composition (especially salinity, but also acidity, oxygen levels, and dissolved matter); pressure; density; and light levels.

Some organisms must also be finely tuned to survive rapid changes in some of these characteristics. For example, organisms that live in estuaries and other coastal environments must be able to manage rapid fluctuations between salty and fresh water.

The surface and deep layers ordinarily do not mix, but in certain places they do. Those locations—called **upwellings** and **downwellings**—are very important for driving the global circulation of seawater, as you will learn later in this chapter.

Ocean Currents

In 1492, when Christopher Columbus set sail across the Atlantic Ocean in search of China, he took an indirect route. On the outward voyage, he sailed southwest toward the Canary Islands and then west on a course that carried him to the Caribbean Islands, where he first sighted land. In choosing this course, he was following the path of the prevailing winds and surface ocean currents instead of fighting the westerly winds and currents at 40°N latitude. (**Westerly** means flowing *from* the west, and **easterly** refers to currents and winds that blow from the east.) On the return trip, he sailed a more northerly route in order to take advantage of the westerly winds and currents at that latitude. His route is shown by the dotted black arrows in the top portion of **Figure 12.4**.

Surface ocean currents, like those Columbus followed, are set in motion by the prevailing winds. The surface of the ocean creates friction when the wind passes over it, with the result that the wind literally "drags" or "pushes" the surface water along. For this reason, these currents only extend to about 50 to 100 meters deep and are confined to the surface zone. Surface currents are part of the reason that the surface layer of the ocean is well mixed.

The pattern of water flow in the deep ocean is quite different from that of surface currents (**Figure 12.5**). Differences in temperature and salinity—which change the water's density—drive this circulation pattern, and the current directions are further controlled by the Coriolis force (discussed later in the chapter). The scientific name for the global deep ocean current system is the **thermohaline circulation** because it is driven by variations in temperature (*thermo*) and salinity (*haline*).

> **thermohaline circulation** The deep-ocean global "conveyor belt" circulation, driven by differences in water temperature, salinity, and density.

The global thermohaline circulation moves continuously around the globe, so it has no starting point or ending point, but we can visualize it as beginning in the far northern part of the Atlantic Ocean. Water off the coast of Greenland in the North Atlantic is very cold; it is also salty because it has had fresh water removed from it to form sea ice. This

Surface ocean currents • Figure 12.4

Sailors have long been aware of the prevailing currents in the ocean. Christopher Columbus used the North Atlantic current to good advantage in 1492. Surface ocean currents in the northern hemisphere tend to curve to the right (clockwise), whereas in the southern hemisphere, they curve to the left (counterclockwise).

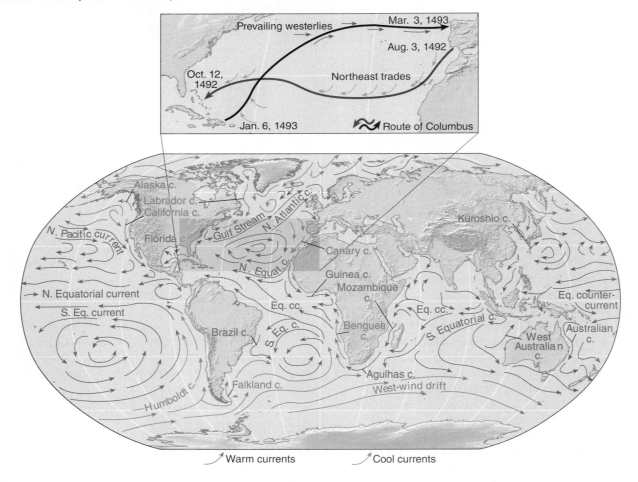

The ocean conveyor belt • Figure 12.5

Vertical motions and differences in temperature, salinity, and density drive the conveyor belt movement of the global thermohaline circulation. It takes about 1000 years for water to complete one circuit of this global flow pattern.

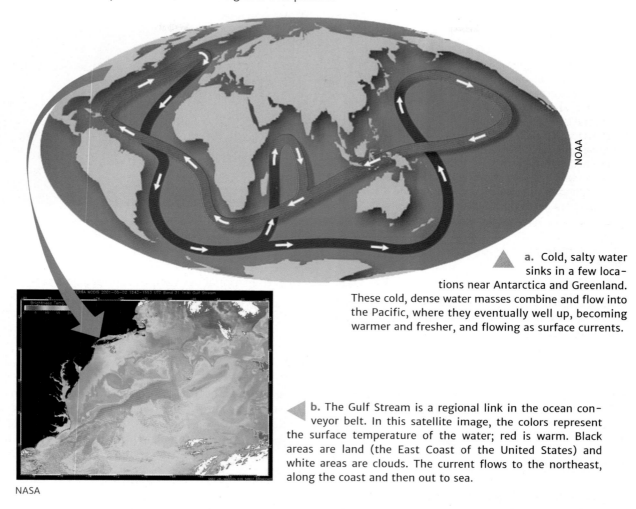

a. Cold, salty water sinks in a few locations near Antarctica and Greenland. These cold, dense water masses combine and flow into the Pacific, where they eventually well up, becoming warmer and fresher, and flowing as surface currents.

b. The Gulf Stream is a regional link in the ocean conveyor belt. In this satellite image, the colors represent the surface temperature of the water; red is warm. Black areas are land (the East Coast of the United States) and white areas are clouds. The current flows to the northeast, along the coast and then out to sea.

water is therefore very dense, and it sinks to form a deep mass of cold, dense water called **North Atlantic Deep Water (NADW)**.

The mass of cold, salty, dense water from the North Atlantic moves slowly along the bottom of the ocean. In the South Atlantic it mixes with another mass of cold, salty, dense water, known as **Antarctic Bottom Water (AABW)**. The current of combined water masses flows across the seafloor and northward into the Pacific. In the Pacific Ocean to the west of South America the cold water wells up, becoming shallower and warmer.

The shallower, warmer currents eventually flow through the Indian Ocean, back into the Atlantic, and toward the north, where they are largely responsible for maintaining a mild climate in Europe. The warm **Gulf Stream** current is part of this northward flow. By the time the water reaches the North Atlantic, it begins to cool and sink, creating another downwelling mass of NADW. Because of its continuous, repetitive nature, this circuit has been called "the great ocean conveyor belt." It is also referred to as the **global overturning circulation**. It takes about 1000 years for water to complete the circuit, but this is the main mechanism whereby the deepest ocean water is connected to the shallow ocean and the atmosphere. Finding out more about the zones and currents of the ocean is one of the main goals of the *Okeanos Explorer*, a research vessel operated by the National Oceanographic and Atmospheric Administration (NOAA); see *Where Geologists Click* to learn more about this and other NOAA programs.

NOAA Ocean Explorer

The National Oceanic and Atmospheric Administration is an authoritative source for all sorts of information about the ocean and atmosphere, as well as fisheries, coastal zones, weather, and climate. One interesting thing you can learn about on their website is the *Okeanos Explorer*, a U.S. Navy vessel that has been converted and deployed for the sole purpose of scientific exploration and discovery to advance our understanding of the ocean.

Courtesy NOAA

OCEAN EXPLORER

Home | Explorations | Okeanos Explorer | Education | Technology | History | Multimedia | Fun & Facts | Office Home

The ROV team aboard the *R/V Walton Smith* collaborates with the mission scientists collecting video and still images that will be used to chacterize habitat and provide clues to population connectivity in the study area.

STOP CONCEPT CHECK

1. **What** are two possible origins of Earth's water?
2. **What** are two processes that add salts to, and two processes that remove salts from, seawater?
3. **What** are the name and physical characteristics of the temperature zone in the ocean that is transitional between the surface and deep zones?
4. **How** do surface currents differ from deep ocean currents?

WHERE OCEAN MEETS LAND

Learning Objectives

1. **Explain** how tides, plate tectonics, and climatic change can affect sea levels.
2. **Describe** how waves and longshore currents transport sediment.
3. **Identify** common types of shorelines, coastal landforms, and reefs.

The majority of the world population lives within 100 kilometers of a coastline. This reflects our dependence on the ocean, especially the rich resources in coastal zones. However, the concentration of large numbers of people in coastal areas means that the coastal environment must absorb the impacts of a wide range of human activities. It also means that human vulnerability to hazards can be particularly high in coastal zones; for example, infrequent events such as large storms can cause major loss of life and damage to property.

If you visit almost any coastline on two occasions one year apart, you will see changes. Sometimes the changes are small, but often they are substantial. Large sand dunes may have shifted. Sand may have built up behind barriers or may have been eroded away. Steep sections of coastline may have collapsed. Channels may have broken through from the sea to lagoons on the landward side, where there were no channels before. The energy driving these continual changes comes from storms and the waves that accompany them.

Changes in Sea Level

Water plays a powerful role in shaping coastlines. Before describing the landforms that result from the water's action, we will describe the processes themselves, which operate on very different time scales. On a very long time scale, over many thousands of years, sea level can rise or fall by hundreds of meters. On a shorter time scale—twice a day—tides produce changes in water level that can amount to several meters in certain places. On the shortest time scale, ocean waves constantly stir up the sediment along the coast, and, especially during storm season, waves batter the coastline and can produce dramatic effects.

Global Volume Changes One of the most important factors in determining the long-term position of the shoreline is the volume of the ocean. Geologists use the term **eustatic** (from the Greek for "true standing") to refer to global sea level determined by the volume of water in the ocean, as opposed to local variations that may be caused by rising or sinking land along coastlines.

Eustatic sea level is strongly tied to global climatic change. When the climate warms, water stored on continents in glaciers and ice caps melts and returns to the sea. This causes a worldwide rise in sea level. Conversely, during cold

It has been suggested that humans migrated across a "land bridge" from Asia into the western hemisphere. The green, yellow, brown, and white regions on these diagrams are above sea level.

a. About 20,000 years ago, during the most recent ice age, sea levels were about 120 meters lower than they are today. This caused the emergence of the land bridge between Asia and North America.

b. Sea level has risen since the melting of glaciers after the last ice age ended. Today Asia and America are separated by an 85-kilometer-wide stretch of sea called the Bering Strait.

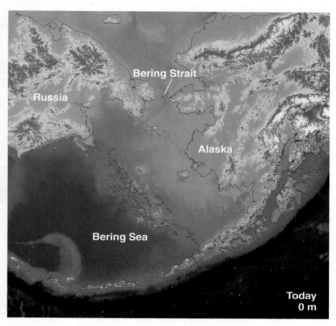

Manley, W.F., 2002, Postglacial Flooding of the Bering Land Bridge: A Geospatial Animation: INSTAAR, University of Colorado, v1, http://instaar.colorado.edu/QGISL/bering_land_bridge

climatic periods, glaciers and ice caps expand, and water is withdrawn from the ocean and stored on land (in the form of ice); this results in a drop in sea level. Currently, global warming is suspected to be responsible for a worldwide rise in sea level of approximately 2.4 millimeters/year. Such a trend is nearly imperceptible on the scale of a human lifetime, but over geological time it may account for great change in the position of a shoreline (**Figure 12.6**).

Tides   From a human perspective, a very obvious change in sea level occurs due to the effect of **tides**. The gravi-

> **tides** A regular, daily cycle of rising and falling sea level that results from the gravitational action of the Moon, the Sun, and Earth.

tational attraction of the Moon makes ocean water bulge toward the Moon on the side of Earth nearest the Moon. There is also a bulge away from the Moon on the opposite side, whose origin is the inertial force (the same force that pulls the string of a yo-yo tight if you swing it around your finger). The Sun also affects the tides, but because it is so much farther away than the Moon, its tide-producing force is only about half as strong.

To visualize how tides work, consider the tidal bulges oriented with their maximum height lying along a line running through the center of Earth and the center of the Moon.

Whereas Earth rotates around its axis, the tidal bulges remain stationary, opposite the Moon. Thus, any given coastline will move eastward through both tidal bulges each day. Every time a landmass encounters a tidal bulge, the water level along the coast rises. As Earth rotates, the coast passes through the highest point of the tidal bulge, causing a high tide. Then the water level begins to fall until it passes through the lowest point, causing a low tide.

Along most coastlines, two high tides and two low tides are observed each day. However, the shape of a coastline can greatly influence the tidal **runup height**, the highest elevation reached by the incoming water. Narrow openings into bays, rivers, estuaries, and straits can amplify normal tidal fluctuations. At Minas Basin in the Bay of Fundy in Nova Scotia, a **tidal range** (the difference between high and low tide) of up to 16 meters has been reported (see *What a Geologist Sees*). The bay is very long and narrow, which causes the incoming tide to rush in, forming a steep-fronted wall of water called a **tidal bore** that can move faster than a person in average physical condition can run.

Earth–Moon–Sun tidal interactions affect the solid body of Earth as well, causing periodic inward and outward fluctuations. This is one reason why the shape of Earth is closer to an oblate ellipsoid or spheroid than it is to a true sphere. These solid-body tides are one source of heating inside the planet (see *Remember This!*). They gradually slow Earth's

What a Geologist Sees

What Causes Tides?

The tidal range in the Bay of Fundy in eastern Canada is the largest in the world (**Figure a**). These fishing boats are grounded at low tide. At high tide, the water will rise to the level where the posts in the photograph change color.

A geologist visiting the Bay of Fundy would realize that the Moon's gravitational attraction and the inertia of the rotating Earth−Moon system combine to produce this tidal variation. As shown in this sketch (**Figure b**), the two forces stretch Earth's ocean water into an oblong shape, with bulges directed toward and away from the Moon. The bulges remain essentially stationary while Earth rotates through them, creating two high tides and two low tides per day.

High-tide water level

Richard Nowitz/NG Image Collection

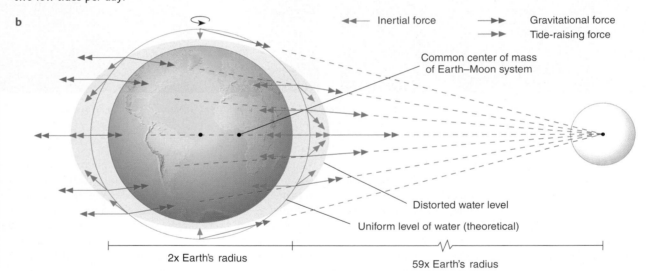

Inertial force   Gravitational force
Tide-raising force

Common center of mass of Earth–Moon system

Distorted water level

Uniform level of water (theoretical)

2x Earth's radius   59x Earth's radius

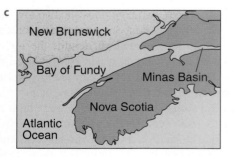

New Brunswick

Bay of Fundy   Minas Basin

Nova Scotia

Atlantic Ocean

But that's not the whole story. A geologist would know that local topography strongly affects both the timing and size of the tides. The tides in the Bay of Fundy are so high because the frequency of the tides closely matches the natural period of oscillation of water in the long, thin bay, especially in Minas Bay where the highest tides occur (**Figure c**). It is like sloshing the water in a bathtub: If you move back and forth at just the right frequency, the water will spill over the sides.

THINK CRITICALLY

Does Earth cause tides on the Moon?

rotation because the tidal bulge tends to get ahead of the Moon. This means that the Moon pulls slightly backward on it. The effect is very small but significant on a geological time scale. In the early Phanerozoic Eon, the day was about 22 hours long, and there were nearly 400 days in a year.

REMEMBER THIS! Can you recall the other sources for Earth's internal heat? You can remind yourself by looking back again at *The Age of Earth* in Chapter 3.

A **rogue wave** is a wave that is unusually high compared to its surroundings.

a. This rogue wave off the shore of South Carolina was about 18 meters high— about as tall as a six-story building.

NOAA

b. On this radar image of the sea surface, in the center of the white bar you can see a dark trough that goes down more than 10 meters below sea level, adjacent to a bright crest that reaches more than 15 meters above sea level. A ship caught in the trough would have seen a wall of water more than 25 meters high. The cross section (inset) shows that this rogue wave was quite localized; waves all around it are less than 10 meters from trough to crest.

Aug 20, 1996

Overhead view of ocean surface (satellite radar)

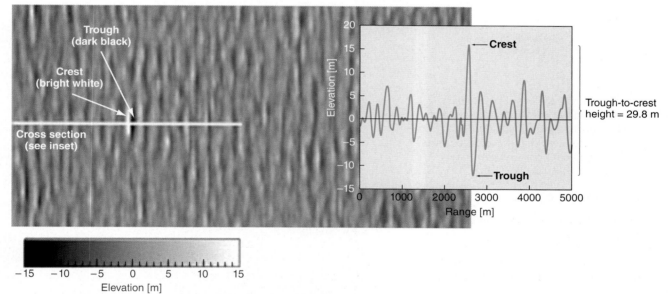

Waves

Like surface ocean currents, ocean waves receive energy from wind. The size of a wave depends on how fast, how far, and how long the wind blows across the water surface. A gentle breeze blowing across a bay may ripple the water or form low waves less than 1 meter high. In contrast, storm waves whipped up by intense winds over several days may tower over ships unfortunate enough to be caught in them (**Figure 12.7**). Waves generated by a storm can travel great distances. For example, surfers in California keep an eye on the weather report for storms far away in the tropical Pacific because they know that a good storm creates a "swell" that will arrive at their shores several days later.

Wave Action along Coastlines As a wave approaches the shore, it undergoes a rapid transformation. In deep water, a buoy or a parcel of water makes circular loops as the waves pass by. But in shallower water, the circular loops become flatter (**Figure 12.8a**). Where water depth becomes less than half a wavelength (the crest-to-crest length of the wave), the increasingly shallow seafloor interferes with wave motion and distorts the wave's shape. The wave height increases, and the wavelength decreases. Now the front of the wave is in shallower water and is also steeper than the rear. Eventually, the front becomes too steep to support the advancing wave. As the rear part continues to move forward, the wave collapses, or breaks—hence the term **breakers**, referring to a line of breaking waves (**Figure 12.8b**).

When a wave breaks, the motion of the water instantly becomes turbulent, like that of a swift river. **Surf** is found in the **surf zone** between the line of breakers and the shore. Each wave finally dashes against the rocks or rushes up a sloping

> **surf** The "broken," turbulent water found between a line of breakers and the shore.

Waves change form as they travel from deeper to shallower water.

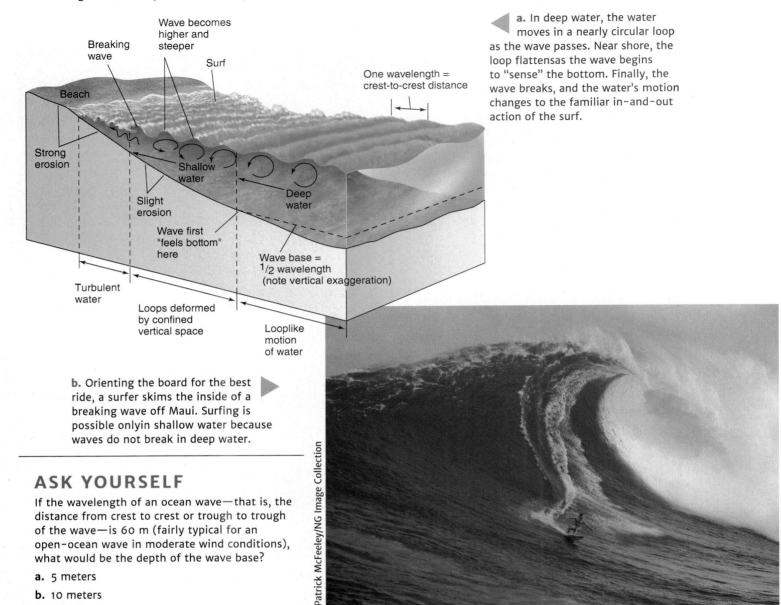

a. In deep water, the water moves in a nearly circular loop as the wave passes. Near shore, the loop flattens as the wave begins to "sense" the bottom. Finally, the wave breaks, and the water's motion changes to the familiar in-and-out action of the surf.

b. Orienting the board for the best ride, a surfer skims the inside of a breaking wave off Maui. Surfing is possible only in shallow water because waves do not break in deep water.

Patrick McFeeley/NG Image Collection

ASK YOURSELF

If the wavelength of an ocean wave—that is, the distance from crest to crest or trough to trough of the wave—is 60 m (fairly typical for an open-ocean wave in moderate wind conditions), what would be the depth of the wave base?

a. 5 meters

b. 10 meters

c. 20 meters

d. 30 meters

e. 60 meters

beach until its energy is expended; then the water flows back toward the open sea. Water that has piled up against the shore returns seaward in an irregular and complex way, partly as a broad sheet along the bottom and partly in localized narrow channels known as **rip currents** that can sweep unwary swimmers out to sea. Experienced swimmers know that a rip current is not wide; by swimming sideways to the current, rather than against it, they can get out of trouble.

A wave approaching a coast generally does not encounter the bottom simultaneously all along its length. When a segment of a wave touches the seafloor, that part of the wave slows down. Gradually the trend of a wave becomes realigned to parallel the contours of the seafloor. This process, **refraction**, causes a series of waves approaching a shoreline at an angle to change their direction of movement (see *Remember This!*).

REMEMBER THIS! The word *refraction*, used in the context of water waves, means "bending"—just as it does in the context of seismic-wave refraction or light-wave refraction. You can review this and other wave-related terminology by looking back at Chapter 5, *Studying Earth's Interior*.

Erosion and Transport of Sediment by Waves

Surf is a powerful erosive force because it possesses most of the original energy of the waves that created it. Wave erosion takes place not only at sea level but also below sea level and—especially during storms—above sea level. In the surf zone, rock particles are worn down, becoming smoother, rounder, and smaller. Through continuous rubbing and grinding with these particles, the surf scours and deepens the bottom. Onshore, the surf acts like a saw cutting horizontally into the land. Its energy is eventually consumed in turbulence, in friction at the bottom, and in the movement of sediment thrown up from the bottom.

Two processes, one on land and one underwater, transport the sediment: the longshore current and beach drift.

Most waves reach the shore at an oblique angle (**Figure 12.9a**). Part of the force of an incoming wave is oriented perpendicular to the shore; this produces the crashing surf. Another component of the wave motion is oriented parallel to the shore. The parallel component sets up a **longshore current**. While surf erodes sediment at the shore, the longshore current moves the sediment longitudinally in the surf zone.

> **longshore current** A current within the surf zone that flows parallel to the coast.

Meanwhile, on the exposed beach, incoming waves produce an irregular pattern of water movement along the shore. Because waves generally strike the beach at an angle, the **swash** (uprushing water) of each wave travels obliquely up the beach before gravity pulls the water down (**Figure 12.9b**). This zigzag movement of water carries sand and pebbles first up and then down the beach slope.

Longshore current and beach drift • Figure 12.9

Longshore currents transport sediment parallel to the shoreline.

a. A longshore current is generated as waves approach a beach at an oblique angle. Such a current can transport considerable amounts of sediment along a coast.

b. Surf swashes obliquely onto a Brazilian beach and forms a series of arc-shaped cusps. A grain of sand moves along a zigzag path, as successive waves wash up on the shore at an angle and retreat back downslope in a direction nearly perpendicular to the shoreline.

Carl & Ann Purcell/© Corbis

Successive movements of this type gradually transport sediment along the shore, causing **beach drift**. The greater the angle of waves to the shore, the greater the rate of drift. Marked pebbles have been observed to drift along a beach at a rate of more than 800 meters per day.

The processes of erosion and deposition along a coast are anything but steady. A single winter storm can erode cliffs or beaches more than a full year's worth of ordinary surf. The balance between erosion and deposition can change with the seasons. Along parts of the Pacific Coast of North America, winter storm surf tends to carry away fine sediment and the beach becomes narrow and steep. In calm summer weather, fine sediment drifts in and the beach assumes a gentler profile.

Human actions also can shift the balance between erosion and deposition, as you learned in the case of the Chandeleur Islands. When a seawall interrupts the flow of sediment along the coastline, for example, the beach builds up on one side of the seawall but erodes away on the other side because the longshore current no longer

brings in enough material to replenish the eroded sediment (**Figure 12.10**).

Shorelines and Coastal Landforms

The end result of the constant interplay between erosional and depositional forces along coastlines is a wide variety of shorelines and coastal landforms. Their forms depend on the geological processes at work, the susceptibility to erosion of coastal rock, and the length of time these processes have been operating. Eustatic changes in sea level can also influence the development of coastal features. Many coastal landforms show clear signs of different sea levels at different times in the past (**Figure 12.11**).

Despite the variability of coasts and shorelines, three basic types are most common: the rocky (cliffed) coast, the lowland beach and barrier island coast, and the coral reef. Each one has a particular set of erosional and depositional landforms.

Rocky Coasts   The most common type of coast, comprising about 80% of ocean coasts worldwide, is a rocky, or cliffed, coast. When a cliffed coast is seen in profile,

Engineering the shoreline • Figure 12.10

In Ocean City, Maryland (right), the construction of a jetty has caused sand to accumulate and make the beach wider. Just south of Ocean City, Assateague Island in Virginia (left) has been deprived of the sand that the longshore current would have deposited on its shore. Thus the beach on Assateague is retreating inland.

Ocean City

Direction of longshore current

Jetty

Sand accumulates on the up-current side of the jetty

James P. Blair/NG Image Collection

The coast of New Zealand at Tongue Point has two terrace-like landforms called **benches**. They were elevated above sea level by two stages of tectonic uplift. You can see two other common features of rocky coasts: headlands that jut out into the sea and small "pocket" beaches that form in the bays between the headlands.

G.R. Roberts/The Natural Sciences Image Library

wave-cut cliff   A coastal cliff cut by wave action at the base of a rocky coast.

the usual elements are a vertical or overhanging **wave-cut cliff** and a horizontal wave-cut bench at its base, both products of erosion. As the upper part of the cliff is undermined, it collapses, and the resulting debris is redistributed by waves. An undercut cliff that has not yet collapsed may have a well-developed notch at its base. The bench may be covered by sand, or the bedrock may be exposed, especially at low tide.

If the coast has been uplifted by tectonics, a wave-cut bench and its sediment cover can be lifted up out of the water and become a marine terrace. In some locations, you can see two or more terraces ascending out of the ocean like a giant staircase (see Figure 12.11).

The rocky character of cliffed coasts may be misleading to people looking for a dramatic home site. They see a rocky cliff as a sign of permanence and stability, whereas in fact quite the reverse is the case. Shorelines with cliffs are susceptible to frequent landslides and rock falls as erosion eats away at the base of a cliff. Roads, buildings, and other structures built too close to such cliffs can be damaged or destroyed when sliding occurs (**Figure 12.12**).

Beaches and Barrier Islands Beaches are a striking feature of many coasts. Most people think of a beach

as the sand surface above the water along a shore. Actually, a **beach** also includes sediment in the surf zone, which is underwater and therefore continually in motion. At low tide, when a large part of a beach is exposed, onshore winds may blow beach sand inland to form belts of coastal dunes.

beach   Wave-washed sediment along a coast.

A landform commonly associated with beaches is the **barrier island** (**Figure 12.13**). Sand dunes are typically the highest topographical points on a barrier island. Barrier islands are found along most lowland coasts; the Atlantic and Gulf coasts of the United States consist mainly of a series of barrier beaches ranging from 15 to 30 kilometers in length and 1.5 to 5 kilometers in width, located 3 to 30 kilometers offshore. Examples include Coney Island, New York, the Outer Banks of North Carolina, and the Chandeleur Islands in Louisiana.

barrier island   A long, narrow, sandy island lying offshore and parallel to a low-land coast.

Barrier islands are topographically low, so they are very susceptible to flooding. During a major storm, surf washes across the low places and erodes them, cutting **tidal inlets** that may remain open permanently. At such times, fine sediment is washed between the barrier island and the mainland. Because of this deposition and erosion of sediment, the length and shape of barrier islands are always changing.

Waves crashing upon a shoreline can undercut the cliff.

Millionaire's folly

Cliff collapses when undercut rock can no longer support it

Undercutting by wave action

a. Waves have undercut the base of this cliff, leading to collapse of the slope beneath the building.

Area of collapse

Richard Reid/NG Image Collection

b. Houses dangle on the edge of a cliff in Pacifica, California, after winter storms caused a section of cliff to collapse. Note the rubble on the beach and the scar on the cliff where the debris slide occurred.

Unfortunately, the ever-changing nature of barrier island coasts conflicts with our desire to erect permanent buildings on them. Property owners often protect their properties with artificial seawalls, which, though they may serve as a local fix, only hasten the erosion or deposition processes elsewhere on the coast.

Barrier island beaches typically exhibit depositional landforms such as **spits** (elongated ridges of sand or gravel that project from land into the open water of an embayment along the coast), **tombolos** (spit-like ridges of sand and gravel that join an island to the mainland), and **bay barriers**, which may completely close off the mouth of a small bay. A well-known example of a large, complex spit is Cape Cod, Massachusetts.

The elongated bay lying inshore from a barrier island or other low, enclosing strip of land is called a **lagoon** (**Figure 12.13c**). Lagoons are commonly fed by **estuaries**, the wide, fan-shaped mouths of rivers in the tidal zone where fresh water and salt water meet. Lagoons and estuaries are important habitats for a wide variety of plants and animals. They also play an important role in the protection of mainland shorelines because they serve as buffers against storm waves. Human activities can also adversely affect these sensitive environments (see the *Case Study*).

Coral Reefs Many of the world's tropical coastlines consist of limestone **reefs** built by vast colonies of organisms, principally corals, which secrete calcium carbonate (the main chemical constituent of limestone) as their skeletal material. Reefs are built up very slowly over thousands of years. Each of the tiny coral animals deposits a protective layer of calcium carbonate; over time the layers build up, forming a complex reef structure.

> **reef** A hard structure on a shallow ocean floor, usually but not always built by coral.

There are three main types of coral reef (**Figure 12.14**). **Fringing reefs** form coastlines that closely border the adjacent land. **Barrier reefs** are separated from the land by a lagoon. The Great Barrier Reef off Queensland, Australia, is a famous example of a major barrier reef. Sometimes the land against which the reef originally formed erodes or subsides to the point where it no longer emerges above sea level. This often happens when midocean volcanoes with fringing reefs become dormant or extinct. The result can be an **atoll**, the third main type of reef.

Reefs are highly productive ecosystems that support a diversity of marine life forms (see **Figure 12.14d**). They also perform an important role in the recycling of nutrients in shallow coastal environments. They provide physical barriers that

Barrier islands, spits, and lagoons • Figure 12.13

Barrier islands and spits are common depositional landforms along shorelines.

a. This aerial view of the Outer Banks in North Carolina shows a series of barrier islands. The action of wind and waves constantly pushes the sediment toward the mainland (top left in this photo).

Cotton Coulson/NG Image Collection

David Alan Harvey/NG Image Collection

b. Salishan Spit in Oregon, shown here, is attached to the mainland at one end, while the other end terminates at a tidal inlet.

c. Spits and barrier islands often create a sheltered lagoon on the landward side. This lagoon is on Cayo Costa Island in Florida.

Raymond Gehman/NG Image Collection

spit

tidal inlet

The Chandeleurs and the *Deepwater Horizon* Oil Spill

The Chandeleur Islands can't win. After decades of sediment-starvation from engineering of the Mississippi River, and massive storm-surge damage by Hurricane Katrina in 2005, the barrier islands were hit again on April 20, 2010, when the BP *Deepwater Horizon* oil rig exploded in a fiery inferno. The damaged well released almost 5 million barrels (about 780 million liters) of crude oil into the Gulf of Mexico.

It took months to stop the leaking oil, which caused extensive damage to coastal and marine plants, wildlife, habitat, and fishing and tourism. The cleanup effort, deploying more than 28,000 people, involved controlled burn-offs; skimming and suctioning of oil from the surface; chemical dispersants; floating containment booms; and sand barriers along shorelines.

What was the ultimate fate of those 5 million barrels of oil? A team of scientists has been trying to answer this question. Some oil washed up on nearby shores, including the Chandeleur Islands (**Figures a** and **b**). Some was collected or dispersed by various cleanup methods. A large portion evaporated or sank to the bottom of the Gulf, where its fate remains uncertain. The pie chart (**Figure c**) shows an early estimate of the fate of the oil as of August 2010, by the NOAA Office of Response and Recovery for the *Deepwater Horizon*/BP Oil Spill.

Crude oil varies widely in composition, with thousands of hydrocarbon compounds, many toxic. Spilled oil behaves differently, depending on weather, wave, and wind action, depth and temperature of the water, nature of the shoreline, and other factors. Add a few technical complexities such as the great depth of the well head in this case, throw in the urgency associated with fragile ecosystems, and you get an idea of how challenging large oil spills can be.

a

Mark Ralston/AFP/Getty Images, Inc.

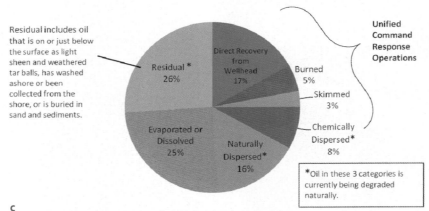

b

Courtesy NOAA

Deepwater Horizon Oil Budget

Based on estimated release of 4.9m barrels of oil

Residual includes oil that is on or just below the surface as light sheen and weathered tar balls, has washed ashore or been collected from the shore, or is buried in sand and sediments.

Residual * 26%

Direct Recovery from Wellhead 17%

Burned 5%

Skimmed 3%

Chemically Dispersed* 8%

Evaporated or Dissolved 25%

Naturally Dispersed* 16%

Unified Command Response Operations

*Oil in these 3 categories is currently being degraded naturally.

c

THINK CRITICALLY

What kinds of problems do you think might occur with an oil spill or leak in very deep water, as compared to a shallow-water spill? What about a cold-water spill versus a warm-water spill?

Coral reefs · Figure 12.14 _____

Coral reefs are highly productive ecosystems.

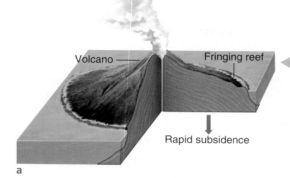

a. A fringing reef forms against the shores of an active volcanic island.

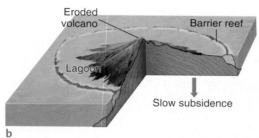

b. As the volcano becomes dormant or extinct, it begins to erode and subside. The reef is now separated from the coastal land by a lagoon, becoming a barrier reef.

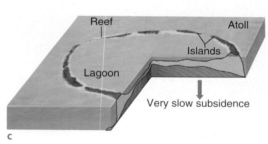

Digital Vision/Getty Images, Inc.

c. Once the land has eroded and subsided below sea level, an atoll remains.

d. Reef-building corals provide complex habitat choices and typically host an abundant diversity of life.

dissipate the force of waves, protecting the ports, lagoons, and beaches that lie behind them, and are an important aesthetic and economic resource.

Corals require shallow, clear water in which the temperature remains above 18°C but does not exceed 30°C. Coral reefs therefore are formed only at or close to sea level and are characteristic of warm, low latitudes (although there are other reef-building organisms that can survive in colder waters). Corals also favor places where there is deep-sea upwelling that provides abundant nutrients, normal salinity—not too salty, not too fresh—and an absence of sediment being deposited from large streams.

In recent years a pervasive problem has been **coral bleaching**. The causes of coral decline are numerous and not completely understood. Because of their very specific requirements, coral reefs are highly susceptible to damage. For example, changes in suspended sediment in the water as a result of coastal erosion or storm wave action can change the light level and clog coral polyps. Corals can be killed by natural causes, such as hurricanes, but the reef usually recovers from them over the long term. Anthropogenic injuries, such as scarring from boats that run aground on the reef, are much harder for coral to recover from. Recently, scientists have suspected that the absorption of atmospheric carbon dioxide by the ocean is changing the composition—mainly the acidity—of ocean water. This may be having a negative impact on corals, which are showing signs of damage in many parts of the world ocean. The decline of coral health in the Florida Keys is discussed in **Amazing Places**.

The Florida Keys Reef

The world's third-longest coral barrier reef, and the only living coral reef in the continental United States, runs parallel to the Florida Keys, just offshore, for 320 kilometers. Corals have skeletons that are made of calcium carbonate. They are limestone right from the start and gradually add to the landmass of the continent.

a. In the Florida Keys Reef, you can find a variety of corals, such as the fire coral and the mustard hill coral in the foreground, and the brain coral in the background.

b. When the water gets too warm, coral polyps expel the symbiotic algae that give them their bright colors. Bleached coral is not necessarily dead, but will soon die without its algae. The white parts of the staghorn coral in this photo are bleached; the brown parts are still healthy.

Stephen Frink/Alamy

Thomas K. Gibson/Florida Keys National Marine Sanctuary

Courtesy Phillip Dustan, College of Charleston

c. Here you can see how part of Carysfort Reef, part of the Florida Keys reef system, progressed from a healthy state in 1975 to a sick one in 1985, and by 1995 it was almost completely dead. By 2000, the reef had lost 90% of its original coral cover.

THINK CRITICALLY

Which human activities do you think could cause damage to corals, given their specific requirements for water temperature and light levels?

STOP CONCEPT CHECK

1. **Why** are the heights of the tides not the same in every location?

2. **How** do waves in deep water behave differently from waves in shallow water?

3. **Why** do jetties and seawalls on one part of a beach often have adverse effects on other parts?

THE ATMOSPHERE

Learning Objectives

1. **List** the main chemical constituents of Earth's atmosphere.

2. **Describe** the main characteristics of the four layers of Earth's atmosphere.

3. **Explain** how the Sun's heat and Earth's rotation affect the movement of air.

Atmosphere is the generic term for a gaseous layer that surrounds a planet or other celestial body. When Earth was formed some 4.56 billion years ago, it was surrounded by an envelope of gaseous components. This **primary atmosphere** was lost early in Earth's history—stripped away by the intense solar wind associated with the young Sun. Earth evolved a new, **secondary atmosphere** through volcanic outgassing of some of the volatile constituents encased in its interior, with some additional water and other volatile material contributed by incoming comets (**Figure 12.15**).

> **atmosphere** The envelope of gases that surrounds a planet.

The atmosphere and hydrosphere have evolved chemically over Earth's history, in close partnership with the biosphere and the geosphere. The early atmosphere had a very different composition and was not "breathable" in the sense that we know it today. The advent of a breathable atmosphere with available oxygen took hundreds of millions of years and depended on the activity of photosynthetic organisms such as algae. You will learn more about these chemical changes and about how the atmosphere and hydrosphere were influenced by the origin and evolution of life in Chapter 15.

Composition of Earth's Atmosphere

Many planets and even some moons have atmospheres, but **air** is the gaseous envelope that surrounds one planet in particular: Earth (see Figure 12.15).

> **air** The mixture of 78% nitrogen, 21% oxygen, and trace amounts of other gases, found in Earth's atmosphere.

Air is an invisible, normally odorless mixture of gases and suspended particles. Two components of air are highly variable in concentration: aerosols and water vapor. **Aerosols** are liquid droplets or solid particles that are so small that they remain suspended in the air. Water droplets in fogs are liquid aerosols. Some examples of solid aerosols are tiny ice crystals, smoke particles from fires, and sea-salt crystals from ocean spray.

Water is always present in the air, but in varying amounts expressed by the **humidity** of the air. On a hot, humid day in the tropics, as much as 4% of the air by volume may be water vapor. On a crisp, cold day, less than 0.3% may be water vapor. Note that 100% **relative humidity**, a term that you might hear in a weather report, does not mean the air is 100% water vapor! It simply means that the air contains as much water vapor as it can carry at that particular temperature. The temperature at which the relative humidity is 100% is called the **dew point**.

Because the water vapor and aerosol contents of air vary so widely, the relative amounts of the remaining gases are reported as if the air were entirely lacking in water vapor and aerosols. When these two components are ignored, the relative proportions of the remaining gases in the air—termed **dry air**—are essentially constant. As shown in **Figure 12.16**, three gases—nitrogen (78%), oxygen (21%), and argon (0.93%)—make up 99.96% of dry air by volume. The remaining gases (carbon dioxide, 0.035%; neon, 0.0018%; and six others) are present in very small quantities. However, some of these minor gases are profoundly important for life on Earth because they absorb certain wavelengths of sunlight. They act both as a warming blanket and as a shield against deadly ultraviolet radiation.

Oxygen and carbon dioxide in the atmosphere are constantly being removed or replenished by plants and animals, through chemical processes such as the weathering of rock and formation of soil. Gases also cycle from the atmosphere to the ocean and back again, passing through the ocean surface. Further recycling of volatile constituents occurs through geological processes such as volcanism and subduction, which link the atmosphere and hydrosphere to the geosphere. If anything happens to affect the rates of any of these processes, the chemical makeup of the atmosphere will change.

Layers in the Atmosphere

The characteristics of the atmosphere are not constant throughout its depth. When sunlight hits the top of the atmosphere, about 30% of it is reflected back into space, but the remaining 70% is absorbed by the atmosphere itself and by the ocean, land, and biosphere. The absorbed solar energy warms Earth's surface, which in turn warms the bottom portion of the atmosphere. Eventually, all of this energy is re-emitted in the form of long-wavelength infrared radiation, back to outer space. However, as the sunlight passes through the atmosphere, water vapor and some of the minor gases absorb certain wavelengths of solar radiation, which raises the temperature of the air.

The atmosphere that we have today is a secondary atmosphere, and it has evolved chemically over the course of Earth's history.

Where did the air come from?
Earth's **primary atmosphere** was lost—blown away by a strong solar wind. Volcanic emissions brought to the surface volatile constituents that had been trapped inside the planet. Eventually, the planet cooled sufficiently that it was able to retain this envelope of gases, the **secondary atmosphere.**

Breathable air
It took billions of years before the atmosphere contained enough "free" oxygen to be "breathable" as we now know it. This change involved the removal of carbon and the production of oxygen, both of which were dependent on life. Mats of photosynthetic cyanobacteria, like the one shown here, were key players in the production of a breathable atmosphere. A wolf spider is crawling across the mat.

Richard Bizley/Photo Researchers, Inc.

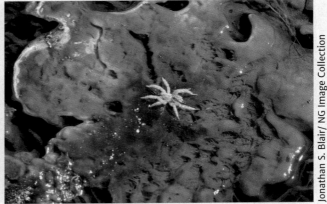

Jonathan S. Blair/ NG Image Collection

A portrait of Earth's atmosphere
This spectacular photograph, from the International Space Station over the Pacific Ocean in 2003, shows the troposphere, the bottom layer of the atmosphere, as a thin blue band above the horizon. Anvil-shaped clouds in the foreground are thunderstorms. Their shape is caused by warm air in the clouds that have reached the top of the troposphere.

Courtesy NASA

THINK CRITICALLY

If the atmosphere changed chemically over the course of Earth's history, would this also have caused changes in the hydrosphere, particularly the ocean?

What air is made of • Figure 12.16

Air contains two substances whose concentration varies from place to place and time to time: water vapor and aerosols. The rest of the atmosphere consists primarily of nitrogen and oxygen, with small amounts of other gases.

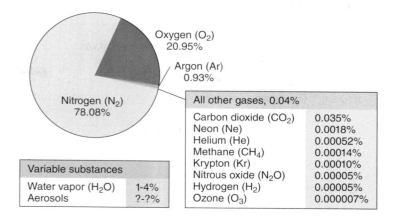

All other gases, 0.04%	
Carbon dioxide (CO$_2$)	0.035%
Neon (Ne)	0.0018%
Helium (He)	0.00052%
Methane (CH$_4$)	0.00014%
Krypton (Kr)	0.00010%
Nitrous oxide (N$_2$O)	0.00005%
Hydrogen (H$_2$)	0.00005%
Ozone (O$_3$)	0.000007%

Variable substances	
Water vapor (H$_2$O)	1-4%
Aerosols	?-?%

Scientists have identified four major atmospheric layers with distinct temperature profiles (**Figure 12.17**). In the lowest level, temperature drops rapidly with increasing altitude because the atmosphere is warmed from below, by Earth's surface. Several reversals in the temperature profile occur at higher altitudes, defining the **pauses** that separate each layer from the next. The air in the outermost layer is so tenuous that this zone is defined by rocket scientists (though not by geologists) to be part of "space." NASA awards a space-flight badge to anybody who flies above 80 kilometers.

Four major layers • Figure 12.17

Temperature varies with altitude in the atmosphere, defining the four major layers and the pauses that separate them.

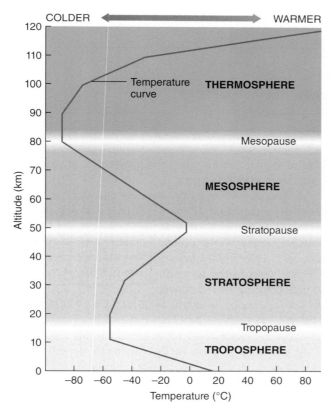

The Troposphere and Greenhouse Effect Most humans, with the exception of military pilots and astronauts, never fly outside the troposphere. The **troposphere** contains 80% of the actual mass of the atmosphere, including almost all of the water vapor and clouds. The thin blue layer of atmosphere shown in Figure 12.15c is mainly the troposphere.

troposphere The lowest layer of Earth's atmosphere, extending (variably) to about 15 kilometers in altitude.

Although very little mixing occurs between the troposphere and the stratosphere, the troposphere itself is constantly moving and thoroughly mixed by winds. The troposphere is also where almost all weather-related phenomena originate. The dynamic state of the troposphere arises because it is heated from below, as mentioned previously. Warm air rises, so the air at the bottom of the troposphere, constantly supplied by heat from the surface, is always in motion.

The troposphere contains most of the heat-absorbing gases (called **radiatively active gases**, or **greenhouse gases**) that play a role in warming Earth's surface. The most important greenhouse gas is water vapor. Another very important greenhouse gas is carbon dioxide, and yet another is methane, the main constituent of natural gas. Greenhouse gases intercept and absorb some of the outgoing infrared terrestrial radiation and prevent it from escaping, sort of like the glass of a greenhouse does (**Figure 12.18**); therefore, this natural atmospheric process is called the **greenhouse effect**. Without the greenhouse effect, the surface of Earth would be a cold and inhospitable place. However, it is a matter of serious concern that the concentration of greenhouse gases in

greenhouse effect The absorption of long-wavelength (infrared) energy by radiatively active gases in the atmosphere, causing heat to be retained near Earth's surface.

the atmosphere is steadily increasing as a result of human industrial activity. We will explore this phenomenon and its potential impact on the global climate system in greater detail in Chapter 14.

Process Diagram

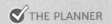

How a greenhouse works • Figure 12.18

The glass in a greenhouse (**Figure a**) works by trapping warm air underneath the glass. Radiatively active, or "greenhouse," gases in the troposphere (**Figure b**) work in a similar way, but instead of physically trapping the outgoing warmed air, the gases absorb infrared radiation, warming the air and the surface.

a.   b.

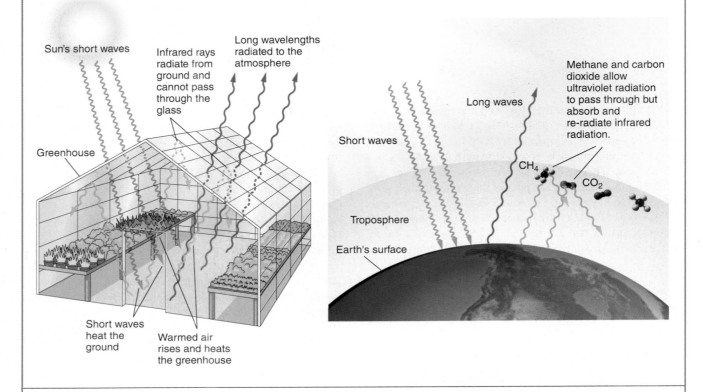

THINK CRITICALLY

Do you think Earth's greenhouse effect would be stronger over land or over the ocean?

The Stratosphere and the Ozone Layer The **stratosphere** contains 19% of the atmosphere's total mass,

> **stratosphere** The layer of Earth's atmosphere above the troposphere, extending to about a 50-kilometer altitude.

which means that the troposphere and the stratosphere combined contain 99% of the atmosphere. Beyond the stratosphere are the **mesosphere** and **thermosphere**, which together comprise only 1% of the mass of the atmosphere. The three outer layers of the atmosphere play very important roles for life on Earth despite their relatively small masses (when compared to the troposphere). Oxygen in various forms in all of these layers absorbs harmful ultraviolet rays coming from the Sun (**Figure 12.19**). The gas ozone (O_3) in the stratosphere, present in tiny but vital amounts, absorbs the most dangerous of the short-wavelength ultraviolet rays.

In recent years scientists have become very concerned about the destruction of the stratospheric **ozone layer** by chemical pollutants (**Figure 12.20**). Among these pollutants are chlorofluorocarbons (CFCs), which were formerly an ingredient in aerosol sprays

> **ozone layer** A zone in the stratosphere where ozone is concentrated.

but were banned by an international treaty in 1996. Although it is still too early to be certain, there are signs that the destruction of ozone is abating as a result of this action taken by the global community. Perhaps, in the future, this will be cited as an example of a successful environmental intervention. To see maps and animations showing changes in the ozone hole over time, see *Where Geologists Click*.

A shield against radiation • Figure 12.19 _____

Ultraviolet radiation from the Sun can be harmful or lethal; generally speaking, the shorter the wavelength, the more harmful the radiation. Fortunately, the atmosphere protects us from almost all these rays because they are absorbed by three kinds of oxygen—O, O_2, and O_3 (ozone).

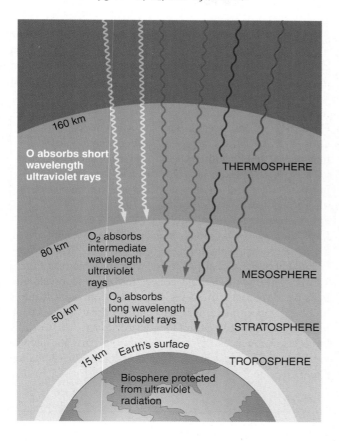

160 km

O absorbs short wavelength ultraviolet rays

THERMOSPHERE

80 km

O_2 absorbs intermediate wavelength ultraviolet rays

MESOSPHERE

O_3 absorbs long wavelength ultraviolet rays

50 km

STRATOSPHERE

15 km   Earth's surface

TROPOSPHERE

Biosphere protected from ultraviolet radiation

Movement in the Atmosphere

Two things energize the atmosphere: the Sun's heat and Earth's rotation. Because Earth is nearly spherical, the Sun does not warm every place on Earth equally. In places where the Sun is directly overhead, the incoming rays are perpendicular to the surface, and a maximum amount of heat is received per unit area (about 1366 watts per m^2). Because of the curvature of Earth's surface, at all other locations the surface is at an angle to the incoming rays; therefore, these locations receive less heat per unit of surface area. As well, Earth's axis of rotation is tilted by 23.5° with respect to the plane of its passage around the Sun. This means that the northern and southern hemispheres receive direct sunlight at different times of the year, creating the seasons.

The atmosphere and ocean act to redistribute this uneven heat, mainly through winds and ocean currents. Air in the atmosphere and water in the ocean absorb heat and move it from the equator—where the input of solar heat is greatest—toward the poles, where it is least.

The heating of Earth's surface causes convection currents in the atmosphere. The convection cells consist of

The ozone "hole" • Figure 12.20 _____

In 1985, scientists discovered that a previously unnoticed gap in the ozone layer was forming over Antarctica during the southern spring. (A smaller hole also formed over the Arctic Ocean.) The gap has grown larger in area, with more severe depletion at the center. This image shows the ozone hole (blue) in September 2006—the largest ever recorded. (Source: NASA Ozone Hole Watch.)

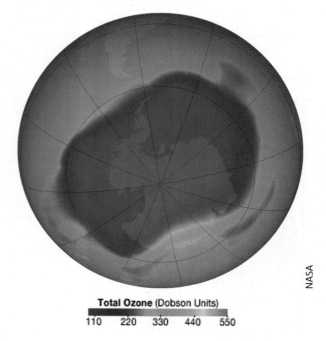

NASA

Total Ozone (Dobson Units)

110   220   330   440   550

enormous volumes of moving air, called **air masses**. Heated air near the equator expands, becomes lighter (less dense), and rises. Near the top of the troposphere, the air mass spreads outward toward the poles. As the upper air travels northward and southward toward the poles, it gradually cools, becomes heavier, and sinks. Upon reaching the surface, this cool air flows back toward the equator, warms up, and rises again, thereby completing a convective cycle (see *Remember This!*). In reality, it is not quite so simple: The global circulation organizes itself into three major sets of convection cells, which interlock like gears (**Figure 12.21**).

> **REMEMBER THIS!** Can you remember the other major context in which we discussed the process of heat transfer by convection? Review this by returning to *A Mechanism for Plate Motion*, Chapter 4. What are the differences and similarities in convection in very different examples?

When an air mass rises, it leaves a region of low **atmospheric pressure** at the surface. Atmospheric pressure, or **air pressure**, is a measure of how much of the mass of the atmosphere overlies a particular location. A low-pressure area has less atmospheric mass overlying it; a high-pressure area has more atmospheric mass overlying it. In the parts of convection cells where the air is denser and is descending from aloft, a region of high atmospheric pressure is formed

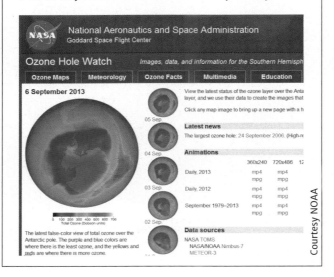
at the surface. This difference between high-pressure and low-pressure areas, caused by rising and falling air, adds to the dynamic nature of the lower atmosphere. Air always moves away from a zone of high atmospheric pressure and toward a zone of low atmospheric pressure. This **pressure gradient** is thus a force that causes air to move, creating **wind**.

wind Air in motion.

The Coriolis Force If Earth did not rotate, air currents in the atmosphere would simply flow to the north at high altitude and to the south along the surface, moving between the equator and the poles in a simple convection cell. But Earth does rotate, and its rotation complicates the convection currents in the atmosphere (as well as in the ocean). The **Coriolis force** causes anything that moves freely with respect to the rotating Earth (including both water and air) to veer off a straight path. In the northern hemisphere, the Coriolis

Coriolis force An effect due to Earth's rotation, which causes a freely moving body to veer from a straight path.

force causes a moving mass to veer toward the right, and in the southern hemisphere toward the left. The effect strongly influences the global pattern of wind systems (see Figure 12.21), causing the simple convection cells to break into belts of convecting air masses. These are consistent features of Earth's atmosphere, and they have a great influence on both day-to-day weather and long-term climate. The Coriolis force also influences the pattern of ocean currents, including both surface currents and the deep ocean thermohaline circulation.

Global atmospheric circulation • Figure 12.21

Huge convection cells transfer heat from the equator, where the input of solar energy is greatest, toward the poles, where solar input is least. Because Earth is rotating, the flow of air toward the poles and the return flow toward the equator are constantly deflected sideways.

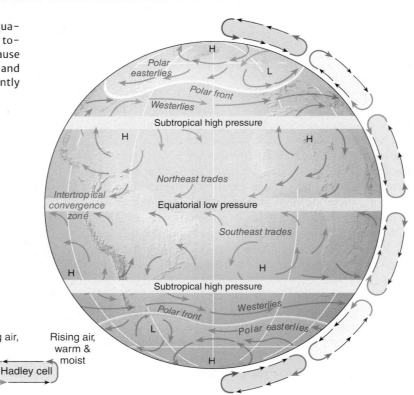

Descending air, cold & dry — Polar cell

Rising air, warm & moist — Ferrel cell

Descending air, cool & dry — Hadley cell

Rising air, warm & moist

Wind Systems The Coriolis force breaks up the flow of convective air between the equator and the poles into three major belts or cells. A large belt of circulating air lies between the equator (0°) and about 30° latitude in both the northern and southern hemispheres. Warm air rises at the equator, creating a low-pressure zone called the **intertropical convergence zone** or **ITCZ** (**Figure 12.22**). The ITCZ is characterized by cloud cover because the rising warm air cools and precipitates moisture. It rises to the top of the troposphere and begins to flow toward the poles, but it veers off course as a result of the Coriolis force. By the time the high-altitude air mass reaches latitude 30° (N and S), it has cooled and therefore sinks. The descending air flows back across Earth's surface toward the equator. As it flows, the land and sea warm the air so that it eventually becomes warm enough to rise again.

The low-latitude cells (from 0° to 30°N and 0° to 30°S) created by this circulation pattern are called **Hadley cells**. The returning surface winds of Hadley cells are deflected by the Coriolis force so that they are northeasterlies in the northern hemisphere (i.e., flowing from the northeast toward the southwest), whereas in the southern hemisphere they are southeasterlies. Flowing to the west along the equator, these are called the **trade winds**. Their consistent direction and flow, combined with their influence on surface currents in the ocean, carried trade ships across the tropical ocean at a time when winds were the chief source of navigational power (see Figure 12.4).

Another belt of convecting air cells, called the **polar cells**, lies over the polar regions. In a polar cell, frigid air flows across the surface, away from the pole and toward the equator, slowly warming as it moves. When the polar air reaches about latitude 60°N or 60°S, it has warmed sufficiently to rise convectively high into the troposphere and flow back toward the pole, where it cools and descends again, thereby completing the convection cell. Because of the Coriolis force, the cold air that flows away from the poles is deflected to the right, giving rise to a wind system called the **polar easterlies**.

Between the Hadley cells and the polar cells, a third, but less well-defined, set of convection cells called **Ferrel cells**

> **trade wind**
> Northeasterly and southeasterly equatorial wind systems.

Trade winds • Figure 12.22

Trade winds are the returning near-surface air flow in the Hadley cells, diverted by the Coriolis force so that they flow toward the west, just to the north and south of the equator.

a. The intertropical convergence zone, where the trade winds of the northern and southern hemispheres merge, is clearly visible in this satellite photograph. Warm, rising air near the equator causes ocean water to evaporate and form a nearly perpetual band of clouds.

b. The continual blowing of the east-to-west (easterly) trade winds has caused this tree on the island of Aruba, to lean far to one side.

Courtesy NASA

miralex/iStockphoto

is located in the midlatitudes, between about latitude 30° to 60°N and 30° to 6°S. In these midlatitude cells, deflection of air by the Coriolis force creates winds that blow from the west in the northern hemisphere. These winds, labeled "westerlies" on Figure 12.21, are called **jet streams**—very rapid winds that flow in narrow channels between the Ferrel cells and the Hadley cells.

The presence of the jet streams explains why weather systems in the continental United States and southern Canada generally move in from west to east. The polar easterlies, which blow from east to west between the polar cells and Ferrel cells in both hemispheres, are also jet streams. You can think of jet streams as being like "ball bearings" between the Hadley and Ferrel cells, and between the Ferrel and polar

cells. These circulation patterns will become clearer if you take some time to study Figure 12.21.

STOP CONCEPT CHECK

1. **What** are the two components of air that vary significantly in concentration from day to day and place to place?
2. **What** are the most important characteristics of the two lowest layers of Earth's atmosphere?
3. **What** are trade winds, westerlies, and polar easterlies, and what are their physical causes?

WHERE OCEAN MEETS ATMOSPHERE

Learning Objectives

1. **Describe** some of the major interactions between the atmosphere and the ocean, and how they regulate global climate.
2. **Explain** how hurricanes and other tropical cyclonic storms result from atmosphere–ocean interactions.
3. **Outline** what happens during an El Niño event.

The surface of the ocean is an interface—a boundary between the two great fluid reservoirs of this planet. Through this boundary the atmosphere and ocean are linked, acting in tandem as one great system to control both climate and weather. **Climate** is an average of weather patterns over a long period, generally on a regional or global scale. The processes we think of as **weather**—wind, rain, snow, sunshine, storms, and even floods and droughts—are temporary local variations against the more stable, longer-term background of climate.

We will look much more closely at global climate systems in Chapter 14. For now, let's consider the roles of the atmosphere and the ocean in regulating climate and driving weather systems. Then we will examine two important weather phenomena that illustrate how this interaction operates.

Ocean–Atmosphere–Climate Interactions

Much happens at the ocean's surface, the dynamic interface between atmosphere and ocean. Of course, the water is constantly in motion, broken by waves and moved by winds

and currents. People and animals use this surface for transport and for gathering resources. Materials also move from one reservoir to the other across the interface. For example, sea spray allows salt particles to move from the ocean to the atmosphere, where they are transported by wind and eventually deposited on land. Dust and particulate pollutants similarly are blown by the wind and deposited from the atmosphere onto the surface of the ocean. On a grand scale, ocean–atmosphere interactions and circulation patterns are largely responsible for controlling the great variety and range of climatic conditions on this planet.

Some of the most important material transfers that happen across the ocean–atmosphere interface occur in the vapor phase. For example, water leaves the ocean and moves to the atmosphere by evaporation—the breaking away of water molecules from the ocean's surface. Carbon dioxide (along with other gases) is absorbed by ocean water across this interface, which allows the ocean to act as a sink for excess carbon dioxide from the atmosphere. This is a crucial process in controlling the carbon content of the atmosphere, and therefore plays a crucial role in the greenhouse effect; it also has implications for the composition (mainly the acidity) of ocean water.

Heat also is exchanged across the ocean–atmosphere interface. This exchange is extremely important in the regulation of Earth's global climate system since these two fluid bodies are responsible for transporting heat from the equator to the poles. The ocean differs greatly from the land in the amount of heat it can store. When the Sun's rays strike the land, only the top meter or so is warmed. Below the top few meters, rock temperatures are controlled by the geothermal gradient; at any given depth, the temperature is roughly constant year round. In the ocean, however, mixing by currents and waves means the Sun's heat affects much more than just the surface layer.

Water has a high **heat capacity** (an indicator of a material's ability to store heat) compared to many terrestrial materials, which contributes to its temperature stability. Both the ocean and the atmosphere are also affected by water's **latent heat**—the energy that the ocean absorbs when water evaporates, and releases when water freezes. When water evaporates from the ocean, it carries some of the Sun's heat energy with it into the atmosphere, leaving the ocean water slightly cooler and the lower part of the atmosphere slightly warmer. The reverse happens when water freezes: It releases its latent heat and maintains the temperature of the water around it. These processes, together, greatly reduce the amount of variation in ocean temperatures (**Figure 12.23**). The stability of ocean temperature also means that there is a much more pronounced seasonal change in temperature between summer and winter over the land than over the ocean.

The temperature and moisture of air masses are strongly influenced by the characteristics of the surface over which the air is flowing, as you can see clearly in Figure 12.23. The ocean influences the temperature and moisture content of the lower atmosphere, which in turn moderates the climate of coastal areas. Along the Pacific Coast of Washington and British Columbia, for example, winter air temperatures seldom drop to freezing, whereas inland temperatures plunge to −30°C or lower.

Even if you live far from the ocean rather than in a coastal zone, you feel the ocean's influence on a regular basis, courtesy of atmospheric circulation. For example, in eastern North America, the muggy weather and thunderstorms of summertime originate with water that evaporated off the Gulf of Mexico. The monsoon rains in India, nor'easters off the coast of New England, and winter storms in the Pacific Northwest and the Prairies—all of these are weather systems that are transported by circulation in the atmosphere, from the ocean to the land.

Tropical Cyclones

One weather phenomenon that clearly demonstrates the interaction between ocean and atmosphere is cyclonic storms. There are many different types of **cyclones**, distinguished by where they form, how they develop, and their characteristics of temperature, air pressure, wind speed, and geographic

> **cyclone** A wind system that is circulating around a low-pressure center.

The global air temperature distribution • Figure 12.23

This map shows the range in average daily air temperature over both land and sea. There is a broader range of temperatures over land (in red, orange, and yellow) than over water (in blues).

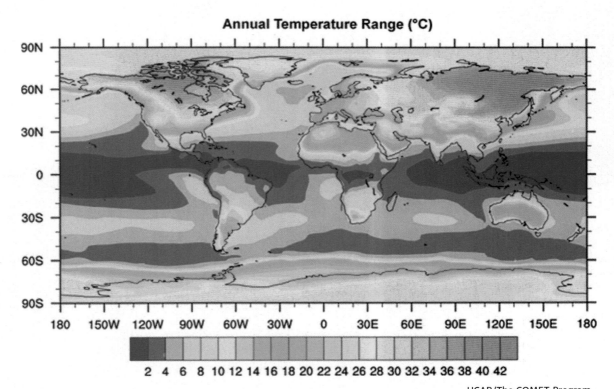

UCAR/The COMET Program

extent. The most intense and typically the most damaging are **tropical cyclones**, which are called **cyclones** if they form over the Pacific Ocean, **typhoons** if they form over the western Pacific or Indian Ocean, and **hurricanes** if they form over the Atlantic Ocean.

Cyclones circulate counterclockwise in the northern hemisphere and clockwise in the southern hemisphere, as dictated by the twin forces of air pressure gradient and Coriolis force. Air naturally moves into a low-pressure center; in general, the greater the pressure drop, the more vigorous the wind speeds. Meanwhile, the Coriolis force deflects the pathway of the air to the right in the northern hemisphere and to the left in the southern hemisphere. The end result is a cyclonic wind system, rotating around the low-pressure center.

One type of cyclone is an **extratropical** ("outside of" the tropics) or **midlatitude cyclone**. These form between 30° and 60° N and S, as a result of the interaction between warm and cold air along the polar fronts. They are large in geographic extent—up to 2000 kilometers across—and tend to last many days. This type of cyclone is responsible for most weather events in the midlatitude regions of the world. They also can spawn more local, intense weather systems, such as **thunderstorms** and **tornadoes**.

Hurricanes, typhoons, and cyclones are intense tropical cyclonic storms that start as wind systems gently circulating over warm ocean water. Hurricanes generally start to form in the eastern Atlantic, near Africa (**Figure 12.24**). To develop, they require a warm sea-surface temperature (at least 26.5°C). Warm ocean water is drawn upward into the low-pressure center, where it evaporates and then re-condenses. This releases latent heat and energizes the storm, which may then develop into a hurricane. Hurricanes and

On the track of a hurricane • Figure 12.24

Hurricanes draw their energy from warm surface water in the ocean.

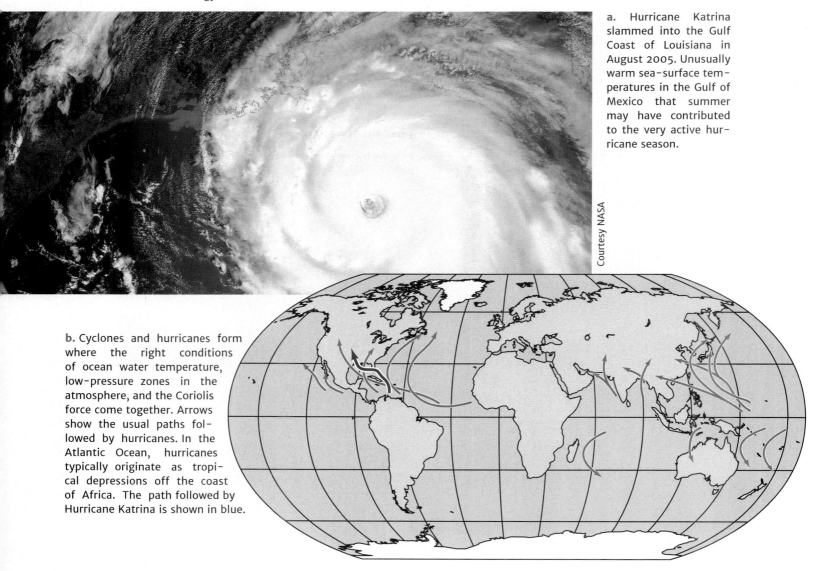

a. Hurricane Katrina slammed into the Gulf Coast of Louisiana in August 2005. Unusually warm sea-surface temperatures in the Gulf of Mexico that summer may have contributed to the very active hurricane season.

Courtesy NASA

b. Cyclones and hurricanes form where the right conditions of ocean water temperature, low-pressure zones in the atmosphere, and the Coriolis force come together. Arrows show the usual paths followed by hurricanes. In the Atlantic Ocean, hurricanes typically originate as tropical depressions off the coast of Africa. The path followed by Hurricane Katrina is shown in blue.

other cyclonic storms can be generated only in latitudes where the Coriolis force is strong enough for cyclonic circulation to develop—that is, higher than about latitude 5° N or S. The Coriolis force is zero at the equator, which means that hurricanes cannot form there.

A hurricane, by definition, has wind speeds greater than 119 kilometers/hour. (At lower wind speeds, it would be called a **tropical storm** or **tropical depression**.) Because a hurricane draws its energy from warm ocean water, its wind speeds will diminish and the hurricane will dissipate once it moves onshore, away from its energy source. For this reason, most hurricane wind damage occurs near the coast. Winds are usually accompanied by torrential rain and sometimes by **storm surge**, a local, exceptional flood of ocean water onto coastal areas. The center (or **eye**) of a hurricane is a region of very low air pressure, which causes the surface of the ocean to bulge upward locally. Hurricane-force winds drive the high seas onshore, and extensive flooding can result. Storm

surge caused the massive devastation in New Orleans and coastal areas like the Chandeleur Islands during Hurricane Katrina in 2005, and flooded parts of New Jersey and New York during post-tropical Hurricane Sandy in 2012.

El Niño and La Niña

Another important weather phenomenon that highlights the complex nature of the interactions between atmosphere and ocean is **El Niño** (**Figure 12.25**).

Roughly every four to seven years, a mass of unusually warm water appears off the coast of South America in the Pacific Ocean. Fish populations decline; warm-water organisms foreign to these waters begin to appear; and the trade winds slacken. Peruvians refer to this pattern as El Niño, because

> **El Niño** A regional weather system that involves unusual warming of equatorial Pacific surface water.

La Niña and El Niño • Figure 12.25

El Niño and La Niña are contrasting phases in a complex reversing wind system that occurs in the equatorial Pacific.

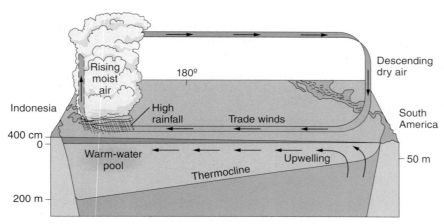

Normal conditions in the tropical Pacific

La Niña

a. In a "normal" or La Niña year, persistent trade winds blow westward across the tropical Pacific from the zone of upwelling water off Peru. The warm water collects in a large pool above the thermocline in the western Pacific. The moist maritime air rises and cools, bringing abundant rainfall to Indonesia and feeding the Asian monsoon.

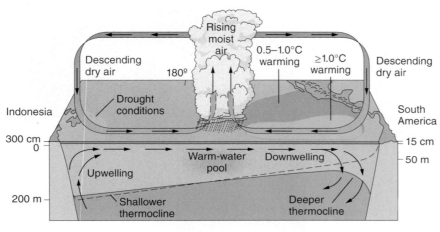

El Niño conditions in the tropical Pacific

El Niño

b. During El Niño, the air pressure difference between the eastern and western Pacific decreases, causing the trade winds to weaken or reverse. Rising warm, moist air greatly increases rainfall in the mid-Pacific, while descending cool, dry air brings drought conditions to Indonesia and Australia. Surface waters in the eastern Pacific are unusually warm, shutting off the supply of nutrients from upwelling deep, cold water. During a strong El Niño year, weather is disrupted over more than half of the planet.

it commonly appears at Christmas time (*El Niño* refers in Spanish to "the Christ child"). Coincident with Peruvian El Niño conditions, very heavy rains fall in normally arid parts of Peru and Ecuador; Australia experiences drought conditions; anomalous cyclones appear in Hawaii and French Polynesia; the seasonal rains of northeastern Brazil are disrupted; and the Indian monsoon may fail to appear. During exceptional El Niño years, weather patterns over much of Africa, eastern Asia, and North America are affected.

El Niño has been experienced by generations of Peruvians, but its broader significance as a coupled atmosphere–ocean phenomenon has been recognized only recently. Normally, there is a gradient from a high-pressure zone in the eastern tropical Pacific to a low-pressure zone in the western Pacific. This pressure difference causes the trade winds to blow toward the west (thus they are easterlies, blowing from the east) because air always moves from an area of high atmospheric pressure toward an area of lower atmospheric pressure. In the western Pacific the warm, moist air rises, causing cloudiness and rain in the area of Indonesia. During these normal years (called **La Niña** when the conditions are particularly strong), the easterly trade winds push the warm surface water toward the western Pacific, allowing deep, cold water from the Southern Ocean to well up to the surface along the coast of South America (**Figure 12.25a**).

When the atmospheric pressure difference at the surface is large (high in the east, low in the west), the trade winds blow strongly toward the west; when the pressure difference is small, however, the trade winds weaken. An El Niño event begins when the air pressure difference becomes small and the trade winds weaken, or even reverse. Without the strong easterly trade winds to push warm surface water away from the equatorial coast of South America, the upwelling of cold, deep water is suppressed (**Figure 12.25b**). Anomalously warm surface water accumulates in the central and eastern Pacific, near South America. The zone of high rainfall that is normally situated near Indonesia shifts toward the central Pacific, bringing drought conditions to Indonesia.

The effects of major El Niño events are felt over at least half of the planet. Weather impacts that are felt in regions far from the equatorial Pacific are mostly caused by jet streams being pushed out of their normal pathway. A major area of current research interest centers on identifying the factors that trigger El Niño events, so that the onset can be detected as early as possible. Understanding El Niño and La Niña requires scientists to consider the atmosphere and ocean as one great, interlocked system.

STOP **CONCEPT CHECK**

1. **What** are three ways that the atmosphere and ocean exchange materials?

2. **Where** do hurricanes and other tropical cyclonic storms get their energy?

3. **Why** does the upwelling of cold, deep water from the Southern Ocean fail to occur along the Pacific Coast of South America during an El Niño event?

SUMMARY

 THE PLANNER

1 The Ocean   314

- There has been an ocean on this planet for at least 4.0 billion years. The water in the ocean may have condensed from steam produced by primordial volcanic eruptions, or some of the water may have been delivered to the planet's surface via cometary impacts.

- Earth's water is contained mainly in four great, interconnected basins, which form the **world ocean**. The size, distribution, and topography of these basins are largely controlled by plate tectonic processes.

- Seawater ranges in **salinity** from 3.3 to 3.7% and varies measurably from place to place. Freezing and evaporation make the water saltier, whereas rain, snow, and river flow make it less salty.

- The water in the ocean forms layers based on density, which is controlled by temperature and salinity. The water in the surface layer, from the surface to a depth of about 100 meters, is relatively warm and moves in broad, wind-driven currents. The water in the deep layer moves in great, slow, global currents of the **thermohaline circulation**, driven by differences in temperature and salinity as shown in the diagram.

The ocean conveyor belt • Figure 12.5

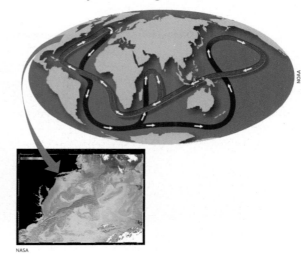

2 Where Ocean Meets Land 320

- The ocean's level varies over a wide range of time scales and for various reasons. Worldwide changes in sea level due to the melting or growth of polar ice sheets take place over thousands of years. Local changes due to the **tides** occur twice a day along most coasts.

- When a wave moves onto the shore, its motion is distorted, as the shallow bottom interferes with the circular motion of water in the wave. It eventually breaks, creating turbulent **surf**. Much of the resulting erosion and transport of sediment is accomplished by **longshore currents** in the surf zone, as shown in the diagram, and by **beach drift** (on land).

Longshore current and beach drift · Figure 12.9

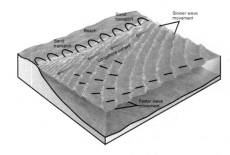

- Shorelines are highly variable, but three basic types are most common: rocky coasts and **wave-cut cliffs**, lowland **beaches** and **barrier islands**, and coral **reefs**. Shorelines and coastal landforms are shaped by a combination of erosive and depositional processes. Storms and artificial structures often accelerate the process of coastal erosion.

3 The Atmosphere 333

- The composition of **air**, excluding water vapor and aerosols, is 99.96% by volume nitrogen, oxygen, and argon. This is the particular mix of gases that makes up the **atmosphere** of Earth.

- Air temperature changes markedly as one moves upward from the surface. As a result, there are four distinct layers in the atmosphere, each with a distinct temperature profile, as shown in the diagram. From the bottom up, they are the **troposphere**, the **stratosphere**, the mesosphere, and the thermosphere. The troposphere contains most of the gases that play a role in Earth's **greenhouse effect**. The **ozone layer**, which protects life on Earth by absorbing harmful incoming ultraviolet radiation, is a concentration of O_3 in the stratosphere.

Four major layers · Figure 12.17

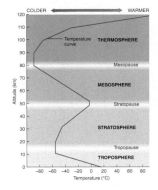

- The amount of heat energy from the Sun reaching Earth's surface is greatest near the equator and least near the poles. **Winds** result from the unequal distribution of energy and the consequent differences in atmospheric pressure. Convection currents move heat from the equator toward the poles. Earth's rotation produces the **Coriolis force**, which causes winds to veer to the right in the northern hemisphere and to the left in the southern hemisphere. One result is the easterly **trade winds** that blow in equatorial regions.

4 Where Ocean Meets Atmosphere 340

- Climate is the average or "normal" weather for a particular location, over a long time.

- The heat-absorbing capacity of the ocean combines with circulation in the atmosphere to control the variety and distribution of Earth's climatic zones.

- **Cyclones** are wind systems that circulate around centers of low atmospheric pressure. Tropical cyclones draw their energy from warm surface water, illustrating the interaction between ocean and atmosphere.

- **El Niño** is an important weather system that involves complex interactions between the ocean and the atmosphere. El Niño events, as shown in the diagram, which can affect the weather over half of the globe, are triggered by variations in atmospheric pressure, which cause weakening of the trade winds and anomalies in equatorial sea-surface temperatures.

La Niña and El Niño · Figure 12.25

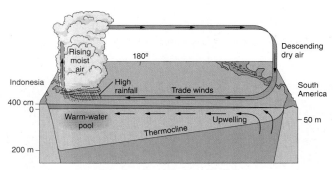

Normal conditions in the tropical Pacific

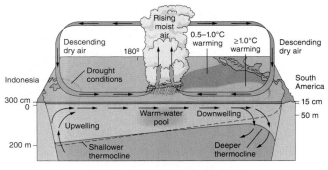

El Niño conditions in the tropical Pacific

KEY TERMS

air   333

atmosphere   333

barrier island   327

beach   327

beach drift   326

Coriolis force   338

cyclone   341

El Niño   343

greenhouse effect   335

longshore current   325

ozone layer   336

reef   328

salinity   316

stratosphere   336

surf   323

thermohaline circulation   318

tides   321

trade wind   339

troposphere   335

wave-cut cliff   327

wind   338

world ocean   314

CRITICAL AND CREATIVE THINKING QUESTIONS

1. Compare Earth's atmosphere with what is known about the atmospheres of other planets. How does its composition differ, and why? Why do some planets have dense atmospheres and others have nearly none? Does Jupiter's Great Red Spot have any analogues on Earth?

2. During the early Tertiary Period, North and South America were not connected. How might that have changed the global pattern of ocean circulation? How would this in turn have affected global climate? Do some library research and suggest some tests for your hypothesis.

3. Visit a shoreline. If possible, visit the same spot on the shoreline on two or more occasions, with some time between visits. What kinds of coastal landforms do you observe? What kinds of changes can you notice from one visit to the next?

4. Rock of Permian and Triassic ages in both North America and western Europe record the existence of desert conditions. What might have caused the deserts to form?

5. Geological evidence indicates that the atmosphere of early Earth was free of oxygen. What constraints might that have had on early life?

6. Compare the major surface ocean currents (Figure 12.4) to the global atmospheric circulation patterns (Figure 12.21). Describe the similarities that you note between oceanic and atmospheric circulation in the North and South Atlantic basins.

Surface ocean currents • Figure 12.4

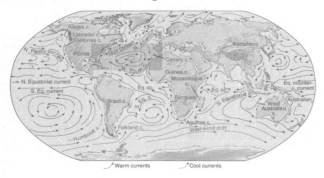

Global atmospheric circulation • Figure 12.21

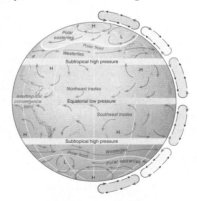

WHAT IS HAPPENING IN THIS PICTURE?

This is a satellite image of tropical cyclone Edzani, in January 2010.

NASA

THINK CRITICALLY

Can you tell whether Edzani was in the northern or southern hemisphere, just by looking at the picture? Think about how the Coriolis force would influence the flow of air into the low-pressure center of the storm. (Look it up online to see if you guessed the hemisphere correctly.)

SELF-TEST

(Check your answers in Appendix D.)

1. Which of the following processes increases the salinity of seawater?

   a. freezing

   b. rain, snow, and river runoff

   c. evaporation

   d. Both a and c are correct.

2. Which of the following processes decreases the salinity of seawater?

   a. freezing

   b. rain, snow, and river runoff

   c. evaporation

   d. Both a and c are correct.

3. The water in the _____ extends to a depth of 100 meters, is relatively warm, and moves in broad, wind-driven currents.

   a. deep zone

   b. surface layer

   c. thermocline

   d. transition zone

4. Deep ocean currents are more influenced by the _____ of the water than by wind directions.

   a. density

   b. temperature

   c. salinity

   d. All of the above answers are correct.

5. In coastal regions, the ocean can act to _____.

   a. increase average temperatures of the land

   b. decrease average temperatures of the land

   c. induce ice formation

   d. moderate temperatures of the land

6. Which of the following statements about global sea level is correct?

   a. Global sea level is constant over both human and geological time.

   b. Global sea level can vary tens to hundreds of meters over geological time.

   c. Large variations in global sea level can be an effect of climate change.

   d. Both b and c are correct.

7. This diagram depicts the forces involved with the generation of tides on Earth. Label the diagram with the following terms:

distorted water level   common center of mass of
inertial force   Earth–Moon system

gravitational force   uniform level of water (theoretical)

                     tide-raising force

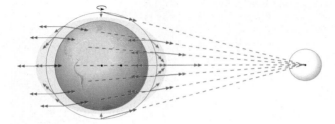

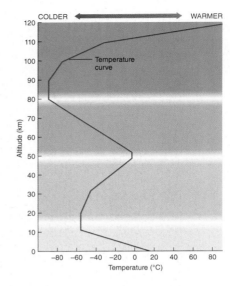

8. Shorelines are highly variable, but three basic types of coastlines are most common. Which of the following is *not* a common type of coastline?

a. rocky coasts and wave-cut cliffs

b. trenches

c. lowland beaches and barrier islands

d. coral reefs

9. This block diagram shows the beach and shore environment. Place arrows on the diagram, showing the direction of longshore current and sand transport. Be sure to label each of the sets of arrows.

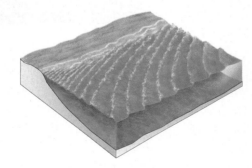

10. _____ is the most abundant chemical constituent of Earth's atmosphere.

a. Oxygen

b. Carbon dioxide

c. Argon

d. Nitrogen

e. Water vapor

11. This diagram shows a graph of temperature variations vertically through the atmosphere. Label the diagram with the following terms:

thermosphere   tropopause

stratosphere   mesopause

troposphere   stratopause

mesosphere

12. The atmosphere contributes to the warming of Earth's surface _____.

a. by trapping ultraviolet rays in the troposphere

b. by focusing the Sun's rays through refraction

c. through evaporation, which causes heating of the surface

d. by absorbing and reradiating infrared radiation

13. The atmosphere can shield organisms from harmful _____ rays from the Sun, as they are absorbed by O, O_2, and O_3 (ozone).

a. infrared

b. ultraviolet

c. gamma

d. neutron

14. The movement of air masses is a result of _____.

a. differential heating of the curved Earth by the Sun

b. the deflection of moving air masses by Earth's rotation

c. the seasonal melting of ice in the polar regions

d. Both a and b are correct.

e. Both b and c are correct.

15. Subtropical high pressure is created by _____.

a. descending cool and dry air at the juncture of a Ferrel cell and Hadley cell

b. rising warm and moist air at the juncture of a polar cell and Ferrel cell

c. rising warm and moist air at the juncture of a Ferrel cell and Hadley cell

d. descending cool and dry air at the juncture of a polar cell and Ferrel cell

THE PLANNER

Review the Chapter Planner on the chapter opener and check off your completed work.

13 CLIMATIC EXTREMES: DESERTS AND GLACIERS

Carsten Peter/NG Image Collection

John Burcham/NG Image Collection

Global Locator

Aurora Peak Alaska

NG Maps

HARSH LANDSCAPES

The Mandara Lakes in Libya are stunning (see inset). The water is as flat as a mirror, reflecting a turquoise sky. The palm trees are dwarfed by the nearby dunes of the Sahara Desert. It is easy to see why early explorers were drawn to the harshness of the desert: Its vastness, its sense of danger, and the life-giving beauty of its oases make human undertakings seem trivial by comparison.

Explorers of another stripe, like this mountaineer exulting at the summit of Aurora Peak in Alaska (main photo), are fascinated by the world's icy wildernesses. This mountaineer is looking at Black Rapids Glacier. Almost every description of the Sahara Desert could also apply to this landscape: abstract, beautiful, immense, dangerous, remote, and vulnerable.

For geologists, deserts and glaciers are linked by more than the beauty of their abstract landscapes; they are the results of extreme climates—the extremes of dry and cold, linked together through the processes of our global climate system. The erosional power of wind and ice, which play lesser roles elsewhere, are dominant in these regions. In this chapter, we will look closely at the geological processes that operate in the locations that are characteristic of these climatic extremes.

DESERTS AND DRYLANDS

Learning Objectives

1. **Identify** five different types of deserts.

2. **Explain** how the wind shapes desert surfaces through abrasion and deflation.

3. **Describe** the structure and formation of dunes and other desert landforms.

REMEMBER THIS! Do you remember the three major sets of convection cells that make up the global atmospheric circulation system? They are shown along the edge of Figure 13.1, and you can review their names and characteristics by looking back at *The Atmosphere* in Chapter 12.

Convection in the atmosphere creates global belts of rising and falling air masses, resulting in three belts of high rainfall and four of low rainfall (**Figure 13.1**). High-rainfall belts are regions of **convergence**, where warm, moist air masses meet and rise. These belts lie along the equator and along the polar fronts, at 50°N and 50°S latitudes, resulting in warm–humid (equatorial) and cold–humid (polar front) climate zones. Low-rainfall belts are regions of **divergence**, where cool, dry air masses sink downward. These belts lie in the two polar regions and in the subtropical regions at 30°N and 30°S latitudes, creating two dry climate subtropical regions and two dry, cold polar climates (see *Remember This!*).

Types of Deserts

The word *desert* literally means "deserted region." However, irrigation is changing the meaning by making deserts suitable for agriculture and therefore habitable. **Desert** is now defined in terms of precipitation: Deserts form in **arid** lands, which receive less than 250 millimeters of precipitation per year, covering 25% of Earth's land area outside of the polar regions. In addition, there is a smaller percentage of **semiarid** land in which the annual rainfall ranges between 250 and 500 millimeters.

> **desert** An arid land that receives less than 250 millimeters of rainfall or snow equivalent per year and is sparsely vegetated unless it is irrigated.

Arid and semiarid lands, collectively known as **drylands**, are characterized by a lack of available water.

The world's deserts • Figure 13.1

This map shows the distribution of arid and semiarid climates and the major deserts associated with them. Many of the world's great deserts are located where belts of dry air descend along the 30°N and 30°S latitudes. Notice also that regions of cold, descending air also surround both of the poles. (Compare to Figure 12.21.)

- Hot arid (desert) climates
- Semiarid climates
- Cold (polar desert) climates

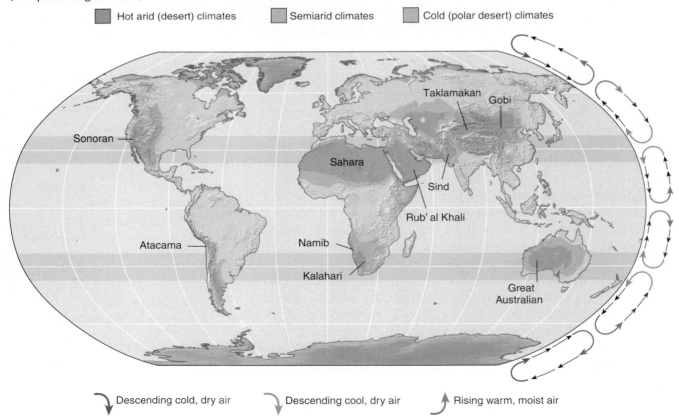

- Descending cold, dry air
- Descending cool, dry air
- Rising warm, moist air

This is not just measured in terms of low precipitation but also the balance between precipitation and evaporation. If evaporation (i.e., water losses from the system) exceeds precipitation (i.e., water inputs into the system) on a regular basis, then water availability will be low.

Deserts can be separated into five categories, of which we have already mentioned two. The most extensive, the **subtropical deserts**, are associated with the two belts of low rainfall near the 30°N and 30°S latitudes (as shown in Figure 13.1). These include the Sahara, Kalahari, and Great Australian deserts. Despite being covered by ice, **polar deserts** receive as little precipitation as subtropical deserts and are considered to be "frozen" deserts. Because the precipitation comes in the form of snow that never gets a chance

to melt, polar deserts gradually build up a thick ice sheet. Antarctica is technically the world's largest desert.

The other three categories of desert are less related to global air circulation patterns and more related to local geography. They are **continental interior deserts**, **rainshadow deserts**, and **coastal deserts** (**Figure 13.2**). Later in the chapter, we will take a closer look at the unique environment of the polar desert. For now, let's focus on the geological processes that characterize the world's hot deserts.

Wind Erosion

As discussed in Chapter 7, wind is an important agent of erosion, transport, and deposition. Processes related to wind—

Hot deserts • Figure 13.2 _____

Aside from the great frozen polar deserts, most arid regions are hot.

a. Subtropical desert: The Sahara is the greatest of the world's subtropical deserts. Here, a camel caravan crosses the desert in Libya.

b. Inland continental desert: Mongolian nomads transport their belongings through the Altai Mountains, which border on the Gobi Desert. Inland continental deserts receive little rain because they are far from the ocean.

Carsten Peter/NG Image Collection

Dr. Cynthia M. Beall & Dr. Melvyn C. Goldstein/NG Image Collection

c. Rainshadow desert: A rainshadow desert forms when a mountain range creates a barrier to the flow of moist air, causing a zone of low precipitation on the downwind side of the range. Death Valley, seen here, lies on the landward side to the east of the Sierra Nevada, the tallest mountain range in the continental United States.

d. Coastal desert: Baja, California, the long, narrow peninsula in Mexico just south of its border with the United States, is a coastal desert. Coastal deserts occur along the **margins** of continents where cold, upwelling seawater cools the air, decreasing its ability to form precipitation.

Marc Moritsch/NG Image Collection

Annie Griffiths Belt/NG ImageCollection

aeolian (or *eolian*) processes—are particularly effective as agents of erosion in arid and semiarid regions.

Windblown Sediment

Sediment carried by the wind tends to be finer than that moved by water or ice. Because air is far less dense than water, particles moved by air are much smaller than particles moved by water flowing at the same velocity. Typically, the largest particles that can be lifted in the airstream are grains of sand (**Figure 13.3**).

Although smaller in size, the particles in windblown sediment are similar to those in water-borne sediment in the way they travel. The largest grains are transported by **surface creep**. As wind speed increases, smaller grains may be bumped or lifted into the air, where they experience **saltation**. Finer dust-sized particles may be carried aloft to heights of a kilometer or so, where they can travel along in **suspension** as long as the wind keeps blowing. Such particles can be carried all the way across the ocean.

> **surface creep** Sediment transport in which the wind causes particles to roll along the ground.
>
> **saltation** Sediment transport in which particles move forward in a series of short jumps along arc-shaped paths.
>
> **suspension** Sediment transport in which the wind carries very fine particles over long distances and periods of time.

Mechanisms of Wind Erosion

Flowing air erodes the land surface in two ways. The first, **abrasion**, results from the impact of wind-driven grains of sand. Abraded rock acquires distinctive, curved shapes and a surface polish (**Figure 13.4**). A bedrock surface or stone that has been abraded and shaped by windblown sediment is a **ventifact** ("wind artifact"). When preserved in sedimentary strata, ventifacts can tell geologists the direction of prevailing winds in the past.

> **abrasion** Wind erosion in which airborne particles chip small fragments off rocks that protrude above the surface.

The second important wind erosional process is called **deflation** (see Figure 13.4). Deflation on a large scale takes place only where there is little or no vegetation and where loose particles are fine enough to be picked up by the wind. It is especially severe in deserts but can occur elsewhere during times of drought, when no vegetation or moisture is present to hold soil particles together. Continued deflation sometimes leads to the development of **desert pavement**; most of the fine particles are removed, leaving a continuous pavement-like covering of coarse particles.

> **deflation** Wind erosion in which loose particles of sand and dust are removed by the wind, leaving coarser particles behind.

Movement of sediment by wind • Figure 13.3

Wind, like water, moves grains by creep, saltation, and suspension (Compare to Figure 7.11.).

a. Under conditions of moderate wind speed, sand grains larger than 500 micrometers (500 μm, or 0.5 mm) move by surface creep, while smaller grains (70–500 μm) move by saltation. Still finer particles (20–70 μm) are carried aloft in suspension, by turbulent eddies. (Compare to Figure 7.11.)

b. Fast wind speeds cause movement of grains by saltation. Impacted grains bounce into the air and are carried along by the wind. Gravity pulls them back to the land surface where they impact other particles, repeating the process.

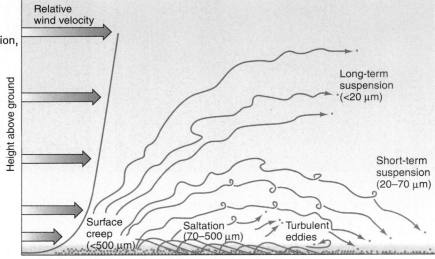

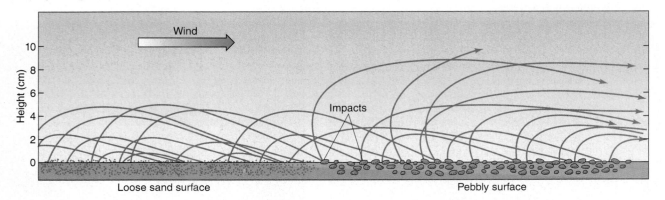

Process Diagram

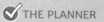 ✓ THE PLANNER

How wind shapes surfaces • Figure 13.4

The two main mechanisms of wind erosion are abrasion and deflation.

From abrasion to ventifact

a. Windblown sand peppers the upwind side of an exposed rock, eventually abrading it to a smooth, inclined surface. ▼

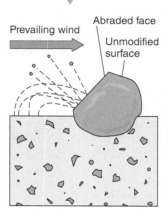

Prevailing wind

Abraded face

Unmodified surface

b. Ventifacts, each with at least one smooth, abraded surface facing upwind, litter the ground near Lake Vida in Victoria Valley, Antarctica. ▼

Courtesy Stephen C. Porter

From deflation to desert pavement

c. These drawings and accompanying photos show how the progressive removal of sand from sediment with different-sized particles can lead to the formation of desert pavement.

Deflation

Deflation

No further deflation

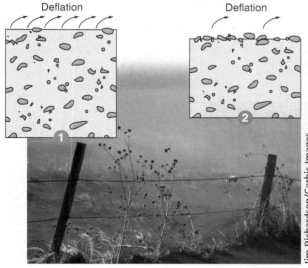

Jim Richardson/Corbis Images

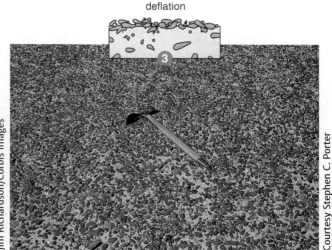

Courtesy Stephen C. Porter

▲ In the first photo, deflation is in progress in a plowed field in eastern Colorado.

▲ The second photo shows desert pavement in Searles Valley in California. One hypothesis for its formation is that the gravel is too coarse for the wind to move, and the pavement is formed by deflation of fine-grained material. A second hypothesis is that a layer of gravel on the surface traps wind-transported dust.

THINK CRITICALLY

What clues could you use to determine whether a rock has been weathered by wind or by water?

Deserts and Drylands **353**

Desert Landforms

Desert landforms can be either erosional or depositional, or a combination of both. Wind erosion is at its most effective in deserts, where conditions are dry and vegetative cover is minimal. Because windblown sediment is typically fine, sediment that is picked up by wind may eventually be deposited quite far from its source. For example, distinctive reddish dust particles carried from the Sahara Desert by winds have been identified in the soils of Caribbean islands, in the ice of Alpine glaciers, in deep-sea sediment, and in the tropical rainforests of Brazil.

Water also plays an important role in shaping the desert landscape, through infrequent but intense rainfall on surfaces with little protective cover. However, the most distinctive and characteristic landform found in deserts is eolian in origin: dunes.

Dunes Although little is known about how **dunes** begin, it is likely that they start where some minor surface irregularity or obstacle distorts the flow of air. Upon encountering an impediment, the wind sweeps over and around it but leaves a pocket of slower-moving air immediately downwind. In this pocket of low wind velocity, sand grains moving with the wind drop out and begin to form a mound. The mound in turn influences the flow of air over and around it and may continue to grow into a dune.

A typical dune is asymmetrical, with a gentle windward slope (the side facing toward the wind) and a steep leeward face (the side facing away from the wind). Pushed by the wind, sand moves by surface creep and saltation up the gentle windward slope (**Figure 13.5**). When it reaches the top,

> **dune** A hill or ridge of sand deposited by winds.

Process Diagram

THE PLANNER

How sand dunes form • Figure 13.5

Dunes result from the transport and deposition of windblown sand.

a. This cross section through a sand dune shows the typical gentle windward slope (facing into the wind) and the steep slip face (facing away from the wind). The solid lines inside the dune show old slip faces.

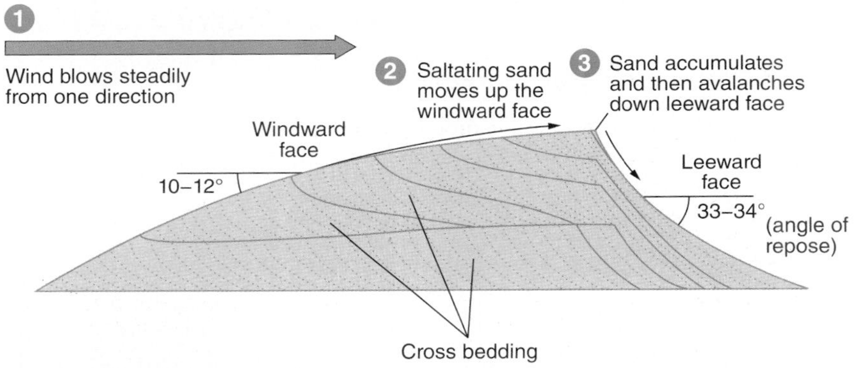

1. Wind blows steadily from one direction
2. Saltating sand moves up the windward face
3. Sand accumulates and then avalanches down leeward face

Windward face
10–12°
Leeward face
33–34° (angle of repose)

Cross bedding

b. Similar patterns of cross bedding in ancient sandstones from Utah tell us that this was a sandy, windswept desert during the Jurassic Period.

THINK CRITICALLY

From the orientation of the cross bedding in the rock formations in Utah, can you tell which way the wind was blowing when the sand was originally deposited?

© Corbin17/Alamy

The shape, size, and behavior of a dune are a function of the three factors shown in the triangle: sand, wind, and vegetative cover.

If the wind regularly blows in several different directions, it piles the sand up into stationary **star dunes**, such as these in the Empty Quarter (Rub' al Khali) of Saudi Arabia. ▶

George Steimetz/Corbis Images

◀ Crescent-shaped dunes called **barchans** are very mobile. They are formed when the wind blows predominantly in one direction (the "horns" of the crescent point downwind). The dunes shown here are in Reserva Nacional de Paracas, Atacama, Peru.

George Steinmetz/NG Image Collection

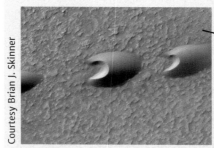

Courtesy Brian J. Skinner

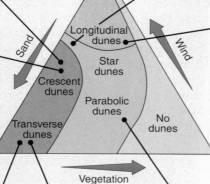

Marc Moritsch/NG Image Collection

▲ **Longitudinal dunes**, like these in Death Valley, run parallel to the prevailing winds. They form in deserts with meager sand supply and in areas with bidirectional winds that push first on one side of the dune and then on the other.

©John S. Shelton/University of Washington Libraries, Special Collections

▲ Mars is a dusty, windy planet. These giant Martian barchans were photographed from an orbiting space vessel.

George Steinmetz/NG Image Collection

▲ When there is a copious sand supply, barchan dunes can merge and form **transverse dunes**, such as these in the Empty Quarter. They are oriented perpendicular to the prevailing winds.

NASA

▲ This field of transverse dunes in Victoria Crater, Mars, was explored by *Opportunity*, one of two robotic vehicles on Mars. The edge of the crater has been modified by mass wasting and wind erosion.

▲ Coastal regions, where moist wind off the ocean allows vegetation to grow, are a typical environment for **parabolic dunes**. The arms, stabilized by vegetation, point upwind (opposite to barchan dunes).

Triangle diagram labels: Sand, Wind, Vegetation, Longitudinal dunes, Star dunes, Crescent dunes, Parabolic dunes, Transverse dunes, No dunes

THINK CRITICALLY

Why is there an area labeled "No dunes" in the bottom right-hand corner of the triangle?

the sand cascades down the steep leeward slope, also called the **slip face**. The slip face is always on the leeward side, so we can tell which way the wind was blowing from the asymmetrical form of the dune. Crisscrossed strata within the dune, called **cross beds**, are former slip faces. These can be preserved as cross-bedded strata in sedimentary rock derived from former sand dunes, as discussed in Chapter 8.

The sliding sand on a slip face comes to rest at the **angle of repose**, the steepest angle at which loose particles will come to rest. The angle of repose varies for different materials, depending on factors such as the size and angularity of the particles. For dry, medium-sized sand particles, it is about 33–34°; the angle is generally steeper for coarse materials such as gravel and gentler for fine materials such as silt.

On Earth, three factors control the shape and behavior of a dune: the wind conditions, the amount of vegetation cover, and the characteristics and quantity of sand available. These three factors are shown schematically in the triangle in **Figure 13.6** along with photos of common types of dunes. Clearly, if there is no sand, or if there is plenty of vegetative cover to anchor sediment in place, dunes will not form. Some types of dunes tend to remain stationary. Others may migrate over long distances, and they can cause severe degradation and loss of agricultural productivity when they invade non-desert lands. This is part of the process of **desertification**.

Dunes are known to form on at least one other planet in our solar system: Mars. There, where there is no vegetative cover, the kinds of dunes observed are barchan and transverse, two of the kinds of dunes controlled principally by sand supply.

Other Desert Landforms Contrary to popular belief (and many Hollywood movies), most deserts do not consist of endless expanses of sand dunes. Only one-third of the Arabian Peninsula, the sandiest of all dry regions, and only one-ninth of the Sahara Desert are covered with sand dunes. The remaining land area is either crossed by systems of stream valleys or covered by alluvial fans. Running water, therefore, is important in both erosion and deposition in deserts, just as it is in rainy regions.

Some desert landforms arise from the combined action of wind and water. One such landform occurs when a resistant stratum is underlain by a softer, more easily eroded stratum that is removed and carried away; in North America, they are called **hoodoos** (**Figure 13.7**). Other landforms characteristic of desert regions, such as steep-sided but flat-topped **buttes** and table-like **mesas**, also result from a combination of water and wind erosion of bedrock, where a resistant layer overlies an easily eroded unit.

In some deserts, wind and water erosion are enhanced by the effects of frost wedging (Chapter 7). It may seem odd that frost wedging could be important in a desert environment, but conditions in deserts often fluctuate widely between daytime, when the Sun is strong and temperatures are high, and nighttime, when temperatures can dip below freezing. If water that has seeped into cracks is repeatedly frozen and thawed, day after day, the cracks will widen and the rock will be opened to further weathering by wind and water.

Rainfall in a desert region typically falls in brief, intense downpours that occur during a short rainy season. The rapid

Hoodoos • Figure 13.7

Weathering and erosion of differentially resistant strata by the combined action of wind, water, and frost wedging create interesting desert landforms.

a. These hoodoos are part of the distinctive landscape of the Alberta Badlands near Drumheller, in Canada.

b. Hoodoos are formed when erosion removes easily eroded strata underlying a more resistant layer. In desert environments where nighttime temperatures fall below freezing, frost wedging can be an important agent of mechanical erosion, prying apart the rock and opening it to further wind and water action.

By Gorgo [Public domain], via Wikimedia Commons

Plateau

Fin

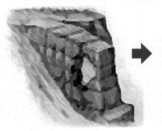

Window

Hoodoos

Running water can be as important as wind in shaping both erosional and depositional landforms in deserts, especially following infrequent but intense storms.

Courtesy Stephen C. Porter

B.A.E./Alamy

a. After a storm, a flash flood thunders down this arroyo on the Navajo reservation in Arizona, cutting deeply into land that lacks vegetative cover. As the floodwater subsides, sediment is deposited across the alluvial floor of the canyon.

b. When an arroyo drains from an upland area into an open desert floor, the stream loses flow velocity and deposits its sediment load in a broad alluvial fan. This large fan extends from the Altun Mountains into the Taklamakan Desert, China.

runoff erodes steep-sided canyons, called **arroyos**, into the landscape (**Figure 13.8a**). These are likely to be dry most of the year but are subject to flash floods during the wet season. When water in an arroyo leaves an upland region and enters the flat desert floor, the flow velocity drops dramatically. The water loses its ability to transport sediment, and drops its load of sand and gravel in an **alluvial fan** (**Figure 13.8b**). If canyon openings are closely spaced along the base of a mountain range, the alluvial fans sometimes coalesce into a broad alluvial apron called a **bajada**.

STOP CONCEPT CHECK

1. **Why** is a desert more likely to develop in the subtropics than in the tropics?

2. **What** are the main mechanisms of wind erosion, and how do they work?

3. **What** three variables control the formation of the five main types of sand dunes?

DESERTIFICATION AND LAND DEGRADATION

Learning Objectives

1. **Clarify** the differences between desertification and land degradation.

2. **Suggest** approaches that can slow or reverse desertification and land degradation.

Deserts are constantly changing—migrating, growing, or shrinking. **Desertification** of nondesert lands can result from natural environmental processes (mainly climatic change) or from human activities, or from a combination of the two. To distinguish between natural and anthropogenic desertification, the United Nations Environment Programme and others who work in dryland

> **desertification** Invasion of desert conditions into nondesert areas.

land degradation
Land damage or loss of productivity caused by human activity, which may lead to the advance of desert conditions into nondesert areas.

management prefer to use the terms land degradation and **accelerated desertification** in reference to changes that result partially or primarily from human activity. Not all land degradation leads to desertification; for example, chemical contamination of soil is also a form of land degradation.

Ever-Changing Deserts

In the region south of the Sahara lies a drought-prone belt of dry grassland known as the **Sahel**. There the annual rainfall is normally only 10 to 30 centimeters, most of it falling during a single brief rainy season. In the early 1970s, the Sahel experienced the worst drought of the 20th century. For several years in a row, the annual rains failed to appear, causing the adjacent desert to spread southward by as much as 150 kilometers. The drought extended from the Atlantic Ocean to the Indian Ocean, and it affected a population of at least 20 million.

Naturally occurring processes involving fluctuations in both precipitation and temperature have caused the Sahara Desert to advance and retreat many times over the past 10,000 years. However, the results of the drought were intensified by the fact that between about 1935 and 1970, the human population of the region had doubled, and the number of domestic livestock also increased dramatically. This resulted in severe overgrazing, and the grass cover was devastated by the drought. Millions of people suffered from thirst and starvation. The overgrazing is continuing today, leaving the Sahel at risk for another devastating famine if the dry weather should return.

The major signs of desertification include lower water tables, higher levels of salt in water and topsoil, reduction in surface water supplies, unusually high rates of soil erosion, and destruction of vegetation. Areas that are the most susceptible to desertification, whether by natural or human causes, are shown in the *Case Study*. Most are semiarid fringe lands adjacent to the world's great deserts. In many of these places, humans have lived successfully in a semiarid environment for centuries; what has changed is an explosion in the size of the population and the adoption of agricultural practices that may not be suited to that part of the world.

One of the best-known examples of accelerated desertification occurred in the United States and southern parts of Canada during the mid-1930s, when huge dust storms swept across the Great Plains and drove many farm families off their land. John Steinbeck, in his award-winning novel *The Grapes of Wrath*, described this resettlement, the largest forced migration in the country's history. The Southern Plains came to be called the "Dust Bowl," and historians refer to that period as the Dust Bowl years.

The Dust Bowl had both natural and human causes. Like the Sahel famine, it was triggered by a multiple-year drought. The effects of the drought were exacerbated by decades of poor land-use practices. The grasses that originally grew on the prairies had protected the rich topsoil from wind erosion. However, settlers gradually replaced those tall grasses with plowed fields and seasonal grain crops, which left the ground bare and vulnerable for part of the year.

Mitigating Land Degradation

Today, improved farming and irrigation practices have greatly reduced the risk of similar catastrophes. In both the United States and Canada, the Dust Bowl experience led to the establishment of soil management agencies at both the federal and state/provincial levels. Some programs and incentives for farmers to adopt better soil management practices that were started just after the Dust Bowl continue even today. One of the biggest changes in agriculture in the Great Plains since the 1930s has been the extensive use of groundwater for irrigation, which can help to stabilize the topsoil (**Figure 13.9**). A drawback of irrigation, however, is the potential for depletion of groundwater resources (see *Remember This!*).

> **REMEMBER THIS!** How does groundwater flow in the subsurface, and how long does it take to replenish an aquifer that has been depleted? You can remind yourself about these processes by revisiting *Fresh Water Underground*, in Chapter 11.

Stabilizing soil • Figure 13.9

These fields in Kansas use central-pivot irrigation, which minimizes evaporative loss of water and gives the fields of wheat, corn, and sorghum their distinctive circular shapes. The protection afforded by irrigation comes at a cost, though: It is slowly depleting the High Plains Aquifer, which underlies much of the Midwest.

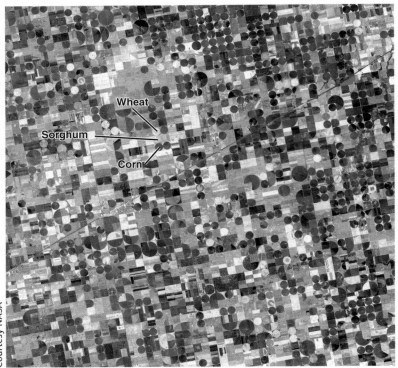

Courtesy NASA

The Sahel and the Dust Bowl

Land degradation and resulting desertification can happen anywhere that inappropriate land uses cause stress that exacerbates the effects of natural climatic change.

This happened in the North American Prairies during the 1930s Dust Bowl. Shown here (**Figure a**), a massive dust storm closed in on Stratford, Texas, on April 18, 1935. Within a few minutes, the town would be enveloped in pitch darkness, and it would be impossible to see even the house in the foreground of this photo. The dust resulted from prairie lands being laid open to the elements by plowing. In the Sahel region of Niger (**Figure b**), a herd of goats grazes on pasture at the edge of the desert. As the goats consume the remaining grass and bushes, the dunes of the desert will inevitably advance. Advances and retreats of the Sahara Desert in this region, caused by natural climatic changes, have been exacerbated by overly stressful use of the land.

Global Locator

Texas

NG Maps

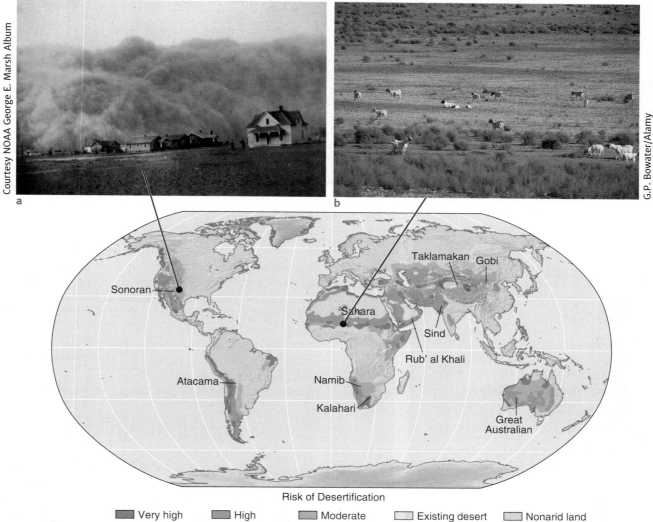

Courtesy NOAA George E. Marsh Album

a

G.P. Bowater/Alamy

b

Risk of Desertification

■ Very high   ■ High   ■ Moderate   ☐ Existing desert   ☐ Nonarid land

c

This map (**Figure c**) identifies some of the world's great deserts and regions that are most at risk of desertification today.

THINK CRITICALLY

Could something like the Dust Bowl happen in North America today? What safeguards are in place to prevent it? Do you think they are adequate?

How can desertification be halted or reversed? The answer lies largely in understanding the geological principles involved and in applying measures designed to reestablish a natural balance in the affected areas. Soil management techniques are widely known and readily available; they simply need to be applied more aggressively. These techniques include crop rotation, windbreaks, contour plowing and terracing of steep slopes, low-till and no-till farming, and reforestation of vulnerable lands. Geologists and soil scientists can identify and map soils that are unsuitable for agriculture. Land-use planners can eliminate the incentives to exploit arid and semiarid lands beyond their capacity.

The preservation of productive lands is essential to maintaining the world's food production capacity at the level needed for an increasing population. You can learn much more about how the nations of the world are cooperating to protect productive lands from erosion and desertification by visiting the website of the United Nations Convention to Combat Desertification (see *Where Geologists Click*).

STOP CONCEPT CHECK

1. **What** are the main causes and signs of desertification and land degradation?
2. **How** can farmers and others address the problems of land degradation?

Where Geologists CLICK

United Nations Convention to Combat Desertification

The United Nations Convention to Combat Desertification (UNCCD) was established in 1994 as a legally binding international agreement to promote sustainable land management in drylands. Some of the most vulnerable ecosystems and communities are located in the world's drylands. Learn about UNCCD's partners and projects at this website.

GLACIERS AND ICE SHEETS

Learning Objectives

1. **Distinguish** between the different kinds of glaciers and ice formations.
2. **Describe** how ice in a glacier changes form, accumulates, ablates, and moves.
3. **Identify** several kinds of landforms created by glacial erosion and deposition.

Desertification can be an expression of natural climatic change, but another climate battle is played out in the vast deserts of the polar ice sheets. The expansion and shrinking of glaciers and ice sheets, both in the polar regions and in more temperate alpine settings, are expressions of the complex interplay between temperature and precipitation in the global climate system, which we investigate in greater detail in Chapter 14.

The existence of glaciers and ice sheets is linked to interactions among several parts of the Earth system: tectonic forces that produce high, mountainous areas; the ocean, a source of moisture; and the atmosphere, which delivers moisture to the land in the form of snow. We now turn our attention to the great polar deserts and other parts of the **cryosphere**. One very important source of information about this dynamic and rapidly changing system is the National Snow and Ice Data Center (see *Where Geologists Click*).

> **cryosphere** The perennially frozen part of the hydrosphere.

Components of the Cryosphere

Annual precipitation (snowfall) is generally very low in polar regions because the air is too cold to hold much moisture. The small amount of snow that does fall doesn't usually melt because summer temperatures stay very low. In areas where more snow falls each winter than melts during the following summer, the covering of snow gradually grows thicker. As the snow accumulates, its increasing weight causes the snow at the bottom to compact into a solid mass of ice. When the accumulating snow and ice become so thick that the pull of gravity causes the frozen mass to move, a **glacier** is born.

> **glacier** A semipermanent or perennially frozen body of ice consisting largely of recrystallized snow, which moves under the pull of gravity.

Where Geologists CLICK

National Snow and Ice Data Center

The National Snow and Ice Data Center (NSIDC) is a collaborative organization that involves NASA, NOAA, and numerous researchers with scientific expertise on anything and everything to do with the cryosphere. They provide a range of datasets and products relevant to the monitoring and understanding of Earth's snow and ice cover. Some interesting programs include the Antarctic Glaciological Data Center, ELOKA (Exchange for Local Observations and Knowledge of the Arctic), and a great online archive of glacier photographs.

Ice caps that occur at high latitudes are worth special mention. An **ice sheet** is the largest type of glacier on Earth, a continent-sized mass of ice that covers all or nearly all the land within its margins. At present, ice sheets are found only in Greenland and Antarctica, though they have been much more extensive in the past. They contain 95% of the world's glacier ice (and 70% of the world's fresh water). They are so thick and heavy that some of the land underneath Antarctica has actually been pushed below sea level (**Figure 13.10**).

Ice shelves are thick sheets of floating ice hundreds of meters thick that adjoin glaciers on land. They are constantly replenished by land-based glaciers and also lose ice when large pieces called **icebergs** break off from them.

In contrast, **sea ice** is a form of ice cover that never touches land at all, but forms by the direct freezing of seawater. Antarctica is surrounded by sea ice, which in wintertime roughly doubles the apparent area of the continent. For hundreds of years, most of the Arctic Ocean has been covered by sea ice year-round. Now, however, climate change has led to accelerated melting of sea ice and the opening of the Northwest Passage (see *Amazing Places*).

Glaciers are cold because they consist primarily of ice and snow. However, scientists have found that by drilling holes through glaciers interior temperatures are not all the same. Some glaciers are warmer than others, and a difference in temperature influences the behavior and movement

Welcome to Antarctica • Figure 13.10

The East Antarctic Ice Sheet covers most of the continent of Antarctica, and the West Antarctic Ice Sheet overlies a volcanic island arc and the surrounding seafloor. In this satellite image, you can also see four ice shelves that occupy large bays. Glaciers that flow down from the mainland feed these shelves.

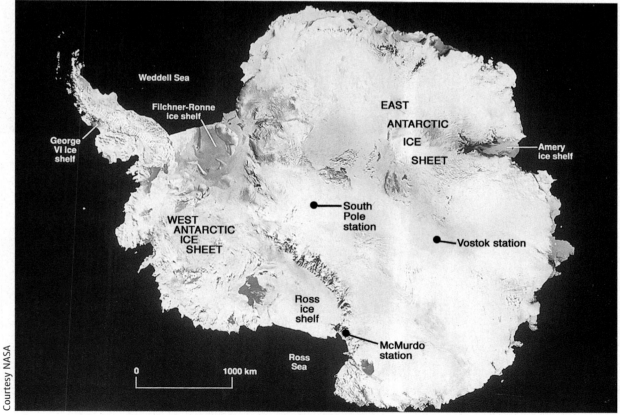

of the ice. In one kind of glacier, the ice is near its melting point throughout the interior. These glaciers, called **temperate glaciers**, form in low and middle latitudes. Meltwater and ice can exist together at equilibrium in temperate glaciers. At high latitudes and high altitudes, where the mean annual temperature is below freezing, the temperature in the glacier remains low, and little or no seasonal melting occurs. Such a cold glacier is commonly called a **polar glacier**. The five main types of glaciers are illustrated in **Figure 13.11**.

Amazing Places

✓ THE PLANNER

The Northwest Passage

The Northwest Passage connects the Atlantic to the Pacific Ocean, winding among the islands of the Canadian Arctic Archipelago in the Arctic Ocean (**Figure a**). The Vikings are known to have sailed to the far northern Arctic Ocean on early fishing expeditions; however, in the 1500s the Little Ice Age (Chapter 14) caused sea ice to expand greatly, blocking any subsequent sea travel through the Arctic until the end of the 19th century.

Throughout those ice-blocked centuries, European explorers were drawn to the Northwest Passage, mounting expeditions in hopes of discovering an efficient trade route to the Orient. The most famous is the ill-fated Franklin Expedition, which left England in 1845. After becoming ice-bound, Captain John Franklin and all 128 crew were lost. The ships are still sought today, and grim theories abound as to what actually happened to the crew.

The first explorer to sail the whole route was Norwegian Roald Amundsen in 1903, in a small herring boat called Gjøa (**Figures b, c**). From then until the early 2000s, only a handful of boats managed to make it all the way through the Passage without the assistance of icebreakers. In recent years, however, climatic warming has greatly accelerated the loss of sea ice in the Arctic. The first commercial vessel sailed through in 2008, and many other vessels, both large and small, have now made the journey (**Figure d**).

The opening of the Northwest Passage to shipping and other sea traffic brings the possibility of oil spills and other forms of pollution in the Arctic Ocean, including the transfer of invasive species between the Atlantic and Pacific. Sovereignty issues also muddy the waters; Canada claims sovereignty over the waters of the Northwest Passage, but the United States, Russia, and Denmark have contested this claim.

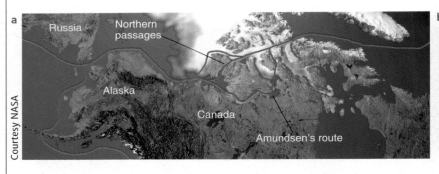

Courtesy NASA

National Library of Norway

NOAA Photo Library

© Mark Peterson/Corbis

Global Locator

Arctic Ocean

NG Maps

THINK CRITICALLY

What are some of the environmental implications of having ships move through the Northwest Passage? What about the economic and political implications?

The five main types of glaciers are shown here.

a. A **cirque glacier**, such as this one in Montana's Glacier National Park, occupies a bowl-shaped depression on a mountainside and typically serves as the source for a valley glacier.

Melissa Farlow/NGI mage Collection

c. An **ice cap** covers a mountaintop (or low-lying land in the polar regions) completely and usually displays a radial-outward-flow pattern. In this aerial photograph, the Greenland Ice Cap surrounds the Nunatak Mountains.

©Marli Bryant Miller

d. When a glacial valley is partly filled by an arm of the sea, the valley is called a **fjord**, and the glacier is a **fjord glacier**. Such glaciers often give rise to icebergs that break off and float away. This is the Sawyer Glacier in Alaska.

Alaska Stock Images/NG Image Collection

b. Valley glaciers flow down valleys and are fed either from cirque glaciers or ice caps. This valley glacier is in Alaska's Wrangell Saint Elias National Park.

Thomas Kitchin & Victoria Hurst/ AllCanada Photos/Corbis Images

e. When a glacier flows all the way out of the mountains and onto the surrounding lowlands, it is called a **piedmont glacier**. The Columbia Glacier in Alaska starts as a valley glacier and then spreads out as a piedmont glacier.

Taylor Kennedy– SitkaProductions/NG Image Collection

ASK YOURSELF

Which one of the following types of glaciers would most typically form in a coastal environment?

a. piedmont glacier

b. fjord glacier

c. cirque glacier

d. valley glacier

e. ice cap

Ever-Changing Glaciers

Although we have defined a glacier as a semipermanent or perennially frozen body of ice, glaciers are constantly changing in several ways. For example, the snow that falls on the surface of glaciers gradually changes into ice. Glaciers also shrink and grow in response to seasonal changes in temperature and precipitation. The ice in a glacier also moves, slowly but surely, under the influence of gravity. This movement is usually slow but in some circumstances can be surprisingly rapid. Changes in climatic conditions also cause the margins of glaciers to advance or retreat. Let's take a closer look at some of the processes of change in glaciers.

How Glaciers Form Newly fallen snow is very porous and is easily penetrated by air. The presence of air in the pore spaces allows the delicate points of each snowflake to **sublimate** (change from solid directly to vapor, without melting). The resulting water vapor crystallizes in tiny spaces in the snowflakes, eventually filling them. In this way, the ice crystals in the snow pack slowly become smaller, rounder, more compact, and denser, until the pore spaces between them disappear (**Figure 13.12**). Snow that survives for a year or more becomes more compact as it is buried by successive snowfalls. As the years go by, the snow gradually becomes denser and denser, until it is no longer penetrable by air and becomes **glacier ice.** This process may take decades in the case of temperate glaciers to millennia in the case of polar ice sheets.

Further changes take place as the ice is buried deeper and deeper. As snowfall adds to the glacier's thickness, the increasing pressure causes the small grains of glacier ice to grow. This increase in size is similar to what happens when fine-grained rock recrystallizes as a result of metamorphism (see *Remember This!*). Ice is, in fact, a mineral, and therefore glacier ice is technically a rock. However, the properties of this rock are very different from those of any other naturally occurring rock because of its very low melting temperature and its unusually low density. Ice floats in water because it is only nine-tenths as dense as water.

How Glaciers Grow and Shrink The mass of a glacier constantly changes as the weather varies from season to season and with local and global climatic changes over time. In a way, a glacier is like a checking account. Instead of being measured in terms of money, the balance of a glacier's account is measured in terms of the amount of snow deposited, mainly through snowfall in the winter, and the amount of snow (and ice) withdrawn, mainly through melting during the summer. The additions are collectively called **accumulation**, and the losses are collectively called **ablation** (**Figure 13.13**).

Near the top, or **head**, of the glacier is an accumulation zone, where snow turns into glacier ice. Near the end, or **terminus**, of the glacier, more ice is rapidly lost to evaporation and melting than is replaced by snow. The total added to the account at the end of a year—the difference between accumulation and ablation—is a measure of the glacier's **mass balance**. When the ice budget of the glacier as a whole runs a deficit, the glacier decreases in thickness, and the terminus is likely to retreat (especially if the deficit continues for several years in a row). Conversely, when it runs a surplus, the glacier grows, and the terminus is likely to advance.

How Glaciers Move According to our definition, a glacier moves because of the pull of gravity. How can we detect this movement? One method is to carefully measure the position of a boulder on its surface relative to a fixed point beyond the glacier's edge. If you measure the boulder's position again a year later, you will find that it has moved "downstream," usually by several meters. Actually, it is the ice that has moved, carrying the boulder along.

From snow to ice · Figure 13.12

As a new snowflake is slowly converted into a granule of glacier ice, it loses its delicate points through evaporation and recrystallization and becomes much more compact.

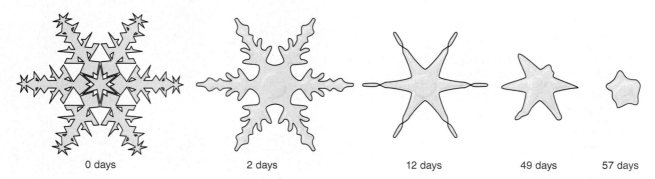

| 0 days | 2 days | 12 days | 49 days | 57 days |

This cross section of a valley glacier shows what happens inside. Accumulation near the glacier's head is offset by ablation at the surface and near the terminus.

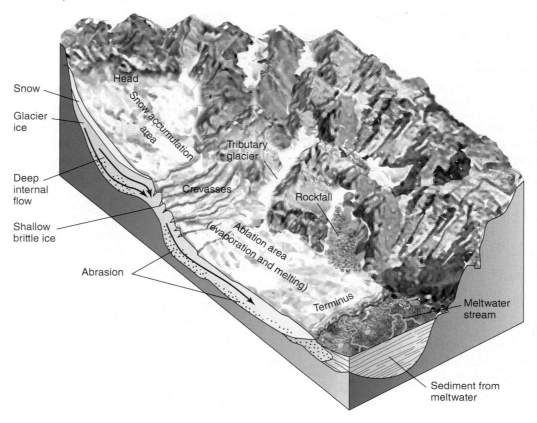

Snow
Glacier ice
Deep internal flow
Shallow brittle ice
Abrasion

Head
Snow accumulation area
Tributary glacier
Crevasses
Rockfall
Ablation area (evaporation and melting)
Terminus
Meltwater stream
Sediment from meltwater

Measurements of velocity show that the ice in the central part of the glacier moves faster than the ice at the sides and that the uppermost layer moves faster than the lower layers. This is similar to what happens to water flowing in a stream (see Chapter 7), though it occurs much more slowly; in most glaciers, flow velocities range from a few centimeters to a few meters a day. It may take hundreds of years for an ice crystal that fell as a snowflake at the head of a glacier to reach the terminus and melt. The glacier ice moves in two basic ways: by internal flow and by basal sliding across the underlying rock or sediment.

As the weight of overlying snow and ice in a glacier increases, individual ice crystals are subjected to higher and higher stress. Under this stress, ice crystals deep within the glacier undergo very slow movements, called **creep**, along internal crystal planes (**Figure 13.14**). As the compacted, frozen mass moves, the crystal axes of the individual ice crystals are forced into the same orientation and end up with their internal crystal planes oriented in the same direction.

In contrast to the deep parts of a glacier, where ice flows by internal creep, the surface portion has relatively little weight on it and is brittle. When a glacier passes over a change in slope, such as a cliff, the surface ice cracks as tension pulls it apart. When the crack opens up, it forms a **crevasse**, a deep, gaping fissure in the upper surface of a

glacier (**Figure 13.15**). Thus, ice moves in a glacier through a combination of ductile deformation at depth and brittle deformation at the surface—a pattern not dissimilar to the pattern seen in deformation of rock (see *Remember This!*).

REMEMBER THIS! Do you remember the important differences between ductile and brittle deformation? These differences apply to deformation in ice, as well as in rock. You can review this material by looking back at the section on *Rock Deformation* in Chapter 9.

Sometimes ice at the bottom of a glacier slides across its bed (the rock or sediment on which the glacier rests). This is called **basal sliding**. In temperate glaciers, meltwater at the base can act as a lubricant. Basal sliding may account for up to 90% of total observed movement in such a glacier, with the remaining 10% being internal flow. In contrast, polar glaciers are so cold that they are frozen to their beds; they seldom move by basal sliding, and all movement is by internal flow.

On infrequent occasions, a glacier may seem to go wild when ice in one part of the glacier begins to move rapidly downslope, producing a chaos of crevasses and broken pinnacles. Rates of movement have been observed that are up to 100 times those of ordinary glaciers. These episodes

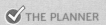

How ice deforms and flows internally • Figure 13.14

The two main processes that produce changes in a mass of ice are recrystallization and internal flow.

Recrystallization

a. A deep ice core from Russia's Vostok Station penetrates the East Antarctic Ice Sheet to a depth of 2083 meters. Microscopic examination of samples from different depths in the core show progressive increase in the size of ice crystals, the result of recrystallization as the thickness and weight of overlying ice slowly increased with time.

THINK CRITICALLY

What are the similarities and differences between recrystallization and internal flow in glaciers, and recrystallization and development of foliation and schistosity during metamorphism (Chapter 10)?

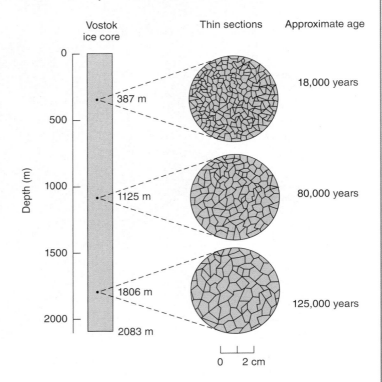

Internal flow

b. Through a combination of recrystallization and slippage along crystal lattice planes, randomly oriented ice crystals are reorganized by stress so that their internal crystal planes are parallel.

c. The ice creeps (slips) along its internal aligned crystal lattice planes, in a process very similar to playing cards in a deck of cards sliding past one another.

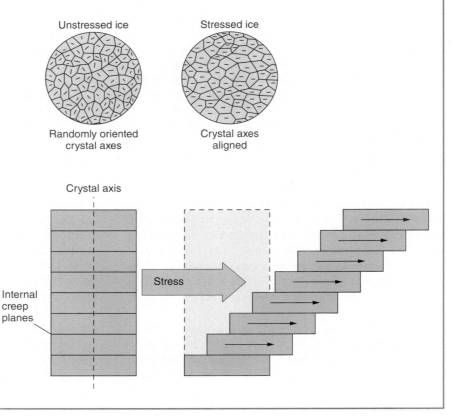

Crevasses: Brittle deformation • Figure 13.15

Deep fissures in the ice, called crevasses, open up as a result of stresses in the brittle surface layer of a glacier. The glacier flows in a direction perpendicular to a crevasse.

Glacial flow

Courtesy Stephen C. Porter

are called **surges**, and their causes are not fully understood (**Figure 13.16**). Geologists hypothesize that, in many cases, a buildup of water pressure at the base of the glacier reduces friction and permits very rapid basal sliding. The surge stops when the water finds an exit.

The Glacial Landscape

As glaciers move, they change the landscape by eroding and scraping away material, as well as by transporting and depositing material at their ends and along their margins. In changing the surface of the land over which it moves, a glacier acts like a file, a plow, and a sled. As a file, it rasps away firm rock. As a plow, it scrapes up weathered rock and soil and plucks out blocks of bedrock—glacial erosion. As a sled, it carries away the load of sediment acquired by plowing and filing, along with rock debris that falls onto it from adjacent slopes—glacial deposition. **Figure 13.17** illustrates some of the types of terrain that result from these processes.

Basal sliding and the "galloping glacier" • Figure 13.16

Basal sliding and glacial surges may be initiated when water accumulates at the base of a glacier.

a. The buildup of water pressure lubricates the base and allows the glacier to flow very rapidly, until the water finds a way out again.

b. This is an ice dam at the terminus of the Hubbard Glacier, in Russell Fjord, Alaska. The helicopter hovering in front shows the scale of the wall of ice.

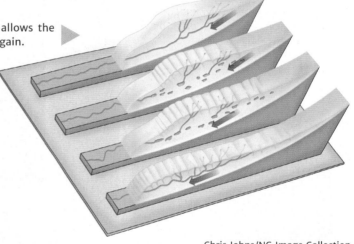

Chris Johns/NG Image Collection

Chris Johns/NG Image Collection

c. In 1988, the ice dam shown in (**b**) broke and the Hubbard Glacier surged through, blocking much of the bay and creating a temporary freshwater lake. This picture was taken shortly after the dam broke.

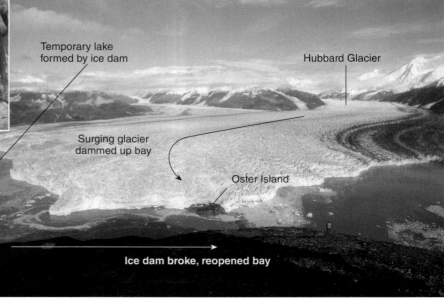

Temporary lake formed by ice dam

Hubbard Glacier

Surging glacier dammed up bay

Oster Island

Ice dam broke, reopened bay

Glaciers create landforms both by erosion and by deposition.

Glacial erosion

◀ **a.** These glacial grooves in Ohio were etched into limestone during the most recent ice age, about 35,000 years ago.

b. Mount Everest, seen here, is the highest point above sea level. It is surrounded by glacially carved features, including deep, bowl-shaped cirques and knife-sharp arêtes. ▶

◀ **c.** The gorgeous Lauterbrunnen Valley in Switzerland has the classic U-shape of a glacial valley. The glacier that formed it no longer exists.

THINK CRITICALLY

Are there any glacial landscapes near where you live? What are two different ways that you could find this out? How would you distinguish glacial landforms from other types of landforms?

Glacial deposition

d. Glacial till can sometimes include very large boulders, such as these boulders in Yellowstone National Park. When they are different from the bedrock, such boulders are called **erratics**.

Raymond Gehman/NG Image Collection

Courtesy Gerald Osborn, University of Calgary

e. This terminal moraine near Mount Robson in British Columbia marks the farthest advance of the glacier at left in the 19th and 20th centuries.

LOOK Die Bildagentur der FotografenGmbH/Alamy

f. The dark stripes running down the center of Kaskawulsh Glacier in the Yukon are part of a medial moraine.

Cary Wolinsky/NG Image Collection

g. The curving ridge of sand and gravel in this photo, now covered by a thin layer of soil and grass, is an esker, in Kettle Moraine State Park in Wisconsin.

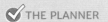
Periglacial Landforms

Looking at this curious hexagonal patterned ground in Beacon Valley, Antarctica, a geologist would suspect that the pattern might somehow be connected with freezing and thawing processes in the soil. Close examination reveals that each hexagon is surrounded by fractures filled by wedges of ice. The geologist realizes that the ice wedges must have formed when water seeped into open cracks in the ground and subsequently froze.

THINK CRITICALLY

Can you think of any other natural environments that have a pattern of hexagonal polygons similar to this one? (*Hint*: We have looked at two others in the book. Did they form in a similar manner?)

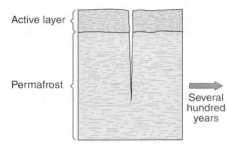

The geologist reasons that the repeated melting and freezing must have continued for a long time to develop such an extensive area of patterned ground. In summer, the crack opens or partially melts, allowing more water to enter. In winter, the ice freezes again. The ice wedge continues to grow as the melting and refreezing cycle repeats hundreds of times. By excavation, the geologist would discover that such wedges can grow as wide as 3 meters and as deep as 30 meters.

Here the geologist examines another periglacial feature called *lithalsa*, or stone rings. They are frost-heaved mounds of stone that have collapsed in the center. These are in the Svalbard Archipelago in the Arctic Ocean (part of Norway). Larger frost-heaved mounds, which can reach up to 600 meters in height, are called **pingoes**.

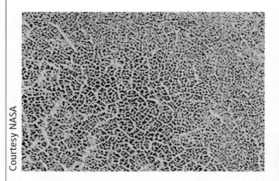

In 2008, a small robot called *Phoenix* landed in a northern region of Mars where the terrain has a curious pattern that geologists thought might be patterned ground like that in Antarctica. To test their hypothesis, they activated a chemical analyzer on *Phoenix* that confirmed the presence of ice in the wedges by baking a soil sample just enough to melt the ice.

Glacial Erosion The base of a glacier is studded with rock fragments of various sizes that are carried along with the moving ice. When basal sliding occurs, small fragments of rock embedded in the basal ice scrape away at the underlying bedrock and produce long, nearly parallel scratches called **glacial striations**. Larger particles gouge out deeper **glacial grooves** (**Figure 13.17a**). Because glacial striations and grooves are aligned parallel to the direction of ice flow, they help geologists reconstruct the flow paths of former glaciers.

Mountain glaciers produce a variety of distinctive landforms. Bowl-shaped **cirques** are found at a glacier's head. Two cirques on opposite sides of a mountain can meet to form a sharp-crested ridge called an **arête**. Cirques developing on all sides of a mountain may carve its peak into a prominent **horn** (like Mount Everest, **Figure 13.17b**).

When glacier ice moves downward from a cirque, it scours a valley channel with a distinctive U-shaped cross section and a floor that usually lies well below the level of tributary valleys (**Figure 13.17c**). Continental ice sheets can gouge the bedrock to form lakes; some examples of very large glacially formed lakes are the Great Lakes, Lake Winnipeg, and Great Bear Lake. Large glaciers and ice sheets are more effective agents of erosion and carve deeper valleys and lakes than small tributary glaciers. At the intersection of a smaller glacier and a larger glacier, there is usually an abrupt change in elevation of the valley floor due to the different depths of erosion.

Glacial Deposition Like streams of water, glaciers carry a load of sediment particles of various sizes. Unlike a stream, however, a glacier can carry part of its load at its sides and even on its surface. A glacier can carry very large rocks and small fragments side by side. When deposited by a glacier, the mixed rocky fragments (called glacial **till**) are not sorted, rounded, or stratified the way stream deposits usually are. In most cases, the boulders and rock fragments in a till are different from the underlying bedrock (**Figure 13.17d**).

> **till** A heterogeneous mixture of crushed rock, sand, pebbles, cobbles, and boulders deposited by a glacier.

The boulders, rock fragments, and other sediment carried by a glacier may be deposited along its margins or at its terminus. These form ridges called moraines. Specifically, **lateral moraines** form along the edges, a **terminal moraine** forms at the terminus (**Figure 13.17e**), and a **recessional moraine** forms as a glacier melts and recedes. If two glaciers converge, they may trap lateral moraines between them, forming a ridge of material that rides along the middle of the ice

> **moraine** A ridge or pile of debris that has been, or is being, transported by a glacier.

stream, called a **medial moraine** (**Figure 13.17f**). Geologists have used the locations of glacial moraines in the United States and Canada to determine how far the glacier ice cover extended over North America during the last ice age.

The sinuous deposit shown in **Figure 13.17g** may look perplexing at first: It seems like an upside-down stream bed embossed upon the landscape. What could create such a feature? We have already mentioned that the bottoms of some temperate glaciers contain meltwater. This water may form a stream that tunnels through the glacier. (Such streams can sometimes be seen emerging from the terminus of an active glacier.) Like any other stream, it deposits sediment. If the glacier subsequently retreats, that sediment is left behind in a raised bed called an **esker**, like the one shown in the photo.

The retreat of a glacier can leave behind a terrain full of pits and pockmarks from abandoned blocks of ice embedded in the glacial debris. These subsequently melt, and the depressions left behind are called **kettles**. Many kettles fill with water to form kettle ponds and lakes. One famous example of a small kettle pond is Walden Pond, immortalized by the writer Henry David Thoreau.

Periglacial Landforms Land areas that are near or adjacent to glaciers are referred to as **periglacial** (from the Greek *peri*, "around"). Periglacial landscapes have distinctive landforms of their own, which result principally from intense frost action and a large annual range in temperatures. The most common type of landscape in present-day periglacial regions is **tundra**, a treeless biome that experiences long winters and very short summers, and is characterized by poorly developed soils and low, scrubby vegetation. Tundra is usually underlain by a layer of permafrost. During the short summer, the ice in permafrost melts only in a thin layer near the surface, called the **active layer**. The freeze–thaw cycle produces characteristic geological formations called **ice wedges** and **patterned ground** (see *What a Geologist Sees*).

> **permafrost** Ground that is perennially below the freezing point of water.

STOP **CONCEPT CHECK**

1. **How** do polar glaciers differ from temperate glaciers?
2. **What** has to happen for a glacier to advance or retreat?
3. **What** is significant about terminal moraines?

SUMMARY

1 Deserts and Drylands   350

- The term **desert** refers to arid lands where annual rainfall is less than 250 millimeters. Five types of deserts have been identified: subtropical, continental interior, rainshadow, coastal, and polar. Subtropical and polar deserts result from the global wind patterns that create dry high-pressure air masses around 30°N and 30°S and at the poles, as shown in the map. The other three kinds of deserts result from more local geological conditions.

The world's deserts · Figure 13.1

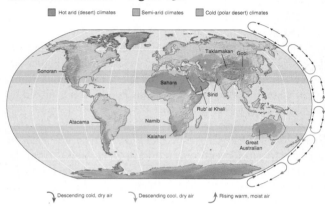

- Eolian (wind) erosion is particularly effective in arid and semiarid regions. Wind moves particles through **surface creep, saltation**, and **suspension**. Flowing air erodes the land surface through the processes of **abrasion** and **deflation**.

- **Dunes** are hills or ridges of sand deposited by winds. They are asymmetrical, with a gentle slope facing the wind and a steeper slip face on the leeward side. Common types of dunes are barchan, transverse, star, parabolic, and longitudinal. The type of dune that will form in a given place depends on the amount of sand, the wind conditions, and the amount of vegetation.

- Contrary to the popular image of a desert, the majority of desert lands are not covered by sand. Water erosion is an important geological process in deserts. Flash floods carve deep canyons called arroyos and create depositional landforms such as alluvial fans.

2 Desertification and Land Degradation   357

- **Desertification** involves the invasion of desert conditions into nondesert lands, which can result in accelerated soil erosion, decline in water tables, and loss of agricultural productivity. Desertification can be caused by natural environmental changes or by human activities and can lead to famines affecting millions of people.

- When deserts advance as a result of poor land-use practices, it is referred to as **land degradation** or accelerated desertification.

- Appropriate land use, the application of simple soil management approaches, and carefully designed irrigation (see photo) can prevent or mitigate many of the negative consequences of desertification.

Stabilizing soil · Figure 13.9

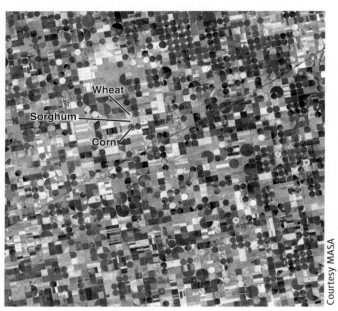

Courtesy MASA

3 Glaciers and Ice Sheets   360

- The perennially frozen part of the hydrosphere is called the **cryosphere**. It includes **glaciers** on land as well as sea ice. Glaciers come in several varieties and can form either in polar regions or at high altitudes in temperate regions. Most of the world's fresh water is locked in vast ice sheets in Antarctica and the North Pole region.

- Glacier ice is formed by the compaction of grains of snow and recrystallization of small ice crystals into larger ones—processes that are similar to lithification and metamorphism in ordinary rock. The mass of a glacier can change from season to season and year to year through accumulation and ablation, as shown in the diagram. Accumulation (by new snowfall) predominates at the head of the glacier, and ablation (by melting) predominates at the terminus.

A glacier has a budget · Figure 13.13

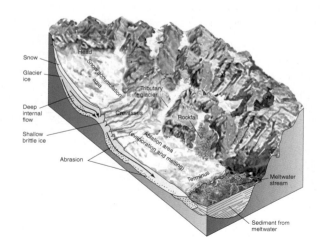

- Just like ordinary rock, glacial ice can move by either ductile or brittle deformation. The internal movement is ductile and aligns the ice crystals in the direction of flow. Brittle deformation occurs when a glacier goes over a change in slope, opening up fissures called crevasses. At the bottom of a glacier, where basal sliding occurs, small fragments of rock embedded in the ice scrape away at the underlying bedrock, producing glacial striations and grooves.

- In mountainous regions, glaciers produce a variety of distinctive erosional landforms, such as cirques, arêtes, and U-shaped valleys. Common periglacial features include **permafrost** and patterned ground, which are formed by the repeated freezing and thawing of groundwater.

- Glacial deposits often consist of unsorted **till**. A **moraine** is a ridge or pile of debris being carried along by a glacier or deposited along its edge or terminus. When a glacier retreats, the moraine is left behind. Such deposits are useful for identifying the previous extent of glaciers that have retreated or disappeared. Other features often left behind by retreating glaciers are kettle lakes and elevated eskers.

KEY TERMS

abrasion   352

cryosphere   360

deflation   352

desert   350

desertification   357

dune   354

glacier   360

land degradation   358

moraine   371

permafrost   371

saltation   352

surface creep   352

suspension   352

till   371

CRITICAL AND CREATIVE THINKING QUESTIONS

1. We have discussed the connection between large atmospheric circulation patterns and the occurrence of subtropical deserts. What climatic and atmospheric processes contribute to the formation of rainshadow deserts, coastal deserts, and continental interior deserts?

2. Investigate the current status of drought and land degradation in the Sahel or elsewhere. Can you find any information about soil erosion control techniques or other methods that are being used to combat desertification?

3. Investigate the history of soil conservation programs and organizations that emerged from the experiences of the Dust Bowl years. How have these organizations changed over time?

4. Do some research on the most recent ice age. Do you live in an area that was formerly covered by ice? If so, how thick was the ice?

5. Many glaciers in locations around the world have been retreating at a rapid rate for the past few decades. Why? Is the retreat caused by natural or anthropogenic processes? We will discuss this in greater detail in Chapter 14. Choose one glacier and investigate its current status; find out whether the glacier is advancing or retreating, and how quickly.

6. Consider Figure 13.14a. Notice that the grain sizes in the ice become larger the longer the ice has been buried at depth. This happens as a result of recrystallization of the grains of ice. Now recall the process of recrystallization of mineral grains during lithification (Figure 8.12), and during metamorphism (Figure 10.9, for example). In what ways do you think the three sets of processes are similar or related? In what ways do you think they are different?

How ice deforms and flows internally • Figure 13.14

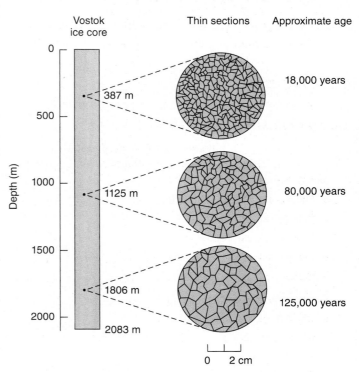

WHAT IS HAPPENING IN THIS PICTURE?

This house was built on top of permafrost in Dawson City, Yukon Territory, Canada.

© imageBROKER/Alamy

THINK CRITICALLY

1. How might warming temperatures affect the permafrost?
2. Why would this cause the surface to buckle and subside?

SELF-TEST

(Check your answers in Appendix D.)

1. _____ and _____ deserts result from the global wind patterns that create dry high-pressure air masses around 30°N and 30°S and at the poles.
   a. Subtropical, continental interior
   b. Subtropical, polar
   c. Subtropical, rainshadow
   d. Continental interior, rainshadow
   e. Continental interior, polar

2. Deflation on a large scale takes place only _____.
   a. where there is little or no vegetation
   b. where loose particles are fine enough to be picked up by the wind
   c. in desert environments

   d. Both a and b are correct.
   e. Both b and c are correct.

3. A typical sand dune _____.
   a. is asymmetrical
   b. has a gentle windward slope
   c. has a steep leeward face
   d. All of the above are correct.

4. Which one of the following is *not* one of the major indicators of desertification?
   a. lower water tables and a reduction of surface waters
   b. increased surface temperatures in summer months
   c. higher levels of salt in water and topsoil
   d. unusually high rates of soil erosion
   e. destruction of vegetation

5. The following diagram depicts dune formation as a function of wind, sand supply, and vegetation cover. Label the diagram with the following terms:

longitudinal dunes   transverse dunes

barchan dunes   parabolic dunes

star dunes

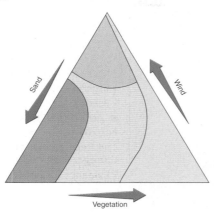

6. Arroyos and bajadas are _____.

a. common products of wind erosion

b. two possible end results of subsidence in desert environments

c. desert landforms created by running water

d. signs of human impact on the desert landscape

7. This diagram shows various glaciers at Earth's surface. Label the illustration with the appropriate terms for the individual glaciers a through e:

cirque glacier   fjord glacier

piedmont glacier   ice cap

valley glacier

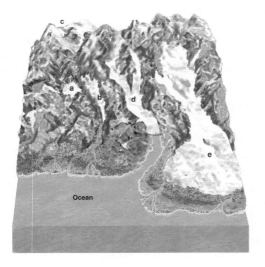

8. In _____, meltwater and ice can exist together in equilibrium.

a. temperate glaciers

b. polar glaciers

c. ice caps

9. In _____, little or no seasonal melting occurs.

a. temperate glaciers

b. polar glaciers

c. ice caps

d. Both b and c are correct.

10. Ice in a glacier typically undergoes both brittle and ductile deformation.

a. true

b. false

11. Glacier ice moves under the influence of gravity through _____.

a. basal sliding

b. internal flow

c. Both a and b occur in all glaciers.

d. Either a or b can occur, depending on the characteristics of the glacier.

12. Which of the following is formed by glacial erosion?

a. striations

b. permafrost

c. eskers

d. till

13. Which of the following is formed by the deposition of glacial sediment?

a. grooves

b. arêtes

c. moraines

d. crevasses

14. This photograph shows a glacial landscape. What is the name for the curving ridge of sand and gravel that dominates the picture?

a. erratic

b. esker

c. kettle

d. terminal moraine

Cary Wolinsky/NG Image Collection

15. The term **periglacial** refers to land that _____.

a. was glaciated in a former time

b. is currently lying underneath glacier ice

c. is near or adjacent to a glacier

d. is at risk of becoming glaciated

THE PLANNER ✓

Review the Chapter Planner on the chapter opener and check off your completed work.

14

EARTH'S CLIMATES: PAST, PRESENT, FUTURE

futureatlas.com

Mario Bono/Shutterstock

FARMING IN THE DESERT

The area surrounding Kufra Oasis in eastern Libya is one of the driest places on Earth—annual rainfall is only about a millimeter. Yet in Kufra there are fields of verdant crops, nurtured by irrigation from groundwater (inset photo, satellite image).

The source of the water is the Nubian Sandstone, host to the largest fossil aquifer in the world. A *fossil aquifer* is no longer recharged by precipitation, but contains ancient water sealed into the rock. The Nubian Sandstone Aquifer underlies approximately 2.2 million square kilometers of the eastern Sahara Desert, including most of Egypt, half of Libya, and large parts of Sudan and Chad. Most of the water entered the aquifer thousands of years ago, when the climate in the Sahara was considerably wetter. The river channels that were once connected to the aquifer system are now dry valleys, called *wadis*.

A tiny amount of recharge infrequently reaches the aquifer, but the rate of withdrawal greatly exceeds replacement. The level of the groundwater is dropping, and eventually Kufra Oasis itself will become dry. The climate of the Sahara region has changed many times in its history, becoming wetter or drier as a consequence of natural forces that affect climate, which you will learn more about in this chapter.

THE CLIMATE SYSTEM

Learning Objectives

1. **Describe** the main components of Earth's climate system.

2. **Identify** the six major climate categories.

Climatically extreme areas such as deserts, glaciers, and polar regions, which we examined in Chapter 13, have taken on special importance in recent years. These extreme environments are particularly sensitive to changes in **climate** and thus are likely to be early indicators of global climatic change, popularly called **global warming**. Global warming is a scientifically complex topic, and it is also politically and emotionally challenging. It is important to emphasize the difference between what we know is happening and what we think is happening—a distinction that is often lost in the doomsday accounts one sees on television, online, and in the press. This is a scientific approach, and it is the approach that we will take in this chapter.

> **climate** The average weather conditions of a location or region over time.
>
> **global warming** Present-day warming of the world's climate that most scientists believe is likely to continue and is at least partly caused by human activities.

In this chapter we investigate the natural causes of climate change, and the evidence demonstrating that climates have changed throughout Earth's history. We look at some of the tools and techniques that scientists use to study climates of the past. We also consider how human activities are affecting the Earth system and, in turn, climate. We start our study of climate by looking at the components of the climate system and the interacting processes and feedbacks that characterize it.

Components of the Climate System

Earth's climate system is complex and is driven by interactions among all of the planet's major subsystems (**Figure 14.1**): atmosphere, hydrosphere (mainly the ocean), cryosphere, geosphere, and biosphere. Most recently, these have been further influenced by processes in the **anthroposphere**, the realm of human activity. The components of the climate system interact so closely that a change in one of them causes changes in the others.

All of the components of the climate system, except the geosphere, are driven by solar energy. Some incoming solar radiation is reflected back to space by clouds, atmospheric pollutants, ice, snow, and other reflective surfaces. The remainder of the incoming solar energy is absorbed, stored, and transferred through various reservoirs in the Earth system. It is subsequently re-emitted at longer wavelengths, from the three great reservoirs—atmosphere, ocean, and land (see *Remember This!*, next page).

Earth's climate system • Figure 14.1

The climate system has five major interacting components: geosphere, atmosphere, hydrosphere, cryosphere, and biosphere. All are influenced by the anthroposphere—the sphere of human activity.

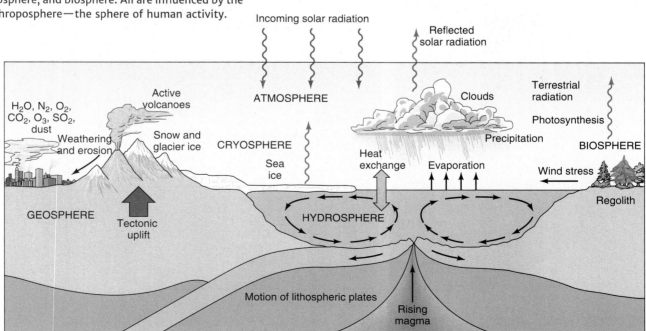

REMEMBER THIS! Can you describe how Earth's natural greenhouse effect works? The radiative balance between incoming and outgoing energy, moderated by the greenhouse effect, is crucial in maintaining a stable global climate. If you need to review, go to *Layers in the Atmosphere*, Chapter 12.

Vegetation is particularly important in the climate system. Plants influence the composition of air by acting as a reservoir for carbon dioxide (a greenhouse gas), and by affecting humidity and local cloud cover. Vegetation also helps determine the reflectivity of the land surface. Its absence can increase wind erosion, which can influence climate by affecting how much dust is in the atmosphere.

The ocean serves as a great reservoir of thermal energy that helps moderate climate, because of its ability to absorb energy and retain it in the form of heat. The ocean also is extremely important in controlling the composition of the atmosphere because seawater contains a large amount of dissolved carbon dioxide. If the balance between oceanic and atmospheric carbon dioxide reservoirs were to change by even a small amount, the radiation balance of the atmosphere would be affected, bringing about a change in world climates.

Finally, the cryosphere—the perennially frozen part of the Earth system—plays a crucial role in the climate system, as you will see in this chapter. The polar ice caps, in particular, help to determine the reflectivity of the planet, serve as an enormous storage reservoir for water, and influence the oceanic thermohaline circulation, all of which are important in regulating climate.

Present-Day Climates

Scientists commonly use variations of the **Köppen system** to describe the present-day distribution of climate zones (**Figure 14.2**). This climate classification system, originally developed by Austrian climatologist Vladimir Köppen, is based on the distribution of native vegetation types. It combines measurements of average temperature and precipitation to define six major climate categories. The principal categories can be refined by modifiers that indicate variations of precipitation, temperature, and seasonality.

The most notable feature of a map showing the world distribution of climate zones is the close link between climate zones and the prevailing wind currents in the global atmospheric circulation system, shown in Figure 12.21. For example, the world's dry climates and deserts are mostly concentrated along the 30°N and 30°S latitudes, where the descending air masses are dry. The wet tropical climates and rainforests of Africa and South America lie near the equator, where we expect lots of warm, moist air.

STOP CONCEPT CHECK

1. **What** are the main components of the Earth system that interact to control climate?

2. **What** factors do scientists use to distinguish the six main climate classifications?

Global climate zones • Figure 14.2

In a simplified version of the Köppen (or Köppen-Geiger) climate classification system, there are six basic climate zones: tropical, dry, temperate–humid, cold–humid, polar, and highland. These zones are strongly related to the global pattern of atmospheric circulation and the distribution of major ecosystems.

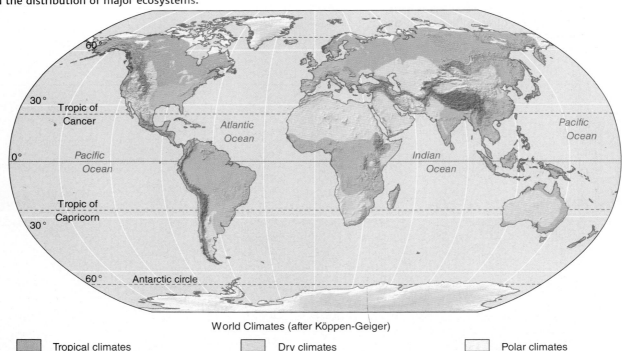

World Climates (after Köppen-Geiger)

Tropical climates
Temperate-humid climates
Dry climates
Cold-humid climates
Polar climates
Highland climates

NATURAL CAUSES OF CLIMATE CHANGE

Learning Objectives

1. **Summarize** the main external factors that cause climate change.

2. **Summarize** the main internal factors that cause climate change.

3. **Explain** how feedbacks contribute to complexity in the climate system.

As discussed in the chapter opener, we know that deserts expand and retreat, and that their climates change as a result of natural causes; they have done so throughout Earth's history (see the *Case Study*). Several natural mechanisms cause changes in global climate, on both short and long time scales. Some of these mechanisms are external to the Earth system, and others are internal. It is important that we understand these natural mechanisms of change, before we go on to consider the human input into climate change.

External Influences on Climate

The Sun, the main source of energy driving Earth's climate system, varies in its total energy output, variously expressed as **solar luminosity** or **radiant flux**, on both long and short time scales. Fluctuations in the energy output of the Sun should result in overall cooling of the planet when the output is low, and warming when the output is high. One problem with this hypothesis is that there is no direct way to measure what the solar output was at times in the distant past, when

---

CASE Study

✓ THE PLANNER

Wetter Times in Wadi Kufra

At Kufra Oasis (see chapter-opening photos), abundant fresh water is stored deep underground in the Nubian Sandstone Aquifer. Geologists have studied the isotopic composition of the water to determine its source and age (i.e., how long it has been underground). They also have sampled woody organic matter from ancient soils (**paleosols**) along now-buried river channels, using carbon-14 analysis to determine the ages of ancient soil surfaces. Through such studies scientists have been able to reconstruct the climatic history of the region.

Present-day groundwater recharge in this extremely arid environment is almost nonexistent; almost all water that falls as precipitation evaporates before it infiltrates. However, there have been at least three significant recharge periods during the Holocene Epoch. These humid periods, called **pluvials**, were characterized by much higher rainfall (300 to 400 mm/yr). The last of the pluvials ended about 3500 years ago, and the Sahara has been drier and hotter since then.

Rainfall during the pluvials supported surface water bodies and lush vegetation. Evidence for wetter periods has been bolstered by discoveries of the remains of large mammals, such as elephants and hippos, which cannot survive in the current arid conditions. The pluvials also supported early humans; satellite images reveal ancient river channels and human artifacts buried under the sand. The nicknames "Wet Sahara" and "Green Sahara" are sometimes used to describe the Neolithic Period (around 9500 years ago), when inhabitants of the Sahara maintained settlements of significant size and carried out farming and cattle herding.

Mike Hettwer

A scientist holds a belly plate from a soft-shelled turtle from the Tenerian culture, which lasted from the 5th to the 3rd millennium BCE. The presence of this animal's remains indicates a much wetter climate at that time.

Cave paintings like this from Adrar Akakus in modern-day Libya, some as old as 12,000 years old, depict palm trees, animals, and activities indicative of a greener and wetter climate, where there is now desert.

age fotostock/SuperStock

Mike Hettwer

The 11-year-old girl in this burial at Gobero, Niger, wears a bracelet on her upper arm that was carved from the tusk of a hippo 4800 years ago. Today hippos live only in much wetter parts of Africa, to the south.

THINK CRITICALLY

How might a scientist begin to figure out whether present-day desertification in regions bordering the Sahara is being caused mainly by natural climatic change or by human mismanagement of land?

glaciation (or glacial period or ice age) A relatively cold period, when Earth's ice cover greatly exceeded its present extent.

interglaciation (or interglacial period) A relatively warm period, when Earth's ice cover and climate resembled those of the present day.

Earth experienced **glaciations** or **interglaciations**. Tests are therefore based on indirect measurements and on computer modeling of solar output, and the results have been contradictory.

In the long term, over the course of solar system history, the Sun's total energy output has increased. Scientists have deduced this on the basis of computer modeling, combined with knowledge about the life cycles of stars similar in mass to our own Sun. Over that same 4.56-billion-year history, however, Earth's overall average surface temperature has decreased significantly. Why is Earth's temperature decreasing, if the main energy input—solar energy—seems to be increasing? This is a paradox that has not yet been resolved. The luminosity of the Sun is a fundamental determinant of Earth's climate, but clearly it is not the only factor.

In addition to long-term changes in luminosity, the Sun exhibits a number of short-term changes that affect the radiative energy output and have direct impacts on Earth, such as solar flare activity. One well-known phenomenon is the cycle of **sunspots**—dark, relatively cool spots that are visible on the surface of the Sun. Sunspot activity varies on a fairly predictable time scale, reaching a peak and then decreasing to a minimum roughly every 11 years. Periods of maximum sunspot activity are associated with intense magnetic activity in the Sun; this, in turn, influences solar convection, leading to higher solar energy output. The result is that periods of minimum sunspot activity are associated with lower solar output.

The relationship between sunspot activity and solar output suggests that periods in which sunspots are at a minimum should correlate with colder temperatures on Earth. It has been challenging to demonstrate this correlation for past climatic events, but one example that is often cited is the so-called **Maunder Minimum**, which lasted from 1645 to about 1717. This was a period of dramatically low sunspot activity; in some years only a few sunspots were observed, compared to the thousands that are more typical. The Maunder Minimum occurred during a prolonged period of unusually cold weather and harsh winters that lasted from the 13th century until the middle of the 19th century. There have been other periods of sunspot minima that appear to correlate with colder-than-normal conditions, but it has been difficult to establish a convincing causal relationship.

The role of solar variability in climate is tempered by many other factors, both external and internal, that contribute to climate change. For example, variations in Earth's orbit affect the climate system (**Figure 14.3**) by influencing how much solar radiation reaches Earth's surface, where, and at what times of year. Changes in the **eccentricity** (departure from circularity) of Earth's orbit, variations in the

degree of **tilt** of the planet's axis of rotation, and **precession** (wobbling) of the axis are all important influences that vary on different time cycles but with great predictability. Sometimes these factors cancel each other out; at other times, they align in such a way that incoming solar radiation is minimized or maximized. The times and magnitudes of these variations, called **Milankovitch cycles**, can be calculated to a high degree of certainty, and they correspond fairly closely to the timing of past glacial and interglacial cycles (shown in **Figure 14.3d**).

Milankovitch cycles The combined influences of astronomical–orbital factors that produce changes in Earth's climate.

Internal Influences on Climate

External factors such as the Sun's output and Earth's orbital variations set the stage for our climate system, but many internal factors moderate these influences.

Atmospheric Filtering The first obvious candidate for an internal influence on climate is the atmosphere. Solar radiation must pass through the atmosphere before it reaches Earth's surface, and it passes through again—this time as terrestrial radiation—on its way back to outer space.

As you learned in Chapter 12, gases in the atmosphere interact with both incoming solar radiation and outgoing terrestrial radiation, reflecting, refracting, and scattering some of it, and absorbing some of it in particular wavelengths. Radiatively active gases, mainly in the troposphere, selectively absorb radiation in the infrared wavelengths, causing a layer of warmed air to accumulate close to the surface (see Figure 12.18); this is the greenhouse effect, which warms the surface of the planet sufficiently to support life as we know it.

The most important of the naturally occurring greenhouse gases, by far, is water vapor. Other important contributors to the natural greenhouse effect include carbon dioxide (CO_2), methane (CH_4), and nitrous oxide (NO_2), all of which are minor constituents of the atmosphere but very important in terms of their contribution to Earth's radiation balance.

The greenhouse gas composition of the atmosphere is controlled by many natural processes, including seasonal and long-term variations in photosynthesis, variations in forest cover and soil moisture, decay of organic matter, and burial (or exposure) of seafloor sediment. Another important factor is volcanic gas, of which both water vapor and carbon dioxide are major components. Vast lava outpourings have occurred at times in the geological past, and geologists have hypothesized that these could have raised the carbon dioxide content of the atmosphere to as much as 20 times the current level. If this hypothesis is correct, then the geosphere and the atmosphere are linked dynamically in their contribution to the greenhouse effect and climate change.

Process Diagram

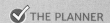
THE PLANNER

How orbital changes influence climate · Figure 14.3

Three kinds of orbital change combine to affect Earth's climate. These external factors interact to control how much sunlight reaches Earth at any given time.

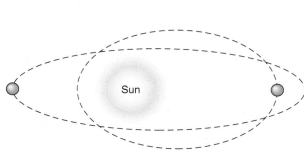

Change in eccentricity of orbit

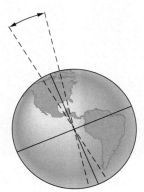

Axial tilt change

Precession (wobble)

a. Change in eccentricity of orbit
Earth's orbit becomes more and less elongate, varying on a period of about 100,000 years.

b. Axial tilt change
Earth's axis changes its tilt, varying on a period of about 41,000 years.

c. Precession (wobble)
Earth's axis wobbles in a circle, with a period of about 26,000 years.

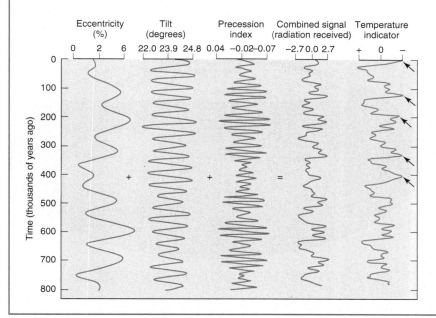

d. Combined effect
These curves show variations in eccentricity, tilt, and precession during the past 800,000 years. Their combined signal (second curve from the right) shows the amount of radiation received on Earth over time. The combined signal closely matches the curve at the far right, which indicates temperature. This supports the hypothesis that Earth's orbital changes influence the timing of glaciations (arrows).

THINK CRITICALLY

What other influences do orbital variations exert on climate, weather, light levels, and seasonality on Earth?

Reflectivity   Another factor that controls how much solar radiation reaches and interacts with Earth's surface is the **albedo** of both the atmosphere and the materials of the surface (**Figure 14.4**). Ice and snow are high-reflectivity surfaces; forests, rock, soil, and water are generally low-reflectivity surfaces. Human-made surfaces such as

> **albedo**   The reflectivity of a surface, as a percentage of the total reflected radiation.

cities, buildings, and pavement vary quite a lot, but overall they tend to be fairly reflective. When radiation strikes highly reflective surfaces, it is scattered and reflected back to space, instead of being absorbed and heating the surface materials. When the world enters a glacial age, large areas of land and water are progressively covered by snow and ice. Their highly reflective surfaces scatter the incoming radiation, leading to further cooling of the surface and the lower atmosphere.

Surface albedo · Figure 14.4

Land, water, snow, ice, and human-made surfaces all have characteristic reflectivities.

HIGH ALBEDO (Snow, Ice, Sand) ↑ ↑ ↑

LOW ALBEDO (Forests, Water) ↑ ↑ ↑

George Ostertag/SuperStock

The atmosphere and cloud tops also reflect a portion of incoming solar radiation, intercepting it before it even reaches the surface. **Aerosols**—extremely fine, suspended particles of dust, volcanic ash, ice, pollutants, and other substances—can cause dramatic changes in atmospheric albedo. Large explosive volcanic eruptions can eject huge quantities of fine ash and sulfur into the atmosphere, creating a veil of sulfate aerosols that encircles the globe (**Figure 14.5**). The aerosols scatter incoming solar radiation, resulting in the cooling of Earth's surface. Volcanic dust settles out rather quickly, generally within a few months to a year; however, tiny droplets of sulfate, produced by the interaction of volcanic sulfur gases and other atmospheric components, can remain in the upper atmosphere for years. These aerosols scatter the Sun's rays and increase the reflectivity of clouds; therefore, explosive, sulfur-rich volcanic eruptions are strongly connected with global cooling.

Clouds influence both the albedo and the heat-retaining capacity of the atmosphere (**Figure 14.6**). Different clouds contribute in different ways. The reflectivity of different cloud types varies dramatically, from about 10% to about 90%. This variation results from differences in thickness, as well as the size and abundance of water droplets and other particles (aerosols) that make up the cloud. Wispy, high-altitude clouds warm the surface by trapping warm air underneath them. Thick, low-altitude clouds trap some heat, but they cool the surface by increasing the reflectivity of the atmosphere.

Volcanoes and climate · Figure 14.5

Major volcanic eruptions can cause an aerosol veil that leads to global cooling.

a. Mount Pinatubo, a stratovolcano in the Philippines, erupted violently in 1991, producing a sulfur-rich aerosol haze that encircled the globe. The color scale on this diagram shows atmospheric sulfur dioxide in parts per billion, after the eruption; the warmer colors indicate higher levels of sulfur.

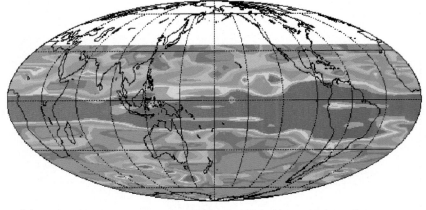

b. Sulfate aerosols from the eruption of Mount Pinatubo caused a global decrease in temperature of at least 0.4°C, and more in the northern hemisphere.

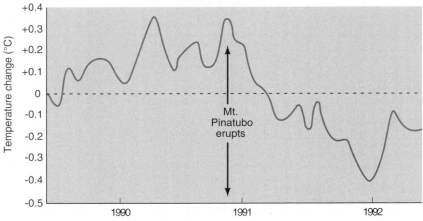

Process Diagram

How clouds influence climate • Figure 14.6

Different types of clouds have differing impacts on surface temperature.

a. High-altitude cirrus clouds: Net effect = warming

High-altitude, wispy clouds have low albedos; they allow the Sun's shortwave radiation to pass through (red arrows). They absorb outgoing longwave radiation (yellow arrows), re-radiating some of it back to the surface and thus contributing to greenhouse warming.

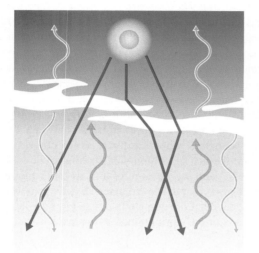

b. Low-altitude stratocumulus clouds: Net effect = cooling

Low-altitude stratocumulus clouds are thicker and less transparent than high-altitude clouds. They have higher albedos and reflect incoming solar energy (red arrows) back to outer space. They trap outgoing longwave energy (yellow arrows) and send it back to the surface, which contributes to greenhouse warming. The effectiveness of their high reflectivity means that the net effect is cooling.

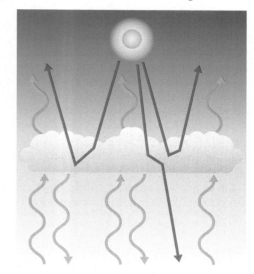

NASA image courtesy Jeff Schmaltz, MODIS Rapid Response Team at NASA GSFC

NASA

THINK CRITICALLY

Clouds of any type tend to have higher albedos than the surfaces beneath them. What would be the climatic implications if cloud cover were to increase over high-albedo areas like deserts or the polar ice caps? What about low-albedo surfaces, like forests or the ocean?

Changes in Ocean Circulation The global circulation of the world ocean plays an important role in the climate system. The thermohaline circulation system links the atmosphere with the deep ocean, by way of the ocean's surface layer (see *Remember This!*). Warm surface water moving northward into the North Atlantic in the Gulf Stream releases heat to the atmosphere by evaporation, maintaining the relatively mild climate of northwestern Europe. As a result of evaporation, the remaining water becomes cooler and more saline—and therefore denser. Cold, saline water sinks to produce North Atlantic Deep Water in the northern hemisphere and Antarctic Bottom Water in the southern hemisphere, kick-starting the deep-water parts of the thermohaline circulation. The locations where this sinking occurs are surprisingly limited because the conditions that produce the necessary cold, dense water are very specific.

> **REMEMBER THIS!** Do you remember how the ocean's global conveyor-belt circulation system works, and how it links the deep ocean to surface water and to the atmosphere? If you would like to review, you can look back at Figure 12.5 and the section *Ocean Currents* in Chapter 12.

Consider what would happen if this system closed down. If the water of the North Atlantic were to become warmer or fresher, for example, such that North American Deep Water failed to form, the thermohaline circulation could be disrupted, bypassing the northern part of the Atlantic Ocean altogether. This would effectively shut down the warm Gulf Stream Current, plunging the coastal areas of North America and western Europe into a deep freeze. You might recognize this as the scenario in the 2004 science fiction movie *The Day After Tomorrow*.

Once the Gulf Stream portion of the thermohaline circulation is cut off, the expanding sea-ice cover in the North Atlantic and extensive ice sheets on the adjacent continents would cause the climate to become increasingly cold. Thus, changes in the thermohaline circulation system may help explain why Earth's climate system appears to fluctuate between two relatively stable modes—one in which the ocean conveyor system is operational (interglaciation) and one in which it has shut down (glaciation).

In the film *The Day After Tomorrow*, the change from interglacial to glacial happens over the course of a few days, an impossible time scale in the real world. However, over the past decade or so, considerable interest has been focused on fluctuations of climate that start and end abruptly, last only a few hundred to a thousand years, and recur at intervals much shorter than the tens of thousands of years that we commonly associate with major glaciations. A rapid cooling interval of this type appears to have happened between 11,000 and 10,000 years ago, when Earth was in the process of emerging from the last glaciation. This cold episode lasted about 1300 years, and scientists refer to it as the **Younger Dryas event** (**Figure 14.7**). The Younger Dryas was not unique; it now appears that the climate fluctuated rapidly in and out of glacial conditions during much of the last ice age.

Younger Dryas cold snap • Figure 14.7 _____

The Younger Dryas event was a rapid cooling event that happened between 11,000 and 10,000 years ago.

a. In full-glacial conditions, plants that are currently limited to polar and high-altitude regions could move into forests in northwestern Europe. Among these is *Dryas octopetala*, shown here. A large amount of *Dryas* pollen is found in deposits dating from the Younger Dryas event.

b. Measurements of oxygen isotopes (an indicator of temperature) in sediment from a Swiss lake (left) and an ice core from the Greenland ice sheet (right) show that both the onset and the end of the Younger Dryas were rapid. At the end, the climate of Greenland warmed by about 7°C in just 40 years.

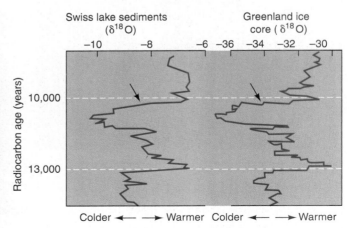

Note: $\delta^{18}O$ is a scientific notation which indicates the ratio of stable isotopes ^{18}O:^{16}O.

Plate Tectonics Global oceanic circulation is directly influenced by the geographic distribution of continents and ocean basins, which in turn influence climate. For example, the Middle Cretaceous Period (about 100 million years ago) had one of the warmest climates in Earth's history, with an average global temperature at least 6°C warmer than today. Sea level was 100 to 200 meters higher, and warm, shallow seas covered many continental coastal areas. The continents were clustered together, with an enormous world ocean covering more than half of the globe. This dramatically affected the thermohaline circulation and, in combination with a high level of atmospheric carbon dioxide (possibly from extremely vigorous volcanic emissions), profoundly influenced the global climate.

Another example of geographic and tectonic influences on climate is the Isthmus of Panama, a narrow strip of land that joins North America and South America (**Figure 14.8**). The land of the isthmus was pushed above sea level about 3 million years ago, during the Pliocene Epoch, as a result of the collision of the Pacific and Caribbean plates. Before then, water circulated freely through an oceanic "gateway" between the Pacific and Atlantic basins. The temperature of the ocean overall was much warmer than it is presently, which likely contributed to a rise in global surface temperature that culminated about 55 million years ago in an event termed the **Paleocene-Eocene Thermal Maximum**. Plant and animal remains typical of redwood and cypress forests and dating from that time have been found in the cold, treeless tundra of the High Arctic, providing evidence of temperate or even tropical climates in northern locations (see *Amazing Places*). The gradual rising of the land bridge eventually blocked the circulation of ocean water between the basins. Warm water flowing from the Caribbean (on the Atlantic side), instead of passing through to the Pacific, was diverted, flowing to the north alongside North America. This warm current eventually became the Gulf Stream.

So ice leads to more ice, and bare ground leads to more bare ground. Glaciations last for many thousands of years, but they may start and stop rapidly. Clouds can cool the Earth's surface, but they also can warm the surface. Volcanic eruptions can cause global cooling by ejecting volcanic dust and sulfur aerosols, but they can also cause global warming by adding greenhouse gases to the atmosphere. All of this may seem confusing and contradictory, but this kind of complexity is quite typical of the climate system. When one part of a delicately balanced system is changed, the effects and readjustments—both complementary and contradictory—are propagated throughout the system. The challenge in understanding the climate system is to determine which response will dominate when changes occur. To get a better handle on this issue, we need to consider the role of feedbacks in the climate system.

Feedbacks

The recognition of abrupt climatic shifts shows how much scientists still have to learn about the global climate system. What makes Earth's climate system even more challenging

Closing the ocean gateway • Figure 14.8 _____

The connection between the Atlantic and Pacific has changed as a result of plate tectonics, with enormous impacts on oceanic circulation.

a. Surface waters flowed freely from the Pacific into the Atlantic 10 million years ago via an oceanic gateway known as the Central American Seaway. ▼

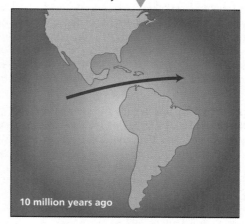

10 million years ago

b. About 5 million years ago, the Pacific and Caribbean plates began to converge. The resulting rise of the Isthmus of Panama restricted water exchange between the Atlantic and Pacific basins. The warm Gulf Stream current began to flow northward along the eastern coast of North America. ▼

5 million years ago

c. Today, the Isthmus of Panama completely blocks the flow of water between the Atlantic and Pacific in this region, and the strong Gulf Stream is responsible for the mild climate in the North Atlantic. ▼

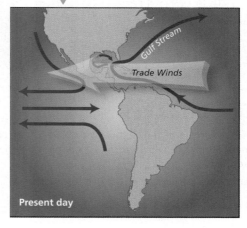

Present day

Fossil Forests of the High Arctic

Axel Heiberg Island and Ellesmere Island, in Nunavut's Qikiqtaaluk Region in the far north of Canada, are cold, wind-swept, and treeless. Since the 1980s, scientists have been studying an amazing collection of fossilized remains on these islands. Actually, they are more like mummified remains, since entire plants, wood (**Figure a**), leaf litter, seeds, and cones have been preserved without the mineral replacement that technically characterizes fossilization (see Chapter 15).

The preserved remains include the stumps and root systems of tall trees (**Figure b**), including redwood, cypress, oak, pine, and sycamore—trees that could not survive in the current tundra conditions. Also present are the remains of ferns and flowering plants, tortoises, snakes, and even crocodiles (**Figure c**), hippos, and tapirs. Axel Heiberg, Ellesmere, and other locations in Canada's High Arctic were covered by many generations of lush forests and wetlands during the warm Eocene Epoch, about 45 million years ago.

The Eocene climate in the High Arctic was probably similar to that of present-day temperate rainforests of the Pacific Northwest—perhaps even as warm as the wetland forests of Florida (**Figure d**). At high latitudes there is constant daylight in the summer and 24-hour darkness in the winter—an interesting survival challenge for the plants and animals that inhabited these regions during the Eocene.

Global Locator

Ellesmere Island

Axel Heiberg Island

NG Maps

One might be tempted to think that plate tectonics simply rearranged the landmasses, moving Axel Heiberg and Ellesmere from more southern latitudes to their present-day polar locations; however, paleomagnetic studies show that their locations have been relatively stable for the past 45 million years. Evidence suggests, instead, that the polar climate and global ocean temperatures were much warmer at that time than at present.

The government of Nunavut is considering establishing a park to protect the extraordinary fossil forests of the High Arctic. The proposed name for the park is Napaaqtulik, which means "where there are trees" in the Inuktitut language.

a

Hemis/Alamy

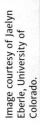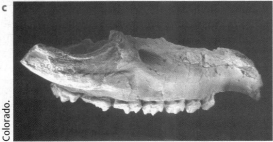

c

Image courtesy of Jaelyn Eberle, University of Colorado.

b

Image courtesy of Jaelyn Eberle, University of Colorado.

d

Comstock Images/Getty Images, Inc.

ASK YOURSELF

The fossil forests of the High Arctic thrived in an environment similar to which of the following modern-day environments:

a. temperate rainforests of the Pacific Northwest

b. tropical rainforests of South America

c. Antarctica

d. a dry *wadi* in the Sahara Desert

e. Greenland

Both positive and negative feedbacks are common in the climate system. These two scenarios begin with a premise of some climatic warming. Compare these scenarios to Figure 14.6.

a. In this negative feedback cycle, initial warming leads to increased evaporation and cloud cover. If the clouds are primarily low-altitude clouds that reflect incoming solar radiation. the surface will cool.

Negative feedback cycle

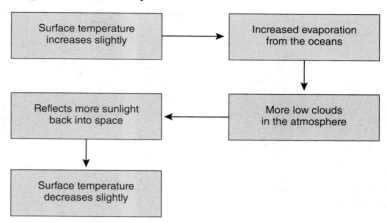

b. In this positive feedback cycle, initial warming leads to increased evaporation and more atmospheric water vapor. Water vapor, an effective greenhouse gas, causes additional warming. If the clouds are high-altitude clouds that allow solar radiation to pass but trap outgoing terrestrial radiation, further warming occurs.

Positive feedback cycle

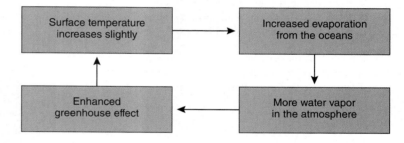

> **feedback** A cycle in which the output from a process becomes an input into the same process.

is that the interacting components are linked by **feedbacks**, both positive and negative.

A **negative feedback** occurs when a system is stabilizing or self-limiting (**Figure 14.9a**). In this case, the system's response to a change is in the opposite direction from the initial input. For example, if the global surface temperature warms, evaporation would be expected to increase. This would lead to more water vapor in the atmosphere and thus to more cloud cover. If these were low clouds that raise the albedo of the atmosphere and block incoming solar radiation, the surface temperature would cool down again. The response of the system is in the opposite direction to the initial change, and the process is self-limiting.

In contrast, a **positive feedback** is self-perpetuating and self-reinforcing—what we might refer to as a "vicious cycle." The system's response to a change, in this case, is in the same direction as the initial input (**Figure 14.9b**). For example, if the global surface temperature were to become warmer, evaporation—and thus water vapor in the atmosphere—would be expected to increase. Water vapor is a highly effective greenhouse gas, so an increase would lead to further warming, more evaporation, more water vapor,

and still more warming. This is thought to be one of the most significant positive feedbacks in the climate system.

There are many positive feedbacks in Earth's climate system. It is important to understand that while positive feedbacks are self-reinforcing, they don't always act to reinforce warming. For example, an ice-covered surface increases albedo, reflecting solar radiation and further cooling the surface; this is a positive feedback. If some ice melts, revealing an underlying surface of bare rock or water, the darker material will absorb more solar radiation, warming the surface and leading to further melting of ice; this is also a positive feedback.

Feedbacks make Earth's climatic processes extremely challenging to disentangle. For example, if there were an increase in evaporation (as explored in Figure 14.9), which type of cloud would mainly be formed—the warming kind (high altitude) or the cooling kind (low altitude)? Or would both responses occur, with one overpowering the other? These are the types of research issues that climatologists are attempting to resolve as they struggle to improve our understanding of the processes that control Earth's climate.

The global **carbon cycle** has many feedbacks that affect climate (**Figure 14.10**) on a

> **carbon cycle** The set of processes by which carbon cycles from reservoir to reservoir through the global environment.

Carbon in various forms constantly cycles among the atmosphere, hydrosphere, biosphere, crust, and mantle. The global carbon cycle has a fundamentally important influence on climate.

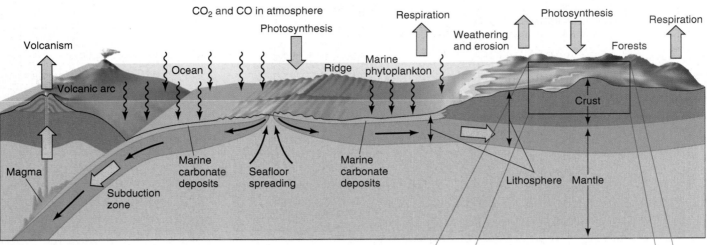

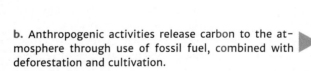 **a.** Carbon enters the atmosphere through volcanism, weathering, biological respiration, and decay of organic matter. Photosynthesis incorporates carbon into the biosphere, from which it can become part of the crust if buried with accumulating sediment. Subduction carries carbon from the oceanic crust into the mantle.

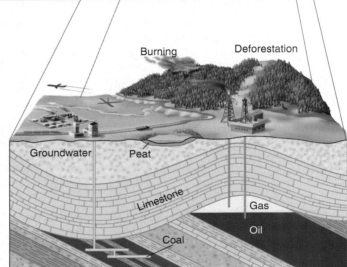

b. Anthropogenic activities release carbon to the atmosphere through use of fossil fuel, combined with deforestation and cultivation.

variety of time scales. For example, seafloor spreading regulates atmospheric CO_2 by controlling the rate of volcanism and, therefore, the production of volcanic CO_2. During periods of intense tectonic activity, volcanic emissions contribute large quantities of CO_2 to the atmosphere; during periods of tectonic quiescence, volcanic emissions are less. The metamorphism of carbon-rich sediment and limestone carried downward in subduction zones is an additional and possibly larger source of atmospheric CO_2 that is controlled by the tectonic cycle.

Carbon dioxide is also removed from the atmosphere by the weathering of surface rock. As you learned in Chapter 7, rainwater combines with CO_2 to form carbonic acid (H_2CO_3), which causes chemical weathering of silicate rock. The weathering products are carried to the ocean by streams, where marine organisms use the carbonate and silica to build their shells or skeletons. When they die,

their remains accumulate on the seafloor and are buried, stored as sediment, and perhaps even converted into rock by lithification (see *Remember This!*). Weathering of rock, therefore, is a negative feedback in the climate system; it removes carbon from the atmosphere and stores it for a long time. This **sequestration** of carbon helps move the global climate system toward an equilibrium condition.

> **sequestration** Long-term storage of a material, in isolation from the atmosphere.

> **REMEMBER THIS!** What is the name given to sediment that originates from the accumulation of carbonaceous remains on the ocean floor? What rock type would it become, upon lithification? Refer to *Biogenic Sediment* and *Biogenic Sedimentary Rock* in Chapter 8 to review.

One major source of uncertainty in the carbon cycle lies in the response of terrestrial ecosystems to a warmer global climate. Increased CO_2 in the atmosphere leads to enhanced growth of vegetation, which removes CO_2 from the atmosphere through photosynthesis—a negative feedback. However, warmer conditions can lead to an increase in soil respiration, resulting in increased movement of CO_2 and CH_4 to the atmosphere—a positive feedback. In balance, it appears that a warmer climate could decrease the ability of the land to act as a storage reservoir and a sink for carbon, therefore contributing to a positive feedback cycle.

> **reservoir** A place in the Earth system where a material is stored for a period of time.
>
> **sink** A reservoir that takes in more of a given material than it releases.

The ocean, too, is crucial as a sink for atmospheric carbon dioxide. If the atmospheric concentration of CO_2 increases, the uptake of CO_2 by ocean water should also increase. However, warmer conditions decrease the ability of the ocean to absorb CO_2. An additional complexity is that as the ocean takes in CO_2 the water becomes more acidic, as discussed in Chapter 12. A more acidic ocean would be less capable of absorbing atmospheric CO_2.

In the deep ocean, methane (CH_4) is stored, frozen into molecules of ice in seafloor sediment. An enormous volume of methane—perhaps more than 6 trillion tons—is trapped in this form, called **gas hydrates**. If ocean water warms, even by a small amount, the ice that traps this vast quantity of methane could melt, allowing it to bubble out. This could lead to a significant positive feedback because methane is a potent greenhouse gas (many times more powerful than carbon dioxide). Its release into the atmosphere would cause warming, potentially leading to further warming of ocean water—another positive feedback. In fact, such a feedback process is thought to have been a factor in causing the Paleocene-Eocene Thermal Maximum.

STOP CONCEPT CHECK

1. **What** do Earth's orbital cycles have to do with climate?
2. **What** are the four most important radiatively active gases in the natural greenhouse effect?
3. **What** is the difference between a negative feedback and a positive feedback?

THE RECORD OF PAST CLIMATE CHANGE

Learning Objectives

1. **Summarize** the tools and approaches used to study paleoclimates.

2. **Describe** the trends in Earth's climate over the past few million years, the past few thousand years, and the past few hundred years.

Before we can understand the human role in climate change, present or future, we must first look back in time and find out how Earth's climate has changed over geological history. Geologists and climatologists use many different tools and approaches to study ancient climates. The evidence of past temperature fluctuations, glaciations, and other climatic changes comes from multiple sources; no single source is definitive.

Evidence of Climate Change

Last winter may have been colder than the winter before, or last summer may have been wetter than the previous summer, but such observations do not mean that the climate is changing. The identification of real climatic change must be based on a shift in average conditions over a span of many years. Several years of abnormal weather may not mean that a change is occurring, but a **trend** that persists for more than a decade may signal a shift to a new climate regime.

> **trend** A long-term or underlying pattern in a time series of data.

Today, changes in the atmospheric conditions that define weather and (in the longer term) climate are carefully tracked and measured on an almost continuous basis, at many locations around the world. However, such instrumental tracking has been recorded systematically for only the past century or so. Let's take a look at the records of past climate change (summarized in **Figure 14.11**), and then consider how scientists have managed to extend those records even farther back, into deep prehistoric time.

Figure 14.11 highlights three very important points. First, change is the norm, not the exception, in our climate system. No matter how much global warming occurs in the next century, it is unlikely to show up as more than a barely perceptible blip on any of these graphs. Second, the overall trend in temperature in the Cenozoic Era has been downward. The current global warming episode will do nothing to change that. Third, superimposed on the overall trend of cooling is a series of glaciations, each lasting about 100,000 years, followed by warm interglacial periods. We are currently near the peak of a warm interglacial cycle. In 50,000 years or so, Earth will probably experience another ice age.

This graph shows estimates of global surface temperatures over the past 60 million years (**Figure a**), the past 10 million years (**Figure b**), the past 150,000 years (**Figure c**), and the past 130 years (**Figure d**). The graphs in **a**, **b**, and **c** are based on data from seafloor sediment; **d** is based on instrumental weather records.

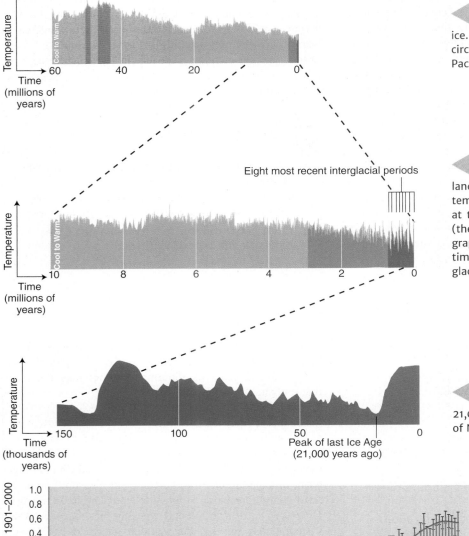

a. 60 million years ago to present
Earth's surface was largely free of ice. Sea levels were higher, and seawater circulated freely between the Atlantic and Pacific.

b. 10 million years ago to present
As plate motions moved the major landmasses near their present locations, temperatures fell and glaciers appeared at the poles. In the past 800,000 years (the dark blue band in the temperature graph), the climate has fluctuated eight times between ice ages and warm interglacial periods.

c. 150,000 years ago to present
At the peak of the last ice age, 21,000 years ago, glaciers blanketed most of North America.

d. 130 years ago to present
With the average temperature for the 20th century as a baseline for comparison, Earth is now warmer than it has been at any time in the past 100,000 years, and it is roughly the same temperature as it was in the last interglacial period, 120,000 years ago.

Historical Records of Climate In some places, instrumental records of weather conditions have been maintained for a century or more, which is long enough to see if there have been any significant shifts or emerging trends in climate. One of the longest continuous records comes from Great St. Bernard Hospice in the Alps, where the Augustinian friars have recorded temperature since the 1820s and snowfall since the 1850s. The temperature pattern demonstrated by the instrumental record from the Alps is representative of other parts of the northern hemisphere, where average temperatures experienced a fluctuating rise after the 1880s to reach a peak in the 1940s (Figure 14.11d). Thereafter, average temperatures declined slightly until the 1970s, when they again began to rise. In the 1990s, the 2000s, and 2010s, we have repeatedly seen some of the highest values ever recorded.

The Geological Record of Climate Historical instrumental records represent only a tiny fraction of the evidence of climate change; the majority comes from the geological record. Scientists have long puzzled over geological features that seem out of place in their present climate. In the chapter opener and the *Case Study* about Wadi Kufra, you learned that many times in the past the climate in the Sahara region has been much more humid than it is at present. In *Amazing Places* you learned that ancient tropical forests are preserved as fossils in the High Arctic. On the other hand, fossilized plant remains in the temperate north-central United States show that this region formerly resembled arctic landscapes like those now seen in far northern Canada.

All of these and many other lines of evidence demonstrate that **paleoclimates** in many localities differed dramatically from their present-day climates. Throughout Earth's history, change has been the norm in the climate system rather than the exception.

> **paleoclimate** The climate of an ancient time.

Climate Proxies

The fossil record provides a broad, sweeping overview of climatic changes over vast spans of time, and historical instrumental measurements provide specific, detailed information about recent variations. What is needed is a record of climatic change that is more specific and detailed than the fossil record, but extends farther back in time than recent historical records.

Fortunately, **climate proxy records** can fill this gap by providing evidence of year-to-year or season-to-season variability in specific locations over the course of human history,

> **climate proxy record** Records of natural events that are influenced by, and closely mimic, climate.

and much longer. A "proxy" is a replacement or stand-in, so a climate proxy is something that "stands in" for direct measurements of weather conditions. We look for processes that were operating at a specific time in the past, were controlled by some aspect of the weather (temperature and precipitation are the most common), and for which a record has been kept (either by nature or by people). Although lacking the precision of instrumental data, climate proxy records can add up to a detailed picture of local, regional, and global climate trends.

Human Records of Climate-by-Proxy One approach to climate proxies is to look at historical records of events and processes that were controlled by weather conditions. For example, just about everything related to farming, fishing, and harvesting is controlled by temperature and precipitation. These activities are important for human well-being, so people have been keeping track of them for a long time—more than 1000 years, in some cases. Three examples of climate proxies in human historical records are shown in **Figure 14.12**. Other useful records include variations in the

height of the Nile River at Cairo, the quality of wine harvests in Germany, the date of blooming of cherry trees in Japan, and variations in wheat prices in Europe (because the price is controlled by the quantity and quality of the harvest, which in turn is controlled by climate).

Even the longest human historical records go back only 1000 years or so. To extend our use of climate proxies farther into the past, we must rely on nature's own record of climate, preserved by processes such as the deposition of annual or seasonal growth rings. To use this approach, there must be a mechanism for determining the date of the natural record; without this mechanism, we would end up with a record of changes in climate, but no way to determine when the changes actually occurred. Let's look at a few of the most useful natural climate proxies.

Ice Core Data Probably the most important source of information about paleoclimates is preserved in thick deposits of ice that make up the polar ice sheets (mainly Greenland and Antarctica) and lower-latitude alpine glaciers. Ice cores (**Figure 14.13a**) drawn from these glacial deposits provide nearly continuous records of weather conditions, some extending to hundreds of thousands of years before the present. The information preserved in the ice is revealed by the chemical analysis of oxygen isotopes from the ice.

Isotopes are naturally occurring variations of elements, which differ just slightly from one another in mass but not in other chemical characteristics (see *Remember This!*). For example, oxygen has three naturally occurring isotopes—^{16}O, ^{17}O, and ^{18}O. Of these ^{18}O is the heaviest; it behaves chemically just like the others, but it is preferentially concentrated during processes influenced by mass, such as evaporation and precipitation. Normal water, H_2O, contains all three of the naturally occurring isotopes of oxygen (and typically two naturally occurring isotopes of hydrogen).

> **REMEMBER THIS!** Do you remember how an atom, an element, an isotope, an ion, and a compound differ from each other? If you need to remind yourself, look back at *Elements and Compounds* in Chapter 2.

Many of the natural processes that separate and differentially concentrate isotopes are temperature-dependent—that is, they are influenced by variations in temperature. Sampling and analysis of the isotopic composition of any material that was affected by a temperature-dependent process, and that was in equilibrium with its surroundings, can reveal the past temperature history of that material. Numerous isotopes are useful in paleoclimate analysis; however, water is so ubiquitous and so closely tied up with climatic processes that oxygen isotopes from H_2O are the most widely used for this purpose. Measurements of oxygen isotopes in glacier ice enable scientists to calculate the air temperature when the snow that later was transformed into ice accumulated at the glacier surface. Other isotopic measurements reveal how much of Earth's global water budget was locked up in glaciers at various times in the past.

Climate proxies give scientists information about how the climate has changed over time. The records can be kept by humans or by nature, but a crucial aspect is the ability to attach dates to the phenomena.

Natural records of climate
Natural climate proxies help scientists extend temperature records back thousands of years, and even millions of years before the present.

a. Glacier ice forms from snow, which is deposited in annual layers, as seen here in Glacier Bay National Park, Alaska.

b. The width of annual tree rings varies with growing conditions, including sunlight, temperature, and precipitation.

Jon Arnold Images Ltd./Alamy

GYROPHOTOGRAPHY/amanaimagesRF/Getty Images

d. Seafloor sediment contains fossils of tiny sea organisms, foraminifera, which once lived in surface waters. These microfossils contain abundant information about the chemistry and temperature of the ocean. ▼

Photo from Rob Dunbar and Glen Shen

c. The growth of some corals produces structures similar to the annual rings of trees. Analyzing the chemical composition of the coral can provide a temperature record.

NASA Images

100 µm

e. Fossil pollen can be used to re-construct past vegetation and climate. This is a scanning electron microscope photograph of a grain of *Drymiswinterii* pollen (42 µM), from a tree that is native to temperate rainforests.

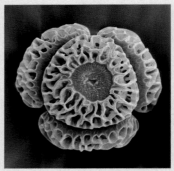

R.E. Litchfield/Photo Researchers

ASK YOURSELF

What characteristics are important, for a natural or human process to serve as a climate proxy?

a. It must be controlled by or mimic some aspect of climate.

b. It must retain some form of record of interaction with climate.

c. It must add annual or seasonal records of interactions with climate.

d. There must be a way to assign a numerical date to the record.

e. All of the above are necessary, in order for a natural or human process to serve as a climate proxy.

Human records of climate

Human records of climate proxies span from the present to more than 1000 years ago.

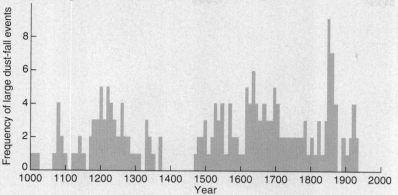

ChinaFotoPress / Getty Images, Inc.

f. The frequency of major dust-fall events in China is useful as a proxy because a dusty atmosphere is indicative of a cold, glacier-dominated climate.

g. The severity of winters in England is based on the number of mild or severe months experienced.

Nigel Hicks/NG Image Collection

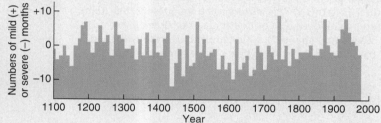

h. The number of weeks per year during which sea ice reached the coast of Iceland is a record that fishers have kept for almost 1000 years.

David Astley

Comparing climate proxies to instrumental measurements

Borehole temperatures (Huang et al. 2000) Glacier lengths (Oerlemans 2005b)
Multiproxy (Mann and Jones 2003a) Multiproxy (Moberg et al. 2005a)
Multiproxy (Hegerl et al. 2006) Tree rings (Esper et al. 2002a)
Instrumental record (Jones et al. 2001)

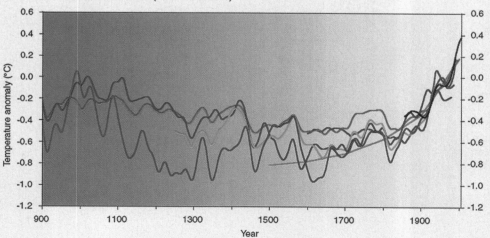

i. In this graph of surface temperature in the Northern Hemisphere, instrumental measurements are shown by the black curve (starting in the mid-1800s). The other curves are reconstructions based on various climate proxies. All curves show that temperatures during the last few decades of the 20th century were higher than during any comparable period in the past 1000 years.

Isotopic analysis of ice cores from glaciers and polar ice caps can provide a record of temperature at the time when the snow fell.

a. Scientists recover a core of ice that will be used for isotopic studies of paleoclimate. Cores from the Greenland and Antarctic Ice Sheets have yielded the most data, but studies on ice cores from midlatitude glaciers have also been extremely important.

Peter Essick/Aurora Photos Inc.

b. Ice core data from Antarctica show a reconstruction of temperature, in terms of the difference from present-day temperature, going back 420,000 years (Δ, the Greek letter delta, stands for "change"). This temperature reconstruction is based on analysis of oxygen isotopes from the ice.

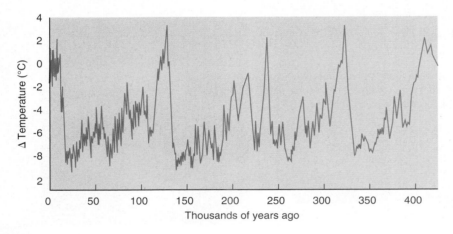

c. The temperature reconstruction shown here, also from Antarctica, is based on the analysis of deuterium (an isotope of hydrogen) in ice cores from Antarctica. Peaks on the graph indicate warm interglacial periods. This record has now been extended to 740,000 years before the present.

THINK CRITICALLY

One of the most interesting challenges in paleoclimatology has been to explain slight mismatches in timing (called **asynchronicity**) between major climatic events recorded in ice cores from Antarctica and Greenland. Can you think of any reasons why a "global" change in climate might be recorded slightly earlier at one pole than at the other?

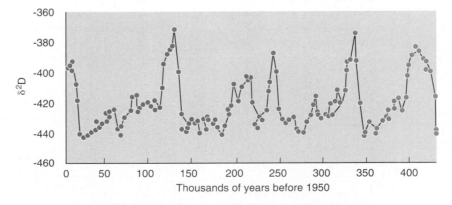

Note: δ²D refers to variation in deuterium, a stable isotope of hydrogen.

A crucial feature of ice core analysis is that glacier ice is laid down in annual layers (as shown in Figure 14.12a; also see *Remember This!*). By counting the annual layers, scientists can count back in time to attach dates to the temperature determinations. Without the layering, ice core data would be of much less use, since there would be no precise time scale attached to the temperature changes. Scientists have been able to correlate ice core data from several different locations around the world, contributing to our understanding of paleoclimates on a global scale.

> **REMEMBER THIS!** How does snow become glacier ice? To review this question, turn to *Glaciers and Ice Sheets* in Chapter 13. Can you see how the trapping of air bubbles occurs?

Some isotopic variations in glacier ice from ice cores provide information about fluctuations in the air temperature near the glacier surface (**Figure 14.13b, c**). Other variations in ice cores and in isotopic studies of marine sediment reveal changes in ice volume on a global scale. Traditionally, Antarctica and Greenland have been the principal sources for ice core data, but to get a truly global perspective, scientists need to combine multiple records from various areas. Recently, more attention has been focused on retrieving paleoclimate records from high-altitude, low-latitude temperate glaciers, many of which are disappearing.

Another particularly useful aspect of ice core analysis is that small bubbles of air are trapped in the glacier ice during its transformation from snow to ice. These provide samples of the ambient air at the time the snow fell, and they can be extracted and chemically analyzed to determine the composition of the atmosphere at that time. This makes an extremely powerful dataset; we can not only decipher what the climate was like in the past but also learn the chemistry of the atmosphere at that time (see *What a Geologist Sees*).

Samples from Antarctica and Greenland have shown that the atmosphere contained far less carbon dioxide and methane during glacial ages than during interglacials. Calculations suggest that the low levels of these two important greenhouse gases during glacial times can account for nearly half of the ice age temperature lowering. In contrast, the rapid increase of atmospheric carbon dioxide in our time is unprecedented in the ice core record and implies that an unusual warming is in progress.

Isotopic analysis of ice has been central in establishing the global paleoclimatic record, but other Earth materials also serve as climate proxies. Groundwater, sediment, shells, and bones, for example, also undergo processes that are influenced by temperature, and preserve the distinctive isotopic signature of their surroundings. As long as they can be dated, these materials also can be useful as climate proxies.

Annual Layers Many organisms deposit annual growth rings and are therefore potentially useful as climate proxies. For example, a tree living in middle latitudes typically adds a growth ring each year (as you saw in Figure 14.12b, the width and density of which reflect the local climate. Many species live for hundreds of years; a few, like the Giant Sequoia and Bristlecone pine of the California mountains, live for thousands of years.

In marine environments living corals and similar organisms, such as coralline red algae, also deposit annual or seasonal growth rings (as shown in Figure 14.12c). These organisms equilibrate to the water in which they grow, so their chemical composition changes in response to the composition and temperature of the water. From their annual growth rings, scientists can obtain a record of changes in water temperature spanning thousands of years.

Deep-sea and lake-bottom sediments accumulate in layers, year by year. Sediment cores can provide some of the best indirect evidence of past climatic changes over time. Seafloor sediment contains abundant fossils of tiny sea creatures called foraminifera (which you first encountered in Chapter 8, in the context of biogenic sediments). These microfossils (Figure 14.12d) equilibrate with the water around them, preserving a chemical record of past climatic changes.

Plant pollen fossils like those shown in Figure 14.12e also contribute greatly to our knowledge of past climatic conditions. A sample of bog or lake sediment typically yields a vast number of pollen grains that can be identified by type, counted, and analyzed statistically. In any given layer within a sediment core, the pollen grains reveal the assemblage of plants that flourished near the site when the enclosing sediment layers were deposited. The precipitation and temperature at the site of a similar modern plant assemblage can be used to estimate the climate represented by the fossil assemblage.

Earth's Past Climates

By using climate proxies and other evidence of past climates preserved in the geological record, scientists have established a detailed chronology of climatic changes over Earth's long history. Let's summarize these changes, starting with the most recent millennium and moving backward in time.

Climate of the Past Millennium An episode of mild climate during the Middle Ages, called the **Medieval Warm Period**, eventually gave way to a colder period, when temperatures in western Europe averaged 1 to 2°C lower. Scientists refer to this as the **Little Ice Age**, and it is discernible as a tiny dip in the temperature reconstruction in Figure 14.11c. The Maunder Minimum, the period of unusually low sunspot activity mentioned previously in this chapter, occurred during the last part of the Little Ice Age, perhaps exacerbating the colder-than-normal conditions.

In western Europe, the Little Ice Age lasted from about 1300 until the 1800s, and was characterized by unusually snowy winters; cool, wet summers; and expansion of sea ice in the North Atlantic. By the early 17th century, advancing glaciers were overrunning farms in the Alps, Iceland, and Scandinavia. During the worst years of that century, sea ice completely surrounded Iceland, causing fisheries to fail. Erratic weather led to crop failures, rising grain prices, and famines, which resulted in large-scale emigrations of Europeans to North America. Thus, many Canadians and Americans owe their present nationality to the Little Ice Age climate.

What a Geologist Sees

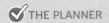 THE PLANNER

Climate Data in Ice Cores

©AP/Wide World Photos

Data retrieved from ice cores provides some of the most powerful data for geologists who want to learn about past climates. This geologist is holding an ice core that was extracted from a depth of 3000 meters in the Antarctic Ice Cap. The ice is estimated to be one million years old. The core will be cut into thin slices which will be examined under a microscope.

This is a thin slice of the ice core, prepared for microscopic study. Tiny bubbles of air were trapped in the pore spaces when flakes of snow recrystallized to form this glacierice. When the ice is melted under controlled conditions in a laboratory, the chemical composition of the "fossil air" can be analyzed.

SPL/BRITISH ANTARCTIC SURVEY/ Photo Researchers, Inc.

The results of analyzing the fossil air are shown below. The geologist will be particularly interested in the concentrations of the greenhouse gases carbon dioxide and methane in the air bubbles. The curve labeled $\delta^{18}O$ refers to the oxygen isotopic composition of the ice, which provides a proxy for temperature.

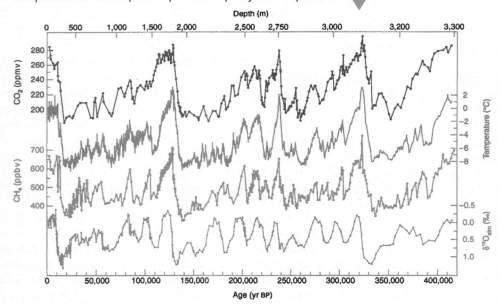

The geologist sees that at times when temperature was low, CH_4 and CO_2 were also low, and at times when temperature was high, CH_4 and CO_2 were also high. This is a chicken-and-egg question: Were temperatures low because the greenhouse gas concentrations were low, or were the greenhouse gas concentrations low because temperatures were low? Scientists do not yet have the answer to this question.

THINK CRITICALLY

How could a geologist determine the age of the "fossil air" trapped inside an ice core?

Little Ice Age conditions persisted until the middle of the 19th century, when a general warming trend caused mountain glaciers to retreat and the North Atlantic sea ice to retreat northward. Minor fluctuations of climate have continued to take place since then, but the overall trend of warming brought conditions that were increasingly favorable for crop production at a time when the human population was expanding rapidly and entering the industrial age.

The Last Glaciation   The last time Earth's climate was dramatically different from what it is now was during the last glacial period. The last glaciation, which started about 70,000 years ago and ended about 10,000 years ago, was the most recent of a long succession of glaciations in the Pleistocene Epoch. To reconstruct the climate of this latest ice age, scientists have relied on analyses of periglacial features, glacier ice, and sediment that contain isotopic and fossil evidence of paleoclimate.

In the popular imagination, glacial ages were times when temperatures were very cold, perhaps rivaling those in Antarctica today. Although such extreme cold did exist in some regions, in other places the average temperatures at the culmination of the last glaciation were not very different from what they are now. In the tropics, temperatures were about the same as they are today. In midlatitude coastal regions, temperatures on land were generally reduced by about 5 to 8°C, whereas in continental interiors, reductions of 10 to 15°C occurred (**Figure 14.14**).

During the last glaciation, the climate of the northern middle and high latitudes became so cold that a vast ice sheet formed over central and eastern Canada and expanded southward toward the United States and westward toward the

North America in the last glaciation • Figure 14.14

This map shows North America about 20,000 years ago, during the last glaciation. Coastlines lie farther seaward because sea level was lower by about 120 meters. Sea-surface temperatures are based on analysis of microfossils in deep-sea cores. Circled numbers show the estimated temperature lowering, relative to present temperatures, at selected sites, based on climate-proxy evidence.

THINK CRITICALLY

Why would temperature reductions during the last glaciation have been greater in continental interiors compared to coastal regions?

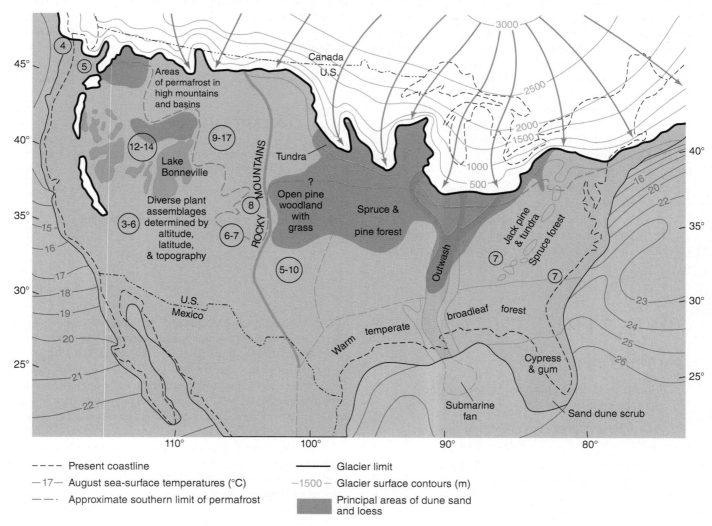

---- Present coastline

—17— August sea-surface temperatures (°C)

– – – Approximate southern limit of permafrost

——— Glacier limit

—1500— Glacier surface contours (m)

Principal areas of dune sand and loess

Rocky Mountains. Other great ice sheets formed over the mountains of western Canada, northern Europe, and northwestern Asia. As ocean water evaporated and was deposited as snow on the growing ice sheets, world sea level fell to about 120 meters below the present level. This changed the shapes of coastlines and continents. The great ice sheets of Greenland and Antarctica spread across the adjacent, exposed continental shelves. Large glacier systems formed in the Alps, Andes, Himalayas, and Rockies, and on isolated peaks and mountain ranges scattered through all latitudes. Some scientists postulate that an ice shelf may have completely covered the Arctic Ocean, extending into the North Atlantic.

At the height of the glacial age, the middle latitudes were both windier and dustier than they are today. Glacial-aged aeolian deposits of fine sediment called loess (Chapter 8) are found south of the ice limit in the midwestern United States, where cold winds flowing south from the ice mass picked up fine sediment from the floodplains of glacial meltwater streams and carried it further south. The same happened in Central Asia and western Europe. In each of these regions, successive layers of loess are separated by soils that formed during the interglacial periods.

In many arid and semiarid regions, including the Sahara, the Middle East, southern Australia, and the American Southwest, the shift to cooler glacial-age climates resulted in the enlargement of existing lakes and rivers or the creation of new ones. Some of this condition may have been caused by increased precipitation, but evidence in some locations actually points to reduced precipitation during glacial times. An alternative explanation is that lower temperatures led to reduced evaporation.

The glacial ages witnessed major changes not only in the cryosphere, hydrosphere, and atmosphere but also in the biosphere. Pollen studies show that in glacial times, the vegetation distribution was quite different from what we see today. About 20,000 years ago, a belt of tundra existed immediately south of the glacier margin, and today's grasslands of the Great Plains were mostly open pine woodlands. The changes accompanying the advance and retreat of the ice sheets were dynamic and complicated; both plant and animal species were displaced in various directions, forming ecological communities that are unknown on the present landscape.

Pleistocene and Older Glacial Ages   As recently as a few decades ago, it was thought that Earth had experienced only four glacial ages. This traditional view was discarded when studies of deep-sea sediment disclosed evidence of a long succession of glaciations during the Pleistocene. Paleomagnetic dating (Chapter 3) of deep-sea cores shows that during the past 800,000 years, there have been eight such episodes. All the available evidence shows that in the Pleistocene Epoch as a whole (the past 1.8 million years), about 30 glacial ages are recorded.

Ancient glaciations, identified mainly by rock of glacial origin and associated polished and striated rock surfaces, are known from farther back in Earth's history as well. The earliest glaciation dates to about 2.4 billion years ago, in the early Proterozoic, and evidence of other glacial episodes has been found in rock of late Proterozoic, early Paleozoic, and late Paleozoic age (see the geological time scale in Figure 3.6). During the late Paleozoic (Carboniferous and Permian) glaciation, 50 or more glacial advances and retreats are believed to have occurred. The geological record is fragmentary and not always easy to interpret, but evidence suggests that Earth's land areas must have had a very different relationship to one another during the late Paleozoic glaciation than they do today. In the Mesozoic Era, glaciation of similar magnitude apparently did not occur, consistent with geological evidence that points to a long interval of mild temperatures both on land and in the ocean.

STOP **CONCEPT CHECK**

1. **What** are the most important sources of evidence about changes in Earth's climate over time?
2. **How** do scientists use ice cores to learn about past climates?
3. **How** many major glaciations occurred during the Pleistocene Epoch?

PREDICTING THE FUTURE

Learning Objectives

1. **Examine** the evidence for anthropogenic climate change.
2. **Describe** the probable effects of continued global warming in the next century.
3. **Summarize** the major uncertainties in predicting future climate change.

Earth's climate has changed dramatically in the past and will continue to change. However, the causes of change are complicated, and this makes it difficult to predict how the climate will change and at what rate. Furthermore, in the past two centuries, a new component has been introduced: an industrialized human population that is now capable of significantly affecting the climate not only locally but globally.

That the world's climates can change measurably within a human lifetime (whether by natural or human causes) is a relatively new realization. With this realization has come increasing concern about the impacts of such changes on nature and on society. Scientists continue to grapple with the challenges of measuring the changes, separating short-term fluctuations from long-term trends, and disentangling natural influences from human influences.

Because the stakes in predicting future climate change are so high—for the environment, the economy, and society as a whole—it is important to distinguish between what we know with a high degree of certainty, what we think we know but with somewhat less certainty, and what we recognize as true uncertainties.

What We Know

The chemistry of Earth's atmosphere has changed as a result of human activity, particularly since the Industrial Revolution; this fact is not controversial. Some of these **anthropogenic** changes have resulted from the emission of gases that are of wholly synthetic origin, such as chlorofluorocarbons (see *Remember This!*). Other changes have resulted from human activities that cause the mobilization of naturally occurring compounds, such as sulfur and carbon compounds from the burning of fossil fuels.

> **REMEMBER THIS!** Chlorofluorocarbons (CFCs) are synthetic chemicals that contribute to the breakdown of ozone in the stratosphere. As it turns out, CFCs are doubly damaging because they are also greenhouse gases! To review the role of ozone and the impacts of CFCs in the atmosphere, look back at *Layers in the Atmosphere*, Chapter 12.

Among these compounds, the greenhouse gases have received particular scientific and public attention over the past two decades because their atmospheric concentrations are rising. While it may be troubling, in itself, that human action has had a measurable effect on the chemistry of the atmosphere, our real concern in this chapter is with the impact of these changes on the stability of Earth's climate system.

When considering the human contribution to the greenhouse effect, also known as the **anthropogenic greenhouse effect** (or **accelerated,** or **enhanced, greenhouse effect**), we are primarily concerned with carbon dioxide (CO_2) because of the magnitude of our emissions and methane (CH_4) because of its extreme efficiency as a greenhouse gas.

> **anthropogenic greenhouse effect** The portion of greenhouse warming that results from human activities rather than from natural processes.

The first indisputable evidence of an anthropogenic effect on atmospheric chemistry with the potential to affect climate was the steady rise in carbon dioxide levels observed over the past 60 years (**Figure 14.15a**). Atmospheric carbon dioxide levels are higher now and rising much more rapidly than at any other time in the past 100,000 years. Samples of ancient air from ice cores show that the preindustrial concentration of CO_2 was about 280 parts per million by volume, a typical value for an interglacial age. The subsequent rapid increase to almost 400 parts per million during the past 200 years is unprecedented in the ice core record and implies that something very unusual is taking place.

Observed changes in atmosphere and ocean chemistry • Figure 14.15

Carbon dioxide is a naturally occurring greenhouse gas, but its atmospheric and oceanic concentrations have increased as a result of human activity.

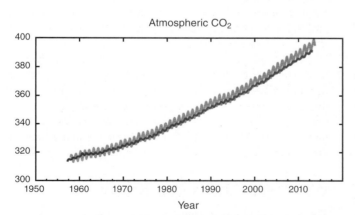

Atmospheric CO_2

a. The concentration of carbon dioxide in the atmosphere (shown here in ppm) has been measured continuously since 1958 at Mauna Loa Observatory in Hawaii (red line). The "zig-zag" pattern reflects seasonal variations in the biological uptake of CO_2 as a result of photosynthesis. The long-term trend of annual average measurements (black line) shows a persistent increase in CO_2.

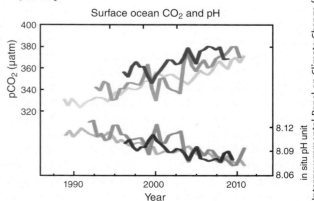

Surface ocean CO_2 and pH

b. When atmospheric CO_2 goes up, more CO_2 moves from the atmosphere into surface ocean water. The blue curves show the increasing partial pressure of CO_2 in surface ocean water. Carbon dioxide reacts with water to form carbonic acid; the more CO_2 dissolved in ocean water, the more acidic the water becomes. The green curves show the declining pH of ocean water.

Figure SPM.4 from IPCC, 2013: Summary for Policymakers. In: *Climate Change 2013: The Physical Science Basis. Working Group I Contribution to the Fifth Assessment Report of the Intergovernmental Panel on Climate Change* [Stocker,T.F., D.Qin, G.-K. Plattner, M.Tignor, S.K.Allen, J.Boschung, A.Nauels, Y.Xia, V.Bex and P.M. Midgley (eds.)]. Cambridge University Press, Cambridge, UK and New York, USA.

Measured surface temperatures are getting warmer.

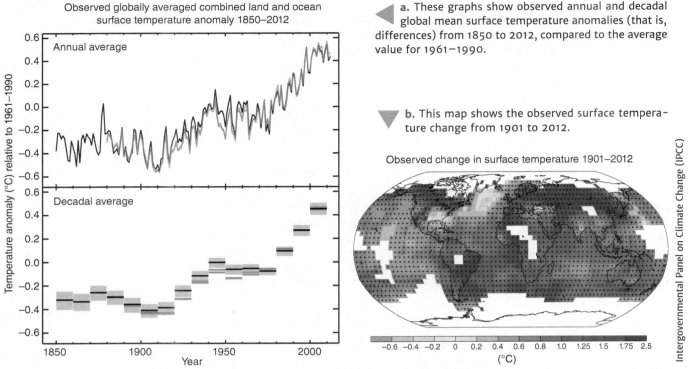

Observed globally averaged combined land and ocean surface temperature anomaly 1850–2012

a. These graphs show observed annual and decadal global mean surface temperature anomalies (that is, differences) from 1850 to 2012, compared to the average value for 1961–1990.

b. This map shows the observed surface temperature change from 1901 to 2012.

Observed change in surface temperature 1901–2012

Intergovernmental Panel on Climate Change (IPCC)

Figure SPM.1 from IPCC, 2013: Summary for Policymakers. In: *Climate Change 2013: The Physical Science Basis. Working Group I Contribution to the Fifth Assessment Report of the Intergovernmental Panel on Climate Change* [Stocker,T.F., D.Qin, G.-K. Plattner, M.Tignor, S.K.Allen, J.Boschung, A.Nauels, Y.Xia, V.Bex and P.M. Midgley (eds.)]. Cambridge University Press, Cambridge, UK and New York, USA.

What is the cause of this increase? Humans now pump almost 35 billion tons of carbon dioxide into the atmosphere each year, much of it from the burning of fossil fuels—more than enough to account for the increase in atmospheric CO_2. Additional contributing factors are widespread deforestation, with its attendant burning and decay of cleared vegetation, and the use of wood for fuel in many underdeveloped countries that have rapidly growing populations.

The various parts of the Earth system are so closely interconnected that a change in atmospheric chemistry of this magnitude has impacts elsewhere in the system, including the ocean. Carbon dioxide is exchanged freely between the atmosphere and the surface waters of the ocean. If CO_2 in the atmosphere increases, we would expect to see an increase in surface ocean water; this is shown in **Figure 14.15b**. Carbon dioxide reacts with water to form carbonic acid, so increased levels of CO_2 in ocean water should cause an increase in the acidity (that is, a decrease in the pH) of ocean water; this, too, is shown in Figure 14.15b. The rising acidity of ocean water has the potential to cause a host of problems for oceanic aquatic life.

Carbon dioxide is not the only cause for concern. Methane gas (CH_4) absorbs infrared radiation 25 times more effectively than CO_2, making methane an important greenhouse gas despite its relatively low atmospheric concentration. The concentration of atmospheric methane has increased by about 160% since the Industrial Revolution (from 700 ppb to about 1811 ppb). The increase essentially

parallels the rise in the human population. This is not surprising, for much of the methane now entering the atmosphere is generated either by biological activity related to rice cultivation or as a by-product of the digestive processes of domestic livestock, especially cattle. The global livestock population has increased greatly in the past two centuries, and the total acreage under rice cultivation has increased more than 40% since 1950.

Logic and past climate records suggest that an increase in greenhouse gases should be accompanied by an increase in temperature. The evidence for this increase in temperature is becoming more conclusive each year (**Figure 14.16**). Globally averaged worldwide temperature records show an increase of 0.85°C from 1880 to 2012, and the first decade of the 21st century is now recognized as the hottest on record.

What We Think We Know

The observed global temperature increase now appears to be having real, observable effects. These include the retreat of glaciers, calving of large icebergs from ice shelves, increased storm activity, drought in some regions, and enhanced intensity of forest fire activity (**Figure 14.17**). No one should try to attribute any individual event specifically to climate change, but trends suggest that they may be the first real indicators of a changing climate system. Certainly, the dramatic increase over the past century in hydrometeorological disasters—that is, hazardous events such as floods and hurricanes, which

Some of the effects of climate change may already be discernible.

a. An 1870 post card shows the position of Rhone Glacier. The modern photo of the glacier in the background, taken in 2006, shows that the ice has retreated dramatically.

© The New York Times/Redux Pictures

b. The pack ice in the Beaufort Sea, off the North Slope of Alaska, now breaks up weeks earlier in the spring than it once did.

Paul Nicklen/National Geographic Creative/Getty Images, Inc.

c. On the West Antarctic Peninsula, the rise in temperatures has led to an influx of gentoo penguins, which prefer warmer subarctic temperatures, and a sharp decline in the numbers of Adélie penguins (shown here).

Ralph Lee Hopkins/NG Image Collection

d. in 2013, Australia experienced its warmest year ever recorded, leading to widespread drought and devastating fires.

Michael Clayton-Jones/The AGE/Fairfax Media/Getty Images

e. No single storm can be attributed to climate change—not even one as devastating as Post-Tropical Storm Sandy—but an increase in the frequency and intensity of storms is an anticipated impact of global warming. This image, taken by NASA's GOES-13 satellite, shows Sandy off the East Coast of the United States on October 28, 2012. It is about to collide with a continental weather system, seen here as a line of clouds running north–south along the Appalachian Mountains.

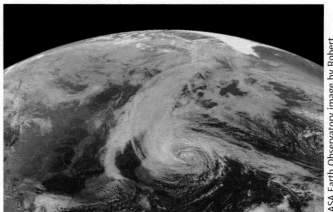

NASA Earth Observatory image by Robert Simmon with data courtesy of the NASA/NOAA GOES Project Science team

arise from processes in the atmosphere and hydrosphere—is widely acknowledged.

Will changes like these continue into the future? It is crucial that we attempt to answer this question. In recent years, climatologists have developed **general circulation models** that have successfully simulated the general character of present-day climates and have greatly improved weather forecasting. These successes, and the availability of ever-more-powerful computing capability, encourage scientists to use such models to obtain a general picture of future climate change.

> **general circulation model** A computer model of the climate system, linking processes in the atmosphere, hydrosphere, biosphere, and geosphere.

General circulation models allow us to incorporate different assumptions about anthropogenic factors that are driving climate change. The models differ in various details, but virtually all scenarios predict a global mean temperature increase that will likely exceed 1.5°C by the end of the 21st century. However, if fossil fuel consumption continues to grow at an increasing rate, atmospheric carbon dioxide will likely double (compared to preindustrial levels) by 2100, if not sooner. If this proves to be the case, climate models predict that average global temperatures could rise between 1.5° and 4.5°C. The increase will not be uniform all over the globe but will be greatest in the polar regions (**Figure 14.18**).

Despite the challenges inherent in climate modeling and data analysis, there is now a strong scientific consensus that (1) human activities have led to increasing atmospheric concentrations of carbon dioxide and other trace gases that have enhanced the greenhouse effect; (2) global mean surface air temperature has increased by up to 0.8°C during the past 100 to 150 years, an increase that appears to be a direct result of the anthropogenic greenhouse effect; (3) during the next century, global average temperature will likely continue to increase; and (4) this increase in mean surface temperature will have ripple effects in other parts of the Earth system.

The most thoroughly reviewed and widely accepted synthesis of scientific information concerning climate change is a series of reports issued by the **Intergovernmental Panel on Climate Change (IPCC)**, established in 1988 by the United Nations Environment Programme (UNEP) and the World Meteorological Organization. The IPCC's *Fifth Assessment Report*, published in 2013, represents the consensus of scientific climate research from around the world.

> **Intergovernmental Panel on Climate Change (IPCC)** An international, interdisciplinary panel of scientists and other experts, established to keep the world community up to date on the science of the global climate system.

The *Fifth Assessment Report* summarizes many thousands of scientific studies; it documents observed trends in surface temperature, precipitation patterns, snow and ice cover, sea levels, storm intensity, and other factors. It also predicts future changes in these and other phenomena, after considering a range of potential scenarios (such as the RCPs shown in Figure 14.18) for future greenhouse gas emissions. The report also addresses the impacts of current and future climate change on wildlife, ecosystems, and human societies, as well as strategies that we might pursue in response to climate change. You can—and should—read this very important document yourself, and other reports produced by the IPCC; they are all available online (see *Where Geologists Click*).

As with all other scientific endeavors, the IPCC must deal in uncertainties; its authors have therefore assigned statistical probabilities to all conclusions and predictions. The language used in the report is extremely specific and careful in expressing degrees of certainty. For example, "virtually certain" indicates 99 to 100% probability, in the likelihood of a given outcome. "Likely" indicates 66 to 100% probability; "very unlikely" indicates 0 to 10% probability; and so on.

In addition, estimates regarding impacts of change on human societies are conservative because scientific conclusions had to be approved by representatives of the world's national governments, some of which are reluctant to move away from a fossil fuel–based economy. Nevertheless, the *Fifth Assessment Report* concludes that "warming of the climate system is unequivocal. . . . The atmosphere and ocean have warmed, the amounts of snow and ice have diminished, sea level has risen, and the concentrations of greenhouse gases have increased" (p. 2).

And what of the human role in climate change? The IPCC has strengthened its wording with each new report. The *Fifth Assessment Report* concludes that "it is *extremely likely* that human influence has been the dominant cause of the observed warming since the mid-20th century" (p. 15). The term *extremely likely* carries the definition of 95 to 100% certainty. Note as well that human activity is cited as the *dominant* cause of warming. No major internationally or nationally recognized scientific organization publicly maintains a position that differs from this conclusion, although some reputable organizations and individuals remain noncommittal.

The Big Uncertainties

It is of obvious importance to human society that it be able to apply the scientific understanding of Earth's climate system to the prediction of future climate changes. However, there are a number of basic uncertainties: Will concentrations of greenhouse gases continue to increase, and, if so, how rapidly? How will the ocean, a major reservoir of heat and a fundamental element in the climate system, respond to climatic changes? Will the thermohaline circulation shut down, as it has done in the past, and what further effects would that have on climate? How will changes affect ice sheets and cloud cover, and how will those in turn affect the planet's albedo? How will soils respond to warming? Will species and ecosystems be able to adapt? How will climatic changes and their impacts differ from region to region? When feedbacks with multiple responses occur, which response will dominate?

These maps show the projected effects of increases in atmospheric carbon dioxide, based on multiple model results.

RCP stands for Representative Concentration Pathway; these are standardized scenarios that are used by all climate modelers. RCP2.6 (left) is a scenario in which atmospheric carbon dioxide peaks and then declines to very low levels. RCP8.5 (right) is a scenario in which carbon dioxide emissions continue to increase over time.

RCP 2.6   RCP 8.5

Change in average surface temperature (1986–2005 to 2081–2100)

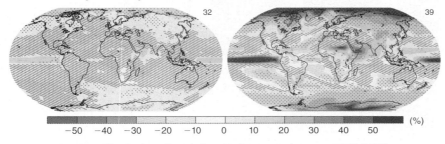

−2 −1.5 −1 −0.5 0 0.5 1 1.5 2 3 4 5 7 9 11 (°C)

a. These maps show projected changes in mean surface temperature for the two RCP scenarios, in 2081–2100, compared to averages for 1986–2005.

Change in average surface precipitation (1986–2005 to 2081–2100)

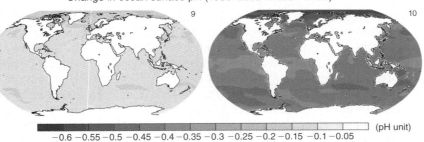

−50 −40 −30 −20 −10 0 10 20 30 40 50 (%)

b. These maps show projected changes in average precipitation for the two RCP scenarios, in 2081–2100, compared to averages for 1986–2005.

Northern Hemisphere September sea ice extent (average 2081–2100)

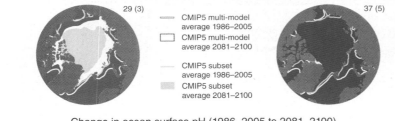

29 (3)

—— CMIP5 multi-model
average 1986–2005

☐ CMIP5 multi-model
average 2081–2100

—— CMIP5 subset
average 1986–2005

☐ CMIP5 subset
average 2081–2100

37 (5)

c. These maps show the projected extent of northern hemisphere sea ice in the month of September, The lines show the averages for 1986–2005, and the filled-in areas show multiple-model projected results for 2081–2100, for the two RCP scenarios.

Change in ocean surface pH (1986–2005 to 2081–2100)

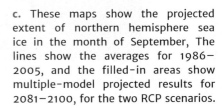

9   10

−0.6 −0.55 −0.5 −0.45 −0.4 −0.35 −0.3 −0.25 −0.2 −0.15 −0.1 −0.05 (pH unit)

d. Projected changes in surface ocean pH (that is, acidity) are shown here for 2081–2100 in the two RCP scenarios, compared to the averages for 1986–2005.

Intergovernmental Panel on Climate Change (IPCC)

Figure SPM.8 from IPCC, 2013: Summary for Policymakers. In: *Climate Change 2013: The Physical Science Basis. Working Group I Contribution to the Fifth Assessment Report of the Intergovernmental Panel on Climate Change* [Stocker,T.F., D.Qin, G.-K. Plattner, M.Tignor, S.K.Allen, J.Boschung, A.Nauels, Y.Xia, V.Bex and P.M. Midgley (eds.)]. Cambridge University Press, Cambridge, UK and New York, USA.

Many of the linkages in the climate system are still poorly understood and therefore difficult to represent accurately in general circulation models. For instance, computer models do not yet adequately portray the dynamics of ocean circulation or cloud formation, two of the most important elements of the climate system. Because of such uncertainties and complexities, scientists are reluctant to make firm forecasts, and they tend to be cautious in their predictions. As discussed previously, to the scientists who carry out this research, uncertainty and the terms they use to describe uncertainty have specific, clearly defined meanings. They represent an appropriate level of acknowledgment of the scientific uncertainty involved in the study of Earth's climate system.

Where Geologists CLICK

The Intergovernmental Panel on Climate Change: *Fifth Assessment Report*

The *Fifth Assessment Report* of the IPCC is readily available online at www.ipcc.ch (click on AR5 Climate Change 2013). This is an extremely important document that you should read for yourself.

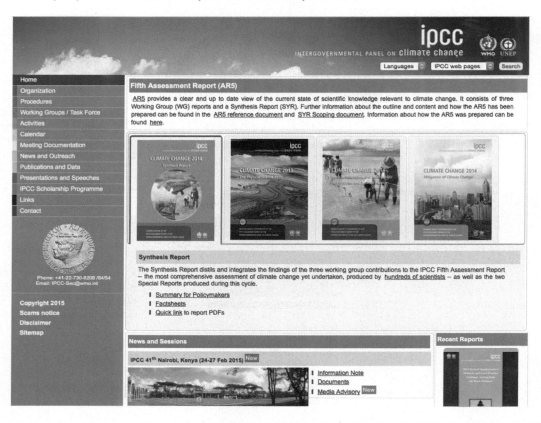

This understandably cautious approach has complicated the public discourse on climate change; it emphasizes the gap between what we know about the Earth system and what we would like to know, and it points to the many challenges that face both the scientists who study global change and the policymakers who must manage it.

The indirect effects of warming are particularly difficult to quantify. Likely impacts include the rising of the sea level due to the melting of land ice; increased intensity of severe hurricanes, typhoons, and the seasonal monsoon in Asia, all of which draw energy and moisture from warm seawater; spread of diseases that thrive in hotter climates, such as malaria; and significant changes in animal and plant populations due to death or migration. Some of the possible effects of global warming are illustrated in **Figure 14.19**.

An increase in global surface air temperature by a few degrees may not sound like much; surely, we can put up with this rather insignificant change. However, the difference in average global temperature between the present and the coldest part of the last ice age was only about 5°C, so a temperature change of even a degree or two could have significant global repercussions. In extracting and burning Earth's immense supply of fossil fuels, people have unwittingly begun a great "geochemical experiment" that is having a significant impact on our planet and its inhabitants. It is extremely important, not only scientifically, but socially, economically, and politically, that we seek and find the answers to questions about future climate change.

Possible effects of global warming • Figure 14.19

Some of the potential impacts of climate change could be devastating.

a. The Maldives and other small-island nations could find themselves underwater if sea levels continue to rise. The Maldives, in the Indian Ocean, are built on coral reefs that grow over time but could not possibly grow fast enough to keep up with a rapid change in sea level. ▼

James L. Stanfield/NG Image Collection

b. The total area affected by monsoon rains, the amount of precipitation, and the length of the monsoon season are all likely to increase as a result of climate change; this could also lead to an increase in flooding in these areas. ▼

© think4photop/Shutterstock

c. In much of the western United States, the freshwater supply is dependent on the melting of the winter snow pack in the Rocky Mountains. A smaller snow pack could cause streams like this one, at the foot of the Sierra Nevada, to dry up earlier each year. ▼

David Clapp/Photolibrary/Getty Images, Inc.

d. It is highly probable that permafrost will disappear altogether from the High Arctic. This will have impacts on buildings and infrastructure. More importantly, it could accelerate the release of carbon from northern soils, causing a positive feedback that could further contribute to warming. ▼

Andrea Pokrzywinski / Wikimedia Commons CC BY 2.0

e. The effect of global warming on crops is difficult to assess. An atmosphere with a higher carbon dioxide concentration could have a fertilizing effect on crops. An extended growing season in areas such as Siberia could also promote agricultural productivity. On the other hand, a hotter, drier climate could be devastating for crops in areas such as this drought-ridden field in Delaware. ▶

© Tony Campbell/Shutterstock

1. **How** have greenhouse gas concentrations in the atmosphere changed since the Industrial Revolution?

2. **What** effects are likely to happen over the next century if, as scientists now believe, Earth is getting warmer?

3. **What** does it mean when scientists use terms such as *probable* and *likely* to describe the potential effects of climate change?

SUMMARY

✅ THE PLANNER

1 The Climate System   377

- Earth's **climate** system is complex, as shown in the diagram. It is driven by interactions among the atmosphere, hydrosphere (mainly the ocean), cryosphere, geosphere, biosphere, and, most recently, the anthroposphere. The components of the climate system interact so closely that a change in one of them causes changes in the others. The main source of energy that drives the climate system is the Sun.

Earth's climate system · Figure 14.1

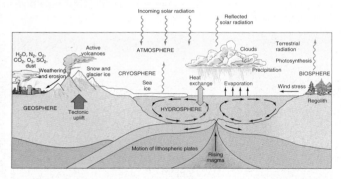

- Climate classification systems such as the Köppen system use average temperature and precipitation measurements and vegetation types to define major climate zones. Climate zones are closely related to global atmospheric circulation patterns.

2 Natural Causes of Climate Change   379

- Climate change is nothing new; it is a fundamental characteristic of the climate system.

- External influences on climate include the Sun's radiative output and cyclical variations in Earth's orbital characteristics, as shown in the diagram. These **Milankovitch cycles** are closely related to the timing of glacial–interglacial cycles.

How orbital changes influence climate · Figure 14.3

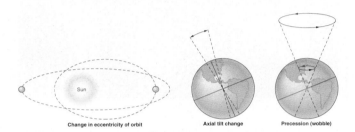

Change in eccentricity of orbit · Axial tilt change · Precession (wobble)

- Internal influences on climate include the filtering capacity and composition of the atmosphere, particularly with regard to greenhouse gas concentrations; the **albedo** or reflectivity of the atmosphere and other Earth surfaces; volcanic emissions; cloud cover; variations in oceanic circulation; and plate tectonics.

- **Feedbacks** are characteristic of the climate system and add to its complexity. Positive feedbacks are self-reinforcing; negative feedbacks are self-limiting. Many important feedbacks in the climate system are related to the global **carbon cycle**, through which carbon moves from one **reservoir** to another. The ocean is a particularly important **sink** for atmospheric carbon. When carbonaceous sediment accumulates on the ocean floor and is lithified to form limestone, the carbon it contains is **sequestered** in a long-term reservoir, isolating it from the atmosphere.

3 The Record of Past Climate Change   389

- Several years of abnormal weather may not mean that a change is occurring in the climate system, but a **trend** that persists for more than a decade may signal a shift to a new climate regime. To understand the significance of modern climate changes, geologists study **paleoclimates**.

- Geologists use a variety of tools and approaches to study paleoclimates, including analysis of fossils, sediment, and ice cores. Ocean sediment contains microscopic fossils, and changes in the proportion of warm-water and cold-water plants reflect the changes in world temperatures. The isotopic composition of ice in ice cores indicates past temperature variations. Ice cores also preserve trapped bubbles of "fossil air" that help scientists determine the concentration of greenhouse gases in the past.

- **Climate proxy records** are records of processes that are controlled or influenced by and that mimic climatic variations. Climate proxies can be tracked in human records or in the geological record, but for a proxy to be useful, it must be possible to attach a date to the record. Isotopic analyses of ice cores provide the most useful and extensive climate proxy record.

- Over the past 1.8 million years, Earth has experienced repeated **glaciations** and warm **interglaciations**. We are now in an interglacial period (as shown in the graph). The last glaciation, or ice age, peaked about 21,000 years ago. The current trend of global warming may create a more pronounced interglacial period but is unlikely to significantly delay the next ice age, which can be expected in 50,000 years or so.

Global surface temperatures, past to present · Figure 14.11

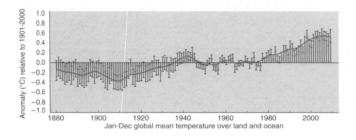

4 Predicting the Future   398

- Greenhouse gases have always affected the climate, but the **anthropogenic greenhouse effect**, caused by greenhouse gas emissions from the burning of fossil fuel and other activities, has arisen only in the past century, as shown in the graph.

- The current expectation of many scientists, through many years of data obtained from **general circulation models**, is that **global warming** will continue through the 21st century and that its extent will depend on human actions to limit the production of greenhouse gases. The **Intergovernmental Panel on Climate Change** keeps the international community up to date on developments in climate science.

- The effects of global warming are so far, and will continue to be, most pronounced in the polar regions, where sea ice is thinning, glaciers are retreating, and ice caps are melting. Worldwide effects in the future may include a rise in sea levels, increases in the severity of weather systems, drought, and changes in animal habitat that will cause some species to die and force others to migrate to new territory.

Observed changes in atmosphere and ocean chemistry · Figure 14.15a

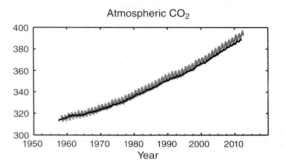

KEY TERMS

CRITICAL AND CREATIVE THINKING QUESTIONS

1. How did sea-surface temperatures at the peak of the last glaciation differ from those of the present? Why do you think some regions of the ocean have shown more change than others? What influence would these changes have had on atmospheric circulation and weather?

2. How can isotopic analyses of deep-sea sediment reveal changes in global ice volumes?

3. At the height of the most recent ice age, vegetation in North America south of the ice front must have been very different from the vegetation today. Do some research and find out what is known of vegetation changes in your area over the past 20,000 years.

4. Choose two human climate proxy records and two natural climate proxy records. Describe in detail how the phenomena are controlled by or mimic climate, what type of climate information can be derived from them, and how long the records have been kept.

5. Find out if your city, state, province, or country has set goals for the reduction of carbon dioxide emissions to limit its contribution to global warming. What steps have been taken to meet these goals?

6. Consider the maps in Figure 14.18 a and b. On the left is RCP 2.6, the "peak and decline" scenario for CO_2 emissions; on the right is RCP 8.5, the "continued high emissions" scenario. Locate your home region on the maps. What do the projections hold for RCP 2.6 in this location? Wetter? Warmer? Cooler? Drier? By how much? How different is the RCP 8.5 projection for this location?

Projected effects of increases in atmospheric CO_2 • Figure 14.18

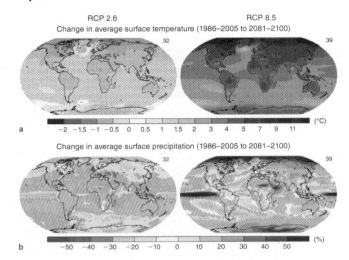

WHAT IS HAPPENING IN THIS PICTURE?

In this "Calvin and Hobbes" comic strip, Calvin tells his pet tiger, Hobbes, about his theory that the days are getting colder because the Sun is going out. Let's call this Hypothesis 1. His father, on the other hand, says the days are getting colder because Earth is getting farther from the Sun—Hypothesis 2. Another reasonable hypothesis is that Earth's axis is tilted, which makes the sunlight less direct in winter—Hypothesis 3.

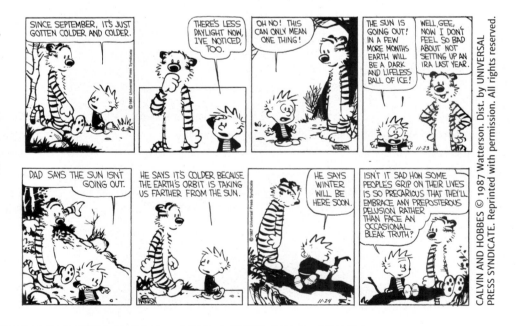

THINK CRITICALLY

1. What scientific tests could you perform to determine why—or, indeed, if—the weather is getting colder?
2. Which explanation do you think is right—Calvin's, his dad's, or Hypothesis 3?

SELF-TEST

(Check your answers in Appendix D.)

1. Which one of the following is an example of climate change?

    a. an extremely hot summer

    b. three very cold winters in a row

    c. a very intense hurricane season

    d. two years of above-normal precipitation

    e. All of these indicate that the climate is changing.

    f. None of these is definitively indicative of climate change.

2. The Köppen climate classification system is based on _____.

    a. variations in oceanic circulation

    b. temperature, precipitation, and vegetation patterns

    c. global atmospheric circulation patterns

    d. paleoclimate records

    e. All of the above answers are correct.

3. The orbital variations that combine to produce Milankovitch cycles are _____.

    a. seasons, day–night cycles, and tides

    b. radiative balance, solar output, and albedo

    c. tilt, eccentricity, and precession

    d. glaciations, interglaciations, and feedbacks

4. Which one of these surfaces would have the highest albedo?

    a. forest

    b. ocean

    c. ice cap

    d. soil

    e. rock

5. This graph of Earth's climate record shows that temperatures have _____ overall, in the past 2 million years.

    a. fluctuated greatly

    b. remained constant

    c. been slowly decreasing

    d. been slowly increasing

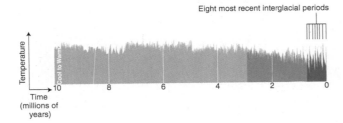

6. Geological studies have revealed a number of natural agents that can act together to cause climate change. Which of the following is not considered a possible cause of climate change?

    a. changes in the composition of the atmosphere

    b. tectonism

    c. interruptions of ocean circulation

    d. changes in solar output

    e. All of the above are considered to be natural causes of climate change.

7. Which of the following would definitely not be useful as a climate proxy for the study of paleoclimate?

    a. growth rings in corals

    b. layered ice from polar regions and glaciers

    c. ocean sea-surface temperature

    d. tree rings

    e. Any of these would likely be useful as a climate proxy.

8. A climate proxy must be influenced by or mimic some aspect of climate and then preserve a record of that climatic influence. What is the other crucial characteristic of a useful climate proxy?

    a. It must be global, rather than local, in its extent.

    b. It must be something that can be duplicated in a laboratory.

    c. It must have occurred in the recent past.

    d. It must be able to have a date attached to it.

9. Imagine this scenario: The climate warms by 1°C. Evaporation of ocean water increases. As a result, cloud cover increases. The clouds that form are mainly stratus clouds, which block incoming solar radiation, cooling the surface. Is this scenario an example of a positive feedback or a negative feedback?

    a. negative feedback

    b. positive feedback

    c. This scenario shows both positive and negative feedback.

    d. This scenario shows neither positive nor negative feedback.

10. Geologists use a number of techniques to study paleoclimates, including data collected from _____.

    a. fossil pollen grains from peat bogs and lakes

    b. seafloor sediment

    c. paleosols

    d. ice cores

    e. All of the above are techniques geologists use to study paleoclimate.

11. What can scientists learn from air bubbles trapped in polar ice, like the ones shown here?

   a. greenhouse gas composition of ancient air

   b. temperature changes over the past few thousand years

   c. variations in snowfall at the poles

   d. date of ice core climate proxy

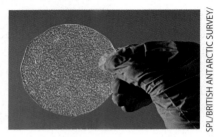

SPL/BRITISH ANTARCTIC SURVEY/
Photo Researchers, Inc.

12. When did the last major glaciation end?

   a. about 1 million years ago

   b. about 10,000 years ago

   c. about 1000 years ago

   d. about 150 years ago

13. What is the cause of the zig-zag pattern seen in the curve on this graph?

   a. human contributions to atmospheric carbon dioxide caused by the burning of fossil fuels

   b. variations in atmospheric carbon dioxide that result from seasonal variations in photosynthesis

   c. regional and global climate change

   d. changes in sea-surface temperature and oceanic thermohaline circulation

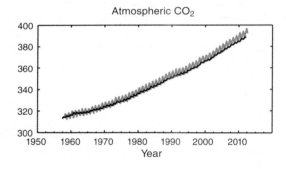

Atmospheric CO$_2$

14. Anthropogenic carbon dioxide in the atmosphere results from the burning of fossil fuels, in addition to some other important sources. How far back does the recent record of atmospheric carbon dioxide measurements extend?

   a. about 1000 years

   b. about 100 years

   c. about 50 years

   d. about 10 years

15. What would be the effects of continued global warming over the next century?

   a. retreat of glaciers

   b. calving of large icebergs from ice shelves

   c. shrinking of some animal habitats

   d. expansion of some animal habitats

   e. All of the above are possible effects of global warming.

THE PLANNER ✓

Review the Chapter Planner on the chapter opener and check off your completed work.

15 A BRIEF HISTORY OF LIFE ON EARTH

courtesy Alan Groves/Art Dinouveau

©AP/Wide World Photos

AN ANCIENT NEST

It has long been accepted that dinosaurs laid eggs, like modern reptiles. However, eggs are fragile and are rarely preserved as fossils, so it has been a slow process to gather evidence about the egg-laying behaviors of dinosaurs. (The main photo is an artist's rendition of a nesting dinosaur.) One of the most challenging aspects is that it is rare to find actual dinosaurs or embryos associated with the eggs, making it difficult to attribute any particular nest to a specific dinosaur species.

A notable case in which it was possible to identify the species associated with a clutch of eggs is the 2-meter-long fossilized dinosaur shown in the inset photo. The 67-million-year-old dinosaur, unearthed in northern China in 1924, is curled protectively around at least 20 eggs.

When the fossil was found, it was not widely accepted that dinosaurs cared for their young, so the name Oviraptor—"egg thief"—was given to the newly discovered species. Much later (in 1994), when an embryo of the same species was found inside one of the eggs, the entire scenario had to be reinterpreted. This fossil, now housed at the American Museum of Natural History in New York and nicknamed "Big Mamma," provides strong evidence that dinosaurs cared for their young.

EVER-CHANGING EARTH

Learning Objectives

1. **Describe** the important changes in Earth's environment over the past 4.6 billion years.

2. **Explain** how photosynthesis adds oxygen to the atmosphere.

3. **Describe** how the oxygen and carbon cycles are connected.

Throughout this book, we have seen evidence that Earth is a place of constant change. Luckily for us, negative feedbacks among the geosphere, atmosphere, hydrosphere, and biosphere moderate these changes. Earth's environments are in a state of **dynamic equilibrium**—ever-changing, but balanced and resilient—so conditions don't swing too wildly, and the planet continues to be habitable.

In this section of the chapter, we present evidence of changes that have occurred throughout Earth's history, with enormous impacts on Earth's **life zone** (introduced in Chapter 1). **Figure 15.1** presents a summary of these changes, which have supported and continue to support life but also

The changing Earth • Figure 15.1

From left to right, this diagram illustrates some of the major events in the history of Earth's surface environment during its first 4.56 billion years.

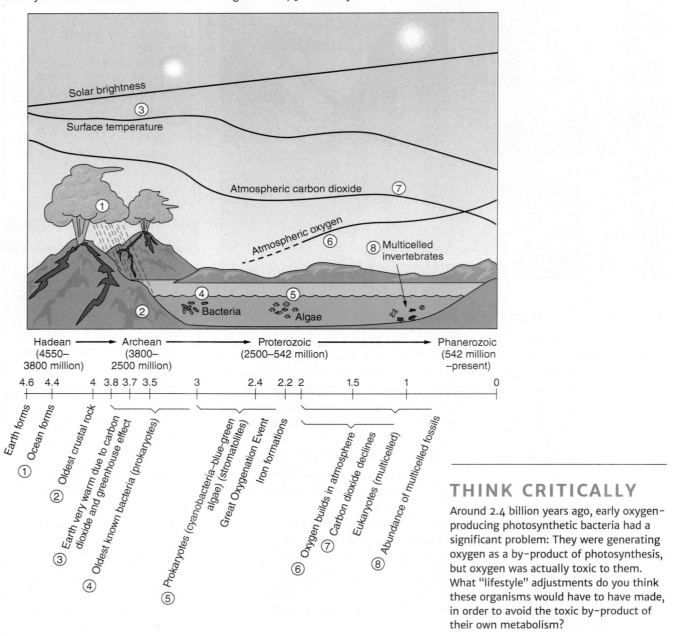

THINK CRITICALLY

Around 2.4 billion years ago, early oxygen-producing photosynthetic bacteria had a significant problem: They were generating oxygen as a by-product of photosynthesis, but oxygen was actually toxic to them. What "lifestyle" adjustments do you think these organisms would have to have made, in order to avoid the toxic by-product of their own metabolism?

have been, to a certain extent, driven by life itself. Remember that the backdrop for all of these changes has been the constant rearrangement of continents and oceans as a result of plate tectonics, which has been operating for at least the past 2 billion years and probably longer.

Early Earth

Compared to the Sun, which is representative of the raw materials from which Earth and the other planets of our solar system formed (see Chapter 1), Earth contains less of some volatile elements, such as nitrogen, argon, hydrogen, and helium. Most of these light elements were lost when the **primary atmosphere**, the envelope of gas that surrounded early Earth, was stripped away by the solar wind, meteorite impacts, or both. Little by little, Earth generated a new, **secondary atmosphere** by volcanic outgassing of volatile materials from its interior (see *Remember This!*).

> **REMEMBER THIS!** Do you remember how Earth's early atmosphere and hydrosphere were formed? You can remind yourself by returning to the sections on *The Ocean* and *The Atmosphere* in Chapter 12.

Volcanic outgassing was then and continues to be the main process by which volatile materials are released from Earth's interior—although it is now occurring at a much slower rate. Early Earth was extremely volcanically active, and outgassing was vigorous. The main chemical constituent of volcanic gas (as much as 97% by volume) is water vapor, with varying amounts of other constituents. However, the planet's surface was very hot—much too hot for liquid water to be sustained, so it was returned immediately to the atmosphere by evaporation.

With no ocean there was certainly no opportunity for life to take hold. But little by little the surface of the planet cooled. By as early as 4.4 billion years ago, liquid water began to accumulate and to persist in surface depressions. This set the stage for life to eventually take hold.

The total volume of volcanic gas released over the past 4 billion years or so accounts quite nicely for the present composition of the atmosphere, with one extremely important exception: oxygen. As you can see in Figure 15.1, Earth had virtually no oxygen in its atmosphere more than 4 billion years ago, but the atmosphere is now approximately 21% oxygen. What is the origin of the oxygenated atmosphere that we have today?

An Oxygenated Atmosphere

Traces of oxygen were probably generated in the early atmosphere through the breakdown of water molecules into oxygen and hydrogen by ultraviolet light (a process called **photodissociation**). Although this is an important process, it doesn't even come close to accounting for the present high levels of oxygen in the atmosphere.

Almost all of the free oxygen now in the atmosphere originated through **photosynthesis** (**Figure 15.2**). ("Free" refers to

> **photosynthesis** A chemical reaction whereby plants use light energy to induce carbon dioxide to react with water, producing carbohydrates and oxygen.

Photosynthesis • Figure 15.2

Photosynthesis, which may have begun on Earth as early as 3.5 billion years ago, allows plants to convert light energy into chemical energy.

a. This pea plant, like all other green, leafy plants, produces oxygen through the process of photosynthesis.

b. The photosynthetic reaction combines carbon dioxide (CO_2) and water (H_2O) to make carbohydrates (molecules containing C, H, and O), which the plant needs to grow. The reaction produces oxygen molecules (O_2), which the plant releases through pores in its leaves. The reaction requires energy from sunlight.

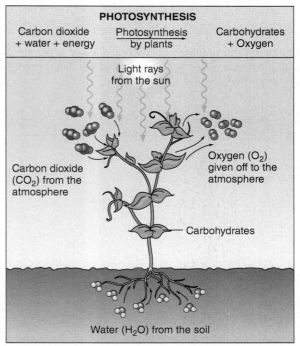

PHOTOSYNTHESIS

| Carbon dioxide + water + energy | Photosynthesis by plants | Carbohydrates + Oxygen |

Light rays from the sun

Carbon dioxide (CO_2) from the atmosphere

Oxygen (O_2) given off to the atmosphere

Carbohydrates

Water (H_2O) from the soil

©CORBIS

oxygen in the form of O, O_2, or O_3—that is, not bonded into a molecular compound with other elements.) Photosynthesis is thought to have originated as early as 3.5 billion years ago; however, early photosynthetic bacteria probably mostly produced sulfur, rather than oxygen, as a by-product of photosynthesis. Oxygen-producing (or **oxygenic**) photosynthesis may have existed for almost as long, but it didn't have a significant impact on the composition of the atmosphere until around 2.5 or 2.4 billion years ago.

Oxygen is a very reactive chemical. Throughout Earth's early history, most of the free oxygen produced by photosynthesis was combined with iron in ocean water to form iron oxide-bearing minerals. The control that oxygen exerted on iron dissolved in the ocean is discussed in Chapter 8's *What a Geologist Sees*. Evidence of the gradual transition from oxygen-poor to oxygen-rich ocean water is preserved in seafloor sedimentary rock: The minerals in seafloor sedimentary rock older than about 2.5 billion years contain reduced (oxygen-poor) iron compounds, whereas in rock younger than about 1.8 billion years, oxidized (oxygen-rich) compounds predominate. Sediment precipitated during the transition period contains alternating bands of red (oxidized iron) and black (reduced iron) minerals. This sediment, originally deposited as chemical sediment on the seafloor, eventually became the rock known as **banded iron formation**.

Evidence for the transition to an oxygen-rich atmosphere comes mainly from marine sedimentary rock, and thus applies specifically to the ocean. Because ocean water is in constant contact with the atmosphere, however, the two systems function together in a state of dynamic equilibrium. This implies that the transition from an oxygen-poor to an oxygen-rich atmosphere also must have occurred during this period. The period from 2.4 to 2.0 billion years ago, during which free oxygen began to build up in the ocean and atmosphere, is known as the **Great Oxygenation Event**, and it dramatically altered the conditions for life on Earth.

Along with the buildup of molecular oxygen (O_2) in the atmosphere came an eventual increase in ozone (O_3). Ozone filters out harmful ultraviolet radiation (Chapter 12), so its accumulation in the stratosphere eventually made it possible for life to flourish in shallow water, and finally on land. This critical stage in the evolution of the atmosphere—when the ozone layer first began to function as an effective ultraviolet filter—was reached between 1100 and 541 million years ago. Interestingly, the fossil record shows an explosive diversification of lifeforms at the same time (the beginning of the Phanerozoic Eon).

Oxygen has continued to play a key role in the evolution and form of life. Over the past 200 million years, the concentration of oxygen has risen from 10% to as much as 25% of the atmosphere, before settling (probably not permanently) at its current value of 21% by volume, in dry air (**Figure 15.3**). This increase has benefited humans and all other mammals because mammals are voracious oxygen consumers. Not only do we require oxygen to fuel our high-energy, warm-blooded metabolism, our unique reproductive system demands even more. An expectant mother's used (venous) blood must still have enough oxygen in it to diffuse through the placenta into her unborn child's bloodstream. It would be very difficult for any mammal species to survive in an atmosphere of only 10% oxygen.

The Other Side of the Oxygen Story

The story of how oxygen accumulated in the ocean and atmosphere begins with photosynthesis, but photosynthesis is only one side of the story. Photosynthesis in the oxygen cycle is balanced by **decomposition**, in which organic carbon combines with oxygen to form carbon dioxide. The oxygen and carbon cycles are coupled together, and they

The oxygen content of the atmosphere • Figure 15.3 _____

Over the past 200 million years, oxygen levels in the atmosphere have increased markedly. The rise of mammals, aided by the demise of the dinosaurs 65 million years ago, may have resulted partly from the plentiful oxygen supply.

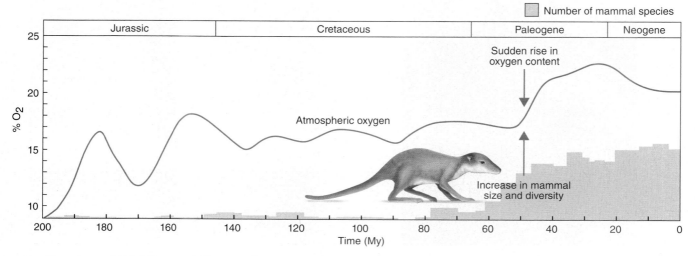

interact throughout the geosphere, atmosphere, hydrosphere, and biosphere.

One of the reasons that oxygen has been able to accumulate in the ocean and atmosphere is that the decomposition side of the oxygen and carbon cycles was suppressed by the burial of organic sediment. If organic matter is buried as sediment before it fully decomposes, its carbon is isolated and it is no longer available to react with the free oxygen in the atmosphere. In that case, there should be a net accumulation of carbon in sediment and a buildup of oxygen in the atmosphere.

What could cause organic matter and its carbon to be buried on such a massive scale? This is where plate tectonics comes into the story. The most likely place for the burial of huge volumes of organic sediment is in the warm, shallow seas along the edges of continents. Organic matter in continental shelf seas is quickly buried by erosion of sediment from rising mountain ranges. The lithosphere, hydrosphere, and biosphere all interacted to isolate carbon, allowing the development of the oxygen-rich atmosphere we breathe today.

The role of life in the chemical evolution of the atmosphere and hydrosphere does not stop with the oxygen and carbon cycles. Nitrogen, carbon, phosphorus, iron, and sulfur also circulate through the Earth system, and their flows are also strongly affected by interactions with living organisms.

The global cycling of water has also played a fundamental role in regulating the conditions for life on this planet. Water is the single most important ingredient for the development and maintenance of life. The history and diversity of life are very much a part of this planet's geological history. There are countless examples of interactions between the biosphere and other parts of the Earth system. Plants and microorganisms accelerate the weathering of rock and formation of soil. Marine organisms sink to the bottom of the sea, where they form sediment that is buried, or turned into limestone. Land plants accumulate, undergoing lithification to form coal. And biologic processes, as we have seen, regulate the composition of the air that we breathe. The study of geology is thus inseparable from the study of life on Earth.

STOP CONCEPT CHECK

1. **Where** did Earth's primary and secondary atmospheres come from?
2. **Why** was there little or no oxygen in the secondary atmosphere early in Earth's history?
3. **What** are the sources of atmospheric oxygen, and what processes remove oxygen from the atmosphere?

EARLY LIFE

Learning Objectives

1. **Explain** how the fundamental requirements for life inform the search for answers about how life originated.

2. **Describe** the major differences between prokaryotic and eukaryotic organisms.

Scientists have not yet found conclusive evidence for life on Earth prior to the early Archean Eon, which began about 4.0 billion years ago. In rock formed about 3.8 billion years ago, isotopic signals from graphite in metamorphosed shale suggest that the carbon in the graphite was once part of living cells.

The environment of Earth before 3.8 billion years ago was absolutely hostile to life as we now know it, with a noxious atmosphere, constant volcanic eruptions, and a very high rate of bombardment by colossal meteorites. Yet a remarkably short time later, by about 3.55 billion years ago, entire colonies of bacterial life forms had developed, as shown by fossils of layered structures of bacterial origin, called **stromatolites** (**Figure 15.4**). How microscopic life emerged and spread so quickly on a previously barren and inhospitable planet is still one of the greatest unsolved mysteries of science.

Life in Three Not-So-Easy Steps

What is a living organism? There is not absolute agreement on this question, but it seems clear that for life to exist at least three fundamental conditions must be met. First, the organic molecules that are the building blocks of life must exist. Second, an organism must have a means of **replication**, to create a more or less accurate copy of itself. And third, it must have a **metabolism**, a means of extracting energy and material sustenance from its environment. In this section we will consider these three steps to life in greater depth.

Earth uses the same set of 20 carbon-based molecules, called **amino acids**, as "building blocks." Furthermore, all known living organisms are made of one or more **cells**, enclosed by a membrane. The cell membrane serves a dual purpose: maintaining a relatively constant chemical environment (or **homeostasis**)

cell The basic structural and functional unit of life; a complex grouping of chemical compounds enclosed in a porous membrane.

within the cell and allowing materials and energy to pass in and out as needed. (Note that this means that cells are open systems—both materials and energy can pass through their boundaries.)

Carbon is essential to life on Earth because carbon atoms can **polymerize** to form very long chains and complex molecules (such as proteins and enzymes), which enable

Stromatolites are bacterial mats; they haven't changed much over the past 2 billion years.

a. These odd-looking bumps in Shark's Bay, Western Australia, are present-day stromatolites, which are formed in warm, shallow seas by photosynthetic bacteria.

b. This 2.2-billion-year-old fossilized stromatolite from Michigan shows a pattern of growth rings that is identical to a cross section of a modern-day stromatolite.

O. Louis Mazzatenta/NG Image Collection

Francois Gohier/Photo Researchers, Inc.

cells to function. The first step in the emergence of life was likely the synthesis of these complex organic chemicals from inorganic ingredients.

However, amino acids and biopolymers do not form by themselves; at a minimum, they require an energy source (**Figure 15.5**). In the 1950s, Stanley Miller showed that it is possible to assemble amino acids out of a mixture of inorganic ingredients by exposing them to an electric spark (as might happen, for example, if lightning struck). However, it is still unclear whether the earliest amino acids really formed this way, and several other hypotheses are still being investigated.

Replication in modern life relies on a truly remarkable mechanism. Every cell nucleus contains a molecule called **DNA** (**deoxyribonucleic acid**). DNA is shaped like a twisted ladder (as shown in **Figure 15.5b**), in which each rung consists of two complementary organic molecules called **nucleotides**, which fit together like a lock and key.

> **DNA** Deoxyribonucleic acid; a double-chain biopolymer that contains all the genetic information needed for an organism to grow and reproduce.

However, DNA is far too complex to have been the first self-replicating molecule. Most experts believe that a simpler, single-stranded molecule called **RNA** (**ribonucleic acid**) must have appeared first, and they have dubbed the hypothetical pre-DNA version of life the "RNA world." But even RNA is too complex and fragile to assemble by itself; proteins are required. How would these proteins work together without DNA or RNA to direct them? This version of a chicken-and-egg paradox has yet to be resolved.

Although present-day organisms use one method of replication exclusively (DNA), several different kinds of metabolism have evolved. Plants obtain energy via photosynthesis. Animals obtain energy from the food they eat, and oxygen is needed to release the energy; this is **aerobic metabolism**. In contrast, many kinds of bacteria have **anaerobic metabolisms**, for example, obtaining energy through the nonoxygenated breakdown of food by the process of **fermentation**. Other one-celled organisms can extract energy directly from hydrogen, sulfur, or salt via **chemosynthesis**. This allows them to survive in high-temperature or high-salinity environments that scientists once considered uninhabitable (see **Figure 15.5c and d**). Such organisms are often called **extremophiles** because they live in conditions that are the extreme end of the chemical and thermal circumstances in which organic molecules can remain chemically stable.

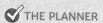
What is life, and how did it originate? There are at least three prerequisites that must be met for any living organism to exist.

The first not-so-easy step: Making organic molecules

a. In the 1950s, Stanley Miller's experiment used a "primordial soup" of methane, ammonia, and hydrogen to create organic amino acids in a flask. Scientists now believe that he used the wrong ingredients: Earth's primitive atmosphere probably consisted mainly of carbon dioxide, water vapor, and nitrogen. No one has yet come up with a convincing mechanism for producing organic molecules out of these ingredients, in conditions that resemble those of early Earth.

O. Louis Mazzatenta/NG Image Collection

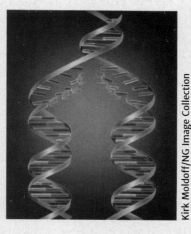

Kirk Moldoff/NG Image Collection

The second not-so-easy step: Replication

b. The two strands of the twisted molecule of DNA are held together by organic molecules called *nucleotides*, which come in complementary pairs. When the two strands are separated, either can act as a template to re-create the other. This allows for the duplication of the genetic information needed for an organism to grow or reproduce.

The third not-so-easy step: Metabolism

The earliest organisms might have been chemosynthetic rather than photosynthetic. Seafloor hydrothermal vents give us an idea of how life might have emerged in the very hot environment of early Earth.

Dr.Verena Tunnicliffe, University of Victoria

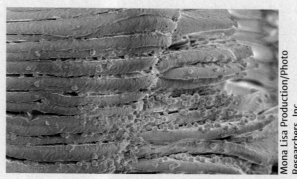

Mona Lisa Production/Photo Researchers, Inc.

c. "Black smokers," such as this vent west of Vancouver Island, Canada, release superheated water and a variety of minerals. Sunlight never penetrates to these depths, so organisms rely on chemosynthesis rather than photosynthesis to obtain energy. The long white-and-red organisms are tube worms.

d. Deep-sea bacteria like these (blue spheres on the surface of a tube worm), extract energy from the chemicals produced by the vent and form the base of a food chain that includes tubeworms, crabs, and shrimp.

ASK YOURSELF

In order for amino acids to form from elements, an energy source is required. Miller used an electric spark. What natural energy source was he trying to imitate?

a. sunlight
b. Earth's internal energy
c. cosmic rays
d. lightning
e. nuclear energy

Archean and Proterozoic Life

Some chemical residues that signal the former presence of life, called **biosignatures**, date as far back as the early Archean Eon (see *Remember This!*). However, the most ancient known fossils (that is, preserved organisms rather than just a trace chemical indication of their former presence) are the remains of microscopic **prokaryotes**. Prokaryotes are still present on Earth today; all bacteria are prokaryotes. They are unicellular (although they may form colonies, they can survive on their own), and they have rudimentary nuclei. The extremophile bacteria shown in Figure 15.5d are part of a particular **domain** of prokaryotes called **Archaea**. Bacteria are extremely well adapted to their own specific environments and are far more numerous than anything else on Earth. Your own body contains 10 times as many bacterial cells as human cells!

> **prokaryote** A single-celled organism with no distinct nucleus—that is, no membrane separates its DNA from the rest of the cell.

> **domain** The broadest taxonomic category of living organisms; biologists today recognize three domains: Bacteria, Archaea, and Eukarya.

> **REMEMBER THIS!** In this chapter we will be making frequent references to the various time units of the geological timescale; do you remember what they are? You can review them by looking back at *The Geologic Column* in Chapter 3.

For the first 2 billion years of life, the fossil record is rather sparse because the only forms of life were microscopic and had no hard parts that could be preserved. However, we do have one important piece of indirect evidence of ancient life. Stromatolites, as you saw in Figure 15.4, are mound-like structures that consist of many thin layers of calcium carbonate. Similar structures can be found today; they are formed in seawater by the action of photosynthetic organisms called **cyanobacteria**. Fossilized stromatolites have been found in rock up to 3.55 billion years old, providing evidence that photosynthesis and the production of oxygen are ancient processes on Earth.

At some time in the Proterozoic Eon, a new kind of life form appeared: **eukaryotes** (from the Greek words meaning "true nucleus"). A eukaryotic cell has a well-defined **nucleus** with an enclosing membrane (**Figure 15.6**). In addition, eukaryotic

> **eukaryote** An organism composed of eukaryotic cells—that is, cells that have a well-defined nucleus and organelles.

Prokaryotes and eukaryotes · Figure 15.6

The two basic cell types are prokaryotic and eukaryotic. Both cells have been stained to enhance their visibility under a microscope.

a. In prokaryotic cells, such as this bacterium, the nucleus is poorly defined and not contained by a membrane.

b. In eukaryotic cells, such as this cell from a plant root, the nucleus and several other structures called *organelles* are clearly defined.

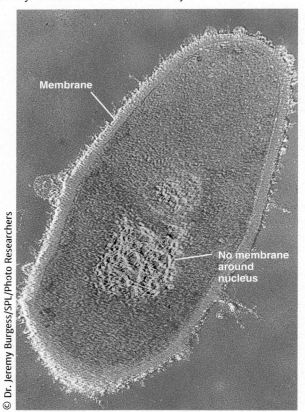

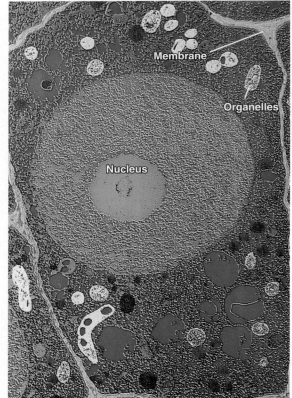

These strangely shaped fossils, specimens of the Ediacara fauna, are the most ancient evidence of multicellular animals.

a. *Mawsonia spriggi* was probably a floating, disc-shaped animal like a jellyfish, 13 centimeters in diameter.

O. Louis Mazzatenta/NG Image Collection

b. *Dickinsonia costata* was a worm-like creature, 7.5 centimeters in diameter.

O. Louis Mazzatenta/NG Image Collection

cells contain a number of smaller structures called **organelles**, some of which are functional bodies and some of which may originally have been prokaryotic bacteria that were engulfed by the larger eukaryotes.

Eukaryotes appeared at least 1.4 billion years ago, and perhaps as much as 2.7 billion years ago. Like most of the other dates in the early history of life, these dates are uncertain because the first eukaryotes were microscopic in size and lacked hard parts and therefore are not well preserved as fossils. It is no accident that they emerged after the transition to an oxygenated atmosphere; they had aerobic metabolisms and thus were better equipped to make use of free oxygen than prokaryotic bacteria had been.

The availability of oxygen as a fuel for metabolism had profound ramifications for early organisms. Aerobic metabolisms are more efficient than anaerobic metabolisms, allowing more energy to be extracted from each molecule of food. Eukaryotic cells grew larger and became more complex than prokaryotic cells. Eukaryotes were also more tolerant of crowding than anaerobic bacteria had been; this allowed them to enter many habitats and develop lifestyles that had not previously been accessible, such as living in large colonies. Although the first eukaryotes were still single-celled organisms, similar to modern slime molds, the stage was set for multicellular life.

The earliest fossils of multicellular eukaryotic organisms appear at the end of the Proterozoic Eon, preserved in rock about 630 million years old. These organisms, which have now been found in a number of locations, are called the **Ediacara fauna** (or Ediacara biota), after the site where they were first discovered, the Ediacara Hills of South Australia. The Ediacara fauna lived in quiet marine bays. They were jelly-like animals with no hard parts, and they were mostly sessile (i.e., could not move about on their own) (**Figure 15.7**).

The Ediacaran organisms represent a huge jump in diversity and complexity from the first unicellular eukaryotes, which appeared at least 800 million years earlier. Scientists still do not know much about what happened during those 800 million years because fossil evidence is sparse and difficult to interpret.

STOP CONCEPT CHECK

1. **What** are the basic building blocks and fundamental processes that must be in place for life to exist?

2. **What** allowed eukaryotic organisms to become more complex than prokaryotes?

EVOLUTION AND THE FOSSIL RECORD

Learning Objectives

1. **Describe** how natural selection provides a means for evolution to occur.

2. **Describe** the most common ways in which organisms can be preserved as fossils.

At the beginning of the Phanerozoic Eon, about 545 million years ago, the fossil record suddenly shows an explosion in the diversity of species. We have explored some of the possible reasons for this explosion: the oxygenated atmosphere, the protective layer of ozone, and the emergence of eukaryotes and then multicellular organisms. At this point, it seems appropriate to pause and describe how new species arise and how they are preserved as fossils.

Evolution and Natural Selection

On December 27, 1831, Charles Darwin set sail from England as an unpaid naturalist and "gentleman's companion" for the captain of the *H.M.S. Beagle*. Trained as a clergyman, Darwin at the time of his departure believed in the biblical account of creation and the fixed nature of species. By the time he returned in 1836, his views had changed considerably, though it is clear from his writings that he still saw the hand of God at work.

Darwin kept scrupulous notes and made paintings and sketches of the plants, animals, and fossils he saw on the voyage. In 1859, long after his return to England, Darwin published his observations and ideas in a book called *On the Origin of Species by Means of Natural Selection* (**Figure 15.8**). He waited so long to publish his findings because he was concerned about the uproar it might—and did—cause.

From the time of William "Strata" Smith, who formulated the principle of faunal and floral succession (Chapter 3), it had been widely recognized that life has changed through time. Darwin was not the first to suggest **evolution** as an explanation for these changes and for the variety and distribution of species on Earth. He was, however, the first to provide such a thorough discussion of the available evidence, gathered during his voyage and examined over the following years (see *Case Study*). Darwin was eventually motivated to publish his ideas when another young British naturalist, Alfred Russel Wallace, independently hit upon the same explanation for how evolution works.

> **evolution** The theory that life on Earth has developed gradually, from simple organisms to more complex organisms.

The theory of evolution, sometimes concisely defined as "descent with modification," rests on a central pillar: that all modern organisms are the descendants of different kinds of organisms that existed in the past. Because the word "theory" is often misunderstood, it is important to emphasize that there is no doubt today among legitimate biologists that evolution does occur; has occurred throughout the history of life on this planet, as confirmed by a wealth of evidence in the fossil record; and has been observed to occur repeatedly in laboratory situations. The question that is still the subject of much discussion and scientific investigation is not *whether* evolution occurs but exactly *how* it occurs (see *Remember This!*).

> **REMEMBER THIS!** Do you remember the difference between a theory and a hypothesis, as they are used in the context of science? You can review the distinctions by looking back at *What Is Geology?* in Chapter 1.

Charles Darwin: Decipherer of evolution's clues • Figure 15.8

Though he was a retiring and unpretentious man, Charles Darwin wrote one of the most controversial and influential books in scientific history, *On the Origin of Species*. Originally printed in a small edition of 1250 copies, his book has been through at least 400 printings and translated into at least 29 languages.

Photo Researchers/Getty Images, Inc.

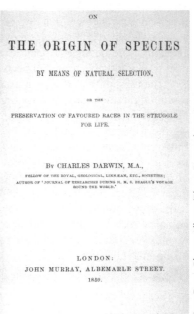

ON

THE ORIGIN OF SPECIES

BY MEANS OF NATURAL SELECTION,

OR THE

PRESERVATION OF FAVOURED RACES IN THE STRUGGLE FOR LIFE.

By CHARLES DARWIN, M.A.,

FELLOW OF THE ROYAL, GEOLOGICAL, LINNÆAN, ETC., SOCIETIES; AUTHOR OF 'JOURNAL OF RESEARCHES DURING H. M. S. BEAGLE'S VOYAGE ROUND THE WORLD.'

LONDON:
JOHN MURRAY, ALBEMARLE STREET.
1859.

Mary Evans Picture Library/Photo Researchers, Inc.

Darwin and the Galápagos Finches

On the Galápagos Islands, Darwin counted 13 species of apparently related birds, all similar to the mainland finch called a grassquit, but with different beak shapes and different diets. What could account for such a dramatic difference in diversity between the islands and the mainland?

Darwin reasoned that long ago, finches from the mainland had colonized the volcanic islands and had subsequently changed as a result of having to adapt to their new environments. Different beak shapes had developed as the birds adapted to different diets. It was a logical idea, but it contradicted the widely believed theological doctrine that no new species had appeared on Earth since creation.

©J. Dunning/VIREO

In Ecuador, on the mainland of South America, there is only one species of finch, this small, seed-eating bird called a grassquit.

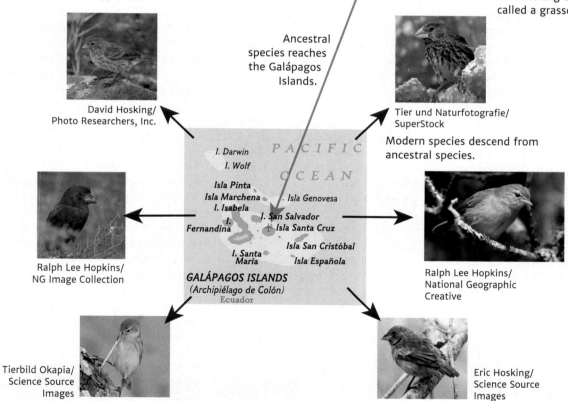

David Hosking/
Photo Researchers, Inc.

Ancestral species reaches the Galápagos Islands.

Tier und Naturfotografie/
SuperStock

Modern species descend from ancestral species.

Ralph Lee Hopkins/
NG Image Collection

Ralph Lee Hopkins/
National Geographic
Creative

Tierbild Okapia/
Science Source
Images

Eric Hosking/
Science Source
Images

GALÁPAGOS ISLANDS
(Archipiélago de Colón)
Ecuador

I. Darwin
I. Wolf
Isla Pinta
Isla Marchena *Isla Genovesa*
I. Isabela
I. *I. San Salvador*
Fernandina *Isla Santa Cruz*
I. Santa *Isla San Cristóbal*
María *Isla Española*

PACIFIC OCEAN

Alison Wright/NG Image Collection

Biologists Peter and Rosemary Grant spent 42 years studying Darwin's finches on isolated Daphne Major island in the Galápagos. Their results strongly support evolutionary theory.

THINK CRITICALLY

Darwin reasoned that the original grassquits that colonized the islands had become stranded and therefore isolated from the population in Ecuador. How might they have become stranded?

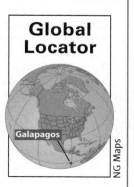

Global Locator

Galapagos

NG Maps

In *On the Origin of Species*, Darwin outlined a hypothesis to explain how evolution occurs, and he called this mechanism **natural selection**. Evolution tells us that populations of organisms have changed over time; natural selection tells us that the changes happen as a result of **adaptation** to changing environmental conditions. When a useful new trait emerges that provides a competitive advantage for an individual—such as, for example, a beak shape that makes it easier for a finch to eat hard-to-crack seeds—that individual will likely experience enhanced survival and reproductive success. If the trait is **heritable** (that is, transmissible from parent to offspring), offspring that inherit the trait also will experience enhanced survival and reproductive success. After several generations, most individuals will have inherited the advantageous trait, and the whole population thus evolves over time.

> **natural selection**
> The process by which individuals that are well adapted to their environment have a survival advantage and pass on their favorable characteristics to their offspring.

It is important to understand that an organism does not develop useful or adaptive traits in response to an environmental constraint or need. Traits occur by chance; some are beneficial and boost an individual's chances of survival; others do not. In Darwin's time it was not known how organisms transmit traits to later generations; now we know that heritable traits are encoded in **genes** on an organism's DNA. Developments in the science of genetics have greatly strengthened the scientific support for natural selection as the mechanism for evolution. The random variation that is essential for natural selection is explained by **mutations** in genes—accidental deletions, transpositions, or substitutions of one nucleotide for another, that allow a new trait to be expressed.

> **species** A population of genetically and/or morphologically similar individuals that can interbreed and produce fertile offspring.

One of Darwin's most important contributions was that he waded into the long-standing debate about how new **species** arise. Among many others, Charles Darwin's own grandfather, Erasmus Darwin, had been involved in this debate. Before Darwin's time, it had been a prevalent idea that each different species was part of a fixed hierarchy of species. Darwin's work contributed significantly to our understanding that species are not fixed and unchanging, but rather that populations change and new species evolve from preexisting ones as a result of natural selection.

When considered over the course of Earth's history, it appears that evolution happens exceedingly slowly; we know of many species that have endured for millions or even hundreds of millions of years. However, the mechanism of natural selection also allows for relatively rapid changes. In modern laboratories, scientists can observe evolution in progress, through the expression of specific inherited traits passed along from generation to generation by organisms that reproduce very rapidly, such as fruit flies.

There is still considerable scientific debate over the relative importance of gradual change versus rapid change in evolution. Darwin favored extremely slow, gradual change, or **gradualism**, whereas the famous evolutionary biologist Stephen Jay Gould, among others, argued for **punctuated equilibrium**, in which species persist for a very long time with few changes and undergo occasional periods of very rapid change. Gould helped to create space for this healthy scientific debate within a firmly Darwinian context, by writing that Darwin "acknowledged the provisional nature of natural selection while affirming the fact of evolution."[*] (Stephen Jay Gould, "Evolution as Fact and Theory," *Discover 2* (May 1981): 34–37; from *Hen's Teeth and Horse's Toes*, New York: W. W. Norton & Company, 1994, pp. 253–262.)

In recent years, scientists also have begun to recognize the importance of occasional catastrophic events. The best-documented example is the meteorite impact that is thought to have wiped out the dinosaurs. These animals died out, in all likelihood, not because they were less well adapted to their environment than other species but because of a chance event that they had never experienced before and had no opportunity to adapt to.

To explore evolution and natural selection in greater detail, and to learn more about Darwin's work while the *Beagle* was in the Galápagos Islands, see *Where Geologists Click*.

Where Geologists CLICK

Charles Darwin Foundation

Galápagos—a volcanic hot spot island chain that is part of Ecuador—is almost synonymous with the work of Charles Darwin in developing the theory of evolution. The Charles Darwin Foundation on the island of Santa Cruz in Galápagos was founded in 1959 with the help of UNESCO (the United Nations Educational, Scientific, and Cultural Organization), and IUCN (the International Union for Conservation of Nature). Foundation scientists and volunteers carry out research on marine and terrestrial organisms and environments, social science problems, invasive species, ecological restoration, conservation, and public outreach.

How Fossils Form

The best evidence for evolution lies in the vast numbers of **fossils** chronicling the succession of species that no longer exist on Earth. Although fossilization can occur in many ways (**Figure 15.9**), it is always a relatively rare event. If a dead animal or plant is exposed to air, running water, scavengers, or bacteria, it will decompose or be eaten, and its parts will be scattered or destroyed.

> **fossil** Remains of an organism from a past age, embedded and preserved in rock.

For an organism to be preserved as a fossil, its remains must be quickly covered by a layer of protective material—usually sand or mud but some-times tree sap, ice, tar, or volcanic ash. Hard parts such as bones, shells, and teeth are less easily destroyed and thus more likely to be preserved than soft or delicate parts such as skin, hair, feathers, or leaves.

Sometimes a deceased organism is preserved with little or no alteration. For example, insects many millions of years old have been trapped in tree sap, which hardens into amber (**Figure 15.9a**). This seals off the specimen from the elements so completely that parts of its original organic matter can still be recovered. Ice and tar are also excellent preservatives. In dry climates, natural mummification can occur, in which the soft parts desiccate and harden before they have a chance to decompose.

More commonly, however, fossils reflect the original shape of an organism but do not contain the original

---

Fossil preservation • Figure 15.9

There are many different ways that the remains of organisms can be preserved as fossils.

▼ **a.** Preservation in amber—fossilized tree resin—has protected the delicate legs and wings of this ancient mosquito, which is more than 24 million years old.

Paul Zahl/NG Image Collection

b. The La Brea Tar Pits are a collection of asphalt seeps in California. The gooey pits trapped both predator and prey species, who may have mistaken their shiny surfaces for water holes. Thousands of fossils of Pleistocene age and younger have been recovered, including saber-toothed cats, dire wolves, horses, ground sloths, and mammoths. Shown ▼ here is an excavation at the Page Museum's Pit 91.

Ryan Miller/Capture Imaging

© Panglossian/Shutterstock

◄ **c.** These fossil ammonites (which lived as long ago as 400 million years) look like shells, but none of the original shell material remains. All molecules of the original shells have been replaced by minerals, in a common fossil-preservation process called *mineralization*.

d. Over many millennia, the woody material in this log from Petrified Forest National Park, Arizona, became mineralized. Although it looks very much like fresh wood, preserved even down to the cellular level, it is now composed ▶ completely of stone.

© Panglossian/Shutterstock

Fossils of bones and other hard parts of organisms are more common, but sometimes more delicate structures and indirect evidence of the organism's presence can be preserved.

a. *Archaeopteryx* (from the Greek for "ancient wing") lived about 150 million years ago and was transitional between dinosaurs and birds. The first fossil ever found of ▽ *Archaeopteryx* was this single feather, found in 1859 in a limestone quarry in Germany.

b. Over 65 million years ago, duck-billed hadrosaurs in what is now Argentina left their tracks in soft, red mud, which turned to rock. The formation of the Andes Mountains tilted the formerly horizontal mud flat to ▽ such an extent that it is now a vertical rock wall.

Mazzetenta O. Louis/NG Image Collection

© Tristan da Cunha/Alamy

materials. Bones and shells, for example, are often replaced, molecule by molecule, by minerals carried in solution by groundwater (**Figure 15.9c**). This process is called **min-eralization**, and the same process creates **petrified wood** (**Figure 15.9d**).

Less commonly preserved are delicate materials like eggshells (as described in the chapter-opener), skin, and feathers (**Figure 15.10a**). **Carbonization** can preserve even delicate leaf structures; it occurs when volatile material in the plant evaporates, leaving behind a thin film of carbon. Some fossilized materials have even been found to contain **melanosomes**—organelles that are responsible for producing color. These are now being used to establish the true color of skin and feathers from organisms that lived millions of years ago.

Some fossils do not preserve any parts of the organism itself. For example, an organism may leave behind an imprint, or a **mold,** in the soft sediment that covered it, as with the

> **trace fossil** Fossilized evidence of an organism's life processes, such as tracks, footprints, and burrows.

Ediacara fauna (shown in Figure 15.7). **Trace fossils** provide indirect evidence of animal life, such as trails, burrows, and footprints (**Figure 15.10b**). Prehistoric animals also left behind fecal droppings; they are called **coprolites** when preserved and fossilized. In spite of their unappealing origin, such fossils can provide useful clues about animals' characteristics, habits, and diets.

STOP **CONCEPT CHECK**

1. **What** is the difference between evolution and natural selection?

2. **Why** do the hard parts of organisms appear more often as fossils than do soft parts, and what are the differences in how they are preserved?

LIFE IN THE PHANEROZOIC EON

Learning Objectives

1. **Describe** the dramatic changes in Earth's biota during the Cambrian Period.

2. **Identify** the requirements for a living organism to survive on land.

3. **Describe** how plants, amphibians, and reptiles met the requirements for surviving on land.

4. **Outline** the most recent evolutionary steps in the development of humans.

5. **Define** mass extinction and identify two theories of what causes such events.

During most of the history of life on Earth—3 billion years of it—the only living organisms were of microscopic size. But about 630 million years ago, with the appearance of larger multicellular animals, the Ediacara fauna, life began to diversify very rapidly into a wide variety of sizes and body types. We will take a whirlwind tour through this phase of the

What a Geologist Sees

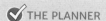 THE PLANNER

Life in the Cambrian Period

Geologists study fossils to learn about the organisms that are preserved—how they were structured, how they moved, and so on. Fossils also reveal much information about the lifestyles of ancient organisms, as well as the environments in which they lived and died.

Courtesy Brian J. Skinner

a. This geologist is holding a fossil of a trilobite, one of the first animals to develop a hard covering, presumably to defend against predators. Trilobites were extremely numerous and long-lasting as a species; they are ubiquitous among Cambrian fossils. This 34-centimeter-long specimen of *Olenellus getzi* was found in Lancaster County, Pennsylvania, and is Lower Cambrian in age.

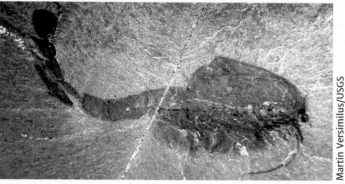

Martin Versimilus/USGS

b. The geologist would immediately see a big difference between the trilobite and this specimen of *Waptia fidensis*, a soft-bodied arthropod from the Burgess Shale of British Columbia. This species did not have a hard shell as the trilobites did, and therefore fossils of it are much rarer. Perhaps *Waptia fidensis* did not have too many predators, so early in the Cambrian Period. As a geologist, what processes do you think needed to occur for the soft parts of this specimen to be preserved in such detail?

THINK CRITICALLY

Despite their efficient defense against predation, trilobites eventually became extinct. However, arthropods (of which *Waptia fidensis* was an early example) have persisted. They are now a hugely diverse family that includes organisms from lobsters and crabs to millipedes and spiders. Some scientists estimate that arthropods account for more than 80% of living animal species. Why have arthropods been so successful overall, compared to trilobites with their heavy defensive armor?

development of life, which continues to the present day (**Figure 15.11**).

The Phanerozoic Eon is named from the Greek *phaneros*, meaning "visible," because it is that part of Earth's history in which evidence of life is abundantly visible. It was no accident that early geologists placed the boundaries of the Cambrian Period where they did; they recognized the appearance of macro-fossils as a significant turning point for life on Earth. The Phanerozoic Eon is divided into three eras: the Paleozoic Era (old life), the Mesozoic Era (middle life), and the Cenozoic Era (recent life).

The Paleozoic Era

The Paleozoic Era started 541 million years ago, with the Cambrian Period. It was a time of incredible diversification of life. Why was this so?

One hypothesis is that sexual reproduction, which developed with the eukaryotes, afforded a more rapid way for new "experimental" forms of life to emerge. Another hypothesis is that there was finally enough oxygen in the atmosphere to support the metabolism of larger organisms. The presence of oxygen led to the development of an ozone layer, which would have shielded Cambrian life forms from harmful ultraviolet radiation. Rising oxygen levels also influenced the biochemistry of calcium phosphate and calcium carbonate in seawater, allowing animals to grow skeletons and/or shells. Another hypothesis is that predation led to the development of protective hard parts, which were readily preserved as fossils. And yet another hypothesis is that extreme climate changes at the end of the Proterozoic Eon led to accelerated evolutionary responses in surviving organisms.

Whatever the reasons, a great many changes began to occur about 541 million years ago, in what has been

---

Geology InSight   Timeline of life • Figure 15.11   ✓ THE PLANNER

The geologic time scale provides a context for our understanding of the origin and evolution of life on Earth.

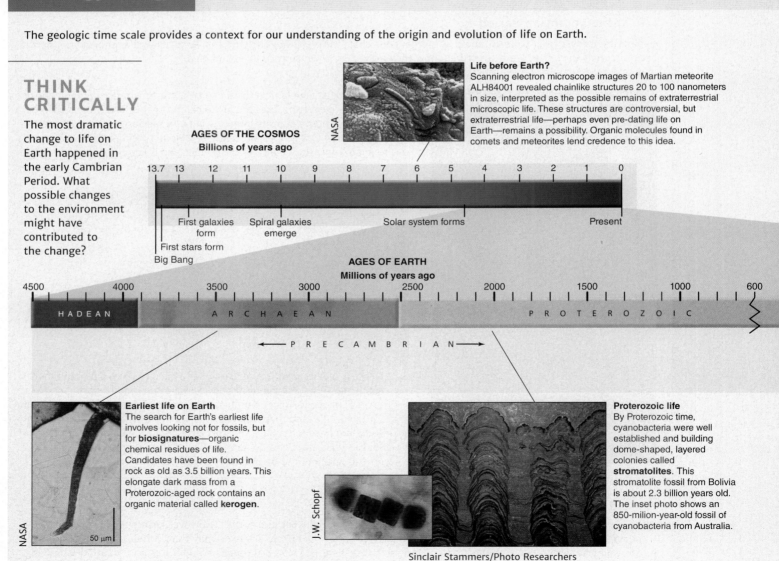

THINK CRITICALLY

The most dramatic change to life on Earth happened in the early Cambrian Period. What possible changes to the environment might have contributed to the change?

Life before Earth?
Scanning electron microscope images of Martian meteorite ALH84001 revealed chainlike structures 20 to 100 nanometers in size, interpreted as the possible remains of extraterrestrial microscopic life. These structures are controversial, but extraterrestrial life—perhaps even pre-dating life on Earth—remains a possibility. Organic molecules found in comets and meteorites lend credence to this idea.

NASA

AGES OF THE COSMOS
Billions of years ago

13.7 13   12   11   10   9   8   7   6   5   4   3   2   1   0

First galaxies form   Spiral galaxies emerge   Solar system forms   Present
First stars form
Big Bang

AGES OF EARTH
Millions of years ago

4500   4000   3500   3000   2500   2000   1500   1000   600

HADEAN   ARCHAEAN   PROTEROZOIC

← P R E C A M B R I A N →

Earliest life on Earth
The search for Earth's earliest life involves looking not for fossils, but for **biosignatures**—organic chemical residues of life. Candidates have been found in rock as old as 3.5 billion years. This elongate dark mass from a Proterozoic-aged rock contains an organic material called **kerogen**.

NASA   50 µm

J.W. Schopf

Proterozoic life
By Proterozoic time, cyanobacteria were well established and building dome-shaped, layered colonies called **stromatolites**. This stromatolite fossil from Bolivia is about 2.3 billion years old. The inset photo shows an 850-milion-year-old fossil of cyanobacteria from Australia.

Sinclair Stammers/Photo Researchers

called the **Cambrian explosion**, or **Cambrian radiation**. Compact animals were evolving to replace the soft-bodied, jelly-like organisms of Ediacaran times. These included trilobites, mollusks (clams and sea snails), and echinoderms (sea urchins). The new animals were equipped with gills, filters for feeding, efficient guts, a circulatory system, and other characteristics that have continued to serve animals well up to the present.

The Cambrian Period also ushered in the development of skeletons, both internal and external. Skeletons gave many organisms a selective advantage, protecting them against predators, against drying out, against being injured in turbulent water, and so on. It is not surprising that hard-shelled organisms, such as trilobites, are better preserved in the fossil record (see *What A Geologist Sees, p. 425*).

However, a wide variety of fossils of soft-bodied creatures also have been found in the Burgess Shale (see *Amazing Places*), and even richer deposits in Chengjiang, China. From these deposits, we now know that every **phylum** in the animal **kingdom** was present in the Cambrian Period, as were a number of phyla that no longer exist. In this sense, the Cambrian marine environment had the greatest diversity of life forms in Earth's history.

> **kingdom** The second-broadest taxonomic category. The six recognized kingdoms are Bacteria, Archaea, and (in the domain Eukaryota) Protista, Plantae, Fungi, and Animalia. The hierarchical subdivisions of a kingdom are phylum, class, order, family, genus, and species.

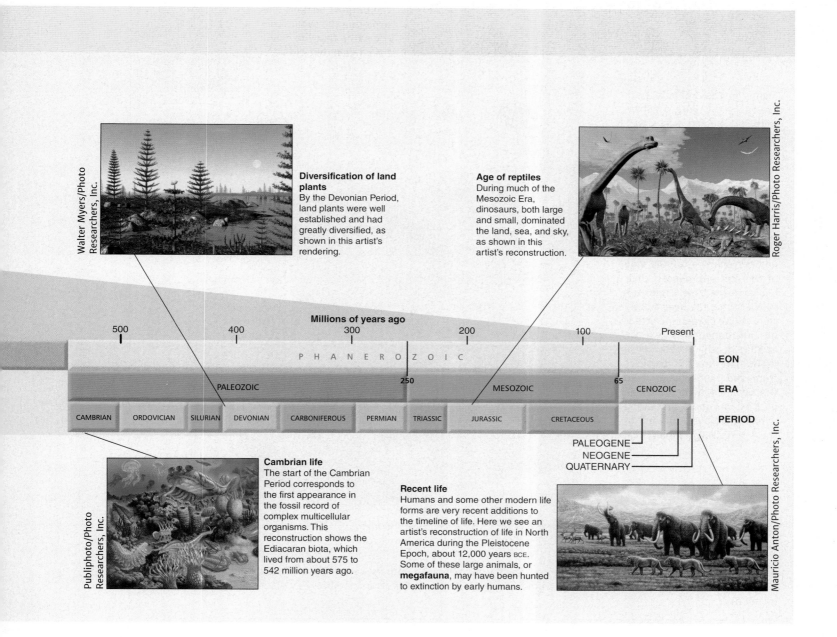

Diversification of land plants
By the Devonian Period, land plants were well established and had greatly diversified, as shown in this artist's rendering.

Walter Myers/Photo Researchers, Inc.

Age of reptiles
During much of the Mesozoic Era, dinosaurs, both large and small, dominated the land, sea, and sky, as shown in this artist's reconstruction.

Roger Harris/Photo Researchers, Inc.

Millions of years ago

500   400   300   200   100   Present

PHANEROZOIC — EON

250 — PALEOZOIC — MESOZOIC — 65 — CENOZOIC — ERA

CAMBRIAN | ORDOVICIAN | SILURIAN | DEVONIAN | CARBONIFEROUS | PERMIAN | TRIASSIC | JURASSIC | CRETACEOUS — PERIOD

PALEOGENE
NEOGENE
QUATERNARY

Cambrian life
The start of the Cambrian Period corresponds to the first appearance in the fossil record of complex multicellular organisms. This reconstruction shows the Ediacaran biota, which lived from about 575 to 542 million years ago.

Publiphoto/Photo Researchers, Inc.

Recent life
Humans and some other modern life forms are very recent additions to the timeline of life. Here we see an artist's reconstruction of life in North America during the Pleistocene Epoch, about 12,000 years BCE. Some of these large animals, or **megafauna**, may have been hunted to extinction by early humans.

Mauricio Anton/Photo Researchers, Inc.

The Burgess Shale

Michael Melford/NG Image Collection

a

In 1909, American paleontologist Charles Walcott discovered the world's preeminent site for Cambrian fossils. The Burgess Shale is about 90 kilometers from Banff, British Columbia. It is a treasure trove for specimens such as this trilobite (**Figure a**), as well as more exotic organisms such as the five-eyed *Opabinia* and others. It was only in the 1970s that paleontologists realized that many of the organisms found there are unrelated to any living animals. They are not only extinct species but members of extinct phyla. Exploring the Burgess Shale is like exploring the evolutionary paths that life could have taken, but didn't.

Global Locator

Yoho National Park

NG Maps

Many of the animals preserved in the Burgess Shale were soft-bodied. Such creatures fossilize only under very special circumstances. This is how scientists reasoned that it happened: The Burgess fauna lived in shallow, oxygen-rich waters atop an algal reef with steep sides (**Figure b**). Periodically, mudslides would sweep some unlucky animals off the side of the reef and deposit their bodies at the base (**Figure c**). At that time, the deep waters were still so oxygen-poor that no microorganisms existed at that depth to decompose them. The fine silt particles from the mudslide encased the bodies and then became lithified into shale, preserving a highly detailed imprint of these surprising animals.

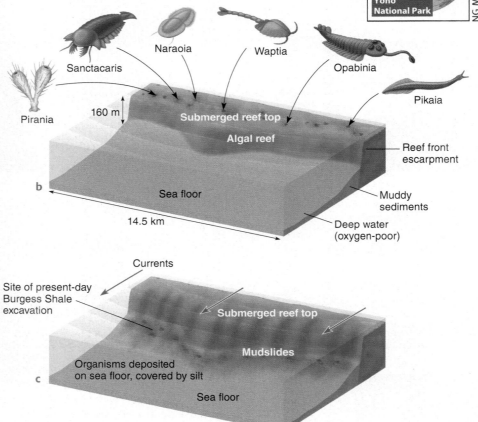

Pirania

Sanctacaris

Naraoia

Waptia

Opabinia

Pikaia

160 m

Submerged reef top

Algal reef

Reef front escarpment

b

Sea floor

Muddy sediments

14.5 km

Deep water (oxygen-poor)

Currents

Site of present-day Burgess Shale excavation

Submerged reef top

Mudslides

Organisms deposited on sea floor, covered by silt

c

Sea floor

THINK CRITICALLY

Some of the organisms preserved in the Burgess Shale were plants, and others were clearly animals; still others appear to have been transitional between plants and animals. How do you think the distinction between plants and animals should be defined?

From Sea to Land

The great proliferation of life in the Cambrian explosion was confined to the sea. In order to spread to land, it was essential for living organisms to meet certain requirements. The first requirement is some means of *structural support*. Whereas aquatic organisms are buoyed by water, land-based organisms must contend with gravity. But because water remains critical to all the chemical processes of life, any land-based organism must maintain an *internal aquatic environment*. Living in an environment surrounded by air, rather than water, the organism must develop some way of *exchanging gases with air* instead of with water. Finally, all sexually reproducing organisms require a moist environment for the reproductive system. The first organisms to overcome these four hurdles were plants.

Plants Evidence suggests that land plants evolved from green algae more than 600 million years ago (**Figure 15.12**). Eventually, during the Silurian Period, **vascular plants** evolved. These plants have structural support from stems and limbs (requirement 1), and they have a set of vessels through which water and dissolved elements are transferred from the roots to the leaves (requirement 2). Gas exchange (requirement 3) occurs by diffusion through adjustable openings in the leaves called **stomata**. When carbon dioxide pressure inside the leaf is high, the stomata open; when it is low, they close. The stomata also close when the plant is short of water, thereby protecting it from drying out.

The means of reproduction in plants (requirement 4) has passed through several evolutionary stages (**Figure 15.13**). The earliest plants were seedless, and some seedless plants still exist, such as mosses and ferns. These can reproduce either sexually or asexually, but for the sexual phase, they require a body of water where the male and female reproductive bodies (**spores**) meet and fuse. Thus mosses and seedless plants in general have always depended on a rather moist environment. Seedless plants reached their peak in the Carboniferous Period, and their fossils created the extensive deposits of coal (carbon-rich sedimentary rock) that gave the period its name.

In the middle Devonian Period, some plants began to evolve their own moist environment to facilitate sexual reproduction. The first plants to do this were **gymnosperms**, including ginkgos and conifers. The female cell of a gymnosperm is attached to the vascular system and therefore has a supply of moisture. The male cell is carried in a pollen grain with a waxy coating. When the two fuse, a **seed** results. The seed contains moisture and a food supply that sustains the growth of the young plant until it can support itself. With the evolution of seeds, vascular plants were able to spread beyond swampy lowlands to other habitats.

> **gymnosperm** A naked-seed plant.

The earliest life on land? • Figure 15.12

The first organisms to colonize the land may have looked like the green algae shown in this photograph. They were the ancestors of modern plants.

Raymond Gehman/NG Image Collection

Arthropods Many of the creatures in the Cambrian seas belonged to the phylum *Arthropoda*, named for their jointed legs. Modern arthropods include crabs, spiders, centipedes, and insects—the most diverse phylum on Earth. They were the first creatures to make the transition from sea to land.

With a few exceptions, early arthropods were small and light. They were covered with a hard shell of **chitin** (a fingernail-like material). Thus, they were well adapted to life on land, in regard to the need for structural support and water conservation. The first arthropods on land were probably centipedes and millipedes, in the Silurian Period. By the Mississippian Period, insects were abundant and included dragonflies with a wingspan of up to 60 cenntimeters (**Figure 15.14**). But for all their success as land creatures, the arthropods have very primitive respiratory and vascular systems. For example, insects breathe through tiny tubes that penetrate their outer coating. This mode of respiration

Many of the structures and reproductive strategies evolved by early plants can still be observed in modern plants.

a. This fossil fern, preserved in shale, is about 300 million years old.

b. Compare the fossil fern (**a**) to a modern fern. This photograph shows the spore-producing organs, the dark spots on the underside of the frond.

c. Naked-seed plants like the gingko developed from seedless plants late in the Devonian Period. These are modern and fossilized ginkgo leaves.

d. Flowers and fruits were an advantageous adaptation for plants because they serve as an incentive for insects to do the work of distributing pollen. This 15-million-year-old fossil of a sweet gum fruit, found in Idaho, is shown next to its modern equivalent.

severely limits the size of an insect and explains why almost all insects are small.

The "blood" of arthropods is simply body fluid that bathes the internal organs; it does not circulate in blood vessels. The fluid is generally kept in motion by a sluggish "heart" that is little more than a contracting tube. However, "primitive" does not mean poorly adapted. The arthropods have branched into more than a million species, and they are

A single wing of the giant dragonfly *Megatypus schucherti* is 16 centimeters long. The largest dragonfly today is only 15 centimeters in total width. This specimen, Lower Permian in age, is from Dickinson County, Kansas.

Courtey Peabody Museum of Natural History, Yale University

nearly indestructible. Who has ever heard of a cockroach having a heart attack?

Fishes and Amphibians The phylum of greatest interest to most of us, because humans belong to it, is the **chordates**. These are animals that have at least a primitive version of a spinal cord (called a **notochord**). Like all the other animal phyla, chordates can be found as fossils of the Cambrian Period, although they are relatively inconspicuous. The earliest so far discovered is *Haikouichthys*, a jawless fish akin to a hagfish or a lamprey that lived 525 million years ago—only 16 million years after the beginning of the Cambrian explosion.

Jawed fish arrived next. With jaws, fish could lead a predatory lifestyle and grow to much larger sizes; the jawless fish had been limited to filtering food out of the water or dredging it from the seafloor. Among the first large jawed fish were sharks and ray-finned fish. The earliest known intact shark fossil is 409 million years old.

The first fish to venture onto land may have been a member of an obscure order called *Crossopterygii*, or lobe-finned fish (**Figure 15.15**). These fish had several features that could have enabled them to make the transition to land. Their lobe-like fins contained all the elements of a quadruped limb. They had internal nostrils, characteristic of air-breathing animals. As fish, they had already developed a vascular system that was adequate for life on land.

Amphibians, the first terrestrial chordates, originated in the Devonian Period. Amphibians have never become wholly independent of aquatic environments because they have not developed an effective method for conserving water. To this day, they retain permeable skins. They have also never truly met the reproductive requirement for life on land. In most amphibian species, the female lays her eggs in water, and the male fertilizes them there after a courtship ritual. The young (e.g., tadpoles) are fish-like when first hatched. Just like the seedless plants, amphibians have kept one foot (figuratively speaking) on land and one foot in the water.

There are a couple of candidates for the first fish whose descendants made the transition from sea to land.

a. The first fish to haul themselves onto land may have been relatives of the coelacanth. When a living coelacanth was caught in the Indian Ocean in 1938, it created a sensation because its entire order, Crossopterygii, had been believed to be extinct. Today's coelacanths, like this one, are exclusively deep-sea creatures.

b. Another candidate for the first fish to move onto the land is the lungfish. Unlike the coelacanth, today's lungfish still survive for short periods on land without water.

Tom McHugh/Science Source

© Hoberman Collection/Corbis

The Mesozoic Era

> **extinction** Permanent disappearance of a species.

The Paleozoic Era closed with the **extinction** of trilobites and a great many other marine creatures. An estimated 96% of all living species disappeared at the end of the Permian Period, in the greatest mass extinction in Earth's history. We will return to the question of mass extinctions at the end of this chapter, but the cause of this extinction remains an enigma that has yet to be solved. The era that followed the Paleozoic, the Mesozoic Era, commenced when all the major landmasses on Earth joined together in the supercontinent Pangaea (see Figure 1.19). Then, in the middle of the era, the supercontinent began to split apart in a process that continues today.

Flowering Plants Whatever caused the great extinction at the end of the Permian Period did not seem to greatly affect plant life on land. Gymnosperms, which had appeared in the Devonian Period, dominated the plant world during the Triassic and Jurassic periods. Gymnosperms,

however, have an important liability: The male cell carrier, the pollen, is spread through the air. This is extremely inefficient; what chance does a pollen grain in the air have of finding a female cell?

Eventually, at the beginning of the Cretaceous Period, **angiosperms**—flowering plants—found a more efficient solution (see Figure 15.13d).

> **angiosperm** A flowering, or seed-enclosed, plant.

For a small incentive, such as nectar or a share of the pollen, insects deliver pollen directly from one flower to another or from one part of a plant to another. After pollination, a plant develops a seed in much the same way as gymnosperms. In many cases, birds and other animals help distribute the seeds by eating a plant's seed-bearing fruits and distributing the seeds in their feces. Flowering plants still dominate land plants today.

Reptiles, Birds, and Mammals The Carboniferous and Permian periods were times when amphibians were abundant. Most families died out in the end-of-Permian extinction. One branch of the amphibians, however, evolved into reptiles—the first fully terrestrial animals. Reptiles were freed from the water by evolving an egg that contained amniotic fluid for the young to grow in and by developing a watertight skin.

These two evolutionary advances enabled the reptiles to occupy many terrestrial niches that the amphibians had not been able to exploit because of their need to live near water. The amniotic egg led to an explosion in reptile diversity, much as the evolution of the jaw had done for fish. Moving out of the Mississippian and Pennsylvanian swamps, some reptiles colonized the land, some moved back into the water, and a few took to the air. Not only did reptiles greatly increase in diversity during the Jurassic Period, they also grew to tremendous size. The dinosaurs were the largest land animals that have ever lived, possibly ranging up to 100 metric tons in weight and 35 meters in length.

Birds first appeared near the end of the Jurassic Period, and they are now considered to be direct descendants of the dinosaurs. An early bird, *Archaeopteryx* (**Figure 15.16a**, next page), would have been classified as a dinosaur if not for the discovery that it had feathers. Even before *Archaeopteryx*, vertebrates had made the transition to the air in the form of pterosaurs—flying reptiles with long wings and tails. Most paleontologists do not consider pterosaurs to be true dinosaurs, although they were very closely related. The detail of the transition from reptiles to birds remains one of the most highly controversial topics in paleontology today.

Mammals are descended from a class of "mammal-like reptiles" that existed as long ago as the Permian Period. The transition from reptiles to mammals is well understood, though perhaps not quite as well understood as the transition from fish to amphibians. It is difficult to pick out a single mammalian adaptation that is comparable in survival value to the jaws of fish, the eggs of reptiles, or the feathers of birds. During the Cretaceous Period, mammals certainly did not outcompete the dinosaurs; they survived by being small and inconspicuous. Some lived in trees (**Figure 15.16b**, next page), avoiding ground-level predation. Some tree-dwelling mammals even experimented with gliding flight as early as 130 million years ago—almost as early as the first birds began flying.

The Cenozoic Era

Evidence suggests that an accidental catastrophe—a giant meteorite impact—was at least partially responsible for the environmental changes that wiped out the great reptiles and 70% of all other species at the end of the Mesozoic Era. The departure of dinosaurs gave mammals a chance to grow larger and to diversify.

In the Cenozoic Era, mammals benefited from the atmosphere's high oxygen level, which is conducive to fast metabolism. Unlike reptiles, whose brain sizes have not grown (relative to their body size), mammals have continued to evolve toward larger brain size throughout the Cenozoic Era. This may be one key to the success of mammals because it has enabled them to diversify their lifestyles to a much greater extent than reptiles ever could.

The Cenozoic was also an important developmental time for land plants. The last frontier for plants—the dry steppes, savannas, and prairies—was not colonized until the Paleogene Period, when grasses evolved. This process involved the assistance of animals, in particular the great grazing herds that lived on all continents except Antarctica.

The Quaternary Period The Quaternary Period is the final major time division of the Cenozoic Era; the present day is part of the Quaternary. During most of the Quaternary Period, the continents have been pretty close to their present-day positions. The most significant characteristic of climate during the Quaternary has been repeated major glaciations. The dramatic swings in climate had a big impact on the survival and adaptation of species during this time (see *Remember This!*).

> **REMEMBER THIS!** Can you remember the major external factors that can lead to a glaciation? You can remind yourself by revisiting *Natural Causes of Climate Change* and *The Record of Past Climate Change* in Chapter 14.

One of the most noteworthy features of life in the Quaternary was the predominance of very large land animals, populating much of Earth. They may have migrated out of Africa and Asia, which today still host some very large species such as elephants and rhinos. During the Pleistocene Epoch, giant sloths, tapirs, saber-toothed cats, dire wolves, bison, mammoths, and mastodons roamed through Europe, North America, and South America, constituting what is known as the **Pleistocene megafauna** (**Figure 15.17**, next page). Even some birds and fish were gigantic during this time period, like the teratorn ("monster bird"), with a wingspan of over 3.5 meters, and the sabertooth salmon, which grew to be well over 2 meters in length. Many of these animals died out during a major extinction event, the exact causes of which are not fully understood; one hypothesis is that they were overhunted to extinction by early humans.

The Human Family From a human point of view, the most remarkable thing that has happened during the Cenozoic Era is the emergence of our own species. Charles Darwin was often accused of fostering the belief that humans are descended from the apes. In fact, the family of humans, *Hominidae*, and the family of apes, *Pongidae*, are both descended from an earlier common ancestor that was neither human nor ape.

The emergence of humans is one of the most complex and controversial fields in paleontology, in part because of gaps in the fossil record and the lack of transitional forms. But it is clear that **hominids**—human-like organisms—are a very recent evolutionary development.

The first hominid that was clearly **bipedal** (i.e., routinely walked upright) was *Australopithecus*, of which the famous fossil "Lucy" is an example (**Figure 15.18**, on p. 435). These hominids were only about 1.2 meters in height but had a brain capacity larger than that of chimpanzees. Their fossils range from about 3.9 million to 3.0 million years in age. From

Early birds and mammals • Figure 15.16

The emergence of birds and mammals involved many new reproductive, morphological, and lifestyle adaptations.

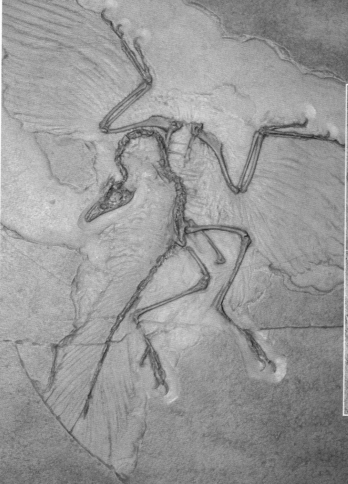

Jason Edwards/NG Image Collection

a. The skeletons and teeth of *Archaeopteryx* were very similar to those of dinosaurs. However, the very detailed impressions of feathers in this fossil identify *Archaeopteryx* as a bird. An *Archaeopteryx* feather is shown in Figure 15.10a.

Courtesy Carnegie Museum of Natural History

b. This shrew-sized *Eomaia scansoria* is the oldest-known fossil of a placental mammal (a mammal that gives live birth). It lived 125 million years ago, during the height of the dinosaur age. The shape of its claws shows that it was a tree-dweller.

Pleistocene megafauna • Figure 15.17

© Stocktrek Images, Inc./Alamy

During the Pleistocene Epoch, enormous animals such as mastodons (shown here), woolly mammoths, saber-toothed tigers, bison, and many others roamed North America, pictured here in an artist's reconstruction. Many species of the Pleistocene megafauna disappeared during a major extinction event, possibly caused by over-hunting by early humans.

Lucy and the ancient human family • Figure 15.18

Human-like Australopithecines walked upright on two feet, lived together in small groups, and looked after their children until well after infancy.

a. This drawing by Michael Rothman depicts a mother and child of the species *Australopithecus afarensis*.

© Michael Rothman

b. This 3.3-million-year-old fossil is the skull of an *A. afarensis* baby, who probably looked much like the child in the drawing.

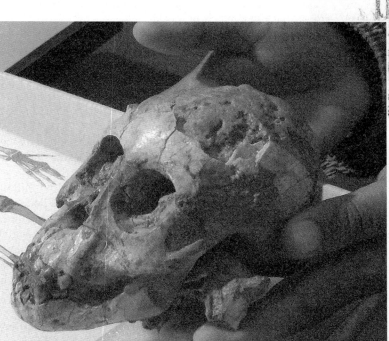

Lealisa Westerhoff/Getty Images

c. From footprints like these, preserved in soft volcanic mud, scientists know that Australopithecines walked upright on two feet. This 70-meter trail includes the footprints of two adults and possibly a child, stepping in the footprints of one of the adults. To the right are footprints of an extinct three-toed horse.

© John Reader/Science Photo Library/Photo Researchers

THINK CRITICALLY

Did ancient humans or human ancestors ever encounter dinosaurs?

the shape of its pelvis and from footprints left in soft volcanic mud, we know that *Australopithecus* walked upright, though its skull looked more apelike than human. Lucy's descendants never spread beyond Africa, and they disappeared altogether about 1.1 million years ago.

Genus Homo *Homo erectus*, one of the first species of our own genus (*Homo*), was more widely traveled than *Australopithecus*. Fossils of *Homo erectus*, dating back about 1.8 million years, have been found in Africa, Europe, China, and Java (**Figure 15.19**). An earlier species called *Homo habilis* is believed to have mastered the use of stone tools as far back as 2.4 million years ago, and toolmaking is a distinguishing feature of the genus *Homo*. The earliest known (thus far) species of the genus *Homo*, called *Homo gautengensis*, was discovered in 2010; this species may represent a link to the earlier Australopithecines.

Homo erectus disappeared 300,000 years ago and was replaced by *Homo neanderthalensis* ("Neanderthal man") no later than 230,000 years ago. The poor fossil record between 400,000 and 100,000 years ago has made it difficult for scientists to determine exactly how this transition occurred. We hypothesize from burial sites that Neanderthals might have practiced some form of religion. Because of similarities in teeth and brain size (slightly larger than our own), some experts have argued that Neanderthal was part of our own species; however, recent DNA studies suggest that *Homo sapiens* is not a direct descendant of Neanderthals. The Neanderthals disappeared about 30,000 years ago and were replaced rather suddenly by the biologically modern people, the first indisputable members of our own species, *Homo sapiens*.

Rewriting human history? • **Figure 15.19** ————

The human lineage is extremely complicated, but this 1.8-million-year-old *Homo erectus* skull found in 2013 in the Republic of Georgia suggests that it may be simpler than originally thought. The top half of the skull looks quite different from the bottom half (not pictured here); they might previously have been interpreted to be from two different species had they not been found together in this remarkably complete fossil skull.

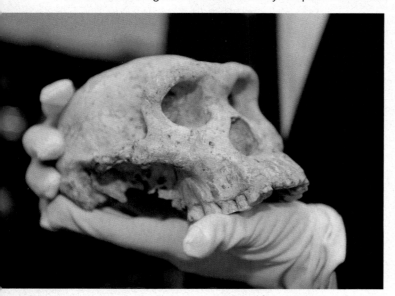

Vano Shlamov/AFP/Getty Images

Did *Homo sapiens* evolve from the Neanderthals, or were they a distinct species? What happened during the 5000-year period when both kinds of humans were alive and overlapped geographically in Europe? Did the modern *Homo sapiens* kill the Neanderthals? These and many other questions await answers as paleontologists continue to look for clues in the fossil record.

Mass Extinctions

Species extinctions have happened throughout the history of life on this planet; in fact, by far the majority of species that have ever lived are now extinct. Scientists refer to this as **background extinction**. At several places in the fossil record of the Phanerozoic Eon, however, paleontologists have found abrupt and profound changes in the fossil assemblage—not just in one location but worldwide; and not just affecting one species, but vast numbers of species in geologically short periods of time. These dramatic changes record **mass extinctions**. For geologists, mass extinctions are a convenience because they can be used to delineate so many of the time periods in the geologic column, but they are also a conundrum: What could possibly cause most of the species on Earth to become extinct in a geologically short period of time?

> **mass extinction** A catastrophic episode in which a large fraction of living species become extinct within a geologically short time.

The most famous mass extinction occurred 65 million years ago, at the end of the Cretaceous Period (the boundary between the Mesozoic and Cenozoic eras). It is sometimes called the **K–T extinction** (K stands for Cretaceous, and T stands for Tertiary, an old term for the period immediately following the Cretaceous). Paleontologists estimate that around 70% of all species, including the dinosaurs, died out during this extinction. Many of the species that survived must also have come perilously close to extinction.

In the past quarter-century, scientific opinion has coalesced around the hypothesis that the end-of-Cretaceous extinction was at least partly caused by environmental changes that resulted from the impact of a large meteorite with Earth (**Figure 15.20**). When it was proposed by Walter and Luis Alvarez in 1980, the meteorite-impact theory was highly controversial, but many lines of evidence now support it (**Figure 15.21**). We can be reasonably certain now that the events described in Figure 15.20 did happen, although we cannot be absolutely certain that this event killed all the dinosaurs.

One of the remaining problems with the meteorite impact theory is that the great end-of-Cretaceous extinction was not unique, nor was it even the most dramatic of all extinctions. As mentioned earlier in this chapter, the most devastating mass extinction occurred 245 million years ago, at the end of the Permian Period, when an estimated 95% of all species died out. There have been at least 5 and possibly as many as 12 mass extinctions during the past 250 million years. Some of them can be linked to massive meteorite impacts, but others cannot. Several other known craters on Earth rival the

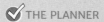

How the dinosaurs died...? • Figure 15.20

About 65 million years ago, a meteorite as large as Mount Everest struck Earth. The impact site is now covered by younger sedimentary rock, but satellite images reveal a faint circular depression around its edge, and drilling has confirmed that the rocks were shattered by a great impact. The crater is named Chicxulub (pronounced "tjik-zuh-lub") after a Mayan town near the impact site.

1 The Chicxulub meteorite struck in the ocean, offshore from Mexico's Yucatán Peninsula, blasting a crater 180 kilometers across.

2 The impact ejected massive amounts of water and debris far into the atmosphere. The blast wave killed plants and animals all over the western hemisphere.

3 As broiling-hot debris from the impact rained down, forests ignited, creating continent-wide forest fires. Soot from the fires started by the impact debris may have remained in the atmosphere for months, or even years, blocking the sunlight and halting photosynthesis all over the world.

4 A year after the impact, algae and ferns may have begun to grow again, but the forests were still bare.

THINK CRITICALLY

How do you think animals like mammals and marine shelled organisms survived this event, whereas the dinosaurs did not?

size of the Chicxulub crater, yet the ages of the craters do not correlate well with the dates of other mass extinctions.

On the other hand, some scientists have pointed out that a strong correlation exists between the eruption of flood basalts and mass extinctions. The end-of-Cretaceous boundary lies very close in time to the eruption of the Deccan Traps in India, and the Permian extinction occurred around the time of the largest known flood basalts, the Siberian Traps (**Figure 15.22**).

Impact evidence • Figure 15.21

Evidence of meteorite impacts can be found all over the world in rock units marking the end of the Cretaceous Period.

a. This layer of whitish clay in Colorado is about 2 centimeters thick. Similar layers of the same age are found in many locations, but are thickest closer to the impact site. Above the clay is a thinner layer that contains shocked quartz grains and is enriched in iridium, an element that is rare on Earth but more common in meteorites. Dinosaur fossils occur below the clay layer but not above.

b. In strata just above the impact layer, representing materials deposited after the meteorite impact, fern spores are much more prevalent than angiosperm pollen—a sign of a newly regenerating plant community.

Jonathan Blair/NG Image Collection

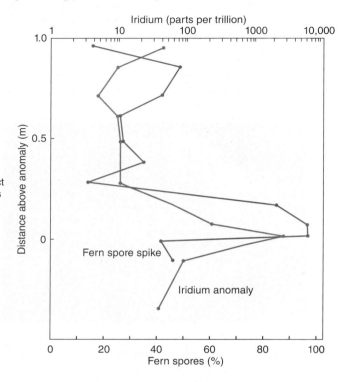

Volcanism and mass extinctions • Figure 15.22

Several of the world's largest flood basalt deposits formed at roughly the same time as mass extinctions occurred. Scientists are still debating whether, and how, an enormous lava flow in one region could cause mass extinctions all over the world. (My = millions of years before present.) (*Source*: Courtesy Dr. Richard Ernst.)

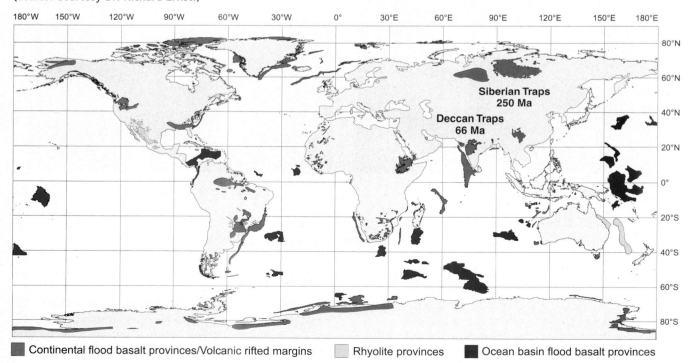

■ Continental flood basalt provinces/Volcanic rifted margins   ☐ Rhyolite provinces   ■ Ocean basin flood basalt provinces

This map of the human "footprint," developed by the Wildlife Conservation Society, is based on population density and land use. The areas least impacted by humans are shown in green.

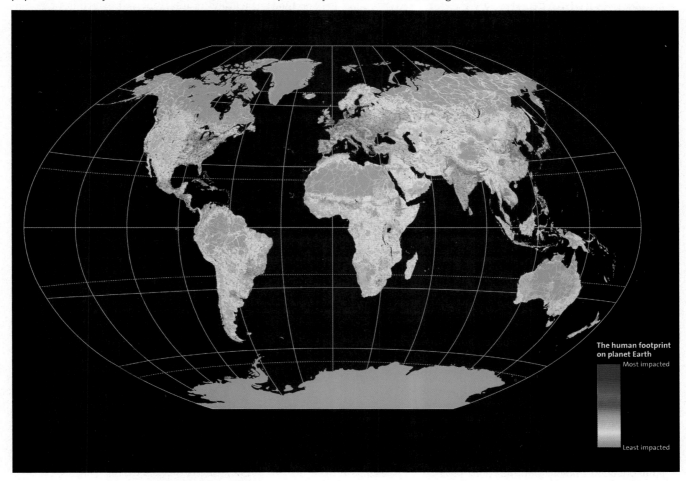

The human footprint on planet Earth

Most impacted

Least impacted

Perhaps massive outbreaks of volcanism, producing worldwide climate change, are the "normal" agent of mass extinctions, and the end-of-Cretaceous meteorite was merely an interloper that happened to strike Earth. The study of mass extinctions and the role that impacts may have played in them continues to be an area of active research. It is especially appropriate today because the human footprint on planet Earth is so heavy (**Figure 15.23**) that the current rate of species extinctions now rivals the rate of extinctions during the previous die-offs.

 CONCEPT CHECK

1. **What** are some of the possible reasons for the explosion of animal diversity in the Cambrian Period?

2. **How** have plants adapted to life on land, particularly in their reproductive systems?

3. **What** are the major milestones in the evolution of chordates?

4. **Why** is it inaccurate to say that humans descended from apes?

5. **Summarize** the evidence that suggests that a meteorite impact killed the dinosaurs.

1 Ever-Changing Earth 412

- The history of life is intertwined with that of the atmosphere and hydrosphere. Earth's early atmosphere consisted primarily of water vapor, carbon dioxide, and nitrogen, the products of outgassing from volcanoes.

- Oxygen gradually accumulated over more than a billion years, primarily through the process of **photosynthesis** as shown in the diagram (shown below). Photosynthesis, a reaction by which plants convert carbon dioxide and water into carbohydrates, is by far the most important source of oxygen in our atmosphere.

Photosynthesis · Figure 15.2

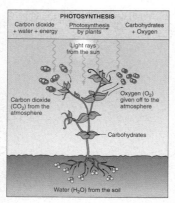

- The buildup in oxygen was accompanied by a buildup of ozone in the upper atmosphere. Earth's land surfaces were probably uninhabitable until the ozone layer began blocking harmful ultraviolet radiation from the Sun.

- Living plants produce oxygen. When dead organisms decay, the bacteria that decompose them consume oxygen and release carbon dioxide. This cycle maintains the balance of oxygen in the atmosphere and hydrosphere. Nevertheless, atmospheric oxygen levels have fluctuated dramatically over geologic time. One reason this can occur is the burial of organic matter before it has completely decomposed. Plate tectonics can accelerate the rate of burial of organic matter and thereby affect the composition of the atmosphere.

2 Early Life 415

- The minimum requirements for life are metabolism and a means of replication. All life on Earth is based on a small set of carbon-based building blocks called amino acids. Also, all living organisms use **DNA**, a biopolymer, to copy genetic information. However, different organisms have evolved different kinds of metabolism, and this is one reason that life is able to flourish in a great variety of environments.

- The fundamental unit of life is the **cell**, which has two fundamental varieties: **prokaryotes** and **eukaryotes**. Eukaryotic cells enclose their DNA within a membrane, whereas prokaryotic cells lack a well-defined nucleus.

- Biologists have classified all living organisms into three **domains**—Bacteria, Archaea, and Eukarya. The first two domains are prokaryotes, which are exclusively single-celled organisms. Prokaryotes evolved long before eukaryotes. Eukaryotes evolved at least 1.4 billion years ago and can be either one-celled or multicellular.

- The most ancient fossils are about 3.5 billion years old, although chemical evidence of the presence of life is preserved in rock considerably older than this. The best pieces of evidence for early life are fossilized **stromatolites**, thick mats of one-celled organisms that can still be found in some places today (see photo). Most other fossils of early life are microscopic, and consequently they are hard to find and difficult to interpret. The earliest known fossils of large multicellular organisms date back 635 million years.

An ancient life form · Figure 15.4

3 Evolution and the Fossil Record 420

- As a result of **evolution**, all present-day organisms are descendants of different kinds of organisms that existed in the past. The mechanism by which evolution occurs is **natural selection**, in which well-adapted individuals tend to have greater survival and more breeding success and thus pass along their traits to later generations.

- New **species** may emerge slowly, as the environment changes gradually over time, or quickly, when a beneficial mutation appears or when a population moves to a new habitat. It is not clear which process is more common.

- Organisms can be preserved as **fossils** in many different ways. The body may be kept essentially intact (see photo), or its shape may be preserved while minerals replace its contents. Some organisms leave behind evidence, such as molds of footprints or **trace fossils**, without leaving behind any body parts.

Fossil preservation · Figure 15.9

4 Life in the Phanerozoic Eon   425

- The Cambrian Period, at the beginning of the Phanerozoic Eon, was a time of explosive diversification of life forms. Several factors may have contributed to the Cambrian explosion: the emergence of multicellular life (just before the Cambrian Period), the protective ozone layer, the rise in oxygen levels, and the ability to form shells.

- All of the extant phyla in the animal **kingdom**, as well as several extinct phyla, emerged during the Cambrian Period. All of the Cambrian fauna were aquatic, and some had hard internal or external skeletons. In order to colonize land, plants and animals had to develop a means of structural support, an internal aquatic environment, and a way of exchanging gases with the atmosphere. For sexual reproduction, a moist environment was also essential.

- The earliest land plants were seedless plants, such as ferns. The next major event in the plant kingdom was the emergence of **gymnosperms**, or naked-seed plants, which flourished during the age of dinosaurs. **Angiosperms**, or flowering plants, developed last, with a much more efficient reproductive system, facilitated by insect pollination.

- The earliest land animals were arthropods (a phylum that includes insects). Fish first ventured onto land during the Devonian Period and eventually gave rise to the amphibians. These, however, were limited in their geographic range because they still required water to spawn.

- Reptiles evolved a watertight skin and eggs that could be incubated outside water. This freed them from dependence on watery environments. Both mammals and birds descended from reptiles, by different evolutionary pathways.

- Mammals have existed since the Jurassic Period. It was apparently the disappearance of the dinosaurs, along with a rise in atmospheric oxygen, that gave mammals the opportunity to diversify and increase in size. Hominids are a very recent family of mammals, which appeared within the last 3.9 million years. Anatomically modern humans appeared only 30,000 years ago. Scientists are not certain whether Neanderthals, which died out around the same time, were a distinct species.

- **Extinction** is a common phenomenon in the geologic record, but several geologic time periods are delineated by **mass extinctions** in which a large proportion of species died out within a geologically short period. The causes of mass extinctions are not thoroughly understood, but most scientists now believe that the end-of-Cretaceous extinction, in which the dinosaurs died out, resulted from a meteorite impact as shown below. Other mass extinctions may have been caused by volcanism.

How the dinosaurs died...? · Figure 15.20

KEY TERMS

CRITICAL AND CREATIVE THINKING QUESTIONS

1. Recall from Chapter 1 (see Figure 1.16) that Earth and Venus are so similar in size and overall composition that they are almost "twins." Now that you know about the evolution of life on Earth and its relationship to the chemistry of our atmosphere, see if you can answer these questions:

Why did these two planets evolve so differently? Why is Earth's atmosphere rich in oxygen and poor in carbon dioxide, whereas the reverse is true on Venus? What would happen to Earth's oceans if Earth were a little bit closer to the Sun?

Earth and its closest neighbors • Figure 1.16

In spite of their similar origins, Venus, Earth, and Mars have profound geologic differences that have made Earth the only one that is hospitable for life.

Visible light / *Cloud-penetrating radar* — Venus | Earth | Mars

	Venus	Earth	Mars
Atmosphere	97% carbon dioxide; temperature averages a blistering 480°C (hot enough to melt lead)	78% nitrogen, 21% oxygen; average temperature 14.6°C	96% carbon dioxide; thin and insufficient to retain much heat; average temperature –63°C; temperatures usually too low to melt water ice (0°C)
Hydrosphere	Exists only as vapor in the atmosphere due to high temperatures	Contains water as solid, liquid, and vapor	Water cannot exist in liquid form on the surface due to low temperatures and pressure
Biosphere	None	Only known biosphere	None known

(Inset left–top: NASA; left–bottom: Courtesy NASA; middle: Courtesy NASA; right: Courtesy NASA)

---

2. One popular criticism of the theory of evolution by natural selection was the paucity of transitional form. However, *Archaeopteryx* was such an organism. In what ways did it resemble its dinosaur predecessors? In what ways was it like or unlike modern birds?

3. Another common criticism of Darwin's theory was its alleged inconsistency with the biblical account of creation. Yet Darwin himself was a Christian, and many scientists since Darwin have had no difficulty reconciling the evidence for evolution with their religious beliefs. Investigate how they have done so. Do you personally feel that evolution by natural selection conflicts with your religious beliefs?

4. What do you think might have happened to mammals if the end-of-Cretaceous extinction had not wiped out the dinosaurs?

5. Use the graph from Figure 15.3 to determine the highest level of atmospheric oxygen (O_2, by volume %) ever in Earth's history. When did this happen (by year, and by geologic period)?

The oxygen content of the atmosphere • Figure 15.3

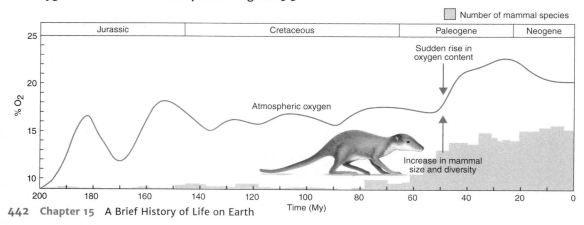

Number of mammal species

Jurassic | Cretaceous | Paleogene | Neogene

Sudden rise in oxygen content

Atmospheric oxygen

Increase in mammal size and diversity

% O_2

Time (My)

WHAT IS HAPPENING IN THIS PICTURE?

In this fossilized bird and frog, found in the Messel Oil Shale near Darmstadt, Germany, the animals' soft tissues, such as feathers and skin, are exceedingly well preserved. (Note the faint imprint of the frog's skin around its bones, for example.)

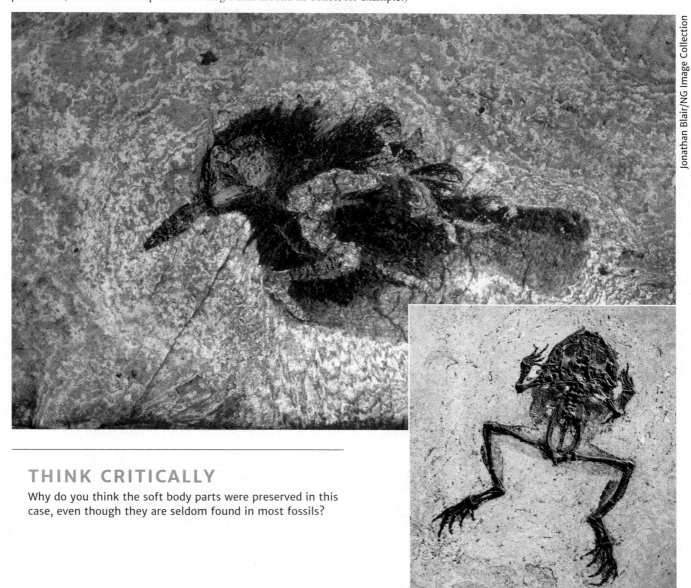

Jonathan Blair/NG Image Collection

THINK CRITICALLY

Why do you think the soft body parts were preserved in this case, even though they are seldom found in most fossils?

SELF-TEST

(Check your answers in Appendix D)

1. Which one of the following statements best describes changes in Earth's environment over the past 4 billion years?

   a. Solar brightness and oxygen generally increased, while surface temperature and atmospheric CO_2 decreased.

   b. Solar brightness and oxygen generally decreased, while surface temperature and atmospheric CO_2 increased.

   c. Solar brightness and surface temperature generally increased, while oxygen and atmospheric CO_2 generally decreased.

   d. Solar brightness and surface temperature generally decreased, while oxygen and atmospheric CO_2 generally increased.

2. Photosynthesis is fundamentally important to life on Earth. On this diagram, label the inputs and outputs of the photosynthetic process, using the following terms:

   carbon dioxide, CO_2 light rays

   water, H_2O carbohydrates

   oxygen, O_2

3. Although scientists cannot be certain why atmospheric oxygen levels increased, they hypothesize that atmospheric oxygen has increased over time _____.

   a. because of a continued increase in the number of photo-synthetic organisms

   b. because of increased rates of seafloor spreading

   c. because organic matter is buried before it decomposes, reducing the formation of carbon dioxide (CO_2)

   d. All of the above statements are correct.

4. The minimum requirements for life are _____.

   a. photosynthesis and a means of replication

   b. mobility and a means of replication

   c. metabolism and a means of replication

   d. mobility and metabolism

5. Two cells are shown in these photographs. One is from a prokaryotic organism and the other from a eukaryotic organism. Label structures in each of the cells with the following terms and then label each cell either *prokaryotic* or *eukaryotic*.

   organelles   nucleus

   cell membrane

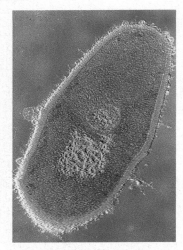

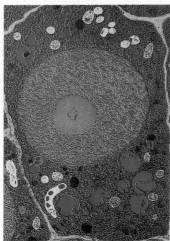

6. _____ is an example of anaerobic metabolism.

   a. Chemosynthesis

   b. Photosynthesis

   c. Fermentation

   d. Both a and b are correct.

   e. Both a and c are correct.

7. Natural selection is the process by which _____.

   a. individuals migrate to environments better suited to survival of the species

   b. individuals adapt to their environment over time

   c. well-adapted individuals pass on their survival advantages to their offspring

   d. All of the above are correct.

8. As a mechanism for evolution, natural selection requires the passing on of specific traits from one generation to the next. These specific traits may reflect _____ passed on through an organism's _____.

   a. genetic mutations; metabolism

   b. genetic mutations; DNA

   c. genetic mutations; RNA

   d. metabolism; DNA

   e. metabolism; RNA

9. How are organisms preserved as fossils within the rock record?

   a. through the preservation of the organism in substances such as sap, tar, or ice

   b. through minerals replacing the contents of the dead organism (mineralization)

   c. by the leaving of impressions, molds, or footprints

   d. through mummification, in especially dry environments

   e. All of the above are methods through which organisms could be preserved as fossils.

10. Which of the following hypotheses do scientists think best explains the explosion of life forms represented by the Cambrian fossil record?

   a. Sexual reproduction began in the early Cambrian Period, leading to a greater diversity of living organisms.

   b. An oxygen-rich atmosphere allowed for the metabolism of larger organisms.

   c. Predation began in the early Cambrian Period, leading to the development of many more organisms with shells and skeletons that might be better preserved in the fossil record.

   d. Extreme climatic changes at the end of the Proterozoic Eon led to accelerated evolutionary responses in surviving organisms.

   e. All of the above hypotheses are considered valid by scientists today.

11. Which of the following is not a requirement for a living organism to survive on land?

   a. structural support

   b. a means of locomotion

   c. an internal aquatic environment

   d. a mechanism of exchanging gases with the air

   e. if sexually reproducing, a moist environment for the reproductive system

12. Vascular plants exchange gas with the air by _____.

   a. diffusion through adjustable openings in the leaves called *stomata*

   b. decay of leaves

   c. photosynthesis

   d. All of the above are correct.

13. Reptiles were freed from the water by _____.

   a. evolving an egg that contained amniotic fluid for the young to grow in

   b. developing a watertight skin

   c. developing a warm-blooded metabolism

   d. Both a and b are correct.

   e. Both b and c are correct.

14. Of the five species from the family *Hominidae* listed here, which one is likely the earliest species from the genus to which *Homo sapiens* belongs?

   a. *Australopithecus afarensis*

   b. *Homo erectus*

   c. *Homo neanderthalensis*

   d. *Homo gautengensis*

   e. *Homo habilis*

15. Mass extinctions on Earth may be correlated with _____.

   a. massive eruptions of flood basalts

   b. the impact of massive meteorites

   c. widespread glaciation

   d. Both a and b are correct.

   e. Both b and c are correct.

THE PLANNER

Review the Chapter Planner on the chapter opener and check off your completed work.

16 UNDERSTANDING EARTH'S RESOURCES

Stephanie Maze/NG Image Collection

James P. Blair/NG Image Collection

A GOLD RUSH

Serra Pelada—or "bald mountain"—is 430 kilometers south of the mouth of the Amazon River on the edge of the Brazilian jungle and difficult to reach. Here, in January 1979, a child found a small gold nugget in the river mud. A geologist was consulted, and subsequently a rich ore deposit was identified. Word of the find leaked out, and by the end of 1979 tens of thousands of gold seekers had found their way to Serra Pelada. A gold rush was underway.

Miners worked claims 2 meters by 3 meters, the size of one of the pedestals in the photograph. They carried the ore out on their backs. Injury and death were common. Rewards came in the form of nuggets (inset photo), and eventually an estimated 360 tons of gold were recovered.

Why are people willing to risk life and limb for gold? Gold is rare. It lasts because it doesn't tarnish, corrode, or dissolve in common liquids, and its value ensures that owners take very good care of it. Because gold is carefully guarded, we can estimate how much has been mined in human history: about 200,000 tons. If all of this gold were stacked on a football field, it would make a pile only 1.75 meters high—not much of a return on 17,000 years of work!

RENEWABLE AND NONRENEWABLE RESOURCES

Learning Objectives

1. **Describe** how the use and overuse of resources has affected some past civilizations.

2. **Explain** the difference between renewable and nonrenewable resources.

3. **Identify** nonrenewable resources that are crucial to modern society.

From the time our ancestors first picked up conveniently shaped stones and used them for hunting and skinning wild animals to the present day, humans have relied on a bountiful Earth to supply a seemingly endless flow of useful materials. Today it is hard to imagine life without myriad such resources making life easier and more convenient. But, as you will learn, history suggests that there may be limits to the bounty.

Natural Resources and Ancient History

Silent and inscrutable after 10 centuries, the giant stone heads of the island of Rapa Nui, also known as Easter Island (**Figure 16.1**) are the principal remains of a civilization that once flourished on this remote outpost in the South Pacific. The Rapa Nui people transported hundreds of the megaliths, called *moai*, over hilly terrain, from the quarry where they were carved to their final locations. Some archaeologists believe that the inhabitants used tree trunks and ropes to roll the stone figures across the land.

Just as interesting as the questions of how and why the Rapa Nui transported the *moai* is the reason they stopped. Scientists have found that palm trees grew on Easter Island until around 1500, when the last of the palm trees disappeared. In one version of Rapa Nuit history, the islanders cut down every last tree, leaving the ground bare and vulnerable to rapid erosion. As a result of the loss of the trees, the Rapa Nui lost not only the ability to transport megaliths but possibly also the resources necessary to sustain their civilization, which was decimated by famine and warfare over the next century.

The decline of past civilizations is an endlessly fascinating and endlessly controversial topic. No civilization's decline can be attributed to a single cause. Nevertheless, a common thread runs through the stories of many societies that flourished and then collapsed. That thread is the depletion of **natural resources**.

> **natural resource** A useful material that is obtained from the lithosphere, atmosphere, hydrosphere, or biosphere.

Rapa Nui megaliths • Figure 16.1

The Polynesians who erected these stone heads called *moai* on Easter Island (Rapa Nui) may have unwittingly sowing the seeds of their own culture's demise. One interpretation of Rapa Nui history suggests that they stripped the island of its palm trees, using the trunks to roll the megaliths into place.

© Lisa Strachan/Shutterstock

On Rapa Nui the critically important resources were trees, a biological resource, and soil, an Earth resource.

Another critical Earth resource is water. In the area that is now present-day Libya, the Garamantian culture arose in the Sahara Desert around the same time as the Roman Empire, and it prospered for about 1000 years, despite the nearly complete lack of rainfall. The Garamantes survived by tapping into immense underground aquifers and transporting the groundwater through a channel of aqueducts called *foggara* (**Figure 16.2**). Unfortunately, around 500 CE, they apparently reached the end of their technological ability to retrieve groundwater. The *foggara* had been depleted, and their cities became ghost towns.

Resource Replenishment and Depletion

Like the societies of the Rapa Nui and the Garamantes, every human society depends on natural resources. Besides the most fundamentally important resources that support life—

Ghost town in the Sahara • Figure 16.2

The Garamantians, ancient inhabitants of Libya, seem to have depleted an essential resource: water.

Victor Paul Borg/Alamy

a. These are the remains of Garama, an ancient city in the Sahara Desert, abandoned about 1500 years ago. The city was the center of Garamantian culture from 500 BCE to 500 CE; as many as 10,000 people lived here.

Foggara

©Nick Brooks

b. The large population was supported by a vast underground network of *foggara*, or aqueducts, whose openings to the surface can still be seen.

soil, water, and air—Earth's resources include building materials, metals, fertilizers, fuel, and gemstones. Biological resources include crops, wild plants, and animals. Many

> **renewable resource** A resource that can be replenished on the scale of a human lifetime.

of these resources are **renewable** or replenishable on a humanly accessible time scale, if they are managed carefully. Even though we may consume a food crop each season, a new crop grows during the following season. A layer of soil lost to erosion will eventually be regenerated through the physical, chemical, and biological processes of soil formation. Groundwater drawn from wells may eventually be replenished by rainwater.

But what does it mean to say that these resources are replenished or regenerated "eventually"? Some resources take a very long time to regenerate—longer than humans are willing or able to wait. For example, the aquifers under the Sahara Desert formed tens of thousands of years ago, when the climate was moister than it is today, and they will not be replenished until the climate changes again, perhaps tens of thousands of years from now. For practical purposes, we consider these to be **nonrenewable resources**.

> **nonrenewable resource** A resource that cannot be replenished or regenerated on the scale of a human lifetime.

Resources such as coal, oil, copper, iron, gold, and fertilizers are mined from mineral deposits. Mineral deposits are known to be forming today, but the rate of formation is exceedingly slow. For example, it may take 600,000 years for a large copper deposit to be formed. From a human point of view, all mineral resources are one-crop resources, and Earth's supply of those "crops" is fixed. One of the defining characteristics of nonrenewable resources is that they are constantly being depleted as we use them.

Humans are the first and only species to routinely use nonrenewable resources. It does not seem to be in our nature to stop. However, history suggests that we should use such resources very judiciously and monitor how much we have left. That is what the Rapa Nui and the Garamantes failed to do. After the cultures that produced the *moai* and the *foggara* died out, their descendants had to adapt to the new conditions. The Easter Islanders developed new rituals that allocated their limited food resources. The inhabitants of the Sahara developed a nomadic lifestyle that was not dependent on the extraction of deeply buried groundwater. Early European settlers in North America began smelting and processing iron in the early 1600s, almost as soon as they arrived in the New World (see *Amazing Places*, next page).

Like our ancestors and ourselves, our descendants will be fundamentally dependent on the availability of critical Earth resources. They may have to make serious changes in their lifestyles if critical resources become even scarcer.

Resources and Modern Society

In our world of the 21st century, there are now 7.1 billion human inhabitants, and the population is growing larger by millions each year. Each of us uses—directly or indirectly—a very large amount of material derived from nonrenewable **mineral resources**. Nearly every chemical element is used in one way or another, and they are extracted from more than 200 different minerals (see *Remember This!*). Without them, we could not build planes, cars, televisions, or computers.

> **REMEMBER THIS!** Can you recall how many minerals are known to scientists, altogether? Refer back to Chapter 2, *Mineral Families*, to remind yourself.

Amazing Places

Saugus Iron Works

Just a few kilometers northeast of the center of Boston, Massachusetts, is the Saugus Iron Works, a National Historical Site that was the first integrated iron works in North America. It is a remarkable place.

The Massachusetts Bay Colony grew rapidly during the 1630s, as immigrants arrived. The English Civil War (1642–1651) slowed trade across the Atlantic Ocean, and the colonists soon found it necessary to start smelting and processing iron in order to have a supply of the iron articles they needed. In the swamps at the mouth of the Saugus River, the colonists found a supply of bog iron ore. This soft, spongy material is hydrous iron oxides (limonite) precipitated from iron-bearing waters by oxidation.

Using water power (**Figure a**) from the Saugus River to pump bellows (**Figure b**), they started smelting iron in the first blast furnace in 1646. For fuel they used charcoal produced from the hardwood forests of the region. Two skilled metallurgists were brought from Europe, and they soon had a forge operating so that the iron could be forged into useful tools. Other facilities followed: a rolling mill for making sheets and rods, a shearing device for cutting sheets, and a drop-hammer weighing 500 pounds for pounding hot iron into desired shapes.

The iron works closed in 1668, when the local bog-iron ore ran out. While it lasted, the Saugus operation was equal to the best iron works in Europe, and it was a training ground for skilled iron workers who eventually helped to found America's iron and steel industry. Much is known about the Saugus Iron Works because there are contemporary written records, and the site was intensively investigated during archaeological excavations between 1948 and 1953. What you see today are probably the most detailed and accurate reconstructions of a 17th-century iron works anywhere in the world.

a

Global Locator

Saugus (Ma)

NG Maps

© G.E. Kidder Smith/CORBIS

b

Bill Brooks/Alamy

THINK CRITICALLY

Why was iron a critical resource for the early settlers in North America?

Industry would collapse, and living standards would deteriorate dramatically. We could not distribute electric power or build tractors to till fields and produce food. The metals needed to build machines for manufacturing, transportation, and communications are nonrenewable resources, extracted from the ground.

We are equally dependent on **energy resources**. Imagine what life would be like if we had to rely entirely on human muscle power. If a healthy adult rides an exercise bike that drives an electric generator hooked to a light bulb, the best an average person can do in a nonstop eight-hour day of pedaling is to keep a 75-watt bulb burning. In North America, the same amount of electricity can be purchased from a power company for about 10 cents. Viewed in this way, we can see that human muscle power is puny. Over many thousands of years, our ancestors found ways to supplement muscle power. At first, they did this by domesticating beasts of burden such as horses, oxen, camels, elephants, and llamas. They later learned to make sails to use wind power, dams to use water power, and engines to convert the heat energy of wood, oil, and coal into mechanical power.

Today we use supplementary energy in every part of our lives, from food production and transportation to housing and recreation. North Americans are among the world's

Per capita energy use differs dramatically from one country to another.

a. An average American uses energy, directly or indirectly, at a rate equivalent to burning 150 75-watt light bulbs every minute of every day. (Canadians, with their cold winters, use even more energy.) Here a highway sign admonishes Los Angeles commuters, "Don't be fuelish—be carpoolish."

b. Haiti uses the least energy per capita of any country in the western hemisphere—the equivalent of about 1.5 light bulbs per inhabitant. In the town of La Victoire there are no cars in evidence, and only one television for the whole town. The photographer reported, "Sometimes it even works."

Michael Nichols/NG Image Collection

James P. Blair/NG Image Collection

biggest energy consumers (**Figure 16.3**). Whereas soil and water were the most critical nonrenewable resources for earlier civilizations, our society's weakest link may be its excessive dependence on nonrenewable energy sources. How and whether we can reduce this dependence is both a political problem and a social problem. Geology plays an important role in three ways: identifying new supplies of traditional resources, allowing us to estimate how much we have left, and evaluating the consequences of using new and unconventional resources.

STOP **CONCEPT CHECK**

1. **How** can the loss of resources affect the stability of a society?

2. **Why** is the distinction between renewable and nonrenewable resources so important?

3. **What** are some of the ways that modern society is dependent on nonrenewable resources?

FOSSIL FUELS

Learning Objectives

1. **Describe** the formation of peat and coal.

2. **Identify** the main sources of petroleum.

3. **Describe** some important nontraditional sources of petroleum and natural gas.

4. **Discuss** the world's reliance on fossil fuels.

People make use of both nonrenewable and renewable energy sources. Everywhere in the world, even in the least-developed countries, nonrenewable sources

fossil fuel Combustible organic matter that is trapped in sediment or sedimentary rock.

supply at least half of the energy used (**Figure 16.4**), and the main nonrenewable source of energy—by far—is **fossil fuels**.

Fossil fuels are animal or plant remains that have been buried and trapped in sediment or sedimentary rock and have undergone chemical and physical changes during and after burial. All fossil fuels are composed primarily of **hydrocarbon** (hydrogen + carbon) **compounds**. Because fossil fuels are derived from the altered remains of plants or animals, their energy content is derived originally from the Sun, via photosynthesis. The principal fossil fuels are peat, coal, oil, and natural gas. The kind of sediment, the specific type of organic matter, and the postburial changes that occur determine which type of fossil fuel is formed.

Peat and Coal

Organic matter that accumulates on land comes from trees, bushes, and grasses. These land plants are rich in organic compounds that tend to remain solid after burial. In water-saturated places such as swamps and bogs, the remains accumulate to form **peat**.

peat A biogenic sediment formed from the accumulation and compaction of plant remains from bogs and swamps, with a carbon content of about 25%.

In the United States, fossil fuels (oil, natural gas, and coal) account for 83% of the energy used. The large amount of lost energy—approximately half, as shown in the upper right—arises both from wasted energy and from the fundamental physical limits on the efficiency of any heat engine.

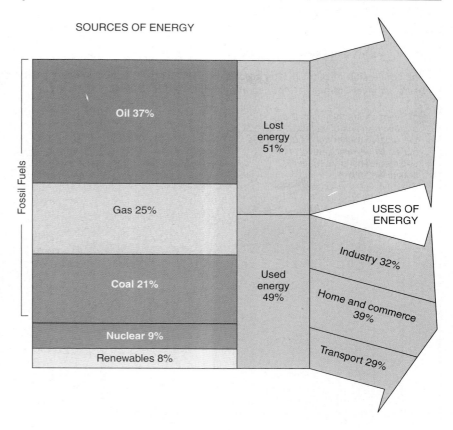

SOURCES OF ENERGY

Fossil Fuels

Oil 37%

Gas 25%

Coal 21%

Nuclear 9%

Renewables 8%

Lost energy 51%

Used energy 49%

USES OF ENERGY

Industry 32%

Home and commerce 39%

Transport 29%

> **coal** A combustible rock (50 to 95% carbon), formed by the compression, heating, and lithification of peat.

Peat is the initial stage in the formation of **coal** (**Figure 16.5**). As layers of peat are compressed and heated by being buried under more and more sediment, water and gaseous compounds such as carbon dioxide (CO_2) and methane (CH_4) escape. The loss of these constituents leaves a higher proportion of carbon in the residue, and carbon is what we want for burning—the higher the carbon content, the greater the **rank** of the coal. The lowest rank of coal is called **lignite**, and **anthracite** is the name for the highest rank of coal. Much of the world's coal is **bituminous coal**, intermediate between lignite and anthracite. Anthracite is so changed from its original form that it is considered a metamorphic rock (see *Remember This!*).

> **REMEMBER THIS!** Can you explain why peat is considered to be a sediment, lignite and bituminous coal are sedimentary rock, and anthracite is a metamorphic rock? If not, you can remind yourself about the differences by reviewing Chapter 2, *Rock: A First Look.*

Coal occurs in strata (miners call them seams) along with other types of sedimentary rock, mainly shale and sandstone. Anthracite occurs with slate—low-grade metamorphic rock. Coal seams tend to occur in groups. For example, 60 seams

of bituminous coal have been found in western Pennsylvania. This abundant coal powered Pittsburgh's steel mills and made it into the "Steel City."

Peat (**Figure 16.6**) and coal have been forming more or less continuously since vascular plants first appeared on Earth about 450 million years ago. However, the size of peat swamps has varied greatly throughout Earth's history, and therefore the amount of coal formed has also varied. By far the largest amounts of peat swamp formation occurred on Pangaea during the warm Carboniferous and Permian periods, 360 to 245 million years ago. The great coal seams of Europe and eastern North America formed from peat deposited at that time, when the swamp plants were different from today and included giant ferns and scale trees. A second great period of peat formation peaked during the Cretaceous Period, 144 to 65.5 million years ago. During this period, the plants of peat swamps were flowering plants, much like those found in swamps today.

The luxuriant growth needed to form thick and extensive coal seams is most likely to occur in a tropical or semitropical climate. We can therefore deduce that either the global climate was warmer in the past or the lands where these seams occur were once in the tropics. Probably both conditions were involved. Coal deposits that were formed in warm low-latitude environments but are now in frigid polar lands provide compelling evidence that plate tectonics moves continents around. The many places where coal is found in

Process Diagram

How coal is formed • Figure 16.5

The conversion of plant matter to coal, or **coalification**, happens over a period of millions of years, as layers of peat are buried and compressed by overlying sediments.

1 Swamps are thick with the organic remains of vegetation. As the organic matter decomposes, it is buried by more vegetation and sediment. The plant matter is converted into peat.

2 As the thickness of overlying sediment increases over time, causing higher pressures and temperatures on the organic layer, water and other volatile components are expelled.

3 By the time a layer of peat has been converted into coal, its thickness has been reduced by 90 percent, most of the volatile components are gone, and carbon (the heat source) has been greatly concentrated.

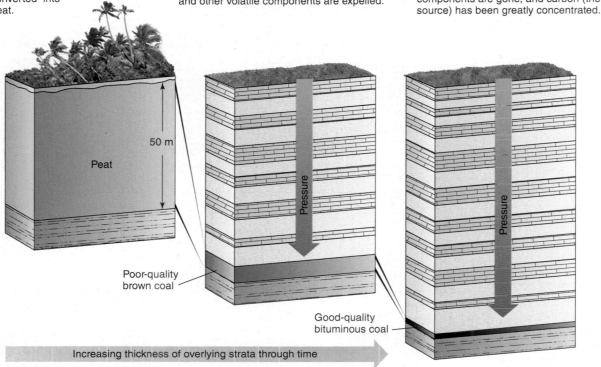

50 m

Peat

Poor-quality brown coal

Pressure

Good-quality bituminous coal

Pressure

Increasing thickness of overlying strata through time

THINK CRITICALLY

If coal and diamond are made from the same element, carbon, why won't you ever find a diamond in a coal deposit?

For peat's sake • Figure 16.6

Robert Sisson/NG Image Collection

A peat cutter harvests peat from a bog in Ireland. When dried, peat provides fuel for heat and cooking. It is higher in energy content than firewood but lower than coal. If the peat cutter could wait a few million years, he could harvest much higher-energy coal.

Coal seams are associated with swampy environments—past and present.

a. The largest coal mine in the western hemisphere is located in Gillette, Wyoming. In the Cretaceous Period, when these coal deposits were being formed, this area was covered with swamps and the climate was subtropical.

b. Okefenokee Swamp in Florida and Georgia is a modern-day example of a peat swamp. Given a few million years and the right conditions, this peat swamp will one day turn into a coal seam.

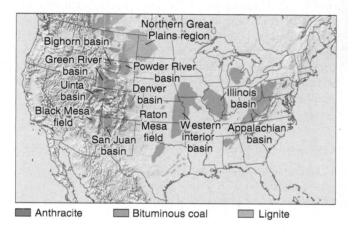

Anthracite — Bituminous coal — Lignite

c. All of the coal deposits shown on this map were once swamps, resembling the Okefenokee Swamp.

the United States today provide an excellent example (**Figure 16.7**). Today peat formation is occurring in wetlands such as the Okefenokee Swamp in Florida and Georgia and the Great Dismal Swamp in Virginia and North Carolina.

Petroleum

In the ocean, microscopic phytoplankton (tiny floating plants) and bacteria are the principal sources of organic matter in sediment. However, the chemicals found in these organisms differ from those in land plants. When buried and compressed under the right conditions, they are slowly transformed into **petroleum**.

petroleum Naturally occurring gaseous, liquid, and semisolid substances that consist chiefly of hydrocarbon compounds.

oil The liquid form of petroleum.

Oil first came into widespread use in about 1847, when a merchant in Pittsburgh started bottling and selling oil from natural seeps. Five years later, a Canadian chemist discovered that heating and distilling oil yields kerosene, a liquid that could be used in lamps.

Kerosene lamps quickly replaced whale oil lamps and greatly reduced the use of candles in household lighting. Soon oil wells were being dug by hand near Oil Springs, Ontario. In 1859, the first commercial oil well was drilled in the United States (**Figure 16.8**), and a modern industry was born.

The modern use of **natural gas** started with an accidental discovery at Fredonia, New York, in 1821, when an ordinary water well began to produce bubbles of a mysterious gas. The gas was accidentally ignited and produced a spectacular flame. Wooden pipes were installed to carry the gas to a nearby hotel, where it was used in gaslights. Though rarely used today, gaslights preceded the electric light bulb, and many people considered them to be superior to early light bulbs.

natural gas The gaseous form of petroleum.

Today, petroleum products are used for a wide variety of purposes in addition to their main use as fuel for heating and operating vehicles and machines. Different components of petroleum are used in fertilizers, lubricants, asphalt, and the most ubiquitous material in contemporary life, plastic (**Figure 16.9**).

The first commercial oil well • Figure 16.8

On August 27, 1859, Edwin Drake's drill "struck oil" in a deposit 21 meters underground in Titusville, Pennsylvania. This shed at Drake's Well Museum is a reconstruction of the world's first commercially productive oil well.

H. Mark Weidman Photography/Alamy

Deposits of petroleum are nearly always found in association with sedimentary rock that formed in a marine environment. When marine microorganisms die, their remains settle to the bottom and collect in the fine seafloor mud, where they start to decay. The decay process quickly uses up any oxygen that is present. The remaining organic material is thereby preserved without decaying and is covered with more layers of mud and decaying organisms. The increasing heat and pressure associated with burial initiate a series of complex physical and chemical changes, called **maturation**, which break down the solid organic material and turn it into liquid and gaseous hydrocarbons.

The temperature and depth conditions under which maturation takes place are referred to as the **petroleum window**. The specific conditions of maturation and the composition of the starting materials determine whether the breakdown products will be oil, natural gas, or another type of hydrocarbon (**Figure 16.10**). While maturation is proceeding, the sediment itself is turned into rock, such as shale or limestone. A rock in which organic material has been converted into oil and natural gas is called a **source rock**. Oil and gas occupy more volume than the original solid organic matter, so the conversion process creates internal stresses that cause small fractures to form in the source rock, and the fractures allow a small fraction of the oil and gas to escape into adjacent, more porous **reservoir rock**.

One raw material, many uses • Figure 16.9

Crude oil consists mostly of hydrocarbons—molecules that contain carbon and hydrogen but no oxygen. At an oil refinery, the oil is distilled into heavier and lighter components. Hydrocarbons with fewer carbon atoms generally have lower boiling points and are useful as fuels. The sizes of the trucks are proportional to the yield.

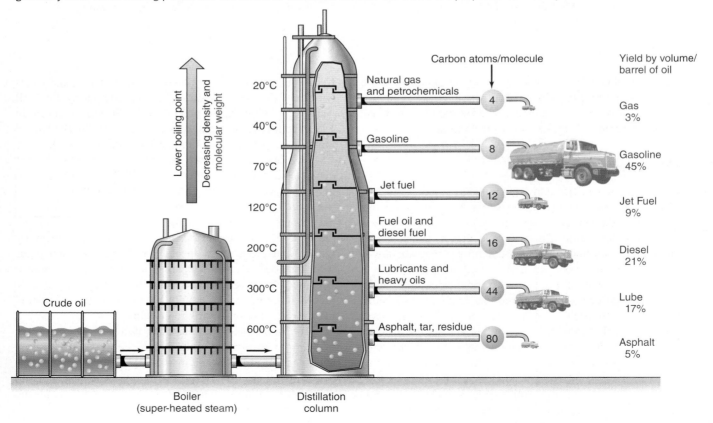

The petroleum window • Figure 16.10

This diagram shows the regions of depth and temperature in which organic matter is converted to oil and gas and at which trapping occurs.

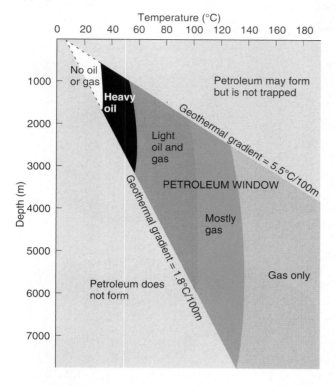

Oil and natural gas are light, so they slowly migrate toward the surface. If nothing stops this slow percolation, they will eventually reach the surface and evaporate into the atmosphere. It is estimated that 99.9% of the petroleum in the world escapes this way.

However, sometimes the migrating oil and gas encounter an obstacle—a layer of impermeable rock that prevents it from reaching the surface. This is a **cap rock**, and shale is the most common rock type. A geological situation that includes a source rock to contribute organic material, a reservoir rock in which the oil accumulates, and a cap rock to stop the migration is referred to as a petroleum trap (or **hydrocarbon trap**). The natural gas lies on top of the oil, because it is the least dense; water, typically salty, lies at the bottom because it is the densest of the fluids beneath the cap rock. Several types of petroleum traps are known (**Figure 16.11**); recognizing and finding them is the job of a petroleum geologist.

> **petroleum trap** The combination of a source rock, a reservoir rock, and a cap rock, which serves to trap and store oil and natural gas in the subsurface.

> **tar sand** A sediment or sedimentary rock in which the pores are filled by dense, viscous, asphalt-like oil.

Nontraditional Hydrocarbons

Oil that is too viscous (thick) to be readily pumped is called **heavy oil**, or **tar**. Tar sands are an in-creasingly important source of oil. The world's largest-known deposits are in Alberta, Canada (**Figure 16.12a**); geologists have estimated that the Alberta tar sands contain as much as 2 trillion barrels of oil. (The world's annual oil production is about 31 billion barrels.) Sandstones in this region are cemented together by tar. To soften and extract the tar, workers cook the sandstone with hot water and steam inside a rotating drum. Once extracted, the big organic molecules in the tar must be refined and reduced to the smaller molecules in gasoline and other useful petroleum products.

Most of the oil in a source rock does not migrate into traditional oil traps but remains in the source rock, trapped in tiny openings, or tightly bonded to the surrounding mineral grains, or both. To extract oil from these formerly inaccessible deposits, a technique has been developed in which fracturing is induced in the source rock by the introduction of a pressurized fluid. The hydrocarbon material flows more readily through these fractures into the extraction well, where it can be withdrawn by pumping. This approach is called **hydraulic fracturing**, or fracking. Fracking has come under intense scrutiny lately because of its potentially negative environmental impacts, which can include contamination of groundwater, noise pollution, and oil leakage.

> **fracking** Induced hydraulic fracturing, in which a pressurized fluid is injected into a well to create tiny fractures, facilitating the withdrawal of tightly held hydrocarbons such as heavy oil.

Another unconventional form of petroleum is a wax-like organic substance called **kerogen**, which comes from very fine-grained sedimentary rock such as shale. If burial temperatures are not high enough to form oil and natural gas from organic matter in the sediment, kerogen is formed instead. If the kerogen is mined and heated, it breaks down and forms oil and gas. To be worth extracting, kerogen in oil shales must yield more energy than the amount needed to mine and heat it. The world's largest deposit of oil shale is found in Colorado, Wyoming, and Utah (**Figure 16.12b**). The U.S. Geological Survey estimates that these deposits, if mined and processed, could yield about 3 trillion barrels of oil.

> **oil shale** A fine-grained sedimentary rock with a high content of kerogen.

Most natural gas is produced from fields that also produce oil, the amount of each commodity depending on the depth and temperature reached by the source bed. Note in Figure 16.10 that when temperature and depth are great enough, gas is the only product formed in a source bed. It has been known for nearly a century that gas is present in source beds, but conventional vertical drilling did not yield a profitable return. In recent years, gas has been recovered by a technology called horizontal drilling, developed for drilling from deep-water platforms, and often combined with fracking. Gas-rich source beds are deep extensions of source beds that produced oil at shallower depths, so **shale gas**, as this product has come to be called, is generally found in areas that already have a history of petroleum production.

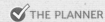
This figure illustrates six geological circumstances in which oil can become trapped. Each trap requires a source rock to contribute organic matter, a reservoir rock to store the oil (usually with natural gas and salty water) in its pores, and a cap rock to prevent further migration of the oil and loss to the atmosphere.

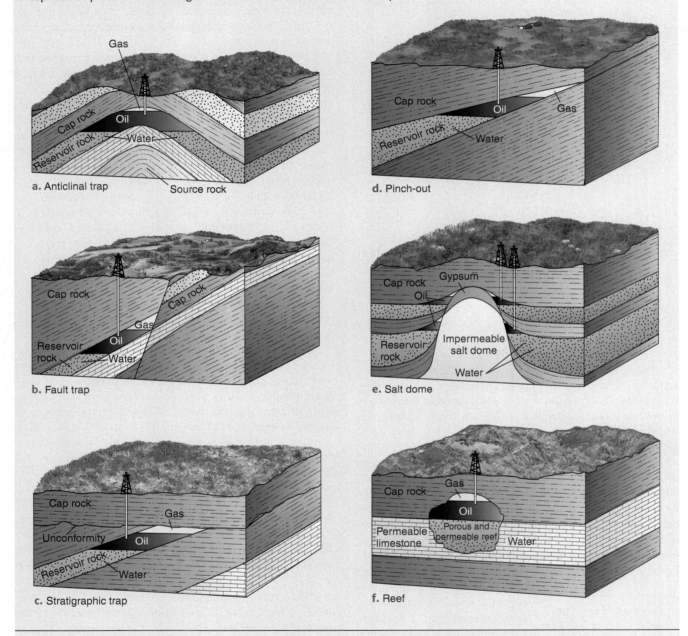

a. Anticlinal trap

b. Fault trap

c. Stratigraphic trap

d. Pinch-out

e. Salt dome

f. Reef

THINK CRITICALLY

The water that is associated with oil deposits is usually salty. Some oil deposits are even associated with salt deposits (as shown in Figure 16.11e). Why would this be?

Coal beds are another newly discovered, unconventional source for natural gas. Coal mines have long been understood to be dangerous because the coal contains methane gas that can be accidentally ignited and cause an explosion. Coal may appear to be a tight solid, but it actually contains myriad micropores, and methane is present in all the pores. In recent years, it has been found possible to drill into coal seams to create small fractures into which the gas can migrate and be recovered. It is estimated that about 25% of the gas produced in the United States now comes from coal beds and shale.

Tar sands and oil shales host unconventional fossil fuel resources.

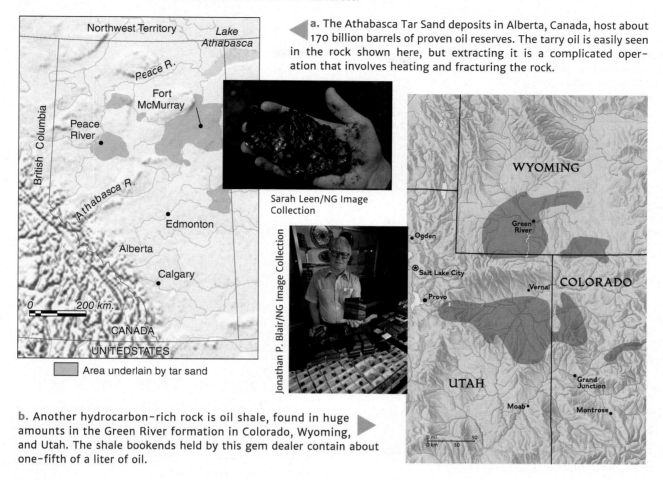

a. The Athabasca Tar Sand deposits in Alberta, Canada, host about 170 billion barrels of proven oil reserves. The tarry oil is easily seen in the rock shown here, but extracting it is a complicated operation that involves heating and fracturing the rock.

Sarah Leen/NG Image Collection

Jonathan P. Blair/NG Image Collection

b. Another hydrocarbon-rich rock is oil shale, found in huge amounts in the Green River formation in Colorado, Wyoming, and Utah. The shale bookends held by this gem dealer contain about one-fifth of a liter of oil.

Relying on Fossil Fuels

Because most of us grew up in an oil-powered economy, it is easy to forget just how recent our dependence on oil is. **Figure 16.13** shows the history of energy consumption and the changing character of the world's energy "mix." Until 1860 or so, the world ran mainly on energy provided by wood; from then until World War II, coal was the dominant energy source. The huge increase in demand for energy after World War II has mostly been filled by oil and natural gas. The ability to discover new fossil fuel deposits to meet these increasing demands was greatly improved by the advent of new technologies for exploration, including seismic studies, satellite imagery, computer modeling, and digital recording methods.

Despite our improved ability to locate and retrieve fossil fuels, we cannot ignore the fact that they are nonrenewable resources. Most projections indicate that world production of oil will peak and begin to decrease before the year 2020. What will happen then? One possibility is that, as in the 1970s, increased efficiency and conservation measures will reduce the demand for energy. There will presumably be an increased contribution from so-called nontraditional sources of oil and gas, including tar sands and oil shales. Coal is still abundant in the United States, but it is unlikely to replace oil because it creates more severe air pollution. Some researchers are working on new technologies for cleaner-burning coal. However, to fulfill the worldwide demand for energy in a reliable, affordable, and environmentally acceptable manner, it will be necessary to place greater emphasis on other sources of energy besides fossil fuels.

STOP **CONCEPT CHECK**

1. **What** is the origin of the energy in a fossil fuel?
2. **What** kinds of organisms provide the source material for coal?
3. **What** kinds of environments lead to the formation of petroleum?
4. **Describe** the history of oil's rise to prominence in the world energy mix.

The history of world energy consumption shows oil's rise to prominence. The brief decline in energy use in the late 1970s and early 1980s resulted from the energy crises of 1973 and 1979, when the Organization of the Petroleum Exporting Countries (OPEC) cut production, prices rose, and industrialized countries attempted to conserve energy.

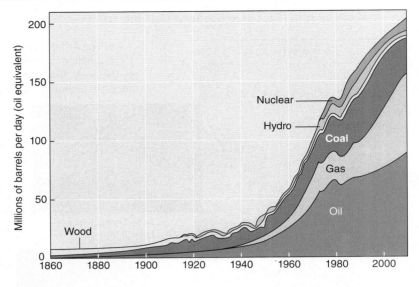

RENEWABLE ENERGY RESOURCES

Learning Objectives

1. **Explain** why biomass, wind, and wave energy are indirect forms of solar energy.

2. **Describe** how nuclear and geothermal power work, and identify their advantages and disadvantages.

Each of the world's 7.1 billion people uses energy at an average rate of approximately 2370 watts, for a total rate of 16.6×10^{12} watts. However, this is only a minute fraction of the amount of energy that enters the Earth system, primarily from the Sun (**Figure 16.14**). It is clear, then, that we are not about to run out of energy in an absolute sense. The question is whether we are clever enough to learn how to use alternative sources of energy rather than rely so heavily on nonrenewable fossil fuels.

The potential alternatives to fossil fuels are largely renewable; they come from solar, biomass, wind, wave, tidal, hydroelectric, nuclear, and geothermal sources. Some of these, including wind and wave energy, are essentially indirect expressions of the Sun's energy and thus are perpetually renewable, or inexhaustible. Sources that derive their energy directly or indirectly from the Sun will not be exhausted as long as the Sun continues to shine. Tidal energy, too, will continue as long as Earth rotates and we have a Moon. Fuel wood and animal waste, the traditional sources for biomass power, is renewable as long as the materials are not harvested too quickly. New biomass fuels like ethanol also come from a variety of renewable sources, such as corn. Nuclear power is technically nonrenewable, but the amount of energy available is so vast that it is, for all practical purposes, inexhaustible.

Power from Sun, Wind, and Water

Solar energy reaches Earth from the Sun at a rate more than 10,000 times greater than the sum of all human energy demands. The hyperabundance of solar energy makes it a very logical candidate for the power source of the future. However, the reality is that the solar future is still far away. Solar energy is best used for direct heating at or below the boiling point of water, as in greenhouses, space heating, and solar water heaters. But it will make a significant dent in our energy budget only if we can convert it directly into electricity. Unfortunately, the best available solar PVC or **photovoltaic cells** (**Figure 16.15**) are still too costly and too inefficient for many uses; you will find them in common use for small everyday items, such as solar-powered calculators. Photovoltaic technology is constantly improving, however, and the cost of energy generated in this manner is decreasing.

Plants are very efficient converters of solar energy. Our oil-based economy runs on the energy stored by plants millions of years ago. However, living and recently living plant matter also contains stored solar energy—which, unlike fossil fuels, is renewable. **Biomass energy** derived from fuel wood was the dominant source of energy until the end of the 19th century, when it was displaced by coal.

> **solar energy** Radiant light and heat energy from the Sun.

> **biomass energy** Any form of energy that is derived more or less directly from plant life, including fuel wood, peat, animal dung, agricultural wastes, and biofuels from various sources.

Earth's primary energy inputs are the Sun, geothermal energy, and tides. Solar energy—at 173,000 terawatts—is overwhelmingly dominant.

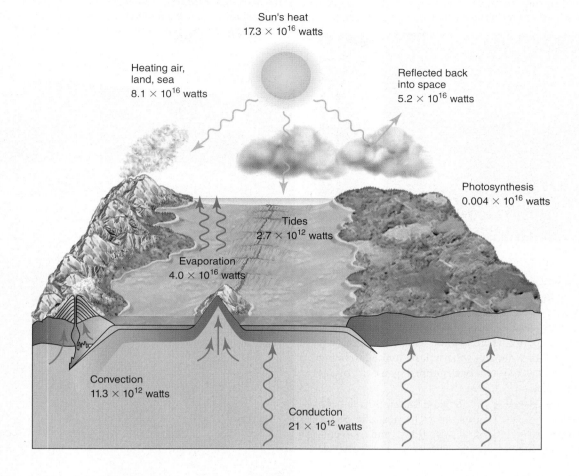

Sun's heat
17.3×10^{16} watts

Heating air,
land, sea
8.1×10^{16} watts

Reflected back
into space
5.2×10^{16} watts

Photosynthesis
0.004×10^{16} watts

Tides
2.7×10^{12} watts

Evaporation
4.0×10^{16} watts

Convection
11.3×10^{12} watts

Conduction
21×10^{12} watts

Solar energy • Figure 16.15

These solar panels were installed on the roof of San Francisco's Moscone Convention Center in 2004. With 5400 solar panels generating 825,000 kilowatt-hours of electricity per year—enough to power 100 homes—it is the largest city-owned solar installation in the United States.

Sarah Leen/NG Image Collection

Biomass fuels are still widely used throughout the world, particularly in less developed countries, where the cost of fossil fuel is very high in relation to income. The conversion of organic wastes and crops like corn and sugar cane into fuels like ethanol or diesel, termed **biofuels**, is an increasingly popular source of fuel for vehicles and equipment.

Wind energy is an indirect form of solar energy, because the heating of land and ocean creates the giant convection cells that drive global wind systems (see Chapter 12). For thousands of years, wind has been used as a source of power for ships and windmills. Today, huge windmill "farms" are being erected in particularly windy places (**Figure 16.16**), to convert wind energy into useful power. In Denmark, wind turbines supply almost 30% of all electrical power used in the breezy coastal country; the goal is for wind energy to account for 50% of electricity production by 2020. Although windmills are still expensive, it seems likely that their cost will soon be competitive with the costs of coal-burning electric power plants.

> **wind energy** Energy derived from the movement of air; an indirect form of solar energy.

Wind energy • Figure 16.16

The wind turbines at this wind farm at Tehachapi Pass, California, generate clean electricity by harnessing the energy of the wind to turn an electric generator. Wind farms can operate only where steady surface winds prevail year-round.

Marc Moritsch/NG Image Collection

One challenge for both wind and solar power is intermittency—the fact that the wind is not always blowing and the Sun is not always shining when customers need the energy. Engineers need to design efficient and economical ways to store the energy when it is not needed and release it when it is needed, or wind and solar will be limited to being components in a power system backstopped by a coal, oil, or nuclear power plant.

hydroelectric energy Electricity generated by running water.

Several methods have been proposed to harness the power of waves, tides, and sea currents. However, **hydroelectric energy** is at present the only form of water-derived power that meets a significant portion of the world's energy needs. To convert the power of flowing water into electricity, it is necessary to build dams (**Figure 16.17**). The flowing water is used to run turbines, which in turn convert the energy into electricity. The ultimate sources of hydroelectric energy are the Sun, which powers the hydrologic cycle, and gravity, which causes the water behind the dam to fall and release its stored potential energy.

The total recoverable energy from the water flowing in all of the world's streams is estimated to be equivalent to the energy obtained by burning 15 billion barrels of oil per year. Thus, even if all the potential hydropower in the world were developed, it could not meet all of today's energy needs. Another problem is that reservoirs eventually fill up with silt, so even though the source is inexhaustible, dams and reservoirs have limited lifetimes.

One energy source that will undoubtedly play a larger role in the future is hydrogen, which can be used to power **fuel cells**. Like batteries, fuel cells depend on chemical energy. But unlike batteries, they are easily replenished with new fuel. The only waste product produced by a hydrogen fuel cell is water (H_2O), so it is very clean compared with fossil fuels. However, the downside to fuel cells is that there is no

Hydropower • Figure 16.17

The Hoover Dam straddles the Colorado River in Arizona and Nevada. Behind it lies Lake Mead, created by the construction of the dam. Water from the lake flows through the hydroelectric power station seen in the foreground. The gravitational force of the running water turns a turbine to generate electricity.

© Andrew Zarivny/Shutterstock

place to "mine" hydrogen. It can be extracted by separating water into hydrogen and oxygen, but the separation process uses up just as much energy as it produces. Hence hydrogen cannot really be thought of as a fuel in its own right but as a way of storing energy that is produced in some other way (perhaps with solar or nuclear power). Even so, there is a great deal of excitement these days about the "hydrogen economy," and future developments will be worth watching.

Nuclear and Geothermal Power

Of the alternative power sources mentioned earlier, **nuclear energy** is probably the only one with the potential to completely replace fossil fuels. However, it faces serious drawbacks that have so far prevented it from reaching that potential.

nuclear energy Energy derived from the binding energy in the nuclei of atoms; fission (splitting of atoms) is the most common source.

Present-day nuclear reactors exploit an energy-producing process called radioactive decay (see *Remember This!*). Two isotopes of uranium, a radioactive element, occur naturally in certain minerals and can be mined and used as fuel for nuclear reactors. In a nuclear reactor, purified and concentrated uranium fuel is augmented by purifying and concentrating the isotope uranium-235, and then it is bombarded with neutrons to stimulate the process of **fission**—the splitting of the uranium atom into two products of smaller mass. Under precisely controlled conditions, this gives rise to a **chain reaction** of atomic fission that sustains itself as long as there is enough uranium fuel present (see the *Case Study*). An uncontrolled chain reaction would cause a nuclear explosion. But if the reaction proceeds under control, a great deal of useful energy can be generated.

> **REMEMBER THIS!** Scientists make use of this same process, radioactive decay, to determine the age of a rock formation. Can you recall how this process works? Refer back to Chapter 3, *Numerical Age* to review radioactive decay.

The fissioning of just 1 gram of uranium-235 produces as much heat as the burning of 2 million grams (or 13.7 barrels) of oil. This vast difference in energy content means that nuclear energy is essentially limitless, even though it comes from a nonrenewable resource. In principle, it would also be possible to extract energy from the process of **fusion**, in which two atomic nuclei are forced to combine. Fusion occurs naturally in the core of the Sun, at extremely high temperatures and pressures; so far, experiments to duplicate the process in more ordinary conditions have been only partially successful.

Another source of useful power is **geothermal energy**,

geothermal energy Energy from Earth's interior.

which comes from Earth's interior. Geothermal energy is produced by the radioactive decay of uranium, thorium, and other radioactive isotopes, as well as the slow escape of heat from Earth's core. As explained in Chapters 4 and 6, this is the energy source that powers plate tectonics and volcanic eruptions. It has been utilized for heat and power generation in locations where it is easily tapped, including New Zealand, Italy, Iceland, and the United States.

Traditional geothermal energy comes from **hydrothermal reservoirs**, underground systems of hot water or steam that circulate in fractured or porous rock. To be used efficiently, hydrothermal reservoirs should be 200°C or hotter, and this temperature must be reached within 3 kilometers of the surface. Therefore, most of the world's hydrothermal reservoirs are close to the margins of tectonic plates, where hot rock or magma can be found close to the surface. The Geysers geothermal installation in northern California—the largest producer of geothermal power in the world—is a hydrothermal reservoir system.

New approaches to the use of geothermal energy involve taking advantage of the temperature difference between the surface and the subsurface. In winter conditions, the ground surface is much colder than the subsurface, which is insulated from seasonal temperature changes; in summer, the reverse is true. Making use of this temperature differential, **ground-source heat pumps** can extract energy quite efficiently and are now being used for space heating and cooling, district heating and cooling, and water heating.

 CONCEPT CHECK

> 1. What is the ultimate source of energy in wind and waves?
> 2. What are some of the environmental drawbacks to nuclear power?

MINERAL RESOURCES

Learning Objectives

1. **Summarize** some of the important ways that new mineral resources can be identified.

2. **Identify** six ways in which mineral deposits are formed.

3. **Describe** the connection between plate tectonics and the locations of mineral deposits.

4. **Discuss** the potential for global depletion of resources.

The number and diversity of minerals and rocks that provide materials used by humans is so great as to defy attempts to organize them conveniently. Nearly every kind of rock and mineral can be used for something (**Figure 16.18**); however, we only mine about 200 different minerals and about a dozen types of rock. Mineral resources that are most valuable also tend to be rare. **Metallic mineral resources** are mined specifically for the metals that can be extracted from them. Examples are zinc, a valuable plating metal, extracted from the mineral sphalerite (ZnS), and lead, used in

metallic mineral resources Deposits that are mined specifically for the extraction of metals.

What Should Be Done with Nuclear Waste?

Approximately 17% of the world's electricity is derived from nuclear power. In several European countries, the production of nuclear power is rising rapidly because these countries have very limited fossil fuel supplies. The nuclear industry has been dogged by concerns about safety. Two accidents in particular have raised concernc. First, in

April 1986, a meltdown occurred in a reactor at Chernobyl, Ukraine, killing about 50 people and releasing radioactivity over a wide area. Second, on March 11, 2011, a 9.0 earthquake near Tohoku, Japan, caused a tsunami that crippled the Fukushima Daiichi plant, damaging three reactors, and causing causing explosions and radioactive emissions.

◀ **A tremendous source of energy?**
In a chain reaction, a neutron strikes a uranium nucleus and causes it to split into smaller nuclei. The process releases two more neutrons, which can go on to collide with more uranium nuclei. Each time a uranium nucleus splits, it releases heat. An atomic power plant uses that heat to generate steam, which turns turbines that generate electricity.

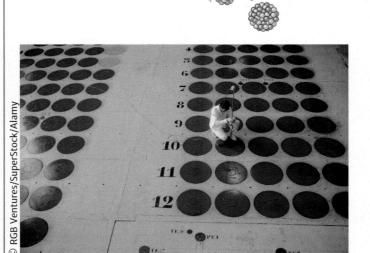

Smaller nucleus

Other particles and energy

Neutron

^{235}U ^{235}U ^{235}U

Smaller nucleus

© RGB Ventures/SuperStock/Alamy

David Howells/Corbis Images

▲ In the United States, nuclear waste is presently stored at 125 temporary sites in 39 states. No permanent storage site has been built. In 2002, the U.S. government designated Yucca Mountain in Nevada, shown here, as a permanent storage site. However, in 2011 the funding was terminated, effectively closing the site. The reason for closure, according to the Government Accounting Office, was for political, not technical or safety reasons.

▲ **. . . Or a tremendous source of toxic waste?**
Nuclear reactors produce radioactive waste that must be isolated from human contact for thousands of years. Here, a technician uses a radiation detector at a waste storage site in France where reprocessed waste from 10 reactors is stored for five years before final disposal.

THINK CRITICALLY

What specific characteristics would you look for in a permanent nuclear waste repository site? Think about the geological characteristics of the site, as well as geographical, biological, and technological factors.

Some mineral products used in everyday life • Figure 16.18

We rely on mineral resources, both metallic and nonmetallic, and every aspects of our daily lives in modern society.

Sand, gravel, stone, brick (clay), cement, steel, tar (asphalt); silica (for glass)

Iron and steel, copper, lead, tin, cement, asbestos, glass, tile (clay), oil (for plastic)

Mineral pigments (e.g., iron, zinc, titanium), and fillers (e.g., talc, mica, asbestos)

Iron, copper, many rare metals; silica (for glass); clay (for ceramic)

Mineral fertilizers; processed, packaged, and delivered by machines made of metal

> **nonmetallic mineral resources** Deposits that are mined for the properties of the minerals they contain, rather than for metals that could be extracted.

automobile batteries, extracted from the mineral galena (PbS). **Nonmetallic mineral resources** are mined for their properties as minerals, not for the metals they contain. Examples are salt, gypsum, and clay.

The branch of geology that is concerned with discovering new supplies of useful minerals is **economic geology**. Economic geologists, with specialists from a variety of subdisciplines such as exploration geology, geochemistry, and structural geology, seek mineral deposits from which the

> **ore** A deposit from which one or more minerals can be extracted profitably.

desired minerals can be recovered least expensively. To distinguish between profitable and unprofitable deposits, we use the word **ore**. The difference

depends on the extraction cost of the mineral and how much people are prepared to pay for it. A formerly unprofitable deposit may become a profitable ore if extraction technology improves, new uses are identified for the mineral, or the mineral becomes scarce enough that the price increases.

Looking for Mineral Resources

Mineral resources are nonrenewable and can be exhausted through mining. Economically exploitable minerals are localized in distinct areas within Earth's crust, as a result of plate tectonic processes (**Figure 16.19**). The uneven distribution of exploitable deposits means that no nation is self-sufficient in mineral supplies. For example, the United States has little or no aluminum, manganese, nickel, or chromium and must import most of what is used.

Because minerals are nonrenewable, countries that can meet their needs for a given mineral today may not

World map of mineral resources • Figure 16.19

Mineral deposits occur throughout the world, but no single country is entirely mineral self-sufficient. Even mineral-rich nations like the United States and Canada must depend on tiny Jamaica for aluminum to feed their smelting industries.

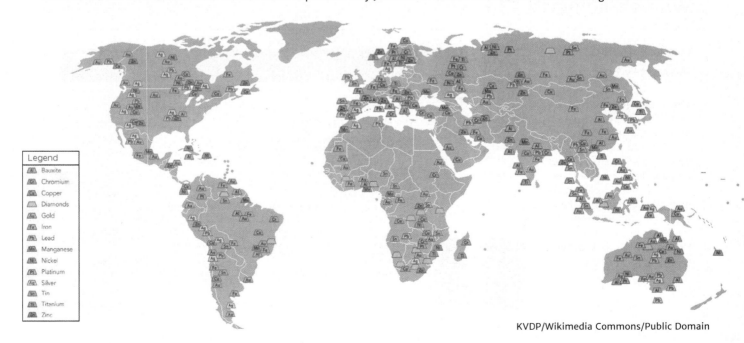

Legend
- Bauxite
- Chromium
- Copper
- Diamonds
- Gold
- Iron
- Lead
- Manganese
- Nickel
- Platinum
- Silver
- Tin
- Titanium
- Zinc

KVDP/Wikimedia Commons/Public Domain

be able to do so in the future. An example is England, one of the first industrialized nations. During the 19th century, England was a great mining nation, producing and exporting such materials as tin, copper, tungsten, lead, and iron. Today, the known deposits of those minerals have been exhausted. The pattern followed by England—intensive mining followed by depletion of the resource, declining production and exports, and increasing dependence on imports—has been repeated often enough that geologists can estimate the remaining effective-lifetime of a given mine or mineral resource. Such projections are necessarily tentative; it is especially difficult to anticipate whether new deposits will be discovered.

Over the past few decades, there has been a shift of mineral exploration and production away from industrialized nations and toward the less developed parts of the world. This shift will undoubtedly continue; as you can see in Figure 16.19, there are many nations of the world whose mineral resources are relatively unexploited. This doesn't mean that there are no more mineral deposits to be found in industrialized countries, but geologists will have to develop new exploration techniques. When new deposits are found, they will have to be exploited with minimal environmental degradation.

The Formation of Mineral Deposits

Minerals can become concentrated into locally enriched deposits as a result of igneous, metamorphic, and sedimentary processes and various combinations of these processes. Some of the most important ore-forming processes are illustrated in **Figure 16.20**. Extensive information is available online concerning the status of mineral resources and exploration; one comprehensive source is the U.S. Geological Survey's Mineral Resources Program (see *Where Geologists Click*).

Hydrothermal Deposits   Hydrothermal mineral deposits are formed when minerals precipitate from hot water solutions that carry dissolved loads of soluble materials, usually including a variety of metals. These **hydrothermal solutions** frequently deposit their mineral loads in cracks in the rock, creating mineral veins like the one in Figure 16.20a. Such mineral deposits usually contain many different ores. For example, 90% of the silver produced in the United States is a by-product of copper mined from hydrothermal deposits. In many cases, the ore mineral is not visible to the naked eye.

In recent years, geologists have gotten a chance to see hydrothermal deposits forming right before their eyes in three distinct locations: a desert valley, a shallow sea, and a midoceanic rift zone (see *What a Geologist Sees*, p. 468). The valuable minerals that are deposited by heated solutions on the seafloor are interlaid with and conformable with seafloor sedimentary strata, but they are technically deposited by hydrothermal processes rather than by sedimentary processes. They are called **stratiform deposits** to illustrate this distinction; these deposits are *like* sedimentary strata in some ways, but they are not formed by sedimentary processes.

Metamorphic and Metasomatic Deposits   Both contact metamorphism and regional metamorphism (Chapter 10) can give rise to concentrations of minerals

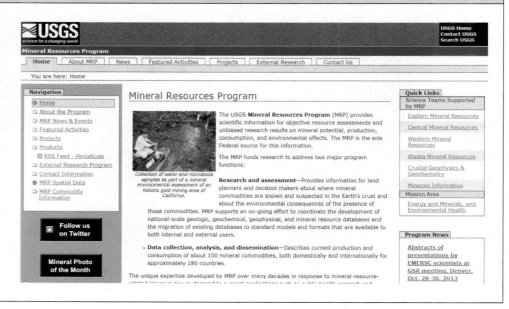

Where Geologists CLICK

USGS Mineral Resources Program

The U.S. Geological Survey Mineral Resources Program provides scientific information needed to assess the quality and availability of mineral resources, as well as carrying out research on mineral production, consumption, and environmental impacts—not just in the United States but around the world.

in economically valuable deposits. Recrystallization and the large grain sizes associated with high-grade regional metamorphism provide one mechanism by which metamorphism can concentrate materials. The famous garnet deposits of the Adirondacks in New York, with individual crystals the size of a fist and larger, are one example of an ore deposit hosted by high-grade, regionally metamorphosed rock.

Contact metamorphism, and particularly the fluids expelled during metasomatism, also can lead to the redistribution and concentration of materials into economically valuable mineral deposits, as shown in Figure 16.20b. Hot metasomatic fluids pick up soluble materials from rock or magma, carry them away by percolation through the surrounding rock, and re-deposit them when different conditions of temperature or chemistry are encountered. In this way, metasomatic deposits and hydrothermal deposits can be closely related.

Magmatic Deposits

Igneous processes can lead indirectly to the formation of mineral deposits, by producing hot metasomatic and hydrothermal fluids that carry soluble materials out into the surrounding country rock. Igneous processes related to melting and crystallization also can lead more directly to the formation of mineral deposits. For example, fractional crystallization (Chapter 6) occurs during the solidification of a magma body, when minerals crystallize one at a time, in sequence, from the magma. In some circumstances, early-crystallizing minerals can become isolated from the remaining melt, usually by sinking, flotation, or filtering, and may thereby become concentrated in zones or layers. Commercially valuable ores that arise in magmatic deposits include chromium, which is used to make steel tougher, and titanium, a corrosion-resistant metal that is lighter and stronger than steel.

Sedimentary Deposits

Processes involved in the formation, transportation, and deposition of sediment can lead to the concentration of minerals in economically valuable deposits, through a variety of mechanisms.

Evaporites are one type of sedimentary mineral deposit (shown in Figure 16.20d). Evaporation is a form of chemical sedimentation, in which materials carried in solution are concentrated in a layer on the surface when a lake or shallow sea dries up. Probably the most well-known examples of evaporite deposits are halite (common salt), gypsum, and borax. Some evaporite deposits can be mined at the surface; in other cases, the deposits have been covered over by millennia of sedimentation and must be mined underground. Salt, as a rock, has a low specific gravity; this means that it is typically buoyant, relative to overlying rock units. The

buried layer of salt flows very slowly toward the surface, pushing up the overlying layers of rock to form a dome-shaped deposit. Salt domes are often associated with oil, because both materials are concentrated in shallow marine environments.

Placer deposits are formed by sedimentary processes related to erosion and deposition of sediment. Placers always consist of minerals that originated somewhere else and were transported from their original site by water. They are specifically associated with minerals that have a high specific gravity, such as gold and platinum. More than half of the gold recovered in human history has come from placers; some gemstones, like emeralds and diamonds, also can be concentrated in placer deposits. Placer ores accumulate in places such as sandbars (shown in Figure 16.20e), where flowing water slows down and loses its carrying power, depositing its sediment load (see *Remember This!*). The ore minerals become concentrated because they are heavier than surrounding minerals and sink to the bottom. Minerals can be separated and concentrated by density in any location where water has a winnowing effect on sediment, such as a beach with breaking waves; that's why you will typically find a black layer if you dig down into beach sand—it is a layer of the relatively heavy mineral magnetite, concentrated by the winnowing action of waves.

> **REMEMBER THIS!** Where does flowing water slow down, lose energy, and deposit its load? A review of *How Water Affects the Land* in Chapter 11 will tell you where to look for placer deposits.

Our final type of sedimentary mineral deposit, a **residual deposit**, consists of minerals that are left behind and concentrated by chemical weathering of a host rock (see Chapter 7). Rainwater that infiltrates the ground picks up soluble substances and carries them downward as it flows through the aerated zone. This process, called **leaching**, is a normal part of the formation of soil horizons. It leaves behind zones or layers that are depleted in soluble materials. Upon reaching the saturated zone, conditions of temperature, chemistry, and pH may change dramatically, and materials carried in solution may be precipitated in a zone of enrichment. Metals or other valuable materials that were dissolved in the solution may be enriched in this way—often just above or below the water table or wherever the ground chemistry undergoes a distinct change (as shown in Figure 16.20f). The most well-known ore that forms as a residual deposit is bauxite, the main source for aluminum.

Mineral deposits can form in many ways. They are classified by the processes by which the ore minerals are concentrated.

Courtesy Brian J. Skinner

a. Hydrothermal Delicate sheets of native gold were deposited in the center of a quartz vein, at Burgin Hill Mine, California, when heated fluids circulated into a cooler region and the metals came out of solution.

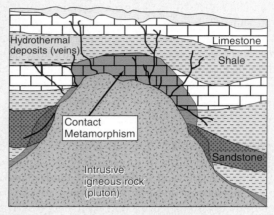

Hydrothermal deposits (veins)
Limestone
Shale
Contact Metamorphism
Sandstone
Intrusive igneous rock (pluton)

Magma chambers are a common source for heat and hot fluids that can lead to the formation of hydrothermal and metasomatic ore deposits. Hot fluids can alter rock by contact metamorphism and metasomatism, concentrating minerals in distinct zones.

William Sacco

b. Metamorphic This rock is from a metamorphic mineral deposit at the Tempiute Mine in Arizona. The ore minerals are sphalerite (brown, lower left), pyrite (gold colored), and scheelite (pale grayish brown, lower right), a tungsten mineral.

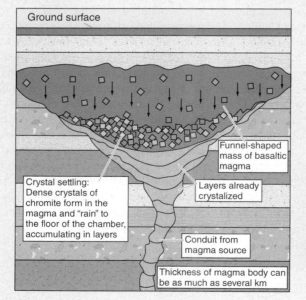

Ground surface

Crystal settling: Dense crystals of chromite form in the magma and "rain" to the floor of the chamber, accumulating in layers

Funnel-shaped mass of basaltic magma

Layers already crystalized

Conduit from magma source

Thickness of magma body can be as much as several km

Courtesy Brian J. Skinner

c. Magmatic Fractional crystallization in magma can concentrate minerals. In this outcrop at Dwars River in South Africa, layers of pure chromite (black), the main ore mineral for chromium, used in steel production, are sandwiched by layers of plagioclase feldspar.

Chromite crystallizes first in the fractional crystallization of basaltic magma. Chromite crystals are denser than the magma, so they may sink to the bottom and accumulate in an almost pure layer.

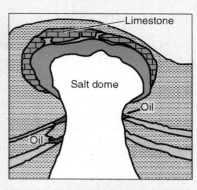

Salt is a low-density rock. If a salt layer becomes buried under sedimentary strata, it will slowly flow upward as a consequence of its own buoyancy relative to the overlying rock. This is why underground salt deposits typically occur in the form of domes.

▲ **d. Sedimentary** Evaporite deposits, such as this salt pan in Death Valley, California, form when lake water or seawater evaporates, leaving behind its dissolved material. Household products such as baking soda and borax come from lake evaporites. Death Valley itself was briefly mined for borax from 1883 to 1888.

THINK CRITICALLY

Which of these types of mineral deposits would be influenced by climatic processes during formation? Which ones are formed deep underground, where they are isolated from the influence of climate?

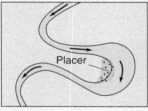
Inside meander loops

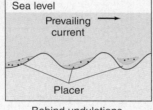
Behind undulations on ocean floor

Dense ore minerals, such as gold, platinum, and diamond, accumulate in locations where sediment is deposited by moving water, typically where the flow energy decreases suddenly.

▲ **e. Placer** The world's richest-known gold deposit, in Witwatersrand, South Africa, is a placer deposit that was formed about 2.7 billion years ago. The layer of conglomerate under the hammer was once a loose layer of pebbles that was washed downstream, along with the gold it contains, from a source vein that has never been found.

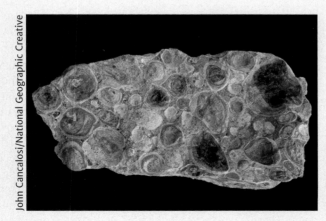

▲ **f. Residual** In this bauxite, a residual ore sample from Queensland, Australia, rounded masses of aluminum hydroxide (gibbsite) are embedded in a matrix of iron and aluminum hydroxides.

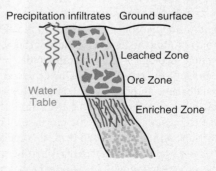

Chemical weathering of rock can concentrate insoluble minerals in residual deposits by dissolving and carrying away the more soluble materials, re-depositing and concentrating them elsewhere.

Observing the Formation of Hydrothermal Mineral Deposits

For many years, geologists speculated about how hydro-thermal mineral deposits might have formed; then three discoveries changed everyone's ideas. First, in 1962, oil prospectors in the Imperial Valley of southern California, unexpectedly tapped into superheated (320°C) brine at a depth of 1.5 kilometers **Figure a**).

Geologists noticed that as the brine flowed upward, it cooled and deposited minerals it had been carrying in solu-tion. Over a period of three months, more than 1.5 tons of copper minerals and half a ton of silver minerals were deposited in this manner. Geologists quickly realized that the same process could happen naturally under the right circumstances, confirming the long-held hypothesis that hydrothermal deposits are formed by deposition from hot brines.

Two years later, in 1964, oceanographers found a series of hot, dense brine pools at the bottom of the Red Sea (**Figure b**). Like the Imperial Valley brine, this water is trapped in a graben, formed in this case over the spreading center be-tween the African and Arabian plates. When geologists took samples from the bottom of the brine pools, they found metal-rich sediment that contained ore minerals with sig-nificant concentrations of silver, gold, cobalt, and other valuable materials. In other words, they found a stratiform mineral deposit of hydrothermal origin in the process of formation.

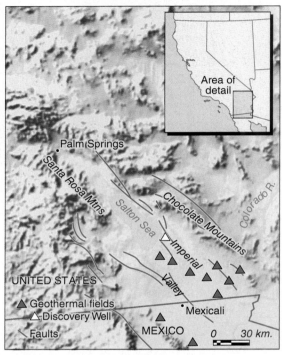

a

Plate Tectonic Controls on Ore Deposits

To a certain extent, the distribution of mineral resourc-es can be linked to specific tectonic environments. This permits economic geologists to identify locations where certain types of mineral deposits are most likely to be found (**Figure 16.21**). However, the correlation is not nearly as precise or as reliable as we would like, which is why we still need exploration geologists to go out to the sites.

Many kinds of mineral deposits occur in groups, forming what exploration geologists call **metallogenic provinces**. These are regions of the crust within which mineral deposits occur in unusually large numbers. Metallogenic provinces form as a result of either climatic (as in the formation of bauxite deposits in the tropics) or plate tectonic processes. For exam-ple, both magmatic and hydrothermal deposits typically form near present or past plate boundaries. This is hardly surprising, as the deposits are related directly or indirectly to igneous ac-tivity, and most igneous activity is related to plate tectonics.

Likewise, some energy resources are concentrated in particular tectonic environments. Geothermal energy is closely related to active plate boundaries and other locations where heat flow is high. Fossil fuels occur in environments where organic-rich sediments accumulated long ago—for-mer terrestrial swamp environments for peat and coal, and former marine sedimentary basins for oil and natural gas.

Will We Run Out?

Are there enough mineral and energy resources available on this planet to raise the living standards of all people to the levels they desire? The answer to this question is not clear. Many geologists are concerned that shortages of non-renewable resources will eventually hamper development. Unfortunately, there is no sure way to know exactly how much of any mineral or energy resource remains to be found.

At present, it appears that shortages of energy resources are more likely to affect us in the short run than are shortag-es of metallic minerals. The production of both energy and mineral resources impacts local geology and the environ-ment. These changes to land, water, and often atmosphere are all too often in the form of pollution or ecological deg-radation. These negative aspects of resource production can be minimized but not entirely eliminated; there are already cases in which rich deposits have been left alone because

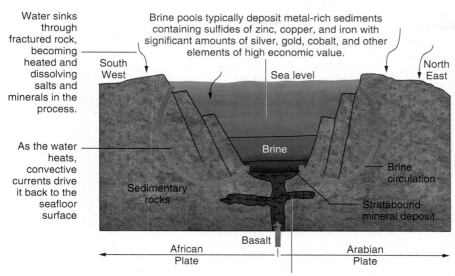

Water sinks through fractured rock, becoming heated and dissolving salts and minerals in the process.

Brine pools typically deposit metal-rich sediments containing sulfides of zinc, copper, and iron with significant amounts of silver, gold, cobalt, and other elements of high economic value.

South West

Sea level

North East

As the water heats, convective currents drive it back to the seafloor surface

Brine

Brine circulation

Sedimentary rocks

Stratabound mineral deposit

Basalt

African Plate

Arabian Plate

The hot, dense brine forms a stratified layer at the base of the seawater column.

b

Image courtesy of UCSB, Univ. S.Carolina, NOAA

c

Finally, in 1978, geologists in deep-diving submarines discovered 320°C hot springs emerging from the ocean floor in a "black smoker" vents at a midocean ridge in the Pacific (**Figure c**). Around the hot springs lay a blanket of sulfide minerals. Again, they had found a modern hydrothermal ore deposit forming before their eyes. Today we refer to these submarine hydrothermal deposits as massive sulfide deposits.

THINK CRITICALLY

In what other modern geological environments are ore deposits of different types currently being formed?

Plate tectonics and minerals • Figure 16.21

Many materials are concentrated in particular plate tectonic settings. Try to identify the ore-concentrating processes that are occurring in each of the tectonic settings illustrated here.

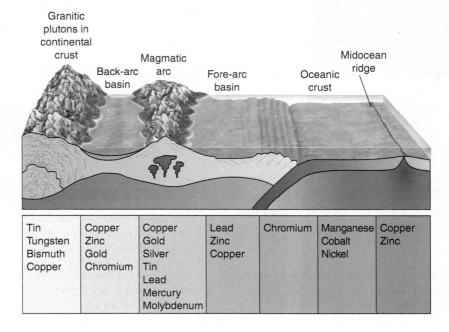

Granitic plutons in continental crust

Back-arc basin

Magmatic arc

Fore-arc basin

Oceanic crust

Midocean ridge

Tin Tungsten Bismuth Copper	Copper Zinc Gold Chromium	Copper Gold Silver Tin Lead Mercury Molybdenum	Lead Zinc Copper	Chromium	Manganese Cobalt Nickel	Copper Zinc

mining would cause unacceptable environmental degradation. What effect these kinds of concerns will have on the long-term supplies of resources remains to be seen.

Throughout the history of energy and mineral exploration, geologists have continually refined and improved the techniques used to locate new deposits, and engineers have refined and improved production techniques. Much ingenuity has been expended in bringing mineral and energy resource production to their present state. By a combination of new discoveries by geologists, new extraction and processing technologies, and careful use and conservation practices, it is likely that Earth's mineral and energy resources can be extended far into the 21st century. However, in the deep future—by the end of the 21st century and beyond—our descendants may face some very difficult choices, as the Easter Islanders did in the 1500s. At the very least, they will have to manage Earth's resources very differently from how we and our predecessors have managed them.

STOP CONCEPT CHECK

1. **What** are some of the approaches that economic geologists use to locate new mineral deposits?

2. **How** are hydrothermal, metasomatic, and magmatic mineral deposits similar and how are they different?

3. **What** is a natural tectonic setting for magmatic mineral deposits?

4. **Which** type of Earth resource, in general, is in more critically short supply at the moment: mineral resources or energy resources?

SUMMARY

✓ THE PLANNER

1 Renewable and Nonrenewable Resources 447

- **Natural resources** can be either **renewable** or **nonrenewable**. Biological resources are mostly renewable, whereas Earth's resources, particularly minerals and fossil fuels, are mostly nonrenewable (see photo). A resource such as soil or groundwater is considered nonrenewable if it cannot be replenished on the scale of a human lifetime.

How much energy do we use? • Figure 16.3

Michael Nichols/NG Image Collection

- Past civilizations have gone through major upheavals when they ran out of a nonrenewable resource. The most likely shortages to face our civilization in the near future are shortages of energy resources.

2 Fossil Fuels 450

- Currently, most of the world's energy needs are met by **fossil fuels**, which are nonrenewable resources. These resources form over the course of millions of years through the burial and chemical alteration of animal and plant remains.

- The major types of fossil fuel are **peat**, **coal**, **petroleum**, and **natural gas**. Peat and coal are formed through the compression and heating of land plants in swampy or boggy conditions, with higher grades of coal being formed by deeper burial. Although peat swamps continue to exist today, the most prolific periods for the production of peat were the Carboniferous and Permian periods, when warm and moist conditions prevailed over most of Europe and North America.

- Petroleum and natural gas are formed by the compression and heating of the remains of marine organisms. They are volatile materials and will escape to the atmosphere, if not held underground by a petroleum trap like the one shown in the figure. Petroleum consists of a variety of hydrocarbon molecules, which contain hydrogen and carbon but no oxygen. The **oil** component of petroleum can be refined into gasoline or kerosene, and it is also the raw material for plastics. Molecules with more carbon atoms tend to be heavier, less volatile, and more useful as lubricants, while the molecules with fewer carbon atoms (including natural gas) are lighter and more useful as fuel.

Traps for oil and gas • Figure 16.11

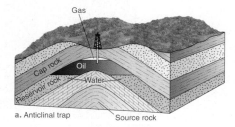

a. Anticlinal trap

- Nonconventional sources of oil include **tar sand**, which is already economically important in Canada, and **oil shale**. These require more intensive processing to yield their oil, including **fracking**, but the deposits are so vast that they may become economically important in the future as the price of conventional oil rises.

3 Renewable Energy Resources 458

- By far the greatest source of energy available at Earth's surface comes from solar radiation. However, humans are so far able to capture only a minuscule fraction of that energy. Direct **solar energy** remains too expensive for electric generation in most places, although it is well suited for heating.

- **Wind energy** and **biomass energy** can be considered indirect versions of solar energy. They are renewable, but at present they provide only a small fraction of our energy. Biomass (primarily wood) was the world's leading source of energy until the late 1800s, when it was replaced by coal; it is reemerging now as a source of power, through new biofuels.

- **Hydroelectric energy**, derived from running water, is a proven energy source in North America. It is not capable of significant further growth. Hydroelectric energy is generated when water flows over a dam and drives the turbines of a power station.

- **Nuclear energy**, provided by the radioactive decay of uranium as shown in the diagram, is virtually limitless and probably the only resource that could in theory replace fossil fuels. In Japan and certain European countries, it is already a major and growing source of energy. However, in North America it faces a serious waste disposal problem and public fears about its safety.

Chain reaction · Case Study

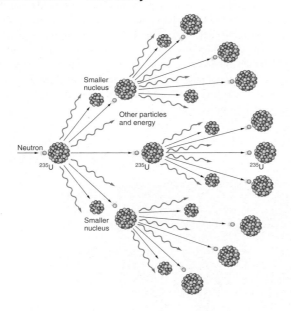

- **Geothermal energy**, powered by the heat radiating from magma chambers and recently solidified volcanic rock, is plentiful in certain locations near tectonic plate boundaries. More recently, ground-source heat pumps have allowed for the simple exploitation of the temperature difference between the surface and subsurface, in most locations, for the extraction of useful power.

4 Mineral Resources 461

- Economic geologists search for new mineral deposits and assess how long they are likely to last. Not all mineral deposits can be mined profitably; those that can are called **ores**. About 200 minerals are mined in the world today. **Nonmetallic mineral resources** are as critical for modern life and technology as are **metallic mineral resources**.

- Mineral deposits form when natural processes concentrate a valuable material in one location. Hydrothermal deposits occur when superheated water cools rapidly and dissolved minerals precipitate from it. Metamorphic and metasomatic deposits occur as a result of regional or contact metamorphism. Magmatic deposits can result from crystallization. Sedimentary deposits include the salts left behind by evaporating water from a lake or shallow sea. Placer deposits form when mineral-bearing rock is eroded, transported, and deposited by water, as shown in the diagram. Residual deposits consist of materials that are carried and re-deposited by percolating rainwater during chemical weathering.

How minerals are formed: Placer deposits · Figure 16.20

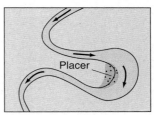

Inside meander loops

- The locations of many ore-forming processes are controlled by plate tectonics. An understanding of an area's geological history can guide economic geologists to promising locations. For example, magmatic mineral deposits are most likely to be found near present or former plate boundaries, and oil and gas are typically found in former marine sedimentary basins.

- New discoveries and new technologies can prolong to some extent our supply of nonrenewable resources. However, in the long run, society must confront the challenge of managing Earth's finite resources.

KEY TERMS

biomass energy   458

coal   451

fossil fuel   450

fracking   455

geothermal energy   461

hydroelectric energy   460

metallic mineral resources   461

natural gas   453

natural resource   447

nonmetallic mineral resources   463

nonrenewable resource   448

nuclear energy   460

oil   453

oil shale   455

ore   463

peat   450

petroleum   453

petroleum trap   455

renewable resource   448

solar energy   458

tar sand   455

wind energy   459

CRITICAL AND CREATIVE THINKING QUESTIONS

1. Investigate how geophysicist M. King Hubbert predicted in 1956 that annual oil production would peak in the early 1970s (the actual peak in the U.S. occurred in 1971). Also, investigate the debate over whether the same predictive technique can be applied to world oil supplies. When do you think world oil production will reach its peak? Or has it done so already?

2. Many hydrothermal mineral deposits of copper, gold, silver, and other metals have been found in the countries bordering the Pacific Ocean. Can you offer an explanation for this remarkable concentration? If you were part of a team of exploration geologists looking for large copper deposits, where would you focus your search?

3. Given that we are now dependent on nonrenewable resources of energy and minerals and that the world's population continues to increase, how do you think human societies will adjust in the future? Do we have a resource problem or a population problem (or both)?

4. Some people think that sustainable development is not a useful concept because it may be impossible to implement—or even to define—in the case of nonrenewable resources. Others think that it is an extremely important concept, if only because it makes us think about the needs of future generations in planning resource management. What do you think?

5. Smelting, refining, and processing plants are sometimes located near mineral deposits—but not always. For example, there are many aluminum smelting plants in Canada and the United States, even though there are almost no significant Al deposits in these countries. Why is it worthwhile for Canada and the United States to have aluminum smelting plants, even if they have no Al deposits? Can you find other examples of mineral deposits shown on this map, in countries that don't carry out very much mineral processing? What are some of the economic, political, geological, social, and geographical circumstances that would lead countries to produce minerals that must be exported for processing?

World map of mineral resources • Figure 16.19

KVDP/Wikimedia Commons/Public Domain

WHAT IS HAPPENING IN THIS PICTURE?

An abandoned salt mine in Germany, which lies 1 kilometer underground, has become a repository for the casks of spent nuclear fuel shown in this picture.

Emory Kristof/NG Image Collection

THINK CRITICALLY

What are some of the characteristics that might make an old salt mine a good place to store nuclear waste?

SELF-TEST

(Check your answers in Appendix D.)

1. Which of the following statements is incorrect?

   a. The depletion of natural resources apparently led to the collapse of some ancient civilizations.

   b. Nonrenewable resources are never replenished.

   c. Renewable resources must be managed so that they are not used at a rate that is greater than the rate of renewal or replenishment of the resource.

   d. Groundwater is, in principle, a renewable resource, but once depleted, it may take a very long time to be replenished.

2. _____ is an example of a nonrenewable resource.

   a. Petroleum

   b. Wind power

   c. Tidal power

   d. Solar power

3. _____ is an example of a renewable resource.

   a. Hydroelectric power

   b. Nuclear power

   c. Coal

   d. Natural gas

4. This diagram shows the proportion of energy resources used in the United States today. The sources of energy have been listed for you. Label the right side of the graph to show lost and used energy. What are the three main categories for the used energy? What is the main form of the lost energy?

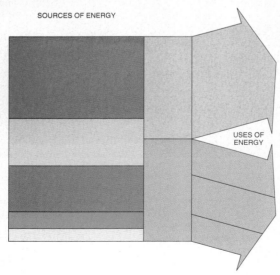

SOURCES OF ENERGY

USES OF ENERGY

5. _____ forms through the compression heating and lithification of plant-rich sediment.

   a. Petroleum

   b. Coal

   c. Biomass energy

   d. All of the above answers are correct.

6. _____ forms from the decomposition of ancient plankton buried in marine sediment.

   a. Petroleum

   b. Coal

   c. Biomass energy

   d. All of the above answers are correct

7. This diagram is a graph showing world energy consumption over time. Complete the graph by labeling the fields showing the proper distribution of types of energy consumed.

   oil   wood

   nuclear   hydroelectric

   coal   gas

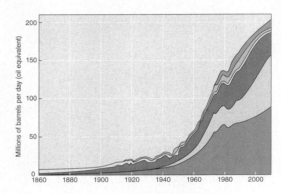

8. _____ is technically a nonrenewable resource, but the amount of energy available is so vast that it is, for all practical purposes, inexhaustible.

   a. Geothermal energy

   b. Nuclear power

   c. Biomass energy

   d. Solar power

   e. Wind energy

9. Which of the following renewable resources derives its energy from the Sun?

   a. wind energy

   b. wave energy

   c. biomass energy

   d. All of the above resources derive their energy from the Sun.

10. Why doesn't solar energy play a more significant role in the production of electricity?

    a. With even the most current solar photovoltaic technologies, it is still relatively costly to produce electricity.

    b. There is not enough energy in sunlight to help with our current levels of consumption.

    c. Current photovoltaic technologies do not allow for electricity production at high enough voltages.

    d. It can be challenging and costly to install solar technologies on existing buildings.

11. Which of the following statements about nuclear power is (are) correct?

a. Nuclear power is one of the few energy sources with the potential to completely replace fossil fuels.

b. Nuclear reactors generate waste that must be isolated from human contact for thousands of years.

c. Approximately 17% of the world's electricity is currently generated by nuclear power.

d. Nuclear power is generated through a controlled reaction of fission decay.

e. All of the above statements are correct.

12. _____ is the branch of geology that is concerned with discovering new supplies of useful minerals.

a. Geophysics

b. Environmental geology

c. Physical geology

d. Economic geology

e. Mineral geology

13. What is the difference between an ore and a mineral deposit?

a. There is no difference.

b. Ore deposits are mineral deposits that contain metals.

c. Ore deposits are mineral deposits that can be profitably mined.

d. Ore deposits are mineral deposits that have formed under high temperature.

14. _____ deposits are formed when minerals precipitate out of hot water solutions.

a. Hydrothermal

b. Metamorphic

c. Placer

d. Sedimentary

e. Magmatic

15. This diagram shows a cross section through Earth's crust across a number of tectonic settings. Draw an arrow from each of the metallic resources listed below to the location where it can be found.

copper   gold

manganese   chromium

lead

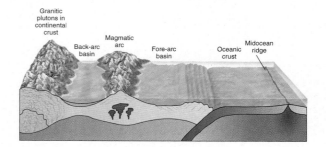

THE PLANNER ✓

Review the Chapter Planner on the chapter opener and check off your completed work.

Commonly Used Units of Measure

LENGTH

Metric Measure

1 kilometer (km)	= 1000 meters (m)
1 meter (m)	= 100 centimeters (cm)
1 centimeter (cm)	= 10 millimeters (mm)
1 millimeter (mm)	= 1000 micrometers (μm) (formerly called microns)
1 micrometer (μm)	= 0.001 millimeter (mm)
1 angstrom (Å)	= 10^{-8} centimeters (cm)

Nonmetric Measure

1 mile (mi)	= 5280 feet (ft) = 1760 yards (yd)
1 yard (yd)	= 3 feet (ft)
1 fathom (fath)	= 6 feet (ft)

Conversions

1 kilometer (km)	= 0.6214 mile (mi)
1 meter (m)	= 1.094 yards (yd)
	= 3.281 feet (ft)
1 centimeter (cm)	= 0.3937 inch (in)
1 millimeter (mm)	= 0.0394 inch (in)
1 mile (mi)	= 1.609 kilometers (km)
1 yard (yd)	= 0.9144 meter (m)
1 foot (ft)	= 0.3048 meter (m)
1 inch (in)	= 2.54 centimeters (cm)
1 inch (in)	= 25.4 millimeters (mm)
1 fathom (fath)	= 1.8288 meters (m)

AREA

Metric Measure

1 square kilometer (km²)	= 1,000,000 square meters (m²)
	= 100 hectares (ha)
1 square meter (m²)	= 10,000 square centimeters (cm²)
1 hectare (ha)	= 10,000 square meters (m²)

Nonmetric Measure

1 square mile (mi²)	= 640 acres (ac)
1 acre (ac)	= 4840 square yards (yd²)
1 square foot (ft²)	= 144 square inches (in²)

Conversions

1 square kilometer (km²)	= 0.386 square mile (mi²)
1 hectare (ha)	= 2.471 acres (ac)
1 square meter (m²)	= 1.196 square yards (yd²)
	= 10.764 square feet (ft²)
1 square centimeter (cm²)	= 0.155 square inch (in²)

1 square mile (mi²)	= 2.59 square kilometers (km²)
1 acre (ac)	= 0.4047 hectare (ha)
1 square yard (yd²)	= 0.836 square meter (m²)
1 square foot (ft²)	= 0.0929 square meter (m²)
1 square inch (in²)	= 6.4516 square centimeter (cm²)

VOLUME

Metric Measure

1 cubic meter (m³)	= 1,000,000 cubic centimeters (cm³)
1 liter (l)	= 1000 milliliters (ml)
	= 0.001 cubic meter (m³)
1 centiliter (cl)	= 10 milliliters (ml)
1 milliliter (ml)	= 1 cubic centimeter (cm³)

Nonmetric Measure

1 cubic yard (yd³)	= 27 cubic feet (ft³)
1 cubic foot (ft³)	= 1728 cubic inches (in³)
1 barrel (oil) (bbl)	= 42 gallons (U.S.) (gal)

Conversions

1 cubic kilometer (km³)	= 0.24 cubic miles (mi³)
1 cubic meter (m³)	= 264.2 gallons (U.S.) (gal)
	= 35.314 cubic feet (ft³)
1 liter (l)	= 1.057 quarts (U.S.) (qt)
	= 33.815 ounces (U.S. fluid) (fl. oz.)
1 cubic centimeter (cm³)	= 0.0610 cubic inch (in³)
1 cubic mile (mi³)	= 4.168 cubic kilometers (km³)
1 acre-foot (ac-ft)	= 1233.46 cubic meters (m³)
1 cubic yard (yd³)	= 0.7646 cubic meter (m³)
1 cubic foot (ft³)	= 0.0283 cubic meter (m³)
1 cubic inch (in³)	= 16.39 cubic centimeters (cm³)
1 gallon (gal)	= 3.784 liters (l)

MASS

Metric Measure

1000 kilograms (kg)	= 1 metric ton (also called a tonne) (m.t)
1 kilogram (kg)	= 1000 grams (g)

Nonmetric Measure

1 short ton (sh.t)	= 2000 pounds (lb)
1 long ton (l.t)	= 2240 pounds (lb)
1 pound (avoirdupois) (lb)	= 16 ounces (avoirdupois) (oz) = 7000 grains (gr)
1 ounce (avoirdupois) (oz)	= 437.5 grains (gr)

1 pound (Troy) (Tr. lb)	= 12 ounces (Troy) (Tr. oz)
1 ounce (Troy) (Tr. oz)	= 20 pennyweight (dwt)

Conversions

1 metric ton (m.t)	= 2205 pounds (avoirdupois) (lb)
1 kilogram (kg)	= 2.205 pounds (avoirdupois) (lb)
1 gram (g)	= 0.03527 ounce (avoirdupois) (oz) = 0.03215 ounce (Troy) (Tr. oz) = 15,432 grains (gr)
1 pound (lb)	= 0.4536 kilogram (kg)
1 ounce (avoirdupois) (oz)	= 28.35 grams (g)
1 ounce (avoirdupois) (oz)	= 1.097 ounces (Troy) (Tr. oz)

PRESSURE

Metric Measure

1 pascal (Pa)	= 1 newton/square meter (N/m^2)
1 kilogram-force square centimeter (kg/cm^2 or kgf/cm^2)	= 1 technical atmosphere (at) = 98,067 Pa = 0.98067 bar
1 bar	= 10^5 pascals (Pa) = 1.02 kilogram-force/ square centimeter (kgf/cm^2 or at)

Nonmetric Measure

1 atmosphere (atm)	= 1.01325 bar = 14.696 lb/in^2 (psi)
1 pound per square inch (lb/in^2 or psi)	= 68.046×10^{-3} atmospheres (atm)

Conversions

1 kilogram-force/ square centimeter (kgf/cm^2 or at)	= 0.96784 atmosphere (atm) = 14.2233 pounds/square inch (lb/in^2 or psi) = 0.98067 bar = 98,067 Pa
1 bar	= 0.98692 atmosphere (atm) = 10^5 pascals (Pa) = 1.02 kilogram-force/ square centimeter (kgf/cm^2)
1Pa = 10^{-5} bar	= 10.197×10^{-6} kgf/cm^2 (or at) = 9.8692×10^{-6} atm = 145.04×10^{-6} lb/in^2 (or psi)
1 atm	= 101,325 Pa 5 1.01325 bar

TEMPERATURE

Metric Measure

0 degrees Celcius (°C)	= freezing point of water at sea level
100 degrees Celcius (°C)	= boiling point of water at sea level
0 degrees Kelvin (K)	= −2273.15°C = absolute zero
1°C	= 1 K (temperature increments)
273.15K	= 0.0° C

Nonmetric Measure

Fahrenheit (°F)	= $(K \cdot 9/5) - 459.67$
Fahrenheit (°F)	= $(°C \cdot 9/5) + 32$

Conversions

degrees Kelvin (K)	= °C + 273.1
degrees Celcius (°C)	= K − 273.15
degrees Fahrenheit (°F)	= $(°C \cdot 9/5) + 32$
degrees Celcius (°C)	= $(°F − 32) \cdot 5/9$

Appendix B   Periodic Table of the Elements

The periodic table lists the known **chemical elements**, the basic units of matter. The elements in the table are arranged left-to-right in rows in order of their **atomic number**, the number of protons in the nucleus. Each horizontal row, numbered from 1 to 7, is a **period**. All elements in a given period have the same number of electron shells as their period number. For example, each atom of hydrogen or helium has one electron shell, while each atom of potassium or calcium has four electron shells. The elements in each column, or **group**, share chemical properties. For example, the elements in column IA are very chemically reactive, whereas the elements in column VIIIA have full electron shells and thus are chemically inert.

Scientists now recognize up to 118 different elements; 92 occur naturally on Earth, and the rest (with the exception of element 117) have been produced synthetically using particle accelerators. Elements are designated by **chemical symbols**, which are the first one or two letters of the element's name in English, Latin, or another language.

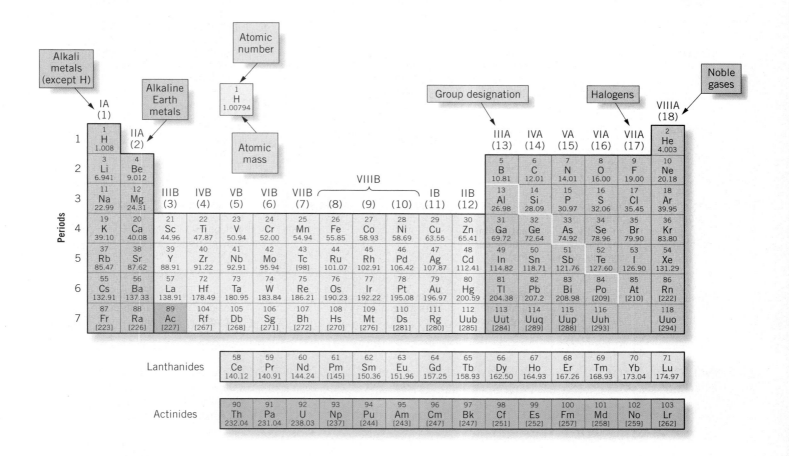

Properties of the common minerals with metallic luster Table C.1

Mineral	Chemical Composition	Form and Habit	Cleavage	Hardness	Specific Gravity	Other Properties	Most Distinctive Properties
Chalcopyrite	CuFeS$_2$	Massive or granular.	None. Uneven fracture.	3.5−4	4.2	Golden yellow to brassy yellow. Dark green to black streak.	Streak. Hardness distinguishes from pyrite.
Copper	Cu	Massive, twisted leaves and wires.	None. Can be cut with a knife.	2.5−3	9	Copper color but commonly stained green.	Color, specific gravity, malleable.
Galena	PbS	Cubic crystals, coarse or fine-grained granular masses.	Perfect in three directions at right angles.	2.5	7.6	Lead-gray color. Gray to gray-black streak.	Cleavage and streak.
Hematite	Fe$_2$O$_3$	Massive granular, micaceous.	Uneven fracture.	5−6	5	Reddish-brown, gray to black. Reddish-brown streak.	Streak, hardness.
Limonite (*Goethite* is most common.)	A complex mixture of minerals, mainly hydrous iron oxides.	Massive, coatings, botryoidal crusts, earthy masses.	None.	1−5.5	3.5−4	Yellow, brown, black, yellowish-brown streak.	Streak.
Magnetite	Fe$_3$O$_4$	Massive, granular. Crystals have octahedral shape.	None. Uneven fracture.	5.5−6.5	5	Black. Black streak. Strongly attracted to a magnet.	Streak, magnetism.
Pyrite ("Fool's gold")	FeS$_2$	Cubic crystals with striated faces. Massive.	None. Uneven fracture.	6−6.5	5.2	Pale brass-yellow, darker if tarnisned. Greenish-black streak.	Streak. Hardness distinguishes from chalcopyrite. Not malleable, which distinguishes from gold.
Sphalerite	ZnS	Fine to coarse granular masses. Tetrahedron shaped crystals.	Perfect in six directions.	3.5−4	4	Yellowish-brown to black. White to yellowish-brown streak. Resinous luster.	Cleavage, hardness, luster.

Properties of rock-forming minerals with nonmetallic luster Table C.2

Mineral	Chemical Composition	Form and Habit	Cleavage	Hardness	Specific Gravity	Other Properties	Most Distinctive Properties
Amphiboles. (A complex family of minerals, *Hornblende* is most common.)	$X_2Y_5SigO_{22}(OH)_2$ where $X = Ca, Na;$ $Y = Mg, Fe, Al.$	Long, six-sided crystals; also fibers and irregular grains.	Two; intersecting at 56° and 124°	5–6	2.9–3.8	Common in metamorphic and igneous rocks. *Hornblende* is dark green to black; *actinolite*, green; *tremolite*, white.	Cleavage, habit.
Apatite	$Ca_5(PO_4)_3$ (F, OH, Cl)	Granular masses. Perfect six-sided crystals.	Poor. One direction.	5	3.2	Green, brown, blue, or white. Common in many kinds of rocks in small amounts.	Hardness, form.
Aragonite	$CaCO_3$	Massive, or slender, needle-like crystals.	Poor. Two directions.	3.5	2.9	Colorless or white. Effervesces with dilute HCl.	Effervescence with acid. Poor cleavage distinguishes from calcite.
Calcite	$CaCO_3$	Tapering crystals and granular masses.	Three perfect; at oblique angles to give a rhomb-shaped fragment.	3	2.7	Colorless or white. Effervesces with dilute HCl.	Cleavage, effervescence with acid.
Dolomite	$CaMg(CO_3)_2$	Crystals with rhomb-shaped faces. Granular masses.	Perfect in three directions as in calcite.	3.5	2.8	White or gray. Does not effervesce in cold, dilute HCl unless powdered. Pearly luster.	Cleavage. Lack of effervescence with acid.
Feldspars: Potassium feldspar (*orthoclase* is a common variety)	$KAlSi_3O_8$	Prism-shaped crystals, granular masses.	Two perfect, at right angles.	6	2.6	Common mineral. Pink, white, or gray in color.	Color, cleavage.
Garnets	$X_3Y_2(SiO_4)_3;$ $X = Ca, Mg,$ $Fe, Mn; Y =$ $Al, Fe, Ti, Cr.$	Perfect crystals with 12 or 24 sides. Granular masses.	None. Uneven fracture.	6.5–7.5	3.5–4.3	Common in metamorphic rocks. Red, brown, yellowish-green, black.	Crystals, hardness, no cleavage.

Appendix C   Tables of the Properties of Selected Common Minerals

Table C.2 (continued)

Mineral	Chemical Composition	Form and Habit	Cleavage	Hardness / Specific Gravity		Other Properties	Most Distinctive Properties
Graphite	C	Scaly masses.	One, perfect. Forms slippery flakes.	1–2	2.2	Metamorphic rocks. Black with metallic to dull luster.	Cleavage, color. Marks paper.
Gypsum	$CaSO_4 \cdot 2H_2O$	Elongate or tabular crystals. Fibrous and earthy masses.	One, perfect. Flakes bend but are not elastic.	2	2.3	Vitreous to pearly luster. Colorless.	Hardness, cleavage.
Halite	NaCl	Cubic crystals.	Perfect to give cubes.	2.5	2.2	Tastes salty. Colorless, blue.	Taste, cleavage.
Kaolinite	$Al_2Si_2O_5 (OH)_4$	Soft, earthy masses. Submicroscopic crystals.	One, perfect.	2–2.5	2.6	White, yellowish. Plastic when wet; emits clayey odor. Dull luster.	Feel, plasticity, odor.
Mica: *Biotite*	$K(Mg, Fe)_3 AlSi_3O_{10} (OH)_2$	Irregular masses of flakes.	One, perfect.	2.5–3	2.8–3.2	Common in igneous and metamorphic rocks. Black, brown, darkgreen.	Cleavage, color. Flakes are elastic.
Mica: *Muscovite*	$KAl_3Si_3O_{10} (OH)_2$	Thin flakes.	One, perfect.	2–2.5	2.7	Common in igneous, and metamorphic rocks. Colorless, pale-green or brown	Cleavage, color. Flakes are elastic.
Olivine	$(Mg,Fe)_2 SiO4$	Small grains. granular masses.	None Conchoidal fracture.	6.5–7	3.2–4.3	Igneous rocks. Olive green to yellowish-green.	Color, fracture, habit.
Pyroxene (A complex family of minerals. *Augite* is most common.)	$XY(SiO_3)_2$ X = Y = Ca, Mg, Fe	8-sided stubby crystals. Granular masses.	Two, perfect, nearly at right angles.	5–6	3.2–3.9	Igneous and metamorphic rocks. *Augite*, dark green to black; other varieties white to green.	Cleavage
Quartz	SiO_2	6-sided crystals, granular masses.	None. Conchoidal fracture.	7	2.6	Colorless, white, gray, but may have any color, depending on impurities Vitreous to greasy luster.	Form, fracture, striation across crystal faces at right angles to long dimension.

Appendix D Self-Test Answers

CHAPTER 1

1 (b), 2 (c), 3 (b), 4 (d), 5 (b), 6 (b), 7 (a), 8 (d), 9 (d), 10 (c), 11 (b), 12 (c), 13 (a), 14 (b), 15 (d).

CHAPTER 2

1 (d), 2 (see Fig. 2.1), 3 (b), 4 (c), 5 (e), 6 (a), 7 (b), 8 (a), 9 (c), 10 (e), 11 (b), 12 (a), 13 (see Fig. 2.14), 14 (c), 15 (b).

CHAPTER 3

1 (a), 2 (c), 3 (c), 4 (c), 5 (c), 6 (see Fig 3.2, Stage 5), 7 (d), 8 (b), 9 (b), 10 (b), 11 (see Fig 3.10), 12 (c), 13 (a), 14 (see Fig. 3.13), 15 (f).

CHAPTER 4

1 (a), 2 (c), 3 (d), 4 (c), 5 (see Fig. 4.5), 6 (a), 7 (see Amazing Places, Fig. A), 8 (b), 9 (c), 10 (a), 11 (d), 12 (e), 13 (c), 14 (see Fig 4.9), 15 (see Fig. 4.9).

CHAPTER 5

1 (c), 2 (b), 3 (d), 4 (b), 5 (a), 6 (d), 7 (d), 8 (see Fig. 5.8), 9 (a), 10 (e), 11 (a), 12 (d), 13 (a), 14 (see Fig. 5.13), 15 (b).

CHAPTER 6

1 (c), 2 (b), 3 (b), 4 (b), 5 (c), 6 (a), 7 (d), 8 (b), 9 (see Figs. 6.20, 6.21), 10 (a), 11 (b), 12 (see Table 6.1), 13 (c), 14 (see Fig 6.23), 15 (b).

CHAPTER 7

1 (See Fig. 7.1), 2 (b), 3 (d), 4 (e), 5 (c), 6 (b), 7 (see Fig. 7.10), 8 (c), 9 (d), 10 (d), 11 (b), 12 (d), 13 (c), 14 (b) 15 (see Fig. 7.15).

CHAPTER 8

1 (a), 2 (b), 3 (b), 4 (c), 5 (a), 6 (b), 7 (b), 8 (a), 9 (e), 10 (c), 11 (c), 12 (See Fig. 8.16)(a), 13 (b), 14 (b), 15 (c).

CHAPTER 9

1 (c), 2 (a), 3 (a), 4 (c), 5 (d), 6 (c), 7 (see Fig. 9.9B), 8 (a), 9 (a), 10 (d), 11 (see Fig. 9.12B), 12 (c), 13 (b), 14 (c), 15 (a).

CHAPTER 10

1 (b), 2 (b), 3 (see Fig. 10.2), 4 (d), 5 (c), 6 (c), 7 (c), 8 (b), 9 (d), 10 (a), 11 (c), 12 (see Fig. 10.12), 13 (a), 14 (see Fig. 10.17), 15 (b).

CHAPTER 11

1 (see Fig. 11.1), 2 (b), 3 (d), 4 (c), 5 (d), 6 (see Fig. 11.6A), 7 (d), 8 (d), 9 (b), 10 (c), 11 (d), 12 (c), 13 (d), 14 (a), 15 (see Fig. 11.16).

CHAPTER 12

1 (d), 2 (b), 3 (b), 4 (d), 5 (d), 6 (d), 7 (see What a Geologist Sees, part B), 8 (b), 9 (see Fig. 12. 9A), 10 (d), 11 (see Fig. 12.17), 12 (d), 13 (b), 14 (d), 15 (a).

CHAPTER 13

1 (b), 2 (d), 3 (d), 4 (b), 5 (see Fig. 13.6), 6 (c), 7 (see Fig. 13.11), 8 (a), 9 (d), 10 (a), 11 (d), 12 (a), 13 (c), 14 (b), 15 (c).

CHAPTER 14

1 (f), 2 (b) (Figure 14.2 is the associated figure), 3 (c), 4 (c), 5 (a), 6 (e), 7 (e), 8 (d), 9 (a), 10 (e), 11 (a), 12 (b), 13 (b) (Figure 14.15A is the associated figure), 14 (c), 15 (e).

CHAPTER 15

1 (a) (Figure 15.1 is the associated figure), 2 (see Figure 15.2B), 3 (d), 4 (c), 5 (see Figure 15.6), 6 (e), 7 (c), 8 (b), 9 (e), 10 (e), 11 (b), 12 (a), 13 (d), 14 (e), 15 (d).

CHAPTER 16

1 (b), 2 (a), 3 (a), 4 (see Figure 16.4), 5 (b), 6 (a), 7 (see Figure 16.13), 8 (b), 9 (d), 10 (a), 11 (e), 12 (d), 13 (c), 14 (a), 15 (see Figure 16.21).

Glossary

abrasion Wind erosion in which airborne particles chip small fragments off rocks that protrude above the surface.

air A mixture of 78% nitrogen, 21% oxygen, and trace amounts of other gases found in Earth's atmosphere.

albedo The reflectivity of a surface, as a percentage of the total reflected radiation.

alluvium Unconsolidated sediment deposited in a recent geologic time by a stream.

angiosperm A flowering, or seed-enclosed, plant.

anthropogenic greenhouse effect The portion of greenhouse warming that results from human activities rather than natural processes.

anticline A fold in the form of an arch, with the rock strata convex upward and the older rock in the core.

aphanitic An igneous rock texture with mineral grains so small they can be observed only under a magnifying lens.

aquiclude A layer of impermeable rock.

aquifer A body of rock or regolith that is water saturated, porous, and permeable.

asthenosphere A layer of weak, ductile rock in the mantle that is close to melting but not actually molten.

atmosphere The envelope of gases that surrounds Earth.

atom The smallest individual particle that retains the distinctive chemical properties of an element.

banded iron formation A type of chemical sedimentary rock rich in iron minerals and silica.

barrier island A long, narrow, sandy island lying offshore and parallel to a low-land coast.

batholith A large, irregularly shaped pluton that cuts across the layering of the rock into which it intrudes.

beach drift The movement of particles along a beach as they are driven up and down the beach slope by wave action.

beach Wave-washed sediment along a coast.

bed load Sediment that is moved along the bottom of a stream.

bedding The layered arrangement of strata in a body of sediment or sedimentary rock.

biogenic sediment Sediment that is primarily composed of plant and animal remains or that precipitates as a result of biologic processes.

biomass energy Any form of energy that is derived more or less directly from plant life, including fuel wood, peat, animal dung, and agricultural wastes.

biosphere The system consisting of all living and recently dead organisms on Earth.

body wave A seismic wave that travels through Earth's interior.

bond The force that holds together the atoms in a chemical compound.

brittle deformation A permanent change in shape or volume, in which a material breaks or cracks.

burial metamorphism Metamorphism that occurs after diagenesis, as a result of the burial of sediment in deep sedimentary basins.

caldera A roughly circular, steep-walled basin atop a volcano.

carbon cycle The set of processes by which carbon cycles from reservoir to reservoir through the global environment.

cave An underground open space; a cavern is a system of connected caves.

cell The basic structural and functional unit of life; a complex grouping of chemical compounds enclosed in a porous membrane.

cementation The process in which substances dissolved in pore water precipitate out and form a matrix in which grains of sediment are joined together.

channel The clearly defined natural passageway through which a stream flows.

chemical sediment Sediment formed by the precipitation of minerals dissolved in lakewater, riverwater, or seawater.

chemical weathering The decomposition of rocks and minerals by chemical and biochemical reactions.

clastic sediment Sediment formed from fragmented rock and mineral debris produced by weathering and erosion.

clay A family of hydrous alumino-silicate minerals; also, tiny mineral particles of any kind that have physical properties like those of clay minerals.

cleavage Breakage of a mineral along preferred planes of weakness.

climate The average weather conditions of a location or region over time.

climate proxy record Records of natural events that are influenced by, and closely mimic, climate.

coal A combustible rock (50 to 95% carbon), formed by the compression, heating, and lithification of peat.

compaction Reduction of pore space in a sediment as a result of the weight of overlying sediment.

compound A combination of atoms of one or more elements in a specific ratio.

compression A stress that acts in a direction perpendicular to and toward a surface.

compressional wave A seismic body wave consisting of alternating pulses of compression and expansion in the direction of wave travel; also called a P wave, or primary wave.

condensation The process by which water changes from a vapor into a liquid or a solid.

conglomerate Clastic sedimentary rock with large fragments in a finer-grained matrix.

contact metamorphism Metamorphism that occurs when rock is heated and chemically changed adjacent to an intruded body of hot magma.

continental collision zone A boundary along which two continental plates converge, resulting in the formation of high mountain ranges.

continental crust The older, thicker, and less dense part of Earth's crust; the bulk of Earth's landmasses.

continental drift The slow lateral movement of continents across Earth's surface.

convection A form of heat transfer in which hot material circulates from hotter to colder regions, loses its heat, and then repeats the cycle.

convergent margin A boundary along which two plates come together.

core Earth's innermost compositional layer, where the magnetic field is generated and much geothermal energy resides.

Coriolis force An effect due to Earth's rotation, which causes a freely moving body to veer from a straight path.

correlation A method of equating the ages of strata that come from two or more different places.

craton A region of continental crust that has remained tectonically stable for a very long time.

creep The imperceptibly slow downslope granular flow of regolith.

crust The outermost compositional layer of the solid Earth; part of the lithosphere.

cryosphere The perennially frozen part of the hydrosphere.

crystal structure An arrangement of atoms or molecules into a regular geometric lattice. Materials that possess a crystal structure are said to be crystalline.

crystallization The process whereby mineral grains form and grow in a cooling magma (or lava).

cyclone A wind system that is circulating around a low-pressure center.

deflation Wind erosion in which loose particles of sand and dust are removed by the wind, leaving coarser particles behind.

delta A sedimentary deposit, commonly triangle-shaped, that forms where a stream enters a standing body of water.

density Mass per unit of volume.

deposition The laying down of sediment, either by physical or chemical processes.

desert An arid land that receives less than 250 mm of rainfall or snow equivalent per year and is sparsely vegetated unless it is irrigated.

desertification Invasion of desert conditions into nondesert areas.

dip The angle between a tilted surface and a horizontal plane.

discharge (1) The amount of water passing by a point on a channel's bank during a unit of time. (2) The process by which subsurface water leaves the saturated zone and becomes surface water.

dissolution The separation of a material into ions in solution by a solvent, such as water or acid.

dissolved load Soluble material that is carried in solution by water.

divergent margin A boundary along which two plates move apart from one another.

divide A topographic high that separates adjacent drainage basins.

DNA Deoxyribonucleic acid; a double-chain biopolymer that contains all the genetic information needed for an organism to grow and reproduce.

domain The broadest taxonomic category of living organisms; biologists today recognize three domains: bacteria, *Archaea*, and eukaryotes.

drainage basin The total area from which water flows into a stream.

ductile deformation A permanent but gradual change in shape or volume of a material, caused by flowing or bending.

dune A hill or ridge of sand deposited by winds.

El Niño A regional weather system that involves unusual warming of equatorial Pacific surface water.

elastic deformation A temporary change in shape or volume from which a material rebounds after the deforming stress is removed.

elastic rebound model A model which postulates that continuing stress along a fault results in a buildup of elastic energy in the rocks, which is abruptly released when an earthquake occurs.

element The most fundamental substance into which matter can be separated using chemical means.

eolian sediment Sediment that is carried and deposited by wind.

epicenter The point on Earth's surface directly above an earthquake's focus.

erosion The wearing-away of bedrock and transport of loosened particles by a fluid, such as water.

estuary A semi-enclosed body of coastal water in which fresh water mixes with seawater.

eukaryote An organism composed of eukaryotic cells—that is, cells that have a well-defined nucleus and organelles.

evaporation The process by which water changes from a liquid into a vapor.

evaporite A rock formed by the evaporation of lakewater or seawater, followed by lithification of the resulting salt deposit.

evolution The theory that life on Earth has developed gradually, from one or a few simple organisms to more complex organisms.

extinction Permanent disappearance of a species.

fault A fracture in Earth's crust along which movement has occurred.

feedback A cycle in which the output from a process becomes an input into the same process.

flood An event in which a water body overflows its banks.

floodplain The relatively flat valley floor adjacent to a stream channel, which is inundated when the stream overflows its banks.

flow Any mass-wasting process that involves a flowing motion of regolith containing water and/or air within its pores.

focus The location where rupture commences and an earthquake's energy is first released.

fold A bend or warp in layered rock.

foliation A planar arrangement of textural features in metamorphic rock that give the rock a layered or finely banded appearance.

fossil Remains of an organism from a past age, embedded and preserved in rock.

fossil fuel Combustible organic matter that is trapped in sediment or sedimentary rock.

fracking Induced hydraulic fracturing, in which a pressurized fluid is injected into a well to create tiny fractures, facilitating the withdrawal of tightly held hydrocarbons such as heavy oil.

fractional crystallization Separation of crystals from liquids during crystallization.

fractional melt A mixture of molten and solid rock.

fractionation Separation of melted materials from the remaining solid material in the course of melting.

general circulation model A computer model of the climate system, linking processes in the atmosphere, hydrosphere, biosphere, and geosphere.

geologic column The succession of all known strata, fitted together in relative chronological order.

geologic cross section A diagram that shows geologic features that occur underground.

geologic map A map that shows the locations, kinds, and orientations of rock units, as well as structural features such as faults and folds.

geology The scientific study of Earth.

geosphere The solid Earth, as a whole.

geothermal energy Energy from Earth's interior.

glaciation (or glacial period or ice age) A relatively cold period, when Earth's ice cover greatly exceeded its present extent.

glacier A semipermanent or perennially frozen body of ice, consisting largely of recrystallized snow, that moves under the pull of gravity.

global warming Present-day warming of the world's climate that most scientists believe is likely to continue and is at least partly caused by human activities.

gneiss (pronounced "nice") A coarse-grained, high-grade, strongly foliated metamorphic rock with separation of dark and light minerals into bands.

gradient The steepness of a stream channel.

greenhouse effect The absorption of long-wavelength (infrared) energy by radiatively active gases in the atmosphere, causing heat to be retained near Earth's surface.

groundwater Subsurface water contained in pore spaces in regolith and bedrock.

gymnosperm A naked-seed plant.

habit The distinctive shape of a particular mineral.

half-life The time needed for half of the parent atoms of a radioactive substance to decay into daughter atoms.

hardness A mineral's resistance to scratching.

high-grade Rock metamorphosed under temperature and pressure conditions higher than about 400°C and 400 MPa.

humus Partially decayed organic matter in soil.

hydroelectric energy Electricity generated by running water.

hydrologic cycle A model that describes the movement of water through the reservoirs of the Earth system; the water cycle.

hydrosphere The system comprising all of Earth's bodies of water and ice, both on the surface and underground.

hypothesis A plausible but yet-to-be-proved explanation for how something happens.

igneous rock Rock that forms by cooling and solidification of molten rock.

infiltration The process by which water works its way into the ground through small openings in the soil.

interglaciation (or interglacial period) A relatively warm period, when Earth's ice cover and climate resembled those of the present day.

Intergovernmental Panel on Climate Change (IPCC) An international, interdisciplinary panel of scientists and other experts, established to keep the world community up to date on the science of the global climate system.

ion An atom that has lost or gained electrons.

isostasy The flotational balance of the lithosphere on the asthenosphere.

isotopes Atoms with the same atomic number but different mass numbers.

joint A fracture in a rock, along which no appreciable movement has occurred.

karst Topography characterized by sinkholes and disrupted drainage patterns, typical in carbonate regions.

kingdom The second-broadest taxonomic category. There are six recognized kingdoms, including animals and plants.

lake A standing body of water with an open surface.

land degradation Land damage or loss of productivity caused by human activity, which may lead to the advance of desert conditions into nondesert areas.

lava Molten rock that reaches Earth's surface.

limestone A sedimentary rock that consists primarily of the mineral calcite.

lithification The group of processes by which loose sediment is transformed into sedimentary rock.

lithosphere Earth's rocky, outermost layer, comprising the crust and the uppermost part of the mantle.

load The suspended and dissolved sediment carried by a stream.

longshore current A current within the surf zone that flows parallel to the coast.

low-grade Rock metamorphosed under temperature and pressure conditions up to 400°C and 400 MPa.

luster The quality and intensity of light that reflects from a mineral.

magma Molten rock that may include fragments of rock, volcanic glass and ash, or gas.

magnetic reversal A period of time in which Earth's magnetic polarity reverses itself.

magnitude A measure of the size or intensity of an event, such as an earthquake.

mantle The middle compositional layer of Earth, between the core and the crust.

marble The product of metamorphism formed by recrystallization of limestone.

mass extinction A catastrophic episode in which a large fraction of living species become extinct within a geologically short time.

mass wasting The downslope movement of regolith and/or bedrock masses due to the pull of gravity.

mechanical weathering The breakdown of rock into solid fragments by physical processes that do not change the rock's chemical composition.

metallic mineral resources Deposits that are mined specifically for the extraction of metals.

metamorphic facies The set of metamorphic mineral assemblages that form in rock of different compositions under similar temperature and stress conditions.

metamorphic rock Rock that has been altered by exposure to high temperature, high pressure, or both.

metamorphism The mineralogical, textural, chemical, and structural changes that occur in rock as a result of exposure to elevated temperatures and/or pressures.

metasomatism The process whereby the chemical composition of a rock is altered by the addition or removal of material by solution in fluids.

meteorite A fragment of extraterrestrial material that falls to Earth.

Milankovitch cycles The combined influences of astronomical-orbital factors that produce changes in Earth's climate.

mineral A naturally formed solid, inorganic substance with a characteristic crystal structure and a specific chemical composition.

molecule The smallest chemical unit that has all the properties of a particular compound.

moraine A ridge or pile of debris that has been, or is being, transported by a glacier.

mudstone A group of very fine-grained, nonfissile sedimentary rock types with differing proportions of silt- and clay-sized particles.

natural gas The gaseous form of petroleum.

natural resource A useful material that is obtained from the lithosphere, atmosphere, hydrosphere, or biosphere.

natural selection The process by which individuals that are well adapted to their environment have a survival advantage and pass on their favorable characteristics to their offspring.

nonmetallic mineral resources Deposits that are mined for the properties of the minerals they contain, rather than for metals that could be extracted.

nonrenewable resource A resource that cannot be replenished or regenerated on the scale of a human lifetime.

normal fault A fault in which the block of rock above the fault surface moves downward relative to the block below.

nuclear energy Energy derived from the binding energy in the nuclei of atoms; fission (splitting of atoms) is the most common source.

numerical age The age of a rock or geologic feature in years before the present.

oceanic crust The thinner, denser, and younger part of Earth's crust, underlying the ocean basins.

oil The liquid form of petroleum.

oil shale A fine-grained sedimentary rock with a high content of kerogen.

ore A deposit from which one or more minerals can be extracted profitably.

orogen An elongated region of crust that has been deformed and metamorphosed through a continental collision.

outcrop A place where bedrock is exposed at the surface.

ozone layer A zone in the stratosphere where ozone is concentrated.

paleoclimate The climate of an ancient time.

paleomagnetism The study of rock magnetism in order to determine the intensity and direction of Earth's magnetic field in the geologic past.

paleontology The study of fossils and the record of ancient life on Earth; the use of fossils for the determination of relative ages.

paleoseismology The study of prehistoric earthquakes.

peat A biogenic sediment formed from the accumulation and compaction of plant remains from bogs and swamps, with a carbon content of about 25%.

percolation The process by which groundwater seeps downward and flows under the influence of gravity.

permafrost Ground that is perennially below the freezing point of water.

permeability A measure of how easily a solid allows fluids to pass through it.

petroleum Naturally occurring gaseous, liquid, and semisolid substances that consist chiefly of hydrocarbon compounds.

petroleum trap The combination of a source rock, a reservoir rock, and a cap rock, which serves to trap and store oil and natural gas in the subsurface.

phaneritic An igneous rock texture with mineral grains large enough to be seen by the unaided eye.

photosynthesis A chemical reaction whereby plants use light energy to induce carbon dioxide to react with water, producing carbohydrates and oxygen.

phyllite A fine-grained metamorphic rock with pronounced foliation, produced by further metamorphism of slate.

plate A large fragment of rigid lithosphere bounded on all sides by faults.

plate tectonics The movement and interactions of large fragments of Earth's lithosphere, called plates.

pluton Any body of intrusive igneous rock, regardless of size or shape.

plutonic rock Igneous rock that solidifies underground, from magma.

polymerization The formation of a complex molecule by the joining of repeated simpler units.

porosity The percentage of the total volume of a body of rock or regolith that consists of open spaces (pores).

precipitation (1) The separation of a solid from a solution. (2) The process by which water that has condensed in the atmosphere falls back to the surface as rain, snow, or hail.

pressure A particular kind of stress in which the forces acting on a body are the same in all directions.

prokaryote A single-celled organism with no distinct nucleus—that is, no membrane separates its DNA from the rest of the cell.

pyroclastic flow Hot volcanic fragments (tephra) that flow very rapidly, buoyed by heat and volcanic gases.

quartzite The product of metamorphism formed by recrystallization of sandstone.

radioactivity A process in which an element spontaneously transforms into another isotope of the same element or into a different element.

radiometric dating The use of naturally occurring radioactive isotopes to determine the numerical age of minerals, rocks, or fossils.

recharge Replenishment of groundwater.

recrystallization The formation of new crystalline mineral grains from old ones.

reef A hard structure on a shallow ocean floor, usually but not always built by coral.

reflection The bouncing back of a wave from an interface between two different materials.

refraction The bending of a wave as it passes from one material into another material, through which it travels at a different speed.

regional metamorphism Metamorphism of an extensive area of the crust, associated with plate convergence, collision, and subduction.

regolith A loose layer of broken rock and mineral fragments that covers most of Earth's surface.

relative age The age of a rock, fossil, or other geologic feature relative to another feature.

renewable resource A resource that can be replenished or regenerated on the scale of a human lifetime.

reservoir A place in the Earth system where a material is stored for a period of time.

reverse fault A fault in which the block on top of the fault surface moves up and over the block on the bottom.

rift valley A linear, fault-bounded valley along a divergent plate boundary or spreading center.

rock A naturally formed, coherent aggregate of minerals and possibly other nonmineral matter.

rock cycle The set of crustal processes that form new rock, modify it, transport it, and break it down.

salinity A measure of the salt content of a solution.

saltation Sediment transport in which particles move forward in a series of short jumps along arc-shaped paths.

sandstone Medium-grained clastic sedimentary rock in which the clasts are typically, but not necessarily, dominated by quartz grains.

saturated zone (or phreatic zone) Water-saturated rock and sediment that underlies the water table.

schist A high-grade metamorphic rock with pronounced schistosity, in which individual mineral grains are visible.

schistosity Foliation in coarse-grained metamorphic rock.

science A systematic approach to studying the natural world.

scientific method The way a scientist approaches a problem; steps include observing, formulating a hypothesis, testing, and evaluating results.

seafloor spreading The processes through which the seafloor splits and moves apart along a midocean ridge and new oceanic crust forms along the ridge.

sediment Rock that has been fragmented, transported, and deposited.

sedimentary rock Rocks that form from sediment under conditions of low pressure and low temperature near the surface.

seismic discontinuity A boundary inside Earth where the velocities of seismic waves change abruptly.

seismic wave An elastic shock wave that travels outward in all directions from an earthquake's source.

seismogram The record made by a seismograph.

seismograph An instrument that detects and measures vibrations of Earth's surface.

seismology The scientific study of earthquakes and seismic waves.

sequestration Long-term storage of a material, in isolation from the atmosphere.

shale Very fine-grained fissile or laminated sedimentary rock, consisting primarily of silt- or clay-sized particles; a fissile mudstone.

shear A stress that acts in a direction parallel to a surface.

shear wave A seismic body wave in which rock is subjected to side-to-side or up-and-down forces, perpendicular to the wave's direction of travel; also called an S wave, or secondary wave.

shield volcano A broad, flat volcano with gently sloping sides, built of successive lava flows.

silicate minerals The most common mineral family in Earth's crust, based on the silica anion.

sink A reservoir that takes in more of a given material than it releases.

sinkhole A dissolution cavity that is open to the sky.

slate A very fine-grained, low-grade metamorphic rock with slaty cleavage; the metamorphic product of shale.

slaty cleavage Foliation in low-grade metamorphic rock, which causes the rock to break into flat, plate-like fragments.

slope failure The falling, slumping, or sliding of relatively coherent masses of rock.

soil The uppermost layer of regolith, which can support rooted plants.

soil horizon One of a succession of zones or layers within a soil profile, each with distinct physical, chemical, and biologic characteristics.

soil profile The sequence of soil horizons from the surface down to the underlying bedrock.

solar energy Radiant light and heat energy from the Sun.

species A population of genetically and/or morphologically similar individuals that can interbreed and produce fertile offspring.

spring A natural outlet for groundwater that occurs where the water table intersects the land surface.

strain A change in shape or volume of rock in response to stress.

stratigraphy The science of rock layers and the process by which strata are formed.

stratosphere The layer of Earth's atmosphere above the troposphere, extending to about 50 km altitude.

stratovolcano A volcano composed of solidified lava flows interlayered with pyroclastic material. Such volcanoes usually have steep sides that curve upward.

streak A thin layer of powdered mineral made by rubbing a specimen on an unglazed fragment of porcelain.

stream A body of water that flows downslope along a clearly defined natural passageway.

stress The force acting on a surface, per unit area, which may be greater in certain directions than in others.

strike The compass orientation of the line of intersection between a horizontal plane and a planar feature, such as a rock layer or fault.

strike-slip fault A fault in which the direction of the movement is mostly horizontal and parallel to the strike of the fault.

structural geology The study of stress and strain, the processes that cause them, and the deformation and rock structures that result from them.

subduction zone A boundary along which one lithospheric plate descends into the mantle beneath another plate.

subsidence A drop in the surface of the land.

surf The "broken," turbulent water found between a line of breakers and the shore.

surface creep Sediment transport in which the wind causes particles to roll along the ground.

surface runoff Precipitation that drains over the land or in stream channels.

surface wave A seismic wave that travels along Earth's surface.

suspended load Sediment that is carried in suspension by a flowing stream of water or wind.

suspension Sediment transport in which the wind carries very fine particles over long distances and periods of time.

syncline A fold in the form of a trough, with the rock strata concave upward and the younger rock in the core.

system A portion of the universe that can be isolated for the purpose of observing and measuring change.

tar sand A sediment or sedimentary rock in which the pores are filled by dense, viscous, asphalt-like oil.

tectonic cycle Movements and interactions in the lithosphere by which rocks are cycled from the mantle to the crust and back; this cycle includes earthquakes, volcanism, and plate motion, driven by convection in the mantle.

tension A stress that acts in a direction perpendicular to and away from a surface.

theory A hypothesis that has been tested and is strongly supported by experimentation, observation, and scientific evidence.

thermohaline circulation The deep-ocean global "conveyor belt" circulation, driven by differences in water temperature, salinity, and density.

thrust fault A reverse fault with a shallow angle of dip.

tides A regular, daily cycle of rising and falling sea level that results from the gravitational action of the Moon, the Sun, and Earth.

till A heterogeneous mixture of crushed rock, sand, pebbles, cobbles, and boulders deposited by a glacier.

topographic map A map that shows the shape of the ground surface, as well as the location and elevation of surface features, usually by means of contour lines.

trace fossil Fossilized evidence of an organism's life processes, such as tracks, footprints, and burrows.

trade wind Northeasterly and southeasterly equatorial wind systems.

transform fault margin A fracture in the lithosphere where two plates slide past each other.

transpiration The process by which water taken up by plants passes directly into the atmosphere.

trend A long-term or underlying pattern in a time series of data.

troposphere The lowest layer of Earth's atmosphere, extending (variably) to about 15 km in altitude.

turbidity current A turbulent, gravity-driven flow consisting of a mixture of sediment and water, which conveys sediment from the continental shelf to the deep sea.

unconformity A substantial gap in a stratigraphic sequence that marks the absence of part of the rock record.

uniformitarianism The concept that the processes governing the Earth system today have operated in a similar manner throughout geologic time.

viscosity The degree to which a substance resists flow; a less viscous liquid is runny, whereas a more viscous liquid is thick.

volcanic rock Igneous rock that solidifies on or near the surface, from lava.

volcano A vent through which lava, solid rock debris, volcanic ash, and gases erupt from Earth's crust to its surface.

water table The top surface of the saturated zone.

wave-cut cliff A coastal cliff cut by wave action at the base of a rocky coast.

weathering The chemical and physical breakdown of rock exposed to air, moisture, and living organisms.

wind Air in motion.

wind energy Energy derived from the movement of air; an indirect form of solar energy.

world ocean The interconnected body of salt water that covers 71% of Earth's surface.

zone of aeration (or vadose zone) Soil and sediment above the water table, which holds both air and moisture.

Chapter 4

Amazing Places: Hawaii Center for Volcanology.

Chapter 5

Figure 5.1: Map and table courtesy of the USGS National Earthquake Information Center.

Chapter 6

Figure 6.10: Myers, Bobbie, and Driedger, Carolyn, 2008, Geologic hazards at volcanoes: U.S. Geological Survey, Figure 6.11: Reproduced/modified by by permission of America Geophysical Union.

Chapter 9

Amazing Places: Price, R.A. (2012): Cordilleran Tectonics and the Evolution of the Western Canada Sedimentary Basin; in Geological Atlas of the Western Canada Sedimentary Basin, G.D. Mossop and I. Shetsen (comp.), Canadian Society of Petroleum Geologists and Alberta Research Council, URL <http://www.ags.gov.ab.ca/publications/wcsb_atlas/atlas.html>, July 27, 2014.

Chapter 12

Figure 12.2: NASA Ozone Watch, Figure 12.5: National Oceanic and Atmospheric Administration Paleoclimatology Program/Department of Commerce.

Chapter 13

Figure 13.5: Reprinted with permission from Springer Sciene and Business Media, Figure 13.6: Adapted from John T. Hack, The Geographical Review, vol. 31, fig. 19, page 260 by permission of the American Geographical Society, What a Geologist Sees: Adapted from Springer Science and Business Media, Amazing Places: NASA.

Chapter 14

Figure 4.3: Courtesy of Nigel Calder, Figure 4.8: Illustration by Jack Cook © Woods Hole Oceanographic Institution, Figure 4.9: Reprinted with permission from Understanding and Responding to Climate Change, 2008 by the National Academy of Sciences, Courtesy of the National Academic Press, Washington, D.C., Figure 14.16: IPCC, 2013: Summary for Policymakers. In: Climate Change 2013: The Physical Science Basis. Contribution of Working Group I to the Fifth Assessment Report of the Intergovernmental Panel on Climate Change [Stocker, T.F., D. Qin, G.-K. Plattner, M. Tignor, S.K. Allen, J. Boschung, A. Nauels, Y. Xia, V. Bex and P.M. Midgley (eds.)]. Cambridge University Press, Cambridge, United Kingdom and New York, NY, USA., Amazing Places: © 2014 Polar Field Services, Inc.

Chapter 15

Figure 15.1: MACKENZIE, FRED T., OUR CHANGING PLANET: AN INTRODUCTION TO EARTH SYSTEM SCIENCE AND GLOBAL ENVIRONMENTAL CHANGE, 4th Edition, © 2011. Reprinted by permission of Pearson Education, Inc., Upper Saddle River, NJ, Figure 15.3: "The Rise of Oxygen Over the Past 205 Million Years and the Evolution of Large Placental Mammals"/ Science 30/ Falowski/ Sep 2005/ Vol 309/ no. 54770 (pg. 2202-2204).

Chapter 16

Figure 16.13: © 2009 International Union of Geological Sciences - ALL RIGHTS RESERVED WORLDWIDE: Figure 1, TWO CENTURIES OF FOSSIL FUEL PROTECTION EPISODES, VOL 12, NO. 4, 1989.

Index